CONTENTS

W9-CBK-904

FROMMER'S

COMPREHENSIVE TRAVEL GUIDE

SWITZERLAND & LIECHTENSTEIN '92-'93

by Darwin Porter
Assisted by Danforth Prince

PRENTICE HALL TRAVEL

NEW YORK • LONDON • TORONTO • SYDNEY • TOKYO • SINGAPORE

FROMMER BOOKS

Published by Prentice Hall General Reference
A division of Simon & Schuster Inc.
15 Columbus Circle
New York, NY 10023

ISBN 0-13-327313-X
ISSN 1044-2294

Manufactured in the United States of America

FROMMER'S SWITZERLAND & LIECHTENSTEIN '92-'93

Editor-in-Chief: Marilyn Wood
Senior Editors: Judith de Rubini, Pamela Marshall, Amit Shah
Editors: Alice Fellows, Paige Hughes, Theodore Stavrou
Assistant Editors: Suzanne Arkin, Peter Katucki, Lisa Renaud, Ellen Zucker
Contributing Editors: Jane Jaffin, Alan LaDuca
Managing Editor: Leanne Coupe

LIST OF MAPS

INFLATION ALERT

In researching this book I have made every effort to obtain up-to-the-minute prices, but even the most conscientious researcher cannot keep up with the inevitable price changes. As we go to press, I believe we have obtained the most reliable data possible. Nonetheless, in the lifetime of this edition—particularly its second year (1993)—the wise traveler will need to allow for a certain increase in prices, although Switzerland, compared to the rest of the world, keeps its prices relatively stable.

A DISCLAIMER

Although every effort was made to ensure the accuracy of the prices and travel information appearing in this book, it should be kept in mind that prices do fluctuate in the course of time, and that information does change under the impact of the varied and volatile factors that affect the travel industry.

CHAPTER 1

GETTING TO KNOW SWITZERLAND

Switzerland has a rich cultural life, with many fine museums and theaters and with orchestras of world renown, but most people visit the country for its superb, even majestic, scenery—alpine peaks, mountain lakes, and lofty pastures. As important as Geneva, Zurich, St. Moritz, and other obvious tourist centers are, they do not convey the full splendors of Switzerland. To experience these, you must venture deep into "William Tell" country, into the heart of Switzerland.

The Federal Republic of Switzerland covers 15,941 square miles and has more than 6.6 million inhabitants. It has four recognized national languages—German, French, Italian, and Romansh, a Romance dialect. Many of its people, however, speak English, especially in the major tourist regions. You will find the Swiss hospitable, restrained, and peace-loving. Switzerland's neutrality allowed it to avoid the wars that devastated its neighbors twice in this century. It also enabled it to achieve financial stability and prosperity.

Switzerland occupies a position on the "rooftop" of the continent of Europe, with the drainage of its mammoth alpine glaciers serving as the source of such powerful rivers as the Rhine and the Rhône. The appellation "crossroads of Europe" is fitting, as all rail lines, road passes, and mountain tunnels seem to lead to Switzerland. From the time that the Romans crossed the Alps and traversed Helvetia (the ancient name for part of today's Switzerland) on their way to conquests in the north, the major route connecting Northern and Southern Europe has been through Switzerland. The country's ancient roads and paths were eventually developed into modern highways and railroad lines.

The main European route for east-west travel also passes through Switzerland, between Lake Constance and Geneva, and intercontinental airports connect the country with cities all over the world. London and Paris, for instance, are less than 2 hours away by air.

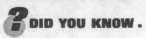

DID YOU KNOW . . . ?

- More than 3½% of the working population of Switzerland is employed in the banking industry.
- As a financial center, Switzerland ranks in importance behind only New York, London, and Tokyo.
- Since the late 18th and early 19th centuries, there has been no foreign invasion of Swiss territory, despite the devastating conflagrations that surrounded it.
- Until the early 19th century, Switzerland was the most industrialized country in Europe.
- Famous for its neutrality, Switzerland once was equally known for providing mercenaries to fight in foreign armies. (The practice was ended by the constitution of 1874, with the exception of the Vatican's Swiss papal guard, dating from 1505.)
- In 1986 the Swiss electorate voted against membership in the United Nations.
- Switzerland drafts all able-bodied male citizens between the ages of 20 and 50 (55 for officers). These soldiers, who continue to live at home, form a reserve defense corps that (in theory) can be called to active duty at any time.
- With its four major language groups, Switzerland effectively contradicts the axiom that a national identity cannot exist without a common language.

The tourist industry as we know it started in Switzerland, and the tradition of welcoming visitors is firmly entrenched in Swiss life. The first modern tourists, the British, began to arrive "on holiday" in the 19th century, and other Europeans, as well as a scattering of North Americans, followed suit. The "nation of hotel keepers" now hosts some 20 million foreign visitors every year. Swiss catering, based on many years of experience, has gained a worldwide reputation, and the entire country is known for its efficiency and its cleanliness.

1. GEOGRAPHY, HISTORY & POLITICS

GEOGRAPHY

The Swiss landscape has been shaped by glaciation. Glaciers hollowed out the valleys and led to the creation of numerous lakes, which are a major feature of the Swiss scenery.

The Swiss plateau, set between the mountain chains of the Jura and the Alps and extending from Lake Geneva in the southwest to Lake Constance in the northeast, represents about 30% of the country's surface area. The country's main cities and industries are concentrated on this plateau, making Switzerland one of the world's most densely populated countries. Most of the Swiss live in this zone, with half the population based in the major urban areas of Geneva, Lausanne, Basel, Bern, Olten, Aarau, Zurich, and Baden. The plateau is also the country's center of agricultural production.

Population growth has inevitably left its mark on areas that would otherwise have been rich in nature. The country's population centers are constantly expanding and are linked to each other by an increasingly dense network of roads. Sadly, such expansion leaves less and less land available for agriculture, vegetation, and wildlife.

As the weekend begins, long lines of vehicles head toward the Jura and the Alps. The Jura, which covers about 10% of the Swiss landmass, consists of long folds of limestone. Although industrialized, the region has large expanses of rolling hills and forest, interspersed with wide valleys and narrow gorges. Part of the Swiss consciousness, the Jura foothills and the Alps are within 2 hours' drive or train ride from almost everywhere on the plateau.

Within its borders, Switzerland has nearly every variety of landscape, vegetation, and climatic condition known in Europe. Only a few dozen miles, as the crow flies, separate the lowest point in Switzerland, the shores of Lake Maggiore (approximately 580 feet above sea level), where palm trees thrive in a Mediterranean climate, from the highest, the Dufourspitze (Dufour Point, 15,217 ft. above sea level), in the Monte Rosa range, where the climate is one of eternal snow and ice.

Before British climbers discovered the charms of Switzerland's mountains in the mid-19th century, local people avoided the sheer rock faces and deserts of ice that dominate many of the country's high altitudes. Residents of the milder valleys believed that the heights were inhabited by demons who would pelt with stones anyone daring to climb up to them. Such fears have long disappeared, but the locals still retain a great respect for the mountains, as their rites and customs show. The Alps have become the main tourist attraction of Switzerland, with about a hundred peaks above 12,000 feet. Some 1,800 glaciers offer the sight of an awesome and sometimes-savage virgin nature, almost untouched since the last glacial period 20,000 years ago, despite human incursions. The view south from the Jungfraujoch, the highest rail station in Europe, is one of windswept rock and ice, chillingly majestic and dramatically memorable.

The Swiss Alps form the centerpiece of Europe's alpine range. They are broken by the great valleys of the Rhône (in the canton of the Valais) and the Rhine (in the canton of the Graubünden), as well as by many lateral valleys. To the north, the alpine chain ends in the Bernese Alps (Finsteraarhorn) and to the south in the Valais Alps (the Monte Rosa range). To the east, the Alps end at Piz Bernina. Within the canton of Ticino, which on the map looks like a triangular section of northern Italy, Switzerland also possesses part of the southern face of the Alps as well.

REGIONS IN BRIEF

Zurich Close to the northern borders of Switzerland, Zurich is the country's largest city, spreading across 36 square miles, with a population of 380,000. The fiscal and business center of the country, it was also the political capital until 1848, when the honor was transferred to Bern.

The Bernese Oberland Switzerland's best-known alpine holiday region is named after its largest city, Bern, the capital. Known for the beauty of its mountains, it includes many famous resorts, the largest of which is Interlaken (popular mainly in the summer). At its higher altitudes, where the snowfall is more consistently excellent, you'll find such wintertime ski resorts as chic and elegant Gstaad, Grindelwald, Kandersteg, Mürren, and Wengen.

IMPRESSIONS

Switzerland is simply a large, humpy solid rock, with a thin skin of grass stretched over it.
—MARK TWAIN, A TRAMP ABROAD, 1880

SWITZERLAND & LIECHTENSTEIN

GERMANY

Schaffhausen

Rhine River

THURGAU

Bodensee (Lake Constance)

Lindau

Winterthur

Bregenz

ZÜRICH

St. Gallen

Zürich

APPENZELL

Appenzell

Lake Zürich

ST. GALLEN

AUSTRIA

Walensee

LIECHTENSTEIN

Vaduz

Lake Zug
Zug
ZUG

Lucerne

Schwyz

Glarus

Glarus Alps

Bad Ragaz

Lake Lucerne

WALDEN

GLARUS

Klosters

WALDEN
LDEN

URI

Flims

Chur

Valbell
Lenzerheide

Arosa

Davos

Rhaetian Alps

GRISONS & THE ENGADINE

Splügen

Savognin

Zuoz

Airolo

St. Moritz

Samedan
Pontresina

Faido

Silvaplana

Inn River

TICINO

Lepontine Alps

Locarno
Ascona

Bellinzona

Brissago

Lugano

Gandria
Morcote

Lake
Como

Lake
Maggiore

Lake
Lugano

Varese

Bergamo

ITALY

Northeastern Switzerland   Relatively neglected by the average tourist, this region is separated from southern Germany and Austria by the waters of the Rhine and by Lake Constance. Its tourist highlights include St. Gallen, a lace-making center and the economic centerpiece of the region, certain sections of the valley of the Rhine, and the Rhine Falls, near Neuhausen.

Basel and the Jura   In northwestern Switzerland, Basel, the capital of this region, is an ancient university and trading center on the Rhine, set midway between French Alsace and the Jura canton in Switzerland. The Jura is a range of "folded" limestone ridges set between two great rivers, the Rhône and the Rhine. Both of these rivers, during part of their courses, form some of the most historic political boundaries of Western Europe.

The Valais   This is the rugged valley of the upper Rhône, encompassing such legendary geographic attractions as the Matterhorn and the Great St. Bernard Pass. Equally divided between French- and German-speaking residents, it is rich in nostalgia and folklore. Its most famous ski resort is Zermatt.

Lausanne and the Shores of Lake Geneva   Called Lac Léman by the Swiss, Lake Geneva is the largest freshwater body in central Europe, embracing some 225 square miles. It is partially fed by the alpine waters of the Rhône and is emptied by a continuation of the same river, which eventually pours into the Mediterranean beside the coastline of southern France. Lausanne, considered the cultural center of its region, is the second-largest city on Lake Geneva and the fifth-largest in Switzerland.

Geneva   Geneva is distinctly different from the rest of Switzerland and culturally more attuned to France (especially Paris). Switzerland's second-largest city, it is built on the Rhône, at the lower end of Lake Geneva, and is bordered on three sides by French territory. A center of world banking and commerce, it is celebrated for its prosperity, elegance, and sophistication. Geneva is also the site of many world organizations, such as the Red Cross, and major international conferences.

Lucerne and Central Switzerland   The heartland of Switzerland, this region takes in four different cantons: Lucerne, Uri, Unterwalden, and Schwyz (from which the country's name is derived). The region's only major city is Lucerne, a medieval town made famous in the 19th century as a resort. It sits at the northern edge of the famous lake that bears its name. Despite Switzerland's wealth of comparable attractions, Lucerne is the Swiss city that most North Americans prefer to visit, even if they have to skip Geneva or Zurich.

The Grisons and the Engadine   This area is the largest and most easterly of the cantons of Switzerland. It is also one of the least densely populated, taking in about 140 square miles of glaciers and legions of jagged and wind-swept mountain peaks. Its capital is Chur, the oldest town in Switzerland, but most visitors bypass it as they head to the ski resorts of Arosa, Klosters, and Davos. The Engadine stretches for 60 miles, from the Maloja Plateau to Finstermünz. The region's chief attraction is St. Moritz, the glamorous winter resort favored by the late shah of Iran and many other luminaries.

IMPRESSIONS

Every object in Switzerland has more than gratified our expectations, except the glaciers.
—WILLIAM COXE, *TRAVELS IN SWITZERLAND*, 1791

The Ticino Comprising the Italian-speaking part of Switzerland, the Ticino is the most southerly, and therefore the warmest, of the country's regions. Not surprisingly, it is the object of the retirement dreams of many residents in the northerly cantons. The region includes the major cities of Lugano and Locarno, which share, respectively, the lakes of Lugano and Maggiore with Italy. The Italian influence is most strongly felt in the region's relaxed tempo of life.

HISTORY

AT THE CROSSROADS OF EUROPE Despite its image as an often placid neutral, Switzerland has a fascinating history of external and internal conflicts. Its strategic location, at the crossroads of Europe, made it an irresistible object to empire builders from Roman times. There is even evidence that prehistoric tribes struggled to hold tiny settlements along the great Rhône and Rhine rivers.

The first identifiable occupants were the Celts, who entered the alpine regions from the west. The Helvetii, a Celtic tribe, inhabited a portion of the country that became known as Helvetia. The tribe was defeated by Julius Caesar when it tried to move into southern France in 58 B.C. The Romans conquered the resident tribes in 15 B.C., and peaceful colonization continued until A.D. 455, when the barbarians invaded, followed later by the Christians. Charlemagne (742–814) conquered the hodgepodge of small states, or cantons, that occupied the area now known as Switzerland and incorporated them into his realm, which later became the Holy Roman Empire. After several battles, the land fell under the domination of the Hapsburgs in 1291.

BIRTH OF THE CONFEDERATION The Swiss have always guarded their territory jealously. In 1291 an association of three cantons formed the Perpetual Alliance—the nucleus of today's Swiss Confederation. To be rid of the grasping Hapsburgs, the Confederation in 1439 broke free of the Holy Roman Empire. It later signed a treaty with France, a rival power, agreeing to provide France with mercenary troops. This led to Swiss fighting Swiss in the early 16th century. The agreement was ended around 1515, and in 1516 the confederates declared their complete neutrality.

During the 16th century, the Reformation and its conflicts of allegiance created deep divisions within the Confederation, but the confederates managed to stay together by adopting a pragmatic approach to their reli-

DATELINE

- **15 B.C.** The Romans conquer the Helvetii and other resident alpine tribes.
- **A.D. 455** Barbarian invasions begin.
- **742–814** Charlemagne incorporates much of what is now Switzerland into his enormous empire.
- **1291** Three cantons form the Perpetual Alliance, the germ of today's Swiss Confederation.
- **1439** The Confederation breaks free of the Holy Roman Empire (dating from 962).
- **1516** The confederates (*Eidgenossen*) proclaim their neutrality in Europe's conflicts.
- **1798** The French Revolution brings an invasion of radical forces and ideas, and the old Confederation collapses.

(continues)

DATELINE

- **1803** Napoleon Bonaparte establishes a new, 19-canton confederation, with relatively enlightened social policies.
- **1814–15** The Congress of Vienna guarantees the national boundaries and neutrality of Switzerland.
- **1848** The Swiss adopt a federal constitution, still in force today. Bern is recognized as the capital.
- **1914** Switzerland declares its neutrality at the outbreak of World War I.
- **1918** Swiss workers stage the only general strike the country has ever known.
- **1920** Switzerland joins the League of Nations, offering the establishment of a headquarters at Geneva.
- **1939** Fearing an invasion by Nazi Germany, the country orders a total mobilization of its air and ground forces.
- **1939–45** Remaining neutral, Switzerland becomes a haven for

(continues)

gious and political differences. Such approach to national issues, based on compromise, remains one of the cornerstones of the Swiss political system. Later, during the Thirty Years' War (1618–48), the Swiss remained neutral while civil wars flared around them.

INDUSTRIALIZATION AND POLITICAL CRISES
Turning to economic development, Switzerland in the 18th century became the most industrialized nation in Europe. A rapid population growth, however, created social problems, widening the division between the new class of wealth and the rest of the population. Popular uprisings occurred, but it was only after the French Revolution that they had an effect. In 1798, succumbing to the pressures, the Swiss Confederation collapsed like a house of cards.

Under French guardianship, progressives moved to centralize the constitution of the Swiss Republic. This pull toward centralization clashed with the federalist traditions of the semi-independent cantons. In 1803, Napoleon Bonaparte established a confederation, with 19 cantons, but when he fell from power Swiss conservatives revived the old order. Much of the social progress resulting from the Napoleonic period was reversed, and the aristocrats had their former privileges restored to them.

The present Swiss boundaries were fixed at the Congress of Vienna in 1814–15. In 1848 a federal constitution was adopted and the capital established at Bern. The federal state, by centralizing responsibility for such matters as customs dues and the minting of coins, created conditions favorable to economic progress. The construction of a railway network and the establishment of a banking system also contributed to Switzerland's development. Both facilitated the country's export industry, consisting chiefly of textiles, pharmaceuticals, and precision machinery.

NEUTRALITY THROUGH TWO WORLD WARS
During World War I (1914–18), Switzerland maintained its neutrality from the general European conflict but experienced serious social problems at home. As purchasing power fell and unemployment rose dramatically, popular unrest grew. One cause of bitterness was that Swiss men conscripted into the army automatically lost their jobs. In November 1918, workers, dissatisfied with their conditions, called a general strike, the first and only one in Switzerland's history. The strike led to the introduction of proportional representation in elections. In the 1920s a 48-hour workweek was introduced, and unemployment insurance was improved.

In 1920, Switzerland joined the League of Nations and provided space for the organization's headquarters at Geneva. As a neutral member, however, it exempted itself from any military action that the League might take.

In August 1939, on the eve of World War II (1939–45), Switzerland ordered a mobilization of its defense forces, fearing an invasion. But an invasion never came, even though Switzerland was surrounded by Germany and its allies. It proved convenient to all the belligerents to have, in the middle of a continent in conflict, a neutral nation through which they could deal with each other.

The sense of neutrality remains so strong that even as recently as 1986 the Swiss voted, in a national referendum, against membership in the United Nations. Switzerland, however, did join the United Nations Educational, Scientific, and Cultural Organization, contributing to its Third World development funds.

DATELINE

escaping prisoners of war but avoids direct conflicts.
• **1948** Switzerland introduces broad-based social reforms, including the funding of old-age pensions.
• **1986** The Swiss electorate votes against membership in the United Nations.

Switzerland's political isolationism of the postwar years coincided with a period of unprecedented financial and industrial growth. Many social-welfare programs were introduced, unemployment was virtually wiped out, and the country moved into an enviable position of wealth and prosperity.

INTO THE FUTURE Switzerland's main political issue during the 1990s will be the country's relationship to the European Community. The Swiss increasingly recognize the need to participate actively in an interdependent Europe, not just financially but also politically and economically.

POLITICS

Switzerland is a confederation of 3,029 communes, each largely responsible for its own public affairs, including school systems, taxation, road construction, water supply, and town planning. The international sign "CH," found on Swiss motor vehicles, stands for *Confœderatio Helvetica* (Swiss Confederation). Over the centuries neighboring communes bonded together in a confederation of 23 cantons, each canton with its own constitution, laws, and government. They have surrendered only certain aspects of their authority to the Federal Parliament, such as foreign policy, national defense, and general economic policy, as well as matters of finance and civil and penal legislation.

The Federal Parliament of Switzerland consists of a 200-member National Council, elected by the people, and a 46-member Council of States, in which each canton has two representatives. The two chambers constitute Switzerland's legislative authority. The executive body, the Federal Council, is composed of seven members,

IMPRESSIONS

Look at Switzerland. Hundreds of years of peace, and what did it produce? The cuckoo clock!
—ORSON WELLS, *THE THIRD MAN*, 1949

who make decisions jointly, although each councilor is responsible for a different department. The president of the Federal Council, who serves a 1-year term, leads the Confederation as primus inter pares (first among equals).

All Swiss citizens, in general, become eligible to vote on federal matters at the age of 20. Surprisingly, it wasn't until 1971 that Swiss women were granted the right to vote. Voting on local issues continues to be restricted to men in the subdivided cantons of Appenzell and in a few small communes.

Despite its neutrality, Switzerland has compulsory military service. The army, however, is devoted solely to the defense of the homeland. Swiss soldiers are always ready to fight—they keep military gear at home, including a gas mask, rifle, and ammunition. Annual shooting practice is mandatory.

2. SWITZERLAND'S FAMOUS PEOPLE

Ernest Ansermet (1883–1969) Swiss conductor, who achieved fame with Diaghilev's Ballet Russe in 1915. He was known for conducting the works of Debussy, Ravel, and Stravinsky. In 1918 Ansermet founded what was to become one of Switzerland's most respected orchestras, the Orchestre de la Suisse Romande, in Geneva, and introduced many new works that later became famous. He frequently conducted musical tours of the United States.

Arnold Böcklin (1827–1901) A painter, known for his mythical scenes and landscapes, which are displayed in galleries throughout Europe. Among his most famous works are *The Elysian Fields, The Sacred Grove,* and *The Island of the Dead.* Böcklin used color imaginatively and developed his mythological portrayals with great originality.

Le Corbusier (1887–1965) Swiss architect, who helped revolutionize international concepts in city planning and functional architecture. Le Corbusier designed his first house at 18 and later became famous for his buildings in Berlin, Marseille, and other cities. In 1950 he contributed to the design of the United Nations Secretariat Building in New York. He also was in charge of the design of the Visual Art Center at Harvard University. Although famous primarily for his work as an architect (he was reputedly a master at the unusual applications of molded concrete), Le Corbusier was also well known as an abstract painter.

Jean Henri Dunant (1828–1910) Co-winner of the first Nobel Peace Prize, in 1901, this Swiss humanitarian was the founder of the Red Cross. Greatly affected by his role in caring for the injured soldiers at the Battle of Solferino (Italy 1859), he later wrote *A Souvenir of Solferino.* In it he called for an international organization, without political ties, to aid the wounded in future conflicts. His proposal eventually led to the Geneva Convention governing the treatment of combatants and to the establishment of the International Red Cross.

Friedrich Dürrenmatt (1921–90) Swiss playwright, best known for his grotesque farce *The Visit,* which was filmed with Ingrid Bergman and Anthony Quinn. *The Physicists,* a mordant satire, was also acclaimed; in it, Dürrenmatt chose as his theme the danger posed by one person's possession of nuclear and nuclear-related technology.

Leonhard Euler (1707–83) One of the originators of pure mathematics, Euler, who was born in Basel, was invited by Catherine the Great to study and teach in

Russia. He discovered the law of quadratic reciprocity (1772) in the theory of numbers. His study of the lines of curvature (1760) led to the new branch of differential geometry. Euler conducted massive research in algebra, trigonometry, calculus, and geometry and made discoveries in astronomy, hydrodynamics, and optics.

Alberto Giacometti (1901–66) Swiss sculptor, whose works are characterized by surrealistically elongated forms and are filled with what critics have called "hallucinatory moods." During his early career, Giacometti worked as a painter; in later life, he returned to painting, but his works reflected a sculptural quality, according to critics.

Carl Jung (1875–1961) Swiss psychologist and psychiatrist, who became the founder of analytic psychology. An early associate of Freud, Jung developed concepts of extrovert and introvert personalities and of the collective unconscious. Greatly influenced by artistic and archetypal themes held in common by many primitive societies, he stressed an active role for an analyst during the therapeutic process.

Paul Klee (1879–1940) Swiss modernist painter, one of the most influential artists of the 20th century. Combining abstract elements with recognizable images, Klee painted in a style characterized by fantasy figures in line and light colors. His works are displayed in galleries of modern art all over the world. He was also an accomplished musician.

Ulrich Zwingli (1484–1531) Swiss religious reformer. Zwingli was a Catholic priest before becoming a Protestant minister. Enraged by the values of the 16th-century popes, he led the Protestant Reformation in Switzerland from 1519 until his death. The movement was later bolstered by the arrival of John Calvin in 1536. Zwingli translated the Bible into Swiss German and wrote a testament of Protestant teachings, *On the True and False Religion*. His influence helped transform Geneva into central Europe's most stalwart bastion of 16th-century Protestantism. Zwingli died in Kappel, near Zurich, in a religious war between Catholics and Protestants.

3. ART, ARCHITECTURE & LITERATURE

ART

Switzerland's museums and art collections are known throughout the world. Among them are the Public Art Collection in Basel and the Oskar Reinhart Foundation in Winterthur. Also important are the art museums of Zurich, Bern (including the Klee Foundation), and Geneva, as well as the Avegg Foundation in Bern (Riggisberg) and the Foundation Martin Bodmer (Geneva-Cologny). The Swiss National Museum in Zurich contains valuable exhibits on history and archeology. There are also museums of church treasures and ethnological displays. An International Museum of Horology is located at La Chaux-de-Fonds.

Before about the mid-1700s, the Swiss, a sober and matter-of-fact people, did not regard art with the passion that some of their neighbors did. As a consequence, Swiss painters were not as prominent as those of Italy and France. Sculpture and painting were considered secondary to architecture, useful only as embellishments to the major work of art, the building itself.

Among the major Swiss artists are Salomon Gessner (1730–88), who painted landscapes and mythological scenes, and Anton Graff (1736–1813), a portraitist. Johann Heinrich Füssli (1741–1825) studied in England, where he became known as Henry Fuseli; he later was appointed keeper of the Royal Academy in London. He is best remembered for his visionary painting *The Nightmare.*

Angelica Kauffmann (1741–1807) became the country's most acclaimed neoclassical painter, depicting allegorical, religious, and mythological themes.

Arnold Böcklin (1827–1901) also became widely known in his time. The subjects of his paintings were either extremely light, even frivolous, or else morbidly depressing, as exemplified by his *Island of the Deceased.*

Ferdinand Hodler (1853–1918) was one of the first really significant names to emerge within the world of Swiss art. Some critics have suggested that he "liberated" Swiss painting. He made effective use of color and rhythmic tension. His works are displayed in such museums as the National Museum in Zurich and the Museum of Art and History in Geneva. His gargantuan murals, one of which depicts the *Retreat of the Swiss Following the Battle of Marignano,* remain among his best-known works.

During World War I, Zurich was the setting for the launching of dadaism. This nihilistic movement, which lasted from about 1916 to 1922, was influenced by the absurdities and carnage of the war. It was based on deliberate irrationality and the rejection of laws of social organization and beauty.

⊘ **The two most prominent names in Swiss art are Paul Klee (1879–1940) and Alberto Giacometti (1901–66).**

The most famous artist to come out of Switzerland was Paul Klee (1879–1940). He became a member of the Blaue Reiter, the German expressionist movement, and worked at the Bauhaus in Weimar. His work is characterized by fantasy forms in line and light-toned colors. Klee also combined abstract elements with recognizable images. His paintings achieved an effect of vulnerability and extreme sensitivity. Among his better-known works are *Mask of Fear, Man on a Tightrope, Pastorale,* and *The Twittering Machine.*

The most distinguished sculptor to emerge from Switzerland was Alberto Giacometti (1901–66). His metal figures, as lean and elongated as figures from an El Greco painting, can be seen in museums throughout the world. After 1930, Giacometti became closely associated with the surrealist movement. His sculpture, exemplified by *L'Homme qui marche* (Man Walking), is said to represent "naked vulnerability."

Another eminent sculptor, Jean Tinguely (b. 1925), became known for his kinetic sculptures, which he called "machine sculptures" or "metamechanisms." Some of these works, including *Heureka,* are displayed in Zurichhorn Park in Zurich. One of Tinguely's most controversial creations is *La Vittoria,* a golden phallus 26 feet long.

Graphic art is another area in which Swiss have distinguished themselves. Today, Switzerland is a center of commercial art and advertising.

ARCHITECTURE

Switzerland's architecture has been remarkably well preserved. The country offers superb examples of Roman ruins as well as of medieval churches, monasteries, and castles.

The architecture of Switzerland has always been greatly influenced by the aesthetic

IMPRESSIONS

[Switzerland is] that country which a philosopher would perhaps prefer to the rest of Europe.
—EDWARD GIBBON, 1775

---

development of its neighbors. As a result, it does not have a distinctive "national" style—except in its rural buildings, and perhaps its wood-sided chalets, which have been copied in mountain settings throughout the world.

Much of the country's earliest architecture was built by the Romans. The ruins at Avenches (Helvetia's chief town), with their once formidable 4-mile circuit of walls and their 10,000-seat theater, date from the 1st and 2nd centuries. A.D.

Many buildings were created during the Carolingian period, including the Augustinian abbey of St. Maurice in the Valais. Considered the most ancient monastic house in Switzerland, it dates from the early 6th century. The Benedictine abbey on the island of Reichenau was launched around 725, and from the early medieval period until the 11th century it was the major cultural and educational center in the country.

Two of Switzerland's finest examples of Romanesque architecture are the Benedictine abbey of All Saints, at Schaffhausen (1087–1150), and the Church of St. Pierre de Clages (11th to 12th century). The style of these buildings was followed by the Romanesque-Gothic transitional style of the 12th and 13th centuries, as exemplified by the Cathedral of Chur or by the imposing, 5-aisle Minster of Basel.

In the 15th century, Switzerland adopted the Gothic style, as seen in the Cathedral of Notre-Dame at Lausanne and the Cathedral of St. Pierre in Geneva. In 1421 the Minster of Bern was constructed in the "late Gothic" style, with a 3-aisled, pillared basilica; no transepts were added.

With the coming of the Renaissance, there was an increased emphasis on secular buildings. The best town for viewing the architecture of this period is Murten (Morat), with its circuit of walls, fountains, and towers. During the baroque era, no mammoth public buildings were erected. Instead, domestic buildings were adorned with the ornate curves developed in Austria, Italy, and Germany. Many of the elegant town houses that give Bern its distinctive appearance were constructed during this era.

✪ **A distinctive "national" style may be found in Switzerland's rural buildings, especially the wood-sided chalets.**

In the 19th century, impressive mansions were built in the neoclassical style. They were mostly those of prosperous merchants eager to evince their wealth.

In the 20th century, Switzerland produced a major architect, Le Corbusier (1887–1965), whose influence extended around the world. Known for his functional approach to architecture and city planning, Le Corbusier believed in adapting a building to the climate and to the convenience of both its construction and its intended use. The majority of his most significant works were erected abroad, in Berlin, Paris, Bordeaux, and Marseille, among other cities.

The principle of functionalism is evident in Switzerland's rural houses perhaps come closest to having a distinctive style. Each region evolved its own style as it sought to build houses especially suited for retaining heat in the inhospitable, high-altitude Swiss climate. For example, in Appenzell, where it rains a lot, farm buildings were

IMPRESSIONS

[Switzerland is] the land of wooden houses, innocent cakes, thin butter soup, and spotless little inn bedrooms with a family likeness to dairies.
—CHARLES DICKENS

---

grouped into a single complex. In the Emmental district, a large roof reached down to the first floor on all sides of the building. In the French-speaking section of the Valais, wooden houses were built quite tall and were joined by open-sided galleries opening onto a view of the kitchen compounds. In the Engadine, the timbered center of the house was traditionally enveloped by masonry walls, over which was painted the famous *sgraffito* decoration that newcomers find charming.

LITERATURE

Many 19th-century English writers went to Switzerland for inspiration. Prominent among them were Mary Godwin (who wrote *Frankenstein* beside placid Lake Geneva), Lord Byron, Robert Browning, Henry Wadsworth Longfellow, and Charles Dickens. In the 20th century, Thomas Mann, James Joyce, Hermann Hesse, and Vladimir Nabokov were some of the major writers who gravitated to Switzerland.

Of course, Switzerland has fine literature of its own. Because of the country's different languages, much of Swiss literature has had strong connections with literary traditions and styles in Germany and Austria, in France, and in Italy. Literature produced solely in Switzerland, with few international influences, is usually written in the Rhaeto-Romanic group of local dialects, among them Romansh.

The first writings about Switzerland were in Latin. Caesar's *Commentaries* included the first description of Helvetia (part of present-day Switzerland) and its inhabitants. Later, native Swiss humanists wrote about their country. The most notable was Ägidius Tschudi, magistrate of Glarus, who composed a *Helvetian Chronicle* in the 16th century; it was printed in 1732 in Basel. Friedrich Schiller drew material from it for his drama *William Tell*.

It wasn't until the 18th century that Swiss literature became defined as such. The most important works—except for those by the Geneva-born Rousseau—were written in German. Among them the most famous is the *Codex Manesse*, first published in 1732 (the manuscript is preserved in Heidelberg). It is a collection of the works of 30 different poets, known collectively as the Minnesingers. In the 19th century, Switzerland's national man of letters, Gottfried Keller, made the *Codex* the subject of one of his Zurich novellas.

Writers who emerged in the 18th century include Albrecht von Haller (1708–77), who wrote voluminous works on physiology and other scientific subjects, and Johannes von Müller (1752–1809), whose *History of the Swiss Confederation* inspired Schiller to write *William Tell*. Johann Heinrich Pestalozzi (1746–1827), an educational reformer, wrote about ordinary village life in such stories as *Leonard and Gertrude*.

✪ **Swiss playwrights Friedrich Dürrenmatt (1921–90) and Max Frisch (1911–91) achieved world acclaim for their works.**

In the 1800s two Swiss works were translated around the world. They were

Heidi (1880), by Johanna Spyri, and *The Swiss Family Robinson* (1813), by Johann David Wyss.

Jeremias Gotthelf (pseudonym for Albrecht Bitzius, 1797–1854), a native of the walled city of Murten, wrote simple, sensitive stories of everyday peasant life that inspired key figures of the romantic movement.

Jacob Christoph Burckhardt (1818–97), one of the preeminent historians of the 19th century, is famous for his great classic *The Civilization of the Renaissance in Italy* (1860). He also wrote a study of the age of Constantine the Great. Burckhardt's emphasis on the cultural interpretation of history influenced the German philosopher Friedrich Nietzsche.

Gottfried Keller (1819–90), novelist, poet, and short-story writer, reigned supreme over Swiss literature in the latter part of the 19th century. His works, particularly *Der grüne Heinrich* (Green Henry) and *People of Seldwyla,* are still popular throughout the German-speaking world.

The last German-language poet of international reputation born in Switzerland was Carl Spitteler (1845–1924), whose major allegorical work, *Olympischer Frühling* (Olympian Spring), published before World War I, argued for the need of ethics in the modern world. Spitteler was awarded the Nobel Prize for literature in 1919.

French-Swiss literature is dominated by two towering figures, Jean-Jacques Rousseau (1712–78), the father of continental romanticism and author of *The Social Contract* and the autobiographical *Confessions,* and Germaine (Madame) de Staël (1766–1817), who conducted a famous salon in Paris. During the French Revolution, de Staël sought refuge at the family estate at Coppet, on the shore of Lake Geneva. Her principal work, *De l'Allemagne* (On Germany, 1810), was an encomium of German romanticism. In 1811 she was exiled from France by Napoleon, who objected to the book; she found comfort in her marriage to a young Swiss officer more than 20 years her junior.

In the 20th century, two Swiss literary figures have gained an international following. One is Friedrich Dürrenmatt (1921–90), who is known mainly for his plays *The Visit* and *The Physicists*. The other is Max Frisch (1911–91), who has achieved a place in contemporary German literature with his plays, among them *Andorra* and *The Firebugs,* and his novels. His most famous novel is *Stiller,* a trenchant critique of Swiss smugness and isolationism.

Within the French tradition, Jacques Chessex (b. 1934) has distinguished himself. In 1973 he won the prestigious Paris-based Prix Goncourt for his novel *L'Ogre.*

4. RELIGION, MYTH & FOLKLORE

RELIGION The Protestant Reformation created bitter conflicts in Switzerland between those cantons defending papal Catholicism and those embracing the new creed of Protestantism. Ulrich Zwingli, who, like Martin Luther, had converted from

IMPRESSIONS

No money, no Swiss.
—JEAN RACINE, *LES PLAIDEURS* (THE LITIGANTS), 1668

the Catholic faith, led the Swiss Reformation, beginning in 1519. He translated the Bible into Swiss-German and reorganized church rituals. The Protestant movement was spurred by the arrival in Geneva, in 1536, of John Calvin, who was fleeing Catholic reprisals in France.

Geneva became one of the most rigidly puritanical strongholds of Protestantism in Europe, fervently committed to its self-perceived role as the New Jerusalem. The spread of Calvinism led to the coining of the French term "Huguenot," a corruption of the Swiss word *Eidgenosse* (confederate).

After Zwingli died in a religiously motivated battle in 1531, the famous Swiss spirit of compromise came into play and a peace treaty was signed, allowing each region the right to practice its own faith. Today, 55% of the Swiss define themselves as Protestant, 43% as Roman Catholic, and 2% as members of other faiths.

MYTH The story of William Tell is part of the world's mythology. It relates that sometime in the early 1300s Tell, together with his young son, visited the town of Altdorf, in his native canton of Uri. There, he refused to obey a decree by the hated Hapsburg governor, an Austrian named Gessler, that all Swiss citizens remove their hats in the presence of his hat, which was affixed to a pole in the town square. Tell was arrested and, as punishment, was ordered to shoot an apple off his son's head. Mercifully, he scored a bull's-eye.

Gessler found that Tell had two arrows with him and inquired why. Always to the point (a characteristic of the Swiss), Tell told him that if the first arrow had missed its mark, he would have aimed the second arrow at Gessler's heart. Tell was arrested again and sent by boat to a prison on the opposite side of Lake Lucerne. In transit, a violent storm came up, allowing the Swiss hero to overpower his guards and steer the boat to shore and safety. He later returned in triumph to slay the evil tyrant.

◌ The story of William Tell is an allegory of the Swiss struggle for freedom.

First found in a 15th-century ballad, probably the product of an older oral tradition, the tale of William Tell has appeared in many versions, culminating in 1804 in Schiller's moving drama. It is a fitting allegory to describe the tenacity of the Swiss people in their struggle for freedom.

FOLKLORE Swiss traditions, customs, and legends were passed over the centuries, from village to village by word of mouth and then were transmitted over the alpine passes through commerce. One legend concerns a giant named Offerus, who, it is said, once carried the baby Jesus across a mountain stream. The child grew heavier and heavier, until it appeared to Offerus that he was bearing the burden of the world on his back. It was then that the Christ child revealed himself, and Offerus was baptized on the spot. Later canonized by the Roman Catholic Church (and renamed Saint Christophorus—literally, "Christ-bearing"), Offerus became the patron saint of the alpine passes during the medieval era.

Another story concerns Mauritius, ordered by Rome to lead Theban legions into battle against the Christians in Gaul. He is said to have revolted, along with his legions, in the Valais and to have died a martyr's death. In the Valley of the Rhône, the town of St. Maurice (which developed from an early Roman settlement) honors this Roman general, as does St. Moritz, in the Grisons.

Folk tradition lives on in the regional dress of the Swiss, worn usually by those residing in mountain villages. In the Gruyère, the cheese-making district, herdsmen can be seen wearing the *bredzon,* a canvas jacket with puffed sleeves; at Evolène, in the Valais, working women dress in a simple frock, with a red-and-white kerchief at the neck.

In some parts of Switzerland, the life of the people revolves around the movement of cattle from the shelter of the village to the higher alpine pastures once the weather warms. These beasts, their horns beribboned and covered with flowers, become the centerpiece of what some observers have called a celebration of the rites of spring. The sound of cow bells can be heard for great distances across the valleys. In autumn, the return from the Alps, called *le désalpe,* is another tradition.

In the cities, tradition lives on in the various carnivals and festivals, such as the *Knabenschiessen* at Zurich, the Basel Carnival (masked dances and processions), and the Escalade at Geneva. Sports, too, reflect popular tradition, in such games and events as "wrestling on the grass," stone throwing (or flag throwing), and *Hornuss* (a type of cricket), all of which, of course, require the sound of the alpenhorn to make the tradition complete.

5. CULTURAL & SOCIAL LIFE

PEOPLE   Because the country is a patchwork of ethnic and religious groups, Swiss citizens tend to have a natural tolerance of others and an equally strong intolerance for bureaucracy and autocracy. Perhaps as a result, they are polite but reserved.

Three-quarters of Switzerland's 6,674,000 people reside in the central lowlands between the Alps and the Jura; more than two-fifths live in cities and towns of more than 10,000 residents. There are some 400 inhabitants per square mile.

The bulk of Switzerland's income derives from industry, crafts, and tourism, which together employ more than a million people. Only about 7% of the Swiss are engaged in agriculture and forestry, although the country produces about half of its food supply. Switzerland exports engineering, chemical, and pharmaceutical products, as well as world-famous clocks and watches.

The Swiss have a vastly diverse culture. There are four major linguistic and ethnic groups which overlap each other—German, French, Italian, and Romansh. Despite these variations, however, the Swiss have formed a strong national identity.

LANGUAGES   About 70% of the people speak Swiss-German, or Schwyzerdütsch (*Schweizerdeutsch* in standard German); about 20% speak French; and about 9% speak Italian, mostly in the southern Ticino region. Approximately 1% speak Romansh, a Rhaeto-Romanic dialect that contains a pre-Roman vocabulary and a substratum of Latin elements; it is believed to be the language of old Helvetia and is spoken mainly by people in the Grisons. Most Swiss speak more than one of the four languages. Many also speak English.

SOCIAL LIFE   The Swiss work hard, averaging between 2,000 and 2,300 work hours a year. After work, they like to relax, most often with their families. They tend to read newspapers in the evening, sometimes at a café but most often at home.

In German-speaking Switzerland, many families eat their big meal at noon, so dinner is a light affair—perhaps some Rösti (shredded and fried potatoes) with a glass of wine or a mug of beer, along with a plate of cold cuts and sausage. Many families

IMPRESSIONS

[Switzerland is] small, and like everything within it, so clean that you can hardly breathe for hygiene, and oppressive precisely because everything is right, fitting, and respectable. . . . Everything in this country is of an oppressive adequacy.
—MAX FRISCH

don't drink at all, not even socially, and *alkoholfrei* restaurants exist in every city and town.

Switzerland's younger people like to go out in the evening to a beer hall or a movie. Older couples gather with their friends at the occasional raclette party. Most often the social life in a Swiss home is fairly somber; the average citizen retires early and gets up "with the cows."

Nightclubs that open after midnight can be found mainly in the cities, such as Geneva and Lausanne, where the French influence is strong. Switzerland has a scattering of casinos, called *Kursäle* (singular, *Kursaal*), but since the maximum bet allowed is only 5F ($3.65), they're visited rather for whatever shows, programs, or concerts they happen to be offering at the time.

6. PERFORMING ARTS & EVENING ENTERTAINMENT

Towns of even modest size usually have a resident symphony orchestra and a municipal theater. The theater and concert season runs from September through May. In summer, music and film festivals and folklore displays are presented.

MUSIC   It has often been said that there is really no such thing as Swiss music per se, only music in Switzerland performed by Swiss musicians. There is some validity to this view. Except for its alpine melodies and dance music, Switzerland has made only a modest contribution to the world's repertoire.

Switzerland's leading composer in modern times was Arthur Honegger (1892–1955), who is known for his symphonies, among them *La Symphonie Liturgique* and *Deliciae Basilenses,* as well as other orchestral works. Geneva-born Frank Martin (1890–1974) also received acclaim for his symphonic music. He was an exponent of dodecaphony (12-tone music).

Switzerland has several excellent orchestras and opera companies. The Zurich Opera specializes in German-language productions, and the Grand Théâtre de

IMPRESSIONS

The more one sees of Switzerland, the more one is pleased with the country, and the less one is pleased with the inhabitants.
—HENRY MATTHEWS, *DIARY OF AN INVALID,* 1820

Genève, the country's leading opera house, has a predominantly French-language repertoire. The Orchestre de la Suisse Romande, conducted for 50 years by Ernest Ansermet, is the country's best-known orchestra, and the respected Tonhalle Orchester of Zurich has a loyal following.

Local cultural entertainment is highlighted by the folk music and dancing of the alpine regions, which you can also see and hear in the big cities. These include *Kuhreigen* (round dances), yodeling performances, and a style of dance tunes known as *Ländler,* performed by small orchestras, whose members usually appear in regional costumes.

> ✪ **Switzerland's leading 20th-century composer was Arthur Honegger (1892–1955).**

EVENING ENTERTAINMENT Switzerland's cities offer a variety of evening entertainment. In Zurich the traditional stamping grounds for night owls lie around the Niederdorf, a neighborhood within Old Town known for its strip joints, bars, and music halls. There's even a red-light district. Most nightclubs, however, close at 2am, and many of them seem sterile and a bit boring, at least for people who have traveled widely and gone out a bit. Geneva, too, despite its Calvinist traditions, has a sophisticated nightlife.

It might be more interesting, especially if you're a first-time visitor, to patronize some of the local folkloric places, where you can see and hear yodeling and dancing to alpine music. The beer flows in most of these places. Major Swiss cities also have their international-style bars and discos as well.

Theater presentations tend to be in German or French. So unless you speak either language, these shows may not be for you.

Throughout the winter, the après-ski life in Switzerland's high-altitude resorts might best be described as vigorous, with raclette parties, beer drinking in rustic taverns, sleigh rides, and lots of music, much of it brought in by live groups from Great Britain, France, and Germany or from the United States.

Many after-dark rendezvous joints close down in summer. The Swiss prefer to drink outside, under the summer sky, perhaps in some beer garden, rather than being cooped up inside a deliberately darkened disco.

7. SPORTS & RECREATION

Most people associate Switzerland with year-round skiing. In fact, the abundance of magnificent mountain slopes provides facilities for a variety of snow- and ice-related sports. These include cross-country skiing, skating, ice hockey, curling, tobogganing, and ski-bobbing in winter. In addition, the country offers everything from Swiss-style wrestling to "alpine baseball." Winter skiing, however, is still the main attraction, and as a result, winter is considered to be the high season, with higher prices.

SKIING Skiing is big business in Switzerland—an estimated 40% of the tourist dollar is spent on it. There are more than 1,700 mountain railways and ski lifts, and ski schools, ski instructors, and the best ski equipment in the world are available all over the country. Nearly all resorts have ski-rental shops.

The best-known areas for skiing are the Bernese Oberland, the Grisons, and the Valais. (Skiing facilities will be previewed under these individual chapter headings.)

Warning: Always carry plenty of sun screen, even in winter. Otherwise you might get sunburned because of the intense reflection of sunlight off the snow.

Summer skiing is most often called **glacier skiing.** This sport takes place on glaciers that keep their snow even in July and August. (Ski schools and ski lifts are open in summer.) Glacier skiing is best before lunch, especially in the early-morning hours. The best glacier ski resorts are Zermatt, St. Moritz, Engelberg, Saas-Fee, Gstaad, and Pontresina.

Experienced skiers may wish to take a popular spring ski tour, the **Haute Route,** which crosses the French Alps into Switzerland by various routes; it's a week's tour that can usually be made from March to May. Led by a professional guide, skiers stop overnight and for noon rests at cabins maintained by the Swiss Alpine Club (see "Mountaineering," below, for more information on this club).

Cross-country skiing, or *langlauf,* is the fastest-growing sport in Europe, especially at St. Moritz, Pontresina, and Montana. Those who can't downhill ski can participate in this sport. You go at your own speed and are not at the whim of slope conditions. There are no age limits and no charges for use of the well-marked cross-country trails.

From December 16 to March 31 you can get information on conditions in major ski areas in Switzerland by calling the Swiss National Tourist Office snow report (tel. 212/757-6336 in New York City), 24 hours a day.

For the Nonskier Nonskiers are a growing trend at ski resorts. It's estimated that at such fashionable resorts as Gstaad, Pontresina, Arosa, and Davos, one out of two guests is a nonskier. Most resorts offer a host of other activities, such as sunbathing on mountain terraces, walks through forests, nightclubs, sleigh rides, and sightseeing excursions.

CURLING AND SKATING Curling is another "boom" sport in Switzerland. Curling requires team effort, and is particularly popular at Davos, Villars, Gstaad, and Zermatt.

Ice skating is one of the leading winter sports of Switzerland, and nearly all major resorts have natural ice rinks. Also, there are dozens of artificial ones, of which Davos has the best.

GOLF There are 30 golf courses in Switzerland, found at various altitudes ranging from 700 feet above sea level to 6,100 feet (at St. Moritz). You can thus enjoy your game while viewing beautiful scenery and breathing the bracing Swiss air. Visitors are welcome at local clubs, particularly on weekdays. Golf clubs can be rented at the course's pro shop, and you can get instruction to improve your game if you wish. There are also many miniature golf courses.

TENNIS Tennis is popular, and there are many outdoor and indoor courts all over the country, including those at Saas-Fee and Flims. Most resorts have tennis courts, but if your hotel does not, you can probably use a local club for a nominal fee.

WATER SPORTS You'll find opportunities for swimming at all altitudes in Switzerland, both at beaches along lakes and rivers and in pools. Most beaches are open from June to September or even longer in warmer regions, although the water can be cold in any season. More and more of the big hotels provide heated indoor swimming pools. Sailing, waterskiing, windsurfing, and canoeing are all available.

HORSEBACK RIDING Both St. Moritz and Arosa are good places for horseback riding. Switzerland has 230 riding centers that will rent horses, but amateurs should think twice about riding in the snow.

HANG GLIDING This dangerous and expensive sport is one of Switzerland's newest. The mountains and passes are subject to wind currents that may be exciting but are certainly scary, sometimes even for the most experienced gliders.

FISHING Switzerland's abundant rivers, lakes, and streams provide dedicated anglers with plenty of good fishing. Trout are found in most waters up to altitudes of 6,000 feet, and lake trout have been known to weigh 22 pounds. You need a license to fish, but municipal authorities can get you one easily. Regulations vary from place to place, so to be sure you're legal, inquire at a hotel or local tourist office.

CYCLING Riding a bicycle is both a sport and an economical way of touring the country. You can rent one for a small fee at many railroad stations and turn it in at another station. A bicycle can be transported on a passenger train for a nominal fee. You should reserve a bicycle a day or so in advance at the station from which you plan to start.

The Swiss Touring Club (TCS) maintains 10 cycling centers where you can rent bicycles and get brochures and maps of cycling circuits in the environs of each center. The club will direct you along the least-congested routes, taking you through villages and past castles and manor houses that you might not otherwise discover. Even in remote areas you can usually find someone with good enough English to help you if you have a problem or if you're lost. You can call the TCS in Geneva at 022/737-13-36.

HIKING With 30,000 miles of well-marked and well-maintained walking paths, Switzerland is ideal for hikers. The paths lead through alpine valleys, over lowlands, up hills to meadows, or into the heart of the Alps. Whether you choose a gentle walk or a rigorous trek to the high areas, you will see unspoiled beauty, such as alpine meadows with blooming wildflowers. Many hotels offer walking or hiking excursions.

8. FOOD & DRINK

FOOD

Swiss cuisine is a flavorful blend of German, French, and Italian influences, with traditional specialties based on whatever ingredients are readily available within each particular region. In most restaurants and hotel dining rooms today, menus will list a wide array of international dishes, but you should make an effort to sample some of the local fare.

CHEESE Cheese-making is part of the Swiss heritage. Cattle breeding and dairy farming, concentrated in the alpine areas of the country, have been associated with the region for 2,000 years, since the Romans ate *caseus Helveticus* (Helvetian cheese). In fact, the St. Gotthard Pass was a well-known cattle route to the south as far back as the 13th century. The Swiss, who helped develop the American dairy industry, have exported cheese, cattle, and their expertise to the entire world.

Today, more than 100 different varieties of cheese are produced in Switzerland.

The cheeses, however, are not mass produced—they're made in hundreds of small, strictly controlled dairies, each under the direction of a master cheese maker with a federal degree, to ensure that the product is made according to manufacturing standards and is properly cured to produce its own natural, protective rind.

The cheese with the holes, known as Switzerland Swiss or Emmentaler, has been widely copied, since nobody ever thought to protect the name for use only on cheeses produced in the Emme Valley until it was too late. Other cheeses of Switzerland, many of which have also had their names plagiarized, are Gruyère, Appenzeller, raclette, royalp, and sapsago. The names of several mountain cheeses have also been copied, including sbrinz and spalen, closely related to the *caseus Helveticus* of Roman times.

Fondue   Cheese fondue, which consists of cheese (Emmentaler and natural Gruyère used separately, together, or with special local cheeses) melted in white wine flavored with a soupçon of garlic and lemon juice, is the national dish of Switzerland. Freshly ground pepper, nutmeg, paprika, and Swiss kirsch are among the traditional seasonings. Guests surround a bubbling *caquelon* (an earthenware pipkin or small pot) and use long forks to dunk cubes of bread into the hot mixture, stirring them on the bottom of the pot. Other dunkables are chunks of apples and pears, grapes, cocktail wieners, cubes of boiled ham, shrimp, pitted olives, and tiny boiled potatoes. These morsels are usually secured to the fork by spearing a bread cube after them.

Raclette   This cheese specialty is almost as famous as fondue. Popular for many centuries, its origin is lost in antiquity, but the word "raclette" comes from the French word *racler,* meaning "to scrape off." Although originally raclette was the name of the dish made from the special mountain cheese of the Valais, today it describes not only the dish itself but also the cheese varieties suitable for melting at an open fire or in an oven.

A piece of cheese (traditionally half to a quarter of a wheel of raclette) is held in front of an open fire. As it starts to soften, it is scraped off onto one's plate with a special knife. Diners do not wait until everyone is served, as the unique flavor of the cheese is most delicious when the cheese is hottest. The classic accompaniment is fresh, crusty, homemade dark bread, but the cheese may also be eaten together with potatoes boiled in their skins, pickled onions, cucumbers, or small corncobs. You usually eat raclette with a fork, but sometimes you may need a knife as well.

OTHER REGIONAL SPECIALTIES   The country's ubiquitous vegetable dish is *Röchti* or *Rösti* (hash-brown potatoes). It's excellent when popped into the oven coated with cheese, which melts and turns a golden brown. *Spätzli* (Swiss dumplings) often appear on the menu.

Lake fish is a specialty in Switzerland, with *ombre* (a grayling) and *ombre chevalier* (char) heading the list—the latter a delectable but expensive treat. Tasty alpine lake fish include *trout* and fried filets of tiny *perch.*

Country-cured *sausages* can be found at open markets around the country. The best known is called *Bündnerfleisch,* a specialty in the Grisons. The meat, however, is not cured, but dried in the crisp, dry alpine air. Before modern refrigeration this was the Swiss way of preparing meat for winter consumption. Now Bündnerfleisch is most often offered as an appetizer. Order it at one of the belvedere restaurants at the top of a chair lift on some alpine perch.

The *Bernerplatte* is the classic provincial dish of Bern. For gargantuan appetites, it's a version of the Alsatian choucroûte garnie. If you order this typical farmer's plate, you'll be confronted with a mammoth pile of sauerkraut or French beans, topped with pigs' feet, sausages, ham, bacon, or pork chops.

In addition to cheese fondue, you may enjoy *fondue bourguignonne,* a dish that has become popular around the world. It consists of chunks of meat spitted on wooden sticks and broiled in oil or butter, seasoned according to choice. Also, many establishments offer *fondue chinoise,* made with thin slices of beef and Oriental sauces. At the finish, you sip the broth in which the meat was cooked.

Typical Ticino specialties include *risotto with mushrooms* and a mixed grill known as *fritto misto. Polenta,* made with cornmeal, is popular as a side dish. Ticino also has lake and river fish, such as trout and pike. Pizza and pasta have spread to all provinces of Switzerland; if you're watching your centimes, either one is often the most economical dish on the menu.

Salads often combine both fresh lettuce and cooked vegetables, such as beets. For a unique dish, ask for a *Zwiebelsalat* (cooked onion salad). In spring, the Swiss adore fresh asparagus. In fact, police have been forced to increase their night patrols in parts of the country to keep thieves out of the asparagus fields.

The glory of Swiss cuisine is its *pâtisseries,* little cakes and confections served all over the country in tea rooms and cafés. The most common delicacy is *gugelhupf,* a big cake shaped like a bun and traditionally filled with whipped cream.

DRINK

Never order water, beer, or coffee with fondue, unless you want to horrify your Swiss waiter. White wine is the invariable choice of beverage with such a dish. If you don't like white wine, you might get by with kirsch or tea.

There are almost no restrictions on the sale of alcohol in Switzerland, but prices of bourbon, gin, and scotch are usually much higher than those in the United States, and portions can be skimpy.

WINE Swiss wines are superb. Unlike French wines, they are best when new. Many wines, such as those from the Lake Geneva region, are produced for local consumption. Try a local wine with your meal. But as you are unlikely to be familiar with the various selections, ask your headwaiter for advice.

Most of the wines produced in Switzerland are white, but there are also good rosés and fragrant red wines. Most exported wines are produced in Valais, Lake Geneva, Ticino, and Seeland. However, more than 300 small wine-growing areas are spread over the rest of the country, especially where German dialects are spoken.

In the French-speaking part of Switzerland, two of the best wines are the fruity Fendant and the slightly stronger Johannisberg. In the German-speaking part, you might want to sample one of the dry and light reds, which include Stammheimer, Klevner, and Hallauer. In the Italian-speaking Ticino, red merlot is a fruity, ruby-red wine with a pleasant bouquet.

For information on where to look for wines, and advice on taking some home with you, get in touch with the **Swiss Wine Growers Association,** P.O. Box 1346, 4, avenue Avant-Poste, CH-1001 Lausanne, Switzerland (tel. 021/20-32-31).

BEER Swiss beer is an excellent brew; it is the preferred drink in the German-speaking part of the country. The beer varies in quality. If you want to face a mug of *Helles,* you'll be served a light beer; *Dunkles* is dark beer.

LIQUEUR Swiss liqueurs are tasty and highly potent. The most popular are *kirsch* (the national hard drink, made from the juice of cherry pits), and *Pflümli* (made from plums). *Williamine* is made from fragrant Williams pears. *Träsch* is another form of brandy, made from cider pears. In the Ticino, most locals are fond of the fiery *Grappa* brandy, which is distilled from the dregs of the grape-pressing process.

9. RECOMMENDED BOOKS, FILMS & RECORDINGS

BOOKS

GENERAL

Herald, Christopher. *The Swiss Without Halos* (Greenwood Press, 1948; reprinted 1979). Examines certain less frequently publicized aspects of a complicated national character.

Mikes, George. *Switzerland for Beginners* (André Deutsch, 1987). A portrait in broad brushstrokes, touching on almost everything, from the "gnomes" of Zurich to Swiss feminism.

Schrepfer, Margaret. *Switzerland: The Summit of Europe* (Dillon Press, 1989). The author discusses the geography, history, language, family life, religion, and educational system of Switzerland, with special emphasis on the German-speaking parts of the country.

Schweizerische Zentrale für Handelsforderung (Swiss Office for the Development of Trade). *Focus on Switzerland* (1975). A beautiful set of four volumes, covering Switzerland's geography, political evolution, intellectual and artistic life, and economy.

Steinberg, Jonathan. *Why Switzerland?* (Cambridge University Press, 1976). An attempt to describe the "real" Switzerland, which a short-term visitor may miss. One interesting subject covered is Swiss wealth and why, because of it, Switzerland matters.

HISTORY

Allen, C. J. *Swit...rland's Amazing Railways* (Nelson & Co., 1953). Not only do they run on time, but they're considered engineering triumphs as well.

Bonjour, E., H. S. Offler, and G. R. Potter. *A Short History of Switzerland* (Greenwood Press, 1952; updated, 1985).

LITERATURE

Fringeli, Dieter. *Contemporary German-Language Literature in Switzerland* (Pro Helvetia Press, 1971).

Frisch, Max. *I'm Not Stiller,* translated by Michael Bullock London (Pro Helvetia Press, 1959). Originally titled *Stiller* in German, the novel involves a semi-autobiographical character, who, after expatriating himself to America for many years, returns under a pseudonym and denies to everyone his Swiss origins as an exercise in self-discovery. According to one Swiss literary critic, "Frisch is not against Swiss citizenship . . . but . . . against a Swiss nationality that is so monopolistic it hardly permits of a personal identity."

Monnier, Jean-Pierre. *Contemporary French-Swiss Literature,* translated by Douglas J. Gilliam (Pro Helvetia Press, 1975).

Singleton, Esther, ed. *Switzerland as Described by Great Writers* (Dodd, Mead and Co., 1912). Descriptions of Switzerland's landscapes, social structures, and eccentricities by such varied writers as John Ruskin and Victor Hugo.

Waidson, H. M., ed. *Anthology of Modern Swiss Literature* (St. Martin's Press, 1984). An English-language selection of prose and poetry by 70 Swiss authors, representing all four of the linguistic traditions of Switzerland.

POLITICS

Lloyd, William B., Jr. *Waging Peace: The Swiss Experience* (1958; reprinted by Greenwood Press, 1980).
Rappard, William E. *Collective Security in the Swiss Experience* (1948; reprinted by Greenwood Press, 1984).
Siegfried, André. *Switzerland: A Democratic Way of Life* (1950; reprinted by Hyperion Press, 1980).

TRAVEL

Cooper, James Fenimore. *Excursions in Switzerland* (1836; reprinted in Baudry's European Library, 1986, edited by A. W. Galignani and R. Bentley).
De Beer, Sir Gavin. *Early Travellers in the Alps* (1930; reprinted by October House, 1967). Tales of intrepid hill climbers.
Hardyment, Christina. *Heidi's Alp: One Family's Search for Storybook Europe* (Atlantic Monthly Press, 1987). A true account of a mother's exploration of Switzerland with four "Heidi wannabees" (her daughters).
Potter, F. A., ed. *Boswell on the Grand Tour: Germany and Switzerland* (1764; reprinted by McGraw, 1955). Tales of cold climes and warm inns, as well as anecdotes by Boswell, the famous chronicler of 18th-century English mores, during his high-altitude exploits.
Whymper, Edward. *Scrambles Among the Alps in the Years 1860-1869* (reprinted by Ten-Speed Press, 1981). Accounts by the Englishman who climbed the Matterhorn and helped pave the way for the Swiss alpine tourist industry.

FILMS

Since about 1955 some 500 feature films and documentaries have been released in Switzerland, mostly in French or German and often with English subtitles. Among the most recent are:

La Femme de Rose Hill (The Woman of Rose Hill), directed by Alain Tanner (1989). This somewhat daring (for Switzerland) film depicts the story of a black woman's marriage—for better or worse—to a Swiss peasant in the canton of Vaud.
Leo Sonnyboy, directed by Rolf Lyssy (1989). The "saga" of a confirmed bachelor who enters into a marriage of convenience with a Thai go-go dancer, with predictable and rather zany results.
Nouvelle vague (New Wave), directed by Jean-Luc Godard and starring Alain Delon (1990). The point of this film, in the director's own words, is "to discover and describe, in a romantic way, the very source of love."
Reise der Hoffnung (Journey of Hope), directed by Xavier Koller (1990). Tells the tragic story of a Turkish couple who emigrate illegally "to rich Switzerland."
Die zukünftigen Glückseligkeiten (Future Felicities), directed by Fred van der Kooji (1990). Based on a work by the 17th-century philosopher Thomas Hobbes, the

story, which depicts the "horrors of peace going hand in hand with the horrors of war," is updated to the present day.

RECORDINGS

FOLK & "EVERGREEN" MUSIC

As an introduction to Swiss music, you might try *Hello Switzerland,* produced by Tell Recordings. It has medleys performed by Swiss folklore choruses and yodeling duets, as well as selections of alpenhorn festival music. The album *20 Beliebte Melodien* (20 Beloved Melodies), issued by Helvetia Recordings, contains some of Switzerland's most popular folk songs interpreted by yodeling masters Ruedi Rymann, Adolf Stähli, Franz Stadelmann, the Oberhofen Yodeling Club, and the Vreni Jodeling duet. Rymann, Switzerland's greatest yodeler, has an album of his own, *Das Komponisten-Portrait Ruedi Rymann* (Activ Recordings), offering 16 examples of his superior artistry.

For those wishing a little more oompah, there is *Zoge am Boge im Heugade Obe,* compiled by Activ Recordings. Among the songs in the album are "Schwüzergruess" (Swiss Greetings) by the Heidi Wild Chorus, the "Birewegge (Fruitcake) Polka" by the Streichmusik Alder Band, "Zuberhüttefäscht" (Festival of the Mountain Huts) by the Turi Schellenberg Ländlertrio, and a highly danceable melody (the favorite of Swiss bankers at play), "De Senn uf em Tanzbode" (Peasants on the Dance Floor) by the Streichmusik Alder Band.

No one interested in Swiss folk tunes should omit the country's *Handorgan* (accordion) music. An excellent representation is offered by the Käslin Brothers' Handorgan Duet, whose popular foot-twitching melodies—*schottisch* (melodies to accompany a singing trio) and *Ländler* (melodies for a small band)—are recorded on Phonoplay's *Käslin & Käslin.* Among the selections are "Mirabella Fox" and "Ballantine-Whisky Time."

POPULAR

One group whose music carefully mingles the big-band and the Swiss evergreen traditions is the Geschwister Schmid Band, whose "oldies" album *Grüezi, Grüezi* (produced by Gold Records) is played at reunions and ballrooms across the country. More international in scope is an album called *Dixie-Ländler* by the PS Corporation Engadiner Landlerfründa; it charmingly mixes Swiss evergreen music with Dixieland jazz in such selections as "Bless Was a Cow," "Ory's Creole," and "Adelheidi's Lover."

CLASSICAL

The classical tradition in Switzerland has borrowed so heavily from the musical traditions in neighboring countries that it has few exponents of a genuinely Swiss idiom. A notable exception is composer Arthur Honegger—and even he is claimed jointly by the French. His grand and somber choral work, *King David* (composed in 1921), is available in versions recorded by the Orchestre de la Suisse Romande (London Records) and by the Friburg Collegium Musicum (Christophorus Records).

On the other hand, a wealth of musical tradition has evolved around the alpenhorn, a wind instrument that, whether straight or curved into a more efficient spiral, can measure up to 14 feet in length. An excellent compilation of Swiss alpenhorn music is available from Clavex Records, *In Praise of the Alphorn.* It contains 16 pieces by several artists, performing everything from works by Leopold Mozart (1719–87) and S. von Wartensee (1786–1868) to popular alpine tunes.

Another album is *Cor des Alpes/Alphorn* (Disques Office), with master musician Jozsef Molnar (alpenhorn), Gerhard Foerster (organ), and Charles Aeschlimann (flute); it contains a sampling of melodies from the past 200 years of Swiss musical tradition.

ROCK

Yes, Switzerland has rock and roll, too. Among its most popular performers are Polo Hofer and the Schmetter Band, whose best-selling album *Eden* has been released by Soundservice.

PLANNING A TRIP TO SWITZERLAND

This chapter is devoted to the where, when, and how of your trip—the advance planning required to get it together and take it on the road.

After deciding where to go, most people have two fundamental questions: What will it cost? And what's the best way to get there? Chapter 2 answers those questions and provides additional practical information that a visitor to Switzerland will need.

1. INFORMATION, DOCUMENTS & MONEY

INFORMATION

SWISS NATIONAL TOURIST OFFICE You can get the latest tourist information before you leave home from the nearest branch of the Swiss National Tourist Office. In the United States the SNTO has offices at: 608 Fifth Avenue, New York, NY 10020 (tel. 212/757-5944); 150 North Michigan Avenue, Chicago, IL 60601 (tel. 312/630-5840); 260 Stockton Street, San Francisco, CA 94108 (tel. 415/362-2260); or 222 North Sepulveda Boulevard, Suite 1570, El Segundo, CA 90245 (tel. 213/335-5980). In Canada the SNTO has an office at 154 University Avenue, Suite 610, Toronto, ON M5H 3Y9 (tel. 416/971-9734).

OTHER INFORMATION SOURCES Other useful sources are newspapers and magazines. To find the latest articles on your choice of destination, go to your library and ask for the *Reader's Guide to Periodical Literature*—look for listings under "Switzerland" or under the city or cities you intend to visit.

You may also want to contact the U.S. Department of State for background bulletins. Contact the Superintendent of Documents, **U.S. Government Printing**

Office, Washington, DC 20402 (tel. 202/783-3238), for a list of the background materials available.

A good travel agent can also be a source of information. If you decide to consult one, make sure that the agent is a member of the American Society of Travel Agents (ASTA). If you get poor service from an agent, you can complain to the **ASTA Consumer Affairs Department,** P.O. Box 23922, Washington, DC 20006.

DOCUMENTS
PASSPORTS & VISAS

Every traveler entering Switzerland must have a valid passport, although it is not necessary for North Americans to have a visa if they do not stay longer than 3 continuous months. For information on permanent residence in Switzerland and work permits, contact the nearest Swiss consulate.

SECURING/RENEWING A PASSPORT   In the United States, citizens 18 and older who meet the requirements are granted a 10-year passport. For an application, go to a U.S. post office or federal court office. In addition, there are federal passport agencies in 13 cities that you can visit in person. These include New York, Washington, D.C., Stamford (Conn.), Seattle, Philadelphia, San Francisco, New Orleans, Boston, Honolulu, Chicago, Los Angeles, Miami, and Houston. Youths under 18 are granted a 5-year passport. Children under 13 must have their parents apply for their passport, and teenagers 13 to 16 must also have a parent's permission before applying for a passport. If your passport is 12 years old or older, or was granted to you before your 16th year, you must apply in person at a passport agency, post office, or federal or state court office. Otherwise, you can renew it by mail for $42, or for $27 if you are under 18.

In applying for a passport, you must complete a government passport application form and provide proof of U.S. citizenship—a birth certificate or naturalization papers. An old passport (providing it's not more than a vintage 12 years) is also accepted. You should also have identification with your signature and photograph, such as a driver's license. You'll also need two identical passport-size photographs. You'll wait the longest to receive your passport between mid-March and mid-September; in winter it usually takes only about 2 weeks by mail. Passports can sometimes be issued in an emergency, providing you present a plane ticket with a confirmed seat.

In Canada, citizens seeking a passport may go to one of the nearly two dozen regional offices in such cities as Ottawa and Montréal. Alternatively, you can mail an application to the Passport Office, Section of External Affairs, Ottawa, K1A 0G3. Post offices have application forms. Passports cost Can$25; proof of Canadian citizenship is required, along with two signed identical photographs. Passports have a 5-year validity.

In Great Britain, citizens may apply at one of the regional offices in Liverpool, Newport, Glasgow, Peterborough, and Belfast, or in London if they reside there. You can also apply in person at a main post office. The fee is £15, and the passport is good for 10 years. Documents required include a marriage or birth certificate. Two photos must accompany the application.

In Australia, locals apply at the nearest post office. Provincial capitals and all big cities such as Sydney or Melbourne have passport offices. The fee is Aus$76. The passport is valid for 10 years. Those under 18 may apply for a 5-year passport for Aus$31.

In New Zealand, citizens may go to the nearest New Zealand consulate or passport office to obtain an application and file in person or via mail. Proof of citizenship is required, and the passport is good for 10 years. The fee is NZ$55.50.

In Ireland, you should write in advance to the Passport Office, Setanta Centre, Molesworth Street, Dublin 2, Ireland (tel. 01/780-822). The cost is IR£35. Applications will be sent by mail, outlining requirements and procedures to follow. Irish citizens living in North America can contact the Embassy of the Republic of Ireland, 2234 Massachusetts Avenue NW, Washington, DC 20008 (tel. 202/462-3939). The embassy can issue a new passport or direct you to one of the three North American consulates that have jurisdiction over a particular region. The cost of an Irish passport, if arranged by mail through Irish consulates, is US$65. If a citizen applies in person, there is a discount of $5.

DOCUMENT PROTECTION   Before leaving your country, you should make two copies of your most valuable documents, including your passport, in case the originals are lost or stolen abroad. Make a photocopy of the inside page of your passport, the one with your photograph. Also, make copies of your driver's license, international driver's license, airline ticket, strategic hotel vouchers, and any other sort of identity card that might be pertinent, such as a youth hostel card. If you're on medication, you should also make copies of prescriptions. Place one copy in your luggage (presuming you're carrying the original on your person) and leave the other copy at your home.

SWISS CUSTOMS

You can take personal effects into Switzerland, such as clothing, toilet articles, sports gear, photographic and amateur movie or video cameras (including film), music instruments, and camping equipment. Medicine must be for your personal use only. You can also take 2 U.S. quarts of alcohol up to 15% proof or 1 quart more than 15% proof. You are also allowed 400 cigarettes, 100 cigars, or 500 grams of tobacco if you're flying in from outside Europe. Those entering from other European countries are allowed 200 cigarettes, 50 cigars, or 250 grams of tobacco.

MONEY

The prices you'll come across in Switzerland are at least as high as those found in the United States. Nevertheless, this book, even as it documents the best hotels, restaurants, and attractions in Switzerland, will try to help you stretch your dollar power—to show you that you don't need to pay scalper's prices for charm, top-grade comfort, and gourmet food. They reflect a standard of living that's among the highest in the world.

There are many bargains, only don't expect to find them in the expensive cities of Zurich and Geneva or in such favored resorts as St. Moritz and Arosa. If you're watching your budget, try to stay in small villages, such as Klosters, on the periphery of celebrated resorts.

CASH/CURRENCY   The basic unit of Swiss currency is the **Swiss franc (F),** which is made up of 100 centimes. Banknotes are issued in denominations of 10, 20, 50, 100, 500 and 1,000 francs, and coins are minted as 5, 10, 20, and 50 centimes, and 1, 2, and 5 francs.

TRAVELER'S CHECKS   Before leaving home, purchase traveler's checks and arrange to carry some ready cash. (U.S. citizens should take about $200 in cash as a safeguard against unforeseen problems.)

THE SWISS FRANC & THE U.S. DOLLAR

At this writing, US$1 = approximately 1.37 Swiss francs (or 1 franc = 73¢), and this was the rate of exchange used to calculate the dollar values given in this chapter (rounded off). The exchange rate fluctuates from time to time and thus may not be the same when you travel to Switzerland. Therefore, the following table should be used only as a guide:

F	US$	F	US$
1	.73	30	21.90
2	1.46	40	29.20
3	2.19	50	36.50
4	2.92	75	54.74
5	3.65	100	72.99
6	4.38	125	91.24
7	5.11	150	109.49
8	5.84	200	127.74
9	6.57	250	182.48
10	7.30	300	218.98
15	10.95	400	291.97
20	14.60	500	364.96
25	18.25	600	437.96

American Express (tel. toll free 800/221-7282 in the United States and Canada) is the most widely recognized traveler's check abroad; the agency imposes a 1% commission. Checks are free to members of the American Automobile Association.

Bank of America (tel. toll free 800/227-3460 in the United States; or call 415/624-5400 collect from Canada) also issues checks in U.S. dollars for a 1% commission everywhere but in California.

Citicorp (tel. toll free 800/645-6556 in the United States; or call 813/623-1709 collect from Canada) issues checks in U.S. dollars, British pounds, or German marks.

MasterCard International (tel. toll free 800/223-9920 in the United States; or call 212/974-5696 collect from Canada) issues checks in about a dozen currencies.

Barclays Bank (tel. toll free 800/221-2426 in the United States and Canada) issues checks in both U.S. and Canadian dollars and British pounds.

Thomas Cook (tel. toll free 800/223-7373 in the U.S.; or call 212/974-5696 collect from Canada) issues checks in U.S. or Canadian dollars or British pounds. It's affiliated with MasterCard.

Each of these agencies will refund your checks if they are lost or stolen, provided you can produce sufficient documentation or their serial numbers. Of course, your documentation should be carried in a safe place—never along with your checks. When purchasing checks from one of the banks listed, ask about refund hotlines; American Express and Bank of America have the greatest number of offices around the world. Purchase checks in a variety of denominations—$20, $50, and $100.

Swiss banks may ask up to 5% to convert your checks into francs. Note, also, that you always get a better rate if you cash traveler's checks at the banks issuing them: VISA at Barclays, American Express at American Express, and so forth.

CREDIT CARDS Credit cards are in wide use in Switzerland. Both American Express and Diners Club are widely recognized. If you see the Eurocard sign or Access displayed at an establishment, it means that the establishment accepts MasterCard.

Credit cards can save your life when you're abroad, sparing your valuable cash and giving financial flexibility for large purchases or last-minute changes.

Of course, you may make a purchase with a credit card thinking that the amount in local currency will be converted into dollars at a certain rate, only to find that the dollar has declined by the time your bill arrives and you're actually paying more for what you purchased. But that is the chance you take. It can also work in your favor.

CURRENCY EXCHANGE

Despite the status of the U.S. dollar as the most widely distributed currency in the world, many hotels in Switzerland will not accept a dollar-denominated check; and if they do, be assured that they'll deduct some substantial conversion charges. In some instances, you can pay with countersigned traveler's checks or perhaps with the imprint on a credit card; but if you're prepaying a deposit, say, on a hotel reservation, it's cheaper and easier for all concerned if you pay with a check drawn on a Swiss bank.

The easiest way to arrange for a transaction of that kind is through a large commercial bank with a correspondent relationship in Switzerland. One such organization is **Ruesch International,** 1350 Eye Street, Washington, DC, 20005 (tel. 202/408-1200, or toll free 800/424-2923). Fully endorsed by many of the Swiss-based organizations recommended in this guidebook, Ruesch performs a wide variety of conversion-related tasks, usually for only $2 (U.S.) per transaction.

If you need a check payable in Swiss francs, call Ruesch's toll-free number, describe what you need, and note the transaction number given to you. Mail your dollar-denominated personal check (payable to Ruesch International) to its office in Washington, D.C. Upon receipt, the company will mail a check denominated in Swiss francs for the financial equivalent, minus the $2 charge, payable at any branch of the Swiss Bank Corporation, one of Europe's fiscal giants. The company also sells traveler's checks denominated in Swiss francs. It will mail brochures and information packets upon request.

WHAT WILL IT COST?

Switzerland is one of the most expensive countries in the world. In Geneva or Zurich, for example, two people in a double room can spend $240 and up a night in a hotel rated expensive, $100 to $180 in a moderately priced establishment, and $65 to $85 in a hotel judged inexpensive. Likewise, dinner in an expensive restaurant will cost at least $50 per person without wine, or $35 in a medium-priced establishment. Any dinner $25 or under is considered inexpensive.

If you want to see the country without breaking your travel budget, you will need to cut short your stay in these cities and spend more time in regional capitals, such as St. Gallen in the northeast, where you can reduce your travel costs from 20% to 40%. To keep costs trimmed, try to avoid expensive luxuries (in Switzerland that means whisky and taxis, among other items). You can purchase a moderately priced rail pass and see a good part of provincial Switzerland in a short time.

Generally, you get good value for your money in Switzerland, where the inflation rate remains low. Hotels are clean and comfortable, and restaurants offer a good cuisine, with ample portions. The trains run on time, and they're fast; and most service personnel treat you with respect, even though they may not be overfriendly.

Many people visit Switzerland just for its winter sports. The most expensive resorts are St. Moritz, Verbier, Gstaad, Davos, and Arosa. You can still enjoy winter fun, all at a moderate cost, if it's not important to you to be seen in chic places. At about two-thirds the price—or even less—you can patronize some of the less fabled winter spots. This guide previews dozens of winter resorts where the skiing is spectacular but the prices aren't.

WHAT THINGS COST IN ZURICH — US$

Taxi from the airport to the city center	32.00
Average tram ride within the city limits	.85
Local telephone call	.35
Double room at Baur au Lac (deluxe)	315.00
Double room at the Hotel Glockenhof (moderate)	190.00
Double room at the Hotel Bristol (budget)	103.00
Lunch for one, without wine, at Mère Catherine (moderate)	18.00
Lunch for one, without wine, at Augustiner (budget)	14.60
Dinner for one, without wine, at Nouvelle (deluxe)	90.00
Dinner for one, without wine, at Ribó (moderate)	35.00
Dinner for one, without wine, at Le Dézaley (budget)	20.00
Glass of wine	2.75
Coca-Cola	2.10
Cup of coffee	1.75
Roll of 100 ASA color film, 36 exposures	4.50
Admission to the Kunsthaus Museum	2.90
Movie ticket	9.00
Theater ticket (at Theater am Hechtplatz)	18.25

WHAT THINGS COST IN LUCERNE — US$

Average taxi ride	8.00
Local telephone call	.25
Double room at the Carlton Hotel Tivoli (deluxe)	235.00
Double room, with bath, at the Continental & Park (moderate)	103.00
Double room, without bath, at the Pension Villa Maria (budget)	59.00
Continental breakfast for one in a hotel	8.50
Lunch for one at Chez Marianne (deluxe)	32.00
Lunch for one at Eichhof (moderate)	17.50
Lunch for one at Wiener Café (budget)	13.15
Dinner for one, without wine, at Old Swiss House (deluxe)	40.15
Dinner for one, without wine, at China Restaurant (moderate)	25.55
Dinner for one, without wine, at Wirtshaus Galliker (budget)	20.00

	US$
Pint of beer (draft pilsner)	4.65
Coca-Cola	1.90
Cup of coffee	1.60
Roll of Kodacolor film, 36 exposures	4.00
Admission to Kunstmuseum	2.90
Movie ticket	8.50

2. WHEN TO GO

CLIMATE The temperature range is about the same as in the northern United States, but without the extremes of hot or cold. Summer temperatures seldom rise above 80°F in the cities, and the humidity is low. Because of clear air and lack of wind in the high alpine regions, sunbathing is possible even in winter. In southern Switzerland the temperature is mild year round, allowing subtropical vegetation to grow.

For a driving tour of Switzerland, June is the ideal month, followed by either September or October, when the mountain passes are still open. In summer the country is often overrun with visitors.

Switzerland's Average High & Low Temperatures (°F)

		Jan	Feb	Mar	Apr	May	June	July	Aug	Sept	Oct	Nov	Dec
GENEVA	High	40	43	50	59	67	74	77	76	70	58	47	40
	Low	29	31	36	41	49	56	59	58	54	45	38	32
INTERLAKEN	High	36	43	50	59	67	72	74	72	68	59	47	38
	Low	23	27	32	38	43	50	54	52	49	41	34	27
LUCERNE	High	43	43	50	58	65	70	76	77	70	52	47	41
	Low	34	32	36	40	49	52	58	59	54	41	38	32
LUGANO	High	43	49	56	63	70	77	81	81	74	61	52	45
	Low	29	31	38	45	50	58	61	59	56	47	38	32
MONTREUX	High	47	46	49	58	65	70	77	76	70	56	49	41
	Low	36	32	36	41	50	54	59	61	56	43	40	32
ST. MORITZ	High	29	34	38	45	50	59	63	61	58	50	38	31
	Low	11	13	18	25	32	40	41	41	38	31	22	14
ZERMATT	High	26	26	27	36	46	52	58	53	52	38	33	26
	Low	20	19	19	28	36	42	48	44	42	32	27	20
ZURICH	High	36	41	50	59	67	74	77	76	68	58	45	38
	Low	27	29	34	40	47	54	58	56	52	43	36	29

Current Weather Conditions American Express Travel Related Service Company provides hourly updated reports on current weather conditions and 3-day forecasts for more than 600 cities in Europe. For Switzerland, dial 1-900/WEATHER (there's a charge for the call) and press the first three letters of the desired city: BAS (Basel), BER (Bern), GEN (Geneva), LUC (Lucerne), STM (St. Moritz), or VAD (Vaduz, Liechtenstein).

HOLIDAYS The legal holidays in Switzerland are New Year's (Jan 1-2), Good Friday, Easter Monday, Ascension Day, Whit Monday, Bundesfeier (the Swiss "Fourth of July"; Aug 1), and Christmas (Dec 25-26).

SWITZERLAND CALENDAR OF EVENTS

The festivals mentioned below, unless otherwise specified, fall on different dates every year. Inquire at the Swiss National Tourist Office or at local tourist offices for an updated calendar.

JANUARY TO MARCH

☐ **Vogel Gryff Festival** (The Feast of the Griffin), Basel. The "Wild Man of the Woods" appears on a boat, followed by a mummers' parade. Mid-January.
☐ **Basler Fasnacht,** Basel. Called "the wildest of carnivals," with a parade of "cliques" (clubs and associations). First Monday after Ash Wednesday.
☐ **Hornussen** ("meeting on the snow"), Maloja. A traditional sport of rural Switzerland. Mid-March.

APRIL TO JUNE

☐ **Primavera Concertistica Music Festival,** Locarno. Beginning a series of music concerts lasting through October. Mid-April.
☐ **Corpus Christi.** Solemn processions in the Roman Catholic regions and towns of Switzerland. End of May.
☐ **Fête à Lausanne,** Lausanne. Beginning of international festival weeks of music and ballet. Mid-June.

JULY TO SEPTEMBER

☐ **Wrestling and Alpine Headmen's Festival** of central Switzerland, Schwyz. July 1.
☐ **William Tell Festival Play,** Interlaken. Performances of the famous play by Schiller. End of July through August.
☐ **International Music Festival,** Lucerne. Concerts, theater, art exhibitions. Mid-August.
☐ **À la rencontre du monde,** Fribourg. International folklore festival. September 1.

OCTOBER TO DECEMBER

☐ **Wine Growers' Festival,** Lugano. A parade marks harvest time. October 6.
☐ **Zibeemärit,** Bern. The famous "onion market" fair. Mid-November.
☐ **Christmas Festivities.** Ancient St. Nicholas parades and traditional markets are

staged throughout the country to mark the beginning of Christmas observances. Major one at Fribourg. Mid-December.

GENEVA
CALENDAR OF EVENTS

AUGUST

☐ **Fêtes de Genève.** Highlights are flower parades, fireworks, and live music all over the city. Early August.

SEPTEMBER

☐ **Festival du Bois de la Batie.** Attracts thousands of young people who listen to live pop and rock groups. Early September.

DECEMBER

✪ *L'ESCALADE   A festival commemorating the failure of the duke of Savoy's armies to take Geneva by surprise on the night of December 11–12, 1602. Brigades on horseback in period costumes, country markets, and folk music are interspersed with Rabelaisian banquets, fife-and-drum parades, and torchlight marches.*

Where: Old Town provides the best vantage point. When: 3 days and nights nonstop in mid-December. How: A schedule of Escalade events is available at the Geneva Tourist Office's information service at Gare de Cornavin.

ZURICH
CALENDAR OF EVENTS

APRIL

✪ *SECHSELÄUTEN   ("Six O'Clock Ringing") A centuries-old guild parade marking the arrival of spring. Members of various guilds in folkloric costumes, along with children's parades celebrate the event, which is climaxed by the burning of Böögg, a straw figure symbolizing winter.*

Where: The Zurich Tourist Office will trace the parade route on a map. Böögg is burned at 6pm on Sechseläutenplatz, near Belevueplatz. When: Third Monday of April. How: A street event open to everyone (no tickets required).

JUNE

☐ **International Zurich June Festival.** Concerts, performances, art exhibits, and masters classes. Sometime in June.

3. HEALTH & INSURANCE

HEALTH

VACCINATIONS Medical care and health facilities in Switzerland are among the best in the world. As a result, no endemic contagious diseases exist. Swiss authorities, however, require immunization against contagious diseases if you have been in an infected area during the 14-day period immediately preceding your arrival in Switzerland.

MEDICATIONS Take along an adequate supply of any prescription drugs that you need, as well as a written prescription that uses the generic name—rather than the brand name—of the drugs (in general, French and German, not U.S., drugs are available in Switzerland). Also, consult your local pharmacist about taking with you over-the-counter drugs, such as Metamucil. Put together your own personal medical kit: aspirin, Band-Aids, nose drops, first-aid cream, insect repellant, and the like. If you're affected by the motion of a plane or train, include some motion-sickness medicine as well.

Be sure to carry your vital medicines and drugs with you in your carry-on luggage, in case your checked luggage is lost.

COMMON TRAVEL AILMENTS Travelers, no matter what country they visit, should exercise caution with respect to what they eat and drink. In Switzerland the tap water is generally safe to drink, but don't drink out of mountain streams or rivers—regardless of how clear and clean they appear to be. Sometimes travelers find that a change in sleeping patterns or a change in diet will lead to diarrhea or constipation. If an attack of diarrhea occurs, drink plenty of fluids (mineral water is recommended) to avoid dehydration, increase your intake of salt to help your body retain fluids, and eat only simply prepared foods, such as plain bread, boiled vegetables, and broth (avoid dairy products, except yogurt). If you experience constipation, eat a high-fiber diet and drink plenty of mineral water; avoid large meals and don't drink wine.

FINDING A DOCTOR If a medical emergency arises while you're in Switzerland, your **hotel staff** can usually put you in touch with a reliable doctor. If it can't, then call your country's **embassy or consulate;** each maintains a list of suitable English-speaking doctors.

Before you leave home, you can obtain a list of English-speaking doctors in Switzerland from the **International Association for Medical Assistance to Travelers (IAMAT),** with offices in the United States at 417 Center Street, Lewiston, NY 14092 (tel. 716/754-4883), and in Canada at 188 Nicklin Road, Guelph, ON N1K 1B5 (tel. 519/836-0102).

MEDIC ALERT If your medical condition is chronic, talk to your doctor before taking an international trip. If you have a specific condition—epilepsy, heart affliction, diabetes, allergies to certain drugs—always wear a Medic Alert identification tag: It will immediately alert any doctor to the nature of your trouble. The tag also provides the number of Medic Alert's 24-hour hotline so that a foreign doctor can obtain your medical records. For a lifetime membership, the cost is a well-spent $30. Contact the **Medic Alert Foundation,** P.O. Box 1009, Turlock, CA 95381-1009 (tel. toll free 800/432-5378).

INSURANCE

GENERAL TRAVEL INSURANCE Insurance needs for the traveler fall into three broad categories: (1) health and accident, (2) trip cancellation, and (3) lost luggage.

Before setting out to purchase any travel insurance, review your current homeowner's, automobile, and medical insurance policies, and also check the contracts of any credit cards you use and the membership contracts of all automobile and travel clubs to which you belong—you may already have adequate coverage for your needs.

Many credit-card companies insure their users in case of a travel accident, providing that the travel cost was paid with their card. Sometimes fraternal organizations have policies that protect members in case of sickness or accidents abroad.

Incidentally, don't assume that Medicare is the answer to illness in Switzerland. It covers U.S. citizens who travel south of the border to Mexico or north of the border to Canada. Canadians, however, are generally protected with their health insurance plans in their individual provinces.

Many homeowner's insurance policies cover theft of luggage during foreign travel and loss of such documents as your Eurailpass, passport, and airline ticket. Coverage is usually limited to about $500. To submit a claim on your insurance, remember that you'll need police reports or a statement from a local medical authority that you did, in fact, suffer the loss or experience the illness for which you are seeking compensation. Such claims, by their very nature, can be filed only when you return from Switzerland.

Some insurance policies, on the other hand—and these are the types you should have—provide advances in cash or arrange transferrals of funds so that you won't have to dip into your precious travel funds to settle medical bills.

If you have booked a charter flight and then suddenly cancel your trip, you will probably have to pay a cancellation fee, even if your cancellation is due to an unforeseen crisis. You can, however, get insurance against such a possibility. Some travel agencies provide this coverage. Often flight insurance against a canceled trip is written into tickets paid for by credit cards from such companies as VISA or American Express. Many tour operators and insurance agents provide this type of insurance for a reasonable additional supplement.

Among the companies offering such policies are:

Travel Guard International, 1145 Clark St., Stevens Point, WI 54481 (tel. toll free 800/826-1300 in the United States), offers a comprehensive 7-day policy that covers basically everything: emergency assistance, accidental death, trip cancellation and interruption, medical coverage abroad, and lost luggage. The cost of the package is $52. There are restrictions, however, which you should understand before you accept the coverage.

Travel Insurance Pak, Travelers Insurance Co., 1 Tower Square, 15 NB, Hartford, CT 06183-5040 (tel. 203/277-2318, or toll free 800/243-3174), offers illness and accident coverage, costing from $10 for 6 to 10 days. For lost or damaged luggage, $500 worth of coverage costs $20 for 6 to 10 days. You can also get trip cancellation insurance for $5.50.

Mutual of Omaha (Tele-Trip), 3201 Farnam Street, Omaha, NE 68131 (tel. 402/345-2400, or toll free 800/228-9792), charges $3 and up a day (with a 10-day minimum) to provide foreign medical coverage up to $50,000. The company features global assistance and maintains a 24-hour hotline. It also offers trip cancellation insurance, lost or stolen luggage coverage, the standard accident coverage, and other policies.

TRAVEL ASSISTANCE Several companies offer policies to cover travelers stranded abroad in some emergency; each maintains a toll-free 800 number for out-of-state callers. Some are:

HealthCare Abroad (MEDEX), 243 Church Street NW, Suite 100D, Vienna, VA 22180 (tel. 703/255-9800, or toll free 800/237-6615). One policy, good for 10 to 90 days, costs $3 a day and includes accident and sickness coverage of $100,000. Medical evacuation is also included, along with a $25,000 accidental death or dismemberment compensation. Trip cancellation and lost or stolen luggage can also be written into this policy at a nominal cost.

WorldCare Travel Assistance Association, 605 Market Street, Suite 1300, San Francisco, CA 94105 (tel. 415/541-4991, or toll free 800/666-4993), features a policy covering 9 to 15 days and costing $105, that includes trip cancellation, lost or stolen luggage, legal assistance, and medical coverage and evacuation.

Access America, 600 Third Avenue (P.O. Box 807), New York, NY 10163-0807 (tel. 212/949-5960, or toll free 800/955-4002), has a 24-hour hotline in case of an emergency. This is a good company for those wanting family or individual policies. Medical coverage for 9 to 15 days costs $49 for $10,000 of coverage. If you want medical plus trip cancellation, the charge is $89 for 9 to 15 days. A comprehensive package for $111 grants 9 to 15 days of blanket coverage, including $50,000 worth of death benefits.

4. WHAT TO PACK

The Swiss, in their choice of attire, are both stylish and conservative. In Geneva or Zurich, locals go to the office, to a restaurant, or to the theater wearing well-tailored suits and smart yet simple dresses. You can follow their lead. Men will feel comfortable in suits or sports jackets of a weight appropriate to the season (ties are advisable in the poshest places). Women will fit in whether they wear suits, skirts, or dresses. The watchword is understatement. You can even wear your designer jeans—but not, of course, everywhere.

In deciding what clothes to take with you on a trip, you should consider, first, where you're going and, second, at what time of year. Obviously, you'll need to pack different suitcases for a winter ski holiday in the Swiss Alps and a summer visit to the Ticino. Here are some guidelines:

Always pack as lightly as possible. Sometimes it's hard to find a porter or a baggage cart in railroad and airline terminals. Also, airlines are becoming increasingly strict about how much luggage passengers can take aboard—not only carry-on items but checked suitcases as well—particularly when flights are fully booked (or overbooked). Checked baggage may not exceed 62 inches (width plus length plus height) or weigh more than 70 pounds. Carry-on luggage may not exceed 45 inches and must be able to fit under the passenger's seat or in the bin above.

The general rule in packing is to include four of everything: four pairs of socks or stockings, four pairs of slacks or four skirts or dresses, four shirts or blouses, and four sets of underwear. At any given moment, at least two of these will be either in need of washing or in the process of drying after you've washed them. (Since it's not always possible to get pressing done at hotels, be prepared to wash your lightweights in your bathroom and hang them up to dry overnight.) Often you'll have to wrap semiwet clothes in a plastic bag as you head for your next destination.

Take at least one outfit for chilly weather and one outfit for warm weather. Even in the summer you may suddenly experience chilly weather while driving in the Alps; conversely, in the Ticino in the middle of February you may find yourself feeling overdressed in your woolens. Also, whatever the season, take a raincoat and an umbrella with you. Finally, take along two pairs of shoes for walking in the street during the day; you may get your shoes soaked and need that extra pair.

You should have a wardrobe that travels well. For sightseeing, wear casual clothes and comfortable shoes (especially if you plan to take several of the recommended walking tours). Don't plan to tour Switzerland in a pair of shorts—you'll be denied entry to some of the country's prime attractions, churches and cathedrals, if you're so attired. Modesty also dictates that you always wear a cover-up when you leave the beach to promenade along lakeside quays.

If you plan to visit casinos or posh nightclubs, dress up. For women, that means casually chic—perhaps a cocktail dress.

5. TIPS FOR SPECIAL TRAVELERS

FOR THE DISABLED   In making travel arrangements in Switzerland, you may find the following information useful:

* A fact sheet and special hotel guide for the disabled is available from the Swiss National Tourist Office.
* On Swiss trains, wheelchair passengers travel in a special section of the passenger car. Certain trains cannot accommodate them there, in which case they would travel in a specified area of the luggage car.
* Hertz Rent-a-Car offers minibuses accessible to wheelchair passengers. Arrangements should be made well in advance with Hertz AG, Lagerstrasse 33, 8021 Zurich (tel. 01/241-8077).
* A car-rental company for wheelchair-bound drivers is **Schweizerische Paraplegiker Vereinigung** (Swiss Paraplegic Association), Langsagestrasse 2, 6010 Kriens (tel. 041/42-11-07).

There are many agencies that provide advance data to help you plan your trip. One is the **Travel Information Service,** Moss Rehabilitation Hospital, 12th Street and Tabor Road, Philadelphia, PA 19141 (tel. 215/456-9900), which charges $5 a package for its data. Each package contains the names and addresses of accessible hotels, restaurants, and attractions, often provided by travelers themselves.

You may want to subscribe to **The Itinerary,** P.O. Box 2012, Bayonne, NJ 07002-2012 (tel. 201/858-3400), at $10 a year. This bimonthly travel magazine is filled with news about travel aids and special tours for the handicapped, as well as information on accessibility and other matters.

You can also obtain a free copy of **Air Transportation of Handicapped Persons,** published by the U.S. Department of Transportation. Write: Free Advisory Circular No. AC12032, Distribution Unit, U.S. Department of Transportation, Publications Division, M-4332, Washington, DC 20590.

There are several tours specifically for disabled visitors. To obtain the names and addresses of the operators of such tours, contact the **Society for the Advancement of Travel for the Handicapped,** 347 Fifth Avenue, New York, NY 10016 (tel. 212/447-7284); send a stamped self-addressed envelope. Yearly membership dues in the society are $40 ($25 for seniors and students).

You may also consider the **Federation of the Handicapped,** 211 West 14th Street, New York, NY 10011 (tel. 212/206-4200), which offers summer tours for members, who pay a yearly fee of $4.

For the blind, the best source of travel information is the **American Foundation for the Blind,** 15 West 16th Street, New York, NY 10011 (tel. toll free 800/232-5463). Among the information provided are the requirements that various countries have for allowing in seeing-eye dogs. The federation also issues identification cards for those who are legally blind for a $6 fee.

FOR SENIORS Many discounts are available for seniors (women over age 62 and men over 65). Be advised, however, that you often have to be a member of an association to obtain certain discounts.

Some 450 hotels in almost 200 Swiss towns and resorts offer special off-season rates for seniors. When making a reservation, you should indicate that you are a senior and present your passport or ID card at the hotel desk upon arrival. A special guide, **"Season for Seniors,"** listing all the participating hotels can be obtained from the Swiss National Tourist Office.

For $1 you can get a booklet **"Travel Tips for Senior Citizens"** (#8970), published by the Superintendent of Documents, U.S. Government Printing Office, Washington, DC 20402 (tel. 202/783-5238). Another useful publication is **"101 Tips for the Mature Traveler,"** distributed free by Grand Circle Travel, 347 Congress Street, Suite 3A, Boston, MA 02210 (tel. 617/350-7500, or toll free 800/221-2610).

SAGA International Holidays, 120 Boylston Street, Boston, MA 02116 (tel. toll free 800/343-0273), is well known for its all-inclusive tours for seniors (60 and over). It includes insurance in the net price of any of its tours. Membership is $5 a year.

The best organization for seniors in the United States is the **American Association of Retired Persons (AARP),** 1909 K Street NW, Washington, DC 20049 (tel. 202/872-4700). Members are offered discounts on car rentals, hotels, and airfares, even sightseeing in some cases. AARP travel arrangements, featuring senior discounts, are handled by American Express. In the U.S. telephone toll free 800/927-0111 for land arrangements or 800/745-4567 for cruises. Flights to various destinations are handled by either of these toll-free numbers.

Information on travel for seniors is also available from the **National Council of Senior Citizens,** 1331 F Street, NW, Washington, DC (tel. 202/347-8800). A nonprofit organization, the council charges a membership fee of $12 ($16 for couples), for which you receive a monthly newsletter containing travel tips. Reduced discounts on hotel and auto rentals are also provided.

FOR SINGLES The 1990 U.S. census showed that 77 million Americans over age 15 are single. A major company that matches single travelers with like-minded companions is **Travel Companion,** P.O. Box P-833, Amityville, NY 11701 (tel. 516/454-0880). The German-born founder, Jons Jurgen, charges $36 to $66 for a 6-month listing of potential companions (of either sex). Members fill out a form stating their preferences. Write for an application and more information.

Singleworld, 401 Theodore Fremd Avenue, Rye, NY 10580 (tel. 914/967-3334, or toll free 800/223-6490), is a travel agency that operates tours geared to solo travel. Two basic types of tours are available: youth-oriented tours for people under 35 and jaunts for those of any age. Annual dues are $25.

Another agency to check is **Grand Circle Travel,** 347 Congress Streets, Boston, MA 02210 (tel. 617/350-7500, or toll free 800/221-2610), which offers escorted tours and cruises for retired people, including singles. Once you book a trip, you become a member and receive vouchers providing discounts for future trips.

FOR FAMILIES   If you're planning to take your family abroad, you'll have to do some planning. If you have a small child, you may want to discuss your vacation plans with your family doctor. In the meantime, make a note to take along such standard home medical supplies as children's aspirin, a thermometer, and Band-Aids.

If you want the airline to provide a special menu for your children, you must request it at least 24 hours in advance. If your child requires baby food, take along your own and ask a flight attendant to warm it to the right temperature.

Take along a "security blanket" for your child. This may be any object—a pacifier, a favorite toy—that, by its familiarity, will be a comfort to the child amid the strange surroundings.

You will need to pack some protection against the sun, especially in summer if you're visiting alpine resorts, where the noonday sun can be intense. A sun umbrella, may be enough for tiny tots; the rest of the family will need sunscreen and sunglasses.

Arrange ahead of time for such necessities as a crib, bottle, warmer, and car seat if you're driving anywhere (in Switzerland, small children aren't allowed to ride in the front seat). Find out if the place you intend to stay stocks baby food; if it doesn't, take some with you and plan to buy some abroad in supermarkets.

Draw up rules for your family to follow during your vacation. The rules should be flexible, of course—after all, this is a trip for fun. But guidelines on bedtime, eating, keeping tidy, staying in the sun, even shopping and spending, can help make everyone's vacation more enjoyable.

Baby-sitters can be found at most hotels. Try to secure one who has at least some knowledge of English.

For $35, **Family Travel Times** will send you 10 issues of a newsletter about traveling with children. Subscribers can call in with travel questions from Monday through Friday 10am to noon eastern standard time (later in the West). Contact TWYCH (which stands for "Travel with Your Children"), 80 Eighth Avenue, Suite 1807, New York, NY 10011 (tel. 212/206-0688).

A hotel guide, **"Hotels Specially Suited for Families,"** is published by the Swiss Hotel Association and is available from the Swiss National Tourist Office. It lists more than 100 hotels in the country catering to families. These hotels have a supervised children's playroom, a play area or garden, a children's menu served before normal mealtimes, and organized family activities.

Note: In Switzerland, children under age 16—if accompanied by at least one adult—travel free on national rail lines. This family travel plan is valid for the purchase of Swiss Passes, Swiss Flexi Passes, Swiss Cards, and point-to-point tickets (see Section 8, "Getting Around," below).

FOR STUDENTS   Students can avail themselves of several travel discounts through the **Council on International Educational Exchange (CIEE),** 205 East 42nd Street, New York, NY 10017 (tel. 212/661-1414). The CIEE provides details about budget travel, study abroad, working permits, and insurance. It also sells helpful publications, including the *Student Travel Catalogue* ($1), and issues the International Student Identity Card (ISIC) for $10.

To keep costs bone-trimmed, you may want to join the **International Youth Hostel Federation (IYHF).** Many countries have branch offices; in the United States it's **American Youth Hostels (AYH),** P.O. Box 37613, Washington, DC 20013-7613 (tel. 202/783-6161). Membership costs $25 annually ($10 if you're under 18).

Some 15 organizations offer educational as well as leisure tours to individual students and groups. Ask the Swiss National Tourist Office for a fact sheet, **"Student/Youth Tour Operators and Organizations."**

6. ALTERNATIVE/SPECIALTY TRAVEL

In the 1990s a new trend has appeared among inveterate travelers—travel with a clearly defined goal. There is also a greater demand for organizations that can provide like-minded companions for such travel. Some of the major organizations offering specialty travel are cited below.

Note that the inclusion of an organization in this section should not be interpreted as a guarantee of that organization's credit worthiness or competency.

SPORT AND RESORT VACATIONS Spas Switzerland has 22 resorts with natural curative springs. Most of these spas, which have been approved by the Association of Swiss Health Spas and the Swiss Society of Balneology and Bioclimatology, include a medical examination, along with thermal baths and excursions, in their package plans for visitors. Many of them are open all year.

The following agencies will provide you with information about spa vacations: **Health and Fitness Vacations,** 100 North Biscayne Boulevard, Miami, FL 33132 (tel. 305/379-8451); **Health and Pleasure Tours, Inc.,** 165 West 46th Street, New York, NY 10036 (tel. 212/586-1175); **Odyssey Travel Ltd.,** 2050 Chestnut Street, San Francisco, CA 94123 (tel. 415/567-9164); **Ring International,** P.O. Box 118, Novato, CA 94947 (tel. 415/892-3966); **Selective Tours of Switzerland,** 301 East 48th Street, New York, NY 10017 (tel. 212/758-4275, or toll- free 800/223-6764). You can also request information from **Swissair,** Tours Dept., 608 Fifth Avenue, New York, NY 10020 (tel. 212/995-4400, or toll free 800/221-6644, 800/522-9606 in New York State).

Mountaineering There are mountain-climbing schools in Andermatt, Champéry, Crans, Davos, Les Diablerets, Fiesch, La Fouly, Glarus, Grindelwald, Kandersteg, Klosters, Meiringen, Pontresina, Riederalp, Saas-Fee, Saas-Grund, Schwende, Täsch, Zermatt, and Zinai. Guides are available at many other resorts.

The 75,000-member **Swiss Alpine Club (SAC),** founded in 1863, promotes mountaineering and ski tours in the high mountains. Although its primary function is to organize alpine rescue services, it also lobbies politically to protect the alpine ecology. Working closely with its equivalent clubs in Austria, Germany, France, and Italy, the club has built mountain huts at strategic spots throughout the country. The huts are modest, with bunk rooms sleeping 10 to 20 people. The average rate for a night's lodging (without food) is 30F ($21.90) daily for nonmembers and 20F ($14.60) for members. Also, there are comfortable hotels and inns at favorable altitudes for alpine treks, many on high peaks and passes.

Membership is limited to applicants over age 18 and is granted for a minimum period of 2 years. Applications should include a passport-size photo and a check in the amount of 105F ($76.65) for the first year's membership and 70F ($51.10) for each year after that. Funds should be drawn on a Swiss bank (to obtain a check drawn on a Swiss bank, contact Ruesch International; see Section 1, "Information, Documents & Money," above).

Mail your application to Edmond Krieger, Swiss Alpine Club, Sektion Zermatt,

Postfach 1, CH-3920 Zermatt, Switzerland. For telephone or printed information, contact the Swiss Alpine Club, Geschäftsstelle, Helvetiaplatz 4, CH-3005 Bern, Switzerland (tel. 031/43-36-11). Membership includes a subscription to the organization's German-language magazine, *Die Alpen,* and discounted overnight accommodations at mountain shelters owned by the club. New members planning to hike extensively in the Swiss Alps are advised to purchase independent insurance, arranged through the SAC, to cover mountain rescue service by helicopter if necessary. The annual premium for such insurance is 20F ($14.60) per person.

Walking Tours The Swiss rigorously maintain their belief in the physical and mental benefits of walking. They have more than 33,000 miles of marked trails in a labyrinth of walkways throughout the country.

Anyone interested in a walking tour of Switzerland can obtain information from **Wander Tours, Inc.,** P.O. Box 8607, Somerville, NJ 00876 (tel. toll free 800/282-1808). Established in 1989 by Bob and Laurie Zubritsky, Wander Tours offers two week-long walking itineraries of Switzerland during the summer (July and August). The tours, which are conducted personally by the Zubritskys, consist of no more than 15 participants between 20 and 55 years, and last about 4 hours each day, covering between 8 and 12 miles, depending on the terrain. Participants' luggage is transported ahead to unpretentious local inns, and participants themselves can at any time opt to continue any leg of the transit by train, meeting the rest of the group for dinner at the end of the day. The cost for the land-based arrangements is $875 per person, double occupancy, with a supplement for single occupancy of about $75. The tours include 6 nights' accommodation, most meals, and transportation within Switzerland.

CULTURAL EXCHANGE   Meet the Swiss An excellent program that seeks to match Swiss and foreign families of similar backgrounds is "Meet the Swiss," sponsored by the **Zurich Tourist Office,** Bahnhofplatz 15 (tel. 01/211-40-00). I recently tested the program. A few days after applying (it takes at least 3 days for the tourist office to set up a visit), I was invited into the home of a Swiss writer and his family; he was working on a biography of Carl Jung. The enjoyable evening was topped off with coffee, Kirschwasser, and a homemade dessert; the family even gave me some white chocolate to take back to my hotel. The next day, reciprocating, I sent flowers.

Servas Servas, 11 John Street, New York, NY 10038 (tel. 212/267-0252), is a nonprofit international network of travelers and hosts (*servas* means "to serve" in Esperanto). Its goal is to bridge the cultural gap through personal interaction between people of diverse backgrounds. Servas travelers are invited to stay in a private home, normally without charge, for a maximum of 2 days. Visitors pay a $45 annual membership fee, fill out an application, and are interviewed for suitability by one of more than 200 Servas interviewers throughout the country. They then receive a Servas directory listing the names and addresses of prospective hosts.

International Visitors Information Service For $6, this organization will mail to you a booklet listing opportunities for contact with local residents in foreign countries. Switzerland is featured. You should make out your check to Meridian House IVIS. Contact the International Visitors Information Service, 733 15th St. NW, Suite 300, Washington, DC 20005 (tel. 202/783-6540).

EDUCATIONAL An international series of programs for people over age 50 who want to combine travel with learning is offered by **Interhostel,** developed by the University of New Hampshire. Sponsored trips, normally lasting 2 weeks, are led by a university faculty or staff member and are arranged in conjunction with a host university or cultural institution. They involve cultural and intellectual activities, such as field trips to museums. For information, contact the University of New Hampshire, Division of Continuing Education, 6 Garrison Avenue, Durham, NH 03824 (tel. 603/862-1147).

In Switzerland, Interhostel has a 2-week program in Leysin, hosted by the American College of Switzerland. Participants stay on campus at what was once a grand hotel and sanitorium, and attend lectures on the French-speaking sections of Switzerland, covering their culture, politics, economics, and history.

A similar program, operating in conjunction with **Franklin College** of Indiana, is in Lugano. The focus here, however, is on the Italian section of Switzerland. Participants, who likewise remain at the college, take a 2-day field trip to Milan. For information, write to the Admissions Office, Franklin College, 501 East Monroe Street, Franklin, IN 46131 (tel. 317/738-8000).

OVERSEAS PROGRAMS FOR STUDENTS The best source of information for students is the **Council on International Educational Exchange (CIEE)**, 205 East 42nd Street, New York, NY 10017 (tel. 212/661-1414). In addition to offering information about work and study programs abroad, it also arranges low-cost travel opportunities. Request a copy of its 455-page *Work, Study, Travel Abroad: The Whole World Handbook* ($11.95 postage paid).

VACATIONS FOR SENIORS One of the most dynamic educational organizations for seniors is **Elderhostel**, 75 Federal Street, Boston, MA 02110 (tel. 617/426-7788). Established in 1975, Elderhostel maintains an array of liberal-arts programs in Europe. The cost of each program includes airfare, tuition (most courses last 3 weeks), accommodations (in student dormitories or modest inns, or even, perhaps, with a private family), and all meals. No homework or grades are given, yet the experience is definitely academic. Applicants must be over age 60 (if two apply as a couple, only one member need meet the age requirement). Call or write for a free newsletter and a list of upcoming courses and destinations.

If you're between 50 and 86 and need a travel companion, then **Golden Companions**, P.O. Box 754, Pullman, WA 99163 (tel. 509/334-9351), may be the answer. The service was founded in 1988 by Joanne R. Buteau, a research economist and writer. It enables members to meet potential travel companions through a confidential mail network. Once they have "connected," they make their own travel arrangements. The annual membership fee of $85 includes a subscription to a bimonthly newsletter, *The Golden Traveler,* which outlines travel discounts and home exchanges.

HOME EXCHANGES One of the most exciting trends recently has been the home-exchange approach to travel, whereby, say, the Behr family of Zurich exchange their home, and perhaps even their automobile, with the Brier family of Boston. Home exchanges cut costs. You don't pay hotel bills, and you can also save money by shopping in markets and eating in. One potential problem, though, is that you may not get a home in the area you request.

World Wide Exchange, 1344 Pacific Avenue, Suite 103, Santa Cruz, CA 95060 (tel. 408/425-0531), is one of several home-exchange agencies. For $45 a year, you can list your home and receive three booklets of listings.

Vacation Exchange Club, 12006 111th Avenue, Suite 12, Youngstown, AZ 85363 (tel. 602/972-2186), has many listings for Switzerland. The annual dues of $24.70 entitles subscribers to receive spring and winter listings; they can also place a listing in one of the directories. Subscribers can pay $16 for the booklets only.

International Home Exchange Service, P.O. Box 190070, San Francisco,

CA 94119 (tel. 415/435-3497), charges $35 for three directories annually. The fee includes a listing in one of them. Seniors get a 20% discount.

7. GETTING THERE

Switzerland is situated at the center of Europe. As a result, it is a focal point for international air traffic. The busy intercontinental airports of Zurich and Geneva can be reached in about 8 jet hours from the east coast of North America and in less than 2 hours from London or Paris. The country is also the crossroads of Europe—all rail lines, road passes, and mountain tunnels lead to it. Similarly, the main European route for east-west travel passes through Switzerland, between Lake Constance and Geneva.

BY PLANE

THE MAJOR AIRLINES

Several U.S.-based airlines compete intensely for the popular transatlantic run between North America and the cities of Zurich and Geneva. A highly recommended newcomer to the scene is **American Airlines** (tel. toll free 800/433-7300), which began making major inroads into the European market in 1982 and now services some of the busiest capitals of Europe. The airline makes frequent nonstop flights to Zurich from both New York and Chicago, with an impressive program of rewards for frequent fliers.

Pan American (tel. toll free 800/221-1111) flies nonstop to Zurich from New York four to seven times weekly, depending on the season. **TWA** (tel. toll free 800/221-2000) can arrange two or three daily connections between New York and Zurich, with a change of aircraft in such cities as Paris. Some travelers opt for passage on **Swissair** (tel. toll free 800/221-4750), which flies nonstop daily from New York to Zurich and Geneva, and from Chicago and Boston to Zurich. It also has nonstop service from Atlanta to Zurich 6 days a week.

REGULAR FARES Most airlines operate on similar fare plans. American Airlines, for example, divides its year into three seasons—low, shoulder, and high. Dates for each of the airlines vary (a fact you can sometimes use to your advantage), but the lowest (low-season) fares are usually offered between October and mid-December and again between Christmas and late March. Fares are slightly higher during shoulder season (May and either September or October, depending on the airline). High-season fares apply the rest of the year. Regardless of which season ticket you select, you should make your reservation as far in advance as possible.

American's lowest regular fare, called an **Advance Purchase Excursion (APEX)** fare, requires that passengers reserve and pay for a round-trip ticket at least 30 days in advance. The lowest APEX fares are for those who fly Monday through Thursday, and they must plan to stay a minimum of 7 days and return within 21 days. Currently, this reduced-fare ticket round-trip from New York to Zurich costs $772 to $1,080 per person, depending on the season.

An unrestricted ticket in **economy class** from New York to Zurich currently costs $2,392 year round. Prices for economy tickets with booking or length of vacation restrictions vary throughout the year. However, if you cannot qualify for the APEX fare, you may be able to buy a less expensive economy-class ticket—some

FROMMER'S SMART TRAVELER: AIRFARES

1. Consider landing in Zurich and ending your sojourn in Basel or Geneva. Most airlines, including Swissair, allow such choice of itinerary, even with the lowest airfares, at no additional charge. You'll save surface transit time between the cities as well.
2. Some airlines, including Swissair, offer a free round-trip train connection from Geneva or Zurich to the country's capital, Bern, as an incentive to tourists to visit one of Switzerland's most charming cities.
3. Flying to Basel requires a connecting flight through either Geneva or Zurich, but some airlines will provide that connection free if you've flown transatlantic. Ask when you book your ticket.
4. Airfares are lowest in midwinter (Nov 1 to Dec 14 and Dec 25 to Mar 21). They are slightly higher during shoulder season (mid-Mar to late May and all of Oct).
5. Seniors (whom Swissair and American define as 62 and older) receive a 10% discount on midweek travel on any of these airlines' promotional economy fares, but only between October and April and not during Christmastime.
6. For anyone 24 and younger, some airlines (including Swissair and American) offer reduced fares that can be confirmed only 72 hours or less prior to departure on either leg of the flight. There's no penalty for last-minute cancellation.
7. You'll be rewarded with reduced rates if you fix your travel dates at least a month in advance.
8. For economy, consider buying all the parts for your vacation in a single transaction. Arrange your airfare, hotel accommodations, car or rail reservations, and connecting flights with a single all-purpose agency.

economy-class seats are always sold for low fares as a promotion. These tickets may be released at any time when there is a large inventory of unsold seats, so you should call daily to find out if any of these less expensive tickets are available.

More expensive than economy class is **business class,** and the highest regular fare is **first class.** In the last two, the amenities are increased accordingly, the food is better, and the seats are more comfortable. All three regular fares can be booked at the last minute, and you can depart and return when you wish, without restrictions.

OTHER AIR-TRAVEL POSSIBILITIES

Because promotional and other fares change all the time, some of the following air-travel possibilities may at times offer good value and at other times be comparable to the fares offered by travel agents or the airlines.

BUCKET SHOPS A bucket shop (once a pejorative term, now a somewhat accepted label) acts as a clearinghouse or consolidator for blocks of tickets that airlines discount and consign during slow travel periods. Tickets can cost 20% to 35% less than the full fare. Terms of payment can vary—anywhere from 45 days prior to departure date to last-minute sales offered in an attempt to fill a half-empty craft.

Bucket shops can be found from coast to coast. Here are some recommendations to get you started. Look for the ads in your local newspaper's travel section.

Maharaja Travel, 393 Fifth Avenue, New York, NY 10016 (tel. 212/213-2020, or toll free 800/223-6862), offers tickets to 400 destinations worldwide.

Access International, 101 West 31st Street, Suite 1104, New York, NY 10001 (tel. 212/333-7280, or toll free 800/827-3633), which specializes in discount tickets to the major cities of Europe, just may be the country's biggest consolidator.

Out west you can try **Sunline Express Holidays, Inc.,** 607 Market Street, San Francisco, CA 94105 (tel. 415/541-7800, or toll free 800/877-2111); or **Euro-Asia, Inc.,** 4203 East Indian School Road, Suite 210, Phoenix, AZ 85018 (tel. 602/955-2742, or toll free 800/525-3876).

CHARTER FLIGHTS Strictly speaking, a charter is a one-time-only flight between two predetermined points, for which the aircraft is reserved months in advance. Before paying for a charter, check the restrictions on your ticket or contract. You may be asked to purchase a tour package and pay far in advance; if you cancel, you'll pay a stiff penalty (or forfeit the ticket entirely). Some charter ticket sellers offer an insurance policy for a legitimate cancellation (like hospitalization or a death in the family). Be aware that a charter might be canceled if the plane is not full.

One reliable charter-flight operator is **Council Charters,** run by the Council on International Educational Exchange, 205 East 42nd Street, New York, NY 10017 (tel. 212/661-0311, or toll free 800/223-7402), which arranges charter seats on regularly scheduled aircraft.

You might also consider **Balair** 608 Fifth Avenue, Suite 803, New York, NY 10020 (tel. 212/581-3411, or toll free 800/872-8800), the all-charter division of Swissair. Unfortunately, it flies to Switzerland only in the summer from New York, San Francisco, Miami, and Bangor, Me.—and only on certain days of the week. Balair's prices can be about 20% less than the cheapest APEX tickets on regularly scheduled airlines.

REBATORS Rebators offer services sometimes similar to those of travel agents. They pass along to the passenger a part of their commission, although many of them assess a fee for their services. A rebator may sell you a discounted travel ticket and also offer discounts on hotels and car rentals. Most discounts range from 10% to 25%, plus a $20 handling charge.

Among the major rebators are: **Travel Avenue,** 641 West Lake Street, Suite 201, Chicago, IL 60606-3691 (tel. 312/876-1116, or toll free 800/333-3335); **The Smart Traveller,** 3111 SW 27th Avenue, Miami, FL 33133 (tel. 305/448-3338, or toll free 800/226-3338 in Florida and Georgia only); and **Blitz Travel,** 8918 Manchester Road, St. Louis, MO 63144 (tel. 314/961-2700).

STANDBY If you're a spontaneous traveler with no schedule demands and you don't mind hanging around the airport, then a standby fare may be for you. Your departure will depend on whether a seat opens up at the last minute. Most airlines do not offer standby seats to Switzerland, although some have standbys to other major European destinations, such as London and Vienna, from which train or bus connections can be made to Switzerland.

GOING AS A COURIER Couriers are hired by overnight air-freight firms hoping to skirt the often-tedious Customs delays on the other end that regular cargo faces. For the service, the courier pays the firm a fee much lower than the cost of the ticket, and sometimes may fly free. Don't worry, the service is legal—you won't be asked to haul in illegal drugs. Also, you don't actually handle the merchandise you're "transporting"; you just carry a document (a shipping invoice) to present to Customs when you arrive.

This cost-cutting technique is not for everyone—there are lots of restrictions and courier opportunities are hard to come by. You're allowed only one piece of carry-on luggage; your checked-baggage allowance is used by the courier firm to transport its cargo. Also, you fly alone; family or friends must make other arrangements.

Check with **Halbart Express,** 147-05 176th Street, Jamaica, NY 11434 (tel. 718/656-8189 daily from 10am to 3pm) or **Now Voyager,** 74 Varick Street, Suite 307, New York, NY 10013 (tel. 212/431-1616 daily from 11:30am to 6pm). An automatic telephone-answering system announces last-minute specials and the firm's fees for the round-trip. Courier services are also listed in the *Yellow Pages* or in advertisements in newspaper travel sections.

BY TRAIN

FROM PARIS   The classic rail link on the continent is from Paris to Switzerland. The *train à grande vitesse* (high-speed train, or TGV) makes the run to Geneva, Bern, Lausanne, and other cities both fast and efficient. Each day, for example, five TGVs leave Paris's Gare de Lyon for Geneva and four trains leave for Lausanne; trip time to both cities is 3½ hours. As part of the EuroCity link, a TGV train departs from Paris daily for Neuchâtel and Bern, where links can be made to the other major Swiss cities, including Zurich. Before you go, you can obtain further information from **Rail Europe,** 226-230 Westchester Avenue, White Plains, NY 10604 (tel. 914/682-5172).

FROM LONDON   Rail links are also good from London to Switzerland.

Via the Hook of Holland   The standard EuroCity express route is to set out from London's Liverpool Street Station, sail from Harwick to the Hook of Holland, and then proceed by train via Cologne, Germany, to either Basel or Zurich. Once there, you can find rail links to the rest of Switzerland.

Across the Channel Through Paris   It's also possible to take the rail link from London across the English Channel to Paris, where you can make connections to Switzerland. If you depart London at 10am you can be in Geneva or Lausanne before 10pm on the same day. The quickest way to reach Paris, however, is to take the Citylink rail–hovercraft–rail service, run by Hoverspeed, from London's Victoria Station to Paris's Gare du Nord. In crossing the Channel, you go from Dover to the French port of Boulogne, where you hop aboard the French Turbotrain for a quick ride to Paris. For information before you go, contact either Rail Europe or **BritRail Travel International,** 1500 Broadway, New York, NY 10036 (tel. 212/575-2667).

BY BUS

International bus service to Switzerland is limited. Most buses carrying visitors to Swiss destinations are on organized coach tours. From London, **Euroways Eurolines Ltd.,** 52 Grosvenor Gardens, London SW1W 0UA (tel. 071/730-0202), has about four departures a week during the summer, running a coach via Paris to Geneva. Most buses depart London in the midafternoon and arrive in Geneva the following morning.

BY CAR

Situated in the middle of the continent, Switzerland has a network of express highways linking it with other European countries. You can drive all the way from Britain to Switzerland by taking a northerly route through Belgium or the Netherlands and then Germany. British motorists prefer such an express auto route, which is free, rather than going through France and paying expensive toll charges.

The route through France is also much slower. It begins a few miles south of Calais and leads directly to the Périphérique (ring road) around Paris, where you can take the Autoroute du Soleil to Switzerland. In Britain the best connection for those planning a road link across France is from Portsmouth to Le Havre.

From the south of Germany, Autobahn E35 leads directly into Basel. From Basel, head east to Zurich on E60.

8. GETTING AROUND

BY PLANE

Switzerland does not have an abundance of airports, partly because of the terrain in much of the Alps and partly because of the Swiss people's own resistance to having a plethora of planes disturb their peace and quiet. To compensate, Switzerland has one of Europe's best railway systems, linking every major city in the country. A good example is Bern, the capital; it relies almost exclusively on rail transport from Zurich, Geneva, and Basel for its air connections to the rest of the world. (There is a small airport at Bern, but it's capable only of accommodating propeller aircraft, usually from medium-sized cities in France and Germany.)

If you want to fly within Switzerland, or from Switzerland to about 30 regional cities in Austria, Italy, Germany, or France, **Crossair** (tel. toll free 800/221-4750), a regional airline operated by Swissair, schedules flights from and to Lugano, Bern, Geneva, Basel, and Zurich.

BY TRAIN

The Swiss Federal Railway is noted for its comfort and cleanliness. Most of the electrically operated trains have first-class and second-class compartments. International through trains link Swiss cities with other European centers. Intercity trains coming from Holland, Scandinavia, and Germany require a change at Basel's station, where a connection is usually available on the same platform. Most intercity trains offer the fastest connections, and as trains leave the Basel station hourly, you don't have to wait there very long.

It is advisable to purchase transportation tickets for Europe before leaving home, especially when your itinerary is specific and complicated. All tickets are available from your travel agent or from the Swiss National Tourist Office (see "Information" in Section 1, "Information, Documents & Money," above).

SWISS PASS/SWISS FLEXIPASS The most practical and convenient ticket for your trip to Switzerland is the **Swiss Pass,** which entitles you to unlimited travel on the entire network of the Swiss Federal Railways, as well as on lake steamers and most postal motor coaches linking Swiss cities and resorts. This pass also permits you to purchase transportation tickets at a reduction of up to 50% for excursions to mountaintops. The Swiss Pass is issued at half price to children ages 6 to 15.

With a Swiss Pass, you don't need to plan in advance. Just get on a train, boat, or postal bus, show your card to the ticket collector, and enjoy your trip. You'll never have to wait long for your next link.

A variation of the Swiss Pass is the **Swiss Flexipass,** of which there are several kinds. A 3-day pass—valid for any 3 days within a 15-day period—costs $199 for first class and $129 for second class. An 8-day pass goes for $239 for first class and $159 for second class, a 15-day pass is $289 for first class and $189 for second class, and a 1-month pass costs $389 for first class and $269 for second class.

For information, call 01/211-50-10 in Zurich.

SWISS REGIONAL PASSES One of the finest transportation bargains is the regional pass, such as that offered in the Bernese Oberland. If you plan to devote 4 or 5 days to a region of Switzerland, you will find this pass a great savings.

The Bernese Oberland Regional Pass, for example, costs only 110F ($80.30), for 5 days of rail travel. Should you stay on 10 more days, you may, with this pass, purchase rail tickets at half price. If you're taking a lot of train rides in the area, you'll virtually pay for the cost of the pass in just 1 day of travel. Inquire at the nearest train station about special regional passes, which differ from area to area.

HALF-FARE TRAVEL CARD (SWISS CARD) The half-fare card, called the Swiss Card, entitles you to purchase an unlimited number of regular transportation tickets, both round-trip and one way, at half the fare on all scheduled service by rail, postal bus, and lake steamer. Some mountain railroads grant only 25% reductions. One month of second-class travel costs $79; for first-class travel it's $109. You must know at the time of purchase the day you want the half-fare card to become valid. For information, call 01/211-50-10 in Zurich.

EURAILPASS The Eurailpass entitles North American residents to unlimited first-class travel over the 100,000-mile national railroad networks of Western European countries, except Britain, and including Hungary in Eastern Europe. It is also valid on some lake steamers and private railroads. A Eurailpass may be purchased for as little as 15 days or as long as 3 months.

The Eurailpass, which is ideal for extensive trips, eliminates the hassles of buying tickets—just show your pass to the ticket collector. You should note, however, that some trains require seat reservations. Also, many of the trains have *couchettes,* or sleeping cars, for which an additional fee is charged.

The pass cannot be purchased in Europe, so you must secure one before leaving on your trip. It costs $390 for 15 days, $498 for 21 days, $616 for 1 month, $840 for 2 months, and $1,042 for 3 months. Children under 4 travel free if they don't occupy a seat (otherwise, they pay half fare); children under 12 pay half fare.

If you're under 26, you can obtain unlimited second-class travel, wherever Eurailpass is honored, on a **Eurail Youthpass,** which costs $425 for 1 month, $560 for 2 months. In addition, a **Eurail Youth Flexipass** offers 15 days of unlimited second-class travel in a 3-month period for $340. It also offers 30 days of unlimited second-class travel in a 3-month period for $540.

Travel agents or national European rail offices will provide further information about these passes. For general brochures, write to **Eurailpass,** P.O. Box 325, Old Greenwich, CT 06870-0235.

Eurail Saverpass Groups of three or more people can purchase a pass for 15 days of discounted travel in first class for $298. To be entitled to the discount, the members of a group must travel together. The Saverpass is valid all over Europe from April 1 and again from September 30.

Eurail Flexipass This pass, good for unlimited first-class travel, offers 5 days of travel during a 15-day period for $230, 9 days of travel during a 21-day period for $398, and 14 days of travel in 1 month for $498.

 THE GLACIER EXPRESS Perhaps the most famous of Switzerland's railway lines, the *Glacier Express* connects the highest peaks and glaciers of the southeastern Alps around St. Moritz and Chur with those of the southwestern

Alps around Zermatt. When the train link opened in 1928, the danger of winter blizzards and snow drifts required that many of the most isolated mountain bridges be dismantled every October and then reassembled the following May. As a result, in the winter trains were rerouted on a lengthy detour through Zurich and northern Switzerland. In 1982 an 8-mile-long tunnel was drilled beneath the Furka mountain, and today trains run without interruption across the mountains in both summer and winter.

The route is one of the most spectacular in the world, with 91 viaducts and tunnels and 291 bridges along the way. There's a daily train between the regions in the winter; in the summer, with its longer hours for viewing, there are two and sometimes three daily trains.

The trip from Zermatt to St. Moritz takes 8 hours and costs $127 in first class and $81 in second class. Many travelers disembark in the medieval city of Chur; this trip takes 6 hours and costs $101 in first class and $65 in second class. From Chur, convenient connections can be arranged to Davos and all points east, especially towns in Austria.

Advance seat reservations are required for the comfortably upholstered coaches (with restaurant cars). Note that the Swiss Pass will cover the full fare on the *Glacier Express,* but because part of the route is administered by a different organization from the rest of the Swiss Rail network, holders of any travel pass in the Eurailpass family (including Youthpasses and Flexipasses) will be charged about half the total fare.

For more information, contact any Swiss National Tourist Office, or the Swiss Center, at 608 Fifth Avenue, New York, NY 10020 (tel. 212/757-5844).

BY BUS

The extremely dense network covered by the Swiss postal buses is useful for trips into the mountains. Hopping on one of the popular yellow buses is a much safer and more comfortable way of seeing the Alps than trying to do your own driving in those regions. The buses will carry you from the railroad station to remote valleys and across the great alpine passes.

A **Postal Coach Holiday Season Ticket,** available at any office of the Swiss Postal Passenger Service, provides half-fare travel for 1 year on all scheduled Swiss postal bus lines. The price is 110F ($80.30) per person. Of greater interest to visitors are the monthly passes, which sell for 65F ($47.45) per person. Hand baggage weighing up to 110 pounds can be taken on a postal bus free. For information call 01/463-8666 in Zurich or contact the Swiss National Tourist Office.

BY CAR

Switzerland provides a system of well-constructed roads and superhighways. Travel is made easy by clear road signs. Alpine passes are not difficult to cross, except in snowstorms, when they may shut down suddenly. Special rail facilities are provided for drivers wishing to transport their cars through the alpine tunnels of the Albula, Furka, Lotschberg, and Simplon. A timetable, showing the various fares and rates, is available from the Swiss National Tourist Office.

AUTOMOBILE PERMIT   Apart from the auto and train tunnel trips mentioned above, and a toll on the road through the Great St. Bernard Tunnel, there are no toll roads in the country. Instead of tolls, Switzerland levies a single annual fee of 30F ($21.90) per car, or 60F ($43.80) for trailers, motor homes, and RVs, for use of the nation's super-highways; when the fee has been paid, a permit sticker is affixed to the car. Drivers of cars without the permit sticker face a fine of more than twice the permit's cost.

Rental cars in Switzerland come with the permit, but vehicles rented in other countries may not have one. Permits are available at border crossings and are valid for multiple reentries into Switzerland within the licensed period. To avoid waiting in a long line at border crossings, you can buy the sticker permit in advance at the Swiss National Tourist Office in Italy, Austria, or Germany (it is not sold in France). Note that if you drive into Switzerland on a secondary road, you do not need a permit sticker—but if you drive on a Swiss super-highway without one, you face that heavy fine.

CAR RENTALS Many foreign visitors prefer the freedom and flexibility of driving their cars. Several American companies cooperate with European affiliates to guarantee prompt delivery of a rental car. One of the most reliable firms is **Budget Rent-a-Car** (tel. toll free 800/472-3325); its prices are competitive with those offered by **Avis** (tel. toll free 800/331-2112) and **Hertz** (tel. toll free 800/654-3001). All three companies offer a discount if you prepay your rental 21 days or more in advance, but getting a refund because of a sudden change of plans or schedules may cost you a penalty of $50 or more. So consider paying the slightly higher prices for reservations that need to be made only 2 days in advance.

As an example, Budget offers one-way rentals between any two of its more than 60 Swiss offices at no additional charge. You can thus rent a car in Geneva, say, and return it in Zurich before flying home. A wide range of vehicles is offered. An Opel Corsa or a Ford Fiesta, suitable for up to four passengers, goes for 346F ($252.55) per week, with unlimited mileage. In a more opulent category, an automatic-transmission Opel Vectra or Ford Sierra shoots up to 625F ($456.20) per week. Note that there is no tax on car rentals in Switzerland.

Collision Damage Waiver Most car companies will offer you optional collision insurance, called a collision damage waiver. Depending on the value of the car, each of the companies charges between 20F and 24F ($14.60 and $17.50) per day for this policy, which in most cases will cover your financial responsibility for any damage to your car. Without it, you'll be responsible for the cost of repairs up to 4,000F ($2,919.60) at Budget and up to four times that amount at Avis.

You might be able to avoid buying this insurance if you pay for the car rental with a credit card. Certain credit-card companies include this coverage when the car is paid for on that card; check with your credit-card company to determine the extent of any collision-damage coverage that may be offered.

RVS/CARAVANS Europeans are fond of touring by recreational vehicle (RV) during the summer. The Swiss call it "caravanning." Campgrounds are available in all major Swiss tourist regions (local tourist offices will direct you to the nearest sites).

For more details about traveling by RV, before you go contact **Foremost Euro-Car,** 5430 Van Nuys Boulevard, Van Nuys, CA 91401 (tel. toll free 800/272-3299).

GAS The cost varies across the country. Gas stations are usually open daily from 8am to 10pm. U.S. gasoline credit cards, generally, are not accepted for payment.

DRIVER'S LICENSE U.S. and Canadian driver's licenses are valid in Switzerland, but if you're at least 18 and touring Europe by car, you should probably invest in an international driver's license. In the United States you can apply for one at any local branch of the **American Automobile Association (AAA);** for a list of local branches, contact the AAA's national headquarters, 1000 AAA Drive, Heathrow, FL 32746 (tel. toll free 800/AAA-HELP). Include two 2-by-2-inch photographs, a $10 fee, and a photocopy of your state driver's license. Canadians can get the address of the nearest branch of the **Canadian Automobile Club** by phoning its national office (tel. toll free 800/336-HELP).

Note that your international driver's license is valid only if it's accompanied by your home state or provincial driver's license.

In Switzerland, as elsewhere in Europe, in order to drive a car legally you must have in your possession an international insurance certificate, known as a **Green Card (Carte Verte)**. The car-rental agency will provide one as part of your rental contract.

DRIVING RULES   The legal minimum age for driving in Switzerland is 18. Note, however, that car-rental companies often set their own minimum age, usually above 18.

Drive on the right side of the road and observe the speed limit for passenger vehicles; it is 120kph (about 75 m.p.h.) on super-highways, 80kph (about 50 m.p.h.) on other highways, and 50kph (about 30 m.p.h.) in cities, towns, and villages, unless otherwise posted.

When driving through road tunnels, turn on and dim your headlights, as required by law. Do not pass another car from the right, even on super-highways. Always wear your seatbelt. Do not permit children under 12 to ride in the front seat. And, needless to say, do not drive if you have been drinking; driving while under the influence of alcohol is a serious offense in Switzerland.

BREAKDOWNS/ASSISTANCE   The Automobile Club of Switzerland and its branch offices will assist motorists at all times. For help, contact **Automobil-Club der Schweiz,** 39 Wasserwerkgasse, CH-3000 Bern 13 (tel. 031/22-47-22), or **Touring Club Suisse,** 9 rue Pierre-Fatio, CH-1211 Genève 3 (tel. 022/37-12-12).

If you have a breakdown, dial 140 for help. To learn of road conditions, call 163. Mountain roads have emergency call boxes.

MAPS   The best maps, available at major bookstores, are *Michelin 427 Switzerland* and the various Michelin regional road guides. An excellent map for those who plan extensive touring is published by *Hallwag* (1:303000). Local tourist offices provide city maps.

BY BOAT

In the summer passenger boats sail romantically on Switzerland's major lakes and rivers. More than 100 boats, with accommodations for 60,000 passengers, operate on the lakes and along stretches of the Rhine and the Aare; most of them have excellent restaurants. Evening trips, with music and dancing, are popular. The old paddle-steamers on the lakes of Brienz, Geneva, Lucerne, and Zurich, dating from before World War I, are particularly attractive and romantic.

Remember that your Swiss Pass or Swiss Card (half-fare travel card) entitles you to unlimited travel on lake steamers.

The timetable comes in three different paperback volumes: one for buses; another for trains, cable cars, and boats; and a third for international connections into Switzerland. The cost of the set is $30. The timetable is available exclusively from **Avos Travel,** 608 Fifth Avenue, New York, NY 10020 (tel. 212/245-1150).

HITCHHIKING

Hitchhiking, or "autostopping," as the Swiss call it, is legal in Switzerland (but it is prohibited on motorways, or express highways). Hitchhikers generally regard Switzerland as one of their favorite places in Europe. Of course, the neater you look, the better will be your chances of getting a lift.

ORGANIZED TOURS

People planning their first trip to Europe understandably have many questions: How do I plan my trip to be sure of seeing the most outstanding sights of a country? How much of a problem will I have in trying to get from place to place, complete with luggage? Am I too old to embark on such a journey? How will I cope with a foreign language?

The answer to all these questions is simple: Go on a good vacation tour whose organizers will look after your needs from the moment you arrive at the airport to the time you depart for the return flight home. Booking a tour is almost always cheaper than the cost of exploring a country on your own and gives the advantage of including a running commentary on sights and monuments. Moreover, you save on both transportation and meals.

There are many different tour operators eager for a share of your business, but one of the most unusual is **Abercrombie & Kent International, Inc.,** 1520 Kensington Road, Oak Brook, IL 60521 (tel. 708/954-2944, or toll free 800/323-7308), a Chicago-based company established some 30 years ago. It specializes in deluxe 10-day tours of Switzerland by train, which, despite all the extras they offer, still cost less than any personally arranged tour would.

Abercrombie & Kent's "Great Switzerland Express" tour is a carefully organized rail trip through the tourist gems of Switzerland. Tour members spend the night either in the mountains (at such resorts as Zermatt and St. Moritz) or beside one of the country's lakes. Only the finest hotels are selected, each a historic legend and usually the very best in its town or region. Among the stops along the tour are Lugano, Lake Como, Montreux, Lausanne, Geneva, Bern, and Zurich, as well as Liechtenstein. Tours depart in June, July, and September; the cost is $3,640 per person, double occupancy, with a supplement of about $300 for single occupancy. Included in the price are daily Swiss-style buffet breakfasts, at least seven other meals (usually elegant European dinners in formal dining rooms or cozy mountain inns), first-class rail transport throughout the country (including an on-board bellboy, who makes transport of luggage and exchanges at railway stations especially easy for the elderly or handicapped), a boat journey across Lake Geneva, entrance fees to museums, sightseeing commentaries by a multilingual guide, and assistance with the tasks of checking in and out.

Another company offering organized visits to Switzerland is **American Express Vacations, Inc.,** P.O. Box 5014, Atlanta, GA 30302 (tel. toll free 800/241-1700), one of the biggest tour operators in the world. Its 14-day tour of "Romantic Europe" includes alpine destinations in Italy, Austria, Switzerland, and Germany. Hotels are first class, rather than deluxe, and travel is usually by motorcoach. The Swiss itinerary begins with a visit to Innsbruck, Austria, and takes in Davos, Lugano, and Lucerne.

SUGGESTED ITINERARIES

IF YOU HAVE 1 WEEK For a visitor in a rush, the classic tour of Switzerland is to drive from German-speaking Zurich to French-speaking Geneva, or vice versa, along the way taking in the country's scenery—an alpine landscape of snow-covered mountains, lakes, and lush valleys. For those, however, who want to see more than just highway scenery, the following itineraries are recommended:

Days 1 and 2: Figure on losing the first day just flying into Zurich and settling into a hotel. Day 2 can be spent touring the attractions of Zurich, as outlined in Chapter 3.

Days 3 and 4: On the third day, head south from Zurich along Route N3, staying on the west side of Lake Zurich. Near Wadenswil (the signs to Lucerne are clearly marked), head west to Lucerne. You'll need at least 2 nights in Lucerne, a favorite of Americans. Spend Day 4 touring Lucerne by paddle-steamer and taking cable cars or funiculars to mountain peaks, such as Rigi and Pilatus. This is the heartland of Switzerland.

Days 5 and 6: After 2 nights, head southwest to Interlaken (take N8), the centuries-old tourist capital of the Bernese Oberland. You will go via the Brunig Pass, a distance of only 35 miles (it will seem much longer). Interlaken is mainly a summer retreat, lying between two lakes, Thun and Brienz. People come here to take excursions to the frozen Jungfrau, which, at 11,333 feet, is one of the highlights of Switzerland. After settling into Interlaken, you'll be ready for an early departure to Jungfrau the following morning, returning late that afternoon.

Day 7: Following that, it's an easy, scenic drive northwest to Bern, a distance of 34 miles via Thun along N6. A diplomatic center, and one of Europe's great medieval cities, Bern deserves at least a night's stopover.

IF YOU HAVE 2 WEEKS   Spend the first week as outlined above.

Days 8 and 9: After a night in Bern, you can head southwest to Lausanne, the fifth-largest city in Switzerland, rising in tiers from Lac Léman (Lake Geneva). Take N12 for 56 miles. Lausanne deserves at least 2 days of your time. Most of Day 8 will be absorbed in getting there and settling into a hotel. Spend Day 9 exploring the city's many attractions and visiting Ouchy (see Chapter 8).

Days 10–12: The next day you can head to Geneva, the country's second-largest city, 38 miles west of Lausanne. Take the western route along the northern arc of Lac Léman. You can make the trip in 2 hours, but you'll enjoy it more if you allow at least half a day. Stop for lunch in Nyon. If you take your time and sample the beauty of the towns and villages along the lake, you'll arrive in Geneva in late afternoon. On the 11th day take a boat trip on Lake Geneva and walk the quays, exploring the attractions of this fabulously rich city. Set aside the 12th day for a visit to Mont Blanc, including a cable-car ride to the summit of Aiguille du Midi—at 12,610 feet, one of the all-time greatest alpine panoramas. A border crossing into France will be part of the experience.

Day 13: Drive along Route 21 east across the southern part of Lake Geneva (which is in France) and head for Montreux, the premier resort of the Vaud Riviera. Visit the Château of Chillon, immortalized by Lord Byron in *The Prisoner of Chillon*.

Day 14: From Montreux head south on E62 to Martigny, continuing east to Visp, where transportation connections are made to the popular ski resort of Zermatt. A small village, Zermatt lies at the base of the great Matterhorn, which towers over it at 14,690 feet.

IF YOU HAVE 3 WEEKS   Those with a third week or more to spend in Switzerland might want to consider an excursion from Zurich to Lugano, the capital of the Italian-speaking Ticino. We'll detour through one of the most charming valleys of Europe, the Engadine, whose tourist center is St. Moritz. The 200-mile trip is made significantly more pleasant by the beautiful scenery along the way.

The roads to the Grisons and the Engadine are open year round and are usually filled with skiers driving to such popular resorts as Davos, Arosa, and Klosters. If you're driving in winter, make sure your car has the proper equipment.

Day 15: Take N3 south from Zurich and drive along the southern shores of Lake Zurich and Lake Walen until you come to Chur, a distance of 76 miles. Chur is the capital of the Grisons (see Chapter 11) and the oldest town in Switzerland. You'll have time to walk around the old town and maybe take a scenic drive east to the alpine resort of Arosa, at 6,000 feet. You can spend the night in Chur.

Days 16 and 17: A short drive south from Chur will take you to Valbella/Lenzerheide on Lake Heid, at an altitude of 4,757 feet. After a stop, continue along the same route to Savognin at the mouth of the Val Nandro.

At the famed Julier Pass, you'll be at the main entrance to the Engadine. The first village you'll come to is Silvaplana. Take a short drive east to the more glamorous—and more expensive—St. Moritz. (By the time you reach St. Moritz, you will have covered 126 miles since leaving Zurich. If you drive straight through without stopping, you will be able to reach St. Moritz in 4 hours.

You should stay at least 2 nights in St. Moritz. The following day you can continue your drive up the Engadine Valley, which stretches for 60 miles from the Maloja Plateau, at 5,955 feet, to Finstermünz.

Days 18 and 19: After leaving St. Moritz, head 79 miles south to Lugano. Because of the mountainous roads, the trip takes 4 hours, but the majestic scenery more than compensates for the time. The route takes you into Italy (border formalities are generally relaxed).

Get an early start from St. Moritz and head in a southwesterly direction toward the Maloja Pass, traveling through Vicosoprano. Continue along Route 37 to Chiavenna, crossing into Italy at Castasegna. This is the sunny south—"land where the lemon trees bloom," in Goethe's charming poem. Once you reach Chiavenna, you can travel along a narrow highway, following the western side of Lake Como, toward Lugano. Exit at Menaggio. Once there, head right along Route 340 in the direction of Lake Lugano, passing through charming little villages along the northern shoreline. Make Lugano your base for exploring the Ticino.

Day 20: To leave Lugano, head north along N2 and take the western exit to Locarno, which is the second major resort of Ticino. Save part of your afternoon to drive west along the lake to the old town of Ascona, which many visitors prefer to Locarno itself. Return to Locarno for the night.

Day 21: To return to Zurich at a leisurely pace, take E9 toward the St. Gotthard Pass—one of the most historic and most popular routes in Switzerland. The pass provides a link between the Grisons and the Valais Alps. The road tunnel, which was inaugurated in 1980, is open year round. You can stay overnight at Andermatt, which stands at the junction of four alpine roads. Northern routes to Zurich are clearly marked. In general, count on about 3 to 3½ hours of driving time between the St. Gotthard Pass and Zurich.

9. WHERE TO STAY

HOTELS

Most hotels in Switzerland are clean, comfortable, and efficiently run. On the deluxe level they are among the finest in the world (two in Zurich, in fact, are regarded as the best in Europe). After all, César Ritz came from Switzerland.

FROMMER'S SMART TRAVELER: HOTELS

TIPS FOR VALUE-CONSCIOUS TRAVELERS

1. The price you pay in inexpensive hotels depends on the plumbing. Rooms with showers are much cheaper than those with private baths. Even cheaper is a room with a sink and a *cabinette de toilet* (toilet and bidet).
2. Consider a package tour (or book land arrangements with your air ticket). You'll often pay 30% less than individual "rack rates" (off-the-street independent bookings).
3. Ask about winter discounts. Some hotels won't grant them, but many will, especially if bookings that week were light.

QUESTIONS TO ASK IF YOU'RE ON A BUDGET

1. Is there a surcharge on either local or long-distance calls? Often surcharges are lethal, maybe an astonishing 40%. If so, make your calls at the nearest post office.
2. Is there a garage? What's the charge?
3. Does the hotel include service of 10% or 15% in the rates (*service compris*), or will it be added on at the end of your stay?
4. Are all hotel taxes included in the price or will they be added on?
5. Is breakfast (continental) included in the rates?

There are several kinds and categories of hotels. An *alkoholfrei* hotel is one that doesn't serve liquor. A hotel *garni* is one that serves breakfast and beverages but no other meals. You can judge a hotel (and its prices) by its stars: Five stars signify deluxe; four stars, first class; three stars, superior; and two stars, standard. One star indicates "minimum." A minimum hotel, with the most limited of facilities, can nevertheless be clean and reasonably comfortable; and standard hotels are among the best travel values in the country.

Reservations may be made directly with the hotel, through any recognized travel agency, or through various reservations systems that have toll-free 800 numbers. The hotel is entitled to request a deposit when you make your reservation (the amount will vary from hotel to hotel).

ALTERNATIVES TO HOTELS

BED-AND-BREAKFAST The Swiss concept of a bed-and-breakfast is different from that in the United States and Canada. In Switzerland many bed-and-breakfast places are more like small, cozy hotels than like private homes. Called "E+G Hotels"—a voluntary chain of 220 guesthouses—they are located throughout the country. A folder listing addresses and phone numbers is available from the Swiss National Tourist Office. You may want to join the privately run Bed-and-Breakfast Club in Switzerland. A price-worthy way to travel, it is a source of friendly contacts and cultural exchanges.

PRIVATE HOMES In Swiss mountain and rural areas, a list of private accommodations can be obtained from most local tourist offices. Look for the various signs advertising such an accommodation (generally, a single room): ZIMMER FREI in German, CHAMBRE A LOUER in French, and AFFITASI CAMERA in Italian.

CHALET, HOUSE, AND APARTMENT RENTALS For a list of U.S. agencies handling such rentals, contact the Swiss National Tourist Office. Local tourist offices in Switzerland also provide listings of apartments and chalets to rent. The Swiss prefer to do business in writing rather than on the phone. It is therefore strongly recommended that you write to the home owners; allow about 20 days for a reply.

The best agency for arranging vacation homes in Switzerland is a Swiss-based company, **Interhome,** representing some 20,000 properties. Travelers have easy access to chalets and condos in all the major resort areas—from modest studio apartments at budget prices to luxurious villas with all the modern amenities. The U.S. branch, Interhome, Inc., is at 124 Little Balls Road, Fairfield, NJ 07004 (tel. 201/882-6864). You can contact it for a catalog of vacation homes available in some 80 locations in Switzerland.

FARM VACATIONS A unique way to get to know Switzerland, this program lets you experience firsthand the working world, home life, and food of a Swiss farming family. A brochure, "Swiss Farm Holidays," tells how it's done; it's available from the Swiss National Tourist Office.

YOUTH HOSTELS About 100 youth hostels exist in Switzerland, open to single people or families. Fees range from $5 to $12 per person per night, depending on the hostel. There is no upper age limit, but in peak season members who are 25 and younger have priority. For an International Youth Hostel Card and more information, contact American Youth Hostels, Inc., P.O. Box 37613, Washington, DC 20013-7613 (tel. 202/783-6161).

10. WHERE TO DINE

Breakfast, usually included in the price of your hotel room, will probably be continental style, often served as a buffet. You'll get rolls, butter, preserves, coffee or tea, and some fruit juices. If you order extras—such as orange juice, bacon or ham, and eggs—you may be stuck with a stiff tab.

When in doubt about where to eat, try a railroad-station buffet; it's generally excellent and moderate in price. If you want a fast-food meal, head for a modestly priced *Imbiss,* or snack bar, for open-face sandwiches and other selections.

As a country of cultural diversity, Switzerland offers a wide range of cuisines, mainly French, German, and Italian, along with a few dishes that might be called "national specialties," such as fried potatoes known as Rösti. Most restaurants offer a special of the day, known as a *Tagesteller* or *plat du jour,* which usually represents the best value on the menu.

To cut costs, always ask for the local wine when visiting a particular region. It will

---

IMPRESSIONS

The Swiss managed to build a lovely country around their hotels.
—GEORGE MIKES, DOWN WITH EVERYBODY, 1951

usually be excellent and far cheaper than a wine "imported" to the area. Unlike French wines, Swiss wines are best when new. Swiss beer is also first-rate.

Visitors who eat only kosher food can obtain from the Swiss National Tourist Office a list of Swiss restaurants serving such a cuisine.

From cities to villages, a traveler in Switzerland will find a wide diversity of restaurants, from a country inn to a fashionable five-star establishment opening onto some alpine peak or lake. In winter the Swiss like to gravitate to a cozy, wood-paneled country *Gasthof* (inn), but in fair weather they prefer the lakeside terrace restaurant with its scenic view. Mountain restaurants at high altitudes are popular year round.

Home-style eating places in the Italian-speaking Ticino are known as *grotti*. The most interesting places to dine at in Zurich are the guildhalls. You get history with your cuisine. Geneva is like a Swiss Paris, and the best places for genuine food and atmosphere are the brasseries and bistros of Old Town. In Bern, while exploring the city's medieval origins, you might want to pause for a stein of beer and a hearty Swiss repast in one of the *Bierkeller* (beer cellars).

In any region of Switzerland, you'll find Italian pasta and pizza emporiums, along with American fast-food burgers and such. But you'll also face a sampling of the fares of other nationalities, especially Chinese, Indian, and Greek.

Many places are closed on Sunday. As a rule of thumb, the midday meal is served from noon to 1:30pm and dinner is served from 7 to 9:30pm. Of course, in such big cities as Zurich and Geneva you can dine around the clock. In small villages, early restaurant closings are more common.

Some of the best, most expensive restaurants in Switzerland also have a moderately priced café section serving excellent food, often from the same kitchen. Sometimes the restaurant will be upstairs and the café downstairs, opening onto a boulevard. Of course, you don't get the formal service and rich atmosphere of the main restaurant, but many locals prefer to dine in cafés.

In some restaurants, "cash-register tickets" are placed on your table as you order. For example, you get a separate ticket for each beer ordered or each plate of food. The "damages" are added up on one final bill.

Most restaurants include a service charge of 10% to 15%. If you are pleased with the service, it is still customary to leave a few extra francs.

11. WHAT TO BUY

Swiss goods are of a very high standard and are usually superbly finished. You will find a wide choice of handmade products, from all parts of Switzerland, at the "Swisscraft" shops located across the country. (English, by the way, is spoken in most shops and department stores.)

Typical items to look for are linen, embroideries, fine handkerchiefs, textiles, wood carvings, ceramic arts, toys, dolls, multipurpose Swiss army pocketknives, and music boxes. Of course, there are also the world-famous Swiss watches and clocks to consider if you're pondering a choice of souvenirs; they come in a great variety of designs and prices. If you decide to buy a cuckoo clock, check for the country of origin. Switzerland may be traditionally associated with such clocks, but often the ones you find on sale have been made in Germany's Black Forest—they're fine, but they're not *Swiss* cuckoo clocks.

Other items on your souvenir list may be Swiss chocolates, which are justifiably famous; Swiss brandies, made from a variety of fruits (cherries, grapes, apples, plums) and flavored with alpine herbs; and Swiss pottery, excellent specimens of which can be found in every region.

The major cities and towns all have attractive shopping districts, where you can find high-quality fabrics and the latest in haute couture. Bern, Geneva, and Lausanne have many bookstores and antique shops in their old-town quarters. (Note that while classic antiques are priced beyond the means of the average visitor, rustic Swiss furniture pieces are more moderately priced.)

If you're interested in wood carving, you can visit the famous center in Brienz, attached to the Bernese Cantonal Wood-carving School: Huggler-Wyss, Holz-Bildhauerei, Brunngasse, 3855 Brienz (tel. 036/51-16-79). The best art galleries are in Zurich, Geneva, Lausanne, and Basel. Dealers will ship your purchases to your home.

TAX REFUNDS   Foreign visitors may obtain a refund on the WUST (Merchandise Turnover Tax), amounting to 6.2%, if the purchase exceeds 500F ($364.95) per item. For information on how to get your refund, ask the seller. Most merchants will be quite willing to help with the paperwork.

FAST FACTS: SWITZERLAND

American Express   American Express has offices in Geneva, Zurich, and Bern (see the individual city chapters).

Business Hours   **Banks** are usually open Monday through Friday from 8:30am to 4:30pm (closed on legal holidays). Foreign currency may be exchanged at major railroad stations and airports daily until 10pm. Most **business offices** are open Monday through Friday from 8am to noon and 2 to 6pm. **Shops** are usually open Monday through Friday from 8am to 12:15pm and 1:30 to 6:30pm, and on Saturday from 1:30 to 4pm. In large cities most shops don't close during the lunch hour, although many do so on Monday morning.

Cigarettes   Most popular U.S. brands can be found in Switzerland. However, there are many British- and Swiss-made brands you may want to try, especially if you like a mild cigarette. Cigars and pipe tobacco are also widely available.

Climate   See Section 2, "When to Go," above.

Crime   See "Safety," below.

Currency/Currency Exchange   See Section 1, "Information, Documents & Money," above.

Customs   U.S. residents returning from abroad are allowed to bring back $400 in duty-free items for personal use. To qualify, you must have been outside the United States at least 48 hours and not have claimed an exemption in the previous 30 days. Articles valued in excess of $400 will be assessed at a flat duty rate of 10%. Antiques and original works of art produced 100 years prior to the date that you return to the United States may be brought home duty free, but you must be able to prove their authenticity. Gifts for your personal use, but not for business purposes, may be excluded from the $400 exemption. You can send home unsolicited gifts amounting to a total of $50 per day without declaring them on your Customs form. Liquor is limited to one 32-ounce bottle; tobacco, to 200 cigarettes and 100 cigars. Keep all your receipts for purchases made in Switzerland or elsewhere on your trip abroad, as you may be asked for proof of the prices you paid.

Documents Required   See Section 1, "Information, Documents & Money," above.

Driving Rules   See Section 8, "Getting Around," above.

Drug Laws A word of warning: Penalties for illegal drug possession are more severe in Switzerland than they are in the United States and Canada. You could go to jail or be deported immediately. Note that drug sellers often turn in their customers to the police.

Drugstores Switzerland has excellent pharmacies. Yet, outside the main cities it's hard to get a prescription filled after business hours.

Electricity Switzerland's electricity is 220 volts, 50 cycles, AC. Some international hotels are specially wired to allow North Americans to plug in their appliances, but you'll usually need a transformer for your electric razor, hairdryer, or soft-contact-lens sterilizer. Ask at the electrical department of a large hardware store for the size of transformer you'll need. You'll also need an adapter plug to channel the electricity from the Swiss system to the flat-pronged American system. Don't plug anything into the house current in Switzerland without being certain the systems are compatible.

Embassies and Consulates Embassies are located in Bern, the capital; some nations also maintain consulates in other cities. **United States:** Embassy at Jubiläumsstrasse 93, Bern (tel. 031/43-70-11); consulate in Geneva, at 1–3, avenue de la Paix (tel. 022/733-55-37), and in Zurich, at Zollikerstrasse 141 (tel. 01/55-25-66). **United Kingdom:** Embassy at Thunstrasse 50, Bern (tel. 031/44-50-21); consulate in Geneva, at 37-39, rue de Vermont (tel. 022/734-38-00), and in Zurich, at Dufourstrasse 56 (tel. 01/47-15-20). **Canada:** Embassy at Kirchenfeldstrasse 88, Bern (tel. 031/44-63-81); consulate in Geneva, at 11, chemin du Pré-de-la-Bichette (tel. 022/733-90-00). **Australia:** Embassy at Alpenstrasse 29, Bern (tel. 031/43-01-43). **New Zealand:** Does not have an embassy in Switzerland; consulate-general in Geneva, at 28A, chemin du Petit-Saconnex (tel. 022/734-95-30).

Emergencies Dial 117 for the **police** (emergencies only) and 118 to report a **fire.**

Etiquette The Swiss tend to be polite and reserved, and appreciate foreigners who are the same. Pushing in line is definitely out; loud talk in restaurants is frowned upon. When invited to homes, guests are expected to bring either chocolates or flowers.

Gambling Many Swiss towns and resorts have casinos, but, because of government restrictions, they are less affluent than casinos in other countries. A wide choice of entertainment is offered, including folklore displays. Gambling is restricted to boule games; the maximum bet is 5F ($3.65). The minimum age for gambling in Switzerland is 20.

Gasoline See Section 8, "Getting Around," above.

Hitchhiking See Section 8, "Getting Around," above.

Holidays See Section 2, "When to Go," above.

Information See Section 1, "Information, Documents & Money," above; and individual chapters for local information offices.

Language The three major languages are German, French, and Italian, although most people in the tourist industry speak English. The best phrase books are published by Berlitz: *French for Travellers, German for Travellers,* and *Italian for Travellers*.

Laundry Most hotels will do your laundry for you. To do your own, see listings of self-service laundries in the individual city chapters.

Legal Aid This may be hard to come by in Switzerland. The government advises foreigners to consult their embassy or consulate (see "Embassies and Consulates," above) in case of a dire emergency, such as an arrest. Even if your embassy or consulate declines to offer financial or legal help, it will generally offer advice on how to obtain help locally.

Liquor Laws   The official drinking age is 16. As in many European countries, the application of laws governing drinking are flexible and enforced only if a problem develops or if decorum is broken. Driving while intoxicated, particularly if it results in damage to property or persons, brings swift and severe punishment, involving sizable fines and possible imprisonment.

Mail   Post offices in large cities are open Monday through Friday from 7:30am to noon and 1:45 to 6:30pm, and on Saturday from 7:30 to 11am. If you have letters forwarded to a post office to be collected after you arrive, you'll need a passport for identification. The words *"Poste Restante"* must be clearly written on the envelope. Letters not collected within 30 days are returned to the sender. It costs 1.10F (82¢) to send an airmail postcard to Canada and the United States. Airmail letters weighing up to 10 grams cost 1.40F ($1.10) to Canada and the United States.

Maps   See "By Car" in Section 8, "Getting Around," above.

Newspapers/Magazines   Most Swiss papers are published in German, French, or Italian. Most news kiosks in major cities stock the British dailies, plus the latest editions of the *International Herald Tribune,* which, although edited in Paris, is printed in Zurich. The latest copies of *Time* and *Newsweek* or other U.S. and British magazines are also widely available, often at your hotel.

Passports   See Section 1, "Information, Documents & Money," above.

Pets   Dogs and cats brought into Switzerland from abroad will require a veterinary certificate stating that the animals have been vaccinated against rabies not less than 30 days and not more than 1 year prior to entry into the country. This regulation also applies to dogs and cats returning after a temporary absence from Switzerland, but is not applicable to animals transported through the country by rail or air traffic.

Photographic Needs   Every major town in Switzerland has outlets selling and processing popular brands and sizes of film. In alpine resorts most outlets develop and make black-and-white prints, but color shots usually have to be mailed to city labs for processing.

Police   Dial 117 for emergencies.

Radio/TV   Television programming is in German, French, or Italian, but often films in English are shown, with the local language appearing as subtitles. Most hotels have radios, on which you can hear British news broadcasts at certain times, even English programs broadcast by Swiss Radio International, a shortwave service coming from Bern. The BBC can often be picked up on transistor sets, as can the American Forces Network.

Rest Rooms   Most Swiss public rest rooms are clean and modernized. However, in this multilingual country you'll have to know what you're looking for. Depending on which part of Switzerland you find yourself in, public rest rooms may be WC (water closet), *Toiletten, toilettes,* or *gabinetti.* Women's rooms may be identified as *"Damen"* or *"Frauen," "Signore"* or *"Donne," "Femmes"* or *"Dames";* and men's rooms may be labeled *"Herren"* or *"Männer," "Signori"* or *"Uomini," "Hommes"* or *"Messieurs."* Public rest rooms can be found at bus stations, railway terminals, and cable-car platforms. If these aren't handy, use the rest rooms in cafés. Most public lavatories are free, but have a 20-centime or 50-centime piece ready just in case.

Safety   Crimes of violence, such as muggings, are rare in Switzerland. It is generally safe to walk the streets of cities day and night. The most common crime reported by visitors is a picked pocket. Often the pickpockets are not Swiss but visitors to the country or newly arrived, unemployed immigrants. It used to be safe to leave your ski equipment atop cars, but no more.

Taxes   No taxes are added to purchases in Switzerland. Swiss merchants pay tax to the government, and the percentage is included in the price marked on any object.

In addition, foreign and Swiss drivers entering Switzerland are required by law to purchase a windshield sticker for 30F ($21.90), valid for travel on Swiss roads for 1 year. Without a sticker, you can be subject to a 60F ($43.80) fine. Stickers are sold at all Customs posts upon entering Switzerland.

Telephone/Telex/Fax   The telephone system is entirely automatic and connects the entire country. Helpful numbers to know are: 111 for directory assistance, 120 for tourist information or in winter for snow reports, 140 for help on the road, 162 for weather forecasts, and 163 for up-to-the-minute information on road conditions. Hotels add substantial service charges for calls made from your room; it's considerably less expensive to make calls from a public phone booth. It is possible to call your home collect.

To use a coin-operated telephone, lift the receiver and insert 40 centimes (35¢) to get a dial tone. Be sure to have enough coins on hand, as you must insert more for each message unit over your initial deposit. (If you insert more coins than necessary, the excess amount will be returned.) A pay phone will accept up to 5F ($3.65).

To make a local call, dial directly after you hear the dial tone (no area code needed); for other places in Switzerland, dial the area code and then the number. To call a foreign country, dial the code of the country first, then the area code, and then the number.

Faxes and telexes are usually sent at your hotel for a moderate surcharge, or you can go to the local post office.

Time   Switzerland's clocks are 6 hours ahead of eastern standard time in the United States, and 1 hour ahead of Greenwich mean time.

Tipping   A 15% service charge is automatically included in all **hotel and restaurant** bills, although some people leave an additional tip if the service has been exceptional. For **taxis**, a tip is usually included in the charges (a notice will be posted in the cab).

Tourist Offices   See Section 1, "Information, Documents & Money," in this chapter; and specific cities throughout this book.

Visas   See Section 1, "Information, Documents & Money," above.

Water   Tap water is safe to drink in all Swiss towns and cities. But don't drink from rivers or mountain streams, regardless of how clean the water may appear.

Yellow Pages   Unless you command a knowledge of German, French, or Italian, you may not know what you are looking up in the yellow pages of the phone directories. You can ask someone at your hotel to locate a particular service for you.

CHAPTER 3

ZURICH

Zurich is the largest city in Switzerland and one of the most beautiful cities in Europe. It still retains much of its 19th-century charm. The city is situated on the northern shore of Lake Zurich in the heart of Helvetia. It is big enough to offer all the amenities to visitors, yet small enough to discover on your own.

Zurich is the capital of a canton of the same name that joined the Swiss Confederation in 1351. Most of the city's 380,000 residents speak a form of German called Schwyzerdütsch (Schweizerdeutsch, in standard German). A former seat of the Reformation, Zurich is staunchly Protestant (some say Puritan).

Zurich began as a textile center and has become heavily industrialized. Its skies are not polluted, however, because the factories run on electricity. Zurich is also a center of international finance; the headquarters of five major banks are on Bahnhofstrasse. Bankers are sometimes referred to as gnomes because banks store mountains of gold in underground vaults.

Zurich produces one-fifth of the nation's income, but it's far from a dreary city of commerce. It has been a great center of liberal thought, attracting Lenin, Carl Jung, James Joyce, and Thomas Mann. The dadaist school was founded here in 1916. The increase of visitors in the last two decades has spurred the development of a more lively nightlife and entertainment scene.

1. ORIENTATION

ARRIVING

BY PLANE   Kloten Airport (tel. 816-25-34), the international airport of Zurich, is the biggest airport in Switzerland and the most popular gateway to the country. It's among the 10 busiest airports in Europe.

WHAT'S SPECIAL ABOUT ZURICH

Ace Attractions

☐ The quays of Zurich, promenades along Lake Zurich and the Limmat River, the most famous being Limmatquai, in the heart of the city.

☐ Altstadt (Old Town), on both sides of the Limmat, filled with cobblestone streets, old squares, and winding alleyways.

Religious Shrines

☐ Fraumünster Church, from the 12th century, noted for its chapel and stained-glass windows by Chagall.

☐ Grossmünster (the cathedral), whose legendary founder was Charlemagne; the parish church of Zwingli, the reformer.

Museums

☐ The Swiss National Museum, providing the largest and most comprehensive view of Swiss history. Some of its religious artworks date from the 9th century.

☐ The Museum Rietberg, one of the most important collections of non-European art on the continent.

☐ The Fine Arts Museum, an excellent assemblage of art from the Middle Ages to Rodin and Giacometti.

Shopping

☐ If only for window-shopping, Bahnhofstrasse is one of Europe's most elegant shopping streets, filled with luxurious merchandise.

Excursions

☐ A summertime boat ride on Lake Zurich, one of the most beautiful lakes in Europe.

Kloten is located far away from the center of Zurich; the 7-mile trip by taxi costs 43F to 50F ($31.40 to $36.50). The train service offered by Swiss Federal Railways is much cheaper; for 4.60F ($3.40), you'll be delivered in fewer than 10 minutes to the Zurich Hauptbahnhof, the main railway station. The train runs every 20 to 30 minutes from 5:30am to 11pm. You can also take bus no. 68 (Zurich Airport–Seebach), but you'll have to change to tram no. 14 to get to the center of town.

BY TRAIN Trains leave Gare de l'Est in Paris daily at 5:04pm, reaching Zurich at 11pm. Another train departs from Paris at 7:30am daily, going via Basel, with an arrival in Zurich at 1:23pm. From Munich the *Gottfried Keller Express* departs daily at noon, with a 4:21pm arrival in Zurich. The *Bavaria* leaves Munich daily at 6pm, arriving in Zurich at 10:21pm.

Arrivals are at the Zurich Hauptbahnhof (tel. 211-50-10).

BY BUS Zurich's bus routes function only as feeder lines from outlying suburbs (which lie off the train lines) into the vicinity of the town's railroad station.

BY CAR From Basel take N3 east; from Geneva take N1 northeast, going via Bern, where you will connect with E4 and E17 heading east into Zurich.

IMPRESSIONS

Zurich's relationship to the world is not of the spirit, but of commerce.
—C. J. JUNG

BY BOAT   The **Zurichsee-Schiffahrtsgesellschaft,** Mythenquai 333 (tel. 482-10-33), offers regularly scheduled modern passenger ships as well as old steamers plying both sides of Lake Zurich. The service is operated from Easter to October, going from Zurich as far as Rapperswil.

TOURIST INFORMATION

The **Zurich Tourist Office,** Bahnhofplatz 15 (tel. 01/211-40-00), is at the main railway station. It's open March through October, Monday through Friday from 8am to 10pm and on Saturday and Sunday from 8am to 8:30pm; November through February, Monday through Thursday from 8am to 8pm, on Friday from 8am to 10pm, and on Saturday and Sunday from 9am to 6pm. There's a branch office at the airport (tel. 816-40-81), open daily from 8am to 8pm.

CITY LAYOUT

Zurich is situated on both shores of the Limmat River where it flows from the northern end of Lake Zurich. The Sihl River, a tributary of the Limmat, also flows through the city, and quays line the riverbanks and the lake. The city spreads across a ravine in the eastern hills between the wooded slopes of the Zürichberg and the Käferberg hills into the Glatt River valley.

Zurich might be said to have begun at the **Lindenhof,** which is where you, too, might begin your orientation to the city. This square is the architectural center of historic Zurich. From here, you can survey the city as it rises on both banks of the Limmat from **Bahnhofbrücke** (*Brücke* means "bridge") to **Quailbrücke.** Between these two bridges are four other spans over the river: Muhle-Steg, Rudbrunbrücke, Rathausbrücke, and Münsterbrücke.

Below this square runs **Bahnhofstrasse,** one of the most elegant and expensive shopping streets in the world. It begins in the west, at the **Hauptbahnhof,** the railway station, opening onto Bahnhofplatz, and runs east to the lake. It crosses **Paradeplatz,** a converging point for trams and the modern center of the city. From Paradeplatz you can continue east, passing Fraumünster church and crossing Münsterbrücke to reach the right bank of the river. Here, the narrow streets of the **Limmatquai** are the second-best place in the city to shop. Running parallel to Limmatquai is **Niederdorfstrasse,** in the so-called red-light district of Zurich.

Old Town, or **Altstadt,** developed in the early medieval period and is focused on Lindenhof, Fraumünster, Grossmünster, and St. Peter's. It expanded to **Weinplatz,** the oldest market square, and **Strehlgasse.** By the 11th century the city continued its development on the right bank with such centers as **Kirchgasse** and **Neumarkt.**

NEIGHBORHOODS IN BRIEF   Zurich is divided by the Limmat River into two general areas.

   West Bank of the Limmat   This district is dominated by Bahnhofplatz, center of rail connections, and Bahnhofstrasse, which is the main commercial and banking thoroughfare. This is the Zurich world of high finance and elegant shops. The venerable Fraumünster, on Fraumünsterstrasse, dominates the west bank.

   East Bank of the Limmat   Opposite the Fraumünster, on the other side of the river, rises Grossmünster, on Grossmünsterplatz; its two Gothic towers are an east-bank landmark. The historic guildhalls of Zurich, such as the Zunfthaus zur Saffran, rise on the east bank of the river. So, too, does the Rathaus, the city's town hall, completed in 1698. On the east bank you can explore the eastern part of Altstadt, strolling along Neumarkt, one of the best preserved of the old streets. The area beyond is Niederdorf, the center of the town's "hot spots."

FINDING AN ADDRESS In a system that developed during the Middle Ages, all Swiss cities, including Zurich, begin their street-numbering system with the lowest numbers closest to the center of town. In Zurich, the center is the Hauptbahnhof. All even numbers lie on one side of the street and all odd numbers are on the other.

MAPS The best map of Zurich, published by Falk, is a pocketsize *Stadtplan* (city plan) with an index. Copies are available at various newsstands and at any bookstore. Try the **Travel Book Shop,** Rindermarkt 20 (tel. 252-38-83).

2. GETTING AROUND

Zurich is an easy city to navigate. The trams (streetcars) and buses are reliable and can take you to most areas you wish to visit.

BY PUBLIC TRANSPORTATION The public transport system of Zurich is operated by **VEZ Züri-Linie,** or Zurich Public Transport (tel. 211-50-10 for information). The modern and extensive network of trams and buses (there is no subway) runs daily from 5:30am to midnight. You should have to wait no longer than 7 minutes at rush hours. Most trams and buses originate at the Zurich Hauptbahnhof, in the heart of the city.

Tickets are purchased from automatic vending machines located at every stop. You must have a ticket *before* you get on a vehicle; if you're caught without one, you'll pay a fine of 30F ($21.90).

For a trip of up to five stops the **fare** is 1.50F ($1.10) for short rides and 2F ($1.45) for longer journeys. Visitors can get the most for their money by ordering a *Tageskarte* (one-day ticket), costing 5F ($3.65), which allows you to travel on all city buses and trams for 24 hours.

BY TAXI Traveling by taxi is very expensive. Therefore, use taxis as a last resort. The only good thing about them is that the service charge is included in the fare. The basic charge is 5F ($3.65), plus 2.40F ($1.80) per kilometer (tip included). Call 44-44-41 for **Taxi-Zentrale Zurich.**

BY CAR I don't recommend attempting to see Zurich by car—the city is too congested and parking is too scarce. Save the car for exploring the environs.

Parking You should get a street plan (see "Maps" in Section 1, "Orientation," above), which indicates parking garages by a "P" sign; a similar leaflet is available from the Zurich police. Some hotels have their own parking garages, for which there is an extra charge; others, especially those in congested Old Town, do not. You'll have to inquire at your hotel for the location of the nearest public garage likely to be open at the time of your arrival.

Rental Cars All the major car-rental firms are represented in Zurich, with offices at Kloten Airport and downtown, including **Avis,** Gartenhofstrasse 17 (tel. 242-20-40); **Budget Rent-a-Car,** Lindenstrasse 33 (tel. 47-17-47); and **Hertz,** Lagerstrasse 33 (tel. 242-84-84).

BY BICYCLE If you're energetic, bicycling is a good way for you to get around Zurich, especially in the outlying areas. Bicycles can be rented at the baggage counter of the railway station, the Hauptbahnhof (tel. 211-50-10), for 12F ($8.75) per day.

ON FOOT This is the only real way to explore Zurich. Zurich and its quays are ideal for walking, and many of the places of interest, such as the sights of Altstadt on both sides of the Limmat, are conveniently grouped together. Take a walking tour for a general overview, and then go inside any buildings or attractions that interest you.

 ZURICH

American Express The office at Bahnhofstrasse 20 (tel. 211-83-70) is open Monday through Friday from 8:30am to 5:30pm and on Saturday and Sunday from 9am to noon.

Area Code Zurich's telephone area code is 01.

Baby-sitters Call **Kady** (tel. 211-37-86) for an English-speaking baby-sitter. The **Jelmoli Department Store,** Bahnhofstrasse 69 (tel. 220-44-11), has child-care facilities.

Bookstores A good one, with a wide selection of English titles, is **Daeniker's Bookshop,** In Gassen 11 (tel. 211-27-04), between the Limmat River and Paradeplatz. Excellent for travel guides of all kinds is the **Travel Book Shop,** Rindermarkt 20 (tel. 242-38-83), whose well-traveled owner, Gisela Treichler, is a specialist in travel to both central Europe and central Asia.

Business Hours **Banks** are open Monday through Wednesday and Friday from 8:15am to 4:30pm and on Thursday from 8:15am to 6pm. Two well-known banks are the Union Bank of Switzerland, at ShopVille (tel. 234-11-11), and the Swiss Bank Corporation, Bahnhofstrasse 70 (tel. 211-31-71). For hours of **offices and shops,** see "Fast Facts: Switzerland" in Chapter 2.

Car Rentals See Section 2, "Getting Around," above.

Climate Summers in Zurich are not as warm as on the French Riviera, but the lake is usually warm enough to swim in during July and August. Many days are chilly, and spring and fall can be quite cold. In winter the temperature rarely goes below zero. The average temperature in January is 30°F; in July the average is only 61°F. On cloudy days the view of the Alps is obscured.

Consulates If you lose your passport or have another emergency, go to the **U.S. Consulate,** Zollikerstrasse 141 (tel. 55-25-66). The **Consulate of the U.K.** is at Dufourstrasse 56 (tel. 47-15-20). Canadians and Australians should contact their respective embassies in Bern, and New Zealanders should apply to their consulate-general in Geneva (see "Fast Facts: Switzerland" in Chapter 2).

Currency See Section 1, "Information, Documents & Money," in Chapter 2.

Currency Exchange Most banks and travel agencies will exchange money for you. There's also an exchange office at the Zurich Hauptbahnhof, the main railway station, open daily from 6:30am to 11:30pm.

Dentist Emergency dental problems can be solved by calling 255-11-11. An appointment with an English-speaking dentist can be arranged for you.

Doctors Get in touch with the **Universitätsspital** (University Hospital), Rämistrasse 100 (tel. 255-11-11).

Drugstores For an all-night drugstore, go to the **Bellevue Apotheke,** Theaterstrasse 14 (tel. 252-44-11).

Emergencies Call the **police** at 117. For **first aid,** phone 47-47-00; for the **City Ambulance Service,** dial 361-61-61. There is an accident department at the **Cantonal University Hospital,** Schmelzbergstrasse 8 (tel. 255-11-11).

Eyeglasses Your eyeglasses can be replaced or repaired at **Götte's,** Bahnhofstrasse 98 (tel. 211-37-80).

Hairdressers and Barbers Women do not need a reservation at **Gidor,** Theaterstrasse 8 (tel. 251-90-18). Men can get their hair cut at the Hauptbahnhof, the rail station.

Holidays See Section 2, "When to Go," in Chapter 2.

Hospitals See "Doctors" or "Emergencies," above.

Information See "Tourist Information" in Section 1, "Orientation," above.

Laundry/Dry Cleaning One of the best self-service laundries is **MM Speed-Wash,** Müllerstrasse 55 (tel. 252-99-14), near Stauffacher Strasse and Helvetia Platz. It's open Monday through Saturday from 7am to 10pm and on Sunday from 10:30am to 10pm. A 24-hour, express dry-cleaning service is offered by **Texsana,** Baselstrasse 50 (tel. 493-14-12).

Libraries The main branch of the **Pestalozzi Library** (Zurich's public library) is at Zähringerstrasse 17 (tel. 261-78-11), open daily from 10am to 7pm.

Liquor Laws There is no difference between liquor laws in Zurich and those in the rest of Switzerland. The legal drinking age is 18, but many innkeepers claim that, unofficially, it is more like 16. There are few incidents where anyone is asked for proof of age before receiving a drink in a bar or café. Although the attitude toward drinking is relaxed, imbibers are expected to behave with restraint. This publicly sanctioned indulgence changes instantly the moment drinking is combined with driving, for which penalties are severe.

Lost Property There is a lost property office at Werdmühlestrasse 10 (tel. 216-25-50), open Monday through Friday from 7:30am to 5:30pm.

Luggage Storage/Lockers These are available at several locations throughout the vast Hauptbahnhof (tel. 211-50-10).

Newspapers/Magazines The major newspaper of Zurich is the *Neue Zürcher Zeitung,* in German. The *International Herald Tribune* is printed in Zurich. Several German-language magazines are published in Switzerland, and the latest copies of *Newsweek* and *Time* (European editions) are available at most newsstands and in big-hotel lobbies.

Photographic Needs A wide supply of all types of film is available at **Jelmoli Department Store,** Bahnhofstrasse 69 (tel. 220-44-11). Jelmoli also offers 1-hour developing service at its "Mister Minit."

Police See "Emergencies," above.

Post Office The main post office is the **Sihlpost,** Kasernenstrasse 95-99 (tel. 245-41-11), across the Sihl River from Löwenstrasse; an emergency-service window is always open. Most post offices—listed under "Post" in the phone directory—are open Monday through Friday from 7:30am to 6:30pm and on Saturday from 7:30 to 11am.

Radio/TV The Swiss Broadcasting Corporation (SBC) produces both radio and TV programs in Zurich in German. Nine different radio programs are aired by the SBC, supplemented by Swiss Radio International (SRI). The SBC also has German-language telecasts from Zurich. Via satellite, the country receives many different TV programs from its neighbors.

Religious Services Zurich has some 100 churches and three synagogues. Addresses of churches and service times are listed in the leaflet "Zürcher Kirchen laden ein" (Zurich Churches Invite), available at the tourist office.

Rest Rooms Public toilets are located at all central points, including the Hauptbahnhof and such locations as Bellevueplatz, Paradeplatz, and Heimplatz. They are open daily, generally from 5am to midnight.

Safety Zurich is considered one of the safest cities in Europe, both during the day and at night. The most potentially dangerous place is Niederdorf, the red-light district in Altstadt.

Shoe Repairs Express service is provided on the ground level of **Jelmoli Department Store,** Bahnhofstrasse 69 (tel. 220-44-11).

Taxes A 6.2% VAT (Value-Added Tax) is added to hotel and restaurant bills. There are no other special taxes.

Taxis See Section 2, "Getting Around," above.

Telephone/Telex/Fax A telephone, Telex, and fax office is open at the Zurich Hauptbahnhof, the main railway station, daily from 7am to 10:30pm.

Transit Info For bus and tram information, call 211-50-10.

Weather See "Climate," above.

Yellow Pages A knowledge of German will help you locate individual services.

3. ACCOMMODATIONS

Zurich is an ideal place to get acquainted with Swiss hospitality. Its 120 hotels offer accommodations ranging from the most sumptuous suites in Europe to simple, clean pensions. Even the cheap rooms are clean and well kept. Finding a room can be a problem, however. The top hotels are usually filled with businesspeople: The city frequently hosts conventions and fairs, so you could have trouble finding a room in February. If possible, you should arrive with a reservation.

Some of the establishments recommended below can be reached through toll-free "800" numbers in North America.

In Zurich, hotels rated "Very Expensive" charge $200 to $375 a night for a twin or double room; those considered "Expensive" ask $175 to $275. The "Moderate" range is $130 to $215, and hotels considered "Inexpensive" by Zurich standards ask $75 to $115 for a double. Anything under $75 for a double is definitely "Budget."

Note: Rooms in hotels in the "Very Expensive" and "Expensive" categories all have private baths unless otherwise indicated.

ON THE LEFT BANK

VERY EXPENSIVE

ATLANTIS SHERATON HOTEL, Döltschwieg 234, CH-8055 Zurich. Tel. 01/463-00-00, or toll free 800/325-3535 in North America. Fax 01/463-03-88. 157 rms, 4 suites. A/C MINIBAR TV TEL **Transportation:** Döltschwieg bus from the Hauptbahnhof.

$ Rates (including continental breakfast): 230F–330F ($167.90–$240.85) single; 310F–410F ($226.25–$299.25) double; from 850F ($620.40) suite. AE, DC, MC, V.

Situated in a wooded park at the foot of the Uetilberg, a 15-minute ride from the Hauptbahnhof, the Sheraton provides enough amenities to satisfy all your needs. The lobby area is tastefully decorated in steel grays and reds, with a fireplace and a burnished-metal chimney. The staff is efficient and often includes local musicians who play Swiss band music. The rooms are attractively decorated in shades of gray, with

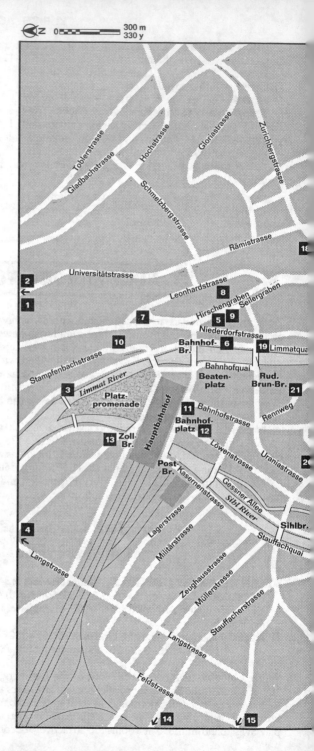

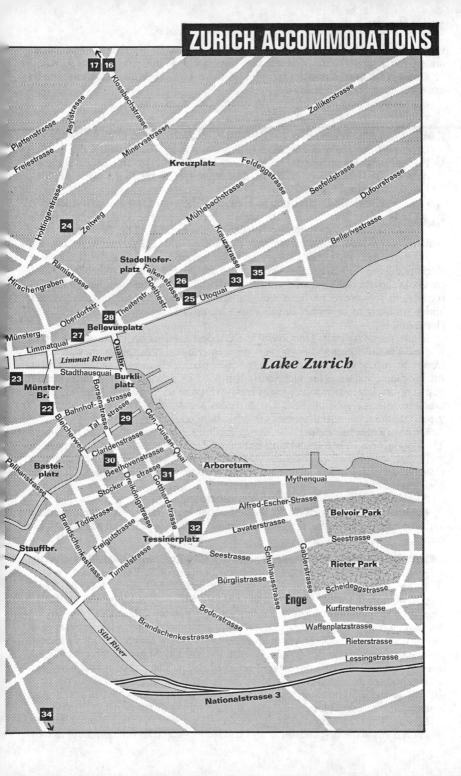

wood details. The least expensive accommodations lie at the far end of an underground tunnel in the "Guesthouse" annex and do not receive room service.

Dining/Entertainment: The in-house disco Le Club is free. The hotel has an excellent international restaurant.

Services: Room service in regular rooms, wake-up calls.

Facilities: Swimming pool, fitness center.

BAUR AU LAC, Talstrasse 1, CH-8022, Zurich. Tel. 01/221-16-50. Fax 01/211-81-39. 139 rms, 16 suites. A/C MINIBAR TV TEL **Tram:** 4.

$ Rates (including continental breakfast): 270F–350F ($197.05–$255.45) single; 430F–510F ($313.85–$372.25) double; from 1,200F ($875.90) suite. AE, DC, MC, V. **Parking:** 25F ($18.25).

⭐ One of the world's great hotels, owned by the same family since it opened in 1844, the Baur au Lac is ideally located at the end of fashionable Bahnhofstrasse, next to the Schanzengraben Canal. The three-story stone building is surrounded by a private park that's filled with red geraniums in summer.

Johannes Baur, the son of an Austrian baker, insisted that the hotel have a view of Zürichsee (Lake Zurich) and the Alps. This quietly elegant Zurich landmark is always stylish. In the late 1800s, members of the Prussian, Russian, and English royal families stayed here. In more recent times it might have been Marc Chagall or John Lennon. Today it's likely to be former British Prime Minister Margaret Thatcher or Plácido Domingo.

Inside, guests are treated to some of the grandest hotel service in Europe. In rooms where Richard Wagner and Franz Liszt once entertained at the piano, they are today treated to Jugendstil glass, tapestries, antiques, marble floors, and Oriental carpets. All bedrooms and suites are luxuriously furnished in individual styles. Suites get the best antiques, but regular rooms might have an Empire style or a style from one of the Louis periods, or even modern. These rooms are an ideal choice for those who appreciate the traditional amenities of a deluxe hotel.

Dining/Entertainment: The dining facilities are among the finest in Zurich. The elegantly rustic, year-round Grill Room is a Zurich institution, especially popular with members of the Swiss business world at noon. Open in winter, the Restaurant Français, decorated in soft salmon tones, offers French cuisine and vintages from the hotel's wine cellar.

Services: Baby-sitting, room service, concierge.

Facilities: The summertime Le Pavillon, open from May to October, provides a 19th-century garden setting for food and drink. Parking is provided, adjacent to the garden.

SAVOY BAUR EN VILLE, Poststrasse 12, CH-Zurich. Tel. 01/211-53-60. Fax 01/221-14-67. 112 rms, 15 suites. A/C MINIBAR TV TEL **Tram:** 4.

$ Rates (including continental breakfast): 320F ($233.55) single; 450F ($328.45) double; from 1,150F ($839.40) suite. AE, DC, MC, V. **Parking:** 25F ($18.25).

The Baur en Ville has been a Zurich landmark since 1923, and after recent renovations it's better than ever. A conservative and refined hotel, it is conscious of its role as one of the premier hotels of Zurich. Its six stories are conspicuously located amid exclusive stores on Paradeplatz. Owned by bankers, the hotel has rooms that are quietly dignified, decorated in a wide range of styles. The public rooms have high ceilings and are decorated either in a somber forest green with wood detailing, or in the case of the main salon, in a vivid scarlet, with white-and-gilt rococo adornment. Some rooms have balconies, with space for sunbathing or for enjoying breakfast.

Dining/Entertainment: The sidewalk café is one of the most popular daytime establishments in the city, and the Savoy Grill is a top-notch French restaurant as well.

Services: Beauty parlor, hairdressing salon, room service.
Facilities: Travel agency, florist, elegant shops.

HOTEL SCHWEIZERHOF, Bahnhofplatz 7, CH-8001 Zurich. Tel. 01/211-86-40. Fax 01/211-35-05. 114 rms. A/C MINIBAR TV TEL **Tram:** 4.
$ Rates (including continental breakfast): 190F–280F ($138.70–$204.35) single; 290F–430F ($211.65–$313.85) double. AE, DC, MC, V.
Located in one of the city's busiest areas, the Schweizerhof is accessible from anywhere in town by tram. The stone building has gables, turrets, and columns and is decorated with flags. Inside, the public rooms are pleasing and unpretentious, painted in clear colors, with clusters of subdued furniture. This is a grand old station hotel in a turn-of-the-century tradition, although recent major renovations have kept the hotel in step with the times. The ideal rooms are the semicircular corner units, which come with a modern bath, radio, and other amenities.
Dining/Entertainment: A French restaurant, well-appointed bar, and Le Gourmet coffee shop are offered.

EXPENSIVE

HOTEL ASCOT, Tessinerplatz 9, CH-8002 Zurich. Tel. 01/201-18-00. Fax 01/202-72-10. 73 rms. A/C MINIBAR TV TEL **Tram:** 6 or 7.
$ Rates (including breakfast): 170F–240F ($124.10–$175.20) single; 240F–350F ($175.20–$255.45) double. AE, DC, MC, V.
Situated in a mixed residential/commercial neighborhood within a 10-minute walk from the lake and Bahnhofstrasse, this establishment is one of the most stylish four-star hotels in Zurich. Originally built in 1954, the Ascot underwent expensive renovations in 1987, transforming its six floors into showrooms of Italian style. Today, even the facade (pink and maroon, with etched and unetched glass) looks new. The lobby has a black-and-white checkerboard floor and mahogany paneling. The more expensive bedrooms have patios, Italian marble baths, intricately crafted paneling made from tropical woods, radios, and other amenities.
Dining/Entertainment: Even if you don't stay here, the bar and French restaurant (the Jockey Club) deserves a visit. Restaurant Fujiya serves a Japanese cuisine.

HOTEL GLARNISCHLOF, Claridenstrasse 30, CH-8022 Zurich. Tel. 01/202-47-47, or toll free 800/528-1234 in North America. Fax 01/201-01-64. 70 rms, 3 suites. MINIBAR TV TEL **Tram:** 13.
$ Rates (including buffet breakfast): 200F ($146) single; 300F ($218.95) double; from 560F ($408.75) suite. AE, DC, MC, V.
Despite its outer appearance, which resembles an anonymous Swiss bank, this hotel is actually warm and inviting, with light-wood paneling, patterned rugs, and elegant armchairs. Part of the Best Western chain, it is conveniently located in the midst of the financial district. The manager offers spacious accommodations with high ceilings. Three deluxe junior suites have whirlpool baths and air conditioning.
Dining/Entertainment: A grill room, snack restaurant, and bar are offered.

NEUES SCHLOSS, Stockerstrasse 17, CH-8022 Zurich. Tel. 01/201-65-50. Fax 01/201-64-18. 59 rms. MINIBAR TV TEL **Tram:** 7, 8, 10, or 13 to Stockerstrasse.
$ Rates (including continental breakfast): 170F–240F ($124.10–$175.20) single; 260F–350F ($189.75–$255.45) double. AE, DC, MC, V.

This hotel is only a few steps from the Kongresshalle and the lake. Joggers and nature lovers will find a handful of lakeside parks nearby. A member of the family-owned Seiler Hotel chain, it is an unobtrusive gray building, with balconies and art deco detailing. Bedrooms provide radios and other amenities.

Dining/Entertainment: The hotel's restaurant, Le Jardin, attracts bankers and other businesspeople at lunch.

HOTEL ST. GOTTHARD, Bahnhofstrasse 87, CH-8023 Zurich. Tel. 01/ 211-55-00. Fax 01/211-24-19. 135 rms, 7 suites. MINIBAR TV TEL **Tram:** 6, 7, 11, or 13.

$ **Rates:** 210F–250F ($153.30–$182.50) single; 310F–380F ($226.25–$277.35) double; from 525F ($383.20) suite. Breakfast 20F ($14.60) extra. AE, DC, MC, V.

A long-time favorite of the Swiss, the St. Gotthard is located on one of the main shopping streets, only a block from the railroad station. All bedrooms have a plush decor. Most of the rooms are air-conditioned.

Dining/Entertainment: The Oyster Bar specializes in lobster flown in from Canada and attracts sophisticated people from all over the city. This and three other cosmopolitan restaurants—the Café St. Gotthard for snacks and pastries, the Prime Grill, and La Bouillabaisse, a French restaurant known for seafood—make the St. Gotthard one of the main attractions on Bahnhofstrasse. The Birdwatchers Club is one of the most fashionable discos in Zurich.

Services: Laundry/dry cleaning, shoeshine and valet service, wake-up calls, and baby-sitting.

Facilities: Safety deposit boxes, sauna, massage, solarium; car-rental desk.

HOTEL TIEFENAU, Steinwiesstrasse 8-10, CH-8032 Zurich. Tel. 01/ 251-24-09. Fax 01/251-24-76. 30 rms. TV TEL **Tram:** 3 or 8.

$ **Rates** (including buffet breakfast): 170F–240F ($124.10–$175.20) single; 240F–350F ($175.20–$255.45) double. AE, DC, MC, V. **Parking:** Free. **Closed:** Several weeks around Christmas.

Set near the Kunsthaus, in a residential section of Zurich's east bank, and a 10-minute tram ride from Bahnhofstrasse, this family-owned hotel evokes a country inn you'd expect to find far from the bustle of Zurich. Its garden contains giant trees and an outdoor café and restaurant terrace overlooking the building's yellow facade and forest-green shutters. Established in 1835, the hotel contains a scattering of antiques and Oriental carpets. The sunny bedrooms are larger than you might have expected, and spotless. The hotel closes for a few weeks at Christmastime.

HOTEL GLOCKENHOF, Sihlstrasse 31, CH-8023 Zurich. Tel. 01/211-56-50, or toll free 800/528-1234 in North America. Fax 01/211-56-60. 108 rms. MINIBAR TV TEL **Tram:** 3, 4, or 15.

$ **Rates** (including buffet breakfast): 170F ($124.10) single; 254F ($185.40) double. AE, DC, MC, V.

This modern hotel is situated halfway between the train station and the lake. There is a spacious lobby with leather-upholstered chairs. Bedrooms are comfortable, with dark carpeting, vanity tables, and an occasional Oriental rug.

Dining/Entertainment: The Glogge-Egge restaurant has a warm atmosphere, created by wooden planks, hanging lights, and lots of brickwork. The café-terrace is in the sunny courtyard.

MODERATE

HOTEL NOVA-PARK, Badenerstrasse 420, CH-8040 Zurich. Tel. 01/

491-22-22. Fax 01/491-22-20. 363 rms, 4 suites. MINIBAR TV TEL **Tram:** 31 or 83.

$ **Rates:** 160F–240F ($116.80–$175.20) single; 205F–285F ($149.65–$208) double; from 450F ($328.45) suite. Breakfast 12F ($8.75) extra. AE, DC, MC, V. **Parking:** 25F ($18.25).

This is the largest four-star hotel in Switzerland—a modern complex adorned with sculpture, paintings, and a dramatic color scheme. Guests have access to a good network of bus and tram lines as the hotel is only 10 minutes from the center of town. The comfortable rooms have radios and audiovisual hookups, which can receive films in seven languages, including English.

Dining/Entertainment: The six restaurants and a disco make this hostelry a popular gathering spot for locals and tourists. Live music is presented nightly in the hotel bar.

Services: Laundry facilities, room service in suites.

Facilities: The largest fitness center in Switzerland with a therapy center.

HOTEL STOLLER, Badenerstrasse 357, CH-8040 Zurich. Tel. 01/492-65-00. Fax 01/492-65-01. 80 rms. MINIBAR TV TEL **Tram:** 2 or 3.

$ **Rates** (including continental breakfast): 180F ($131.40) single; 240F ($175.20) double. AE, DC, MC, V.

Conveniently located near tram lines, this newly renovated hotel puts travelers at ease. The salons are decorated with modern styling and grace. Bedrooms are comfortably furnished and cozy and decorated in harmonious colors. Rooms for nonsmokers are available.

Dining/Entertainment: Guests unwind in the Stoller Bar and later enjoy excellent French food and wines in the Auberge Restaurant. A Stube serves home-style Swiss dishes, and the Stoller Ice Cream Terrace is a summer delight.

HOTEL TRÜMPY, Limmatstrasse 5, CH-8005 Zurich. Tel. 01/271-54-00. Fax 01/272-19-30. 71 rms. TV TEL **Tram:** 3.

$ **Rates** (including continental breakfast): 140F–170F ($102.20–$124.10) single; 170F–220F ($124.10–$160.60) double. AE, DC, MC, V.

The octagonal spires of the National Museum are only a block away from this grand

---

 FROMMER'S COOL FOR KIDS

HOTELS

Hotel Ambassador (see p. 80) The location is safe and central, and rates include a buffet breakfast. Reasonably priced meals are served in a sidewalk café. An extra bed in a room carries a 40F ($29.20) supplement, and a crib can be set up in any room.

Novotel Zurich Airport (see p. 83) Kids delight in the sumptuous buffet breakfast, and for other meals there's a special children's menu. Novotel caters to children, who find games waiting for them in the lobby.

Hotel Tiefenau (see p. 76) Like a country inn tucked away in Zurich, this place offers special menus for children. It also grants them reduced rates. The street is relatively traffic free.

old building near the railroad station. A Swiss flag usually flies over the buff-colored facade, while a canopy shelters the sidewalk café from the sun. The lobby has Oriental rugs and a large stone fountain spewing water from a bas-relief human head. Bedrooms are comfortably appointed and some are decorated in vivid colors. All rooms have soundproof windows and radios. The dining room serves good meals.

INEXPENSIVE

HOTEL BRISTOL, Stampfenbachstrasse 34, CH-8035 Zurich. Tel. 01/ 261-84-00. Fax 01/251-19-51. 55 rms (44 with bath). TV TEL **Tram:** 11 or 14.
$ **Rates** (including continental breakfast): 65F ($47.45) single without bath, 110F ($80.30) single with bath; 90F ($65.70) double without bath, 140F ($102.20) double with bath; 180F ($131.40) triple with bath. AE, MC, V.
For many years, the Hotel Bristol has been one of Zurich's best-known and most successful small hotels. It's on a hill near the main train station, behind the major road to the airport, with a ramp leading to the main entrance. Bedrooms are well maintained, frequently renovated, and simply furnished. No alcoholic beverages are allowed. The hotel has an elevator and a large lounge containing a wide-screen TV. All rooms have radios. Only breakfast is served.

HOTEL KINDLI, Pfalzgasse 1, CH-8001 Zurich. Tel. 01/211-59-17. Fax 01/211-65-28. 22 rms (all with bath). MINIBAR TV TEL **Tram:** 3.
$ **Rates** (including continental breakfast): 120F ($87.60) single; 140F–190F ($102.20–$138.70) double. AE, DC, MC, V.
Ⓢ Located at the end of a steep street in Rennweg (the old town), this 16th-century gray hotel has cozy, well-designed bedrooms, with views of Old Town; each room contains a radio and a fridge. The furnishings are an eclectic mix of antique and contemporary. The owner, Willy Schmid, is a folk singer who, with his orchestra and international singing stars, plays to a full house practically every night (see Section 9, "Evening Entertainment," below).

HOTEL LIMMAT, Limmatstrasse 118, CH-8031 Zurich. Tel. 01/271-52-40. Fax 01/272-86-76. 60 rms (40 with shower or bath). MINIBAR TV TEL **Tram:** 3, 4, or 13 to Limmatplatz.
$ **Rates** (including continental breakfast): 120F ($87.60) single without shower or bath, 150F ($109.50) single with shower or bath; 170F ($124.10) double without shower or bath, 220F ($160.60) double with shower or bath. AE, DC, MC, V.
This recently renovated hotel, in the city center near the railroad station, has added new windows and more rooms with showers and toilets. Its furnishings are modern, and its rooms have VCRs and radios. The hotel has two restaurants, one elegantly decorated, and a bar.

ON THE RIGHT BANK

VERY EXPENSIVE

DOLDER GRAND HOTEL, Kurhausstrasse 65, CH-8023 Zurich. Tel. 01/251-62-31. Fax 01/251-62-31. 187 rms, 11 suites. TV TEL **Tram:** 3, 8, or 15.
$ **Rates** (including continental breakfast): 270F–350F ($197.05–$255.45) single; 400F–510F ($291.95–$372.25) double; from 1,150F ($839.40) suite. AE, DC, MC, V. **Parking:** 25F ($18.25).

✪ I consider this the greatest hotel in Europe—it epitomizes class, style, and comfort. Past clients have included Albert Einstein, Arturo Toscanini, Winston Churchill, and Henry Kissinger. Only 6 minutes from the center of Zurich, the hotel itself is part medieval fortress, part Renaissance château, and part 19th-century palace. The cogwheel funicular that connects the hotel to the center of Zurich is only one of its unusual features. Built on top of a 50-acre wooded promontory, the hotel is located in a conservative residential section of Zurich. It consists of two balconied wings, with half-timbered replicas of watchtowers on the far ends that seem to pivot around an enormous dungeon capped with a soaring copper spire. The hotel is also surrounded by carefully tended gardens. Renovated public rooms include the Gobelin salon, with its enormous and extremely valuable tapestry. The 90-year-old main building contains the original bedrooms; the 60-room annex was added in 1964. Most bedrooms have a minibar and some contain air conditioning.

Dining/Entertainment: The superb French restaurant, La Rotonde, is staffed by a small army of culinary technicians. The hotel also has a 55-seat bar.

Services: A private hotel limousine takes up to six guests from and to the railroad station or airport; 24-hour room service.

Facilities: Funicular (free for guests), sports facilities, five tennis courts, nine-hole golf course, swimming pool (with its own waves), skating rink (in winter).

HOTEL EDEN DU LAC, Utoquai 45, CH-8023 Zurich. Tel. 01/261-94-04. Fax 01/261-94-09. 54 rms, 3 suites. A/C MINIBAR TV TEL **Tram:** 4.

$ **Rates** (including continental breakfast): 230F–250F ($167.90–$182.50) single; 420F–450F ($306.55–$328.45) double; from 900F ($656.90) suite. AE, DC, MC, V.

✪ A grand hotel with an ornamented facade, the Eden du Lac resembles the Paris Opéra, with neoclassical columns, pediments, corner urns, and wrought-iron garlands of fruits and flowers. There is a nostalgic ambience here, thanks to the efforts of the manager, Rudolf A. Bartschi, who is partially responsible for making Swiss hotels the standard of excellence throughout the world. The walk from the hotel to downtown Zurich is like an old-fashioned promenade. Rose-colored bedrooms have many amenities. Accommodations in the rear are less expensive because they lack views of the lake.

Dining/Entertainment: The hotel's French restaurant is one of the finest in Zurich, with service to match. There is also a private hotel bar.

Services: Laundry facilities, room service.

Facilities: Sauna with exit to roof.

HOTEL WALDHAUS DOLDER, Kurhausstrasse 20, CH-8030 Zurich. Tel. 01/251-93-60, or toll free 800/528-1234 in North America. Fax 01/251-00-29. 100 rms, 10 suites. MINIBAR TV TEL **Tram:** 3, 8, or 15.

$ **Rates:** 180F–270F ($131.40–$197.05) single; 270F–410F ($197.05–$299.25) double; from 500F ($364.95) suite. Breakfast 12F ($8.75) extra. AE, DC, MC, V.

Surrounded by forests in the Dolder residential section of Zurich, this hotel offers an experience in country living. The high-rise has balconies, some with awnings, on every floor. Inside, the spacious bedrooms, each with a modern bath, are decorated with comfortable, upholstered sofas and armchairs; their large windows offer views of the lake and the mountains. Doubles are essentially two-room apartments.

Dining/Entertainment: The rustic restaurant has a collection of 19th-century saws and woodworking tools hanging on the walls.

Services: Room service, massages.

Facilities: Sauna, solarium; nearby nine-hole golf course; nearby tennis courts, minigolf course, and indoor and outdoor swimming pool.

HOTEL ZUM STORCHEN, Am Weinplatz 2, CH-8022 Zurich. Tel. 01/211-55-10. Fax 01/211-6451. 79 rms. TV TEL **Tram:** 4 or 15.

$ **Rates** (including continental breakfast): 200F–260F ($146–$189.75) single; 290F–430F ($211.65–$313.85) double. AE, DC, MC, V.

Important visitors to Zurich have enjoyed the hospitality of this hotel for about 635 years. Paracelsus, Burgomaster Pfyffer, envoys of the Swedish king Gustavus Adolphus, Richard Wagner, and Gottfried Keller have all been among the illustrious guests to take advantage of the old Storchen's cuisine, wine cellar, and accommodations. Many Swiss consider this to be the best hotel in Zurich; it is therefore necessary to reserve ahead, especially in summer.

The hotel is undeniably romantic. Supposedly named for the storks that nested on the roof, it sits on a bank of the Limmat looking across the river to the floodlit Rathaus. A favorite feature is the café terrace, cantilevered above the sidewalk on granite columns that are hundreds of years old. From the terrace you'll have a sweeping panorama of Old Zurich without ever having to leave your *Kaffeeklatsch*. A large statue of an enraged stork decorates the facade of Zum Storchen and is visible from the river.

Dining/Entertainment: The Rôtisserie restaurant offers first-class facilities, complete with river views and ornate stucco ceilings. The cocktail bar, filled with pewter tankards, attracts local executives.

EXPENSIVE

HOTEL OPERA, Dufourstrasse 5, CH-8008 Zurich. Tel. 01/251-90-90. Fax 01/251-90-01. 68 rms. A/C MINIBAR TV TEL **Tram:** 2 or 4.

$ **Rates** (including buffet breakfast): 130F–180F ($94.90–$131.40) single; 190F–280F ($138.70–$204.35) double; 230F–320F ($167.90–$233.55) triple. AE, MC, V.

This is a clean, cozy, and efficiently managed establishment, next to the Opera House. It has a large, attractive, carpeted lobby, with an assortment of comfortable armchairs. Top-floor rooms are the best, but all provide most amenities, including soundproofing and radios. There's bus service to Kloten Airport daily every 1½ hours.

HOTEL ZURICH, Neumühlequai 42, CH-8001 Zurich. Tel. 01/363-63-63. 301 rms, 11 suites. A/C MINIBAR TV TEL **Tram:** 3.

$ **Rates** (including breakfast): 190F–260F ($138.70–$189.75) single; 240F–360F ($175.20–$262.75) double; from 800F ($583.90) suite. AE, DC, MC, V.

Situated high above the banks of the Limmat and a short walk across the river from the railroad station, this black-and-white structure is one of the most popular modern hotels in Zurich. The spectacular view from the top of the building encompasses the spires and green parks of downtown Zurich.

The bedrooms are often sunny and well decorated, with strikingly tiled bathrooms and all the modern conveniences you'd expect in a deluxe hotel. The hotel's bars, salons, and restaurants all cater to a sophisticated, international crowd. A swimming pool is on the premises.

MODERATE

HOTEL AMBASSADOR, Falkenstrasse 6, CH-8008 Zurich. Tel. 01/261-76-00. Fax 01/251-23-94. 45 rms (all with bath or shower). MINIBAR TV TEL **Tram:** 4 or 15.

$ Rates (including buffet breakfast): 130F–190F ($94.90–$138.70) single; 190F–290F ($138.70–$211.65) double. AE, DC, MC, V.

The Ambassador offers the best possible view of the lake without actually paying the monstrous "lakeside view" prices. You'll be near the opera and Bellevueplatz, and within one block of the lake. Guests are treated like royalty. The rooms, which are soundproof and contain radios, tend to be irregularly shaped, which lends character. Some contain air conditioning. There is a popular sidewalk café at street level. Families with infants should note that a crib can be set up in any room.

ARC ROYAL COMFORT INN, Leonhardstrasse 6, CH-8001 Zurich. Tel. 01/261-67-10, or toll free 800/228-5150 in North America. Fax 01/251-47-80. 59 rms (all with bath). MINIBAR TV TEL **Tram:** 3.

$ Rates (including continental breakfast): 120F–140F ($87.60–$102.20) single; 160F–180F ($116.80–$131.40) double; 200F ($146) triple. AE, DC, MC, V. **Parking:** 25F ($18.25).

This chain-affiliated Comfort Inn is one of the most modern bed-and-breakfast hotels in downtown Zurich, a 5-minute walk from the rail station. Guests can expect personal attention from staff members. All rooms have modern bathrooms and radios, among other amenities. There's an airport bus service, a round-the-clock Telex service for business clients, and an underground garage nearby for easy parking. There's a special no-smoking floor.

HOTEL FLORHOF, Florhofgasse 4, CH-8001 Zurich. Tel. 01/261-44-70. Fax 01/261-46-11. 33 rms (all with bath). MINIBAR TV TEL **Tram:** 3.

$ Rates (including continental breakfast): 125F–165F ($91.25–$120.45) single; 180F–240F ($131.40–$175.20) double. AE, DC, MC, V.

This former private residence is today a well-run hotel. You'll arrive at a paved walkway leading to the double staircase of a large, blue, patrician house. Inside, the dining room is heated by a blue-and-white Swiss tile oven. Some of the comfortably furnished bedrooms still have their high molded-plaster ceilings.

HOTEL HELMHAUS, Schifflandeplatz 30, CH-8001 Zurich. Tel. 01/251-88-10. Fax 01/251-04-30. 25 rms (all with shower or bath). MINIBAR TEL TV **Tram:** 4 or 11.

$ Rates (including buffet breakfast): 128F–137F ($93.65–$100) single; 170F–208F ($124.10–$152) double. AE, DC, MC, V.

The Helmhaus is one of the best moderately priced hotels in Zurich. Originally built in 1356, this simple, six-story hotel is set on the boatlanding square, a block from the river at the corner of Limmatquai. Shops fill the space on the ground floor. The establishment is extremely well run. Since it was renovated in 1984, many of its comfortable, impeccable rooms contain geometrically patterned curtains and contoured chairs; all have radios and some have air conditioning. Light meals are available between 6:30 and 8:30pm. Shuttle-bus service for two people is available between the airport and the city.

INEXPENSIVE

HOTEL DU THEATRE, Seilergraben 69, CH-8023 Zurich. Tel. 01/252-60-62. Fax 01/252-01-54. 60 rms (all with bath). MINIBAR TV TEL **Tram:** 6, 7, or 10.

$ Rates (including continental breakfast): 95F–112F ($69.35–$81.75) single; 130F–160F ($94.90–$116.80) double. AE, DC, MC, V.

The first thing you'll notice about this modern hotel is its emphasis on art. A 20-foot, dramatically colored, intricate metal collage hangs over the facade, while a life-size female nude statue is near the entrance. The soundproof rooms are comfortable and not without their own unusual prints and artwork. The hotel is located near the center of the tram system.

HOTEL KRONE, Limmatquai 88, CH-8001 Zurich. Tel. 01/251-42-22. Fax 01/251-47-63. 26 rms (2 with bath). TEL **Tram:** 4 or 15.
$ **Rates** (including continental breakfast): 60F ($43.80) single without bath, 65F ($47.45) single with bath; 95F ($69.35) double without bath, 105F ($76.65) double with bath. AE, DC, MC, V.

Located only 500 yards from the railroad station and a few steps from Bahnhofstrasse, this early 17th-century building has gone through several renovations. The beige-and-cream interior contains Oriental rugs and detailed woodwork. Some rooms have a view of the Limmat. Nineteen rooms have a minibar.

HOTEL LEONHARD, Limmatquai 136, CH-8001 Zurich. Tel. 01/251-30-80. Fax 01/252-38-70. 12 rms (all with bath). MINIBAR TV TEL **Tram:** 4 or 15.
$ **Rates** (including continental breakfast): 125F ($91.25) single; 150F ($109.50) double. AE, DC, MC, V.
This establishment, owned by the Leonhard family, is located in the old city, 2 minutes' walk from the main railroad station. All the rooms have twin beds, radios, alarm clocks, and safes. There is a typical Swiss restaurant.

HOTEL VORDERER STERNEN, Bellevueplatz, CH-8001 Zurich. Tel. 01/251-49-49. Fax 01/252-90-63. 10 rms (none with bath). **Tram:** 4 or 15.
$ **Rate:** 50F–60F ($36.50–$43.80) single; 70F–80F ($51.10–$58.40) double. Breakfast 12.50F ($9.15) extra. AE, DC, MC, V.
This hotel, on the shore of the lake, faces the famous Bellevueplatz, which has excellent tram connections to every part of the city. It has a street-level restaurant and a garden restaurant with a terrace, one flight up. The clean, simple bedrooms have hot and cold running water and access to shared showers off the hallways.

BUDGET

HOTEL MARTAHAUS, Zähringerstrasse 36, CH-8001 Zurich. Tel. 01/251-45-50. 85 beds (none with bath). **Tram:** 3, 6, 7, or 10.
$ **Rates** (including continental breakfast): 50F ($36.50) single; 76F ($55.45) double; 92F ($67.15) triple; 25F ($18.25) per person in a dormitory. No credit cards.

Because of the Martahaus's popularity with budget travelers, it's often hard to get a room here during the summer. Rooms sleep one, two, three, or six people. Each room has a sink and access to a shower down the hall. The establishment is within walking distance of the main station.

PENSION ST. JOSEF, Hirschengraben 64-68, CH-8001 Zurich. Tel. 01/251-27-57. 60 rms (none with bath). **Tram:** 3.
$ **Rates** (including buffet breakfast): 60F ($43.80) single; 100F ($73) double; 120F ($87.60) triple. No credit cards.

This Catholic pension is especially good for women who are traveling alone. Only a 6-minute walk from the central station, it's clean, comfortable, and strictly run.

AT KLOTEN AIRPORT

HILTON INTERNATIONAL ZURICH, Höhenbuhlstrasse 10, CH-8058

Zurich-Kloten. Tel. 01/810-31-31, or toll free 800/445-8667 in North America. Fax 01/810-93-66. 278 rms, 8 suites. A/C MINIBAR TV TEL **Directions:** See below.

$ Rates (including continental breakfast): 235F–310F ($171.55–$226.25) single; 275F–350F ($200.70–$255.45) double; from 600F ($437.95) suites. AE, DC, MC, V.

Sprawling across several hundred yards of wooded hillsides near Kloten Airport, the Hilton looks like a chain of railroad cars joined together by a sun terrace and the panoramic windows of its restaurant. Many visitors in Zurich prefer its pastoral setting, which, despite the adjacent meadows, is only 15 minutes by taxi or bus (no. 68) from Zurich's downtown train station. Since the airport closes every evening and the rooms are all soundproofed, guests are insulated from the noise of departing jets. The bedrooms are sunny, filled with conservative, modern furniture and all the conveniences you'd expect from an international Hilton.

Dining/Entertainment: Before-dinner drinks are available at the Bonanza Bar, with live piano music, while the hotel coffee shop is suitable for light meals. Many guests prefer Sutter's Grill, with its open grill, copper decor, and meticulous service. For guests seeking a chalet atmosphere, the Taverne provides accordion music.

Services: Bank, car-rental desk, and souvenir shop.

Facilities: A nearly 2-mile outdoor track with 20 exercise or rest stations scattered along the route, and an invigorating fitness program.

Directions: From the main autobahn between downtown Zurich and Kloten Airport, follow the FLUGHAFEN signs and get off at the Glattbrugg /Opfikon/Kloten exit, the last exit before the airport. From there dark-yellow-and-black signs lead to a nearby hill, where the hotel is located.

NOVOTEL ZURICH AIRPORT, Talackerstrasse 21, CH-8152 Zurich-Glattbrugg. Tel. 01/810-31-11. Fax 01/810-81-85. 257 rms (all with bath). MINIBAR TV TEL **Bus:** 68.

$ Rates (including buffet breakfast): 135F–160F ($98.55–$116.80) single; 155F–180F ($113.15–$131.40) double. AE, DC, MC, V. **Parking:** 25F ($18.25).

If your schedule requires that you spend the night near Kloten Airport, this might be an ideal choice. Don't worry about being awakened in the night by the scream of jet engines: Zurich city ordinances prohibit airline departures or arrivals after 11pm. The airport is only 5 minutes away, and you can be in downtown Zurich in just 20 minutes. Opened in 1986, this typical Novotel is known for its streamlined, comfortable rooms and easy check-in. In fact, wheeled carts put guests in control of their own luggage (eliminating tipping).

Dining/Entertainment: In the evening, a piano bar in the lobby attracts the international business crowd. Afterward, guests patronize Le Grill, a good restaurant offering food service daily until midnight. Specialties include a smoked fish plate, dried meat and cheese, and chipped veal in a well-flavored cream sauce served with Rösti. There is also a special children's menu (Novotel, in fact, caters to children, who find games waiting for them in the lobby).

Services: It's a do-it-yourself place—you even wheel your own luggage to the room in a cart.

Facilities: Garage.

AT KÜSNACHT

HOTEL ERMITAGE AM SEE, Seestrasse 80, CH-8700 Küsnacht-Zurich. Tel. 01/910-52-22. Fax 01/910-52-44. 46 rms (all with bath). TV TEL **Transportation:** You'll have to take a taxi.

$ Rates (including continental breakfast): 140F–190F ($102.20–$138.70) single; 220F–270F ($160.60–$197.05) double. AE, DC, MC, V.

⭐ This lakeside country inn is located in the suburb of Küsnacht, 7 minutes by car from the center of Zurich. The hotel is spacious and airy, with panoramic windows. The public rooms contain vivid carpeting, scattered Oriental rugs, and fine furniture. Many of the well-equipped rooms open onto balconies; the most expensive ones offer views of the lake. Guests have use of a private lakefront beach and well-maintained grounds. The French restaurant offers candlelight dinners in an elegant setting every night, and there is also a warmly decorated bar area.

4. DINING

Zurich offers more than 1,200 restaurants, featuring a selection of international and **Swiss specialties.** The local favorite is *Rösti* (potatoes grated and fried). You should also try *Züri-Gschnätzlets* (shredded veal cooked with mushrooms in a cream sauce laced with white wine) and *Kutteln nach Zürcherart* (tripe with mushrooms, white wine, and caraway seed). Another classic dish is *Leberspiesschen* (liver cubes skewered with bacon and sage and served with potatoes and beans). *Zouftschriibertopf* is a potpourri of bacon, grilled meat, and mushrooms.

Among **local wines,** the white Riesling Sylvaner is outstanding. Zurich residents often drink a white Räuschling with fish platters. The light Clevner wines, always chilled, are made from blue Burgundy grapes that grow around the lake. You should be able to order wine by the glass, even in first-class restaurants.

Most places in Zurich prefer a reservation even if they don't require it. The cost of a dinner varies considerably: At restaurants rated "Very Expensive," $100 and up per person; "Expensive," about $50; "Moderate," $35; and "Inexpensive," $25 and under.

ON THE LEFT BANK

EXPENSIVE

NOUVELLE, Erlachstrasse 46. Tel. 462-63-63.
   Cuisine: SWISS. **Reservations:** Required. **Tram:** 9 or 14.
$ Prices: Appetizers 10F–26F ($7.30–$19); main courses 42F–46F ($30.65–$33.60); fixed-price meals 37F ($27) at lunch, 120F ($87.60) at dinner. AE, DC, MC, V.
   Open: Lunch Mon–Fri noon–3pm; dinner Mon–Sat 7–11:30pm.
This restaurant, which counts artists and businesspeople among its clientele, is one of the most talked-about establishments in Zurich. The dining room has brown walls, a high ceiling, and a row of paintings dipicting Maxim's of Paris as it looked a century ago. There are also surrealist paintings by the well-known Zurich artist H. R. Giger.

The menu changes with the season and might include grilled red mullet with Belgian endive and zucchini or a salmon pot-au-feu. Food is presented as an intricate collage, with creatively cut vegetables. The Mediterranean menu includes portions of the finest "products of the sea."

RESTAURANT PICCOLI (ACCADEMIA), Rotwandstrasse 48. Tel. 241-42-02.

Cuisine: ITALIAN. **Reservations:** Required. **Tram:** 3.
$ **Prices:** Appetizers 20F–35F ($14.60–$25.55); main courses 40F–50F ($29.20–$36.50). AE, MC, V.
Open: Lunch Mon–Fri noon–2pm; dinner Mon–Fri 6–10pm. **Closed:** July.

One of the finest and most elegant Italian restaurants in Zurich is owned by Mr. Panardo-Piccoli. The many classic Italian dishes range from Venetian to Neopolitan; specialties include agnolotti alla piemontese and different types of spaghetti, as well as risotto with mushrooms. For a meat course, I recommend the filetto alla napoletana or veal liver alla veneziana. The daily specials might include seasonal game, such as pheasant and partridge.

MODERATE

RIBÓ, Luisenstrasse 43. Tel. 272-48-64.
Cuisine: SPANISH. **Reservations:** Required. **Tram:** 4, 13, or 32.
$ **Prices:** Appetizers 5.50F–10F ($4–$7.30); main courses 18F–36F ($13.15–$26.30). MC, V.
Open: Lunch Mon–Fri 11:30am–2:30pm; dinner Mon–Fri 5:30–11pm. **Closed:** Late Aug to late Sept.

The best Spanish restaurant in Zurich is just off Limmatplatz. You will receive a warm welcome from its English-speaking hosts, Rodolfo Ribó and his wife, Rosita. The small restaurant, decorated like a regional tavern, is known for its cozy atmosphere and well-prepared specialties. I suggest that you begin with a glass of sherry, such as Tío Pepe. Appetizers include garlic soup and Catalán salad with ham, eggs, sardines, olives, tuna, and asparagus tips. For a main course, I recommend the paella (made with chicken, mussels, squid, scampi, and shrimp) or a zarzuela (boiled seafood, fisherman's style).

VELTLINER KELLER, Schlüsselgasse 8. Tel. 221-32-28.
Cuisine: SWISS/ITALIAN. **Reservations:** Recommended. **Tram:** 3.
$ **Prices:** Appetizers 12F–20F ($8.75–$14.60); main courses 18F–36F ($13.15–$26.30). AE, DC, MC, V.
Open: Lunch Mon–Sat 11:30am–2pm; dinner Mon–Fri 6:30–10pm, Sat 6–10pm. **Closed:** July 16–Aug 6.

The Veltliner Keller has served as a restaurant since 1551; before that it was a wine cellar. Located next to St. Peter's Church in Old Town, it has an ancient interior of carved wood. The paneling is a mountain pine called *arve* (grown only in Switzerland). The chef prepares many familiar Swiss specialties, including the classic chopped-veal dish of Zurich. Several Italian dishes are also featured. The macaroni comes with a mixed grill of sausage, liver, veal, kidney, and beef. Ingredients change with the season and might include game, wild mushrooms, and fresh berries from the mountains.

INEXPENSIVE

AUGUSTINER, Augustinergasse 25. Tel. 211-72-10.
Cuisine: SWISS. **Reservations:** Required. **Tram:** 6, 7, 10, or 11.
$ **Prices:** Appetizers 5F–21F ($3.65–$16.35); main courses 15F–45F ($10.95–$32.85); fixed-price meals 18F ($13.15) at lunch, 29.50F–49.50F ($21.55–$36.15) at dinner. AE, DC, MC, V.
Open: Mon–Fri 11am–10pm, Sat 11am–9pm.

Located near the chic shopping district of Bahnhofstrasse, this local secret has an old-fashioned ambience and reasonable prices. The owners offer hearty fare, which

SWITZERLAND

BERN ⭐   Zurich ●

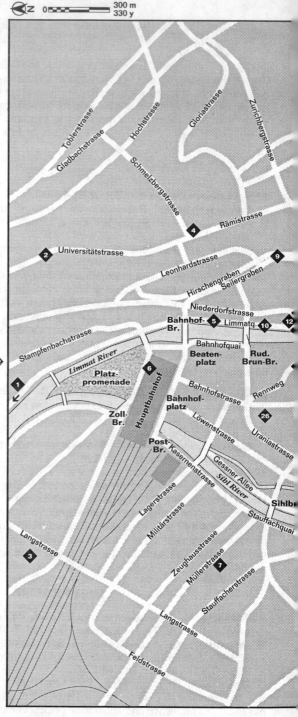

Agnès Amberg **8**
Augustiner **23**
Bierhalle Kropf **21**
Blockhus **18**
California **28**
Casino Zürch Horn **35**
Chez Max **34**
Conti **32**
Dézaley, Le **14**
Fischstube Zürichhorn **33**
Florhof Hotel Restaurant **9**
Haus Zum Ruden **15**
Hiltl Vegi **26**
Jacky's Stapferstube **2**
Jockey Club, The **30**
Kronenhalle **4**
Mère Catherine **17**
Nô Das Köstliche Teehaus **22**
Nouvelle **31**
Odéon, Café-Bar **5**
Piccoli (Accademia) **7**
Ravi's Indian Cuisine **1**
Restaurants Bahnhofbuffet
    Zürich **6**
Ribó **3**
Schober, Conditorei Café **16**
Select, Café **10**
Spaghetti Factory **29**
Sprüngli, Confiserie **27**
Tübli, Le **12**
Veltliner Keller **20**
Zeughauskeller **25**
Zunfthaus Zur Saffran **19**
Zunfthaus Zur
    Zimmerleuten **13**
Zur Munst, Cafeteria **24**
Zur Oepfelchammer **11**

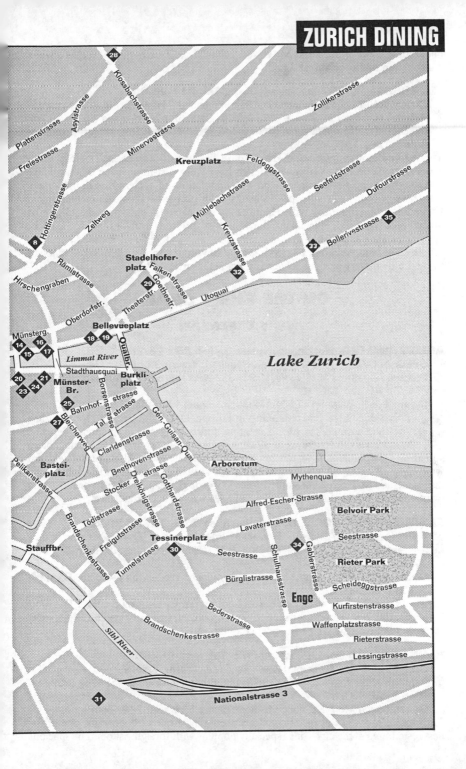

might include the house steak, pot-au-feu, calves' liver, Zurich minced veal in a white wine-cream sauce, or a mixed grill.

ZEUGHAUSKELLER, Am Paradeplatz. Tel. 211-26-90.
  Cuisine: SWISS. **Reservations:** Recommended. **Tram:** 2, 6, 7, 8, 9, 11, or 13.
  $ Prices: Appetizers 4.80F–14.70F ($3.70–$10.75); main courses 7.50F–28.70F ($5.50–$21). No credit cards.
  Open: Daily 11:30am–11pm.
This mammoth restaurant, which dates from 1487, was once an arsenal; its vast dining room seats 200. Large wooden chandeliers hang from cast-iron chains. The walls are decorated with medieval halberds and with illustrations of ancient Zurich noblemen. Generous portions of traditional Swiss dishes are served with steins of local beer. Owners Kurt Andreae and Willy Hammer say that patrons consume some 25 tons of potato salad a year. Hurlimann draft beer is poured from 1,000-liter barrels. Specialties include calves' liver, Wiener Schnitzel, and regional sausages, such as Saucisson of Neuchâtel. For 62F ($45.25) you can order a yard-long sausage—enough to feed four hungry people. Service is quick, efficient, and friendly.

ON THE RIGHT BANK

VERY EXPENSIVE

AGNES AMBERG, Hottingerstrasse 5. Tel. 251-26-26.
  Cuisine: SWISS. **Reservations:** Required. **Tram:** 3 or 8.
  $ Prices: Appetizers 15F–45F ($10.95–$32.85); main courses 46F–75F ($33.60–$54.75). AE, DC, MC, V.
  Open: Lunch Tues–Fri 11:30am–2:30pm; dinner Mon–Sat 6:30pm–12:30am.

This is one of the best restaurants in Europe. Dishes are prepared by an author who has devoted her life to creating and writing about epicurean delights. Sumptuous meals here are as pleasing to the eye as they are to the palate. For an appetizer, I recommend fresh foie gras in a terrine, pâté of duckling, or mussel soup with curry. A salad made with sweetbreads is available in season. Delectable main dishes include St. Pierre farci (stuffed John Dory) de poireaux (leeks) au beurre blanc (white butter), guinea fowl with honey, and sea bass in a saffron sauce.

CASINO ZURICH HORN, Bellerivestrasse 170. Tel. 55-20-20.
  Cuisine: INTERNATIONAL. **Reservations:** Required. **Tram:** 2 or 4.
  $ Prices: Appetizers 22F–38F ($16.05–$27.75); main courses 30F–60F ($21.90–$43.80). AE, DC, MC, V.
  Open: Lunch Wed–Mon 11:30am–2pm; dinner Wed–Mon 6–10pm. **Closed:** Jan 21–Feb 19.
Large and popular, this restaurant has an outdoor terrace right on the lake. The food is excellently prepared and the service is courteous. Try filets of perch Casino style, steak de veau (veal steak), or riz (rice) colonial.

HAUS ZUM RÜDEN, Limmatquai 42. Tel. 261-95-66.
  Cuisine: SWISS. **Reservations:** Required. **Tram:** 4 or 15.
  $ Prices: Appetizers 12F–46F ($8.75–$33.60); main courses 45F–75F ($32.85–$54.75). AE, DC, MC, V.
  Open: Lunch Mon–Sat noon–1:45pm; dinner Mon–Sat 7–9:45pm.
The Gothic room in this historic guild house dating from 1295 contains one of the best restaurants in the city—it's especially popular with foreign visitors. The spacious

yet intimate dining room has an elaborate hardwood ceiling and stone walls, which are decorated with medieval halberds and stag horns. The chef specializes in *cuisine du marché* (market-fresh cuisine). Outstanding dishes include a salad of roebuck and sweetbreads, a soup of saffron-flavored mussels, snails in truffle sauce, and lamb cooked with green peppercorns.

EXPENSIVE

RESTAURANT CONTI, Dufourstrasse 1. Tel. 251-06-66.
Cuisine: ITALIAN. **Reservations:** Required. **Tram:** 2, 4, or 11.
$ Prices: Appetizers 8F–20F ($5.85–$34.60); main courses 26F–45F ($19–$32.85). AE, DC, MC, V.
Open: Lunch Mon–Sat 11am–2pm; dinner Mon–Sat 6–11:30pm. **Closed:** Nov.
This opulent Belle Epoque restaurant lies just behind the Opera House. It is common to eat dinner here, then see a show, and return for dessert and coffee. The carefully chosen menu is based on seasonal specialties. Try a dish of homemade pasta, followed by either scaloppine al limone or entrecôte Robespierre. The meal includes freshwater and ocean fish, followed by a meat dish such as pheasant.

JACKY'S STAPFERSTUBE, Culmannstrasse 45. Tel. 361-37-48.
Cuisine: SWISS. **Reservations:** Required. **Tram:** 9 or 10.
$ Prices: Appetizers 12F–20F ($8.75–$14.60); main courses 25F–36F ($18.25–$26.30). AE, DC, MC, V.
Open: Lunch Tues–Sat 11am–2pm; dinner Tues–Sat 6–11pm.
Well known among the chic crowd, this restaurant serves some of the best beef and veal steaks in town. The owner, Jacky Schlapfer, is a local celebrity. I recommend the veal cutlet or veal shank; the meat is usually braised and priced according to weight. An assortment of fresh mushrooms is also presented. Other superb dishes include the goose liver and the fresh lobster salad. There is a distinguished wine list.

KRONENHALLE, Ramistrasse 4. Tel. 251-02-56.
Cuisine: SWISS/FRENCH. **Reservations:** Required. **Tram:** 2, 4, 5, 8, 9, 11, or 15.
$ Prices: Appetizers 10F–36F ($7.30–$26.30); main courses 20F–60F ($14.60–$43.80). AE, DC, MC, V.
Open: Daily noon–midnight.
This celebrity favorite has attracted such greats as Thomas Mann, James Joyce, Miró, Braque, Picasso, Richard Strauss, and Igor Stravinsky. Modern guests include Plácido Domingo, Catherine Deneuve, and Yves Saint Laurent.
The restaurant is in a five-story, gray Biedermeier building with gold crowns above the six windows on the first floor. Traditional Swiss cuisine and international dishes are served in the three dining rooms. The decor includes original paintings by Klee, Chagall, Matisse, Miró, Kandinsky, Cézanne, Braque, Bonnard, Monet, and Picasso. Regional specialties are served on a trolley and include smoked pork with lentils and bollito misto (boiled beef, chicken, sausage, and tongue). For a main dish, try shredded calves' liver with Rösti or young chicken with rosemary, risotto, and bolets.
In the Kronenhalle Bar the specialty is the Ladykiller. You might also enjoy Bündnerfleisch—thinly sliced, smoked, dried beef. The bar is open daily from 11:30am to midnight.

LE TÜBLI, Schneggengasse 8. Tel. 251-24-71.

Cuisine: CONTINENTAL. **Reservations:** Required. **Tram:** 3.

$ **Prices:** Appetizers 15F–22F ($10.95–$16.05); main courses 20F–42F ($14.60–$30.65). AE, DC, MC, V.

Open: Lunch daily noon–3pm; dinner daily 7–11pm.

This cozy, chic restaurant has fewer than 10 tables. The cuisine is presented in a theatrical style, with top-notch service. Only fresh ingredients are used. The menu changes frequently, but might include duckling with figs, veal cutlet with mushrooms, or baked turbot with herb rice. Wine is sold by the glass.

MODERATE

CALIFORNIA, Asylstrasse 125. Tel. 53-56-80.

Cuisine: AMERICAN. **Reservations:** Recommended. **Tram:** 3, 8, or 15.

$ **Prices:** Appetizers 7.50F–12F ($5.50–$8.75); main courses 18F–41F ($13.15–$29.95); fixed-price lunch 15F ($10.95). AE, DC, MC, V.

Open: Lunch Mon–Fri 11:45am–1:45pm; dinner daily 6:30pm–midnight.

Fashion photographers and models frequently have lunch at this low-key, chic establishment. Almost everyone speaks English, and the accent in food is American—hamburgers, cheesecake, corn on the cob, T-bone steak. This is a fun place, especially in winter.

FISCHSTUBE ZÜRICHHORN, Bellerivestrasse 160. Tel. 55-25-20.

Cuisine: SWISS. **Reservations:** Required. **Tram:** 2 or 4.

$ **Prices:** Appetizers 4.80F–31F ($3.55–$22.63); main courses 19.80F–55F ($14.50–$40.15). AE, MC, V.

Open: Daily 11:45am–10:30pm. **Closed:** Oct–Apr.

Ideal on a summer evening, this seafood restaurant with outdoor tables is built on pilings over the lake. The scenery, service, and cuisine are hard to beat. I recommend the lake trout, filet of Dover sole Champs-Elysées, grilled lobster, and sirloin steak Café de Paris.

 FROMMER'S COOL FOR KIDS

RESTAURANTS

Spaghetti Factory (see p. 94) Children delight in the Spaghetti Factory, with its memories of life back home. Pastas come in generous portions and are reasonably priced. Go fairly early in the evening as it's less crowded then.

California (see p. 90) As the evening wears on, this place becomes rather chic. If you go around 6:30 to 8pm for dinner, with children in tow, you can let them enjoy such familiar fare as corn on the cob, hamburgers, and cheesecake.

Restaurants Bahnhofbuffet Zurich (see p. 94) Here is a selection of nine railroad station restaurants, many serving top-notch but moderately priced food. These range from a cafeteria where children delight in ordering Swiss fried potatoes (Rösti) to the Chuechli-Wirtschaft (try the apple fritters with vanilla sauce).

ZUNFTHAUS ZUR SAFFRAN, Limmatquai 54. Tel. 261-65-65.

Cuisine: SWISS. **Reservations:** Required. **Tram:** 4 or 15.

$ Prices: Appetizers 12F–20F ($8.75–$14.60); main courses 26F–42F ($19–$30.85). AE, DC, MC, V.

Open: Lunch daily noon–2pm; dinner daily 6–11:30pm.

Built beside the Limmat in 1740, this building was the headquarters for Zurich's spice merchants and apothecaries. The dining room has an opulent wood ceiling, half columns with gilded capitals, and Voltaire chairs; its tall windows offer a grand view of the Limmat. One of the specialties is Zunfttopf—filet mignon of beef with tomatoes and veal medallions with mushrooms; it's served in old bronze pots with saffron rice. Other dishes include sautéed minced veal with kidney in a mushroom-cream sauce, served with Rösti, and minced calves' liver with butter and fresh herbs.

ZUNFTHAUS ZUR ZIMMERLEUTEN, Limmatquai 40. Tel. 252-08-34.

Cuisine: SWISS. **Reservations:** Recommended. **Tram:** 4 or 15.

$ Prices: Appetizers 8F–20F ($5.85–$14.60); main courses 26F–38F ($19–$27.75). V.

Open: Lunch daily 11am–2pm; dinner daily 6–10pm. **Closed:** Mid-July to mid-Aug.

Dating from 1790, this charming restaurant has intricately carved paneling, high ceilings, and rows of leaded glass. The foundations date from 1336. A flight of baroque stairs leads to the elegant dining room decorated with hunting trophies. A typical meal might include veal liver with bacon and beans, minced veal with a mushroom-and-cream sauce, beefsteak tartare, and sirloin steak, followed by an iced soufflé with Grand Marnier.

ZUR OEPFELCHAMMER, Rindermarkt 12. Tel. 251-23-36.

Cuisine: SWISS/FRENCH. **Reservations:** Required. **Tram:** 4 or 15.

$ Prices: Appetizers 6F–18F ($4.40–$13.15); main courses 16F–45F ($11.70–$32.85); fixed-price lunch 14.50F ($10.60). MC, V.

Open: Lunch Tues–Sat 11:30am–2pm; dinner Tues–Sat 6pm–midnight.

Dating from 1357, this student hangout offers food, wine, and song, often with guitar music. The smoky dining room has carved wooden tables. Gottfried Keller, who lived nearby, dined here. The menu, which is in English, includes air-cured smoked beef, shredded calves' liver in butter with Rösti, and shredded veal Zurich style. For dessert, try the vodka sherbet or apple fritters with a hot vanilla sauce. The owner has a winery and offers several of his own vintages.

INEXPENSIVE

LE DEZALEY, Römergasse 7-9. Tel. 251-61-29.

Cuisine: VAUDOIS. **Reservations:** Required. **Tram:** 4 or 15.

$ Prices: Appetizers 3.50F–23F ($2.55–$16.80); main dishes 8F–36.50F ($5.85–$26.65). AE, DC, MC, V.

Open: Lunch Mon–Sat 9am–2:30pm; dinner Mon–Sat 5pm–midnight.

S This landmark house in the center of town is practically a private club for French-speaking Zurich residents. Its two adjoining buildings date from 1274. Pascal Ruhlé manages the restaurant, which has a French-Swiss ambience. Specialties are from the Vaud region, including cheese fondue, fondue chinoise, and fondue bourguignonne. Favorites include minced liver, kidney with Rösti, and sausages made with leeks. I also like the sliced veal Zurich style. Forty different local wines are offered. The menu is in English.

MERE CATHERINE, Am Rudenplatz. Tel. 262-22-50.
  Cuisine: FRENCH. **Reservations:** Required. **Tram:** 4 or 15.
$ **Prices:** Appetizers 7.50F–15F ($5.50–$10.95); main dishes 12F–30F ($8.75–$21.90); fixed-price Sunday dinner 28F ($20.45). No credit cards.
  Open: Daily 11am–11pm.
This small courtyard nestled among the back streets has quiet café tables, ivy, and plenty of sun. At night, young people in leather and jeans listen to rock music at the marble bar. Behind the bar, a corridor leads to a dim restaurant where French bistro-style food is served. Salade paysanne is the most popular appetizer; the terrines are also good. Specials change daily, but might include stuffed eggplant, fish soup, fried squid, and lamb cutlets in the Provençal style.

RAVI'S INDIAN CUISINE, Rütschistrasse 29. Tel. 361-66-56.
  Cuisine: INDIAN. **Reservations:** Recommended. **Tram:** 33.
$ **Prices:** Appetizers 10F–18F ($7.30–$13.15); main courses 15F–30F ($10.95–$21.90). AE, DC, V.
  Open: Tues–Sun 6–11pm. **Closed:** 3 weeks in Aug.
This restaurant on the northern edge of Zurich is a welcome change from continental cuisine. The chefs come from Bombay and Delhi, and the cuisine is from northern India. Recorded Indian music is played in a room with Mogul-style arched windows and hanging musical instruments. I recommend the marinated shrimp grilled over charcoal or grilled lamb with Indian herbs. Most dishes, laced with pungent herbs and sometimes fiery spices, are cooked in a clay pot.

AT ZOLLIKON

CHEZ MAX, Seestrasse 53. Tel. 391-88-77.
  Cuisine: SWISS. **Reservations:** Required, as far in advance as possible.
  Transportation: Taxi.
$ **Prices:** Appetizers 25F–45F ($18.25–$32.85); main courses 52F–76F ($37.95–$55.45). AE, DC, MC, V.
  Open: Lunch Tues–Sat noon–2pm; dinner Tues–Sat 6:30–11:30pm. **Closed:** July 31–Aug 12.
Located 2½ miles from Zurich in the suburb of Zollikon, this attractive house by the lake is a 12-minute ride from the center of town. Chef Max Kehl designed the decor, blending china and silver with modern art. His cuisine moderne concoctions, containing only fresh ingredients, include truffles with Vacherin cheese and a purée of white eggplant. Typical main courses are crayfish in a cream-and-champagne sauce, duck with black-truffle sauce, and veal filets with a homemade mustard sauce. For desert, choose a soufflé from the chef's repertoire.

SPECIALTY DINING

LOCAL FAVORITES

BIERHALLE KROPF, In Gassen 16. Tel. 221-18-05.

Cuisine: SWISS/BAVARIAN. **Reservations:** Recommended. **Tram:** 2, 8, 9, or 11.

$ Prices: Appetizers 7.50F–15F ($5.50–$10.95); main courses 10F–30F ($7.30–$21.90). AE, DC, MC, V.

Open: Lunch Mon–Sat 11:30am–1:45pm; dinner Mon–Sat 5:45–9:45pm.

Closed: Easter, Dec 25.

Everyone in Zurich, from the most conservative to the most liberal, goes to "Der Kropf" for its generous portions and old-fashioned ambience. The restaurant is in one of the oldest burgher houses in town, a few steps from the Paradeplatz. Its dining room has stained-glass windows, polished paneling, chandeliers, and plaster columns. On the walls hang stag horns and painted hunting scenes. Specialties include chopped veal with Rösti, stewed meats, pork shank, and pot-au-feu Zurich style. For dessert, I recommend Palatschinken or Apfelstrudel.

BLOCKHUS, Schifflande 4. Tel. 252-14-53.

Cuisine: INTERNATIONAL. **Reservations:** Not needed. **Tram:** 2, 4, 8, 11, or 15.

$ Prices: Appetizers 7F–12F ($5.10–$8.75); main courses 13F–36.50F ($9.50–$26.65). No credit cards.

Open: Daily 11am–11:30pm.

You'll get a warm welcome at this typical old Swiss restaurant near Bellevueplatz and Limmatquai. Cheese fondue is the specialty, but other dishes are prepared equally well. These include beefsteak tartar and minced veal with Rösti, Zurich's classic dish. There are five lunch menus.

HOTEL DINING

HOTEL FLORHOF RESTAURANT, Florhofgasse 4. Tel. 261-44-70.

Cuisine: SWISS/FRENCH. **Reservations:** Required. **Tram:** 3.

$ Prices: Appetizers 13F–20F ($9.50–$14.60); main courses 24F–38F ($17.50–$27.75); fixed-price meals 33F ($24.10) at lunch, 54F ($39.40) at dinner. AE, DC, MC, V.

Open: Lunch Mon–Fri 11:30am–2pm; dinner Mon–Fri 5:30–9:30pm.

Ⓢ This small, elegant restaurant is run by the Schilter family in an old patrician house that was renovated in 1973. The menu is carefully chosen. The soups and appetizers are especially good. Appetizers might include risotto with mushrooms or dried prosciutto. For a main dish, I recommend filets of fera (a kind of trout); shrimp Indian style, with rice and curry; calves' brains in butter; and kidneys in mustard sauce There is also a good selection of beef and veal dishes.

THE JOCKEY CLUB, in the Hotel Ascot, Tessinerplatz 9. Tel. 201-18-00.

Cuisine: INTERNATIONAL. **Reservations:** Recommended. **Tram:** 6 or 7.

$ Prices: Appetizers 15F–20F ($10.95–$14.60); main courses 30F–50F ($21.90–$36.50); fixed-price dinner 50F ($36.50). AE, DC, MC, V.

Open: Jockey Club, lunch Mon–Fri 11:45am–2pm; dinner Mon–Fri 6:30–11pm. Turf Bar, daily 11am–11pm.

The Jockey Club, an opulent hotel restaurant, emulates English style with its burnished mahogany paneling, brass rails, and supple leather upholstery. Its specialties include sirloin beef from the trolley (both large and small portions), trout, salmon marinated in anise, a brouillade of chicken livers, Florentine-style monkfish, and filet of beef Stroganoff. The service is impeccable.

In the adjacent Turf Bar, shaped like a horseshoe, mirrored tables reflect a fascinating mural on the ceiling. The bar is a less-expensive version of the Jockey Club restaurant. Live piano music is played from 5:30 to 11pm.

VEGETARIAN

HILTL VEGI, Sihlstrasse 28. Tel. 221-38-70.
  Cuisine: VEGETARIAN. **Reservations:** Not needed. **Tram:** 6, 7, 11, or 13.
$ **Prices:** Appetizers 3.90F–5.20F ($2.95–$3.85); main courses 8.20F–26.50F ($6–$19.35); fixed-price lunch 18F ($13.15). No credit cards.
  Open: Breakfast Mon–Sat 6:30–11am; Sun 9–11am; lunch/dinner daily 11am–9pm.

Founded in 1887, this appealing two-story vegetarian restaurant is clean and orderly. The first story has a rough granite floor and a green wood ceiling. Elaborate salads are presented on a steel rack. The upstairs maroon dining room, with its oversize windows, is sunnier.

The menu includes well-prepared and nutritious salads, hearty soups, and rich desserts. One of the least expensive items on the menu is spaghetti, served five different ways. Many curry dishes are also featured. You can even try a raclette vegi-burger. There are more than two dozen different blends of tea.

DINING CLUSTERS/COMPLEXES

At **Restaurants Bahnhofbuffet Zurich,** Bahnhofplatz 15 (tel. 211-15-10), nine railway station restaurants are offered under one roof. The complex is at the end of Bahnhofstrasse in the heart of Zurich. There is a variety of cuisines as well as costs, and all are open daily from 6am to 11:30pm. The most prestigious restaurant is **Au Premier,** which serves French food in an elegant Belle Epoque atmosphere. A specialty is medallions de filet de veau au citron vert (veal with lime sauce). A la carte meals cost 35F to 75F ($25.55 to $54.75).

Traditional Swiss country cuisine is served in a rustic setting at the wine restaurant **Trotte,** where à la carte meals start at 20F ($14.60). Other restaurants and their specialties include Italian dishes at **Da Capo,** grilled sole or salmon at **Alfred Escherstube,** entrecôte maître d'hôtel at **Le Bistro de le Gare,** roast veal sausage with french fries at the **Cafeteria,** garnished hash-brown potato dishes at the **Brasserie,** and pork Casimir in curry sauce at **Winterthurer Stübli,** and apple fritters with vanilla sauce at **Chuechli-Wirtschaft.**

FAST FOOD

SPAGHETTI FACTORY, Theaterstrasse 10. Tel. 261-80-70.
  Cuisine: ITALIAN. **Reservations:** Not needed. **Tram:** 2, 4, 5, 11, or 15.
$ **Prices:** Main courses 10.50F–23F ($7.65–$16.80).
  Open: Mon–Thurs 8am–2am, Fri–Sat 8am–4am, Sun 11am–2am.

Ignore the corny labels given to the homemade pasta dishes and concentrate instead on their good flavor and relatively low prices (for Zurich). This is one of the few restaurants where you can dine reasonably if you have children in tow. You have a choice of sauces to go with your spaghetti or other pastas, and can also order meat and poultry dishes if you don't want spaghetti. The place gets crowded on Friday and Saturday nights.

CAFÉS

CONDITOREI CAFE SCHOBER, Napfgasse. Tel. 251-80-60.

One of the most select cafés in Zurich is located in Zum grossen Erker (The Great Alcove), a building dating from 1314 that was turned into a confectionery and coffee shop by Theodor Schober after 1875. When the last Schober retired, the well-known meeting place was bought and renovated by Teuscher, the epicurean name in chocolates. The old-fashioned café, with its beautiful lighting fixtures and molded ceilings, is known for its hot chocolate. It also offers an array of homemade pastries, cakes, and ice cream. Prices begin at 3F ($2.20).

Open: Mon–Fri 8am–6:30pm, Sat 8am–5pm, Sun 10am–5:30pm.

CAFETERIA ZUR MÜNST, Münzplatz 3. Tel. 221-30-27.

This unusual coffeehouse with a concrete facade has fanciful chandeliers by Swiss artist Jean Tinguely. They resemble funny creatures—half human, half robot—that spin, wave feathers, and pivot at each other. The coffeehouse is on a quiet street that runs into Bahnhofstrasse. Delectable pastries are served in a chatty atmosphere. Elaborate ice-cream confections cost 6.50F ($4.75), and light meals start at 18F ($13.15).

Open: Mon–Wed and Fri 7:30am–7pm, Thurs 7:30am–9pm, Sat 7:30am–5pm.

CAFE/BAR ODEON, Limmatquai 2. Tel. 251-16-50.

This legendary turn-of-the-century bohemian landmark is a popular singles hangout in the evening. Lenin came here during World War I to make such pronouncements as, "The neutrality of Switzerland is a bourgeois fraud and means submission to the imperialist war." The intimate café is decorated in art nouveau and has banquettes and cubbyholes. It also has a curved bar and many sidewalk tables. Light meals begin at 18F ($13.15); coffee costs 3F ($2.20).

Open: Mon–Sat 7am–2am, Sun 11am–2am.

CAFE SELECT, Limmatquai 16. Tel. 252-43-72.

This restaurant has 350 seats on an outdoor terrace sheltered from noise and traffic by the surrounding buildings. It's a gathering place for the literati and is Zurich's closest rival to the Odéon. No alcohol is served. Coffee begins at 2.80F ($2.10), snacks and light meals range from 12F to 18F ($8.75 to $13.15), and cakes and sandwiches average 4F ($2.90).

Open: Daily 7am–11:30pm.

AFTERNOON TEA

NÔ DAS KÖSTLICHE TEEHAUS, Kuttelgasse 7. Tel. 211-75-50.

This modern tearoom has an understated Japanese decor of potted bamboos, trees, and light-wood furniture. It's on a small street of boutiques in Old Town. There is a complete choice of teas (no alcohol is served). Simple menus range from 12F to 18F ($8.75 to $13.15).

Open: Mon–Wed and Fri 7:30am–8pm, Thurs 7:30am–10pm, Sat 7:30am–5pm.

A PASTRY SHOP

CONFISERIE SPRÜNGLI, Am Paradeplatz. Tel. 211-07-95.

This old-fashioned pastry shop on Bahnhofstrasse, founded in 1836, is comparable to the legendary Demel in Vienna. Many Zurichers remember episodes from their childhood that took place here. A variety of pastries and chocolates are sold on the ground floor. The famous Lindt chocolates and the house specialties are about the best you'll ever find. Light meals begin at 18F ($13.15), but most guests order tea for 2.80F ($2.10). Desserts begin at 3F ($2.20).

Open: Mon–Fri 7am–6:30pm, Sat 7:30am–5:30pm.

PICNIC FARE & WHERE TO EAT IT

In Bahnhofplatz and along Bahnhofstrasse, in the vicinity of the rail station, you can easily find the makings of a picnic. Many small pâtisseries sell delectable confections in the area. You can also patronize numerous Swiss delis, which have a high standard of excellence, especially in their choice of cold cuts. Many of them also sell take-out food, including herring salad or grilled chicken. One such deli is **Coop Super-Center,** Bahnhofplatz (tel. 221-02-75).

For your picnic, you can walk to the termination of **Bahnhofstrasse** which opens onto Lake Zurich. However, be careful to clean up any debris—the Swiss disapprove mightily of littering, and the police will impose fines.

You can also visit **Uetliberg,** southwest of Zurich, the northernmost peak in the Albis ridge (see Section 11, "Easy Excursions from Zurich," below).

RESTAURANTS BY CUISINE

Cuisines and Restaurants	Rating*
AMERICAN	
California (page 90)	M
BAVARIAN	
Bierhalle Kropf (page 92)	I
CONTINENTAL	
Le Tübli (page 89)	E
FISH	
Alfred Escherstube (page 94)	I
FRENCH	
Au Premier (page 94)	M
Hotel Florhof Restaurant (page 93)	E
Kronenhalle (page 89)	E
Le Bistro de la Gare (page 94)	I
Mère Catherine (page 92)	I
Zur Oepfelchammer (page 91)	M
INDIAN	
Ravi's Indian Cuisine (page 92)	I
INTERNATIONAL	
Blockhus (page 93)	M
Casino Zurich Horn (page 88)	VE
Jockey Club/Turf Bar (page 93)	E/M

ITALIAN

Da Capo (page 94)	I
Restaurant Conti (page 89)	E
Restaurant Piccoli (Accademia) (page 84)	E
Spaghetti Factory (page 94)	I
Veltliner Keller (page 85)	M

SPANISH

Ribó (page 85)	M

SWISS

Agnès Amberg (page 88)	VE
Augustiner (page 85)	I
Bierhalle Kropf (page 92)	I
Brasserie (page 94)	I
Cafeteria (page 94)	I
Chez Max (page 92)	VE
Fischstube Zürichhorn (page 90)	M
Haus zum Rüden (page 88)	VE
Hotel Florhof Restaurant (page 93)	E
Jacky's Stapferstube (page 89)	E
Kronenhalle (page 89)	E
Nouvelle (page 84)	E
Trotte (page 94)	I
Veltliner Keller (page 85)	M
Winterthurer Stübli (page 94)	I
Zeughauskeller (page 88)	I
Zunfthaus zur Saffran (page 91)	M
Zunfthaus zur Zimmerleuten (page 91)	M
Zur Oepfelchammer (page 91)	M

VAUDOIS

Le Dézaley (page 91)	I

VEGETARIAN

Hiltl Vegi (page 94)	I

*VE = Very Expensive; E = Expensive; M = Moderate;
I = Inexpensive; B = Budget.

5. ATTRACTIONS

Zurich has a rich history and many reminders of its past. There are 20 museums, nearly 100 galleries, and 24 archives, including one devoted to Thomas Mann. Historic buildings, religious monuments, and quays are worth discovering, as well as the well-preserved homes of rich burghers, lovely parks, and gardens. Museum exhibits range from prehistoric lake dwellers to Charlemagne.

Botanic Garden ①
Fraumünster ⑦
Grossmünster ⑤
Helmhaus ④
Landesmuseum ⑫
Lindenhof ⑩
Münsterhof ⑧
Rathaus ⑥
Rietberg Museum ⑬
St. Peter's Church
  (Peterskirche) ⑨
Urania Observatory ⑪
Wasserkirche ③
Zurich Kunsthaus ②

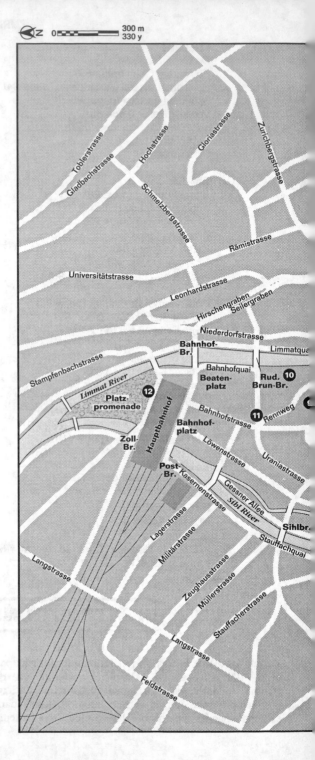

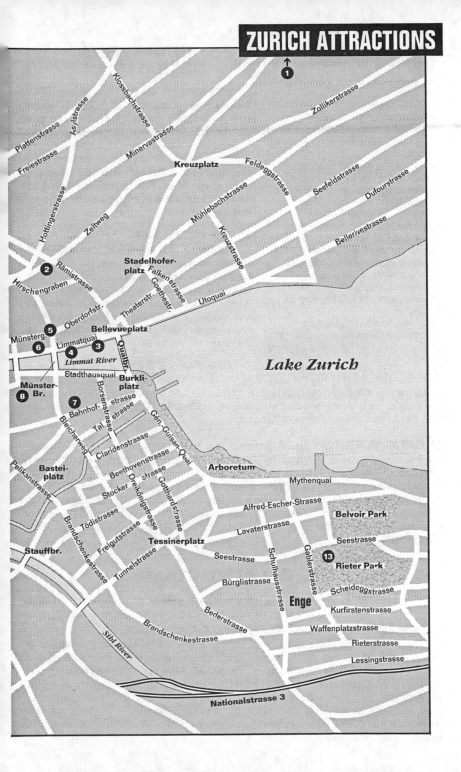

ZURICH ATTRACTIONS

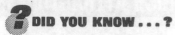

DID YOU KNOW...?

- Lenin sat out part of World War I in Zurich, plotting the Russian Revolution.
- Because of Zurich's proximity to Germany, a few Allied bombs in World War II rained down on it by accident.
- James Joyce wrote much of *Ulysses* in Zurich, not in Ireland.
- Zurich, financial center of stability, gave birth to the revolutionary artistic movement of dadaism, whose aim was to destroy order.
- As you walk down Bahnhofstrasse, you are only a few feet away from where much of the world's gold and silver is stored underground.
- The status of Zurich as a powerful financial capital is little more than a century old.
- Marc Chagall completed the modern stained-glass windows in Fraumünster when he was 83 years old.

SIGHTSEEING STRATEGIES

IF YOU HAVE 1 DAY Take Walking Tour 1 along Bahnhofstrasse to Lake Zurich, where you can board a steamer for a 1½-hour ride on the lake. Return to the shore and visit either the Kunsthaus Museum or the Landesmuseum. In the late afternoon, take Walking Tour 2 through Altstadt, along the famous quays of Zurich and through Old Town, where you might have a raclette dinner in an old tavern.

IF YOU HAVE 2 DAYS Spend the first day as suggested above. In the morning, visit Fraumünster or Grossmünster, the two most famous churches of Zurich. Enjoy lunch in a typical Zurich café. In the afternoon, leave Zurich for Uetliberg, for a spectacular view of the Alps and the city. Have a beer and listen to the oompah band at the Bierhall Wolf in the evening.

IF YOU HAVE 3 DAYS Spend the first 2 days as outlined above. On the third day, see all the attractions you've missed before, including two museums: the Rietberg, with its great non-European art collection, and the Bührle, with its stupendous collection of modern art. Visit the Botanic Garden and the Zoo in the afternoon, if time remains.

IF YOU HAVE 5 DAYS Spend the first 3 days as outlined above. In the morning of the fourth day, go to Winterthur, only a 25-minute ride from Zurich, to see its many attractions, including the Oskar Reinhart Foundation, Am Römerholz, Kunstmuseum, and the Schloss Kyburg. Spend the fifth day exploring the attractions of the environs, including Regensberg, a village nugget from the Middle Ages, about 10 miles from Zurich. In the afternoon, take a lake steamer to Rapperswil, the "town of roses," 19 miles from Zurich. There you can see Rapperswil Castle and other attractions.

THE TOP ATTRACTIONS

THE GREAT CHURCHES

GROSSMÜNSTER, Grossmünsterplatz. Tel. 252-59-49.

This is the Romanesque and Gothic cathedral of Zurich. According to legend, it was founded by Charlemagne, whose horse bowed down on the spot marking the graves of three early Christian martyrs. The cathedral has two three-story towers and is situated on a terrace above Limmatquai, on the right bank. Construction began in 1090 and additions were made until the early 14th century. The choir contains stained-glass windows completed in 1933 by Giacometti. In the crypt is a weather-beaten, 15th-century statue of Charlemagne, a copy of which crowns the south tower.

The cathedral is dedicated to the patron saints of Zurich: Felix, Regula, and Exuperantius. In the 3rd century, the three martyrs attempted to convert the citizens of Turicum (the original name for Zurich) to Christianity. The governor, according to legend, ordered them placed in boiling oil and forced them to drink molten lead. Through the ordeal, they refused to renounce their faith and were beheaded. Miraculously, they still had vitality, enough to pick up their heads and climb to the top of a hill (the present site of the cathedral), where they dug their own graves and then interred themselves. The seal of Zurich honors these saints, depicting them carrying their heads under their arms. The remains of the saints are said to rest in one of the chapels of the Münster (cathedral).

The cathedral was once the parish church of Zwingli, one of the great leaders of the Reformation. He urged priests to take wives (he himself had married) and attacked the "worship of images" and the Roman sacrament of mass. In 1531, Zwingli was killed in a religious war at Kappel. The hangman quartered his body, and soldiers burnt the pieces with dung. The site of his execution is marked with an inscription: "They may kill the body but not the soul." In accordance with Zwingli's beliefs, Zurich's Grossmünster is austere, stripped of the heavy ornamentation you'll find in the cathedrals of Italy.

The view from the towers is impressive. One of them is open May to October in good weather; call to see if the tower is open.

Admission: Cathedral, free; towers, 1F (75¢).

Open: Cathedral, Apr–Sept, Mon–Fri 9am–4pm, Sat 9am–5pm; Oct–Mar, daily 10am–4pm.

FRAUMÜNSTER, Fraumünsterstrasse. Tel. 202-59-21.

This church, with its slender blue spire, is on the left bank overlooking the former pig market, Münsterhof. (Münsterhof is one of the historic old squares of Zurich and is well worth a visit.) A Benedictine abbey was founded at the site in 853 by Emperor Ludwig (Louis the German), the grandson of Charlemagne. His daughter became the first abbess. The present church dates from the 13th and 14th centuries, but the crypt of the old abbey church is preserved in the undercroft.

The chief attractions of Fraumünster are five stained-glass windows—each with its own color theme—designed by Marc Chagall in 1970. They are best seen in bright morning light. The Münster is also celebrated for its elaborate organ. The basilica has three aisles; the nave is in the Gothic style.

IN THEIR FOOTSTEPS

Gottfried Keller (1819–90) Switzerland's national poet and foremost novelist, Keller ranks among the greatest German-language writers of the second half of the 19th century. In his youth he evinced a talent for drawing and studied art in Munich, until poverty forced him to return home. His major novel, *Der grüne Heinrich* (1854–55; *Green Henry*, 1960), which chronicles the development of its hero, has been favorably compared to Goethe's *Wilhelm Meister*. Keller is also known for his short-story collection *People of Seldwyla* (1856–74; English trans., 1929).

• **Birthplace:** Zurich, on July 19, 1819.

• **Residences:** He was born at Neumarkt 27 in Zurich, where his father was a turner, but passed most of his childhood at Rindermarkt 9. At his death he was living at Zeltweg 27.

• **Resting Place:** Sihlfeld Cemetery in Zurich.

From Fraumünster you can cross the **Münsterbrücke,** an 1838 bridge that leads to the Grossmünster. On the bridge is a statue of Burgomaster Waldmann, who was beheaded in 1489; during his rule, the city gained influence over much of the surrounding lands.
Admission: Free.
Open: May–Sept, Mon–Sat 9am–6pm, Sun noon–6pm; Oct–Apr, daily 10am–dusk (about 4–5pm).

PETERSKIRCHE (St. Peter's Church), St. Peterhostatt. Tel. 211-25-88.
Built in the 13th century, St. Peter's on the left bank, south of Lindenhof, is the oldest church in Zurich. It has the largest clock face in Europe—28½ feet in diameter; the minute hands alone are 12 feet long. Inside, the choir is Romanesque, but the three-aisle nave is baroque.
Admission: Free.
Open: Daily 8am–6pm.

THE QUAYS OF ZURICH

The quays of Zurich, with their promenades, are among the city's most popular attractions. The most famous is **Limmatquai,** in the center of Zurich. It begins at the Bahnhof Bridge and extends east to the Rathaus (town hall) and beyond. Many of the quays have lovely gardens. **Uto Quai** is the major promenade along Zurichsee (Lake Zurich), running from Badeanstalt Uto Quai (a swimming pool) to Bellevueplatz and Quai Brücke. The pool is open daily from 8am to 7pm. If you stroll as far as **Mythen Quai,** you'll be following the lake along its western shore and out into the countryside.

THE BEST MUSEUMS

LANDESMUSEUM (Swiss National Museum), Museumstrasse 2. Tel. 221-10-10.
This museum offers an epic survey of the culture and history of the Swiss people. Its collection, housed in a Victorian building behind the Zurich Hauptbahnhof, contains works of religious art, including 16th-century stained glass from Tanikon Convent and frescoes from the church of Mustair. Some of the Carolingian art dates back to the 9th century. The altarpieces are carved, painted, and gilded.
The prehistoric section is also exceptional. Some of the artifacts are from the 4th millennium B.C., when Switzerland was a Roman outpost. There is a large display of Roman clothing, medieval silverware, 14th-century drinking bowls, and 17th-century china, as well as painted furniture, costumes, and dollhouses of various periods. A display of weapons and armor shows the methods of Swiss warfare from 800 to 1800. There's also an exhibit tracing Swiss clock-making from the 16th to the 18th century.
Admission: Free.
Open: Tues–Sun 10am–5pm. **Tram:** 3.

ZURICH KUNSTHAUS (Fine Arts Museum), Heimplatz 1. Tel. 251-67-55.
One of the most important art museums in Europe, the Zurich Kunsthaus is devoted mainly to the 19th and 20th centuries, although the range of paintings and sculpture reaches back to antiquity. The museum was founded in Victorian times and was overhauled in 1976. Today it's one of the most modern and

FROMMER'S FAVORITE
ZURICH EXPERIENCES

Shopping Along Bahnhofstrasse It has been called the most beautiful shopping street in the world, and perhaps it is. Built a century ago on the site of the ancient moat, it's a stroller's paradise. Better window-shop, however, because the price tags are lethal.

Boat Trip on Lake Zurich On a sunny day, this is the best way to spend time in Zurich, sailing on one of Europe's most beautiful lakes on cruises lasting from 1½ to 4 hours. Boats depart from the Bürkliplatz, the lake end of Bahnhofstrasse.

Visiting Uetliberg, Outside the City If the day is sunny, you can take an electric train to this parklike, 2,800-foot hill. Once there, you can wander around, enjoying views of nature and scenic vistas at every turn. It's best to take a picnic.

Meeting a Swiss Family Zurich can seem cold and impersonal unless you get to meet some of the locals. The tourist office will arrange for you to get in touch with a family of your own age and occupation. It's a close-up view of how Zurichers live in their safe, prosperous city.

sophisticated museums in the world, both in its superb lighting and in its arrangement of art.

My favorite exhibits include Rodin's *Gate of Hell,* near the entrance, and the Giacometti wing, showing the artistic development of this amazing Swiss-born artist. The collection of modern art includes works by all the greats—Bonnard, Braque, Chagall, Lipschitz, Marini, Mondrian, Picasso, Rouault. The gallery owns the largest collection outside Oslo of works by the Norwegian artist Edvard Munch. Two old masters, Rubens and Rembrandt, are also represented. To brighten a rainy day, see the pictures by Cézanne, Degas, Monet, Toulouse-Lautrec, and Utrillo.

Admission: 4F ($2.90); special exhibitions 7F–10F ($5.10–$7.30).

Open: Mon 2–5pm, Tues–Fri 10am–9pm, Sat–Sun 10am–5pm. **Tram:** 3, 5, or 8.

RIETBERG MUSEUM, Gablerstrasse 15. Tel. 202-45-28.

The Rietberg contains a stunning collection of non-European art, most of which was assembled by Baron Eduard von der Heydt and donated to the city of Zurich in 1952. The collection is housed in the former Wesendonck Villa, constructed in 1857 by a German industrialist, Otto Wesendonck. Modeled after Villa Albani in Rome, the building is located in a garden in Rieter Park and overlooks Lake Zurich. Richard Wagner came here and fell in love with the hostess, who inspired his tragic opera *Tristan und Isolde.*

The eclectic collection was gathered from the South Sea islands, the Near East, Asia (particularly China, Tibet, and Japan), Africa, and pre-Columbian America. Of all the treasures, my favorite is the *Dancing Shiva,* a celebrated Indian bronze. You should also seek out the votive stelae of the Wei dynasty (dating from the archaic Buddhist period).

Admission: 3F ($2.20).
Open: Tues and Thurs–Sun 10am–5pm, Wed 5–9pm. **Tram:** 6 or 7 from the town center (a 12-min. ride).

ZUNFTHAUS ZUR MEISEN, Münsterhof 20. Tel. 221-28-07.

Across the bridge from the Wasserkirche is one of the famous old guildhouses of the city. It has a wrought-iron gatehouse that opens onto the Münsterhof. The late baroque guildhouse, dating from 1752, is a branch museum of the overstuffed Swiss National Museum. It's devoted mainly to 18th-century Swiss ceramics, the porcelain of Zurich, and several antiques. The beauty of the stuccoed rooms competes with the exhibits.
Admission: Free.
Open: Tues–Sun 10am–noon and 2–5pm. **Closed:** Hols. **Tram:** 3.

MORE ATTRACTIONS

URANIA OBSERVATORY, Uraniastrasse 9. Tel. 211-65-23.

The observatory is halfway between Bahnhofstrasse and the Limmat River on Uraniastrasse. On clear days, you can look through the telescope. There are also exhibits.
Admission: 3F ($1.45) adults, 1F (75¢) children.
Open: Apr–Sept, Mon–Fri 8:30–11pm; Oct–Mar Mon–Fri 8–10pm. **Tram:** 11 or 13.

BÜHRLE MUSEUM, Zollikerstrasse 172. Tel. 55-00-86.

This jewel of a collection is most popular for its French impressionists, including works by Monet, Degas, Renoir, and Manet. The private collection also includes paintings by Rubens, Rembrandt, and Fragonard. There is a limited but very special section devoted to medieval sculpture.
Admission: 6.60F ($5) adults, 3F ($2.20) students.
Open: Tues–Fri 2–5pm. **Tram:** 2 or 4.

BOTANIC GARDEN, University of Zurich, Zollikerstrasse 107. Tel. 385-44-11.

The gardens contain 15,000 living species, including some rare specimens from New Caledonia and Southwest Africa. The herbarium contains more than a million plants. The gardens, owned by the University of Zurich, were laid out on the site of a former private villa.
Admission: Free.
Open: Park, Mar–Sept, Mon–Fri 7am–6pm, Sat–Sun 8am–6pm; Oct–Feb, Mon–Fri 8am–6pm, Sat–Sun 8am–5pm. Greenhouses, daily 9:30–11:30am and 1–4pm. **Tram:** 11 to Hegibachplatz, or 2 or 4 to Hoschgasse. **Bus:** 31 to Hegibachplatz.

COOL FOR KIDS

There are many things to interest children in Zurich. Playgrounds, boat rides, train trips, and the zoo are some of the highlights.

There are 80 **playgrounds** in Zurich. For the one nearest your hotel, inquire either at your hotel or at the local tourist office (see "Tourist Information in Section

1, "Orientation," above). Most **boat trips** leave from the end of Bahnhofstrasse on the right. You might combine a train ride with a trip to an attraction outside of Zurich.

During the off-season, there is a **children's workshop** at the Kunsthaus from October until June, every Wednesday from 2 to 4pm; children 6 to 12 are welcome. Select **theaters** also offer changing programs for children. Ask at the tourist office or get a copy of *Zurich Weekly Official,* available at most newsstands.

Two attractions may be of special interest to children:

ZOOLOGISCHER GARTEN (Zoological Garden), Zurichbergstrasse 221. Tel. 251-71-00.
One of the best-known zoos in Europe, Zurich's Zoological Garden contains some 2,400 animals of about 350 species. It also has an aquarium and an open-air aviary. You can visit the Africa house, the ape house, and the terrariums, along with the elephant house and the giant land turtle house. There are special enclosures for pandas, seals, otters, and snow leopards, and a house for clouded leopards, tigers, Amur leopards, and Indian lions.
Admission: 7.70F ($5.65) adults, 3.85F ($2.90) children.
Open: Summer, daily 8am–6pm; winter, daily 8am–5pm. **Tram:** 6 from the Hauptbahnhof; the zoo is in the eastern sector of the city, called Zurichberg, on a wooded hill.

ZÜRCHER SPIELZEUGMUSEUM (Zurich Toy Museum), Fortunagasse 15. Tel. 211-93-05.
This museum, in one of the oldest parts of the city, contains more than 1,200 antique toys from all over Europe. The collection was amassed by Franz Carl Weber.
Admission: Free.
Open: Mon–Fri 2–5pm, Sat 1–4pm.

SHOPS FOR CHILDREN

Several stores may be fun spots to visit with your kids. The largest toy shop in Europe is **Franz Carl Weber,** Bahnhofstrasse 62 (tel. 211-29-61), named for the famous toy collector. There is also a specialist toy shop, **Pastorini,** Weinplatz 7 (tel. 211-74-26).

The best-stocked children's bookstore in Switzerland is **Kinderbuchladen Zurich,** Grossmünsterplatz 9 (tel. 261-53-50), which carries many books written in English.

SPECIAL-INTEREST SIGHTSEEING

FOR THE LITERARY ENTHUSIAST

THOMAS MANN ARCHIVES, at the Swiss Federal Institute of Technology, Schönberggasse 15. Tel. 362-46-32.
Thomas Mann, the celebrated German writer who won the Nobel Prize for literature in 1929 for such works as *Death in Venice* and *The Magic Mountain,* died in Kilchberg, near Zurich, in 1955. An opponent of the Nazi regime, he had lived outside Germany after 1933—in the United States from 1938 to 1953 and in Switzerland during most of the rest of the period. The archives, located next to the university, contain manuscripts and mementos.

Admission: Free.
Open: Wed–Sat 2–4pm. **Tram:** 6.

FRIEDHOF FLUNTERN (Fluntern Cemetery), Zurichberg district.
James Joyce, the author of *Ulysses,* lived in Zurich from 1915 to 1919, at Universitätsstrasse 38. In 1941 he returned to Zurich from Paris, only a month before his death. Near his tomb is a statue depicting the great Irish writer sitting cross-legged with a book in his hand.
Admission: Free.
Open: May–Aug, daily 7am–8pm; Mar–Apr and Sept–Oct, daily 7am–7pm; Nov–Feb, daily 7am–6pm. **Tram:** 5 or 6.

WALKING TOUR 1 — Bahnhofstrasse

Start: Bahnhofplatz.
Finish: Bellevueplatz.
Time: 1 hour.
Best Times: Monday through Friday from 9am to 5pm or on Saturday from 9am to 1am (when most stores are open)

If you do nothing else in Zurich, walk along the world-famous Bahnhofstrasse. One of the most beautiful shopping streets on earth was built on the site of a "frogs' moat." The street is free from traffic, except for trams.

1. Bahnhofplatz. The site of the Hauptbahnhof, the central railroad station, this is the beginning of Bahnhofstrasse. The square itself is rather drab, but the scenery improves as you go along (the street extends almost a mile to the lake). The Hauptbahnhof was built in 1871. Escalators take you from Bahnhofplatz past an underground shopping mall, ShopVille, to:
2. Bahnhofstrasse. With your back to the railway terminus, you can head up Bahnhofstrasse, which is lined with linden trees, as well as some of the world's most prosperous banks and expensive shops, selling luxury merchandise such as Swiss watches and jewelry.
3. Pestalozzi Park appears on your left, two blocks from Bahnhofplatz, between Schweizergasse and Usterigasse. If it's a sunny day, you can stop here and rest on one of the park benches by a statue of Johann Heinrich Pestalozzi (1746–1827), an educational reformer who had an impact on school standards in the United States.

REFUELING STOP At Bahnhofstrasse 21 is **4. Café Sprüngli,** the most elegant and fashionable place on this chic shopping street to meet for tea and pastries, which are reported to be the best in the city. You can also enjoy daily lunch specials.

Farther along, near Augustinergasse and Pelikan Strasse, you'll see a small pedestrian walkway where you can stop to admire the sculpture in the area.
After you pass St. Peter Strasse and Barengasse, you'll reach:
5. Paradeplatz, the hub of Zurich and the central tram interchange. In the 18th century, it was a cattle market. The square is dominated by the 1876 mansion of Crédit Suisse. East of the plaza is the Hotel Baur-en-Ville, the first hotel constructed in Zurich, in 1838. The facade was reconstructed in 1978.

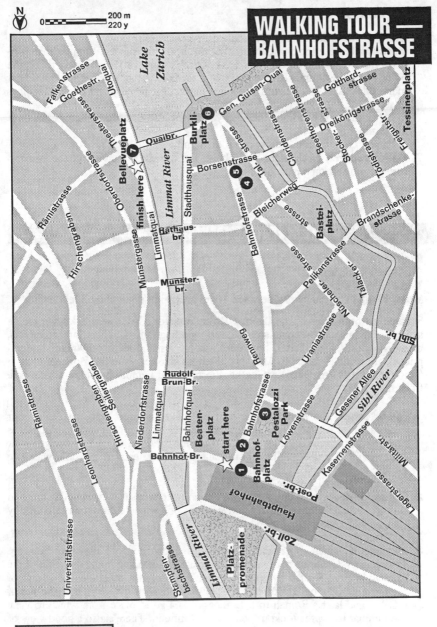

Continue along Bahnhofstrasse until you reach:

6. **Bürkliplatz,** overlooking Quaibrücke, the bridge across the Limmat that connects the left bank with the right bank. On the shore of Lake Zurich, this is the point where the Limmat River empties into the lake. A pint-size vegetable and fruit market flourishes here; there's also a flea market on Tuesday and Friday mornings in summer.

After stopping to admire the lake, you might also consider a boat excursion if it's summer.

If you cross Quaibrücke, you will arrive at:

7. **Bellevueplatz,** on the right bank. Here you can enjoy the view of the lake and river as you rest on a park bench.

WALKING TOUR —— Altstadt

Start: Münsterhof.
Finish: Helmhaus.
Time: 1½ hours.
Best Time: Any sunny day between 10am and 4pm (when there's less traffic).

Situated on both sides of the Limmat River, Altstadt (Old Town) is known for its squares, narrow cobblestone streets, and winding alleys. There are fountains, medieval houses, art galleries, boutiques, quaint restaurants, hotels (many budget-priced), and antique shops. To walk its old streets is to follow in the footsteps of such famous figures as Charlemagne, Goethe, Einstein, and Lenin. The oldest houses date from the 1100s.

1. **Münsterhof,** the former swine market, makes a good place to begin your exploration of Altstadt. This square, on the left bank, is near such landmarks as Fraumünster and the Rathaus. You can reach it by walking along Schlüsselgasse. At Münsterhof 8 is the guildhall Zunfthaus zur Waag, erected in 1637, with late Gothic windows and a gabled facade.

Standing parallel to the Münsterhof is:

2. **Fraumünster,** whose entrance is on Fraumünsterstrasse. A church has stood on this site since 853, when it was a convent for noblewomen. It contains artwork by Chagall and Giacometti, among others.

After the church, your next target can be:

3. **Lindenhof,** which you reach by climbing narrow medieval alleyways from the Fraumünster. Continue north along Schlüsselgasse, heading in the direction of the railroad station. Shaded by trees, the belvedere square of Lindenhof is one of the most scenic spots in Zurich, especially romantic at twilight. Once the site of a Celtic and later a Roman fort, Lindenhof is a good place from which to view the Limmat River; the lookout point has a fountain. There's also a good view of the medieval old quarter, which rises in layers on the right bank.

From Lindenhof, head down Pfalzgasse, forking left onto Strehlgasse to Waggengasse and Rathausbrücke, the city hall bridge spanning the Limmat. You have arrived at:

4. **Weinplatz,** a landmark square. The site of the Corn Exchange until 1620, this is presumably the oldest market square in Zurich. It is named for its 1909 Weinbauer

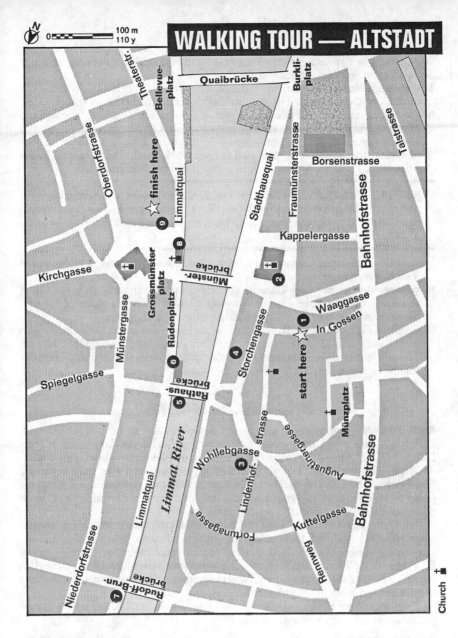

WALKING TOUR — ALTSTADT

0 ⌸⌸⌸⌸ 100 m
110 y

N

Quaibrücke

Theaterstr.
Bellevue-platz
Burkli-platz

Oberdorfstrasse

Borsenstrasse

Stadthausquai

Fraumünsterstrasse

Talstrasse

⭐ finish here

⑨ Limmatquai

Kappelergasse

Bahnhofstrasse

⑧

Kirchgasse

✝ ■

✝ ■

Münster-brücke

✝ ■

Waaggasse

In Gossen

Grossmünster platz

②

① ⭐ start here

Münstergasse

Rüdenplatz

⑥

Storchengasse

④

✝ ■

Münzplatz

Spiegelgasse

Rathaus-brücke

⑤

✝ ■

Limmat River

Wohllebgasse

③

strasse

Lindenhof

Augustinergasse

Bahnhofstrasse

Limmatquai

Fortunagasse

Kuttelgasse

Niederdorfstrasse

Rudolf-Brun-brücke

⑦

Rennweg

Church ✝ ■

ZURICH

Altstadt

① Münsterhof
② Fraumünster
③ Lindenhof
④ Weinplatz
⑤ Rathausbrücke
⑥ The Rathaus
⑦ Café Odeon
⑧ Wasserkirche
⑨ Helmhaus

fountain, which depicts a Swiss wine-grower with a basket of grapes in hand. Most visitors pause to photograph the Flemish-roofed burghers' houses on the opposite bank. Here you can also look at the:

5. Rathausbrücke, spanning the Limmat. The present City Hall Bridge was built in 1878, at the site of the first span in Zurich. Cross the bridge to visit the:

6. Rathaus, the late Renaissance town hall of Zurich, which opens onto Limmatquai. Built in the late 17th century, it has darkly paneled rooms and antique porcelain stoves. Canton councils still meet here in a setting of rich sculptural adornment. The town hall is open on Tuesday, Thursday, and Friday from 10 to 11:30am. Admission is free, but you should tip your guide.

REFUELING STOP   The Belle Epoque **7. Café Odéon,** Limmatquai 2, is the place where Lenin sat out most of World War I, plotting the Russian Revolution. It was also popular with the iconoclastic Dada artists of the same era. Stop for a cup of coffee in a historic setting.

Walk south along Limmatquai until you reach Münsterbrücke, a bridge across the Limmat, the site of:

8. Wasserkirche, or Water Church. This church got its unusual name because it was surrounded by water when it was built in 1479. There is a statue of Zwingli, the famous Swiss reformer. Directly north of the church is the:

9. Helmhaus, Limmatquai 31, built in 1794. It has a fountain hall and a gallery on the second and third floors, where the city shows changing exhibitions of Swiss art. The gallery is open Tuesday through Sunday from 10am to 6pm and also Thursday from 8 to 10pm.

ORGANIZED TOURS

BUS TOURS   The quickest and most convenient way to get acquainted with Zurich is to take a 2-hour motorcoach tour with an English-speaking guide. It costs 22F ($16.05). There are daily departures at 10am and 2pm year round, plus a noon departure daily from May 1 until the end of September and a 4pm daily departure from May until the end of October. The tour takes in the commercial and shopping center and the old town, and goes along the lake for a visit to the Fraumünster Church or one of the historic guildhalls beside Limmatquai.

Another exciting tour is by both coach and aerial cableway. It lasts 2½ hours and costs 30F ($21.90). This tour swings through the Reppischtal-Albispass-Adliswil recreational sector. The highlight is a ride on an aerial cableway, climbing to the Felsenegg at 2,650 feet. From here, there's a panoramic view of the lake and the Alps beyond. The tour also takes in an animal farm and an indoor cactus garden. It leaves daily at 9:30am from May to October.

Tours leave from the tourist office at the main railroad station, and tickets can be purchased at the Zurich Tourist Office.

BOAT TOURS   At some point in your stay you'll want to take a lake steamer for a tour of Lake Zurich. Walk to the end of Bahnhofstrasse and buy a ticket at the pier. In peak season ferries depart about every 30 minutes. A regular round-trip tour of the lake to Rapperswil will cost 20F ($14.60) in second class and 30F ($21.90) in first class. A short trip costs 10F ($7.30).

You might also want to take a boat trip along the Limmat for a close view of Zurich's historic buildings. The boat departs from the Landesmuseum at the Hauptbahnhof and lands at the Zurichhorn. In April and October, departures are every half hour daily from 1 to 6pm; in May, June, and September, daily from 1 to 9pm; and in July and August, daily from 10am to 9pm. The fare is only 10F ($7.30).

WALKING TOURS   One of my favorite tours in Zurich is a 2-hour stroll through the old town with a guide. Meet at 9:30am or 3pm in front of the tourist office at Bahnhofplatz 15. The price is 12F ($8.75) for adults and 6F ($4.40) for children 6 to 12. Between June 1 and September 30, departures are every Tuesday, Thursday, and Saturday.

6. SPECIAL & FREE EVENTS

Many events change from week to week, so pick up a copy of the *Zurich News* at the tourist office for a list of any special exhibitions (usually at museums) or concerts (often at churches) likely to be happening at the time of your visit. Many of these are free, although for special exhibitions you'll often have to pay, but rarely more than 10F ($7.30).

The most famous event in Zurich is **Sechseläuten,** the city's spring festival, beginning on the third Monday in April. Actually it begins the day before, with a children's parade. Various guilds, their members in historical costumes, parade through the city center. At 6pm, Böögg, the straw figure symbolizing winter, is burned at Sechlseläutenplatz at 6pm.

7. SPORTS & RECREATION

Zurichers are not big on spectator sports—they like to get out and perform the sporting activities themselves, getting plenty of fresh air and exercise.

Many of the larger hotels have added swimming pools and tennis courts or handball and racquetball facilities to their attractions. Some have fitness centers, making staying fit while staying in Zurich an inviting possibility.

BEACHES   You can go swimming in Lake Zurich, which has an average summer temperature of 68°F. The finest beach is the **Tiefenbrunnen.** The city and many hotels offer indoor and outdoor **swimming pools.** The pool at Sihlstrasse 71 also has a sauna with its indoor swimming facilities.

GOLF   The two golf courses nearest the center of town are the **Golf and Country Club Zurich,** at Zumikon (tel. 919-00-51), which has an 18-hole, par-72 course, and **Dolder Golfclub,** at Dolder (tel. 251-55-35), with a 9-hole, par-60 course.

HIKING   Zurich has seven "Vita-Parcours," or keep-fit trails. Someone at the Zurich Tourist Office, Bahnhofplatz 15, will map these trails for you.

JOGGING   The nearest woodland jogging route is on the **Allmend Fluntern.** Joggers are also seen frequently along the quays and elsewhere in the city.

SKIING   The closest ski region to Zurich is **Hoch-Ybrig,** about an hour's journey from the Hauptbahnhof. Take the train to Einsiedeln, where you can transfer to a bus to Weglosen and the aerial cableway that will take you to Hoch-Ybrig. Hoch-Ybrig has five ski lifts and two chair lifts.

8. SAVVY SHOPPING

THE SHOPPING SCENE

In the heart of Zurich is a square kilometer (about 25 acres) of shopping, including the exclusive stores along Bahnhofstrasse, previewed in the sightseeing section. Your shopping adventure might begin more modestly at the top of the street, at Bahnhofplatz. Below this vast transportation hub is a complex of shops known as ShopVille.

Most shops are open Monday through Friday from 8am to 6:30pm and on Saturday from 8am to 4pm. Some of the larger stores stay open until 9pm on Thursday, and other shops are closed on Monday morning.

SHOPPING FROM A TO Z

BOOKS

THE TRAVEL BOOK SHOP, Rindermarkt 20. Tel. 252-38-83.
  This shop has a complete selection of travel books, as well as one of Europe's best map collections. Munich-born Gisela Treichler is the owner. Formerly a guidebook writer, she still keeps a finger on the pulse of the travel community by organizing and leading yearly tours. Many of the books are in German, but about half the stock is in English. Maps for trekking and mountaineering from all over the world are also sold.

BUCHHANDLUNG FRIEDRICH DAENIKER, In Gassen 11. Tel. 211-27-04.
  If being in Zurich inspires you to reread excerpts from Carl Jung, this is the place to find them, along with the works of many other authors whose books have been translated into English. In addition to scholarly works, you'll find novels, periodicals, and old-fashioned spellbinders.

DEPARTMENT STORES

GRIEDER LES BOUTIQUES, Bahnhofstrasse 30. Tel. 211-33-60.
  This is one of the best department stores in Switzerland, offering both ready-to-wear and couture by such designers as Ungaro, Scherrer, and Dior. The facility fills two floors of a stone building on Zurich's most fashionable commercial street, where the salespeople tend to be bilingual and formidably well dressed. The accessories, including a wide range of purses, scarves, and leather goods, are well selected.

JELMOLI DEPARTMENT STORE, Bahnhofstrasse 69. Tel. 220-44-11.

 FROMMER'S SMART TRAVELER: SHOPPING

1. Haggle in the open-air flea markets. Depending on how much the owner wants to sell, you can secure some good buys by steady, firm bargaining. Prices in stores are fixed.
2. Don't assume that because a product is made in Switzerland it's cheaper here. Check prices in stores at home before leaving, so that you'll know what is a good buy.
3. Browse through the stores on the right bank, where merchandise is considerably cheaper than it is on the left bank, especially along the fashionable Bahnhofstrasse. Look for the many souvenir and watch shops on Limmatquai.

This Zurich institution has everything a large department store should have, from cookware to clothing. Founded more than 150 years ago by the Ticino-born entrepreneur Johann Peter Jelmoli, the store is a legend in the Zurich business community.

EMBROIDERY

SPITZENHAUS, Börsenstrasse 14. Tel. 211-55-76.
In a city famed for its embroidery, this place is a winner. The helpful salespeople have box after box of the highest-quality products, such as doilies and handkerchiefs, that they will gladly show to you. Much of this exquisite work is done by their families or friends.

FASHIONS

ROMANA BOUTIQUE, Stadhausquai 5. Tel. 211-42-22.
This boutique carries a wide variety of fashionable, discounted European-designer clothes for women. In addition, it offers an assortment of local hand-knit sweaters. The quality of merchandise is outstanding, and the prices are lower than on the nearby Bahnhofstrasse. The obliging staff speaks English.

FOOD

TEUSCHER, Storchengasse 9. Tel. 211-51-53.
Located on a narrow cobblestone street in the old town of Zurich, this surprisingly small store is the original epicurean chocolate shop. You can tell you're in the area by the smell of chocolate truffles, which come in such flavors as champagne, orange, and cocoa.

GIFTS

MEISTER SILBER, Bahnhofstrasse 28A. Tel. 221-27-30.
This elite shop, on the prestigious Paradeplatz in the center of Zurich, has one of

the widest selections of flatware and gift items in Switzerland. The prices are high, but reasonable considering that every article is either exquisitely handcrafted or comes from producers internationally known for quality and fine design.

HANDCRAFTS

HEIMATHUUS, Rudolf Brunbrücke. Tel. 211-57-80.
In 1930, in an effort to help economically distressed areas, a nonprofit society, Schweizer Heimatwerk, was created to keep traditional crafts alive. Today, Heimatwerk shops sell only items designed and made in Switzerland, most of them handcrafted.

Items offered in the 10 Heimatwerk shops include copperware, ceramics, wood carvings, ironwork, jewelry, toys, nave paintings, crystal, tinware, baskets, music boxes, and paper-cutout pictures. Puzzles, games, puppets, even a Noah's ark with its carved wooden animals, are sold here as well.

The headquarters shop and four other outlets of Schweizer Heimatwerk are in Zurich. The prices range from reasonable to expensive. Other branches are at Bahnhofstrasse 2 (tel. 221-08-37), Rennweg 14 (tel. 221-35-73), at the National Museum, and at the Zurich airport in Transit Halls A and B.

LEATHER GOODS

MÄDLER, Bahnhofstrasse 26. Tel. 211-75-70.
Stephanie Mädler and her family have owned this leather-goods shop (now a famous chain) since 1951. The store, which specializes in leather bags and suitcases, has a massively stocked second floor.

LINENS

STURZENEGGER, Bahnhofstrasse 48. Tel. 211-28-20.
This old-fashioned, wood-paneled store is a good place to buy all kinds of delicate hand-embroidered items. A back room contains a variety of intricately patterned tablecloths, placemats, doilies, and napkins. The front room sells blouses, handkerchiefs, shawls, scarves, and children's frocks. Upstairs is a large assortment of nightgowns, pajamas, women's underwear, blouses, and embroidered curtains.

MUSIC

MUSIK HUG, Füsslistrasse 4. Tel. 221-25-40.
This is the largest branch of the best chain of tape and record stores in Switzerland. Conveniently located at the corner of Zurich's commercial centerpiece, the legendary Bahnhofstrasse, it stocks thousands of records and tapes from around the world and has a helpful staff. Its selection of Swiss folkloric music, classical recordings, and modern jazz is especially rich and varied.

SHOES

SCHUHHUAS BALLY CAPITAL, Bahnhofstrasse. Tel. 211-35-15.
This is the place to buy Bally shoes. The prominently situated store is the world's

largest official outlet of this famous Swiss chain. The store carries a complete line of Bally shoes, along with accessories and clothing for men, women, and children.

WATCHES

BEYER, Bahnhofstrasse 31. Tel. 221-10-80.

If your heart is set on buying a timepiece in Zurich, try this well-established store midway between the train station and the lake. Besides carrying just about every famous brand of watch made in Switzerland, such as Rolex and Patek Philippe, it also has a museum in the basement, containing timepieces from as early as 1400 B.C. Exhibitions include all kinds of water clocks, sundials, and hourglasses.

BUCHERER, Bahnhofstrasse 50. Tel. 211-26-35.

A longtime name in the Swiss watch industry, this store also carries an impressive collection of jewelry. Some of the most famous names in watch making are represented with their latest offerings.

9. EVENING ENTERTAINMENT

The city's nightlife is becoming more liberated, but don't expect it to be like Hamburg's Reeperbahn. Most of the nightspots in Zurich close down early, so you should begin early. Concerts, theater, opera, and ballet flourish in Zurich.

THE ENTERTAINMENT SCENE

The highlight of cultural life in Zurich takes place at the Zurich International Festival for 4 weeks in June. International orchestras and concert artists appear here, major exhibitions are launched, and plays (most often in German) are presented. For more details, contact the **International Juni-Festwochen,** Präsidialabteilung der Stadt Zurich, Postfach CH-8002 Zurich (tel. 01/216-31-11).

To learn what special entertainment or presentations are in Zurich at the time of your visit, pick up a copy of *Zurich News,* available free at the tourist office and distributed at the front desks of most hotels.

No special discount tickets are granted, but for regular tickets to operas, theaters, and concerts go to **Billettzentrale (BiZZ** for short), Werdmühleplatz (tel. 221-22-83), open Monday through Friday from 10am to 6:30pm and on Saturday from 10am to 2pm.

The **Zurich Opera** is the most outstanding local company, performing at the Opernhaus. The **Zurich Tonhalle Orchestra,** performing at Tonhalle, also enjoys an international reputation.

THE PERFORMING ARTS

THE MAJOR CONCERT/PERFORMANCE HALLS

OPERNHAUS, Falkenstrasse 1. Tel. 251-69-22.

Near Bellevueplatz, in the center of the city, this concert hall is the home of Zurich's permanent opera company. Dating from the 1890s, it was renovated in 1987.

Wagner conducted two of his operas here, *Tannhäuser* and *The Flying Dutchman*. Today it's also the setting for operettas, classical music concerts, and ballets. The Opernhaus is closed in July and August.

Prices: Tickets, 15F–50F ($10.95–$36.50).

TONHALLE, Claridenstrasse 7. Tel. 201-15-80.

This concert hall, facing Bürkliplatz, is the biggest concert hall in Zurich, with 1,500 seats. It is home to the Zurich Tonhalle Orchestra and the venue for appearances by many internationally known soloists. Recitals and chamber music presentations are also staged here. Try to purchase your tickets as early as possible, because many seats are by subscription. Brahms opened this concert hall in 1895 with a presentation of *Song of Triumph*.

Prices: Tickets, 5F–20F ($3.65–$14.60).

THEATER

Zurich has many well-regarded theaters, but you'll find it difficult to follow the action if you don't know German well.

SCHAUSPIELHAUS, Rämistrasse 34. Tel. 251-11-11.

Schauspielhaus presents classic productions of Shakespeare and Goethe. The ticket office is open Monday through Saturday from 10am to 5pm and on Sunday from 10am to noon. The theater is closed from late June to early September.

Prices: Tickets, 20F ($14.60).

THEATER AM HERCHTPLATZ, Hechtplatz 7. Tel. 252-32-34.

For more experimental works, see a show here. Once again, a grasp of the language is essential. Experimental plays and sometimes cabarets are presented. The location is near Limmatquai and Rathausbrücke.

Prices: Tickets, 25F ($18.25).

VOLKSHAUS, Stauffacherstrasse. Tel. 221-22-83.

Big, splashy musicals are presented here. For tickets and information, visit BiZZ on Werdmühleplatz (see above).

Prices: Tickets, 20F ($14.60).

THE CLUB & MUSIC SCENE

KINDLI SWISS CHALET, Pfalzgasse 1, Rennweg. Tel. 211-41-82.

Most bands that play here specialize in yodeling, although some also play Dixieland jazz or Mozart, complete with alpenhorns and regional costumes. The owners, the Schmid family, perform their unique kind of alpine music. This rustic establishment has pine paneling and timber beams. Dinner is served from 7pm, and the music begins at 8:30pm. Dinner costs around 65F ($47.45), and your first drink runs 10F ($7.30).

Admission: 10F ($7.30) cover for those not having dinner.

BIERHALLE WOLF, Limmatquai 132. Tel. 251-01-30.

This centrally located beer hall offers inexpensive alpine music in a safe atmosphere with a friendly crowd. Folk music is played by an oompah band in regional garb—instruments include guitar, trumpet, accordion, and tub. The large beer hall is decorated with pennants and the flags of the different cantons. Beer is brought in tankards. Live music is presented every day from 4 to 6pm and from 8pm to midnight and every Sunday morning from 10am to noon. During the breaks, slides are shown of alpine scenery. Fixed-price dinners cost 13F to 17F ($9.50 to $12.40); beer runs 5F ($3.65).

Admission: Sun–Thurs 5F ($3.65), Fri–Sat 8F ($5.85).

DAS ROTE HAUS (The Red House), Marktgasse 17. Tel. 252-15-30.

At one time or another during its 700 years, this house was probably painted red, but no one knows when. Set in the rowdiest nightlife center of Zurich, the old town's Niederdorf, the building has played many different roles—it was even a theater for strip acts and cabaret. Today it functions mainly as a disco, with a brief (40-min.) cabaret/circus/vaudeville act that begins every night at 10:30pm. The place is open Monday through Saturday from 9pm to 1am.

Admission: Free, but the first drink costs 17F ($12.40), and each additional drink runs 6F ($4.40) and up.

CASA BAR, Münstergasse. Tel. 261-20-02.

Switzerland's most famous jazz club is also Zurich's oldest, featuring Dixieland and New Orleans–style bands. It's open daily from 8pm to 2am, with a live band playing until midnight.

Admission: Free, but drinking is required; beer costs 8.50F ($6.20).

DANCE CLUBS/DISCOS

MASCOTTE ACTION 1, Theaterstrasse 10. Tel. 252-44-81.

Considered one of the leading discos in the city, this club is known for its energetic dance floor and its bands, which appear only on Thursday. Open every night from 9pm to 2am, it has a futuristic, all-black interior illuminated by modern strobes and by the carefully placed candles burning on the dozens of small tables. Although throughout the week the place welcomes a mixed (and predominantly straight) clientele, every Sunday night the club becomes the almost exclusive domain of Zurich's gay men. Beer costs 7F ($5.10).

Admission: 5F ($3.65).

JOKER/LA BOULE, in Kongresshaus, Gothardstrasse 5. Tel. 202-22-62.

Contained in the city building most frequently used for public meetings (the Kongresshaus), this three-in-one nightclub sets strict standards of respectability for its relatively conservative clientele. Its centerpiece is a small-stakes casino, where roulette tables and blackjack limit bets to 5F ($3.65), so that gambling is an amusement and not a risk-it-all source of pressure. Connected to the casino are two rustically decorated nightclubs, the more unchanging of which is the all-red Joker, where recorded music (mostly from the 1970s) plays without interruption. A few steps away, the all-black La Boule offers a stage, where a frequently changing array of guest bands from around the world (Europe and such Asian countries as Sri Lanka and the Philippines) perform live. All three of this complex's arenas are open Sunday through Thursday from 9pm to 2am and on Friday and Saturday from 9pm to 4am. Beer costs 14F ($10.20); a vodka and tonic, 21F ($15.35).

Admission: 9F–16F ($6.55–$11.70), depending on the night of the week.

THE BAR SCENE

PUBS

OLIVER TWIST PUB, Rindermarkt 6. Tel. 252-47-10.

Although its convivial barmen speak a total of 15 languages (making it probably the most cosmopolitan pub in Zurich), this place is Irish to its very core, with framed photographs of Irish landscapes decorating the paneled walls. There's a charming courtyard with marble pavement and a modern statue of a crouching laborer. Except for special events, no food is served, although the inventory holds more than a dozen kinds of beer (including varieties from the United States and Mexico). Every Saturday night a live musician performs from about 8pm to midnight. Open Monday through Friday from 11:30am to midnight and on Saturday and Sunday from 3pm to 1am. A large beer begins at 5.50F ($4).

JAMES JOYCE PUB, Pelikanstrasse 8. Tel. 221-18-28.

The interior decor of this pub was acquired in the early 1970s by the Union Bank of Switzerland; the furnishings and paneling are from the bar of Jury's, an 18th-century hotel in Dublin that was demolished. The Union Bank reassembled the bar (with slightly more comfortable banquettes) near Bahnhofstrasse to entertain business clients and named it after the famous Dubliner James Joyce, who had described its decor in certain passages of *Ulysses*. The blackboard menu lists daily specials (*plattes*) for 20F to 32F ($14.60 to $23.35), including Irish stew, fish and chips, hamburgers, and fried chicken legs. There's always a good assortment of soups, such as potato with shrimp. Beer costs 3.80F to 6.50F ($2.85 to $4.75). Open Monday through Friday from 11am to midnight and on Saturday from 11am to 6pm.

SWING-SWING, in the Mövenpick Hotel, Regensdorf. Tel. 840-25-20.

A 15-minute drive west of the town center, in the suburb of Regensdorf, this rustic pub is in the basement of a popular hotel. Rustically decorated, with a long bar and a sophisticated sound system, it attracts Swiss of all ages. Taped music (mostly rock) is played by a DJ. Beer costs 8F ($5.85), and mixed drinks run 15F ($10.95) and up. The place is open Monday through Saturday from 9pm to 2am.

Admission: 18F ($13.15).

GAY CLUBS

LES MAINS BLEUES, Kanzleistrasse 15. Tel. 241-73-78.

In the cellar of an older building about a 10-minute walk east of the railroad station, this is not only the premier gay restaurant of Zurich, but it has a bar that is a popular destination in its own right. A meal in the cozy, blue-and-white dining room will cost around 35F ($25.55). The Swiss/Italian menu consists of different variations of veal, shrimp, chicken, and beef dishes. Dinner reservations are recommended. If you visit just for a drink, beer costs 5F ($3.65) and mixed drinks run 13F ($9.50). The restaurant is open daily from 5 to 11pm; the bar daily from 5pm to midnight.

BARFUSSER, Spitalgasse 14. Tel. 251-40-64.

Although more fashionable gay bars have come and gone in Zurich, this is one of the most enduring. Established in the Niederdorf section in 1956, in dark and woodsy premises well worn by the passage of time, it welcomes its greatest percentage of gay clients (predominantly men) after 8pm, with special popularity on Saturday. It's open daily from 3pm to midnight. Beer costs 4F ($2.90) and up.

MASCOTTE ACTION 1, Theaterstrasse 10. Tel. 252-44-81.

Monday through Saturday, the place rocks to a clientele of straight, usually younger, clients. Every Sunday, however, the futuristic, all-black interior is reserved for gay men and their invited guests. Beer costs 7F ($5.10). Hours on Sunday are 9pm to 2am.

Admission: 5F ($3.65).

10. NETWORKS & RESOURCES

FOR STUDENTS Make sure you carry an **International Student Identity Card (ISIC)**, which entitles you to substantial reductions, not only on theater and opera tickets but on officially sponsored tours of Zurich and its surroundings. To get one, take your student credentials to the **Swiss Student Travel Office (SSR)**, Backerstrasse 40 (tel. 241-12-08), where cards are issued. It's open Monday through Friday from 10am to 5pm and on Saturday from 10am to 1pm.

Budget travel, including discounted ski packages, can be arranged at the SSR branch at Leonhardstrasse 10 (tel. 47-29-55), open Monday through Friday from 10am to 6pm.

FOR GAY MEN AND LESBIANS Gay liberation centers include **Schweizerische Organisation der Homosexuellen,** Sihliquai 67 (tel. 42-70-11), a social and information center providing an introduction to male gay life in Switzerland.

For women, there is **Spot 25, Schwul-lesbische Jugendgruppe,** which meets at the same address on Tuesday and Wednesday from 8 to 11pm.

FOR WOMEN **Beratungsstelle INFRA,** Autonomes Frauenzentrum, Mattengasse 27 (tel. 44-88-44), is a social as well as information center for women.

FOR SENIORS Go to the **Zurich Tourist Office,** Bahnhofplatz 15 (tel. 211-40-00), at the main railroad station, and request a copy of "Season for Seniors." This booklet lists some 450 hotels in 200 Swiss towns and resorts that offer special off-season rates for seniors (women over 62 and men over 65).

11. EASY EXCURSIONS FROM ZURICH

Zurich is surrounded by some of the most interesting sightseeing areas in Switzerland. The following are a few of exceptional interest. All these attractions can easily be reached on a short trip from your hotel in Zurich, either by train or by lake steamer.

DAY TRIPS

A few interesting tours—which you can take on your own—make use of funiculars and trains. The **Polybahn funicular** leaves every 3 minutes from Central, the square near Bahnhofbrücke, on Limmatquai. The funicular, operating since 1889 and used daily by students attending the Federal Institute of Technology and the University of Zurich, takes you to the **Poly Terrace,** from which you can view the city and the

Alps. Outdoor performances are held on the terrace, and it's a stopping place for official tours of the city. The Mensa restaurant of the federal institute and its coffee shop are open to the public.

For another interesting trip, take the Dolderbahn for a short aerial cable ride to the **Dolder Recreational Area,** 1,988 feet up above the city. Trains leave every 10 minutes from Römerhofplatz, which you can reach by taking tram no. 3, 8, or 15. The recreational area is open year round and has restaurants, nature trails, old rustic taverns, a path to the zoo, a miniature golf course, and from October to March, a huge ice-skating rink. There is a delightful place to swim, the Dolder Schwimmbad, which is carved into a hillside with a view of Zurich. The swimming area is a 5-minute walk along a forest trail from the end of the cable-car line; follow the signs to Dolder Wellenbad. Admission to the pool, with its artificial waves, is 6F ($4.40). The Dolderbahn ride costs 1.50F ($1.10); buy your tickets from the machine.

If you're looking for rest or recreation close to Zurich, I recommend a trip to **Forch** or **Esslingen** on the Forchbahn, which leaves from the Stadelhofen station. The train takes you out to the green country, where there's a strolling and rambling area with fine views and wooded paths leading down to one of the two lakes, Greifensee or Zurichsee (Lake Zurich). You can take a boat back to town on Lake Zurich. Forchbahn trains run without conductors, so you must buy your tickets from a machine at the stops. A round-trip ticket to Forch costs 7F ($5.10); to Esslingen, 10F ($7.30). For information, call 918-01-08.

I also recommend a visit to **Alpamare,** in the village of Pfäffikon SZ, on Lake Zurich. The recreation area has a heated indoor swimming pool with artificial waves and a slide, and an outdoor thermal pool with underwater music, massage jets, and bubbling water "couches." There are also outdoor thermal baths, containing iodine and brine to relieve rheumatism; a well-equipped playground; a snack restaurant and grills; saunas; and a large solarium. Alpamare is open daily from 10am to 10pm. Admission for 3 hours is 20F ($14.60) for adults and 15F ($10.95) for children 6 to 16. For informaton, call 055/48-32-22.

If you're an admirer of Thomas Mann, I recommend a visit to **Kilchberg,** 4 miles from Zurich, along the southwestern shore of the lake. Mann spent the last years of his life here and was buried on the south side of the small church in the village in 1955. His wife died here in 1980. This town is more famously associated with the 19th-century Swiss author Conrad Ferdinand Meyer.

UETLIBERG

Southwest of Zurich, Uetliberg, the northernmost peak in the Albis ridge, is one of the most popular excursions from the city. Take the mountain railway Uetlibergbahn from the Selnau station in Zurich. A round-trip costs 10F ($7.30) and takes half an hour. You arrive near the Sihl River at an elevation of 2,800 feet.

From the station, you can hike 10 minutes to the summit, where there's a café and restaurant. The tower is a climb of about 170 steps; from the lookout you can see as far away as the Black Forest on a clear day.

WINTERTHUR

This industrial town in the Toss Valley is also a music and cultural center, with an art collection that makes the 25-minute train trip from Zurich worthwhile. Winterthur was once a Roman settlement and became the seat of the counts of Kyburg. It later was a stronghold of the Hapsburgs, until it was sold to Zurich.

Visit on Tuesday or Friday, when the narrow streets of the old town are busy with fruit, flower, and vegetable peddlers. Another exciting time is on the last Saturday of every month, when Swiss from the surrounding countryside sell goods at a flea market. Most attractions are closed on Monday.

WHAT TO SEE & DO

The skyline of Winterthur is dominated by the twin towers of its parish church, the **Stadtkirche,** built from 1264 to 1515 (the towers were added later).

OSKAR REINHART FOUNDATION, Stadthausstrasse 6. Tel. 052/84-51-72.

Oskar Reinhart, a famous collector who died in 1965, willed many of his fabulous artworks to the city. Displayed in the gallery are works of Austrian, German, and Swiss artists, with a fine representation of the Romantic painters, including Blechen, Friedrich, Kersting, and Richter. Many canvases are by Hodler. There are 600 works in all, from the 18th to the 20th century.

Admission: 3F ($2.20) adults, 1.50F ($1.10) children.
Open: Tues–Sun 10am–5pm.

AM RÖMERHOLZ, Haldenstrasse 95. Tel. 052/23-41-21.

Part of Reinhart's collection is displayed in his former home. The art, ranging 500 years from Cranach the Elder to Breughel, can be viewed in intimate rooms throughout the mansion. There are some fine drawings by Rembrandt and El Greco's *Portrait of the Cardinal Inquisitor Don Fernando Niño de Guevara,* circa 1600. Many works are by French painters, including Watteau, Fragonard, and Poussin. Several drawings are by Daumier. Other outstanding artists represented are Delacroix, Manet, Cézanne, van Gogh, Corot, and Renoir. Look for the drawings from Picasso's blue period. There is a small café near the reception desk.

Admission: 3F ($2.20).
Open: Tues–Sun 10am–4pm. **Bus:** 10.

KUNSTMUSEUM, Kunsthaus, Museumstrasse 52. Tel. 052/84-51-62.

Located north of the Stadthaus, this branch of Zurich's fine-arts museum contains an impressive collection of European art and sculpture from the late 19th century to the present. Giacometti and such French artists as Bonnard and Vuillard are well represented. Highlights are works by Van Gogh, Miró, Magritte, Mondrian, Kokoschka, Calder, and Klee. There are sculptures by Rodin, as well as works by Marini and Maillol. The permanent collection is on display from June to August. Temporary exhibits are presented the rest of the year.

Admission: 4F ($2.90).
Open: Tues–Sun 10am–5pm. **Bus:** 3.

SCHLOSS KYBURG

Four miles from Winterthur, Schloss Kyburg is the largest castle in eastern Switzerland, dating from the Middle Ages. The stronghold was the ancestral home of the counts of Kyburg until 1264, when the Hapsburgs took over. It was ceded to Zurich in the 15th century and is now a museum of antiques and armor. There's a good view from the keep. You may also visit the residence hall of the knights, parapet, and chapel.

Admission: 3F ($2.20).
Open: Mar–Oct, Tues–Sun 9am–noon and 1–5pm; winter, Tues–Sun 9am–noon and 1–4pm. **Train:** Kemptthal railroad station (on the Zurich–Winterthur line) or Sennhof-Kyburg (on the Winterthur–Bauma line).

TECHNORAMA OF SWITZERLAND, Technoramastrasse 1. Tel. 052/87-55-55.

The Technorama is a museum of science and industry, with 64,500 square feet of displays, many with tape-recorded explanations. The exhibits show current technological breakthroughs in metallurgy, electronics, physics, and textiles. The Jugendlaber, or youth lab, features 120 experiments. There is a restaurant in the museum; there are also pleasant walkways in the park around the main building. Parents can leave their children (ages 5 to 13) at a supervised Mini-Technorama.

Admission: 10F ($7.30) adults, 6F ($4.40) children.

Open: Daily 10am–5pm. **Closed:** Dec 25. **Directions:** Take Autobahn N1 north of Zurich toward St. Gallen; exit at Ober-Winterthur and drive a mile toward Winterthur. By public transportation, take a train from Zurich to Winterthur, where you switch to a bus marked "Technorama" at the station; buses leave at a quarter to and a quarter past each hour (except noon).

WHERE TO EAT

SCHLOSS WULFINGEN, Wulflingenstrasse 240, Winterthur-Wulflingen. Tel. 052/25-18-67.

Cuisine: SWISS. **Reservations:** Recommended.

$ **Prices:** Appetizers 6.50F–25F ($4.75–$18.25); main courses 32F–45F ($23.35–$32.85); fixed-price meals 22F–28F ($16.05–$20.45) at lunch, 58F–90F ($42.35–$65.70) at dinners. AE, DC, MC, V.

Open: Lunch Wed–Sun noon–2pm; dinner Wed–Sun 6–10pm.

The most romantic place to dine is on the outskirts of town, half a mile north of the center of the village. The rustic stone, stucco, and slate building was built in 1644 and still has many of the original ceramic stoves in the dining rooms. In the summer, owner Rolf Aberli, his charming wife, and his family adorn the intricate shutters of the step-gabled house with garlands. Café tables are set up in front. Specialties include beef in red- and green-pepper sauce with gratin potatoes, sole, turbot, catfish, salmon, giant shrimp, and other seafood. A simpler menu is offered at lunch, including veal stuffed with country ham, a mousse of foie gras served with tiny homemade noodles, and excellent fish dishes.

REGENSBERG

About 10 miles northwest of Zurich and 5 miles north of Regensdorf, the village of Regensberg has preserved its medieval atmosphere. It's a "national trust," which means that nothing can be altered. Easily accessible by car, it's a 20-minute drive from Zurich along the road to Dielsdorf. You can also go by postal bus from Dielsdorf, which is on the Zurich–Oberglatt–Niederweningen railroad line. If you drive, you must park your car outside the town hall and walk into the walled town.

WHAT TO SEE & DO

This village of wine makers and vineyards has well-preserved, half-timbered houses clustered around the main square. The most famous is the **Rote Rose house,** dating from 1540 and containing a little museum of the painter Lotte Günthard. The **village church** dates from the early 16th century.

Dominating the hamlet is a 16th-century **castle** once owned by the Hapsburgs. It was the headquarters of the barons of Regensberg, who ruled the town. From the watchtower, there is a view of the local vineyards and the Lagern hills. On a clear day you can see all the way to Zurich. Today the castle is a children's home.

WHERE TO DINE

GASTHAUS KRONE, Oberburg 81. Tel. 01/853-11-35.
   Cuisine: SWISS/FRENCH. **Reservations:** Recommended.
$ Prices: Appetizers 17F–22F ($12.40–$16.05); main courses 28F–35F ($20.45–$25.55); fixed-price meal 85F ($62.05). AE, DC, MC, V.
   Open: Daily 11am–11pm.

The biggest half-timbered house in the village is considered a citadel of fine cuisine; the excellent local wines alone are worth the 20-minute drive from Zurich. There are several dining rooms, including the local favorite, the Biedermeier salon, whose casement windows overlook the valley. You may dine on the terrace in the summer. The food is exceptional, prepared with some innovative cuisine moderne touches. The service is meticulous.

RAPPERSWIL

A lake steamer from Zurich will take you to the "town of roses," on the northern shore of Lake Zurich, 19 miles away. If you're in Zurich for just a short time and have no other chance to visit the rest of the country, then spend a day going to Rapperswil to see a typical Swiss town.

WHAT TO SEE & DO

The **Rathaus** (town hall), in the main square, dates from 1471. It has a richly embellished Gothic portal. Many of the town's streets date from the Middle Ages.

RAPPERSWIL CASTLE. Tel. 055/27-44-95.
   Built by the young count of Rapperswil when he returned from the First Crusade in about 1200, Rapperswil Castle is an imposing medieval stronghold on a rocky hill, dominating the town. In 1870 it housed the national relics of beleaguered Poland. Today one section is still devoted to Polish art, folklore, and mementos, including those of Copernicus, Chopin, and Kosciuszko.
   Admission: 3F ($2.20).
   Open: Summer, daily 10am–noon and 2–5pm; winter, Sun and hols 10am–noon and 2–5pm, or by special request.

KNIE'S KINDERZOO (Children's Zoo), Strandweg. Tel. 055/27-52-22.
   On the north side of the castle hill is a children's zoo, run by the Knie National Circus; it's on a road that runs along the lake, south of the railroad station. Trained dolphins and other acts perform here. Nearby is the **Hirschgarten** (deer park), in the Linderhof.
   Admission: 6F ($4.40) adults, 3F ($2.20) children 4–14, free for children under 4.
   Open: Daily 9am–6pm. **Closed:** Winter.

HEIMATMUSEUM, Herrenberg. Tel. 055/27-71-64.
   Located east of the parish church, this museum is devoted to local history. It contains Roman artifacts, a weapon collection, paintings, and antiques.
   Admission: 2.50F ($1.85) adults, 1F (75¢) children 6–13, free for children under 6.
   Open: Sat–Thurs 2–5pm. **Closed:** Dec–Easter Sun.

WHERE TO DINE

HOTEL EDEN, Seestrasse 3. Tel. 055/27-12-21.
   Cuisine: SWISS. **Reservations:** Recommended.

$ Prices: Appetizers 7F–20F ($5.10–$14.60); main courses 35F–50F ($25.55–$36.50); fixed-price meals 70F–120F ($51.10–$87.60). AE, DC, MC, V.

Open: Lunch Tues–Sun noon–2:30pm; dinner Tues–Sat 5pm–midnight.

Food connoisseurs from Zurich come to this six-story house (which was built around 1630) to sample the gourmet delicacies. The Ganahi family, which owns the hotel, offers specialties that include fresh goose liver pâté, rack of lamb Eden, baby veal, lobster salad with artichoke hearts, and saltwater fish. Fresh vegetables change with the season. Desserts are consistently excellent.

CHAPTER 4

NORTHEASTERN SWITZERLAND

- **WHAT'S SPECIAL ABOUT NORTHEASTERN SWITZERLAND**
1. **ST. GALLEN**
2. **APPENZELL**
3. **LAKE CONSTANCE**
4. **STEIN-AM-RHEIN**
5. **SCHAFFHAUSEN & RHEINFALL**

In the northeastern region of Switzerland—one of the country's most unspoiled areas—are the beautiful cantons of Appenzell, Glarus, St. Gallen, Schaffhausen, and Thurgau and sights like St. Gallen's Rhine Valley and the Rhine Falls, near Neuhausen. St. Gallen is the region's cultural and economic center, and some of the most splendid orchards in the country dot the shores of Lake Constance.

If economy is a factor in your travel, then you should definitely consider exploring the region, as the prices for food and lodging in its old-world inns are among the lowest in the country.

SEEING NORTHEASTERN SWITZERLAND

Zurich is the traditional gateway for all the cities and towns in this chapter. From it road and railway connections can be made easily with all these points.

IF YOU HAVE 4 DAYS

Day 1: Drive or take the train east of Zurich to St. Gallen for the night.

Day 2: Head south of St. Gallen to explore Appenzell and the attractions in its environs, including Mount Säntis.

Day 3: Drive north to Lake Constance and anchor at one of the resorts along the shoreline, perhaps Arbon.

Day 4: Continue west along the lake to visit Stein-am-Rhein, at the eastern end of the lake, in the morning. Spend the afternoon exploring the Rheinfall outside the medieval city of Schaffhausen, which provides a good place to spend the night.

---

1. ST. GALLEN

53 miles E of Zurich, 97 miles E of Basel

GETTING THERE   By Train   St. Gallen is on the main train lines connecting Zurich with Munich. At least a dozen trains a day arrive from both directions. Trip

WHAT'S SPECIAL ABOUT NORTHEASTERN SWITZERLAND

Great Towns/Villages

☐ Stein-am-Rhein, a small but well-preserved medieval town on the right bank of the Rhine.

☐ Appenzell, famed for its traditional customs and handcrafts and one of the folkloric centerpieces of Switzerland.

☐ St. Gallen, a medieval city of period houses, now the economic and lace-making capital of the region.

Architectural Highlights

☐ The Domkirche at St. Gallen, Switzerland's best example of baroque architecture.

☐ The Munot at Schaffhausen, the only fortress to be based on the theories and illustrations of Albrecht Dürer.

Great Museums

☐ Stiftsbibliothek at St. Gallen, an abbey library with some 130,000 volumes, some of them manuscripts from as early as the 8th century.

Ace Attractions

☐ Mount Säntis, the highest peak in the Alpstein massif (8,200 ft.), with a vast panoramic view of eastern Switzerland; its summit is accessible via cable car.

☐ Lake Constance, with a 162-mile shoreline shared by Switzerland, Germany, and Austria; one of the most mythically rich lakes in Europe.

☐ Rheinfall (Rhine Falls), the most celebrated waterfall in central Europe—Goethe's "source of the ocean" and the setting for some of Wagner's most celebrated operas.

---

time from Zurich is about 75 minutes. St. Gallen is the railway lynchpin for at least four local lines.

By Bus As in most other Swiss cities, bus connections in St. Gallen are meant to supplement railroad service. Buses connect St. Gallen mainly with such outlying villages as Rorschach and Appenzell, with many stops at local villages along the way.

By Car From Zurich head east on N1 (also called E17).

ESSENTIALS The **telephone area code** for St. Gallen is 071. The **St. Gallen Tourist Office** is at Bahnhofplatz 1A (tel. 071/22-62-62).

At 2,200 feet above sea level, this charming valley is one of the primary tourist stops in northeastern Switzerland. St. Gallen, which is the highest city of its size in Europe, is a good base for exploring Lake Constance, Mount Säntis, and the Appenzell countryside. This ancient town in the foothills of the Alps was founded by Gallus, an Irish monk who built a hermitage here in 612. By the 13th century, his "humble cell" had developed into an important cultural outpost. St. Gallen became a free imperial city in 1212, and in 1454 it joined the Swiss Confederation. With a population of some 75,000, St. Gallen is the capital of a canton of the same name.

St. Gallen is the embroidery and lace capital of Europe. It was here that three

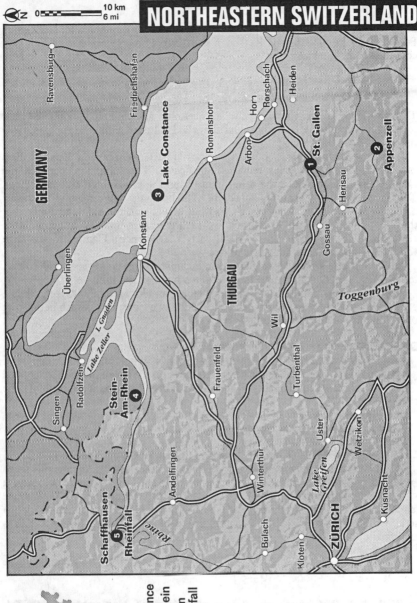

NORTHEASTERN SWITZERLAND

0 — 10 km / 6 mi

N

GERMANY

Ravensburg
Friedrichshafen
Lake Constance **3**
Überlingen
Konstanz
L. Gnaden
Lake Zeller
Radolfzell
Singen
Stein-Am-Rhein **4**
Schaffhausen
Rheinfall **5**
Rhine
Andelfingen
Bülach
Kloten
ZÜRICH
Küsnacht
Lake Greifen
Uster
Wetzikon
Turbenthal
Winterthur
Frauenfeld
Wil
THURGAU
Toggenburg
Gossau
Herisau
St. Gallen **1**
Appenzell **2**
Heiden
Rorschach
Horn
Arbon
Romanshorn

1 St. Gallen
2 Appenzell
3 Lake Constance
4 Stein-Am-Rhein
5 Schaffhausen and Rheinfall

dozen seamstresses worked for a year and a half to make a lace gown for Empress Eugénie, the wife of Napoleon III. Today, most of the embroidery is done by computer-driven machines.

WHAT TO SEE & DO

The **old city** is the main attraction, with its restored half-timbered houses and their turrets and oriels. Wander the lanes and alleys laid out during the Middle Ages; some of them are closed to traffic.

The Protestant Reformation was victorious in St. Gallen, but the **Benedictine monastery at Klosterhof** remained unaffected. The monastery contains the Catholic bishop's residence, the abbey library, and the canton's government offices. This area is also the site of the Domkirche. The buildings that remain of the abbey date from the 17th and 18th centuries. Its walls were razed, and the best view is from the abbey yard, called the Klosterhof. To reach the abbey from Marktplatz in the center of town, take Marktgasse south, past St. Lawrence's Church, to the large Klosterhof. The abbey is built around this yard.

St. Gallen offers many sports facilities, including a scenic 18-hole golf course, tennis courts, riding stables, and three outdoor swimming pools.

Freudenberg, 2 miles south of St. Gallen, at an altitude of 3,000 feet, offers a panoramic view of Mount Säntis, St. Gallen, and Lake Constance (which in this part of the country is known as the Bodensee).

DOMKIRCHE (Cathedral), Klosterhof.

The twin-towered Domkirche at Klosterhof is Switzerland's best example of baroque architecture. It was erected in 1756, on the site of the more celebrated 14th-century Gothic abbey. The interior is also baroque. Be sure to see the chancel.

Admission: Free.
Open: Daily 9am–5pm.

STIFTSBIBLIOTHEK (Abbey Library), Klosterhof 6C. Tel. 22-57-19.

This world-famous library, entered from an inner courtyard, contains some 130,000 volumes, including manuscripts from the 8th to the 12th century. It also displays about 500 books printed in the 15th century. Several Renaissance manuscripts have stunning illustrations. The library hall is built in a charming rococo style, with stucco art and ceiling paintings. A plan of St. Gallen Abbey in 820 is exhibited under glass.

Admission: 4F ($2.90).
Open: May–Oct, Mon–Sat 9am–noon and 2–5pm, Sun 10:30am–noon; Nov–Apr, Tues–Sat 9am–noon and 2–4pm.

TEXTILMUSEUM (Museum of Arts and Trades), Vadianstrasse 2. Tel. 22-17-44.

The museum features the gown of Empress Eugénie. It also holds many other priceless objects, including Coptic textiles from Egyptian tombs, Renaissance Italian lace, 17th-century French silk embroidered vests, and church robes richly embellished with needlework.

Admission: 4F ($2.90).
Open: Summer, Mon–Sat 10am–noon and 2–5pm; winter, Mon–Fri 10am–noon and 2–5pm.

WHERE TO STAY

EXPENSIVE

EINSTEIN HOTEL, Berneggstrasse 2, CH-9001 St. Gallen. Tel. 071/20-00-33. Fax 071/23-54-74. 65 rms (all with bath). MINIBAR TV TEL **Bus:** 1.
$ Rates (including continental breakfast): 190F–240F ($138.70–$175.20) single; 265F–325F ($193.40–$237.20) double. AE, DC, MC, V.
The most desirable hotel in town, the Einstein is near the center of the historic district. Built 150 years ago, it was originally a Swiss embroidery factory. In 1983 it was renovated into a stylish provincial hotel, owned and operated by one of Europe's largest chains, Mövenpick. It has a gray-and-white neoclassical facade and a marble lobby. Live piano music is played in the pub/cocktail bar. Rooms are conservatively furnished and include radios.

HOTEL WALHALLA, Bahnhofplatz, CH-9001 St. Gallen. Tel. 071/22-29-22. Fax 071/22-29-66. 54 rms (all with bath). MINIBAR TV TEL **Bus:** 1.
$ Rates (including buffet breakfast): 140F–160F ($102.20–$116.80) single; 215F–250F ($156.95–$182.50) double. AE, DC, MC, V.
This modernized Best Western is a first-class hotel in the shopping district. It faces the main railroad station and parking garage, about a 3-minute walk from the old town. Many visitors use the Walhalla as a base for excursions to Appenzellerland and the Lake Constance area. The hotel has two restaurants and a bar. The rooms are well furnished and include TVs with multilingual programs and radio alarms.

MODERATE

HOTEL GALLO, St. Jacobstrasse 62, CH-9000 St. Gallen. Tel. 071/25-27-27. 24 rms (all with bath). MINIBAR TV TEL **Bus:** 3.
$ Rates (including buffet breakfast): 140F–150F ($102.20–$109.50) single; 180F–200F ($131.40–$146) double. AE, DC, MC, V.
This hotel is along a busy traffic artery, about a 10-minute walk from the town center. Some of the details of its art nouveau facade are still visible. The recently renovated rooms have tall windows and contain a radio. An attractive restaurant next door, Galletto, is also recommended.

INEXPENSIVE

HOTEL DOM, Webergasse 22, CH-9000 St. Gallen. Tel. 071/23-20-44. Fax 071/23-38-21. 42 rms (all with bath). MINIBAR TV TEL **Bus:** 1.
$ Rates (including continental breakfast): 90F–105F ($65.70–$76.65) single; 135F–160F ($98.55–$116.80) double. AE, DC, MC, V.
This inviting hotel is one floor above street level, near the cathedral of St. Gallen in the center of town. Lendi Silvia and her accommodating staff offer simple rooms with comfortable furniture.

HOTEL EKKEHARD, Rorschacher Strasse 50, CH-9000 St. Gallen. Tel. 071/22-47-14. Fax 071/22-47-74. 34 rms (all with bath). TEL **Bus:** 1.
$ Rates: 85F–110F ($62.05–$80.30) single; 130F–180F ($94.90–$131.40) double. AE, DC, MC.
Located in the center of town, this typical, three-star Swiss hotel is neat and clean. The

rooms are small but pleasant, with functional furniture. There is a wood-trimmed restaurant with modern decor, serving Swiss and continental food at reasonable prices.

WHERE TO DINE

In the restaurants recommended below, as well as in the area's tea rooms and inns, try the famous local sausage, Bratwurst, and St. Gallen's rich regional pastries.

EXPENSIVE

AM GALLUSPLATZ, Gallusstrasse 24. Tel. 23-33-30.
   Cuisine: SWISS. **Reservations:** Recommended. **Bus:** 1.
$ **Prices:** Appetizers 12F–25F ($8.75–$18.25); main courses 25F–45F ($18.25–$32.85); fixed-meal 50F–150F ($36.50–$109.50). AE, MC, V.
   Open: Lunch Sun–Fri noon–2pm; dinner Tues–Sun 6–11pm.

⭐ Am Gallusplatz is one of the most famous restaurants in the old town. Finding it is part of the pleasure of dining here. It's opposite the cathedral, behind a low wall and a pink facade. The gastronomique menu includes seven-course dinners. The menu changes frequently and is based on fresh ingredients. I recommend bouillabaisse "chef," entrecôte Madagaskar, grilled sole and salmon Florentine style, and lamb medallions provençal. For lighter appetites, the wine bar (Weinstube) offers a selection of smaller dishes.

RESTAURANT GALLETTO, St. Jakobstrasse 62. Tel. 25-03-03.
   Cuisine: ITALIAN. **Reservations:** Required. **Bus:** 3.
$ **Prices:** Appetizers 30F–40F ($21.90–$29.20); main courses 50F–80F ($36.50–$58.40); fixed-price meal from 80F ($58.40). AE, DC, MC, V.
   Open: Lunch Tues–Sat 11am–2pm; dinner Mon–Sat 6–11pm. **Closed:** July 20–Aug 10.

Modern and very Italian, this restaurant sports lots of plants, bouquets of flowers, and tempting pastry carts. It's on a busy street, about a 10-minute walk from the historic center of town.

The menu includes an enticing array of antipasti and a wide selection of homemade pasta, including lasagne verde, taglierini with salmon, and ravioli. There are also many excellent veal dishes, including one with porcini mushrooms. Other choices include eggplant parmigiana, veal liver Venice style, and a limited selection of fish, including a mixed fry from the Adriatic.

MODERATE

HOTEL EINSTEIN RESTAURANT, Berneggstrasse 2. Tel. 20-00-33.
   Cuisine: SWISS. **Reservations:** Recommended. **Bus:** 1.
$ **Prices:** Appetizers 12F–22F ($8.75–$16.05); main courses 18F–45F ($13.15–$32.85). AE, DC, MC, V.
   Open: Lunch daily noon–2pm; dinner daily 6–10pm.

One of the finest restaurants in the city is on the fifth floor of the Hotel Einstein. The decor blends rustic timber with marble trim. Specialties include calves' liver with coriander and cider sauce, cream of spinach soup with salmon strips, and filet of sole with artichokes and sherry-flavored butter.

SCHWARTZER BÄREN, Speicherstrasse 151. Tel. 35-30-55.
   Cuisine: SWISS/ITALIAN. **Reservations:** Required. **Transportation:** Take a taxi.

$ Prices: Appetizers 12F–22F ($8.75–$16.05); main courses 25F–38F ($18.25–$27.75). MC, V.

Open: Fri–Tues 11am–11pm.

About a 10-minute drive from the town center, this rustic restaurant serves well-prepared, traditional food with many Italian specialties. The decor includes wrought iron, antiques, and textile wall hangings. Ingredients are always fresh. I recommend the sole with capers and the cutlet of beef with homemade cabbage butter.

STADTKELLER, Spisermarkt, Spisergasse 17. Tel. 22-00-88.

Cuisine: SWISS. **Reservations:** Required. **Bus:** 1.

$ Prices: Appetizers 8F–18F ($5.85–$13.15); main courses 21F–38F ($15.35–$27.75); fixed-price meals 28F–60F ($20.45–$43.80). AE, DC, MC, V.

Open: Lunch Mon–Sat 11am–2pm; dinner Mon–Sat 6pm–2am.

This fashionable spot is located in a busy area of cafés, bars, and boutiques in the center of the old city. A curved flight of stone steps descends to a windowless basement, with flickering candles and a vaulted ceiling. The elegant menu might include fish soup with saffron, sweetbread salad with a morel-flavored vinaigrette, snails in a red wine and butter sauce, sole filets in a tarragon sauce, and smoked salmon. The Bistro à l'Escargot, below, is in the same building.

BISTRO A L'ESCARGOT, Spisermarkt, Spisergasse 17. Tel. 22-00-88.

Cuisine: SWISS. **Reservations:** Recommended. **Bus:** 1.

$ Prices: Appetizers 6F–11F ($4.40–$8.05); main courses 11F–24F ($8.05–$17.50). AE, DC, MC, V.

Open: Lunch Mon–Sat 11:30am–2pm; dinner Mon–Sat 6–11:30pm.

This informal restaurant is situated upstairs from the Stadtkeller. It's brightly illuminated and full of chattering diners. The menu might include snail soup, tripe with Calvados, boiled beef with mustard and onions, and three different varieties of pasta, including spaghetti in a gorgonzola sauce. Specialties include lamb chops provençal, veal scaloppine with Marsala, and pork provençal.

The Schnecken Bar, behind the bistro, is packed with college students every night.

SHOPPING

Many people come to St. Gallen to shop for scarves, handkerchiefs, and table linen. The best place is **Sturzenegger,** St. Leonhardstrasse 12 (tel. 22-78-97), which is a part of a nationwide chain.

Textile factories in the area sometimes have clearance sales, usually in January and July, when visitors can find real bargains.

---

2. APPENZELL

11¼ miles S of St. Gallen, 12 miles SW of Altstätten

GETTING THERE By Train From Zurich you can take a slow local train without transferring; you'll reach Appenzell after about 2 hours. Less time-consuming is to take an express train from Zurich to Gossau, a satellite village of St. Gallen, and transfer to the local train. Trip time from St. Gallen or Gossau to Appenzell on one of the 30 or so daily locals takes about 45 minutes.

By Bus It's a lot more convenient by train. The town's only bus line goes between

Appenzell and St. Gallen, via a meandering path through local villages not serviced by the rail lines. Even worse, from St. Gallen, you'll have to transfer buses in a village called Teufen.

By Car   From St. Gallen, drive south from the city in the direction of Teufen where the road is signposted south to Appenzell.

ESSENTIALS   The **telephone area code** for Appenzell is 071. The **Appenzell Tourist Office** is at Hauptgasse 19 (tel. 071/87-41-11).

In the rolling, verdant foothills of the Alpstein, south of Lake Constance, the Appenzell district retains some of Switzerland's strongest doses of folklore. Its hamlets contain intricately painted houses whose colorful decorations are distinctive to the region. The inhabitants, proud of their cultural distinctions, sometimes wear folk costumes whose ceremonial garb includes an elaborate coiffe with large wings made of a fabric called tulle. Men are known for their rakish earrings (which usually adorn only one ear) and their habit of going barefoot in the summer.

Appenzell is famous for its baked goods and chocolates, for the artists who adhere to a certain school of naïve art (which some observers compare to paintings by the American primitivist Grandma Moses), and for its status as the yodeling headquarters of Switzerland. For centuries the district was relatively isolated from the rest of Switzerland, although today good roads and trusty cable cars ferry sightseers across the otherwise inaccessible terrain.

Appenzell is an excellent base for exploring two nearby peaks, the **Ebenalp** and **Mount Säntis** (see "Easy Excursions," below), and an old but well-preserved village nearby, **Trogen.**

Appenzell's main square, Landsgemeindeplatz, and its main street, Hauptgasse, are lined with traditional painted houses. Here, shops sell the famous embroidery of the area.

WHERE TO STAY

ROMANTIK HOTEL SÄNTIS, Landsgemeindeplatz 3, CH-9050 Appenzell. Tel. 071/87-87-22. Fax 071/87-48-42. 38 rms (all with bath or shower). TV TEL
$ Rates (including continental breakfast): 90F–130F ($65.70–$94.90) single; 145F–220F ($105.85–$160.60) double. AE, DC, MC, V.
This hotel, in the town center, is decorated with dozens of stenciled, symmetrical designs. Its rooms are cozy, many filled with regional antiques. There is a small, Appenzell-style dining room with a wood ceiling and colorful tablecloths. The Heeb family offers a cordial welcome.

HOTEL APPENZELL, Landsgemeindeplatz, CH-9050 Appenzell. Tel. 071/87-42-11. Fax 87-42-84. 16 rms (all with bath). MINIBAR TV TEL
$ Rates (including continental breakfast): 95F ($69.35) single; 160F ($116.80) double. AE, DC, MC, V.
Located on the town's main square, this modern hotel is painted with a combination of whimsical folk colors. The comfortable rooms have conservative, modern walnut furniture and a radio. Bathrooms are lined with travertine marble.

The street-level café, with its outdoor terrace, is open Wednesday through Monday from 7:30am to 11:30pm. Through the café is an elaborately paneled dining room, with walls from a house that belonged to a local doctor (the restaurant bears his name, Hildebrand-Stube). The restaurant is open for lunch Wednesday through Monday from 11am to 2pm and for dinner daily from 5:30 to 10pm.

HOTEL HECHT, Hauptgasse 9, CH-9050 Appenzell. Tel. 071/87-10-25.
Fax 071/87-11-16. 41 rms (36 with bath). TEL
$ **Rates** (including continental breakfast): 85F ($62.05) single without bath, 100F ($73.00) single with bath; 130F ($94.90) double without bath, 160F ($116.80) double with bath. AE, DC, MC, V.

⑤ This 300-year-old hotel, in the center of town opposite the Catholic church, is the biggest alpine inn in Appenzell. The Knechtle family has owned the place for 50 years, keeping it clean, attractive, and conservative. The overall effect is *gemütlich*—cheerful and comfortable. Some of the bedrooms have TVs.

WHERE TO DINE

RESTAURANT SÄNTIS, Landgemeindeplatz 3. Tel. 87-87-22.
Cuisine: SWISS. **Reservations:** Recommended.
$ **Prices:** Appetizers 12F–20F ($8.75–$14.60); main courses 24F–38F ($17.50–$27.75). AE, DC, MC, V.
Open: Lunch daily 11:30am–2pm; dinner daily 6:30–10pm (to 9pm in winter).
Closed: Feb 15–28.
Located on the first floor of the popular Romantik Hotel Säntis, this restaurant offers a view over the elaborately detailed houses of the main square. The menu changes frequently. Typical appetizers include a nourishing bouillon or alpine dried beef garnished with pickles and onions. Main courses might include loin of lamb provençal or roast filet of pork. Some of the meat and fish dishes are accompanied by homemade noodles, served with *al dente* carrots and spinach.

HOTEL HECHT RESTAURANT, Hauptgasse 9. Tel. 87-10-25.
Cuisine: SWISS. **Reservations:** Recommended.
$ **Prices:** Appetizers 8F–20F ($5.85–$14.60); main courses 18F–36F ($13.15–$26.30). AE, DC, MC, V.
Open: Lunch daily 11am–2pm; dinner daily 7–10pm.
Located in the oldest part of town, this restaurant is famous for its excellent cuisine and wine cellar. Cherry paneling and paintings by local artists add a homey touch to the rustic dining room. Appenzell specialties include trout (served au bleu or meunière), rice Casimir, veal with mushrooms in a cream sauce, and filet Gulyas Stroganoff.

EASY EXCURSIONS

EBENALP Visit Ebenalp, 4 miles away, for a spectacular view of the hills and pastures of the Appenzell district. The jagged promontory is at an elevation of 5,400 feet. Wear sturdy walking shoes so that you can walk down to **Wildkirchli**—a chapel in a grotto, inhabited by hermits from the mid-17th to the mid-19th century. Paleolithic artifacts discovered there at the turn of the century indicate that it is the oldest prehistoric settlement found in Switzerland.

To get there, drive to the end of the Weissbad–Wasserauen road, then take a cable car for an 11-minute ride to the summit. The cable car leaves every 45 minutes in season; round-trip costs 15F ($10.95). For information, call 071/88-12-12.

MOUNT SÄNTIS The major attraction in the area is Mount Säntis, the highest peak (8,200 ft.) in the Alpstein massif. It offers a panoramic view of eastern

Switzerland, including the Grisons, the Bernese Alps, the Vorarlberg mountains, Lake Constance, and even Lake Zurich. On a clear day you can see as far as Swabia in southern Germany.

To get there, drive to Schwagalp and take a cable car to the Säntis belvedere. The cable car leaves every 40 minutes year round; round-trip costs 20F ($14.60).

3. LAKE CONSTANCE

Lake Constance is divided into three parts, although the name is frequently applied to the Bodensee, the largest part. At the western end of the Bodensee, the lake splits into two branches: a long fjord, called the Überlingersee, and an irregular marshland, called the Untersee. The Untersee is connected to the rest of the lake by a narrow channel of water, which is actually the young Rhine River. The blue felchen, a pikelike fish found only in Lake Constance, furnishes the district with a tasty and renowned specialty.

The 162-mile-long shoreline of the lake is shared by three countries—Switzerland, Germany, and Austria. The surrounding hills are covered with vineyards and orchards and are dotted with many charming villages. Many vacationers are drawn by the sunny, mild climate and the attractive beaches.

ORIENTATION AND GETTING AROUND   The Swiss gateway to Lake Constance is Rorschach, 7 miles northeast of St. Gallen. You can get there by train either from Zurich in 1½ hours (the train departs every hour) or from St. Gallen in 20 minutes. From Rorschach you can continue on by frequent local trains or buses along the lake to the three other major tourist centers: Arbon, Horn, and Romanshorn. A well-organized network of modern passenger ferries links all these towns along the shore and connects Switzerland with Germany and Austria. The **Rorschach Tourist Office,** Neugasse 2 (tel. 071/41-70-34), provides a frequently changing timetable for all forms of transportation. You can also contact one of the most popular boat lines, **Schiffahrtsbetrieb Rorschach** (tel. 071/41-14-25).

The **telephone area code** for all these towns is 071.

RORSCHACH

This medieval harbor town is located at the foot of the Rorschacher Berg, at the southern tip of the lake. It offers lakeside gardens, an extensive promenade, and facilities for sailing, rowing, swimming, fishing, and windsurfing. Passenger ships pass through on their way to Germany, Austria, and Liechtenstein.

Rorschach's illustrious past is reflected in its buildings, which include the Kornhaus, a granary built in 1746; the former Mariaberg cloister; and 18th-century painted houses with oriel windows along Hauptgasse.

The **Kornhaus,** Hafenplatz (tel. 41-40-62), is now a museum containing prehistoric artifacts, local weaving and embroidery, and an exhibit on the castle of Wartegg. Admission is 3F ($2.20). The museum is open Monday through Saturday from 9:30 to 11:30am and 2 to 5pm, and on Sunday from 10am to noon and 2 to 5pm. It's closed from November to April.

WHERE TO STAY & DINE

PARKHOTEL WALDAU, Seebleichestrasse, CH-9400 Rorschach. Tel. 071/43-01-80. Fax 071/42-10-02. 52 rms (all with bath). MINIBAR TV TEL

$ Rates (including continental breakfast): 158F ($115.30) single; 280F ($204.35) double. MC, V.

This country manor was built after World War II as a private school for boys, then transformed into a modern five-star hotel. The hotel sits on a hill overlooking the lake 4 miles southwest of the center. The interior has paneling and tufted leather banquettes. Rooms contain safes and radios.

Dining/Entertainment: The elegant indoor-outdoor restaurant is known as a glamorous place for businesspeople to entertain clients. Depending on the weather, meals are served in the rear garden or one floor above the reception area. Service is formal and polite; a pianist plays until 11pm. Specialties include veal kidneys with truffles, elegant pasta dishes, goose liver terrine, and a mixed grill with a choice of sauces. Fixed-price lunches start at 45F ($32.85); à la carte dinners start at 75F ($54.75). The restaurant is open daily for lunch from noon to 2pm and for dinner from 7 to 11pm. Reservations are recommended.

Services: Hydrotherapy.

Facilities: Tennis courts, indoor-outdoor pool, fitness center.

HOTEL MOZART, Hafenzentrum, CH-9400 Rorschach. Tel. 071/41-06-32. Fax 071/41-99-38. 30 rms (all with bath). MINIBAR TV TEL

$ Rates (including continental breakfast): 100F ($73) single; 150F ($109.50) double. MC, V. **Parking:** Free.

Opened in 1986, this comfortable hotel, with its own garage, is situated between the main street of town and the lake. The polished granite building has charming rooms, equipped with radios; seven rooms overlook the lake.

The old-world ambience of the hotel's Café Mozart complements its variety of famous pastries. Another specialty is tea—19 varieties, including essence of kiwi, linden blossom, and tea leaves grown on the foothills of Mount Everest. The café also offers simple meals.

HOTEL ANKER, Hafenplatz, CH-9400 Rorschach. Tel. 071/41-42-43. 33 rms (all with bath). TV TEL

$ Rates (including continental breakfast): 75F ($54.75) single; 140F ($102.20) double. AE, DC, MC, V.

If you like boats, you'll love this hotel across the street from the town marina. Built in 1720, the light-gray building has gables, balconies, and a red-tile roof. It's covered with flowers in the summer. The rooms have been modernized.

There are five dining rooms upstairs near the reception desk. I prefer the glass-enclosed terrace overlooking the lake. A typical appetizer is baked Camembert with cranberries and orange sauce. Main dishes include squid in a rémoulade sauce, at least two varieties of trout, salmon with Madeira sauce, and a rijstaffel for two diners. A la carte meals are a good value, beginning at 40F ($29.20). The restaurant is open daily for lunch from 11am to 2pm and for dinner from 5 to 10pm.

HORN

This old fishing hamlet is a 5-minute drive east of Arbon. Set in the canton of Thurgau, it provides an idyllic base for exploring the shores of Lake Constance. The large port of Rorschach is only a 10-minute car or bus ride to the east.

WHERE TO STAY & DINE

HOTEL BAD HORN, Seestrasse 36, CH-9326 Horn. Tel. 071/41-55-11. Fax 071/41-60-89. 44 rms (all with bath). MINIBAR TV TEL

$ Rates: 75F–140F ($54.75–$102.20) single; 140F–260F ($102.20–$189.75) double. AE, DC, MC, V.

This large, ocher-colored hotel is idyllically located in the town center at the end of a small peninsula on the lakefront. It has big windows, gables, a tile roof, rooftop terraces, and an expanse of lawn extending almost to the water. Bedrooms are well furnished and comfortably appointed.

The hotel has three restaurants. I recommend the sunny Captain's Grill with its elegant, nautical decor. Specialties include aiguillettes of pink duck, quenelles of a local fish, scampi with Calvados, and filet of beef with Armagnac. Many dishes are flambéed at your table, including giant shrimp with sherry and filet of pork with gin. A la carte meals start at 50F ($36.50). The restaurant is open daily for lunch from noon to 2pm and for dinner from 6 to 9pm.

ARBON

One of the best spots along the lake is Arbon, the lakefront promenade that offers a view of Constance, the German shore, and the Alps. Facilities include a large boat harbor, swimming pools, and a school for sailing and surfing. **Arbon Castle,** now a local museum, is a medieval stronghold with a 13th-century keep and 16th-century residential wings. The town was built on the site of an ancient Celtic community and was called Arbor Felix by the Romans.

WHERE TO STAY & DINE

HOTEL METROPOLE, on the lakefront, CH-9320 Arbon. Tel. 071/46-35-35. 42 rms (all with bath). MINIBAR TV TEL

$ Rates (including continental breakfast): 110F–130F ($80.30–$94.90) single; 180F–210F ($131.40–$153.30) double. AE, DC, MC, V.

This concrete Best Western hotel, across from the train station, is part of a lakeside complex that exemplifies creative urban planning. The complex includes a department store, a grocery store, and a busy cafeteria. The hotel lobby is Nordic modern, and the rooms are comfortable but plain, each with a loggia and radio. Facilities include a hot whirlpool, sauna, and rooftop swimming pool. The hotel also offers an inviting, dark-toned bar, restaurant, and lakeside café.

HOTEL ROTES KREUZ, Hafenstrasse 3, CH-9320 Arbon. Tel. 071/46-19-14. Fax 071/46-24-85. 28 rms (all with bath) TEL

$ Rates: 60F ($43.80) single; 110F ($80.30) double. MC, V.

Near the departure pier for lake ferries, this stucco house with red shutters and a terrace was built in 1760. The handful of rooms it contains are simple and well scrubbed. You can dine in a glass-enclosed solarium or a cozy pine-paneled room. Specialties include a variety of lake fish. The menu may also offer veal strips with a mushroom-and-cream sauce, calves' liver, and a local favorite—sausage salad. Snacks cost 12F ($8.75); à la carte meals start at 25F ($18.25). The restaurants are open daily for lunch from 11:30am to 2pm and for dinner from 5 to 9pm.

ROMANSHORN

This is the largest port on the lake and the base for Swiss steamers. The resort offers a swimming pool, a sailing school, a waterskiing school, and tennis courts. There is a park as well as a zoo.

A year-round ferry service links Romanshorn with Friedrichshafen, Germany. There, you can visit a castle that served as the summer residence of the Württemberg kings. In the summer, boat trips are organized to Mainau, a German island about 4 miles north of Constance that was once the home of the Grand Duke of Baden.

WHERE TO STAY & DINE

PARK-HOTEL INSELI, Inselistrasse, CH-8590 Romanshorn. Tel. 071/ 63-53-53. Fax 071/63-14-55. 39 rms (all with bath or shower). MINIBAR TV TEL
$ Rates: 85F–133F ($62.05–$97.10) single; 140F–175F ($102.20–$127.75) double. AE, DC, MC, V.

This modern hotel is secluded in a grove of trees in the town center, directly on the lake. Its comfortable rooms—all with radios and safes—offer views of the lawn or the lake; the public rooms are decorated with chrome and plush carpeting. Managed by Anton Stager and his family, the hotel has an informal ambience. There is a sunny, indoor-outdoor café and a more formal rôtisserie.

---

4. STEIN-AM-RHEIN

12 miles E of Schaffhausen, 17 miles N of Winterthur

GETTING THERE By Train Stein-am-Rhein lies midway along the railway link connecting Schaffhausen with Kreuzlingen, on the edge of Lake Constance. From Zurich passengers take an express train to Schaffhausen, then change for a less frequent local train to Stein-am-Rhein; trip time from Zurich is just under 2 hours. There are also good train connections to Stuttgart, Germany.

By Bus The only bus connection to Stein-am-Rhein goes across the border to a German village named Singen, from which there are rail connections to Stuttgart.

By Car From Zurich head north on N1 until a point near Winterthur, where you connect with E41 going north to Schaffhausen. This route becomes N4, connecting with Route 13, heading east toward Stein-am-Rhein.

ESSENTIALS The **telephone area code** for Stein-am-Rhein is 054. The **Stein-am-Rhein Tourist Office** is on Rathausplatz (tel. 054/08-94-21).

Dating from 1094, Stein-am-Rhein is one of the most authentic and best-preserved medieval towns in Switzerland. It's on the right bank of the Rhine, west of the Untersee (an arm of Lake Constance). Nearby was the first Roman bridge ever built over the Rhine.

WHAT TO SEE & DO

Quaint houses line **Rathausplatz** (Town Hall Square) and **Hauptstrasse** (Main Street). Many have oriel windows, rich frescoes, timberwork, and fountains.

The **Historische Sammlung (Historical Museum)** is in the town hall, on Rathausplatz (tel. 41-42-31). The collection includes weapons, banners, and stained glass. Admission is 3F ($2.20). The museum is open Monday through Friday from 10 to 11:30am and 2 to 5pm; closed holidays.

A Benedictine abbey was built on Rathausplatz during the 11th century; it was abandoned, during the Protestant Reformation, in 1524. Today it's the **Klostermuseum St. Georgen (St. George's Abbey Museum)** (tel. 41-21-42), devoted to local history and art. The rooms, because of their rich ceilings, paneling, and 16th-century murals by Thomas Schmid and Ambrosius Holbein, are often more fascinating than the exhibits. Admission to the museum costs 3F ($2.20) for adults, 1.50F ($1.10) for children. The museum is open daily from 10am to noon and 1:30 to 5pm. The restored Convent Church of St. George (a Romanesque basilica built by the Catholics and later transformed into a Protestant church) has sections dating from the 12th century.

WHERE TO STAY

HOTEL CHLOSTERHOF, Hauptstrasse, CH-8260 Stein-am-Rhein. Tel. 054/42-42-42. Fax 054/41-13-37. 68 rms (all with bath). MINIBAR TV TEL
$ Rates: 140F–170F ($102.20–$124.10) single; 190F–270F ($138.70–$197.05) double. AE, DC, MC, V.

The finest hotel in town, situated on the Rhine, east of Rathausplatz, was created from an abandoned shoe factory. Its interior includes an open fireplace and a lobby with a cruciform vault. The hotel attracts foreign visitors during the summer and is a popular conference center off-season. The rooms are stylized; 10 have four-poster beds.

The restaurant, Le Bâteau, offers fine dining amid a nautical decor. Le Jardin is an elegant little in-house bistro. The hotel also has a swimming pool and sauna.

HOTEL-RESTAURANT ADLER, Rathausplatz, CH-8260 Stein-am-Rhein. Tel. 054/42-61-61. Fax 054/41-44-40. 25 rms (all with bath). TEL
$ Rates (including continental breakfast): 70F–95F ($54.75–$69.35) single; 100F–145F ($73–$105.85) double. MC, V. **Parking:** 15F ($10.95) per night.

This simple, comfortable hotel has one of the most flamboyant facades in the old city: It's painted with characters from Rhenish legends, depicting such medieval scenes as a tree of life, martyrs at the stake, and characters groveling before Asian potentates. The hotel has two sections, one dating from 1461 and the other built in 1957. The rooms have a streamlined Nordic design and are equipped with a radio.

HOTEL RHEINFELS, Rathausplatz, CH-8260 Stein-am-Rhein. Tel. 054/41-21-44. Fax 054/41-25-22. 16 rms (all with bath). MINIBAR TV TEL
$ Rates (including continental breakfast): 100F ($73) single; 140F ($102.20) double. No credit cards.

This large building was built in 1448, beside the rapidly flowing Rhine. The hotel is well known for its pleasantly decorated rooms and its river-view terrace restaurant. Upstairs from the restaurant is an antique room with wide, creaking floorboards, massive chandeliers, old portraits, and a collection of medieval armor.

WHERE TO DINE

RESTAURANT SONNE, Rathausplatz 127. Tel. 41-21-28.
Cuisine: SWISS/FRENCH. **Reservations:** Required.
$ Prices: Appetizers 15F–30F ($10.95–$21.90); main courses 35F–50F ($25.55–$36.50). AE, DC, MC, V.
Open: Lunch Fri–Wed noon–2pm; dinner Fri–Wed 6–9pm.

Located near the well-preserved marketplace, the Sonne is one of the most famous restaurants in town. Chef and owner Philippe Combe prepares cuisine moderne for guests in the intimate dining room. Typical dishes include fresh river crabs in a vinaigrette sauce, wild game in a beaujolais sauce (served with wild mushrooms sautéed in butter), and roast hare with mustard sauce. The menu might also include ravioli stuffed with lobster, sea bass with fresh asparagus, and pigeon with truffles. Good wines complement the fine food, and smooth desserts, such as chocolate mousse, provide the perfect finish.

HOTEL RHEINFELS RESTAURANT, Rathausplatz. Tel. 41-21-44.
   Cuisine: SWISS. **Reservations:** Recommended.
$ Prices: Appetizers 5F–15.50F ($3.65–$11.30); main courses 27F–32F ($19.70–$23.35); fixed-price lunch 24F ($17.50). No credit cards.
I've already recommended the hotel that contains this pleasant restaurant. Typical dishes include filets of fera (a lake fish) with lemon and capers, fricasee of Rhenish fish with baby vegetables, hot Bauernschinken (farmer's ham), and grilled veal steak. A "potpourri" of Rheinfels desserts is also offered.

5. SCHAFFHAUSEN & RHEINFALL

32 miles N of Zurich, 17 miles N of Winterthur

GETTING THERE   By Train   Schaffhausen is on all major north-south rail lines between Stuttgart and Milan. There are at least 14 express trains from Zurich every day (trip time is 40 min.).

By Bus   Bus lines link Schaffhausen only to the villages on its periphery.

By Car   From Zurich head north on Route 4 all the way.

ESSENTIALS   The **telephone area code** for Schaffhausen is 053. The **Schaffhausen Tourist Information Office** is at Vorstadt 12 (tel. 053/25-51-41).

A charming little city, Schaffhausen is built on terraces along the steeply inclined right bank of the Rhine. Although many sections of the city are modern and heavily industrialized, Schaffhausen retains its medieval spirit, exemplified by its romantic fountains and old, brown-roofed houses, dotted with oriel windows and decorated with statues in niches. It is a center for visiting the Rhine Falls (Rheinfall), one of the most popular sights in northeastern Switzerland.
   Once ruled by the Hapsburgs, Schaffhausen became an imperial free city and later the capital of a Swiss canton of the same name. Germany borders the canton on three sides, heavily influencing the Teutonic flavor of much of the city's architecture.

WHAT TO SEE & DO

Spend a morning touring **the old town** at your leisure. There is a good view of the town from the battlements of the **Munot,** which dates from 1564. The round fortress has a tower, platform, and parapet walks. It's reached by stairs and has a covered footbridge across the moat. The Munot is the only fortress to be based on a book by Albrecht Dürer, which was published in Nürnberg in 1527. It's open May through September, daily from 8am to 8pm; October through April, daily from 9am to 5pm.
   The crowning glory of the old town is the **Münster (All Saints' Church),** on Münsterplatz. Now Protestant, it was formerly a Benedictine monastery, consecrated in 1052. Its Romanesque architecture is stern and plain. In a nearby small courtyard is

the 15th-century bell that inspired Schiller's poem "Song of the Bell" and the opening of Longfellow's "Golden Legend."

The most charming street is **Vordergasse**, where visitors usually stop to photograph the frescoed Haus zum Ritter, dating from 1485. On Fronwegplatz are two outstanding fountains, from the 1520s. The Rathaus (town hall) was built in 1632.

The ✪ **Museum zu Allerheiligen (All Saints' Museum)**, Baumgarten-strasse (tel. 25-43-77), is one of the most important national museums in Switzerland. The former abbey has exhibits ranging from prehistoric times to the present, including traditional garb of the province, old weapons, and period furnishings. Visit the "Treasury" in the former abbots' salon. The museum is open Tuesday through Sunday from 10am to noon and 2 to 5pm.

RHEINFALL   ✪ The Rheinfall (Rhine Falls) is the most celebrated waterfall in central Europe. It's also the most powerful—700 cubic meters of water per second rush over a width of 150 yards. The water falls 70 feet, a sight that inspired Goethe to liken it to the "source of the ocean." This natural wonder is most spectacular in early summer, when it's fed by mountain snows.

To get to the Rheinfall from Zurich, take a train from the Hauptbahnhof to Neuhausen and get off at the Rheinfall stop. The trip takes less than an hour. It's a 15-minute walk from the train depot at Neuhausen to the waterfall. For a dramatic experience, you can take a 15F ($10.95) boat trip to the rock in the center of the Rheinfall.

You can view the falls from the belvedere of **Laufen Castle** on the left bank. The castle has been converted into a restaurant with a staircase that leads to the view. Bring a raincoat.

You can also take a ferry across the river to Neuhausen and the little castle of **Schlössli-Worth** (tel. 5-40-01), built in the 12th century as a customs post. Today it's a restaurant, open from March to mid-November.

WHERE TO STAY

RHEINHOTEL FISCHERZUNFT, Rheinquai 8, CH-8200 Schaffhausen Tel. 054/25-32-81. 12 rms (all with bath). MINIBAR TV TEL

$ **Rates** (including continental breakfast): 120F–260F ($87.60–$189.75) single; 150F–305F ($109.50–$222.60) double. AE, DC, MC, V.

✪ Located on Freier Platz next to a promenade along the Rhine, this inviting inn was formerly occupied by the fishermen's guild. The Jaeger family converted it to a hotel in 1898. The main public room has a Chinese decor.

The restaurant's cuisine mixes classic European and Asian influences, featuring curried chicken consommé with Chinese ravioli, filet of venison with five Chinese spices and sautéed mustard cabbage, and lobster salad with coriander, Chinese noodles, and creamy sesame sauce. The dishes are rich in taste, texture, and design. The desserts are delicious and beautiful; my favorites include mango with raspberry sauce and a fan of figs, and pineapple with iced vanilla mousse. À la carte meals range from 55F to 90F ($40.15 to $65.70); the fixed-price menu costs 130F ($94.90). The restaurant is open daily for lunch from noon to 2pm and for dinner from 7 to 9:30pm.

HOTEL PARK VILLA, Parkstrasse 18, CH-8200 Schaffhausen. Tel. 054/ 25-27-37. Fax 053/24-12-53. 20 rms (all with bath). MINIBAR TV TEL

$ **Rates** (including continental breakfast): 95F–130F ($69.35–$94.90) single; 120F–180F ($87.60–$131.40) double. AE, DC, MC, V.

This chiseled gray hotel is located near the train station in a park with massive trees. It has towers, steep roofs, and gables with terra-cotta tiles. The interior is as graceful as the exterior is rough. There are crystal chandeliers, a paneled bar, and several public rooms with fresh flowers, comfortable chairs, and oil paintings. A few bedrooms are regally decorated with antiques. There is a well-maintained tennis court behind the building.

HOTEL BELLEVUE, Bahnhofstrasse, CH-8212 Neuhausen am Rheinfall. Tel. 054/22-21-21. Fax 053/22-83-50. 35 rms (all with bath). TV TEL
$ Rates: (including continental breakfast): 82F–100F ($59.85–$73) single; 140F–170F ($102.20–$124.10) double. MC, V.

Perhaps the loviest feature of the Bellevue is its terrace, where you can sip drinks and watch the waterfall beyond. The interior of the hotel is simple and modern. The owner, Thomas Nohava, also has a restaurant with a view of the falls; fixed-price meals start at 30F ($21.90). The Bellevue sits 1¼ miles west of the town center.

WHERE TO DINE

RESTAURANT GERBERSTUBE, Bachstrasse 8. Tel. 25-21-55.
Cuisine: ITALIAN. **Reservations:** Required.
$ Prices: Appetizers 8F–25F ($5.85–$18.25); main courses 18F–35F ($13.15–$25.55). AE, DC, MC, V.
Open: Tues–Sat noon–midnight.

Just west of the Munot, the Guidi family runs the finest Italian restaurant in Schaffhausen. The dining room is in a 16th-century guildhall, which contains a changing exhibition of modern painters. You might begin with the famous egg-and-consommé soup of Rome, stracciatella, following it either with spaghetti or cannelloni or with a veal schnitzel pizzaiola. There are many classic dishes, including chateaubriand with béarnaise sauce and succulent preparations of veal and pasta.

CHAPTER 5

BASEL & THE JURA

- **WHAT'S SPECIAL ABOUT BASEL & THE JURA**
1. **BASEL (BASLE)**
2. **SOLOTHURN**
3. **FRIBOURG**
4. **GRUYERES**
5. **MURTEN (MORAT)**
6. **NEUCHATEL**

Northwestern Switzerland, with its valleys, waterfalls, and old-world villages, is one of the most beautiful regions in the country. The area encompasses the Jura mountain range, Basel, and the surrounding towns. During this part of your journey you'll be zigzagging between two cultures, and the names—for example, Morat in French and Murten in German—will often confuse you. Most of the region has a medieval feel, reflected in the ancient architecture. Some of the towns may already be familiar to you; Gruyères is known for its cheese. Other places, such as the old walled university town of Fribourg and historic Neuchâtel, are also well worth a visit. You will probably be based in Basel (or Basle), which straddles the Rhine, between Alsace in France and the Jura in Switzerland.

The canton of Jura was established in 1979 as the 23rd member of the Confederation. A total of 82 communes make up the canton, with Delemont as its capital. Nearly 88% of the population is Roman Catholic, and French is the predominant language.

Situated between the Rhine and the Rhône, the geological folds and faults of the Jura mountain range form the border of Switzerland and France and extend from Geneva, in the southwest, to Schaffhausen, along the northern border. Very different in height and character from the Alps, the Jura mountains were nevertheless created by the same geological forces. Few peaks exceed 5,500 feet.

Until the advent of modern transportation, farmers of the Jura lived in relative isolation. Today, paved roads and railroads allow visitors to enjoy views of the Alps and the surrounding pastures, pine forests, and valleys. The center of the Swiss watchmaking industry is here. And thriving winter sports resorts can be found throughout the mountains as well, although most of them draw a local rather than an international clientele.

SEEING BASEL & THE JURA

Basel, with its superior air, rail, and bus links, is the traditional gateway to northwestern Switzerland and the Jura mountains. All the major towns in this chapter have excellent rail links (far better than any bus connection). Traveling by car is better, as you can see more of the remote villages and countryside, and the roads are good. You can also take boat trips on the lakes of Neuchâtel and Murten in summer.

WHAT'S SPECIAL ABOUT BASEL & THE JURA

Great Towns/Villages

☐ Basel (Basle), the country's third-largest city, at the "corner" of Switzerland, Germany, and France.

☐ Solothurn, Switzerland's famed baroque town at the foot of the Jura Mountains.

☐ Murten (Morat), beautifully preserved medieval town on the Murtensee.

☐ Gruyères, home of the ancient counts of Gruyères, known for its castle and, more so, for its cheese.

Great Museums

☐ Kuntsmuseum (Fine Arts Museum) at Basel, considered one of the best art museums in the country; filled with "old masters."

Ancient Monuments

☐ Castle of Gruyères, Gruyères, art-filled château, legendary home of the counts of Gruyères.

☐ St. Nicholas's Cathedral, Fribourg, a Gothic pile dominating the medieval quarter.

Cool for Kids

☐ The Zoologischer Garten at Basel, one of the greatest in the world; famed for breeding endangered species.

IF YOU HAVE A WEEK

Day 1: Spend at least one full day and night in Basel to see its major attractions.

Day 2: By rail or car, go to baroque Solothurn.

Day 3: Devote a day to Fribourg, walking the streets of its medieval quarter.

Day 4: Head south to Gruyères for one of the most romantic stopovers in Switzerland.

Day 5: Proceed northwest for a visit to Murten (Morat), a remarkably preserved medieval town on the lake.

Day 6: Moving toward the French border, spend a final night in the ancient city of Neuchâtel.

---

1. BASEL (BASLE)

53 miles NW of Zurich, 61 miles N of Bern

GETTING THERE   By Plane   You can fly to Basel nonstop from New York on **Balair** (tel. toll free 800/TRAV-800), Switzerland's vacation airline and an affiliate of Swissair; it departs from New York's John F. Kennedy Airport every Friday at 4pm and arrives in Basel at 5:15am the following Saturday. Other flights from the United States require a change in Zurich or Paris to a connecting flight on **Swissair** (tel. toll free 800/221-4750).

By Train   Located on the major rail lines between Paris and Zurich, Basel is the most important railroad junction in the Juras. Trip time from Paris is between 4½ and 5 hours, depending on the train; from Zurich an express train can take as little as 1 hour.

By Car Basel is a junction point for highways from all over Europe. From Bern head north on N1, continuing north on N2 at the junction. From Zurich drive west on the same N1, turning north onto N2 at the junction.

SPECIAL EVENTS Basel goes wild during its 3 days of **carnival.** Festivities begin in late February or early March.

The third-largest city in Switzerland, Basel stands on the Rhine at the point where the French, German, and Swiss borders meet. At the entrance to the Swiss Rhineland, Basel is the capital of the half-canton of Basel-Stadt. On its borders are the French Vosges, the German Black Forest, and the Swiss Jura Mountains. Grossbasel, or Greater Basel, lies on the steep left bank, and Kleinbasel, or Lesser Basel, is on the right bank. The old imperial city stood at Grossbasel.

The two parts of the city are linked by half a dozen bridges, plus four ferries powered by river currents. The first bridge, erected in 1225, was for centuries the only one spanning the Rhine; it has been replaced by the present Mittlere Rheinbrücke (Middle Rhine Bridge).

The town was a Roman fort in A.D. 374, named Basilia, and was later ruled by prince-bishops for about 1,000 years. The Great Council met in Basel between 1431 and 1448, during which time a pope was crowned here. After Basel joined the Swiss Confederation, in 1501, it became a Protestant region. At the advent of the Reformation in 1529, it served as a refuge for victims of religious persecution. They flooded in from Holland, Italy, and France, bringing renewed vitality to Basel and laying the foundation for the city's great golden age in the 18th century.

As one of Switzerland's most important cultural centers, Basel saw the development of the printing press and the book trade. Erasmus, the great Dutch humanist and writer, published here, in 1516, the first edition of the New Testament in the original Greek. He is buried in the cathedral. Other Basel residents were the painter Holbein the Younger, who made portraits of Erasmus; the German philosopher Friedrich Nietzsche, who taught at the University of Basel; Theodor Herzl, who addressed the first Zionist World Congress here in 1897; and Jacob Burckhardt, a native, who achieved fame with his history of the Italian Renaissance.

Today the cultural traditions of Basel live on in its many museums (27 in all), art galleries, and schools. The city has become known as an international art and antiquities marketplace. In 1967 its citizens voted by referendum to purchase two well-known works by Picasso, *The Seated Harlequin* and *The Two Brothers*. Picasso was so moved that he donated four other paintings to Basel.

Basel is also a banking and industrial center; it is the headquarters of the Bank for International Settlement. Its chemical and pharmaceutical industry is also one of the most important in the world.

Except at carnival, the citizens of Basel are considered self-restrained and industrious. The German dramatist Rolf Hochhuth has observed: "English understatement looks like megalomania when compared to the people of Basel."

ORIENTATION

ARRIVING If you're flying to Basel, your plane will land at the **EuroAirport/ Basel-Mulhouse-Freiburg Airport** (Balse-Mulhouse in French), which is actually over the border in France, 5 miles northwest of Basel. A city bus runs between the airport and Basel's railroad terminus, departing every 20 to 30 minutes throughout the day; the 15-minute trip costs 1.60F ($1.15) one way. Swiss Customs rarely bothers people crossing the border.

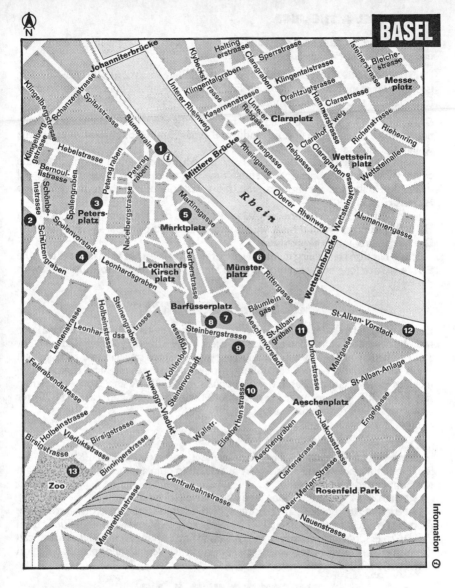

BASEL

Rhein

Johanniterbrücke

Mittlere Brücke

Wettsteinbrücke

Halting erstrasse
Sperrstrasse
Klybeckstrasse
Klingentalgraben
Claragraben
Klingentalstrasse
Isteinerstrasse
Bleichestrasse
Messeplatz
Drahtzugtsrasse
Clarastrasse
Kasernenstrasse
Unterer Rheinweg
Unter er Rebgass
Utengasse
Claraplatz
Clarahof
Richenstrasse
Riehenring
Rheingasse
Rebgasse
Claragraben
Wettstein platz
Oberer Rheinweg
Wettsteinsstrasse
Wettsteinallee
Alemanniengasse

Klingelbergstrasse
Schanzenstrasse
Spitalstrasse
Blumenrain
Hebelstrasse
Klingelberggstrasse
Petersgraben
Bernoullistrasse
Spalengraben
Petersgraben
Nadelbergstrasse
Martinsgasse
Schönbeinstrasse
Peters-platz
Spalenvorstadt
Marktplatz
Rathaus (5)
Leonhardsgraben
Leonhards Kirsch platz
Münster-platz
Schützengraben
Schützengraben
Münster (6)
Rittergasse
Leimenstrasse
Leonhardsstrasse
Steinengraben
Holbeinstrasse
Barfüsserplatz
Bäumleingasse
St-Alban-Vorstadt
Leonhar dss
Steinbergstrasse
Aeschenvorstadt
St-Alban-graben
Stadt-Casino (11)
Kohlenber
Steinenvorstadt
Dufourstrasse
Malzgasse
Feierabendstrasse
Heuwegge-Viadukt
Wallstr.
Elisabethenstrasse
St-Alban-Anlage
Holbeinstrasse
Viaduktstrasse
Birsigstrasse
Binningerstrasse
Aeschengraben
Aeschenplatz
St-Jakobsstrasse
Engelgasse
Birsigstrasse
Zoo
Centralbahnstrasse
Gartenstrasse
Rosenfeld Park
Margarethenstrasse
Peter-Merian-Strasse
Nauenstrasse

Information ⊖

● Basel

★ BERN

SWITZERLAND

Basel Tourist Office (Offizielles Verkehrsbüro Basel) (1)	Münster (6)
Historiches Museum (7)	Museum für Gegenwartskunst (12)
Jüdisches Museum d. Schweiz (4)	Rathaus (5)
Kirschgartenmuseum (10)	Spalentor (2)
Kunsthalle (9)	Stadt-Casino (11)
Kunstmuseum (8)	University of Basel (3)
	Zoologischer Garten (13)

Basel has three **railroad stations**—Swiss, French, and German—making it one of the largest rail junctions in Europe.

INFORMATION   The **Basel Tourist Office,** Blumenrain 2 (tel. 061/261-50-50), is open year round: Monday through Friday from 8:30am to 6pm and on Saturday from 8:30am to 1pm; closed Sunday.

CITY LAYOUT   Basel is divided into two parts by the Rhine: **Kleinbasel** to the north, which is the Rhine port and industrial center, and **Grossbasel,** south of the Rhine, the cultural and commercial center.

High above the south bank of the river, the **Münster** (Cathedral) dominates the city skyline. You may spend your entire time getting to know Grossbasel, the old town. The city has six bridges, the most historic of which is the **Mittlere Rheinbrücke.**

The heart of Basel is **Münsterplatz,** dominated by the Gothic **Rathaus** (Town Hall). Branching off from this square are two of the city's principal shopping arteries, **Gerbergasse** and **Freiestrasse.**

Basel has three remaining medieval gates: the **St. Alban Gate** east of the city, the **Spalen Gate** (one of the finest of its period in Europe), and **St. Johann's Gate** to the west.

GETTING AROUND

Basel has a good, relatively cheap public transportation system. **Bus or tram tickets** must be purchased at a station in advance. Clear maps will help you find your way. For 5.60F ($4.10), you can buy a ticket allowing you unlimited travel in two geographical zones for a 24-hour period. For unlimited travel in four geographical zones, which includes most of Greater Basel, the ticket costs 8F ($5.85). A single, once-only tram ride costs .80F (65¢) for travel beyond more than two stops and 1.60F ($1.70) for travel beyond more than four stops.

FAST FACTS

American Express   The office in Basel, at Aeschengraben 10 (tel. 272-66-90), is open Monday through Friday from 8:15am to 6pm and on Saturday from 9am to noon; closed Sunday.

Area Code   The telephone area code for Basel is 061.

Drugstore   Located in the center of the banking and old town area, **City Apotheke,** Aeschenvorstadt 4 (tel. 272-10-44), is open Monday through Friday from 7:30am to 6:30pm and on Saturday from 8am to 5pm. On weekends and at night, call the **emergency number** in Basel for medical, dental, and pharmacological emergencies: 261-25-15.

WHAT TO SEE & DO

THE TOP ATTRACTIONS

MÜNSTER (Cathedral), Munsterplatz. Tel. 312-32-01.

This red sandstone building towering over the old town was consecrated as far back as 1019. Destroyed by an earthquake in 1356, it was rebuilt along Romanesque and Gothic lines with a green-and-yellow tile roof. The cathedral has functioned as an abbey church since 1528.

The facade is richly decorated, depicting everything from prophets to virgins. The pulpit, which dates from 1486, was carved from a single block of stone. One of its many treasures, at the end of the south aisle, is an 11th-century bas-relief. There's a monumental slab on one of the pillars honoring Erasmus of Rotterdam, who died in Basel in 1536. The church also contains the tomb of Anna von Hohenberg, wife of Rudolf of Hapsburg.

The double cloister is entered on Rittergasse; it was erected in the 15th century on the foundations of the much earlier Roman structure. Visitors will find an excellent view from the twin Gothic towers of the cathedral. There are also two famous views of the cathedral— from the right bank of the Rhine and from the back of the **Pfalz** (palace). This 65-foot terrace also provides a splendid panorama of the Rhine and Germany's Black Forest.

Admission: Cathedral, free; towers, 2F ($1.45).

Open: Easter to mid-Oct, Mon–Fri 10am–6pm, Sat 10am–noon and 2–5pm, Sun 1–5pm; mid-Oct to Easter, Mon–Sat 10am–noon and 2–4pm. **Tram:** 8.

KUNSTMUSEUM (Fine Arts Museum), St. Alban-Graben 16. Tel. 271-08-28.

⭐ This is the best museum in Switzerland, offering one of Europe's most remarkable collections—everything from old masters to 20th-century paintings. You approach the massive building through a courtyard graced with sculptures by Rodin, Calder, and Hans Arp. The collections represent the development of art of the Upper Rhine Valley from the 14th to the 17th century, as well as works by outstanding modern artists.

In addition to paintings by Holbein the Younger, who lived in Basel between 1515 and 1538, and Konrad Witz, the Kunstmuseum has a stunning collection of impressionist and modern art, including works by van Gogh, Picasso, Braque, Klee, Chagall, and Dalí. The largest collection of Légers in the world is here.

Admission: 3F ($2.20); free on Sun.

Open: Tues–Sun 10am–5pm. **Tram:** 6 or 14.

KUNSTHALLE, Steinenberg 7. Tel. 272-08-28.

Located a block away from the Kunstmuseum, this gallery offers experimental works by contemporary artists.

Admission: 6F ($4.40).

Open: Tues–Sun 10am–5pm. **Directions:** Go left from Kunstmuseum on St. Alban-Graben, cross Bankenplatz, and follow Theaterstrasse. **Tram:** 6 or 14.

ZOOLOGISCHER GARTEN, adjoining the Hauptbahnhof. Tel. 281-00-00.

⭐ The Zoologischer Garten, or zoo, is one of the greatest in the world, famous for breeding endangered species in captivity. Located in a park in the middle of the city, it has some 2,000 animals and 600 different species. Trained elephants and sea lions perform tricks. The Vivarium is filled with everything from penguins to reptiles.

Admission: 10F ($7.30) adults, 5F ($3.65) children.

Open: Summer, daily 8am–6:30pm; winter, daily 8am–5:30pm. **Tram:** 6, 10, 16, or 17.

HISTORISCHES MUSEUM, Barfüsserplatz. Tel. 271-05-05.

This former 14th-century Franciscan church, on "Barefoot Square" (named for the unshod friars), contains many relics of medieval Basel. There are magnificent 15th-century tapestries and specimens of ecclesiastical art. One of the best-known sculptures is in the late Gothic style, depicting a babbling king. Its greatest exhibit is a reliquary bust of St. Ursula, in silver and gold, commissioned by the people of Basel to contain the saint's relics.

Admission: 3F ($2.20); free on Sun.

Open: Wed–Mon 10am–5pm. **Tram:** 6 or 14.

HAUS ZUM KIRSCHGARTEN, Elisabethenstrasse 27. Tel. 271-13-13.
Housed in an 18th-century mansion, this museum has an antique watch collection, stunning porcelain displays, toys, and period furnishings, including a kitchen. Look for the Aubusson tapestries.
Admission: 3F ($2.20).
Open: Tues–Sun 10am–5pm. **Tram:** 2.

JÜDISCHES MUSEUM [Jewish Museum of Switzerland], Kornhausgasse 8. Tel. 261-95-14.
This museum displays valuable items connected with Jewish worship, folklore, and history. Items include mementos of the first Zionist World Congress.
Admission: Free.
Open: Mon and Wed 2–5pm, Sun 10am–noon and 2–5pm. **Tram:** 3.

MUSEUM FOR GEGENWARTSKUNST [Museum for Contemporary Art], Alban-Rheinweg 60. Tel. 272-81-83.
This is one of Europe's leading museums of art from the 1960s to the present. It has works by Bruce Nauman, Richard Long, Jonathan Borofsky, Frank Stella, and Donald Judd.
Admission: 3F ($2.20).
Open: May–Oct, Wed–Mon 10am–5pm; Nov–Apr, Wed–Mon 10am–noon and 2–5pm. **Tram:** 6 or 14.

PORT OF BASEL and UNSER WEG ZU MEER [Our Way to the Sea]
Located north of the center of town, the Port of Basel, or Hafen, is the terminus for navigation on the Rhine. Opened in 1924, it is home to many people from all over Europe who live here on barges. From the silo terrace atop a Swiss Navigation Company tower, reached by elevator, you'll have a panoramic view of the Alsace plain and the Black Forest. An adjacent museum contains exhibits on the history of Swiss navigation.
Admission: Tower, 2F ($1.45); museum, 2F ($1.45) adults, 1F (75¢) children under 16.
Open: Tower and museum, daily 10am–noon and 2–5pm. **Tram:** 6 or 14.

MORE ATTRACTIONS

The **Rathaus** (Town Hall), on **Marktplatz,** dominates the market square of Basel. It was built in 1504 in the late Burgundian style, but additions have been made since then. The sandstone building is decorated with shields of the ancient city guildhouses and adorned with frescoes.

You may also want to visit the **University of Basel,** on the south side of Petersplatz. Founded in 1460, it is one of the oldest academic institutions in Switzerland. Its library contains a million volumes, including works by Martin Luther, Erasmus, and Zwingli. It also houses a collection of rare manuscripts. The school's charter was signed by Pope Pius II.

Spalentor (Spalen Gate), west of the university, marks the end of the medieval sector. It is considered one of the most beautiful gates in the country. Built in the 1400s, it was heavily restored in the 19th century. It has a pointed roof and two towers with battlements.

Finally, **Dreiländereck** (Three Countries' Corner), which juts out into the Rhine, is one of Basel's more unusual sites. If you walk around a pylon marking the spot, in just a few steps you can cross from Switzerland into Germany and then into France—and you don't need a passport.

ORGANIZED TOURS

Sightseeing tours of Basel, taking nearly 2 hours, cost 17F ($12.40) for adults and 8.50F ($6.20) for children. Departures are at 10am daily from in front of the Hotel Victoria, Centralbahnplatz 3-4 (tel. 261-55-01), at the railroad station.

From the end of May until the beginning of October, it's also possible to take a **guided stroll** through the old town. Tickets cost 6F ($4.40) for adults and 3F ($2.20) for children. Tours are conducted on Sunday and Monday, departing at 3pm from in front of the cathedral.

At some point you'll want to ride a **ferry,** one of a trio crossing to the right bank of the Rhine. The most interesting of these is the *Münsterfahre,* usually operating from 7am to 7pm throughout the year. A one-way passage for a pedestrian costs 1F (75¢). Once you get off, you can stroll along the Oberer Rheinweg, a river esplanade.

Basel is also a popular embarkation point for **cruises on the Rhine.** In summer, **Basler Personenschiffahrt,** Blumerain 2 (tel. 261-24-00), conducts cruises to Rheinfelden; they cost 22.40F ($16.40) for adults and 11.20F ($8.20) for children.

WHERE TO STAY

It's almost impossible to get hotel reservations during the Swiss Industries Fair, which attracts about a million visitors every spring. Rooms are also impossible to find at carnival time. Hotels then often raise their prices by 25% to 40%.

VERY EXPENSIVE

BASEL HILTON INTERNATIONAL, Aeschengraben 31, CH-4002 Basel. Tel. 061/271-66-22. Fax 061/271-52-20. 217 rms (all with bath), 10 suites. A/C MINIBAR TV TEL **Tram:** 6, 10, 16, or 17.

$ Rates: 185F–240F ($135.05–$175.20) single; 250F–320F ($182.50–$233.55) double; from 390F ($284.65) suite. Breakfast 21.50F ($15.70) extra. AE, DC, MC, V. **Parking:** 25F ($18.25).

Visitors can expect customary Hilton service here. The dramatic black steel-and-glass hotel in the center of town is connected via an underground shopping arcade with the main railway station. It offers tastefully furnished rooms, each containing a radio and other amenities. The hotel is maintained by general manager Urs Hitz and a well-trained multilingual staff.

Dining/Entertainment: The Wettstein Grill, one of the city's best restaurants, entertains many local businesspeople. The coffee shop serves light meals. The hotel has a sophisticated piano bar as well as a Polynesian-style disco.

Services: 24-hour room service.

Facilities: Indoor swimming pool, sauna, massage facilities, conference rooms, underground garage.

HOTEL DREI KÖNIGE, Blumenrain 8, CH-4001 Basel. Tel. 061/261-52-52. Fax 061/261-21-53. 83 rms (all with bath). A/C MINIBAR TV TEL **Tram:** 1, 6, 8, 14, or 15.

$ Rates (including continental breakfast): 193F–295F ($140.60–$215.30) single; 305F–440F ($222.60–$321.15) double. AE, DC, MC, V.

This is the oldest hotel in Switzerland, established in 1026 under the name Zur Blume ("At the Flower"). The white building, situated on the Rhine, contains a guest book (now a museum piece) with the names of Voltaire, Napoleon, Princess (later Queen) Victoria, and Kaiser Wilhelm II. History records that soon after the establishment of the inn, three kings (Conrad II, emperor of the Holy Roman Empire; his son, Henry III; and Rudolf III, the last king of Burgundy) drew up a treaty here that divided western Switzerland and southern France.

A tapestry resembling a Gobelin hangs in the wood-paneled lobby; the bar area is accented with pin lights and brass detail. Some of the rooms have their original ornamentation on the ceilings. All rooms have radios.

Dining/Entertainment: A canopy covers the riverfront café. Dinners are served on the famous terrace overlooking the Rhine.

Services: Room service.

Facilities: Elevator, terrace café, reception and sitting area.

HOTEL EULER, Centralbahnplatz 14, CH-4051 Basel. Tel. 23-45-00. 65 rms (all with bath). MINIBAR TV TEL **Tram:** 6, 10, 16, or 17.

$ Rates (including continental breakfast): 195F–295F ($142.35–$215.30) single; 285F–430F ($208–$313.85) double. AE, DC, MC, V.

The Hotel Euler has everything you'd expect from a grand hotel in Basel. Built in 1865 near the railroad station, it is elegantly detailed in white, with gray stone half-columns. The bedrooms are luxuriously paneled and impeccable.

Dining/Entertainment: The chandeliered dining room serves first-class dinners, while a snack bar offers less formal meals. The bar is richly ornamented with leather and wood.

Services: Baby-sitting, room service.

Facilities: Garden terrace.

EXPENSIVE

HOTEL BASEL, Münzgasse 12, CH-4058 Basel. Tel. 061/261-24-23. Fax 061/261-25-95. 72 rms (all with bath). MINIBAR TV TEL **Tram:** 6 or 14.

$ Rates (including continental breakfast): 130F–175F ($94.90–$127.75) single; 195F–270F ($142.35–$197.05) double. AE, DC, MC, V.

Situated in the old town, this modern building blends in well with its surroundings. Many of its bedrooms are wood paneled; some are under the eaves of the gabled roof. The public rooms are high-ceilinged, with crystal chandeliers. Prices are increased during trade fairs. A café with bright parasols serves drinks and coffee in front of the hotel while a rough-walled Weinkeller and a brasserie offer light snacks or full meals.

HOTEL EUROPE, Clarastrasse 43, CH-4058 Basel. Tel. 061/690-80-80, or toll free 800/44-UTELL in North America. Fax 061/691-82-01. 170 rms (all with bath). A/C MINIBAR TV TEL **Tram:** 2, 6, or 8.

$ Rates (including buffet breakfast): 165F–175F ($120.45–$127.75) single; 230F–250F ($167.90–$182.50) double. AE, DC, MC, V. **Parking:** 25F ($18.25).

Situated on a busy sidewalk, this modern, informal hotel is owned by the ETAP chain. Accommodations are usually compact, with baths tiled in dark colors, radios, and TVs (upon request). Most rooms overlook a quiet garden courtyard.

Dining/Entertainment: Dining and drinking facilities include the Europe Bar, a sidewalk café, and the Bajazzo, a dark restaurant furnished with wooden banquettes and decorated with brilliantly lit murals. A gourmet restaurant, Les Quatre Saisons, is devoted to the fresh produce of each season.

Services: Room service.

Facilities: 130-car underground garage, laundry facilities.

HOTEL INTERNATIONAL, Steinentorstrasse 25, CH-4001 Basel. Tel. 061/281-75-84, or toll free 800/223-5652 in North America. Fax 061/281-76-27. 200 rms (all with bath). A/C MINIBAR TV TEL **Tram:** 10, 16, or 17.

$ Rates: 190F–270F ($138.70–$197.05) single; 260F–375F ($189.75–$273.70) double. Buffet breakfast 25F ($18.25) extra. AE, DC, MC, V. **Parking:** 25F ($18.25).

This is a first-class hotel. The management keeps the hotel spotless and updated, which means replacing furniture when it becomes worn out. Many rooms have a view.

Dining/Entertainment: The Charolaise and the rustic Steinenpick are particularly popular with the Basel business community. A less-expensive tavern on the premises, Kaffi-Mühli, draws a less formal crowd.

Services: Room service, baby-sitting.

Facilities: Gym, sauna, indoor swimming pool, laundry facilities.

HOTEL MERIAN AM RHEIN, Rheingasse at Greifengasse 2, CH-4058 Basel. Tel. 061/681-00-00. Fax 061/681-11-01. 63 rms (all with bath). MINIBAR TV TEL **Tram:** 6 or 14.

$ Rates (including continental breakfast): 130F–145F ($94.90–$105.85) single; 185F–215F ($135.05–$156.95) double. AE, DC, MC, V.

This hotel lies just off the quay where a 13th-century bishop commissioned the construction of the only bridge across the Rhine between Lake Constance and the sea. Located in the oldest part of the city, the Mérian has charm, and updated conveniences such as comfortable beds. Rooms with views of the Rhine are more expensive. The Café Spitz is on the ground floor of the hotel.

HOTEL SCHWEIZERHOF, Centralbahnplatz 1, CH-4002 Basel. Tel. 061/271-28-33. Fax 061/271-29-19. 75 rms (all with bath). MINIBAR TV TEL **Tram:** 6, 10, 16, or 17.

$ Rates (including continental breakfast): 130F–180F ($94.90–$131.40) single; 200F–250F ($146–$182.50) double. AE, DC, MC, V.

Located near the train station, across from a landscaped park, this ornate hotel is six stories high, with a terrace and wrought-iron balconies. It has been in the Goetzinger family for three generations. The salons are decorated with Oriental rugs and some 19th-century antiques, while the bedrooms are modern. The hotel contains a bar and a restaurant.

MODERATE

HOTEL ADMIRAL, Rosentalstrasse 5, CH-4021 Basel. Tel. 061/691-77-77. Fax 061/691-77-89. 130 rms (all with bath). TV TEL **Tram:** 6 or 14.

$ Rates (including continental breakfast): 100F–150F ($73–$109.50) single; 160F–240F ($116.80–$175.20) double. MC, V.

This commercial hotel, next to the Swiss Trade Fair, offers views of the surrounding area. It has a heated outdoor swimming pool on the eighth floor. The sunny bedrooms are decorated in soothing colors and contain radios, among other amenities. The hotel also has a bar and a pleasant restaurant.

CITY HOTEL, Henric-Petri-Strasse 12, CH-4010 Basel. Tel. 061/272-78-11. Fax 061/272-78-81. 85 rms (all with bath). TV TEL **Tram:** 6, 10, 16, or 17.

$ Rates (including continental breakfast): 100F–150F ($73–$109.50) single; 160F–240F ($116.80–$175.20) double. AE, DC, MC, V.

This hotel is located near St. Elisabeth's Church, not far from the railroad station. It's informal and modern, with oversize windows overlooking the street or the tree-filled central garden. The lobby has a gray marble floor and an Oriental rug. Bedrooms are well equipped, with white and natural-grain furniture.

HOTEL DRACHEN, Aeschenvorstadt 24, CH-4010 Basel. Tel. 061/272-

90-90. Fax 061/272-90-02. 40 rms (all with bath). MINIBAR TV TEL **Tram:** 6 or 14.
$ Rates (including continental breakfast): 125F–160F ($91.25–$116.80) single; 190F–225F ($138.70–$164.25) double. MC, V.

Located on a commercial street, close to the Kunsthaus and the old city, this well-established hotel has attracted many repeat visitors. It is artfully maintained by Joe and Pia Dietlin, who offer small but pleasant rooms. Bathrooms are modern and spacious, with dark, checkerboard-tile floors. All units have radios and safes.

HOTEL MÜNCHNERHOF, Riehenring 75, CH-4058 Basel. Tel. 061/691-77-80. Fax 061/641-14-90. 50 rms (40 with bath). TV TEL **Tram:** 1, 2, 6, or 8.
$ Rates (including continental breakfast): 55F–75F ($40.15–$54.75) single without bath, 85F–160F ($62.05–$116.80) single with bath; 80F–140F ($58.40–$102.20) double without bath, 120F–245F ($87.60–$178.85) double with bath. AE, DC, MC, V.

In front of the Swiss Trade Fair and close to the railroad station, the Hotel Münchnerhof is housed in a brownish-ocher building with white trim and small balconies. The attractive interior is traditional. In addition to the hotel, the Früh family also operates the two restaurants, known for their French and Italian cuisine. One of the restaurants has live music.

HOTEL SPALENBRUNNEN, Schützenmattstrasse 2, CH-4051 Basel. Tel. 061/25-82-33. Fax 061/25-00-37. 32 rms (all with bath). MINIBAR TV TEL **Tram:** 6 or 14.
$ Rates (including continental breakfast): 100F–150F ($73–$109.50) single; 160F–240F ($116.80–$175.20) double. AE, DC, MC, V.

This shuttered, gabled house is conveniently located near a tram line, on a public square a few buildings from the Spalentor. Dating from the Middle Ages, it's set in charming surroundings, with a view of a typically Swiss, red-stone fountain. The bedrooms have modern furnishings, with carpeting, tile bath, and a radio. The spacious restaurant is decorated like a nightclub.

INEXPENSIVE

HOTEL KRAFFT AM RHEIN, Rheingasse 12, CH-4058 Basel. Tel. 061/961-88-77. Fax 061/96-43-00. 52 rms (45 with shower). TV TEL **Tram:** 8.
$ Rates (including continental breakfast): 60F–80F ($43.80–$58.40) single without shower, 90F–135F ($65.70–$98.55) single with shower; 110F–180F ($80.30–$131.40) double without shower, 145F–240F ($105.85–$175.20) double with shower. AE, DC, MC, V.

Located across the river from the old town's Rathaus and Münster, the Hotel Krafft am Rhein offers an attractive terrace café overlooking the river. The spacious public rooms are decorated with 19th-century antiques, oversize gilt mirrors, and Oriental rugs. The comfortable, modern rooms often have good views. The Waldmeyer-Schneiter family also manages the well-known restaurant, Zem Schnooggeloch.

HOTEL ST. GOTTHARD, Centralbahnstrasse 13, CH-4051 Basel. Tel. 061/271-52-50. Fax 061/271-52-14. 60 rms (41 with bath). MINIBAR TV TEL **Tram:** 6, 10, 16, or 17.
$ Rates (including continental breakfast): 70F ($51.10) single without bath, 150F

($109.50) single with bath; 100F ($73) double without bath, 240F ($175.20) double with bath. AE, DC, MC, V.

Located opposite the train station, this building has arched canopies stretching above the two doors and three picture windows. The hotel, run by a third generation of the Geyer-Arel family, offers comfortable and safe bedrooms. Some rooms in the main building contain tile baths; others, however, have only sinks. You may prefer a room in the more modern annex. An American restaurant chain operates the dining room and restaurant. The hotel's bar, the Gotthard Club, has a cozy atmosphere.

HOTEL STEINENSCHANZE, Steinengraben 69, CH-4051 Basel. Tel. 061/272-53-53. 44 rms (8 with shower and toilet). **Tram:** 6 or 14.
$ Rates (including continental breakfast): 50F ($36.90) single with sink, 80F ($58.40) single with shower and toilet; 80F ($58.40) double with sink, 110F ($80.30) double with shower and toilet. MC, V.

Located a 10-minute walk from the train station, this modern, five-story hotel has many large windows and a garden. Rooms are simply furnished and sunny. Two rooms have a private phone. Laundry facilities are available.

WHERE TO DINE

Five centuries ago the humanist Enea Silvio de' Piccolomini (who later became Pope Pius II) said about Baslers: "Most of them are devotees of good living. They live at home in style and spend most of their time at the table." Not much has changed.

EXPENSIVE

GOLDEN GATE, Steinengraben 42. Tel. 271-04-13.
   Cuisine: FRENCH. **Reservations:** Required. **Tram:** 6 or 14.
$ Prices: Appetizers 17.50F–50F ($12.80–$36.50); main courses 60F–120F ($43.80–$87.60). AE, DC, MC, V.
   Open: Mon–Sat 9am–midnight.

Golden Gate serves excellent meals. In the summer you can dine in the attractive garden. The Markus Hauenstein family and the accommodating staff serve many French specialties, beginning with feuilletée de saumon, followed by wide-flap mushrooms in the Provençal style. You might also try the escargots Bercy, coquilles St-Jacques, filet of beef Calvados, sole meunière, or veal kidney with mustard sauce.

RESTAURANT STUCKL BRUDERHOLZ, Bruderholzallee 42. Tel. 35-82-22.
   Cuisine: FRENCH. **Reservations:** Required. **Bus:** 15.
$ Prices: Appetizers 18F–25F ($13.15–$18.25); main courses 25F–50F ($18.25–$36.50); fixed-price meals 75F ($54.75) at lunch, from 100F ($73) at dinner, 160F ($116.80) 10-course *menu surprise*. AE, DC, MC, V.
   Open: Lunch Tues–Sat noon–1:30pm; dinner Tues–Sat 6:30–9:30pm.

Located a short distance outside the city limits, Hans and Susi Stuckl's gourmet restaurant is renowned throughout Switzerland. Customers may eat inside or on the backyard terrace, by the garden. The former private residence is decorated with antiques and oil paintings. A favorite room is the Salon Vert, with its green napery, Empire chairs, and light-patterned Oriental rug. There are two other well-furnished dining rooms as well.

Specialties may include a filet of saltwater red mullet with coriander, a terrine of foie gras, a tomato stuffed with frogs' legs and served in a thyme-cream sauce, or a lobster ragoût with truffles and baby leeks. The selle d'agneau (lamb) is cooked with a gratin of green beans, and the sweetbreads are masterful. For dessert I'd suggest a compote of pears or a soufflé made with the fresh fruits of the season.

LA ROTISSERIE DES ROIS, in the Hotel Drei Könige, Blumenrain 8. Tel. 261-52-52.
   Cuisine: SWISS. **Reservations:** Recommended. **Tram:** 1, 6, 8, 14, or 15.
$ **Prices:** Appetizers 15F–25F ($10.95–$18.25); main courses 28F–55F ($20.45–$40.15); fixed-price meal ($64.25). AE, DC, MC, V.
   Open: Lunch daily noon–2:30pm; dinner daily 6:30–10pm.

This elegant restaurant is famous for its riverside terrace, which in midsummer sets tables close to the historic waters of the Rhine. The restaurant offers a sophisticated cuisine du marché. Specialties change with the seasons; you might try warm goose liver with light port wine sauce, guinea fowl with chanterelles, breast of chicken with a leek-flavored cream sauce, mussel soup flavored with saffron, or chateaubriand in a confit of shallots.

SCHLOSS BINNINGEN, Schlossgasse 5 at Binningen. Tel. 47-20-55.
   Cuisine: SWISS/FRENCH. **Reservations:** Required. **Transportation:** Take a taxi.
$ **Prices:** Appetizers 15F–25F ($10.95–$18.25); main courses 35F–60F ($25.55–$43.80). AE, DC, MC, V.
   Open: Lunch Tues–Sat noon–2pm; dinner Tues–Sat 6:30–10pm. **Closed:** July 15–Aug 7.

This 16th-century château and its grounds are owned by the township but managed by independent entrepreneurs. The entrance hall is appropriately baronial, and the grand dining rooms contain an antique loggia (presumably used long ago by chamber orchestras).

The wine cellar is among the best in the region, with at least 50 vintages not listed on the menu (the wine steward will make appropriate suggestions). The menu changes at least three times a year but is likely to include such delectable dishes as a timbale de langoustines with caviar, a selle de chevreuil roti (saddle of roasted roebuck), or fresh lobster, followed by a cold soufflé.

WETTSTEIN GRILL, in the Basel Hilton International, Aeschengraben 31. Tel. 271-66-22.
   Cuisine: SWISS. **Reservations:** Required. **Tram:** 6, 10, 16, or 17.
$ **Prices:** Appetizers: 15F–25F ($10.95–$18.25); main courses 28F–55F ($20.45–$40.15). AE, DC, MC, V.
   Open: Lunch noon–3pm; dinner 7–11pm.

This chic enclave is near the hotel's bar, one flight below street level. Here, some of the greatest culinary creations of the region are served with unobtrusive formality amid a scattering of antique portraits of Swiss heroes. Specialties change with the season. They may include smoked giant shrimp with horseradish, saffron-laced seafood soup, sliced veal in an apple-cream sauce with Calvados, mignon of beef with foie gras, and veal with morels, followed by an elaborate selection of desserts.

MODERATE

CHEZ DONATI, St. Johanns-Vorstadt 48. Tel. 322-09-19.
   Cuisine: FRENCH/ITALIAN. **Reservations:** Required. **Tram:** 15.

$ Prices: Appetizers 5.50F–25F ($4–$18.25); main courses 16.50F–45F ($12.05–$32.85). AE, DC, MC, V.

Open: Lunch Wed–Sun noon–2pm; dinner Wed–Sun 6–10pm. **Closed:** July.

Baslers come here to savor the Italian specialties and the brasserie-style intimacy amid statues and elegant columns. The chef's favorite specialties are homemade lasagne verdi and ravioli ricotta, followed by scaloppine in purgatorio and fegato (liver) alla veneziana. From October to December the chef is able to obtain white truffles, which he uses with style. He also makes a spicy scampi maison.

FISCHSTUBE ZUM PFAUEN, St. Johanns-Vorstadt 13. Tel. 261-32-67.

Cuisine: SWISS. **Reservations:** Required. **Tram:** 6 or 14.

$ Prices: Appetizers 15F–25F ($10.95–$18.25); main courses 30F–42F ($21.90–$30.65). MC, V.

Open: Lunch daily Tues–Sun 11:30am–2pm; dinner daily Tues–Sun 6–10pm. **Closed:** Sun June–Aug, mid-July to mid-Aug.

This restaurant, in a contemporary town house with an understated decor, is known for its fish specialties. Dishes include French preparations of perch, fera, zander, salmon, angler, salmon-trout, and shrimp.

HOTEL DRACHEN RESTAURANT, Aeschenvorstadt 24. Tel. 272-90-90.

Cuisine: INTERNATIONAL. **Reservations:** Recommended. **Tram:** 6 or 14.

$ Prices: Appetizers 10F–22F ($7.30–$16.05); main courses 18F–35F ($13.15–$25.95); fixed-price meal (without dessert) 42F ($30.65). Snack bar, items from 18F ($13.15). MC, V.

Open: Restaurant, lunch daily noon–2pm or later; dinner Mon–Sat 6pm–midnight, Sun 6–9pm. Snack bar, Mon–Sat 7am–midnight, Sun 11am–9pm.

The Hotel Drachen offers a modern decor and some of the finest meals in the city. The international menu has many French dishes. Favorite orders include filet goulash Stroganoff, selle d'agneau (lamb), and veal piccata, along with truite (trout) au bleu. The cellar boasts more than 150 wines. Downstairs, the snack bar serves hot food and drinks.

KUNSTHALLE RESTAURANT, Steinenberg 7. Tel. 272-42-33.

Cuisine: FRENCH/ITALIAN. **Reservations:** Recommended. **Tram:** 6 or 14.

$ Prices: Appetizers 10F–22F ($7.30–$16.05); main courses 18F–32F ($13.15–$23.35). No credit cards.

Open: Main dining room, lunch Mon–Sat noon–2pm; dinner Mon–Sat 6–10pm. Downstairs bar area, Mon–Sat from 8am; food 11am–midnight.

This elegant restaurant, looking out into a garden, has pictures from the Kunsthalle (art gallery) on its walls to complement the chandeliers and handsome rugs. Stone arches lead into the bar area, with murals on the walls. There is also a bar upstairs.

In the main dining room, cold specialties are served on a buffet, while white-jacketed waiters take your orders for hot courses. Selections range from such appetizers as sherry consommé to main dishes like steak or sole with risotto. In the downstairs bar, you can enjoy some of the same specials, as well as omelets and salads.

L'ESCARGOT, Centralbahnstrasse 14. Tel. 271-53-33.

Cuisine: SWISS/FRENCH. **Reservations:** Not needed. **Tram:** 6, 10, 16, or 17.

$ Prices: Appetizers 10F–15F ($7.30–$10.95); main courses 10F–70F ($7.30–$51.10). AE, DC, MC, V.

Open: Lunch Mon–Sat noon–2:30pm; dinner Mon–Sat 6–10:30pm. **Closed:** July.

L'Escargot, one of the best spots in Basel to try la cuisine bourgeoise, is located in a train station, at the bottom of green terrazzo steps. It's warm and cozy, with discreet lighting and illuminated hanging ceramic pots. The bar area is decorated with folkloric illustrations of castles and trees.

Part of the menu is devoted to French regional cooking, including tripe à la mode de Caen and other dishes. The kitchen prepares snails in three different ways. In season you may order roebuck, and all year round you can try such unusual dishes as eggplant gratiné in the Egyptian style. For dessert, I've always enjoyed the Apfelstrudel.

SAFRAN-ZUNFT, Gerbergasse 11. Tel. 261-19-59.
Cuisine: SWISS. **Reservations:** Recommended. **Tram:** 6 or 14.
$ Prices: Appetizers 8F–35F ($5.85–$25.55); main courses 28F–54F ($20.45–$39.40); fixed-price lunch 15F ($10.95) and 25F ($18.25). AE, DC, MC, V.
Open: Lunch Mon–Sat noon–2pm; dinner Mon–Sat 6–10pm.

Outside this medieval stone building, a wrought-iron sign hangs over the street with the restaurant's logo, a gluttonous monk inhaling the aroma from a goblet of wine. Inside, the restaurant is set up in a tavern style, with red-checked tablecloths, wood paneling, and oversize Gothic windows.

Most guests order the fondue Bacchus, with veal and all the condiments. The soups, most often clear broths, are usually good. The kitchen serves more elaborate specialties and elegant appetizers, such as caviar or smoked salmon. You'll regularly find veal steak and chateaubriand on the menu.

SCHLÜSSELZUNFT, Freie Strasse 25. Tel. 261-20-46.
Cuisine: CONTINENTAL. **Reservations:** Recommended. **Tram:** 6 or 14.
$ Prices: Appetizers 12F–20F ($8.75–$14.60); main courses 18F–38F ($13.15–$27.75); three-course fixed-price lunch or dinner 35F–45F ($25.55–$32.85). DC, MC.
Open: Lunch Mon–Sat noon–2pm; dinner Mon–Sat 6–11pm.

This is one of the oldest guildhouses in Basel. The restaurant has a menu with seasonal specialties, offering various types of fish and, in the autumn, venison. Regular specialties include veal curry, tenderloin steak with goose liver and morels, shredded calves' kidney in a Madeira sauce, and shredded veal and kidney in a cream sauce with Spätzli. There are also well-prepared, traditional soups and a fine selection of pasta, including cannelloni au gratin.

ST. ALBAN ECK, St. Albanvorstadt 60. Tel. 271-03-20.
Cuisine: SWISS. **Reservations:** Recommended. **Tram:** 6 or 14.
$ Prices: Appetizers 10F–18F ($7.30–$13.15); main courses 22F–38F ($16.05–$27.75). AE, DC, MC, V.
Open: Lunch Mon–Fri 11:30am–2:30pm; dinner Mon–Fri 6:30–11:30pm.
Closed: July 12–Aug 12.

Set in an antique district filled with architectural charm, St. Alban Eck is a small, intimate restaurant with graceful wooden tables. The building has retained its original stonework and beautiful oak door. Prices range from moderate to expensive. You might want to try filet of perch with almonds, mignons de veau in Calvados, or grilled sole with a rémoulade sauce.

WALLISER KANNE, Gerbergasse 50. Tel. 261-70-17.
Cuisine: SWISS/FRENCH. **Reservations:** Recommended. **Tram:** 1, 4, 8, or 14.
$ Prices: Appetizers 16F–24F ($11.70–$17.50); main courses 30F–60F ($21.90–$43.80); lunch 18F ($13.15). No credit cards.
Open: Lunch Tues–Sat 11:30am–2pm; dinner Tues–Sat 5:30–11pm.

This traditional Swiss restaurant attracts a loyal following of government and business leaders, soccer stars, and local celebrities. A typical meal might start with an hors d'oeuvre of air-dried alpine meat, followed by a veal steak with a savory hollandaise sauce. Swiss Rösti accompany most platters. For dessert, try the Opfelchuechlis (apple fritters) or an excellent chocolate mousse.

INEXPENSIVE

DA ROBERTO, Kuchengasse 3. Tel. 272-46-80.

Cuisine: ITALIAN. **Reservations:** Not needed. **Tram:** 6, 10, 16, or 17.

$ Prices: Appetizers 8F–15F ($5.85–$10.95); main courses 15F–30F ($10.95–$21.90). MC, V.

Open: Lunch daily 11:30am–2pm; dinner daily 5pm–midnight.

Located one block from the central train station, on a narrow side street with lots of activity, this restaurant attracts younger Baslers. Depending on what you order, you can dine here rather inexpensively, enjoying good food, a lively atmosphere, and polite but informal service. There are three separate seating areas, decorated with checked tablecloths and paneled walls. At night the young crowd often drops in for the tasty pizzas, which start at 15F ($10.95). You can also order a daily special, whether a light gnocchi with gorgonzola or filet of beef with fresh mushrooms and homemade fettuccine. Soups are a good buy, as are the spaghetti dishes.

RESTAURANT ELISABETHENSTÜBLI, Elisabethenstrasse 34. Tel. 272-11-05.

Cuisine: SWISS. **Reservations:** Not needed. **Tram:** 6, 10, 16, or 17.

$ Prices: Appetizers 12F–18F ($8.75–$13.15); main dishes 18F–35F ($13.15–$25.55). No credit cards.

Open: Drinks and snacks Mon–Sat 8am–11pm; lunch Mon–Sat 11:30am–2pm; dinner Mon–Sat 6:30–10pm.

The owners prepare well-seasoned budget fare in this charming restaurant. The intimate lighting, green trim, and checkered tablecloths make the whole place cozy. Expect to find the standard Swiss dishes, such as fondue. Little English is spoken here, but the polite staff welcomes foreign customers as well as locals.

RESTAURANT MARKTHALLE, Viaduktstrasse 8. Tel. 272-64-64.

Cuisine: SWISS. **Reservations:** Not needed. **Tram:** 6, 10, 16, or 17.

$ Prices: Appetizers 8F–22F ($5.85–$16.05); main courses 15F–32F ($10.95–$23.35). No credit cards.

Open: Lunch Mon–Sat 11am–2pm; dinner Mon–Sat 5–10pm; Sun 10am–10pm.

This restaurant stands near the central railroad station in the heart of Basel. A long, modern building curves around a busy street corner. Customers can sit on a raised dais, apart from the main room, or at a table in the large room, near the windows. Watch for the daily specials. In season the wild-game dishes might include peppersteak of wild stag prepared hunter's style with homemade Spätzli and mushrooms.

ZUM GOLDENEN STERNEN, St. Albanrheinweg 70. Tel. 272-16-66.

Cuisine: CONTINENTAL. **Reservations:** Recommended. **Tram:** 6 or 12.

$ Prices: Appetizers 8F–15F ($5.85–$10.95); main courses 18F–28F ($13.15–$20.45); fixed-price lunch from 25F ($18.25). AE, DC, MC, V.

Open: Lunch daily noon–2:30pm; dinner daily 6–10pm.

Set on the banks of the Rhine, this is the oldest pub in Switzerland, dating from 1421. Richly decorated with folkloric stencils, stained glass, and carved paneling, it's well known to many different generations of Baslers. The dishes are classic. Appetizers are especially tempting, particularly the smoked eel and smoked trout. I've visited this establishment on several occasions over the years and have always been fond of the terrine maison and the lobster soup. For the main course I'd recommend carré d'agneau (lamb), filet of veal with citron, vol-au-vent, or Hungarian goulash with Spätzli.

SHOPPING

The fashionable shopping street of Basel is Freie Strasse, leading to the market square and town hall.

ANTIQUES

ANTIQUITES M & G. SEGAL, Aeschengraben 14. Tel. 272-39-08.
Founded in 1862, this is one of Switzerland's oldest and most respected antique shops. Furniture, gold and silver articles, faïence, porcelain, and paintings are among the impressive collections of antiques from the 16th to the 19th century. Georges B. Ségal, representing the fourth generation of the founding family, is a renowned dealer, who oversees the shop and an exhibit at the annual fall Swiss Art and Antique Fair.

ART

ERNEST BEYELER GALLERY, Baunleingasse 9. Tel. 272-54-12.
Collectors from all over the world frequent this internationally famous gallery in search of paintings and sculpture.

GALERIE GISELE LINDER, Elisabethenstrasse 54. Tel. 272-83-77.
The average visitors to Basel won't be in the market for an avant-garde painting, but many may be interested in the European art scene as glimpsed at Gisele Linder's gallery. The gallery is at the edge of an inner-city park across from the Basel Hilton, not far from the railroad station. Open Tuesday, Wednesday, and Friday from 2 to 6:30pm, on Thursday from 2 to 8pm, and on Saturday from 10am to 4pm.

COINS

MÜNZEN UND MEDAILLEN A.G., Malzgasse 25. Tel. 272-75-44.
Whether you're looking to buy or to sell, this shop offers a wide selection of coins and medals. The collection includes everything from ancient artifacts to 19th-century pieces.

CHINA & GLASS

FÜGLISTALLER, Freie Strasse 23. Tel. 261-78-78.
Füglistaller, or Fügli, as the Baslers call it, sells the best in European china, glass, and reasonably priced gifts. The beautiful interior design includes a famous staircase and a chandelier.

LEATHER

BALLY CAPITOL ZUM PFLUG, Freie Strasse 38. Tel. 261-18-97.
This store sells shoes and leather goods from the most important shoe manufacturer in Switzerland. The five-story building has big display windows, three-quarter columns, and bas-relief carvings. There is also an exclusive clothes boutique.

LEDER-DROESER, Eisengasse 11. Tel. 261-42-53.

This landmark shop between Marktplatz and the Mittlere Brücke offers a variety of fine leather goods, as well as clothing, umbrellas, foulards, and luggage.

TOBACCO

DAVIDOFF, Aeschenvorstadt 4. Tel. 272-47-50.

This smokeshop stocks a collection of brier-wood and meerschaum pipes, along with cigarettes and cigars from around the world, including Havana.

WATCHES

KURZ, Freie Strasse 39. Tel. 261-26-20.

This store has an impressive display of watches, jewelry, and mantel clocks. It is considered one of the best places in town to purchase a Swiss watch. Stocks are ample.

EVENING ENTERTAINMENT

BORA-BORA DISCO, in the Basel Hilton International, Aeschengraben 31. Tel. 271-66-22.

Located two floors below the lobby, this is a relatively small, plush room with a Polynesian theme. The DJ plays everything from regional music and Mozart to Elvis Presley and disco. It's open on Sunday, Wednesday, and Thursday from 9pm to 2am, and on Friday and Saturday from 9pm to 3am. Drinks begin at 11F ($8.05) each.

Admission: Free.

STADT-CASINO, Barfüssenplatz. Tel. 271-23-23.

Musical acts offered in the Hans-Huber-Saal are frequently televised. You enter through the massive 1930s entranceway. Drinks cost 18F ($13.15) and up.

Admission: Free.

CAFE DES ARTS (Kunsthalle-Garten), Steinenberg 7. Tel. 271-36-19.

This café, one of the finest places in the city for drinks, is in front of the famous Tingueley fountain in the garden of the Kunsthalle. In the summer you might choose one of the café tables in the forecourt, among ivy-covered trellises and modern and classical sculpture. Inside are brass chandeliers and walls covered with risqué art. You'll hear a blend of American pop and rock music. It's open Sunday through Thursday from 9am to midnight and on Friday and Saturday from 9pm to 1am. Wine runs 3.50F ($2.55).

CAFE ATLANTIS, Klosterberg 13. Tel. 272-34-00.

Favored by the city's rock-star hopefuls and college students, this modern hangout has amber windows, beams, and columns, and is open for coffee in the morning. While you're there, be sure to walk up to the second floor, with its psychedelic mirrors, two bars, and red coffee room, for a view of the cathedral. It's open Monday through Friday from 8am to 1am, Saturday from 10am to 2am, and on Sunday from 10am to 1am. Drinks begin about 12F ($8.75).

Admission: About 8F ($5.85), but varies according to the show.

HAZYCLUB, Heuwaage. Tel. 272-99-82.

At this club, live musicians play pop music for the under-35 crowd. There's also a restaurant inside. Open daily from 9pm to 2am. Drinks start at 14F ($10.20).

Admission: Free.

HOTEL EULER, Centralbahnplatz 14. Tel. 272-45-00.

Popular with the international business community, this elegant bar contains a coffered ceiling, crimson fabric, leather chairs and banquettes, wood tables, and small brass lamps. The noise level rarely goes above a murmur. Open daily from 11am to midnight. Drinks begin at 14F ($10.20).

KRONEN BAR, in the Hotel Drei Könige, Blumenrain 8. Tel. 261-52-52.

What's said to be the oldest hotel in Europe is also the host to some of the most avant-garde music in town. The popular piano bar features many American pianists. This spot is decorated with wood paneling and a collection of silk-screened prints. Live music is played Monday through Saturday from 6 to 8pm and 8:30pm to midnight. Hard liquor costs 14F ($10.20) and up.

OLD CITY BAR, in the Basel Hilton International, Aeschengraben 31. Tel. 271-66-22.

This is one of the most elegant and attractive places for a late-night drink or a before-dinner cocktail. The decor is plush, intimate, and low-key, with a pianist thumping out everything from sambas to show tunes. The bar is one floor beneath the Hilton's main lobby, at the bottom of a dramatically curved and illuminated staircase. Open Saturday through Thursday from 11am to midnight and on Friday from 11am to 1am. Drinks run 8F ($5.85).

---

2. SOLOTHURN

27 miles N of Bern, 16 miles NE of Biel

GETTING THERE By Train Solothurn has frequent rail connections to the major cities of Switzerland, including Zurich (65 min.), Geneva (2 hr.), and Biel (1 hr.).

By Car From Bern head north along the N1, veering west at the turnoff to Solothurn.

ESSENTIALS The Solothurn tourist office, the **Verkehrsbüro,** Hauptgasse 69, on Kronenplatz (tel. 065/22-19-26), will provide you with a map and pinpoint several day excursions. The **telephone area code** for Solothurn is 065.

The capital of a canton by the same name, Solothurn, according to a 16th-century rhyme, is "the oldest place in Celtis save Trier." Located on the banks of the Aare, at the foot of the Jura Mountains, it has been fortified many times. Roman inscriptions calling it Salodurum have been found, as have the remains of a Roman castrum.

WHAT TO SEE & DO

Solothurn's **old town** is on the left bank of the river, still partially enclosed by 17th-century walls. Inside are many Renaissance and baroque buildings. Solothurn is called Switzerland's finest baroque town. It was at its peak from the 16th to the 18th century, when it was the residence of the French ambassadors to the Swiss Confederation. Solothurn became part of the Confederation as early as 1481.

The old town is entered through the **Biel Gate,** or the Basel Gate. The heart of the old sector is **Marktplatz,** with its clock tower and produce markets on Wednesday and Saturday morning from 9am to noon. The 15th-century **Rathaus** (town hall) has a notable Renaissance doorway. The two most colorful streets are **Hauptgasse** (Main Street) and **Schaalgasse,** where you'll see many wrought-iron signs and brightly painted shutters.

The baroque **Cathedral of St. Ursus**—said to stand on the spot where its namesake was martyred—dates from the 18th century and has been the seat of the bishop of Basel since 1828. The cathedral, just inside the 16th-century Basel Gate, was constructed by builders from Ticino, which explains its Italian artistry. Try to visit the gardens on the east side.

The **Jesuitenkirche,** or Jesuits' church, on Hauptgasse between the cathedral and the marketplace, dates from 1680 and contains a frescoed, three-bay nave.

MUSEUM ALTES ZEUGHAUS (Old Arsenal), Zeughausplatz 1. Tel. 23-35-28.

Slightly to the northwest of the cathedral stands this museum, which houses one of the largest collections of weapons in Europe. There are fascinating exhibits of medieval weaponry and flags, as well as of Swiss military uniforms.

Admission: Free.

Open: Mar–Oct, Thurs 10am–noon and 2–9pm, Fri–Sun 10am–noon and 2–5pm; Nov–Feb, Tues–Wed and Fri 2–5pm, Thurs 2–9pm, Sat–Sun 10am–noon and 2–5pm.

KUNSTMUSEUM SOLOTHURN (Municipal Fine Arts Museum), Werkhofstrasse 30. Tel. 22-23-07.

Visit this museum if only to see the *Madonna of Solothurn,* by Holbein the Younger. Also outstanding is a 15th-century painting on wood from the Rhenish school, the *Madonna with the Strawberries.* The museum emphasizes Swiss art from the mid-19th century to the present. A collection of excellent works represents the artistry of Buchser, Frolicher, Hodler, Vallotton, Trachsel, Amiet, Berger, and Gubler, among others.

Admission: Optional.

Open: Tues–Sun 10am–noon and 2–5pm.

NEARBY ATTRACTIONS

There are many possible excursions from Solothurn, such as a trip by boat on the Aare River to **Biel,** with a stopover at the **Altreu,** the first stork colony in Switzerland. If you have 2 hours to spare, take the 6-mile run to the **Weissenstein,** one of the country's major attractions—its panoramic view of the Jura is breathtaking. Driving will be difficult, even dangerous, on narrow roads with hairpin curves, so it's best to take the chair lift to the Kurhaus Weissenstein from the Oberdorf station. On a clear day you can see Mont Blanc, Bern, and Neuchâtel Lake.

In fair weather the lift runs Monday through Saturday from 8:30am to 12:30pm and 1:30 to 5:45pm, and on Sunday from 8am to 6pm; in the winter, Monday through Saturday from 9am to noon and 1:30 to 5pm, and on Sunday from 8am to 5pm. The round-trip fare is about 12F ($8.75).

WHERE TO STAY

HOTEL KRONE, Hauptgasse 64, CH-4500 Solothurn. Tel. 065/22-44-12. Fax 065/22-37-24. 42 rms (all with bath). TV TEL

$ Rates (including breakfast): 130F–160F ($94.90–$116.80) single; 160F–210F ($116.80–$153.30) double. AE, DC, MC, V.

The hotel Krone, near the Clock Tower, is one of the oldest inns in the country and basks in its reputation as the hotel where Napoleon's wife, Josephine, stayed for several days in 1811. Run by the Küng family, the inn is a member of Ambassador Swiss hotels and still attracts history buffs. The gilt lettering on the pink facade spells out the name in French—Hôtel de la Couronne. The bedrooms are old-fashioned. The hotel also has a restaurant.

HOTEL/RESTAURANT ROTER TURM, Hauptgasse 52, CH-4500 Solothurn. Tel. 065/22-96-21. Fax 065/22-98-65. 23 rms (all with bath). MINIBAR TV TEL

$ **Rates** (including breakfast): 83F–93F ($60.60–$67.90) single; 135F–165F ($98.55–$120.45) double. AE, DC, MC, V.

Outside this "Red Tower," an illuminated sign spells out the name of the hotel in French. The Lorenz family provides modern, comfortable bedrooms—the largest of which overlook the front square. All rooms have a radio.

On the lobby level is an informal brasserie open throughout the day for drinks, snacks, and meals. The fifth-floor Rôtisserie, however, is far more elegant; it serves lunch from 11:30am to 2:30pm and dinner from 6:30 to midnight daily. Specialties include fresh filet of sole in butter, Italian-style scampi, filets of perch meunière, smoked trout, and veal steak with morels. Reservations are recommended.

WHERE TO DINE

HOTEL KRONE RESTAURANT, Hauptgasse 64. Tel. 22-44-12.
Cuisine: SWISS. **Reservations:** Recommended.
$ **Prices:** Appetizers 15F–22F ($10.95–$16.05); main courses 18F–40F ($13.15–$29.20); fixed-price meal 85F ($62.05). AE, DC, MC, V.
Open: Lunch daily 11am–2pm; dinner daily 6–9pm.

The Hotel Krone is famous for its fine cuisine and wine cellar. Four-course fixed-price meals are served in an elegant beerhall with modern crystal chandeliers, a traditional Swiss decor, and wood tables. The chef has a varied menu, including scampi with crabmeat, filet of sole with riesling, suprême of salmon with champagne, cream of snail soup, and carpaccio. There is also a special children's menu. During the summer, diners may eat in the garden restaurant.

RESTAURANT TIGER, Stalen 35. Tel. 22-24-12.
Cuisine: SWISS. **Reservations:** Recommended.
$ **Prices:** Appetizers 12F–20F ($8.75–$14.60); main courses 18F–38F ($13.15–$27.75); fixed-price meal from 35F ($25.55). MC, V.
Open: Dinner only, Thurs–Tues 5:30–10pm. **Closed:** 2 weeks in Feb.

Set in a historic building near the cobblestone Friedhofplatz, this restaurant offers such specialties as fresh- and saltwater fish, veal steak with aromatic herbs, filet of pork Portuguese style, and calves' liver with Rösti. Try some of the Swiss cheese selections, which include unexported local varieties. In summer, you may dine on the terrace.

---

3. FRIBOURG

22 miles SW of Bern, 33 miles NE of Vevey

GETTING THERE **By Train** Fribourg is on the main railway lines that connect Zurich and Bern with Lausanne and Geneva. Travel time from Lausanne is about 45 minutes; from Bern, about 25 minutes.

By Car From Bern, head southwest on N12; from Vevey, on Lake Geneva, go northeast on N12.

ESSENTIALS The **Office du Tourisme** is at 30, Grand-Places (tel. 037/22-11-56). The **telephone area code** for Fribourg is 037.

SPECIAL EVENTS If your schedule permits, you should try to visit Fribourg during the **international folkloric meeting,** usually held about the beginning of September. Yodeling, wrestling, and a game called *hornussen* dominate the festivities. Note, however, that hotel bookings are difficult to get during the meeting.

Visitors should spend at least a day in this "flower of the Gothic age." Called Freiburg in German, the bilingual town has French names on the left bank of the Sarine River and German names on the right bank.

Once a sovereign republic, Fribourg today has a population of some 40,000, a university, and many other educational institutions.

In a setting between lakes and mountains, Fribourg was founded in 1157. It became a stronghold of Catholicism for centuries and was known for its dyers, weavers, and tanners. In 1481 it became a member of the Swiss Confederation and today it is the capital of a canton of the same name.

The old town ("the Bourg," in French) lies just above the Sarine riverbank and is flanked by the Auge and Neuveville sectors. These, along with the Planche sector on the right bank, form what is known as the Ville Basse (Lower Town).

WHAT TO SEE & DO

Fribourg's major attraction is ☺ **St. Nicholas's Cathedral,** on place Notre-Dame, with its lofty 15th-century Gothic belltower that dominates the medieval quarter. The nave dates from the 13th and 14th centuries, although the choir was reconstructed in the 17th century. The **Chapel of the Holy Sepulcher,** from the 15th century, has some remarkable stained glass and a celebrated organ. The cathedral also has a stunning rose window devoted to the Last Judgment.

In the vicinity of the cathedral are many old patrician houses. Explore this architecturally fascinating part of Fribourg—its Gothic houses, small steep streets, and squares adorned with fountains.

Whether it's called the **Rathaus** (in German) or the **Hôtel de Ville** (in French), the town hall of Fribourg, on route des Alpes, is a notable 16th-century building, with an octagonal clock tower where mechanical figures strike the hours. Outside the town hall, the seat of the parliament of Fribourg, traditionally dressed farmers' wives sell produce on Wednesday and Saturday—the most colorful time to visit the city.

Eglise des Cordeliers, the Franciscan church, another important religious site, is located north of place Notre-Dame (which contains the oldest church in the city, dating from the 12th century). The choir at the Franciscan church is from the 13th century and the nave is from the 18th century. The church has an outstanding wood triptych carved in 1513. Its chief attraction is the splendid altarpiece rising over the main altar, the work of the "Masters of the Carnation," 15th-century artists who signed their works with a white or a red carnation.

The city also has an outstanding art and history museum, the **Musée d'art et d'histoire** or **Museum für Kunst und Geschichte,** 12, rue de Morat (tel. 22-85-71). Housed in an imposing 16th-century former slaughterhouse called the Hôtel Ratze, its treasures include archeological collections of prehistoric, Roman, and medieval objects, as well as a remarkable series of Burgundian belt buckles. The epic sweep of Fribourg's history comes alive in the sculptures and paintings from the 10th to the 20th century. There are also displays on the political, military, and economic life of the canton. Other exhibits include numerous 15th- to 18th-century stained-glass windows and the largest collection in Switzerland of wood sculpture from the first half of the 16th century. The museum is open Tuesday through Sunday from 10am to 5pm (also from 8 to 10pm on Thursday). Admission is 5F ($3.65).

To reach the **upper town** of Fribourg, you can take a funicular. At some point, you'll want to see the **Ponte de Berne,** a covered wooden bridge from 1580.

NEARBY ATTRACTIONS

Fribourg is also the center for some important tours. An 18-mile, 70-minute ride will take you to **Schwarzsee,** or black lake, at about 3,500 feet. This is both a summer and a winter resort (albeit a minor one) known for its beautiful mountain setting.

Another excursion will take you to **Hauterive Abbey** (tel. 037/24-17-83), some 4½ miles southwest of Fribourg. This is a Cistercian abbey, built on a bend of the Sarine River. Its church, dating from the 12th century, has some beautiful 14th-century stained glass and some elaborately carved 15th-century stalls. Visits are possible from Easter until mid-September, Monday through Saturday from 2:30 to 5pm, and on Sunday from 10:45 to 11:30am and 2:45 to 4:45pm; the rest of the year, Monday through Saturday from 2 to 4:30pm and on Sunday from 10:45 to 11:30am and 2 to 4pm.

If you get back in Fribourg by sunset, you can cross the **Zähringen Bridge.** From it you can enjoy a great view of this famous old city.

WHERE TO STAY

EUROTEL FRIBOURG, 14, Grand-Places, CH-1700 Fribourg. Tel. 037/ 81-31-31. Fax 037/23-29-42. 168 rms (all with bath). MINIBAR TV TEL **Bus:** 1 or 2.

$ Rates (including continental breakfast): 120F–160F ($87.60–$116.80) single; 170F–220F ($124.10–$160.60) double. DC, MC, V. **Parking:** 25F ($18.25).

Set high on a cliff a few blocks from the main railroad station, this hotel provides a view of the historic city in the valley below. With easy parking and convenience to Fribourg's modern sector, the Eurotel Fribourg is preferred by many businesspeople. Rooms are spacious and cheerfully decorated. As in other Eurotels, many of the rooms have Murphy beds, enabling occupants to create a sitting room by folding the bed into the wall.

The brasserie restaurant serves American-style beef in a nautical setting; fixed-price meals cost 65F ($47.45). The hotel has a swimming pool, a bar, and a nightclub for dancing.

HOTEL DE LA ROSE, place Notre-Dame, CH-1700 Fribourg. Tel. 037/22-46-07. Fax 037/22-35-66. 40 rms (all with bath). MINIBAR TV TEL **Bus:** 1 or 2.

$ Rates (including breakfast): 95F–125F ($68.35–$91.25) single; 160F–210F ($116.80–$153.30) double. AE, DC, MC.

This hotel occupies a grand sandstone building near the cathedral. The flowered ceiling in the lobby is the hotel's most dramatic feature. On the premises is a pizzeria, plus a café terrace set above the traffic. There is also a bar (the Four Roses) in a 17th-century, cavelike vaulted room. Popular with the under-25 crowd, it has a tiny dance floor; it's open nightly (except Sunday) from 10pm. Bedrooms are modern and comfortably furnished.

HOTEL DUC BERTHOLD, 112, rue des Bouchers, CH-1700 Fribourg. Tel. 037/81-11-21. Fax 037/23-15-87. 40 rms (all with bath). MINIBAR TV TEL **Bus:** 1 or 2.

$ Rates (including breakfast): 98F–120F ($71.55–$87.60) single; 135F–180F ($98.55–$131.40) double. AE, DC, MC, V.

Situated on a busy street alongside the cathedral, this gray-stone and terra-cotta hotel is close to one of the city's major bridges. About half the rooms have been modernized. On the premises are a popular café and brasserie, and an attractive restaurant called La Marmite.

HOTEL ALPHA, 13, rue du Simplon, CH-1700 Fribourg. Tel. 037/22-72-72. 27 rms (all with bath). MINIBAR TV TEL **Bus:** 1 or 2.
$ Rates (including continental breakfast): 56F–62F ($40.85–$45.25) single; 84F–125F ($61.30–$91.25) double. AE, DC, MC, V.

Located near the train station, this modern hotel is one of the best bargains in town. Its reception area is two floors above the ground. Each of the accommodations is simple but adequate. A restaurant and bar on the first landing are independent of the hotel.

WHERE TO DINE

RESTAURANT LA MARMITE, in the Hôtel Duc Bertold, 112, rue des Bourchers. Tel. 81-11-21.
Cuisine: SWISS. **Reservations:** Required. **Bus:** 1 or 2.
$ Prices: Appetizers 10F–28F ($7.30–$20.45); main courses 30F–48F ($21.90–$35.05); fixed-price meals 80F ($58.40). AE, DC, MC, V.
Open: Lunch Mon–Sat 11:30am–2pm; dinner Mon–Sat 6:30–10pm.
This restaurant offers perfect cuisine and a lovely antique decor. It has a ceramic stove, paintings, and intimate lighting. The specialties prepared by chef Rolf Baumann include magret of duckling suprême, exotic mushrooms (Steinpilz) in puff pastry, carré d'agneau (lamb) with a mustard sauce, darne of seabass, and mignons of veal with port.

RESTAURANT FRANÇAIS, 1, place de la Gare. Tel. 22-28-16.
Cuisine: SWISS. **Reservations:** Required. **Bus:** 1 or 2.
$ Prices: Appetizers 15F–22F ($10.95–$16.06); main courses 26F–42F ($19–$30.65); business lunch 40F ($29.20); fixed-price dinner 85F ($62.05). AE, DC, MC, V.
Open: Lunch Mon–Sat 11:45am–3pm; dinner Mon–Sat 7–9:30pm; limited menu to midnight. **Closed:** Sat May–Sept; July 20–Aug 20 (dates may vary).
Here you can order a five-course fixed-price menu, with such specialties as pot-au-feu, filets of pike-perch provençal, fricasee of chicken with cider, veal kidneys with mustard sauce, and a terrine of veal with pistachio and truffles. Main dishes change seasonally.

AUBERGE DE ZÄHRINGEN, route de Zähringen. Tel. 22-42-36.
Cuisine: SWISS. **Reservations:** Required in restaurant; not needed in brasserie. **Bus:** 1 or 2.
$ Prices: Restaurant, appetizers 15F–22F ($10.95–$16.05); main courses 25F–42F ($18.25–$30.65); fixed-price meal 66F ($48.15) at lunch, 78F ($56.95) at dinner. Brasserie, fixed-price meal 30F ($21.90) at lunch, 49F ($35.75) at dinner. AE, DC, MC, V.
Open: Lunch Tues–Sun 11:30am–3pm; dinner Tues–Sat 6:30–9:30pm.
This 17th-century former private residence tends to attract wealthy, seasoned diners. On the ground floor, the dynamic Raemy family has established a brasserie and a more intimate French restaurant. In both, modern paintings by Fribourg artists are displayed. The restaurant offers such seasonal specialties as zander from lac de la Gruyère, rack of rabbit, and pike-perch, plus a ragoût of fresh mushrooms in a Gruyère-cream sauce, wild trout with caviar, and game cock sautéed with fresh

mushrooms. The brasserie has drinks, light meals, and platters of food available during the afternoon.

BUFFET DE LA GARE, 1, place de la Gare. Tel. 22-28-16.
   Cuisine: SWISS. **Reservations:** Not needed. **Bus:** 1 or 2.
$ Prices: Appetizers 10F–18F ($7.30–$13.15); main courses 12F–25F ($8.75–$18.25); fixed-price meal 28F ($20.45). AE, DC, MC, V.
   Open: Lunch daily 11am–2pm; dinner daily 6:15–9:30pm.
Buffet de la Gare contains several dining areas, each worth visiting. You will find a café, snack bar, and a traditional brasserie. At the brasserie, in a decor of polished brass and old-fashioned paneling, you can enjoy tripe milanese, blue trout in butter sauce, and escargots bourguignons; the specialty is lake fish. Meals there are served year round from 11am to 11pm.

---

4. GRUYERES

4 miles S of Bulle, 40 miles SW of Bern, 27 miles E of Palézieux

GETTING THERE   By Train   From either Lausanne or Zurich, most Gruyères-bound passengers transfer at the busy railway junction of Palézieux. From there a secondary railway spur leads to Gruyères, stopping at about 20 other hamlets along the way. Trip time from Zurich to Gruyères is about 4½ hours; from Palézieux to Gruyères, about 1 hour.

By Bus   About seven buses a day connect Gruyères with the rail and bus junction of Bulle, a 10-minute drive to Gruyères' northwest. From Bulle you can make bus connections to Fribourg and rail connections to the rest of Switzerland.

By Car   From Bern, head southwest along N11, taking the southeast turnoff to Bulle; Gruyères is signposted from there.

ESSENTIALS   The **tourist office** (tel. 029/6-10-30) is open Monday through Friday from 8am to noon and 1:30 to 5:30pm. Street names are not used—the village is very small. The **telephone area code** for Gruyères is 029.

This small town, which once belonged to the counts of Gruyères, is known for its castle and its cheese. It is a highlight for anyone taking the "cheese route" through Switzerland. It's also a good base for exploring the district of Gruyère (the region is spelled without an *s*).

In the canton of Fribourg, the little town of Gruyères seems to slumber somewhere back in the Middle Ages. Enclosed by 12th-century ramparts, it is dominated by a castle, where the counts lived from the 12th to the 16th century. Their crest, which bears a crane, is still used in Gruyères.

Cars are forbidden to enter between Easter and the first of November (and on Sunday all year round). You must therefore park your car outside the gates and walk into town.

WHAT TO SEE & DO

If you're here when the tour buses aren't, you'll discover one of the most charming villages on the continent.

At the entrance to the town, at the foot of a hill near the railway station, the Swiss Cheese Union operates a **Model Dairy** (tel. 6-14-10) for demonstration purposes.

Here you can see workers produce the famed Gruyère cheese (a wheel of which weighs 75 lb.), which is a more piquant version of the equally famous Emmenthaler. An audiovisual show reveals how the cheese is made. The dairy is open daily from 8am to 6pm, but it's best to go between 10 and 11am or between 2 and 3pm, when the cheese is actually made.

The traditional lunch in all the restaurants is raclette. A machine is usually placed on your table and you melt and scrape the cheese at your own speed. You can eat right down to the rind, which is crunchy and considered by many to be the best part of the raclette. In the right season, you can finish with a large bowl of fresh raspberries in thick cream.

Switzerland is also famous for its chocolates. At neighboring **Broc,** Peter Cailler-Kohler founded his chocolate factory (tel. 029/6-10-36) in 1898. Conducted tours are possible, but you should consult with the tourist office about times to visit.

You can walk on the cobblestone road to the ✪ **castle of Gruyères** (tel. 6-21-02), passing the house of the famed court jester Chalamala. Dating mostly from the 15th century, the castle, or château, is owned today by the canton of Fribourg. In 1848 the Bovy family of Geneva acquired it and ordered many of its embellishments. Several famous artists, including Corot, lived here. The château is filled with objets d'art, the most outstanding of which are three mourning copes from the Order of the Golden Fleece—part of the bounty grabbed up in the Burgundian wars. The castle is open to the public between June and October, daily from 9am to 6pm; in the winter, daily from 9am to noon and 1:30 to 4:30pm. Admission is 3F ($2.20).

NEARBY ATTRACTIONS

A popular excursion outside Gruyères is to **Moleson-Village,** at about 6,565 feet. It's a 4-mile journey, plus an additional half hour by cable car, which swings up from the village between 8:30am and noon and between 1:30 and 5:30pm; a round-trip costs 22F ($16.05). There's no service from November to mid-December. From the observatory at the peak, you can see the whole Gruyère countryside spread before you. In the winter, Moleson-Village emerges as a fledgling ski resort.

WHERE TO STAY

HOSTELLERIE DES CHEVALIERS, CH-1663 Gruyères. Tel. 029/6-19-33.
Fax 029/6-25-52. 34 rms (all with bath). TV TEL
$ Rates (including breakfast): 115F–135F ($83.95–$98.55) single; 140F–215F ($102.20–$356.95) double. AE, DC, MC, V.

✪ The only Relais & Châteaux hotel in the region, it is set at the end of a private driveway near the main town square. The restaurant section is in a 1950s private villa. The comfortable, conservative bedrooms are situated a few steps away in a more recent addition. The best rooms offer sweeping views of the valley.

Dining/Entertainment: Guests and others are welcome to visit the three elegant dining rooms. The one with the best view is covered from floor to ceiling with garden lattices. The others have a scattering of antiques, Delft tiles, and paneling. Meals are served Thursday through Tuesday from noon to 2pm and 7 to 9pm (closed from mid-January to mid-February). The seasonal menu, with à la carte meals averaging 85F ($62.05), might include filet of turbot with baby onions, veal with an artichoke ragoût, fricasee of pigeon, or a duet of quail cooked in cinders. Reservations are recommended.

HOSTELLERIE DE ST-GEORGES, CH-1663 Gruyères. Tel. 029/6-22-46.
Fax 029/6-33-13. 14 rms (all with bath).

$ Rates (including continental breakfast): 90F–120F ($65.70–$87.60) single; 120F–180F ($87.60–$131.40) double. AE, DC, MC, V. **Closed:** Dec–Feb.

⭐ This peaceful hideaway is acclaimed by many repeat visitors as one of the best places to stay in the region. The building, which dates from the 1500s, offers bedrooms with a radio and other amenities.

Dining/Entertainment: There's a cozy café suitable for drinks, snacks, and light lunches. Many guests prefer the old-world charm of the formal dining room in back, where specialties include filet of beef served on a slate platter, breast of duckling with green peppercorns, and a quiche made with—of course!—Gruyère cheese. Meals generally cost 38F to 48F ($27.75 to $35.05). The restaurant is open daily from 11:30am to 10pm; closed on Monday in the spring and autumn.

HOTEL DE VILLE, CH-1663 Gruyères. Tel. 029/6-24-24. 9 rms (all with bath or shower). TEL

$ Rates (including continental breakfast): 60F–70F ($43.80–$51.10) single; 100F–120F ($73–$87.60) double. AE, DC, MC, V.

Ⓢ Housed in a historic building in the center of the old town, Michel Murith's hotel offers comfortable, pleasantly furnished rooms and a terrace café in front.

An attractive restaurant serves regional specialties such as ham and trout (from an aquarium on the premises).

WHERE TO DINE

RESTAURANT LE CHALET DE GRUYERES. Tel. 6-21-54.
  Cuisine: SWISS. **Reservations:** Recommended.
$ Prices: Appetizers 12F–18F ($8.75–$13.15); main courses 15F–35F ($10.95–$25.55). AE, DC, MC, V.
  Open: Daily 11am–10pm.

Built in 1900, this centrally located wood chalet is a few minutes' walk from the château. The restaurant, which counts former President Jimmy Carter among its customers, has aged timbers, honey-colored planks, and polished farm tools. In the summer, flowers adorn the front balconies. A café is on the lowest floor, and upstairs there's a dining room. The menu includes traditional Swiss dishes such as fondue, raclette, and hot Gruyère cheese on toast with ham, and a "Gruyère platter" piled high with ham, cheese, sausage, and air-dried beef.

---

5. MURTEN [MORAT]

11 miles N of Fribourg, 19 miles W of Bern

GETTING THERE By Train Murten is connected by direct rail line to Fribourg, a 30-minute ride away. About 20 trains a day make the run, stopping off at about half a dozen hamlets along the way. Murten also has good connections to the nearby town of Ins, which lies directly on most of the train routes between Zurich and Paris.

By Boat A restful way to reach Murten is over the lakes that lie to the north and west. Ferries make the water crossing between Neuchâtel and Murten about five times a day throughout the year. It takes about 1½ hours to cross the two lakes (lac de Neuchâtel and Murtensee) and the canal (La Broye) that connects them; the one-way boat fare is 9.40F ($6.85).

In midsummer, a spectacular way to reach Murten is from Biel (Bienne): Between late May and late September, a ferry departs Tuesday through Saturday from the central piers in Biel at 9:50am, arriving in Murten at 12:30pm. One-way transit costs 18.20F ($13.30) and will take you through three lakes (Bielersee, lac de Neuchâtel, and Murtensee) and across the canals connecting them.

By Car   From Bern, head west on Route 10, turning south to Murten at the junction with Route 22.

ESSENTIALS   The **Murten Tourist Information Office** is at Schlossgasse 5 (tel. 71-51-12). The **telephone area code** for Murten is 037.

Of the many old towns in Switzerland, I found Murten one of the most idyllic and beautifully preserved. Its residents speak either French or German, often both. The town lies on what is called the "language demarcation line." Lying on the southern side of Murtensee, which is known in French as lac de Morat, Murten forms a gateway into French-speaking Switzerland. Outside Murten, on June 22, 1476, a fierce battle was fought between the Confederates and Charles the Bold of Burgundy.

WHAT TO SEE & DO

Many houses date from the 15th to the 18th century, and the town itself is surrounded by ✪ **medieval ramparts** with a wall-walk. Today you can stroll along the wall, taking in a view over Altstadt (Old Town) with the castle, lake, and Jura Mountains as a backdrop.

Peter of Savoy was a duke who built the town's **castle** in the 13th century. It's bleak and foreboding, but impressive nevertheless, and from its inner courtyard (which you enter for free) there's a vista of the lake and the Jura foothills.

The main street, **Hauptgasse,** is the major attraction of Murten, running through the center of the old quarter. It leads to the baroque **Bernegate,** which contains one of the oldest clock towers in the country, dating from 1712.

The **Musée Historique,** adjacent to the château (tel. 71-30-00), contains everything from archeological excavations of the city's earliest history to a diorama of the 15th-century Battle of Morat. It's housed in an old mill a few steps from the walls of the château. In the summer, it's open Tuesday through Sunday from 10am to noon and 2 to 6pm; in the winter, Tuesday through Sunday from 2 to 5pm. Admission is 3F ($2.20).

NEARBY ATTRACTIONS

Murtensee, or **lac de Morat,** spread over nearly 10 square miles, has a maximum depth of 150 feet. Between late May and September you can take lake trips on motor vessels and circular tours on the three lakes from Murten to Neuchâtel to Biel (Bienne), with trips through the canals in the Great Marshes. Check with the tourist office for information on these excursions.

WHERE TO STAY & DINE

LE VIEUX MANOIR AU LAC, CH-3208 Murten-Meyriez. Tel. 037/71-12-83. Fax 037/71-31-88. 23 rms (all with bath). MINIBAR TV TEL

$ Rates (including continental breakfast): 100F–160F ($73–$116.80) single; 200F–300F ($146–$218.95) double. AE, DC, MC, V. **Closed:** Mid-Dec to mid-Feb.

★ Located 1½ miles west of the town center (a 5-minute taxi ride from the train station), this gabled, stuccoed building, in an idyllic setting, includes a sun deck and balconies with a view of Lake Morat. The service is impeccable.

Dining/Entertainment: The restaurant, which has a collection of antiques collected from the region, serves excellent food, with a separate menu for meat and fish courses. A fixed-price menu ranges from 55F to 110F ($40.15 to $80.30), and from 45F to 85F ($32.85 to $62.05) if you order à la carte. Reservations are recommended.

HOTEL SCHIFF, Ryf 53, CH-3280 Murten. Tel. 037/71-27-01. Fax 037/71-35-31. 16 rms (all with bath). MINIBAR TV TEL

$ Rates (including continental breakfast): 80F–105F ($58.40–$76.65) single; 140F–190F ($102.20–$138.70) double. Half-board 35F ($25.55) per person extra. AE, DC, MC, V. **Closed:** Mid-Dec to early Feb.

Located at the edge of the lake, near the harbor, this hotel is surrounded by parks and operates a lakeside café. The building, with 19th-century gables and porches, has a modern extension containing well-decorated public rooms. The wallpapered bedrooms are comfortable.

Dining/Entertainment: The hotel's restaurant has large windows offering a view of lawns and chestnut trees down to the lake. Fixed-price lunches cost 42F ($30.65), and there's a six-course fixed-price dinner going for 68F ($49.65). The menu is changed every 2 months; in September, during the hunting season, it features game selections, from wild boar to pheasant. The cuisine is French. There is also a bistro for snacks, as well as a dance club open Tuesday through Sunday.

Services: Laundry, baby-sitting.

Facilities: Open-air parking lot (free) next to the hotel; indoor and outdoor swimming pools a short walk away.

HOTEL WEISSES KREUZ (HOTEL DE LA CROIX BLANCHE), Rathausgasse 31, CH-3280 Murten. Tel. 037/71-26-41. Fax 037/71-28-65. 27 rms (all with bath). TV TEL

$ Rates (including continental breakfast): 70F–100F ($51.10–$73) single; 120F–170F ($87.60–$124.10) double. DC, MC, V. **Closed:** Dec 12–Feb 28.

This is a superb hotel, clean and attractive, with a gracious staff. It is situated on the lake, a 10-minute walk from the train station. The historic buildings—one of which was originally a stable—are set behind a screen of roses on a cobblestone street in the center of the old town. The hotel has a scattering of antiques; bedrooms have either a modern or an antique decor. Every spring, Daniel Bischoff, co-owner and chef, hosts a baroque-music concert series in the large dining room.

Dining/Entertainment: Meals are served in the dining room daily from noon to 2pm and 6 to 9:30pm. A la carte meals begin at 40F ($29.20) and might include an array of local fish dishes, medallions of veal with wild mushrooms, and English-style roast beef.

Services: Room service, laundry.

Facilities: Tennis courts, swimming pool, health club.

HOTEL KRONE (HOTEL DE LA COURONNE), Rathausgasse 5, CH-3280 Murten. Tel. 037/71-52-52. Fax 037/71-36-10. 35 rms (all with bath). TEL

$ Rates (including continental breakfast): 50F–85F ($36.50–$62.05) single; 105F–145F ($76.65–$105.85) double. AE, DC, MC, V. **Closed:** Mid-Nov to mid-Dec.

S This heavily gabled building in the center of town was originally a 15th-century inn. It offers clean accommodations at reasonable prices. The owners, Werner and Christine Nyffeler, are present to assure good service. Half the rooms have a minibar and TV.

The hotel has five different eating areas. You can opt for the street-level pizzeria or the adjacent café/brasserie. A large, sunny, restaurant is one floor above the lobby; it has a salad bar every day, with as many as two dozen varieties of vegetables. A fixed-price meal costs 35F ($25.55). Menu items include filet of beef Stroganoff and filet of trout; prices range from 12F to 45F ($8.75 to $32.85).

---

6. NEUCHATEL

29 miles W of Bern, 19 miles SW of Biel

GETTING THERE   By Train   Neuchâtel lies at the junction of major rail lines linking Geneva with Basel and Zurich with Paris. Travel time to Neuchâtel from Geneva is about 90 minutes; from Zurich, about 2½ hours.

By Boat   Ferries arrive in Neuchâtel about five times a day, winter and summer, from Murten (Morat). The trip—which involves crossing of two lakes (Murtensee and lac de Neuchâtel) and the canal that connects them—takes about 1½ hours. The one-way boat fare is 9.40F ($6.85). For a longer boat itinerary, available only in the summer, see Section 5, "Murten (Morat)," above.

By Car   From Bern, take Route 10 west, then Route 5 south to Neuchâtel.

ESSENTIALS   For more information, contact **Service des Monuments et Sites,** 23, rue du Château (tel. 038/22-36-10). The **telephone area code** for Neuchâtel is 038.

One of Switzerland's most charming towns, Neuchâtel lies at the border of a lake of the same name and at the foot of the green slopes of Chaumont (3,871 ft.). It is the capital of the canton of Neuchâtel, created in 1815 out of a Prussian principality that had joined the Swiss Confederation. The majority of Neuchâtel's population are Protestant and French-speaking (indeed, they are said to speak the finest French in Switzerland). They acquired a fame for watchmaking as early as the 18th century.

Situated at the foot of the Jura Mountains, in the midst of vineyards, Neuchâtel enjoys an idyllic setting. Many of its limestone houses have a distinctive yellow or ocher color, which inspired Alexandre Dumas to describe the town as having been carved out of a "block of butter."

Neuchâtel is a seat of culture and learning. Its university was founded in 1838.

The French influence is evident in architectural styles. Many houses in the old town date back to the 16th century; some were built with defensive towers. The spirit of old Neuchâtel is best seen at the **Maison des Halles,** the market square, where you may want to buy some well-known local cheese, de Jura, to eat later at a picnic around the lake.

No cars are allowed in the center of the old sector.

WHAT TO SEE & DO

The medieval core of Neuchâtel is dominated by three architectural attractions: a castle (château), a collégiale (University Church), and the Prison Tower (Tour des

Prisons). Of the three, the building that has been altered the most over the centuries is the **castle.** Its oldest section, the west wing, was originally built during the 12th century, but most of what you'll see today was added during the 15th, 16th, and 17th centuries. The structure is stern and forbidding; from some of its ramparts, you get a panoramic view of the old town. To visit the castle's interior, apply to the building's concièrge (you'll find him near the gate to the castle, under an archway). Accompanied visits, for a minimum of two or three people, are conducted hourly between 10am and noon and between 2 and 4pm.

Most of the **University Church** was built during the 12th and 13th centuries, though sections of it, most notably the western towers, were a 19th-century embellishment, built when the church underwent (some say suffered) a major overhaul. The building's highlight is found in its Romanesque choir, a monument to the counts of Neuchâtel, created during the 14th century. Adorned with 15 painted effigies of almost-forgotten noblemen, this is considered the most spectacular Gothic memorial in the country. The collégiale is open daily from 8am to 8pm (to 6pm in the winter); admission is free.

Finally, the **Prison Tower** offers a magnificent view. It's open from Easter to the end of September, daily from 8am to 8pm. Admission is .50F (35¢).

The **Griffin Fountain,** from 1664, stands nearby on rue du Château. It's one of the most famous fountains in the country, thanks to Henri II of Orléans, who in 1657 had it filled with 1,300 gallons of red wine to honor his entry into Neuchâtel.

Stroll into the garden of the **Hôtel Du Peyrou,** faubourg de l'Hôpital, dating from 1764. This excellent patrician house was constructed for Du Peyrou, who was a friend of Jean-Jacques Rousseau and published some of his works. *The Bather,* a statue in the pool, is by Ramseyer.

For a great view of the Lake of Neuchâtel and the distant Alps, take a funicular to the Crête du Plan, a height of 1,962 ft. Approach from rue de l'Ecluse, on the border of the medieval sector.

THE MUSEUMS OF NEUCHÂTEL

MUSEE D'ART ET D'HISTOIRE, quai Léopold-Robert. Tel. 20-79-20.

The Museum of Art and History, near the end of quai Léopold-Robert, northeast of the harbor, has an excellent collection of paintings. Many of the works are by local artists of the late 19th and early 20th centuries. You can also see works by Léopold Robert, for whom the quay was named, as well as works by artists painting in Neuchâtel today.

The main attraction of the museum is a 15th-century painting on wood, *The Coronation of the Madonna,* attributed to one of the "Masters of the Carnation." You will find that Neuchâtel's role as a watchmaking city is honored by the museum's clocks and watches. In addition, there is a collection of automata (mechanical figures), including an imaginative, 18th-century trio of figures by a famous local craftsman, Jaquet-Droz.

Admission: 5F ($3.65).
Open: Tues–Sun 10am–noon and 2–5pm. **Bus:** 1 or 6.

MUSEUM OF ETHNOGRAPHY, 4, rue Saint-Nicholas. Tel. 24-41-20.

You can reach the exceptional Museum of Ethnography easily from the castle by heading up rue Saint-Nicholas. The museum takes you on a journey from the mysterious kingdom of Bhutan to Egypt at the time of the pharaohs. On the outer side of the annex is a mammoth fresco, *Conquest of Man,* by Hans Erni.

Admission: 5F ($3.65).
Open: Tues–Sun 10am–5pm. **Bus:** 1.

MUSEE CANTONAL D'ARCHEOLOGIE, 7, avenue Du Peyrou. Tel. 25-03-36.

Near the faubourg de l'Hôpital is the Museum of Archeology. It displays artifacts discovered near the hamlet of La Tene, a late–Iron Age site excavated in 1858 near St. Blaise, at the northern end of the Lake of Neuchâtel. (The archeological site can also be visited.)

Admission: Free.
Open: Tues–Sun 2–5pm. **Bus:** 1.

NEARBY ATTRACTIONS

If you stay in Neuchâtel, you can explore many sights in the environs, especially those that border the lac de Neuchâtel. If you drive 2½ miles northeast of town, you'll reach **La Coudre.** From there you can take a funicular to the top of Chaumont, 3,871 feet. The round-trip fare is 12F ($8.75); the ride each way takes about 15 minutes.

WHERE TO STAY

HOTEL BEAULAC, 2, quai Léopold-Robert, CH-2000 Neuchâtel. Tel. 038/25-88-22. Fax 038/25-60-35. 72 rms (all with bath). MINIBAR TV TEL **Bus:** 1.

$ Rates (including continental breakfast): 110F–160F ($80.30–$116.80) single; 155F–220F ($113.15–$160.60) double. AE, DC, MC, V.

Set near the intersection of quai Léopold-Robert and quai du Port, this comfortable, four-story hotel was designed with an angular modernity that is particularly striking when compared with the 18th-century sandstone buildings surrounding it. Guests can watch the activity at the nearby marina from café tables on the hotel's waterside terrace. The bedrooms are modern. On the premises are three restaurants, one of which, Le Colvert, specializes in fish dishes.

HOTEL CITY, 12, place A. M. Piage, CH-2000 Neuchâtel. Tel. 038/25-54-12. 35 rms (all with bath). MINIBAR TV TEL **Bus:** 1.

$ Rates (including continental breakfast): 80F–100F ($58.40–$73) single; 120F–170F ($87.60–$124.10) double. AE, DC, MC, V.

The hotel, a dignified building erected in the early 1800s, is in the commercial center of town, across the street from Neuchâtel's art nouveau post office. Its owners, Thony and Madelein Blaettler, offer carefully scrubbed rooms with radios and Louis XIV reproductions. Known for its good value and modern accommodations, the hotel welcomes a varied clientele, ranging from foreign diplomats and domestic bankers to budget-conscious travelers. On the premises is one of the city's few Chinese restaurants, as well as a recommended brasserie.

HOTEL DES BEAUX-ARTS, 5-7, rue Pourtalès, CH-2000 Neuchâtel. Tel. 038/24-01-51. 26 rms (15 with bath). TV TEL **Bus:** 1 or 6.

$ Rates (including continental breakfast): 70F ($51.10) single without bath, 85F ($62.05) single with bath; 110F ($80.30) double without bath, 130F ($94.90) double with bath. No credit cards.

This simple concrete hotel, owned by Maria Mutti, is not far from the lake, on a fairly quiet street near the center of town. Built in the early 1970s, it has balconies and two pleasant restaurants.

WHERE TO DINE

LE VIEUX VAPEUR, Port de Neuchâtel. Tel. 24-66-44.

Cuisine: SWISS. **Reservations:** Required. **Bus:** 1 or 6.

$ **Prices:** Restaurant, appetizers 12F–22F ($8.75–$16.05); main courses 18F–42F ($13.15–$30.65). Bar, à la carte from 35F ($25.55). AE, DC, MC, V.

Open: Restaurant, lunch Mon–Sat noon–2pm; dinner Mon–Sat 7–10pm. Bar, lunch Mon–Sat noon–2pm; dinner Mon–Sat 7pm–1:30am. **Closed:** Dec 20–early Jan.

This is a floating restaurant moored beside one of the docks and overlooking colonies of ducks that paddle about searching for table scraps from its kitchens. Inside the restaurant's gleaming hull, a bar ("Le Britchon") has a television set and lots of gleaming brass. It also has a disco with a dance floor, and a nautically decorated restaurant.

If you're looking for a bargain, head below deck to the bar, for grills and spaghetti. More formal meals are served in the restaurant on the upper deck; these might include veal kidneys with juniper berries and mint, mignon of veal stuffed with foie gras and truffles, lake trout with champagne sauce, and grilled John Dory flavored with tarragon.

RESTAURANT CITY, in the Hôtel City, 12, place A. M. Piaget. Tel. 25-54-12.

Cuisine: INTERNATIONAL. **Reservations:** Required. **Bus:** 1.

$ **Prices:** Appetizers 14F–20F ($10.20–$14.60); main courses 25F–35F ($18.25–$25.55). AE, DC, MC, V.

Open: Lunch daily 11:30am–2pm; dinner daily 6:30–10pm.

Set in what was formerly a private walled garden, this establishment combines the best elements of a formal restaurant with those of a brasserie. Its well-prepared meals are a blend of traditional French and regional influences. Thony and Madeline Blaettler draw on century-old family recipes for unforgettable dishes. Perhaps the most unusual dish, the chef's secret, is entrecôte Gerle—a juicy slab of beef laced with a layer of creamy sauce. Other specialties include coq au vin with gratin dauphinoise, chicken with whisky sauce, and filets of palée (a lake fish).

BUFFET DE LA GARE, 1, place de la Gare. Tel. 25-48-53.

Cuisine: SWISS/INTERNATIONAL. **Reservations:** Not needed. **Bus:** 6.

$ **Prices:** Appetizers 2.50F ($1.85); main courses 12F–20F ($8.75–$14.60); fixed-priced lunch 18F ($13.15). AE, DC, MC, V.

Open: Buffet 6am–midnight.

With four distinctly different sections, this is as close to a food factory as you'll find in Neuchâtel. It has a stand-up snack bar in the train station, a catering service, and a less expensive brasserie. At the top of the list, however, is a restaurant with excellent service, an elegant decor, and a chef who takes cooking seriously; its specialties include baby crayfish in saffron, quail mousse, trout garnished with smoked salmon and served with a horseradish mousse, sea trout with grapefruit, and young hare with cabbage leaves.

CHAPTER 6

BERN (BERNE)

Bern, as the capital of Switzerland, is a city of diplomats and the site of international organizations and meetings. It is one of the loveliest and oldest cities in Europe, its origins going back to the 12th century. Much of its medieval architecture has remained untouched, giving Bern the aspect rather of a large provincial town. In 1983 the United Nations declared it a world landmark.

Yet the modern mingles harmoniously with the old in this charming city, as residents discreetly add contemporary-style houses and other structures to their historic environment. Such coexistence between the old and the new is evident also in Bern's status as a university town, with its traditional studies, and as a center of pioneering scientific research.

Bern joined the Swiss Confederation in 1353. In 1848 it became the seat of the federal government, replacing Zurich. The city stands on a thumb of land that is bordered on three sides by the Aare River. Several bridges connect the old part of the city with the newer sections.

Market days in Bern—and thus an ideal time to visit—are Tuesday and Saturday. People from the outlying areas come to town to sell their produce and wares. If you're fortunate enough to arrive on the fourth Monday of November, you'll witness the centuries-old Zwiebelmarkt (Zibelemarit, in the local dialect), or Onion Market. This is the city's last big event before the onset of winter, as residents traditionally stock up on onions in anticipation of the first snows.

Bern is also the center for many excursions, especially to the lakes and peaks of the Bernese Oberland—a vast recreation area only minutes from the capital.

1. ORIENTATION

ARRIVING

BY PLANE The **Bern-Belp Airport** (tel. 54-34-11) is 6 miles south of the city, in the town of Belpmoos. International flights arrive from London, Paris, and Nice, but

✓ WHAT'S SPECIAL ABOUT BERN

Monuments

☐ The Ogre Fountain, with its repre-sentation of a carnival figure, erected about 1544.

☐ The Zytgloggeturm (Clock Tower), the city's western gate from 1191 to 1250, now a gathering point 4 min-utes before each hour, when the chimes start pealing.

Buildings

☐ The Bundeshaus (Federal Palace), the seat of Switzerland's democracy, with its Renaissance-style chambers.

Ace Attractions

☐ The Bärengraben (Bear Pits), where the city's mascots have been fed and admired since the 15th century.

Museums

☐ The Kunstmuseum (Fine Arts Muse-um), famous for its collection of paintings from the 14th to the 20th century, including the world's largest collection of works by Paul Klee.

☐ The Bern Historical Museum, packed with treasures, including the booty captured from the Burgundians in 1476.

Parks and Gardens

☐ The Botanischer Garten, a vast gar-den of exotic plants built on terraces descending to the Aare River.

---

transatlantic jets are not able to land here. Fortunately, it's a short hop to Bern from the international airports in Zurich and Geneva.

Taxis are very expensive, so it's better to take the shuttle bus that runs between the airport and the Bahnhof (train station); it costs 10F ($7.30) one way.

BY TRAIN Bern has direct connections to the continental rail network that includes France, Italy, Germany, and the Benelux countries, even Scandinavia and Spain. The super-fast TGV train connects Paris with Bern in just 4½ hours. Bern also lies on major Swiss rail links, particularly those connecting Geneva and Zurich; each city is only 90 minutes away.

The **Bahnhof,** on Bahnhofplatz, is right in the center of town near all the major hotels. If your luggage is light, you can walk to your hotel; otherwise, take one of the taxis waiting outside the station.

For **information** about tickets and train schedules for the Swiss Federal Railways, call 21-11-11. The office is open daily from 7:30am to 8:30pm.

BY CAR Bern lies at a major expressway junction of Switzerland, with E17 coming in east from Zurich, N2 heading south from Basel, and N12 running north from Lake Geneva.

TOURIST INFORMATION

The **Bern Tourist Office,** in the Bern Bahnhof, on Bahnhofplatz (tel. 031/22-76-76), is open from May to October, Monday through Saturday from 8am to 8:30pm and on Sunday from 9am to 8:30pm; November to April, Monday through Saturday from 8am to 6:30pm and on Sunday from 10am to 5pm. If you need help finding a hotel room, the tourist office can make a reservation for you in a price range you select.

CITY LAYOUT

MAIN ARTERIES AND STREETS   The geography of the city is neatly pressed into a relatively small area, so getting about is quite easy. **Altstadt,** or Old Town, lies on a high rocky plateau that juts out into a "loop" of the Aare River. Most of the major hotels and the outstanding attractions lie within this loop.

Most arrivals are at the Bahnhof on **Bahnhofplatz,** in the center of town. From here you can walk along the major arteries of Bern: **Spitalgasse, Marktgasse, Kramgasse,** and **Gerechtigkeitsgasse.** Major squares include **Theaterplatz,** with its famed Zytgloggeturm or Clock Tower. Adjoining Theaterplatz is **Kornhausplatz** and its much photographed Ogre Fountain. On **Rathausplatz** stands the old Rathaus (Town Hall), seat of the cantonal government.

The three major bridges crossing the Aare into this historic loop are **Kirchenfeldbrücke, Kornhausbrücke,** and **Lorainebrücke.**

FINDING AN ADDRESS   In a system developed during the Middle Ages, Bern begins its street numbering in the center of Altstadt—the numbers increase as they fan out. Even numbers lie on one side of the street, odd numbers on the other.

NEIGHBORHOODS IN BRIEF   Only two of Bern's many neighborhoods are of interest to tourists:

Altstadt   This is the heart of Bern, lying inside a bend of the Aare River. Filled with flower-decked fountains, it encompasses some 3½ miles of arcades and medieval streets, many reserved for pedestrians only. Its main street is Marktgasse, filled with luxury shops and 17th- and 18th-century houses.

South of the Aare   The only other neighborhood in Bern that has much interest to visitors is the sprawling district south of the Aare, reached by crossing the Kirchenfeldbrücke. Here are three major museums, including the Swiss Alpine Museum, the Bern Historical Museum, and the Natural History Museum.

MAPS   You can pick up good local maps at the Bern Tourist Office.

2. GETTING AROUND

BY BUS AND TRAM   The public transportation system, the **Stadtische Verkehrsbetrieb (SVB),** is a reliable, 38-mile network of buses and trams. Before you board, purchase a ticket from the self-service automatic machines at each stop (conductors do not sell tickets). If you're caught traveling without one, you'll be fined 30F ($21.90), in addition to the fare for the ride (single fare is 1.50F or $1.10).

To save time and, possibly, money, you can purchase a **1-day ticket** for 4F ($2.90), which entitles you to unlimited travel on the SVB network during the 24-hour period of your choice. Just get the ticket stamped at the automatic machine before you begin your first trip. One-day tickets are available at the ticket offices at Bubenbergplatz 5 (tel. 22-14-44) and in the underpass of the main railroad station (tel. 22-62-04), as well as at other outlets in the city.

BY TAXI   You can catch a taxi at the public cab ranks, or you can call a dispatcher: **Casinoplatz** (tel. 22-18-18); railway station (tel. 22-18-18); **Weisenhausplatz** (tel. 23-53-53); or **Bundesplatz** (tel. 23-53-53).

BY CAR   This is an impractical way of seeing Bern because of traffic congestion in Old Town, its confusing layout of one-way streets, and its lack of on-street parking. If you have a car, park it in a public garage and explore the city on foot; its miles of arcades were designed to protect pedestrians from rain, snow, and traffic.

   If you want to rent a car to explore the environs, arrangements can be made at **Hertz,** Casinoplatz (tel. 22-33-13); **Europcar,** Laupenstrasse 15 (tel. 25-75-55); and **Avis,** Effingerstrasse 20 (tel. 25-10-25).

BY BICYCLE   Altstadt is compressed into such a small area that it's better to cover it on foot rather than on a bike. Bicycles aren't allowed on the many pedestrians-only streets, anyway.

ON FOOT   This is the only practical means of exploring Altstadt and its many attractions. Many people walk through this section of Bern in about 2½ hours.

   BERN

The following is a quick-reference guide to Bern. For more information, see "Fast Facts: Switzerland" in Chapter 2.

   American Express   The American Express office, Bubenbergplatz 11 (tel. 22-94-01), is open Monday through Friday from 8:30am to 6pm and on Saturday from 9am to noon.

   Area Code   The telephone area code for Bern is 031.

   Baby-sitters   Baby-sitting can be arranged through most hotels. The **Loeb department store,** Spitalgasse 47-51 (tel. 22-71-11), offers a kindergarten for children while you shop. The service is available on Monday from 2 to 5pm and Tuesday through Friday from 9am to noon and again from 1 to 5pm. The fee is 5F ($3.65) for a maximum of 2 hours.

   Bookstores   The best is **Scherz Buchhandlung,** Marktgasse 25 (tel. 22-68-37), which has many titles in English.

   Business Hours   **Banks** are open Monday through Friday from 8am to 4:30pm (on Thursday to 6pm). Most **offices** are open Monday through Friday from 9am to 5pm and on Saturday from 9am to noon.

   Car Rentals   See Section 2, "Getting Around," above.

   Climate   See Section 2, "When to Go," in Chapter 2.

   Currency   See Section 1, "Information, Documents & Money," in Chapter 2.

   Currency Exchange   This is available on the lower level of the Bahnhof, on Bahnhofplatz (tel. 21-11-11), open daily from 6am to 10pm.

   Dentist   Call 22-91-11.

   Doctor   Call 22-92-11.

   Drugstores   If you need a pharmacy, try **Central-Apotheke Volz and Co.,** Zeitglockenlaub 2 (tel. 22-10-94). It's near the Clock Tower in the old city. The staff speaks English and can suggest over-the-counter substitutes for American drugs that may not be obtainable in Europe. It's open on Monday from 1:45 to 6:30pm, Tuesday through Friday from 7:45am to 6:30pm, and on Saturday from 7:45am to 4pm.

Embassies/Consulates If you lose your passport, go to the **U.S. Embassy,** Jubiläumsstrasse 93 (tel. 031/43-70-11). Other embassy addresses are: **Australia,** Alpenstrasse 29 (tel. 031/43-01-43); **Canada,** Kirchenfeldstrasse 88 (tel. 031/44-63-81); **United Kingdom,** Thunstrasse 50 (tel. 031/44-50-21). **New Zealand** citizens should contact their consulate-general in Geneva.

Emergencies Call 117 for the **police,** 144 for an **ambulance,** 118 to report a **fire,** 22-92-11 for a **doctor or dentist,** or 140 for the **road patrol.**

Eyeglasses A large and centrally located optician, **Delta Optik,** Rathausgasse 59 (tel. 21-11-88), can replace both eyeglasses and contact lenses.

Hairdressers/Barbers One of the city's best-known hairdressers is **Erminio,** Laupenstrasse 2 (tel. 25-23-66), a 5-minute walk west of the railroad station. There are separate sections for men and women.

Holidays See Section 2, "When to Go," in Chapter 2.

Hospital The city's largest is **Insel Hospital,** Freiburgstrasse (tel. 64-21-11), the clinic affiliated with the University of Bern.

Information See "Tourist Information" in Section 1, "Orientation," above.

Laundry/Dry Cleaning There's a coin-operated self-service laundry conveniently located near the railway station, the **Bahnhof Duschwasch,** Bahnhofplatz (tel. 22-81-44).

For dry cleaning, a central establishment is **Zytglogge, A.G.,** Kornhausplatz 7 (tel. 22-70-63), a few paces from the town's famous Clock Tower.

Libraries The reading room of the **Swiss National Library,** Hallwylstrasse 15 (tel. 61-89-11), is open Monday through Friday from 9am to noon and 1 to 6pm (on Wednesday to 8pm), and on Saturday from 9am to 2pm.

Liquor Laws The legal drinking age is 18. Never drink and drive in Bern: The penalties are severe.

Lost Property The lost property office at Zeughausgasse 18 (tel. 64-67-72) is open Monday through Friday from 7:30 to 11:30am and 1:45 to 5pm.

Luggage Storage/Lockers Storage facilities are available on the lower level of the Bahnhof, on Bahnhofplatz (tel. 21-11-11).

Newspapers/Magazines Local papers are in German, but copies of the *International Herald Tribune* are available. Most major newsstands, including those at hotels, carry *Time* and *Newsweek.*

Photographic Needs For film and other camera supplies, go to the **Jemoli Department Store,** Marktgasse 10 (tel. 22-61-22), in the center of town.

Police Call 117 in an emergency.

Post Office The **main post office (Schanzenpost),** at Schanzenstrasse 4 (tel. 65-61-11), is open Monday through Friday from 7:30am to 6:30pm and on Saturday from 7:30 to 11am.

Radio/TV The Swiss Broadcasting Corporation (SBC) produces both radio and TV programs in German. Nine different radio programs are aired, supplemented by programs from the Swiss Radio International (SRI). The SBC also has German-language telecasts from Zurich. Bern receives many different TV programs from its neighbors via satellite; ask your hotel which broadcasts it receives.

Religious Services **Protestant** churches in the city center include the cathedral at Münsterplatz (tel. 22-05-72) and Antonier-Kirche (Lutheran), Postgasse 62 (tel. 21-13-91). **Roman Catholic** services are at Holy Trinity Church, Taubenstrasse 4 (tel. 22-24-70), and the Jewish community of Bern meets at the **Synagogue,** Kapellenstrasse 2 (tel. 25-49-92).

Rest Rooms You'll find public facilities in the Bahnhof and in some squares in Old Town.

Safety Bern is considered one of Europe's safest capitals. Nevertheless, you should take the usual precautions; protect your valuables. It is considered safe to walk the streets at night, and crimes against women are rare.

Shoe Repairs   Go to the **Jemoli Department Store,** Marktgasse 10 (tel. 22-61-22), in the center of town.

Taxes   A 6.2% Value-Added Tax (VAT) is included in the price of all goods and services rendered, including hotel and restaurant bills. There are no other special taxes.

Taxis   See Section 2, "Getting Around," above.

Telegrams/Telex/Fax   The Bahnhof (tel. 21-11-11) offers telephone, telegraph, Telex, and fax services Monday through Friday from 6:30am to 10:30pm and on Saturday from 6:30am to 5pm.

Transit Info   Call 21-11-11 for rail information or 65-65-65 for postal-bus information.

Yellow Pages   These won't be much help to you unless you speak German. Your hotel reception desk, however, will usually help you find some particular service.

3. ACCOMMODATIONS

There are accommodations for every budget in Bern. As the federal capital, Bern hosts many conventions and international meetings, and at times its hotels are fully booked. Try to arrive with a reservation.

Altstadt is built on a peninsula so compact that everything—literally—is "around the corner." That means nearly all the hotels, more than 150 restaurants, the major sights, and 3½ miles of arcades for shopping—even the weekly farmers' market and the Houses of Parliament.

Hotels labeled "Very Expensive" charge 280F to 390F ($204.35 to $284.65) per night for a double or twin-bedded room; those rated "Expensive," 130F to 215F ($94.90 to $156.95); "Moderate," 120F to 160F ($87.60 to $116.80); and "Inexpensive," 80F to 115F ($58.39 to $83.95) all with private bath or shower. In the lowest-priced categories, you can save more by taking a room without a bath (but often with a sink).

IN ALTSTADT

VERY EXPENSIVE

BELLEVUE PALACE, Kochergasse 3-5, CH-3001 Bern. Tel. 031/22-45-81. Fax 031/22-47-43. 142 rms, 8 suites. MINIBAR TV TEL **Tram:** 3, 9, or 12.
$ **Rates** (including continental breakfast): 170F–235F ($124.10–$171.55) single; 280F–390F ($204.35–$284.65) double; from 850F ($620.40) suites. AE, DC, MC, V.

This majestic, five-star hotel is next to the Bundeshaus, the seat of the Swiss government. Built in 1913, the gray-stone building has carved Corinthian columns and ornate details; one of the salons has a stained-glass ceiling. The opulent bedrooms are

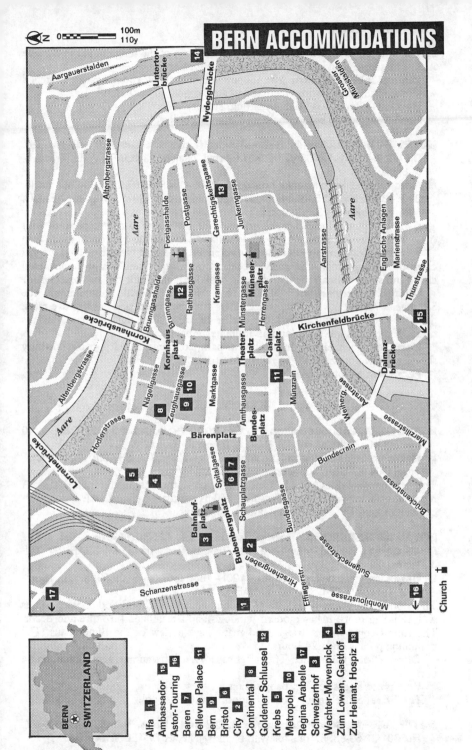

BERN ACCOMMODATIONS

0 ———— 100m
               110y

Alfa **1**
Ambassador **15**
Astor-Touring **16**
Baren **7**
Bellevue Palace **11**
Bern **9**
Bristol **6**
City **2**
Continental **8**
Goldener Schlussel **12**
Krebs **5**
Metropole **10**
Regina Arabelle **17**
Schweizerhof **3**
Wachter-Movenpick **4**
Zum Lowen, Gasthof **14**
Zur Heimat, Hospiz **13**

SWITZERLAND
BERN

Church ✚ ■

large and luxuriously furnished, and some have views of the Jungfrau in the Bernese Alps. The setting is old world, and the service is impeccable.

Dining/Entertainment: The monochromatic dining room has high, arched windows, a sun terrace with green-and-white parasols, and a bar.

Services: Room service, baby-sitting, laundry.

Facilities: Fitness center, indoor swimming pool.

HOTEL SCHWEIZERHOF, Schweizerhoflaube 11, CH-3001 Bern. Tel. 031/22-45-01. Fax 031/21-21-79. 94 rms, 7 suites. MINIBAR TV TEL **Tram:** 3, 9, or 12.

$ **Rates** (including continental breakfast): 230F–280F ($167.90–$204.35) single; 320F–390F ($233.55–$284.65) double; from 1,200F ($875.90) suite. AE, DC, MC, V. **Parking:** 25F ($18.25).

This centrally located hotel managed by the Gauer family is popular with diplomats. It contains many antiques and some of the best decorative art in Bern—18th-century drawing-room pieces, wall-size tapestries, and crystal chandeliers. Each room is uniquely decorated, but all offer comfortably upholstered chairs and sofas, with a fairly good chest, desk, or table. Some are air-conditioned.

Dining/Entertainment: There are several formal restaurants; the Schultheissenstube, my favorite, which offers attentive service and competitive rates; the 16th-century Simmentalerstube; and a Japanese restaurant, Yamato. Jaylin's nightclub provides live music and an intimate ambience.

Services: Valet parking in nearby car park, concierge, laundry, complimentary shoeshine, free porter service to railroad station.

Facilities: Shopping arcade.

EXPENSIVE

HOTEL ALFA, Laupenstrasse 15, CH-3008 Bern. Tel. 031/25-38-66. 40 rms (all with bath). MINIBAR TV TEL **Tram:** 3, 9, or 12.

$ **Rates** (including continental breakfast): 100F–120F ($73–$87.60) single; 130F–160F ($94.90–$116.80) double. AE, DC, MC, V.

This concrete-and-glass hotel is a short distance to the west of the train station. A restaurant occupies an annex. The sunny rooms are attractively decorated, and most contain a radio, TV, alarm clock, phone, and minibar.

HOTEL AMBASSADOR, Seftigenstrasse 99, CH-3007 Bern. Tel. 031/45-41-11. Fax 031/45-41-17. 136 rms (all with bath). MINIBAR TV TEL **Tram:** 9.

$ **Rates** (including buffet breakfast): 120F–150F ($87.60–$109.50) single; 165F–195F ($120.45–$142.35) double. AE, DC, MC, V.

This modern, nine-story hotel is the tallest building in a neighborhood of older houses with red-tiled roofs. It has modern windows and streamlined furniture and decor. The rooms come with a fridge, and many have a view of the Bundeshaus. The swimming pool is open 24 hours.

Dining/Entertainment: The hotel has a French restaurant, a snack bar, and a bar.

Services: Room service, baby-sitting.

Facilities: Sauna, fitness center, indoor swimming pool.

HOTEL BÄREN, Schauplatzgasse 4, CH-3011 Bern. Tel. 031/22-33-67. Fax 031/22-69-83. 57 rms (all with bath). MINIBAR TV TEL **Tram:** 9.

$ **Rates** (including buffet breakfast): 115F–150F ($83.95–$109.50) single; 165F–215F ($120.45–$156.95) double. AE, DC, MC, V.

Conveniently close to the Bundeshaus, the Bären has cozily modern accommodations fitted with contemporary furnishings in warm shades of brown and beige. True to its name, it has filled its lobby with replicas of bears in many manifestations.

HOTEL BERN, Zeughausgasse 9, CH-3011 Bern. Tel. 031/21-10-21. Fax 031/21-11-47. MINIBAR TV TEL **Tram:** 9.

$ **Rates** (including continental breakfast): 115F–150F ($83.95–$109.50) single; 165F–215F ($120.45–$156.95) double. AE, DC, MC, V.

This massive gray hotel, a host to diplomats and business travelers, sits behind one of Bern's most striking art deco facades, gracefully ornamented with arches, columns, and a series of iconoclastic sculptures. Extending from the lobby are seven drinking and dining rooms, each with a different decor. The guest rooms are comfortable and well furnished.

HOTEL BRISTOL, Schauplatzgasse 10, CH-3011 Bern. Tel. 031/22-01-01. Fax 031/22-94-79. 90 rms (all with bath). MINIBAR TV TEL **Tram:** 9.

$ **Rates** (including continental breakfast): 115F–150F ($83.95–$109.50) single; 165F–215F ($120.45–$156.95) double. AE, DC, MC, V.

Set behind a somber neoclassical facade, next door to the Bären, the Bristol has a simple lobby, which sets the tone. It has neither a bar nor a restaurant (so that guests often repair to the Bären for food and drink), but it does boast a sauna on one of the upper floors. Its bedrooms are high-ceilinged and have Nordic-inspired modern furniture.

HOTEL CITY, Bubenbergplatz 7, CH-3011 Bern. Tel. 031/22-53-77. Fax 031/22-06-36. 47 rms MINIBAR TV TEL

$ **Rates** (including continental breakfast): 120F–145F ($80.30–$105.85) single; 175F–195F ($127.75–$142.35) double. AE, DC, MC, V.

Across from the railroad station, this six-story, gray-stone hotel is often booked solid. The modern rooms have simple furniture and are equipped with a radio and a hairdryer. There's a bustling sidewalk café, but there are no restaurants other than the hotel's breakfast room.

HOTEL METROPOLE, Zeughausgasse 28, CH-3011 Bern. Tel. 031/22-50-21. Fax 031/21-11-53. 82 rms (all with bath). TV TEL **Tram:** 9.

$ **Rates** (including continental breakfast): 115F–150F ($83.95–$109.50) single; 165F–215F ($120.45–$156.95) double. AE, DC, MC, V.

Located in the city's center, the Metropole offers comfortable, if small, rooms and a

---

 FROMMER'S COOL FOR KIDS

HOTELS

Hotel Astor-Touring (see p. 184) Children under 6 pay half price, and children under 12 get a 30% discount if sharing their parents' room.

Hotel City (see p. 183) At the railroad station, this hotel has special rates for children sharing their parents' room: 40F ($29.20) for children 10 to 16, 30F ($21.90) for children 4 to 10 and free for infants.

restaurant, the Old Mill, which contains the wheel from an old water mill. The adjacent President Club Bar displays old photographs of nearly forgotten political leaders.

MODERATE

HOTEL ASTOR-TOURING, Zieglerstrasse 66. Tel. 031/45-86-66. Fax 031/46-26-80. 65 rms (all with bath). TV TEL **Tram:** 3.
$ Rates (including continental breakfast): 85F–108F ($62.05–$78.85) single; 120F–160F ($87.60–$116.80) double. AE, DC, MC, V.
This modern, well-maintained hotel is next to the Eigerplatz, a few minutes from the train station. The rooms are fairly spacious and many have balconies. The restaurant serves attractive meals at moderate prices.

HOTEL CONTINENTAL, Zeughausgasse 27, CH-3011 Bern. Tel. 031/22-26-26. Fax 031/22-85-24. 37 rms (all with shower or bath). TV TEL **Tram:** 3 or 9.
$ Rates (including continental breakfast): 88F–140F ($64.25–$102.20) single; 125F–160F ($91.25–$116.80) double. AE, DC, MC, V.
Located near the train station, at the edge of a square with a fountain, this two-star hotel has flower boxes at the windows. The public rooms are unpretentious, and the bedrooms are spacious and modern. A restaurant is attached to the hotel.

HOTEL KREBS, Genfergaasse 8, CH-3011 Bern. Tel. 031/22-49-42. Fax 031/22-10-35. 44 rms (all with shower or bath). TV TEL **Tram:** 3 or 9.
$ Rates (including continental breakfast): 105F ($76.65) single, 155F ($113.15) double. AE, DC, MC, V. **Parking:** 25F ($18.25).
This fully remodeled three-star hotel near the train station shares its ground floor with a store. The rooms are sunny, with attractive furniture. Some are partially paneled.

INEXPENSIVE

HOSPIZ ZUR HEIMAT, Gerechtigkeitsgasse 50, CH-3011 Bern. Tel. 031/22-04-36. 40 rms (17 with bath). TEL **Tram:** 12.
$ Rates (including continental breakfast): 54F ($39.40) single with sink, 74F ($54) single with shower and toilet; 80F ($58.40) double with sink, 104F ($75.90) double with shower and toilet. AE, DC, MC, V.
Set behind a gilded fountain in the old city, the Hospiz zur Heimat is the outstanding budget hotel choice in Bern. It has simply furnished bedrooms with large windows, each with its own flower box. The establishment has a cozy restaurant, which serves nourishing meals (but no alcohol); it is decorated with an enlarged Renaissance map of Bern.

HOTEL GOLDENER SCHLÜSSEL, Rathausgasse 72, CH-3011 Bern. Tel. 031/22-02-16. Fax 031/22-56-88. 29 rms (20 with shower). TV TEL **Tram:** 9.
$ Rates (including continental breakfast): 56F ($40.85) single without shower, 74F ($54) single with shower; 92F ($67.15) double without shower, 110F ($80.30) double with shower. MC, V.
The building housing the hotel dates from the 13th century, when it was used as a stable. Today it looks like a beautifully maintained patrician house. Some of the carpeted bedrooms have wood-paneled walls. The hotel's sidewalk café does a thriving business throughout the summer, and the restaurant (see Section 4, "Dining," below) offers reasonably priced meals.

HOTEL REGINA ARABELLE, Mittelstrasse 6, CH-3012 Bern. Tel. 031/ 23-03-05. 58 rms (36 with bath). TEL **Tram:** 3.

$ Rates: 57F ($41.60) single without bath, 66F–82F ($48.15–$59.85) single with bath; 92F–114F ($67.15–$90.50) double with bath. No credit cards.

Ⓢ This tranquil hotel a 10-minute walk from the train station is surrounded by a lawn with roses; it has a fountain and a sun terrace. Some of its conservatively furnished rooms have Oriental rugs over their parquet floors. The older building has cheaper rooms with shared toilets, although most have a private shower. In the newer building, all rooms have showers and toilets. The management is informal and helpful.

HOTEL WÄCHTER-MÖVENPICK, Genfergasse 4, CH-3011 Bern. Tel. 031/22-08-66. Fax 031/22-32-73. 44 rms (32 with bath or shower). MINIBAR TV TEL **Tram:** 3, 9, or 12.

$ Rates (including continental breakfast): 56F–83F ($40.85–$60.60) single without bath, 100F–125F ($73–$91.25) single with bath or shower; 145F–170F ($105.85–$124.10) double with bath or shower. AE, DC, MC, V.

This four-story corner hotel near the railroad station is efficiently managed by one of Switzerland's biggest hoteliers, the Mövenpick chain. It has a busy sidewalk café, with awnings. The hotel's comfortably furnished bedrooms have a special outlet for North American electrical appliances.

IN SUBURBAN WORB

GASTHOF ZUM LÖWEN, Enggisteinstrasse 3, CH-3076 Worb. Tel. 839/ 83-23-03. Fax 031/839-58-77. 14 rms (all with shower). MINIBAR TV TEL **Transportation:** Take a Worb-bound train east from Bern's Bahnhof.

$ Rates (including buffet breakfast): 75F ($54.75) single; 135F ($98.55) double. AE, DC, MC, V.

Ⓢ This romantic, ivory-covered country inn is in the eastern suburb of Worb, about 20 minutes from the center of Bern by train; it's easily accessible via Route 10. The inn has been in the same family for 11 generations and is now owned by Hans-Peter Bernhard. It is elegantly furnished and has fine examples of craftsmanship. Admire the stairway leading to the reception area from the ground-floor restaurant. The rustic restaurant offers such specialties as mignon de boeuf, entrecôte Café de Paris, and wild game in season. It's open daily for lunch from noon to 2pm and for dinner from 6:30 to 9:30pm; it's closed from mid-July to mid-August. Fixed-price meals range from 35F to 45F ($25.55 to $32.85). The large bar attracts locals. Both establishments are open Monday through Friday.

4. DINING

Bern's cuisine is international. There are dozens of specialty restaurants offering everything from paella to porterhouse, in addition to the famous Swiss potato dish Rösti. The best choice is one of the charming country inns on the outskirts.

Restaurants termed "expensive" charge $50 and up for dinner without wine; those described as "moderate" about $35. Restaurants that charge $25 or under for dinner without wine are considered "Inexpensive," at least in Bern.

IN ALTSTADT

EXPENSIVE

DELLA CASA, Schauplatzgasse 16. Tel. 22-21-42.
   Cuisine: CONTINENTAL. **Reservations:** Recommended. **Tram:** 3 or 9.
 $ Prices: Appetizers 12F–18F ($8.75–$13.15); main courses 22F–42F ($16.05–$30.65). DC, MC, V (upstairs only).
   Open: Lunch Mon–Sat 11am–2pm; dinner Mon–Sat 6–9:30pm. **Closed:** Ground level in July (upstairs dining room remains open).

Entering from under an arcade, you go into a low-ceilinged, paneled room, which is often crowded with chattering diners. (An inner room contains the day's newspapers for those eager to follow the latest political trends and opinions; indeed, the place has been called Switzerland's "unofficial Parliament headquarters.") A quieter, somewhat more formal dining room is found upstairs. The menu features continental and Italian dishes, such as bollito misto, a potpourri of boiled meats. Two of my local favorites are the ravioli maison and the fried zucchini; a popular meat specialty is a filet mignon à la bordelaise with Créole rice.

FROHSINN, Münstergasse 54. Tel. 22-37-68.
   Cuisine: SWISS/ITALIAN. **Reservations:** Required. **Tram:** 3 or 9.
 $ Prices: Appetizers 8F–18F ($5.85–$13.15); main courses 15F–38F ($10.95–$27.75). No credit cards.
   Open: Breakfast/lunch Tues–Sat 8am–2pm; dinner Tues–Sat 6–10pm.

This little restaurant, containing only a dozen tables, stands in the shadow of the Tour de l'Horloge (Clock Tower). It attracts businesspeople, journalists, and politicians as much for its cuisine, which is traditional and innovative, as for its atmosphere. The menu might include goose-liver mousse, liver with Rösti, or filet of beef in a whisky sauce. Other dishes reflect a southern Italian influence. Sabayon with strawberries is a seasonal specialty.

LE MISTRAL, Kramgasse 42. Tel. 22-82-77.
   Cuisine: CONTINENTAL. **Reservations:** Recommended. **Tram:** 3 or 9.
 $ Prices: Appetizers 6F–12F ($4.40–$8.75); main courses 22F–42F ($16.05–$30.65). AE, DC, MC, V.
   Open: Pizzeria, lunch Mon–Sat 11am–2pm; dinner Mon–Sat 6–11pm. Restaurant, dinner only, Mon–Sat 6:30pm–1am.

Named after the cold, violent winds that blow through Provence, Le Mistral consists of a street-level pizzeria and a restaurant in the basement. The pizzeria's specialties include salade niçoise, spaghetti, bolognese, and an array of pizzas, beginning at 11F ($8.05). Tortellini is always a favorite. (In the summer there's a sidewalk café, separated from the light traffic by a row of potted geraniums.)

   The restaurant, decorated to look like a chic stable, serves well-seasoned lamb, veal with morels and cream sauce, fish dishes, and grilled U.S. beefsteaks, including one made with the house special sauce, Le Filet Mistral. For dessert, try crêpes Suzette or sabayon au marsala.

RÄBLUS, Zeughausgasse 3. Tel. 22-59-08.
   Cuisine: FRENCH. **Reservations:** Required. **Tram:** 3 or 9.
 $ Prices: Appetizers 12F–20F ($8.75–$14.60); main courses 25F–38F ($18.25–$27.75). AE, DC, MC, V.
   Open: Lunch Mon–Sat 11am–2pm; dinner Mon–Sat 5pm–midnight.

The premier French restaurant of Bern serves the extravagant specialties of Peter Pulver, the owner and chef. The restaurant is centrally located, near the Clock Tower. Many guests stop for an apéritif in the ground-floor piano bar before proceeding upstairs to the dining room. Specialties include a gratiné of seafood, mignons of veal with morels, Indian-style curried chicken, Chinese fondue, coq au vin with noodles, and veal kidney flambée. For dessert you might try the crêpes Suzette.

MODERATE

ARLEQUIN, Gerechtigkeitsgasse 51. Tel. 22-39-46.

Cuisine: SWISS/ITALIAN. **Reservations:** Recommended. **Tram:** 9.

$ Prices: Appetizers 10F–20F ($7.30–$14.60); main courses 18F–30F ($13.15–$21.90). AE, DC, MC, V.

Open: Mon–Sat 3pm–12:30am.

Bern's society and intelligentsia are attracted to this informal restaurant in the city center. The rustic interior is decorated with art and bronze pieces. Typical Swiss dishes include chicken pâté with morel mushrooms in puff pastry, farmhouse ham and potato salad, and goulash soup. During the summer, tables are set up on the pergola-shaded outdoor terrace.

CHURRASCO, Aarbergergasse 60. Tel. 22-82-88.

Cuisine: ARGENTINIAN. **Reservations:** Recommended. **Tram:** 9.

$ Prices: Appetizers 8F–18F ($5.85–$13.15); main courses 18F–40F ($13.15–$29.20). AE, DC, MC, V.

Open: Sun–Thurs 11:30am–11:30pm, Fri–Sat 11:30am–midnight.

You can imagine yourself in Argentina here. The ranchero decor includes cowhide banquettes, hanging lamps fashioned from pierced tin drums, and rustic accessories of the type you might find on the pampas. A chef dressed like a gaucho grills seasoned meats over a wood fire. Specialties include rumpsteak and entrecôte (in portions labeled medium or *grande*), along with gazpacho, sangría, fried potatoes, and a special blend of coffee.

COMMERCE, Gerechtigkeitsgasse 74. Tel. 22-11-61.

Cuisine: SPANISH. **Reservations:** Required. **Tram:** 12.

$ Prices: Appetizers 5F–17.50F ($3.65–$12.90); main courses 10F–40F ($7.30–$29.20). AE, DC, MC, V.

Open: Lunch Tues–Sat noon–2pm; dinner Tues–Sat 6–9:30pm. **Closed:** Last 3 weeks in July to Aug 7.

This small Spanish tavern near the Fountain of Justice (Gerechtigkeitsbrunnen) attracts many expatriate Spaniards. The decor is Iberian, and the paella is very good. The specialty is scampi prepared in several ways; I also recommend the zarzuela, a Spanish-style bouillabaisse. The rice dishes and salads are all good.

GOLDENER SCHLÜSSEL, Rathausgasse 72. Tel. 22-02-16.

Cuisine: SWISS. **Reservations:** Recommended. **Tram:** 9.

$ Prices: Appetizers 8F–15F ($5.85–$10.95); main courses 15F–28F ($10.95–$20.45). MC, V.

Open: Lunch daily 11:30am–2pm; dinner daily 6–10:30pm; snacks Sun–Thurs 7am–11:30pm, Fri–Sat 7am–12:30am.

As you dine at this very Swiss restaurant, you can relish both the food and the atmosphere. Overhead is the old planking and stonework of the 13th-century building that contains it, and all around you is the bustle of a very busy workaday restaurant. Serving wholesome food in ample portions, the restaurant is on the street level of a budget-priced hotel of the same name (see Section 3, "Accommodations," above). Specialties include a mignon d'agneau au poivre vert (tenderloin of lamb with green-pepper sauce and corn croquettes), or Schweinbratwurst mit Zwiebelsauce (butter-fried sausage with onion sauce) and Rösti.

RESTAURANT HARMONIE, Hotelgasse 3. Tel. 22-38-40.
  Cuisine: SWISS. **Reservations:** Recommended. **Tram:** 9.
$ **Prices:** Appetizers 5F–15F ($3.65–$10.95); main courses 10F–30F ($7.30–$21.90). No credit cards.
  Open: Mon 3–11:30pm, Tues–Fri 8am–11:30pm, Sat 8am–3pm. **Closed:** July.

 Located at the corner of Münstergasse, a few blocks from the Houses of Parliament, this art nouveau charmer evokes 1890s Paris. The owners, Fritz and Marlise Gyger, have operated it since 1981 and have tried to maintain it in the style of their grandparents, who took it over in 1915. Service is efficient, and tables are spaced far enough apart to allow a feeling of intimacy. There are two separate dining rooms and a handful of sidewalk tables set beneath ivy-clad trellises. The menu might include tripe in tomato sauce with Rösti, fresh homemade egg noodles bolognese, or spinach ravioli. Typical lunch dishes include Rösti with ham and eggs, cheese fondue, curried rice, and ratatouille.

INEXPENSIVE

CAFE TSCHIREN, Kramgasse 73. Tel. 22-18-64.
  Cuisine: SWISS. **Reservations:** Not needed. **Tram:** 3 or 9.
$ **Prices:** Light meals from 15F ($10.95). AE, DC, MC, V.
  Open: Mon 11:30am–6:30pm, Tues–Sat 7:30am–6:30pm.
Located under an arcade near the Clock Tower, this café has a vaguely nostalgic wood-paneled dining room and a conservative clientele. There is a Swiss tearoom up a twisting flight of stairs, where you can enjoy light lunches and the luscious chocolate cakes made here.

CONFISERIE FELLER, Marktgasse 31. Tel. 22-58-52.
  Cuisine: SWISS. **Reservations:** Not needed. **Tram:** 3 or 9.
$ **Prices:** Breakfast 7.50F–10F ($5.50–$7.30); salads and platters 13.50F–19F ($9.85–$13.85). No credit cards.
  Open: Mon–Wed and Fri 7:30am–6:30pm, Thurs 7:30am–10pm, Sat 7:30am–5pm.

ⓕ FROMMER'S COOL FOR KIDS
RESTAURANTS

Churrasco (see p. 187) Kids delight in the cowhide ranchero decor, the staff dressed like Argentine cowboys, and the grilled steaks.

Café Tschiren (see p. 188) A very fine place for children, near the Clock Tower. Kids like the low-cost light lunches and the luscious chocolate cakes.

Gfeller am Bärenplatz (see p. 189) This place has practically a different dining section for everyone, including children who enjoy the American-style self-service cafeteria and the pastry buffet.

Set under the busy arcades of a medieval street near the railroad station, this long, narrow café is well known to the daytime shoppers of Bern. There's a bar with leatherette stools and small tables. On a printed card, you can indicate the kinds of salads you prefer, all of which will then be brought to your table assembled on a plate. Service is brisk.

PIAZZA LORENZINI, Marktgasse Passage 3. Tel. 22-78-50.
   Cuisine: TUSCAN. **Reservations:** Required. **Tram:** 3, 5, or 9.
$ **Prices:** Appetizers 5.30F–18F ($3.90–$13.15); main courses 10F–40F ($7.30–$29.20); fixed-price lunch 10.80F ($7.95). AE, MC, V.
   Open: Lunch Mon–Sat 11:30am–2:30pm; dinner Mon–Sat 6pm–12:30am.

This colorful and rustic restaurant serves Tuscan food. The staff offers such specialties as beefsteak Florentine flavored with garlic, coniglio alle erbe con legumi (Tuscan rabbit), and zuppa inglese (trifle).

RATSKELLER, Gerechtigkeitsgasse 81. Tel. 22-17-71.
   Cuisine: SWISS. **Reservations:** Recommended. **Tram:** 9.
$ **Prices:** Appetizers 8F–20F ($5.85–$14.60); main courses 15F–30F ($10.95–$21.90); fixed-price lunch from 22F ($16.05). AE, DC, MC, V.
   Open: Lunch noon–2pm; dinner 6–10pm; light meals 9am–10pm.
This historic establishment has old masonry, modernized paneling, and a battalion of friendly waitresses serving ample portions of food. Specialties include rack of lamb à la diable for two diners, an omelet soufflé aux fruits, veal kidneys Robert, and côte de veau in butter sauce.

SPECIALTY DINING
LOCAL FAVORITES

GFELLER AM BÄRENPLATZ, Bärenplatz. Tel. 22-69-44.
   Cuisine: SWISS. **Reservations:** Not needed. **Tram:** 3 or 9.
$ **Prices:** Appetizers 2.60F–3.80F ($1.90–$2.85); main courses 9.50F–22.20F ($6.95–$16.25); lunches 14.30F ($10.45). No credit cards.
   Open: Daily 10:30am–8pm. **Closed:** Dec 25.
This place serves wholesome meals to a loyal crowd of Bernese. The ground floor is divided into three dining areas. Upstairs is an American-style self-service cafeteria, with large windows opening onto a view of Bärenplatz. There is also a Swiss-style tearoom, as well as a pâtisserie buffet with pastries starting at 4F ($2.90). The restaurant specializes in lunch and early dinners. Portions are large and filling. Try Swiss cheese pie with both Emmental and Gruyère or sauerkraut with smoked pork, bacon, and sausage.

HOTEL DINING

BELLEVUE GRILL, in the Bellevue Palace Hotel, Kochergasse 3. Tel. 22-45-81.
   Cuisine: FRENCH. **Reservations:** Required. **Tram:** 3, 9, or 12.
$ **Prices:** Appetizers 15F–22F ($10.95–$16.05); main courses 22F–45F ($16.05–$32.85). AE, DC, MC, V.
   Open: Dinner only, daily 5:30–11pm. **Closed:** May–Sept.

This intensely formal restaurant is the premier dining room in one of the Swiss capital's finest hotels. A favorite of both diplomats and businesspeople, it serves French specialties with flair. Try the pheasant suprême with foie gras or a grilled American-bred steak with a herb-flavored sabayon.

GRILL SCHULTHEISSENSTUBE, in the Hotel Schweitzerhof, Schwizer-hoflaube 11. Tel. 22-45-01.
 Cuisine: SWISS. **Reservations:** Required. **Tram:** 3, 9, or 12.
$ **Prices:** Appetizers 15F–22F ($10.95–$16.05); main courses 28F–48F ($20.45–$35.05). AE, DC, MC, V.
 Open: Lunch Mon–Sat noon–2pm; dinner Mon–Sat 6:30pm–midnight.

This rustic brown-walled restaurant, on the hotel's second floor, is among the best in the country, according to some critics. The polished paneling, elegant accessories, and horseshoe-shaped bar create an ambience of elite sophistication (the menu cover was designed by Jean Cocteau). My favorite dishes are sea bass with fennel and mignonnettes of lamb flavored with basil. Daily specials include a terrine de foie de canard (duckling) naturelle, lobster soup flavored with tarragon, and blanc de turbot bordelaise.

DINING WITH A VIEW

RESTAURANT LA TERRASSE, in the Bellevue Palace Hotel, Kocher-gasse 3. Tel. 22-45-81.
 Cuisine: CONTINENTAL. **Reservations:** Recommended. **Tram:** 3, 9, or 12.
$ **Prices:** Appetizers 12F–20F ($8.75–$14.60); main courses 18F–38F ($13.15–$27.75). AE, DC, MC, V.
 Open: Lunch daily 11:30am–3pm; dinner daily 6:30–11:30pm.
For a unique gastronomic experience, try the chef's sophisticated *cuisine d'aujourd'hui*. From a terrace high above the Aare River, you can enjoy a spectacular panorama of the Alps. The menu might include turbot in white butter and breast of duckling à l'orange.

AFTER-THEATER SUPPERS

STADTRESTAURANT ZUR MUNZ, in the Bellevue Palace Hotel, Kochergasse 3. Tel. 22-45-81.
 Cuisine: SWISS. **Reservations:** Recommended. **Tram:** 3, 9, or 12.
$ **Prices:** Appetizers 10F–20F ($7.30–$14.60); main courses 18F–42F ($13.15–$30.65). AE, DC, MC, V.
 Open: Daily 8am–11pm.
The refined interior of this bistro is the ideal setting for early-morning coffee, a business lunch, or an after-theater supper. The menu includes fried breast of guinea fowl with mustard and sesame, and young rabbit ragoût with mushrooms and Savoy cabbage.

PICNIC FARE & WHERE TO EAT IT

You can often find the makings for a picnic at one of the food markets of Bern, including the daily **fruit market** on Bärenplatz. On Tuesday and Saturday morning you can also purchase food to go at the markets at Bundesplatz. On Thursday, there is an all-day market at Waisenhausplatz. Otherwise, you can find prepared food at one of the **supermarkets,** Migros or Ryffihof, near the Bahnhof on Bahnhofplatz.
 To enjoy your picnic, head for **Gurten,** Bern's own mountain, which can be reached in 20 minutes on tram no. 9 from the Bahnhof. A combined SVB/

Gurtenbahn ticket includes a funicular ride.

Once at this stroller's paradise you'll find a magnificent viewpoint for looking at the Bernese Alps as you enjoy your picnic. There is also a "children's fairyland."

RESTAURANTS BY CUISINE

Cuisines and Restaurants	Rating*
ARGENTINIAN	
Churrasco (page 187)	M
CONTINENTAL	
Della Casa (page 186)	E
Le Mistral (page 186)	E
Restaurant La Terrasse (page 190)	E
FRENCH	
Bellevue Grill (page 189)	E
Räblus (page 186)	E
Grill Schülteissenstube (page 190)	E
ITALIAN	
Arlequin (page 187)	M
Frohsinn (page 186)	E
Piazza Lorenzini (page 189)	I
SPANISH	
Commerce (page 187)	M
SWISS	
Arlequin (page 187)	M
Café Tschiren (page 188)	I
Confiserie Feller (page 188)	I
Frohssin (page 186)	E
Gfeller am Bärenplatz (page 189)	I
Goldener Schlüssel (page 187)	M
Grill Schultheissenstube (page 190)	E
Ratskeller (page 189)	I
Restaurant Harmonie (page 188)	M
Stadtrestaurant zur Munz (page 190)	E

*VE = Very Expensive; E = Expensive; M = Moderate; I = Inexpensive; B = Budget.

5. ATTRACTIONS

SIGHTSEEING STRATEGIES

IF YOU HAVE 1 DAY   Take a walking tour of Altstadt (Old Town) and visit the mascots of Bern, the bears at the Bear Pit (Bärengraben). Go inside the Cathedral of

St. Vincent (Münster), and see its tympanum or main portal. Stand at the Clock Tower (Zytgloggeturm), the town's west gate since 1191, 4 minutes before any hour and listen to its famous chimes. End your night at the famous Kornhaus Keller, the historic wine cellar of Bern (see Section 9, "Evening Entertainment," below).

IF YOU HAVE 2 DAYS Spend the first day as above. Devote the second day to all that you missed, including the Kunstmuseum (Fine Arts Museum) with its great masterpieces. In the afternoon visit the Botanischer Garten (Botanical Garden) and the Bern Historical Museum on a very busy day.

IF YOU HAVE 3 DAYS Spend your first 2 days as above. In the morning, visit the Swiss Alpine Museum, devoted to the conquests and scientific exploration of the Swiss Alps. Then see the Dählhölzli Zoo (Tierpark). By midday take a trip to Gurten, the mountain of Bern, offering a spectacular view of the Bernese Oberland (an ideal place for a picnic); it's reached by tram no. 9. In the evening, attend a folkloric show, with yodelers, at the Swiss Chalet Restaurant.

IF YOU HAVE 5 DAYS Spend the first 3 days as outlined above. On the fourth day, take an organized tour by rail—call 031/22-12-12 for information. The tour is a high alpine adventure, going by train first through Interlaken, Lauterbrunnen, Wengen, and Kleine Scheidegg, and then over the Jungfraujoch via Grindelwald and Interlaken and back to Bern. Jungfraujoch, at 11,333 feet, has the highest railway station in Europe and offers breathtaking views over glaciers and the Alps, including the so-called Ice Palace. The cost of this excursion is 121F ($88.30) in second class and 142F ($103.65) in first class.

On the fifth day, call the number above to book a "Golden Pass" excursion, which costs 54F ($39.40) per person in second class and 86F ($62.75) in first class. This train ride leaves Bern to visit the villages of the Simmental and the chic resort of Gstaad, before heading along the banks of the Saane River to Montreaux and its historic

---

IN THEIR FOOTSTEPS

Marie Tussaud (1760–1850) Madame Tussaud is a legend today because of her wax figures, which are displayed in London. She created molds from the faces of famous living personages, including Voltaire, Benjamin Franklin, and Sir Walter Scott, and from death masks that she made. Her most famous death mask was of Louis XVI, who was beheaded during the French Revolution.

• **Birthplace:** Born Marie Grosholtz, in Bern, Switzerland, on December 1, 1760.

• **Favorite Haunts:** Paris, where, with her husband, François, she modeled the heads of many of the Revolution's prominent leaders and victims (she herself was imprisoned during the Reign of Terror). London, where, in 1802, she held a successful exhibit of her collection at the Lyceum Theatre.

• **Place of Death:** She died on April 14, 1850, on London's Baker Street, at the site of her collection. (In 1884 her works were moved to Marylebone Road.)

DID YOU KNOW . . . ?

- Bern has the largest covered shopping promenade in Europe, 3½ miles of arcades.
- Some of the most splendid examples of European medieval architecture are found in Bern.
- After a fire in 1405 destroyed what had been a city built almost entirely of wood, the city fathers rebuilt Bern in sandstone.
- Eleven bridges span the Aare River, including one from 1489.
- Bern is the only Swiss city to be listed in its entirety as a world cultural landmark by the United Nations.
- The world's largest collection of the works by Paul Klee is in Bern.
- The bear is the heraldic symbol of Bern.
- Since 1984, Bern has been Europe's "most flower-decorated city."

Château de Chillon. Then it's by train or ship past the vineyards along Lake Geneva to Lausanne and back through the Fribourg region to Bern.

THE TOP ATTRACTIONS

In addition to Bern's major museums and cathedral, there are two other sights that qualify as top attractions.

The **Zutgloggeturm (Clock Tower)** (Zeitglocketurm in standard German), on Kramgasse, was built in the 12th century and restored in the 16th century. Four minutes before every hour, crowds gather for the world's oldest and biggest horological puppet show. Mechanical bears, jesters, and emperors put on an animated performance. Staged since 1530, the act is one of the longest running in show business. The tower marked the west gate of Bern until 1250.

The ✪ **Bärengraben (Bear Pits)**, lying on the opposite side of the river, is a deep, moon-shaped den where the bears, the mascots of Bern, have been kept since 1480. According to legend, when the Duke of Zähringen established the town in 1191, he sent his hunters out into the encircling woods, which were full of wild game. The duke promised to name the city after the first animal slain, which was the Bär (bear). Since then the town has been known as Bärn or Bern. Today, the bears are beloved, pampered, and fed by both residents and visitors (carrots are most appreciated.) The Bear Pits lie on the opposite side of the Nydegg Bridge (Nydeggbrücke) from the rest of Old Town. The bridge was built over one of the gorges of the Aare River; its central stone arch has a span of 180 feet and affords a sweeping view of the city from its center. Below the Bear Pits you can visit the beautiful **Rosengarten** (Rose Gardens), from which there is a great view of the medieval sector and the river.

CATHEDRAL OF ST. VINCENT, Münsterplatz. Tel. 22-05-72.

✪ The Münster is one of the newer Gothic churches in Switzerland, dating from 1421. The belfry, however, was completed in 1893. The most exceptional feature of this three-aisle, pillared basilica is the tympanum over the main portal, which depicts the Last Judgment and has more than 200 figures, some painted. Mammoth 15th-century stained-glass windows are in the chancel. The choir stalls from 1523 brought the Renaissance to Bern. In the Matter Chapel is a remarkable stained-glass window, the *Dance of Death,* constructed in the last year of World War I but based on a much older design. The cathedral's 300-foot-tall belfry dominates Bern and offers a panoramic sweep of the Bernese Alps; to get to the viewing platform, you must climb 270 steps. The vista also includes the old town, its bridges, and the Aare River. Outside the basilica on Münsterplatz is the Moses Fountain, built in 1545.

Admission: Cathedral, free; viewing platform, 2F ($1.45) adults, 1F (75¢) children.

Open: Cathedral, Mon–Sat 10am–noon and 2–4pm, Sun 10am–noon; viewing platform, daily 10:30am–4pm. **Closed:** Mon Nov–Easter. **Tram:** 9.

KUNSTMUSEUM (Fine Arts Museum), Hodlerstrasse 12. Tel. 22-09-44.

⭐ The world's largest collection of works by Paul Klee is the star attraction of this museum. The painter was born in Switzerland in 1879, the same year that the building housing the collection was built. The collection includes 40 oils and 2,000 drawings, gouaches, and watercolors.

The museum also has works by other artists, with emphasis on the 19th and 20th centuries. There is a collection of Italian 14th-century primitives, including Fra Angelico's *Virgin and Child*. Swiss primitives include some from the "Masters of the Carnation." Hodler, the romantic painter, is represented by allegorical frescoes depicting *Day* and *Night*. Impressionists include Monet, Manet, Sisley, and Cézanne, along with Delacroix and Bonnard; and there are typical scenes of Montmartre by Utrillo. Surrealistic painters represented here include Dalí, Seligman, Oppenheim, and Tschumi. There are also works by Kandinsky, Modigliani, Soutine, and Picasso. Constructivist painters include Taueber-Arp, Graeser, Lohse, Bill, Gorin, and Glarner. The museum also has works by contemporary Swiss artists.

Admission: Permanent collection, 3F ($2.20); special exhibitions, 5F–10F ($3.65–$7.30) extra.

Open: Tues 10am–9pm, Wed–Sun 10am–5pm. **Tram:** 9.

NATURHISTORISCHES MUSEUM (Natural History Museum), Bernastrasse 15. Tel. 43-18-39.

This museum, one of the city's best, is often overlooked by visitors. There are excellent exhibits of stuffed African beasts in a simulated natural habitat, Arctic mammals, and local fauna. The most popular display is the reptile collection.

Admission: 3F ($2.20); free on Wed, Sat, and Sun afternoon.

Open: Mon 2–5pm, Tues–Sat 9am–5pm, Sun 10am–5pm. **Tram:** 3 or 9.

MORE ATTRACTIONS

IN TOWN

The town's old but dignified **Rathaus (Town Hall),** on Rathausplatz, is still a center of political life. Built in 1406 in the Burgundian Gothic style and restored during World War II, the town hall has a double staircase and a covered porch.

BUNDESHAUS, Bundesplatz.

This Renaissance building, the Federal Palace, contains the two chambers of Switzerland's Parliament. There is a flower market in front of the building on Tuesday and Saturday morning.

Admission: Free.

Open: Tours given on the hour daily 9–11am and 2–4pm, except when Parliament is in session (no tour Sun 4pm). **Closed:** Public hols. **Tram:** 9.

SWISS PTT MUSEUM, Helvetiaplatz 16. Tel. 62-77-77.

FROMMER'S FAVORITE
BERN EXPERIENCES

The Gurten Connection In just 20 minutes by public transportation, you can leave the center of Bern's train station and be at Mount Gurten, a traffic-free pedestrian's paradise offering a magnificent view of the Bernese Alps. Ask at the station for a combined tram/Gurtenbahn ticket, which includes a funicular ride.

Shopping the Markets of Bern The markets, including the famous November Onion Market, are almost as old as Bern itself. Go to Waisenhausplatz every Tuesday and Saturday morning for the General Merchandise Market; head for Bundesplatz and Bärenplatz on Tuesday and Saturday morning for the fruit, vegetable, and flower market; and be at the cathedral on the first Saturday of every month for the Swiss Handcrafts Market.

Calling on the Bears Nothing is more traditional in Bern than visiting the famous Bear Pits, directly across from Nydeggbrücke. Symbols of the city, the animals flourish in captivity. They're fed carrots, figs, biscuits, and nuts, and they express their gratitude by performing all kinds of acrobatics.

The Post, Telegraph, and Telephone Museum has one of the largest stamp collections in the world. Other displays are devoted to the development of the country's postal and telecommunications systems.

Admission: 2F ($1.45) adults, free for children 15 and under.
Open: Summer, Mon 2–5pm, Tues–Sun 10am–5pm; winter, Tues–Sun 10am–noon and 2–5pm. **Tram:** 3 or 9.

BERNISCHES HISTORISCHES MUSEUM (Bern Historical Museum), Helvetiaplatz 5. Tel. 43-18-11.

This Neo-Gothic structure is built in the style of a 16th-century *Schloss* (castle) and contains many tapestries and antiques. The main attraction, however, is the loot captured from the Burgundians in 1476 at Grandson. These stunning treasures include standards and tapestries that once belonged to Charles the Bold.

Admission: 3F ($2.20) adults, 1.50F ($1.10) children.
Open: Tues–Sun 10am–5pm. **Tram:** 3 or 9.

BOTANISCHER GARTEN (Botanical Garden), Altenbergrain 21. Tel. 65-49-11.

Medicinal and fiber plants, examples of both tropical and subtropical vegetation, woodland and water plants, and a collection of plants from the cold steppes of central Asia are but some of the attractions of this vast garden arranged in descending terraces to the banks of the Aare River. Vegetation from various ecological zones are grown both outdoors and in greenhouses.

Admission: Free.
Open: Mon–Fri 7am–7pm, Sat–Sun 8am–5:30pm. **Tram:** 9.

Admission: 3F ($2.20) adults, 1.50F ($1.10) children.
Open: Tues–Sun 10am–5pm. **Tram:** 3 or 9.

NEARBY ATTRACTIONS

The most spectacular attraction in the immediate vicinity of Bern is the panoramic belvedere at ✪ **Mount Gurten.** It's 1½ miles from Bern on Monbijoustrasse, the road to Thun. At the suburb of Wabern, turn right (the road is marked) toward the funicular platform. It's a 10-minute ride to the summit of Mount Gurten, at 2,815 feet. There is a children's fairyland and a walking area, as well as the lookout point. Round-trip fare on tram no. 9 and the fastest cable railway in Europe is 5F ($3.65) from any stop on the municipal transport system. If you drive to the funicular, where you can park, round-trip passage to the summit costs 4F ($2.90).

KIDS' BERN

The **Dählhölzli Tierpark,** Tierparkweg (tel. 43-06-16), is one of the most interesting zoos in Europe. It offers a complete range of European fauna, from the tiny harvest mouse to the elk and musk oxen. You can admire more than 2,000 animals, including exotic birds, reptiles, and fish in the vivarium. Admission is 5F ($3.65) for adults, 2F ($1.45) for children. The zoo is open in summer, daily from 8am to 6:30pm; in winter, daily from 9am to 5pm. Bus: 18.

Kids also enjoy the **Zytgloggeturm (Clock Tower) and the Bärengraben (Bear Pits).** The **Naturhistorisches Museum,** with its fascinating reptile collection and gallery of stuffed African beasts, is best for a rainy day, and a **picnic at Mount Gurten** is a good way to cap any visit with children to Bern.

SPECIAL-INTEREST SIGHTSEEING

FOR THE SCIENCE ENTHUSIAST Albert Einstein, the great physicist and Nobel Prize winner, lived in Bern from 1902 to 1909—some of the happiest and most productive years of his life. He was working on the Theory of Relativity during that period. His house, at Kramgasse 49, is now occupied by the **Albert Einstein Gesellschaft (Albert Einstein Society)** (tel. 21-00-91). Admission is free, you can visit Monday through Saturday from 10am to 5pm. Tram no. 9 will get you there.

WALKING TOUR — Altstadt

Start: Bahnhofplatz.
Finish: Swiss Parliament.
Time: 2 hours.
Best Time: Any sunny day.

Start at Bahnhofplatz, site of the Bern railroad station, the Bahnhof, facing the:
1. **Hotel Schweizerhof,** a famous landmark hotel, where many ambassadors and presidents have stayed. Opening onto Bahnhofplatz is the:
2. **Church of the Holy Ghost,** or Heiliggeistkirche, dating from 1729 and somehow out of place in such a traffic-congested area. From the church, head east up Spittalgasse, coming first to:
3. **Bagpiper Fountain,** or Pfeiferbrunnen, depicting a player with a bagpipe atop

WALKING TOUR — ALTSTADT

Scale: 0 — 100m / 110y

N

Church ✝■

1. Hotel Schweizerhof
2. Church of the Holy Ghost
3. Bagpiper Fountain
4. Prison Gate
5. Marktgasse
6. Kornhausplatz
7. Clock Tower
8. Kramgasse
9. Zähringer Fountain
10. Albert Einstein's Home
11. Café Tschiren
12. Samson Fountain
13. Justice Fountain
14. Bear Pits
15. Cathedral of St. Vincent
16. Swiss Parliament

a column and capital, which was erected about 1545, presumably by Hans Gieng. Directly east of the fountain, at Bärenplatz, is the:

4. **Prison Gate,** or Käfigturm, dating from the 1200s. It now shelters a tiny museum devoted to the cultural and business life of the city. Continue east along:

5. **Marktgasse,** the main street of Old Town—filled with fashionable shops and florists. Many of its buildings date from the 17th century. The street leads into one of the principal squares of Altstadt:

6. **Kornhausplatz,** site of the Ogre Fountain, which is a representation of a carnival figure, with a pillar and capital erected about 1544. The Kornhaus, an old granary from the 1700s, also stands on the square; today it's a restaurant and wine cellar. Also opening onto this square is the celebrated:

7. **Clock Tower,** or Zytgloggeturm (*Zeitglocketurm,* in regular German), which was the town's west gate from 1191 to 1250. Its chimes start pealing at 4 minutes before every hour. A picture postcard of this scene is the most popular souvenir of Bern. Leaving Kornhausplatz, continue east along:

8. **Kramgasse,** a continuation of Marktgasse, containing many old houses with corner turrets and oriel windows. Another major fountain of Bern stands on this street, the:

9. **Zähringer Fountain,** or Zähringerbrunnen, a monument to the city founder, Berchtold von Zähringen. Here you can see the Bern bear, mascot of the city, along with the Zähringer coat of arms. The pillar, capital, and figure were erected in 1535 by Hans Hiltprand. Continuing, you come to:

10. **Albert Einstein's home,** Kramgasse 49, where, in 1905, the famous physicist wrote his Special Theory of Relativity.

REFUELING STOP At Kramgasse 73, light lunches and luscious pastries are served on the first floor, in the **11. Café Tschiren,** which has the ambience of a Swiss coffeehouse. A twisting flight of stairs leads to a tearoom.

The next fountain encountered on this same street is:

12. **The Samson Fountain,** or Simsonbrunnen, an allegory of strength, with a pillar and capital from 1527 and the figure from 1544.

Continue east along the street, which now changes its name to Gerechtigkeitsgasse. In the center of the street stands yet another famous fountain of Bern, the:

13. **Justice Fountain,** or Gerechtigkeitsbrunnen, an allegory of Justice, with worshipping subjects, including the pope, at her feet. The statue was erected in 1543.

Walk to the end of the street and continue across the river, crossing the Nydeggbrücke, until you reach the famous:

14. **Bear Pits,** or Bärengraben, immediately on your right. The city of Bern is named after the bear, which is its mascot. Bears have been kept in these pits since 1480.

Cross back over the bridge and this time take the street to the left, heading west along Junkerngasse until you reach the:

15. **Cathedral of St. Vincent,** at Münsterplatz. The cathedral's first stone was laid in 1421, but building went on until 1573. From the tower you get a panoramic view of Bern.

After leaving the cathedral, continue west along Münstergasse until you come to Theaterplatz, one of Altstadt's major squares. Continue west in a straight line, following the same street, which has now changed its name to Amthausgasse. You'll then approach Bundesplatz, site of the:

16. **The Federal Palace,** or Bundeshaus (Swiss Parliament). Capped with a massive dome, it was inspired by the Renaissance in Florence. This is the seat of Swiss democracy and one of the nation's symbols.

ORGANIZED TOURS

Highly recommended is the half-day tour that leaves from the tourist office at the main railroad station, the Bahnhof, at Bahnhofplatz. You'll have an English-speaking guide, as the tour takes you through the city's residential quarters, past museums, and down to the Aare River, which flows below the houses of Parliament. You'll see Rose Gardens and the late Gothic cathedral and stroll under the arcades to the Clock Tower. After visiting the Bear Pits, you'll be led through medieval streets of the city and back to the railroad station. Tours are conducted from May to October, daily at 10am and 2pm; in April, Monday through Saturday at 2pm; and from November to March, on Saturday at 2pm. The tour costs 19F ($13.85).

6. SPECIAL & FREE EVENTS

For special events at the time of your visit, see *This Week in Bern,* available at your hotel reception desk or at the tourist office. Dates vary every year for the famous **Shrovetide Carnival** (sometime in Feb or Mar).

In April or May an **International Jazz Festival** is offered, and in July or August a cultural presentation called the **Old Town Summer Festival** is staged.

One of Europe's most famous markets, the **Bern Onion Market,** takes place on November 4.

Details regarding these and other events are available at the Swiss National Tourist Office.

7. SPORTS & RECREATION

The people of Bern are not particularly addicted to spectator sports, but they are very fond of recreational sports in which they supply the action. The vast playground of Europe, the Bernese Oberland, is at their doorstep, and they take advantage of it.

CYCLING TOURS   There are approximately 1,860 miles of roadway in the Bernese Oberland around Bern. Pick up a copy of a bicycle map, outlining the routes, at the tourist office, then rent a bicycle at the Bahnhof (tel. 21-11-11) and set off on your adventure.

FITNESS, SAUNA, SOLARIUM   Go to the **STB Training Center,** Seilerstrasse 21 (tel. 25-02-03), where full facilities are provided to keep you in shape.

GOLF   If you are a member of a golf club back home and have your membership card, you can patronize the **Golf and Country Club** in Blumisberg (tel. 037/36-13-

80), 11 miles west of Bern near Flamatt (on the road to Fribourg). Call for more information.

RAMBLING   It is estimated that there are some 155 miles of marked walking trails in the area around Bern. You can pick up a rambling map at the tourist office.

TENNIS   Courts are available at **Thalmatt,** Mettlenwaldweg 19, Herrenschwaden (tel. 24-14-22).

SWIMMING   The city's best indoor pool, along with a Turkish bath and sauna, are at **Hallenbad,** Maulbeerstrasse 14 (tel. 25-36-56). Hours vary daily. Admission is 3F ($2.20) for swimming; another 11F to 15F ($8.05 to $10.95) is charged for use of the sauna or the Turkish bath.

8. SAVVY SHOPPING

THE SHOPPING SCENE

Stores in the city center are usually open on Monday from 2 to 6:30pm; on Tuesday, Wednesday, and Friday from 8:15am to 6:30pm; on Thursday from 8:15am to 9pm; and on Saturday from 8:15am to 4pm. They're closed Sunday. Some specialty shops have different hours.

SHOPPING A TO Z

ANTIQUES

ALTSTADT GALERIE, Kramgasse 7. Tel. 22-23-81.
   This antique shop has two floors of Swiss chests and tables, many of which are made of pine and come from the Bernese Oberland. Prices are clearly marked. The owner also exhibits works by Swiss painters.

DEPARTMENT STORES

GLOBUS, Spitalgasse 17. Tel. 22-12-55.
   This department store is comparable to Bloomingdale's. It has departments for "everything." Many people from the Bernese Oberland come to Bern just to shop at Globus.

JEMOLI, Marktgasse 10. Tel. 22-61-22.
   This particular branch of the famous department store offers seven floors with 100 different departments. It lies on the main street of Bern. Many Swiss souvenirs, often handcrafts, are offered.

LOEB AG BERN, Spitalgasse 45. Tel. 22-44-55.
   This store, in the center of town, has everything and is a good bet if you forgot to pack some essential item. You can leave your children in the store's kindergarten for up to 2 hours while you shop.

FASHIONS

CIOLINA MODEHAUS, Marktgasse 51. Tel. 22-11-91.
This is a high-fashion women's boutique. Clothes have fine styling but high price tags. It's on the main street.

FEIN-KALLER & CO., Marktgasse 55. Tel. 22-99-51.
This is one of the top stores for men's fashions. Fashions reflect a continental flair. Prices are high, but the quality is first-rate.

JEWELRY

GUBELIN, Bahnhofplatz 11. Tel. 22-54-33.
This is one of the finest jewelry stores in Bern, and one of the most reliable places in which to purchase a genuine Swiss watch. It's just one of seven branches of the oldest jewelry and watch manufacturer in central Switzerland.

LEATHER GOODS

CAPITOL BALLY, Spitalgasse 9. Tel. 22-54-81.
A branch of the famous Swiss shoe manufacturer, the store carries a complete line of Bally's high-quality footwear. Spitalgasse lies right off Bahnhofplatz.

GYGAX MODE IN LEDER, Spitalgasse 4. Tel. 22-25-61.
Gygax Mode is the leading name in leather goods. It sells not only locally produced goods but also some of the best leather items from its neighboring countries. The location is right off Bahnhofplatz.

SOUVENIRS

HEIMATWERK, Kramgasse 61. Tel. 22-30-00.
Located in the arcade of a gray-stone building on a historic street near the Clock Tower, Heimatwerk sells handcrafts from all over Switzerland. Typical items include wood carvings, textiles, music boxes, and jewelry. Wood and ceramic objects are in the basement.

STAMPS

PTT, Zeughausgasse 19. Tel. 62-36-96.
This stamp store is open Monday through Friday from 8:30am to 5:30pm and on Saturday from 8:30am to noon. Here, the philatelist will find the finest collection in Bern, including many rare stamps.

9. EVENING ENTERTAINMENT

Most Bern residents, like the hard workers that they are, get up early on weekday mornings, so they usually limit their evening entertainment to a drink or two at one of the historic cellars, such as the Kornhauskeller or the Klötzlikeller. Nevertheless, the city offers several late-night clubs, with dancing and cabaret, for the nocturnally active international crowd. *This Week in Bern,* distributed free by the tourist office, has a list of cultural events.

THE PERFORMING ARTS

THE MAJOR CONCERT/PERFORMANCE HALLS The Bern Symphony Orchestra, considered one of the finest orchestras in Europe, is conducted by the widely acclaimed Peter Maag. Concerts by the orchestra usually take place either at the **Konservatorium für Musik,** Kramgasse 36 (tel. 22-62-21), or at the **Radio Studio Bern,** Schwarztorstrasse 21 (tel. 46-91-11). Sometimes they are given in churches. Pick up a copy of *This Week in Bern* for details.

Major opera and ballet performances are staged at the **Stadttheater** and the **Theater am Käfigturm.**

THEATER The leading theater in Bern is the **Stadttheater (Municipal Theater),** at Kornhausplatz 20 (tel. 22-07-77). Performances are in German, but even if you don't speak German, you might want to attend an opera or a ballet.

Contemporary plays in German are presented at the **Kleintheater,** Kramgasse 6 (tel. 22-42-42).

DANCE Ballet, cabaret, and many other types of performances are presented at the **Theater am Käfigturm,** Spitalgasse 4 (tel. 22-30-80).

LOCAL CULTURAL ENTERTAINMENT Yodelers and a brass oompah band perform at the **Swiss Chalet Restaurant** in the Hotel Glocke, Rathausgasse 75 (tel. 22-37-71). The dining room is brick with beamed ceilings and red-checkered tablecloths. Oversize cow bells and alpine farm implements hang on the walls. The music begins at 8:30pm on a quiet note as patrons finish their dinner. From 9:30 to 10:30pm there's a concert, with dancing afterward. The kitchen is open until 12:45am—perfect for after-theater snacks. Dinner begins at 40F ($29.20); beer, from 6F ($4.40). Admission is free.

THE CLUB & MUSIC SCENE

KORNHAUS KELLER, Kornhausplatz 18. Tel. 22-11-33.

This former grain warehouse is the best-known wine cellar in the city. The symmetrical stone building, with an arcade on the ground floor, is located in the old city. The cellar seats hundreds of diners in a baronial atmosphere; musical acts are often performed in the evening. The Sunday brunch concert, from 10 to 11:45am, always includes alpine melodies produced by a brass band and accordions. A plate of smoked meats and sauerkraut is the classic dish to order. Hot food is served from 11:30am to 1:45pm and 6:30 to 8:45pm daily. A la carte dinners run 18F to 35F ($13.15 to $25.55), and there's no admission charge.

JAYLIN'S CLUB, in the Hotel Schweizerhof, Bahnhofplatz 11. Tel. 22-45-01.

The most elegant club in town offers live entertainment in a plush, glittering ambience. Located in a prestigious hotel, it attracts patrons from many parts of

Europe, among them visiting heads of state. Musical acts are likely to include American and English jazz groups. The apéritif concert on Saturday from 4 to 7pm is very popular. It's open Monday through Saturday from 9pm to 4am. Admission is 15F ($10.95); free for hotel guests. Drinks begin at 22F ($16.05).

THE BAR SCENE

ARCADY BAR, in the Hotel Schweitzerhof, Schwizerhoflaube 11. Tel. 22-45-01.

Begin your evening with an apéritif here, or drop by later for a nightcap. You'll probably see ambassadors drinking champagne and eating oysters. The elegant decor includes butler's tables and Chinese lamps. You can order snacks, including omelets for 18F ($13.15) and an assiette grisonnaise (a plate of air-dried meats from the Grisons) for 26F ($19). Dress well. The club is open daily from 11am to midnight. Drinks start at 22F ($16.05).

KLÖTZLIKELLER, 62 Gerechtigkeitsgasse. Tel. 22-74-56.

⭐ The oldest wine tavern in Bern is near the Gerechtigkeitsbrunnen (Fountain of Justice), the first fountain you see on your walk from the Bärengraben (Bear Pits) to the Zytgloggeturm (Clock Tower). Watch for the lantern outside an angled cellar door. The well-known tavern dates from 1635 and is leased by the city to an independent operator (a long time ago, the town fathers decreed that only an unmarried woman should get the lease). The menu includes traditional Rösti and Bratwurst with salad and Rösti with ham. You can also order traditional Swiss cheese dishes (raclette, cheese toast, and sliced cheese). Try the wine from the city's own vineyard, at 30F ($21.90) and up per bottle. Open Tuesday through Saturday from 4pm to 12:30am. An à la carte dinner starts at 25F ($18.25).

BELLEVUE BAR, in the Bellevue Palace Hotel, Kochergasse 3. Tel. 22-45-81.

This is the favorite meeting place for international and Bernese businesspeople and politicians. There is piano music in the evening. Seating is available on the terrace in summer. Open daily from 6pm to 2am. Drinks begin at 18F ($13.15).

SPECIALTY BARS & CLUBS

MOCAMBO, Genfergasse 10. Tel. 22-151.

This nightclub combines striptease with disco. The decor includes the the skyline of New York, and the DJ operates out of a pink Cadillac. There are four bars. Open daily from 9pm to 3am. Drinks begin at 18F ($13.15).

Admission: Fri–Sat 22F ($16.05), including one soft drink. Sun–Thurs free.

URSUS CLUB, Junkerngasse 1. Tel. 22-74-06.

Situated near the Bärengraben (Bear Pits), this is one of the leading gay clubs of Bern. Many of the customers are from the Bernese Oberland; some are from the foreign embassies in Bern, so that the place has an international atmosphere. It's open Tuesday through Thursday from 6 to 11:30pm, on Friday from 8:30pm to 12:30am, on Saturday from 8:30pm to 3am, and on Sunday from 5 to 11pm. Beer costs 5F ($3.65).

Admission: Free.

A GAMBLING CASINO

Across the river from the oldest section of Bern, the **Kursaal,** Schanzlistrasse 71-77 (tel. 42-54-66), is the only place in town to gamble. Indeed, it's a great spot for novices to learn gambling, for serious money rarely changes hands here—betting is limited to between 1F and 5F (75¢ and $3.65), as required by Swiss law. There are restaurants, dance halls, and bars. It's open daily from 9pm to midnight and admission is free. Drinks cost 12F ($8.75) and up.

10. NETWORKS & RESOURCES

FOR STUDENTS Make sure you carry an **International Student Identity Card (ISIC),** which entitles you to substantial reductions, not only on theater and opera tickets, but on tourist office–sponsored events. See Chapter 2 for more details.

In Bern, for budget travel tickets and travel discounts, go to **SSR,** Länggasstrasse 32 (tel. 24-03-12), open Monday through Friday from 10am to 6pm.

FOR GAY MEN AND LESBIANS The gay liberation headquarters in Bern is the **Homosexuelle Arbeitsgrupen Bern,** Brunngasse 17 (tel. 22-63-53), which has meetings at this address in the Käfistube on Wednesday, Thursday, Saturday, and Sunday from 7 to 11pm. Special nights are "mixed," but basically this is a men's center.

For information about local events, lesbians can call **SOS telefon** (tel. 22-45-43).

FOR WOMEN Women find Bern and the greater Bernese Oberland a safe destination, where they are relatively free of sexual harassment. The women's center at Bern is **INFRA,** Längmauerweg 1 (tel. 22-17-95), run by OFRA, the local political action group.

FOR SENIORS Go to the tourist office and request a copy of **"Season for Seniors."** This booklet lists some 450 hotels in 200 Swiss towns and resorts, including the Bernese Oberland, that offer special off-season rates for senior citizens (women over 62 and men over 65).

11. EASY EXCURSIONS FROM BERN

EMMENTAL The district of Emmental, in the canton of Bern, just 10 miles or so from the capital, is the pastoral home of the famous hole-filled Swiss cheese. The cheese, called Emmentaler (sometimes spelled Emmenthaler), is made in wheels weighing up to 180 pounds. Even the smallest hamlet has its own cheese maker. Many of the large Bernese farms have been in the same family for generations; most have a main house, or Bauernhaus, and an adjoining *Stöckli,* where the grandparents retire when they get too old to run the farm.

The country inns are known for their good, hearty food and abundant hospitality. Government officials often take special guests outside the city for dinner at one of the local inns.

If you're planning to visit Lake Lucerne after Bern, the quickest way to get there is through Emmental. The scenery is beautiful, for beyond the farms and rolling hills loom the snowy Alps. Burgdorf is the gateway to the district.

Burgdorf This small town in Emmental, northeast of the capital, is reached by fast train service from Bern. It is known for its **castle,** characterized by a trio of towers that have been turned into a historical museum of passing interest. The view of the Bernese Alps is memorable. This large stronghold on an isolated crag dates from the 12th century when it was founded by the dukes of Zähringen, who turned it into one of the country's most formidable bastions of defense. It's open April to October, Monday through Saturday from 2 to 5pm and on Sunday from 9:30 to 11:30am and 2 to 5pm. Admission is 3F ($2.20). Burgdorf also has a late Gothic church, from the end of the 15th century, and many attractive and well-maintained guildhouses.

CHAPTER 7

T E BERNES OBERLAND

- **WHAT'S SPECIAL ABOUT THE BERNESE OBERLAND**
- **1. INTERLAKEN**
- **2. MÜRREN**
- **3. WENGEN**
- **4. GRINDELWALD**
- **5. KANDERSTEG**
- **6. GSTAAD**

The Bernese Oberland is one of the great tourist attractions of the world and one of the best equipped for winter sports. For example, more than 150 installations transport skiers to well-maintained downhill runs. It sprawls between the Reuss River and Lake Geneva, with the Rhône forming its southern border. The area includes two lakes formed by the Aare River, the Thun and the Brienz. The Oberland also takes in the Alps, culminating in the Jungfrau at 13,642 feet and the Finsteraarhorn at 14,022 feet. The canton of Bern, which encompasses most of the area, is the second-largest canton in Switzerland and contains some 100 square miles of glaciers.

The best center for exploring the Bernese Oberland is Interlaken, which is the most popular summer resort. Others, such as Gstaad, Grindelwald, Kandersteg, and Mürren, are both summer and winter playgrounds. You can ski in the mountains during the winter and surf, sail, and waterski on Lake Thun in the summer.

SEEING THE BERNESE OBERLAND

GETTING THERE   Interlaken, along with Bern, is a traditional gateway to the Bernese Oberland and can be your center if you want to see the most dramatic scenic wonders in the canton. About 20 trains from all parts of Switzerland traverse the area, and all the main resorts are linked by rail or cable cars. The four major ski resorts are Gstaad, Mürren, Grindelwald, and Wengen.

IF YOU HAVE A WEEK

Days 1 and 2: Establish your base at Interlaken and use it for exploring the major attractions on Lake Thun and Lake Brienz.
Day 3: While still based at Interlaken, you can pay a visit to the mighty Jungfraujoch.
Day 4: Select one of the ski resorts in the area—especially Mürren, Grindelwald, or Wengen—and use it as a base for exploring some of the natural wonders of the area. More excursions are possible from Grindelwald.
Days 5 and 6: Head for Gstaad, the chicest resort of the Bernese Oberland, for 2 days and nights of fun.

GETTING AROUND   To compensate for the region's almost impossible geography, Swiss engineers have crisscrossed the Oberland with cogwheel railways (some of

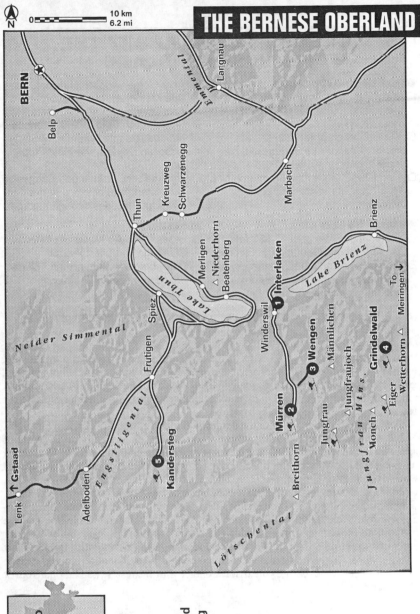

THE BERNESE OBERLAND

0 |▬▬▬▬| 10 km
          6.2 mi

N

BERN ★

Belp

Langnau

Simmental

Kreuzweg

Schwarzenegg

Thun

Marbach

Merligen

△ Niederhorn

Beatenberg

Brienz

Lake Thun

Lake Brienz

Interlaken ❶

Winderswil

To Meiringen →

Spiez

Neider Simmental

Frutigen

△ Männlichen

Wengen ❸

△ Jungfraujoch

Grindelwald ❹

Wetterhorn △

Engstligental

△ Jungfrau

△ Mönch

△ Eiger

Jungfrau Mtns.

Mürren ❷

△ Kandersteg ❺

↑ Gstaad

Adelboden

△ Breithorn

Lenk

Lötschental

SWITZERLAND

★ BERN

The Bernese
Oberland

❶ Interlaken
❷ Mürren
❸ Wengen
❹ Grindelwald
❺ Kandersteg

WHAT'S SPECIAL ABOUT THE BERNESE OBERLAND

Great Towns/Villages
- ☐ Interlaken, a 3-century-old holiday resort and tourist capital of the Bernese Oberland.
- ☐ Gstaad, haven of the rich and famous, set against a backdrop of glaciers and mountain lakes.
- ☐ Grindelwald, called the "glacier village," a major winter and summer mecca.

Natural Spectacles
- ☐ Jungfraujoch, rising to 11,333 feet, the highest railway station in Europe.
- ☐ First, a viewing "table" opening onto the Eiger Peaks, the Wetterhorn, and the Grindelwald Basin.

- ☐ Aare Gorge, wonder of nature, outside Meiringen; gorges cut by the Aare River.
- ☐ Reichenbach Falls, where Sherlock Holmes struggled with Dr. Moriarty in Conan Doyle's *The Final Problem*.
- ☐ Trümmelbach Falls, a good excursion from Interlaken, plunging in five powerful cascades through a gorge.

Museums
- ☐ Swiss Open-Air Museum of Rural Dwellings and Lifestyles, at Ballenberg, an architectural "Switzerland in a nutshell," covering 2,000 acres.

them still driven by steam), aeriel cableways, and sinuous mountain roads, and established scheduled crossings of Lake Brienz by ferry. Though initially confusing, getting to a particular resort is usually part of the fun. The region's busiest railroad junction, and the point where most travelers change trains for smaller railways and the region's short-range bus lines, is Interlaken.

A **transportation pass** for the Bernese Oberland costs 125F ($91.25) for adults. You can also ask for a **Family Card.** This allows children up to 16 years of age—accompanied by at least one parent—to travel free. Young people 16 to 25, if unmarried, pay only half fare if accompanied by at least one parent. The **Regional Holiday Season Ticket** is valid on most railroads, all mountain trains, cable cars, chair lifts, steamers on Lakes Thun and Brienz, and most postal-bus lines in the area. The ticket also qualifies you for a 25% reduction on the Kleine Scheidegg-Eigergletscher-Jungfraujoch railway, the Mürren-Schilthorn aerial cable line, and the bus to Grosse Scheidegg and Bussalp. The ticket, valid for 15 days, can be used for unlimited travel on 5 days of your choice and as a season ticket entitling you to any number of tickets at half fare. You must purchase your Regional Holiday Season Ticket at least 1 week before you arrive. Contact your nearest Swiss National Tourist Office for details.

1. INTERLAKEN

34 miles SE of Bern, 81 miles SW of Zurich

GETTING THERE   By Train   There are several trains daily between Zurich and Interlaken (trip time: 2 hrs.) and between Bern and Interlaken (40 min.). Frequent train service also connects Geneva and Interlaken (2½ hrs).

Although the town has two different railway stations, Interlaken East (Ost) and

Interlaken West, most of the city's center lies near or around Interlaken West. The stations are about 2 miles apart.

By Car   From Bern, drive south on N6 to Spiez, then continue west on N8 to Interlaken.

ESSENTIALS   Information   The **Interlaken Tourist Office** is at Höheweg 37 (tel. 036/22-21-21), in the Hotel Metropole Building. It's open in the summer Monday through Friday from 8am to noon and 2 to 6pm, on Saturday from 8am to noon and 2 to 5pm, and on Sunday from 4 to 6pm; in the winter, Monday through Friday from 8am to noon and 2 to 6pm, and on Saturday from 8am to noon.

Fast Facts   The **telephone area code** for Interlaken is 036. The tourist office (tel. 22-21-21) will help you find a **baby-sitter.** Apotheke Dr. Portmann, Höheweg 4 (tel. 22-34-26), is a convenient **drugstore.**

For **lost and found,** go to the Communal Building at Général-Guisan-Strasse 43 (tel. 21-22-25); for **medical emergencies,** call these numbers: a doctor at 23-23-23 and a hospital at 26-26-26; you will be advised (in English) what to do. You'll find **luggage-storage facilities** at the two major train stations, Interlaken East (tel. 22-30-24) and Interlaken West (tel. 22-35-26); you can leave your luggage for several hours or days.

Interlaken is the tourist capital of the Bernese Oberland. Cableways and cog railways designed for steeply inclined hills and mountains connect it with most of the region's villages and dazzling sights, including the snowy heights of the Jungfrau, which rises a short distance to the south. Excursion possibilities into the rest of the Oberland are both numerous and dazzling.

The "town between the lakes" (Thun and Brienz) has been a holiday resort for more than 300 years. Although it began its prosperity as a summer resort, it has developed into a year-round playground, altering its allure and its role as the seasons change. During the winter, skiers take advantage of the town's low prices. Interlaken charges low-season prices in January and February, when smaller resorts at higher altitudes are charging their highest rates of the year. The most expensive time to visit Interlaken is during midsummer, when high-altitude (and snowless) ski resorts often charge their lowest rates.

An Augustinian monastery was founded at Interlaken in 1130 but was later closed during the Reformation; the ruins can still be seen in a park in the center of town. Tourism to the area can be said to have begun in 1690, when the Margrave Frederic Albert of Brandenburg undertook a journey into the snow-covered rocks of the Jungfrau massif. However, tourism as we know it today dawned at the beginning of the 19th century, when artists and writers (many of them British) were drawn to the town by its scenery. As the country's railroad and steamer services improved, a steady stream of visitors followed, including such notables as Mark Twain, Goethe, Mendelssohn, and representatives from the royal families of Europe.

WHAT TO SEE & DO

SIGHTS   The **Höheweg** covers 35 acres in the middle of town, between the west and east train stations. Once the property of Augustinian monks, it was acquired in the mid-19th century by the hotel keepers of Interlaken, who turned it into a park. As you stroll along Höhenpromenade, admire the famous view of the Jungfrau. Another beautiful sight is the **flower clock** at the Kursaal (casino). You will also see fiacres, the horse-drawn cabs beloved by Edwardians. The promenade is lined with hotels, cafés, and gardens.

Cross over the Aare River to **Unterseen,** built in 1280 by Berthold von Eschenbach. There you can visit the parish church, with its late Gothic tower dating from 1471. This is one of the most photographed sights in the Bernese Oberland. The Mönch appears on the left of the tower, the Jungfrau on the right.

Back in Interlaken, visit the **Touristik-Museum der Jungfrau-Region,** Am Stadthausplatz, Obere Gasse 26 (tel. 22-98-30), the first regional museum of tourism in the country. Exhibitions show the growth of tourism in the region during the past 2 centuries. The museum is open from May to mid-October, Tuesday through Sunday from 10am to 12:30pm and 2 to 5pm. Admission is 3F ($2.20) 2F ($1.45) with a Visitor's Card.

To see the sights of Interlaken, Matten, and Unterseen, while riding in a fiacre, go to Westbahnhof. The half-hour, round-trip tour costs 20F ($14.60) for one person, 25F ($18.25) for two, and 30F ($21.90) for three riders.

Other attractions include animal parks, afternoon concerts, and the delicious pastries sold in cafés. During the summer, visitors can sit in covered grandstands and watch Schiller's version of the William Tell story and the formation of the Swiss Confederation. Lake steamers carry passengers across Lakes Brienz and Thun.

SPORTS   If you need some exercise after a lot of sightseeing and fondue dipping, Interlaken offers many opportunities for sports—sailing, windsurfing, rowing, fishing, golf, tennis, mountain trekking, and glider flying. There is also a swimming pool. More information is available at the tourist office.

Golf   You can play at the Interlaken-Unterseen course (tel. 22-60-22) from April 1 to October 31. The cost is 55F ($40.15) Monday through Friday and 70F ($51.10) on Saturday and Sunday. With a tourist card, the cost is reduced to 45F ($32.85) Monday through Friday and 60F ($43.80) on Saturday and Sunday.

Horseback Riding   There are several bridle paths between Lake Thun and Lake Brienz. The **Voegeli Riding School,** Scheidgasse 66, in Unterseen (tel. 22-74-16), and **Häsler Riding Stables,** Alpenstrasse 21B, in Bönigen (tel. 22-52-70), offer guided rides, costing 25F ($18.25) for 1 hour and 45F ($32.85) for 2 hours.

Swimming   There's a public **indoor pool** (tel. 22-24-16) behind the casino, with a solarium and a fitness room. It's open all year, Tuesday through Friday from 9am to 9:30pm and on Saturday and Sunday from 9am to 6pm. Admission is 6F ($4.40) for adults, 5F ($3.65) for adults with a Visitor's Card, and 3F ($2.20) for children 6 to 16. Children under 6 are admitted free.

Interlaken also has an **open-air pool** with a 33-foot diving board. It's open May to September, daily from 8:30am to 6pm. Admission is 3F ($2.20) for adults, 2.50F ($1.85) for adults with a Visitor's Card, and 2F ($1.45) for children.

Tennis   Use of an indoor court at the **Höhematte** costs 16F ($11.70) per hour, 14F ($10.20) with a Visitor's Card. If you're alone and willing to be matched up with another person, it will cost you half the court fee. For reservations, phone 22-14-72 Monday through Friday from 8am to noon and 2 to 5pm. The courts are open from mid-April to mid-October, Monday through Friday from 8am to 5pm.

WHERE TO STAY

Train arrivals are either at Interlaken East or Interlaken West. If you're loaded with luggage, you'll find a taxi waiting to take you to one of the local hotels or to one of the neighboring resorts, such as Grindelwald. However, after you have been deposited at one of the local hotels, nearly all of which are in the center of Interlaken, you will rarely need a taxi as the town is closely knit and is best explored on foot. Buses are used for connecting the satellite towns and villages or heading to locations on the outskirts, not for traveling about Interlaken center.

VERY EXPENSIVE

GRAND HOTEL BEAU-RIVAGE, Höheweg 211, CH-3800 Interlaken. Tel. 036/21-62-72. Fax 036/23-28-47. 99 rms (all with bath). MINIBAR TV TEL
$ Rates (including buffet breakfast): 200F–220F ($146–$160.60) single; 310F–350F ($226.25–$255.45) double. AE, DC, MC, V. **Parking:** 25F ($18.25).

⭐ This five-star Italian Renaissance hotel, between Höheweg and the Aare River, is one of the grand hotels of Interlaken, renovated in the Belle Epoque style. The central tower has an ascending series of covered loggias decorated with carvings and flowers, a triangular pediment, and a mansard roof. There are two wings with gables and wrought-iron balconies. The renovated rooms are conservatively modern.

Dining/Entertainment: A pianist plays nightly in Le Vieux Rivage. The restaurant, La Bonne Fourchette, offers candlelit dinners by a log fire; it specializes in a cuisine du marché (fresh from the market). A big breakfast buffet is served in L'Ambiance, the biggest restaurant.
Services: Laundry, baby-sitting, room service.
Facilities: Indoor pool, fitness club, sauna.

GRAND HOTEL VICTORIA-JUNGFRAU, Höheweg 41, CH-3800 Interlaken. Tel. 036/21-21-71. Fax 036/22-26-71. 228 rms (all with bath). MINIBAR TV TEL
$ Rates (including buffet breakfast): 250F–295F ($182.50–$215.30) single; 420F–480F ($306.55–$350.35) double. AE, DC, M, V.

⭐ For generations, this grand hotel has been considered one of the most important resort properties of Switzerland. Designed with a richly ornate Victorian styling, it sits right in the town center, at the foot of rigidly symmetrical gardens. It has valuable antiques and one of the best-trained staffs in Interlaken.

Dining/Entertainment: There are two elegant restaurants, three bars (some of which serve snacks), and a disco with live music. One of the bars has comfortable settees.
Services: Room service, baby-sitting.
Facilities: Swimming pool, indoor and outdoor tennis courts, sports facility.

EXPENSIVE

BELLEVUE-GARDEN HOTEL, Marktgasse, CH-3800 Interlaken. Tel. 036/22-44-31. 50 rms (all with bath). TEL
$ Rates (including continental breakfast): 90F–120F ($65.70–$87.60) single; 130F–190F ($94.90–$138.70) double. AE, DC, MC, V. **Closed:** Mid-Oct to first week of Apr. **Parking:** Free.
This updated version of a fortified castle is in a field on the banks of the Aare River, a 3-minute walk from the Westbahnhof. The English-style garden has flowering trees and landscaped walkways—the Fink-Uetz family likes to share a love of nature. The public rooms have comfortable late 19th-century furniture. There is a rustic gazebo next to a wrought-iron fence on the riverbank. The rooms are comfortably furnished and well maintained; TV is available upon request.

HOTEL INTERLAKEN, Höheweg 74, CH-3800 Interlaken. Tel. 036/21-22-11. Fax 036/23-31-21. 60 rms (all with bath). MINIBAR TV TEL

$ Rates (including continental breakfast): 80F–130F ($58.40–$94.90) single; 126F–216F ($91.95–$157.70) double. AE, DC, MC, V. **Parking:** Free.

Byron and Mendelssohn stayed here. The hotel, directly east of the casino, has been gutted and rebuilt since, with a salmon-colored facade sporting baroque touches. The most expensive rooms have a few 19th-century antiques; the rest have conservative, modern furnishings. Amenities include a radio.

Dining/Entertainment: There's a rustic bar, a Swiss-style tavern, and one of the city's only Chinese restaurants.

Services: Laundry.

Facilities: Sauna, garden.

HOTEL KREBS, Bahnhofstrasse 4, CH-3800 Interlaken. Tel. 036/22-71-61. Fax 036/23-24-65. 62 rms (all with bath). TV TEL

$ Rates (including continental breakfast): 100F–130F ($73–$94.90) single; 166F–216F ($121.15–$157.70) double. AE, DC, MC, V.

Located in the shopping district of Interlaken, just off Postplatz, this hotel has a mansard roof, green shutters, and a private garden. There are wooden ceilings and walls and a skillfully crafted wooden staircase leading to the upper floors. The bedrooms are pleasant and comfortable, and some have timbered ceilings.

HOTEL METROPOLE, Höheweg 37, CH-3800 Interlaken. Tel. 036/21-21-51. Fax 036/22-84-87. 100 rms (all with bath). MINIBAR TV TEL

$ Rates (including continental breakfast): 140F–165F ($102.20–$120.45) single; 230F–290F ($167.90–$211.65) double. AE, DC, MC, V. **Parking:** 25F ($18.25).

Americans often prefer this sleek, modern hotel in the center to the aging palaces of Interlaken. The 18-story building was built in 1976 and has been stylishly renovated. It is probably the most up-to-date and best-managed hotel in town. The rooms have plush carpeting, modern furniture, and balconies. The rooms facing south have a spectacular view of Interlaken and the towering mountains.

Dining/Entertainment: The hotel has one of the city's finest restaurants, Le Charolais (see "Where to Dine," below). There are also two medium-priced restaurants serving lunch, as well as a piano bar and an early-evening bar by the pool. The panoramic café is one of the meeting places of Interlaken.

Services: Room service, baby-sitting.

Facilities: Indoor swimming pool, sauna.

HOTEL ROYAL ST. GEORGES, Höheweg, CH-3800 Interlaken. Tel. 036/22-75-75. Fax 036/23-30-75. 152 rms (all with bath). MINIBAR TV TEL

$ Rates: 100F–130F ($73–$94.90) single; 166F–216F ($121.15–$157.70) double. AE, DC, MC, V. **Parking:** 25F ($18.25). **Closed:** Nov–Mar.

This 19th-century hotel, west of the casino, has elaborate confectionery decorations, a gabled red-tile roof, and dozens of small spires. The lower floors have balconies and loggias, with wrought-iron details. The public rooms retain their original rococo splendor. Some of the more expensive bedrooms have original high ceilings; other rooms are modern. The hotel has a salon bar and two restaurants.

STELLA HOTEL, Général-Guisan-Strasse 10, CH-3800 Interlaken. Tel. 036/22-88-71. Fax 036/22-66-71. 30 rms (all with bath), 4 suites. MINIBAR TV TEL

$ Rates (including continental breakfast): 105F–140F ($76.65–$102.20) single; 140F–245F ($102.20–$178.85) double; from 355F ($259.10) suite. AE, DC, MC, V.

The balconies of this hotel, which lies in the center of Rosenstrasse, offer good views of the mountains. In the winter, the white concrete building blends in with the snowy scene around it. Werner and Christine Hofmann-Frei manage the place and are interested in winter sports. Most rooms are furnished in a modern chalet style. There is a rustic piano bar and lounge. The restaurant serves international meals. An indoor swimming pool is on the premises.

MODERATE

HOTEL BEAU-SITE, Seestrasse 16, CH-3800 Interlaken. Tel. 036/22-81-81. Fax 036/23-29-26. 54 rms (42 with bath). TEL

$ **Rates** (including continental breakfast): 50F ($36.50) single without bath, 120F ($87.60) single with bath; 100F ($73) double without bath, 194F ($141.10) double with bath. AE, DC, MC, V. **Parking:** Free.

A short walk from the Interlaken West train station, this hotel is surrounded by spacious gardens with parasol-shaded card tables and chaise longues in the summer. The Ritter family provides a pleasant and relaxing oasis in the middle of town. The hotel has two fine restaurants, the budget-price Stübli and the more elegant and expensive Veranda. The rooms are modern; most of them have a TV and a minibar.

HOTEL BERNERHOF, Höheweg, CH-3800 Interlaken. Tel. 036/22-31-31. Fax 036/22-84-28. 38 rms (all with bath). MINIBAR TEL

$ **Rates** (including continental breakfast): 98F–120F ($71.55–$87.60) single; 150F–180F ($109.50–$131.40) double. AE, DC, MC, V.

Located near the Interlaken West train station, this hotel has an interesting, angled facade. The main salon is vividly decorated with scarlet carpeting and modern chairs with delta-shaped supports. There is an open fireplace in the center. The Hanspeter-Anderegg family offers comfortably furnished rooms with recessed balconies.

HOTEL DU NORD, Höheweg 70, CH-3800 Interlaken. Tel. 036/22-26-31. Fax 036/23-33-37. 56 rms (all with bath). MINIBAR TV TEL

$ **Rates** (including continental breakfast): 95F ($69.35) single; 194F ($141.60) double. Half-board 28F ($20.45) extra. AE, DC, MC, V.

Built at the turn of the century, this yellow hotel borders a wide city park in the town's center. Your host, Reinhard Engel, is sophisticated and warm, and the staff is especially cooperative. Rooms are pleasant and well scrubbed, with modern furniture and radios. The restaurant, Im Gade, is cozy. The street-level bar is a special place, where locals gather to talk. Look for the rack of neckties that are said to have been removed from guests to help them relax.

HOTEL WEISSES KREUZ, Höheweg, CH-3800 Interlaken. Tel. 036/22-59-51. Fax 036/23-35-55. 90 rms (all with shower or bath). TEL

$ **Rates** (including continental breakfast): 100F ($73) single; 160F ($116.80) double. Half-board 28F ($29.45) extra. AE, DC, MC, V.

This inconspicuous hotel is at the end of a row of buildings on the corner of Jungfraustrasse, in the center of Interlaken. The interior is pleasantly decorated with white walls and half-paneling, with a few Oriental rugs. The bedrooms are furnished in a functional style. Managed by the Bieri family, the hotel is open all year.

PARK-HOTEL MATTENHOF, Hauptstrasse, Matten, CH-3800 Interlaken. Tel. 036/21-61-21. Fax 036/22-28-88. 85 rms (all with bath). TV TEL **Bus:** 5.

$ Rates (including half board): 94F–140F ($68.60–$102.20) single; 160F–240F ($116.80–$175.20) double. AE, DC, MC, V. **Parking:** 5F ($3.65).

This large, old-fashioned hotel is in a secluded area at the edge of a forest; you can reach it by heading away from the center toward Wilderswil. The exterior looks like a private castle, with its high, pointed roof, tower, loggias, and balconies. Peter Bühler and his family offer a calm retreat, with terraces, manicured lawns, and panoramic views of the Alps. The salons are warmly decorated and sunny. The hotel's facilities include a swimming pool, a tennis court, play areas, terraces, bars, and restaurants.

INEXPENSIVE

ALFA GARNI, Bernastrasse 7, CH-3800 Interlaken. Tel. 036/22-69-22. 13 rms (10 with bath).

$ Rates (including continental breakfast): 45F ($32.85) single without bath, 80F ($58.40) single with bath; 90F ($65.70) double without bath, 105F ($76.65) double with bath. AE, DC, MC, V. **Closed:** 3 weeks in Jan.

Located near the Interlaken West train station, this villa with gables and turrets was originally a doctor's office and home, built in the 1950s. It is managed by Rolf Schertz and Margaret Weibel. The rooms are well maintained, orderly, and furnished in a modern style. The owners provide thoughtful little touches, such as leaving a chocolate bar on your pillow at night.

DE LA PAIX, Bernastrasse 24, CH-3800 Interlaken. Tel. 036/22-70-44. Fax 036/22-87-28. 45 rms (all with shower or bath). TEL

$ Rates (including continental breakfast): 70F–85F ($51.10–$62.05) single; 90F–140F ($65.70–$102.20) double. AE, DC, MC, V.

This family-run hotel is a pleasant stopover, a block away from the Bahnhof (Interlaken West). You'll recognize it by its ornate roofline, which is gabled and tiled like a house in a Brothers Grimm fairy tale. Gillian and Georges Etterli offer a relaxed atmosphere. The rooms are simply but comfortably furnished; some have a TV.

GASTHOF HIRSCHEN, Hauptstrasse, CH-3800 Matten/Interlaken. Tel. 036/22-15-45. Fax 036/23-37-45. 20 rms (all with bath). TV TEL

$ Rates (including continental breakfast): 85F–110F ($62.05–$80.30) single; 132F–172F ($96.35–$125.55) double. AE, DC, MC, V. **Parking:** Free.

The Graf Sterchi family manages this rustic chalet whose garden terrace opens onto a view of Jungfrau. The Gasthof, on the road to Grindelwald, is open year round. It has a paneled dining room, a less formal bar, and a rear garden. The bedrooms are modernized.

HOTEL LÖTSCHBERG, Bernastrasse, CH-3800 Interlaken. Tel. 036/22-25-45. 25 rms (15 with bath). TEL

$ Rates (including continental breakfast): 64F ($46.70) single without bath, 92F ($67.15) single with bath; 112F ($81.75) double without bath, 152F ($110.95) double with bath. AE, MC, V.

One of the best bargains in town is two blocks from the Interlaken West train station. This baroque hotel, managed by the Hutmacher family, enjoys a lot of repeat business. It's open all year. The rooms are comfortably furnished. There is a reasonably priced restaurant with outside tables.

SWISS INN, Général-Guisan-Strasse 23, CH-3800 Interlaken. Tel. 036/22-36-26. Fax 036/23-23-03. 25 rms (all with shower or bath), 5 apartments. MINIBAR

$ Rates (including continental breakfast): 50F–90F ($36.50–$65.70) single; 85F–140F ($62.05–$102.20) double; from 150F ($109.50) apartment. MC, V. **Parking:** Free.

This small Edwardian inn with balconies and gables offers good value. Mrs. Vreny Müller-Lohner offers tastefully decorated one- to three-room apartments equipped with kitchenettes, minibars, phones, radios, and TVs. They accommodate two to seven guests. The inn has a lounge, a sitting area with a fireplace, and a grill for barbecues in the garden. There are laundry facilities on the premises.

WHERE TO DINE

Most guests dine at their hotels, which partially explains why such a world-famous resort as Interlaken has so few independent restaurants worth noting. Here are several for those who are staying in a *hotel garni* or who want a change of fare.

EXPENSIVE

LE CHAROLAIS, in the Hotel Métropole, Höheweg 37. Tel. 21-21-51.
   Cuisine: SWISS/FRENCH. **Reservations:** Recommended.
$ Prices: Appetizers 12F–22F ($8.75–$16.05); main courses 18F–42F ($13.15–$30.65). AE, DC, MC, V.
   Open: Lunch daily 11:30am–2pm; dinner daily 6:30–9:30pm.

Refined cuisine and superb service are offered at this specialty restaurant. It's located up a flight of stairs from the hotel's lobby. For an appetizer, I recommend terrine of quail. Excellent main dishes include filet of sole with morels, sliced veal with three kinds of mushrooms, grilled lobster with armagnac butter, and medallions of pork flavored with Roquefort.

CHEZ PIERRE, Alpenstrasse 58. Tel. 22-94-22.
   Cuisine: FRENCH. **Reservations:** Required.
$ Prices: Appetizers 15F–25F ($10.95–$18.25); main courses 22F–40F ($16.05–$29.20). AE, DC, MC, V.
   Open: Dinner only, Thurs–Tues 7–9:30pm. **Closed:** Jan.
Here you can order fresh fish from a tank. Other superb dishes include filet of beef with tarragon sauce or roast saddle of lamb provençal. The chef specializes in lobster. A typical meal includes goose-liver terrine, followed by double sirloin steak with mushrooms.

MODERATE

GASTHOF HIRSCHEN, Hauptstrasse, Matten. Tel. 22-15-45.
   Cuisine: SWISS. **Reservations:** Recommended.
$ Prices: Appetizers 10F–15F ($7.30–$10.95); main courses 12F–30F ($8.75–$21.90). AE, DC, MC, V.
   Open: Lunch Thurs–Mon 11:30am–2pm; dinner Wed–Mon 6–9pm.

This hotel's restaurant offers some of the best and most reasonably priced meals in town. The menu is varied and sophisticated. The potato-and-mushroom soup is the finest I've ever tasted. Other appetizers include ravioli filled with crab or a homemade terrine. For a main dish, I recommend sautéed calves' liver, filet of beef bordelaise, beef goulash, broiled trout, or chateaubriand.

RESTAURANT LOTUS, in the Hotel Interlaken, Höheweg 74. Tel. 21-22-11.
   Cuisine: CHINESE. **Reservations:** Recommended.

$ Prices: Appetizers 12F–20F ($8.75–$14.60); main courses 15F–32F ($10.95–$23.35). AE, DC, MC, V.

Open: Dinner only, Thurs–Tues 6–9:30pm.

Chinese cuisine is a pleasant surprise at this conservative Swiss hotel—in fact, it's the only Chinese restaurant in town. Appetizers include spring rolls, fried wonton, and Peking ravioli. The menu is evenly balanced between fish, poultry, and meat dishes, including fish Peking style, duck with Chinese mushrooms, and pork Szechuan. A limited selection of wine is offered.

INEXPENSIVE

PIZPAZ, Bahnhofstrasse 1. Tel. 22-25-33.
   Cuisine: ITALIAN. **Reservations:** Not needed.
   $ Prices: Appetizers 8F–11F ($5.85–$8.05); main courses 11F–22F ($8.05–$16.05). MC, V.
   Open: Tues–Sun 10:30am–1am.

Italian specialties are served at this pizzeria in the center of town. Its many outdoor tables make it a popular place, especially with families. Typical dishes include calves' liver in marsala, osso buco, and at least 20 different pizzas. Gelato misto, a mixed selection of ice cream, is the most popular dessert.

SCHUH, Höheweg 56. Tel. 22-94-41.
   Cuisine: SWISS. **Reservations:** Not needed.
   $ Prices: Appetizers 8F–15F ($5.85–$10.95); main courses 18F–25F ($13.15–$18.25); fixed-price meal from 18F ($13.15). AE, DC, MC, V.
   Open: Lunch Tues–Sun 11am–2pm; dinner Tues–Sun 6–9pm.

This attractive restaurant, confiserie, and tearoom in the center of town has long been known for its pastries. The alpine building has a thick roof arched over the fourth-floor windows, and in back, a sunny terrace with globe lights and a well-kept lawn. The dining room has large windows and a Viennese ambience. A pianist provides music. The Beutler-Kropf family owns this restaurant near the Hotel Victoria.

EVENING ENTERTAINMENT

BARBARELLA, in the Grand Hotel Victoria-Jungfrau, Höheweg 41. Tel. 22-12-38.

It's probably the most urbanized disco in town, with a sophisticated sound system and an impressive array of klieg lights. There is plenty of comfortable seating. Sometimes on Sunday night the disco puts on a brief cabaret act. Drinks begin at 12F ($8.75).
Admission: 10F ($7.30).

HIGHLIFE, Rugenparkstrasse 2. Tel. 22-15-50.

In this high-tech disco, popular music is played in a room of chrome, mirrors, and focused spotlights. It's open daily from 9pm to 3am. Drinks cost about 12F ($8.75).
Admission: Sun–Thurs free, Fri–Sat 10F ($7.30).

SPYCHER, in the Kursaal, Höheweg/Strandbadstrasse. Tel. 22-25-21.

Popular and rowdy, this is a large, rustically decorated restaurant and nightclub, where Swiss folklore music and shows are presented between May and September at

9pm every night except Wednesday. In midwinter, shows are performed only once or twice a week, usually every Monday and Thursday night. Fixed-price meals, ranging from 25F to 35F ($18.25 to $25.55) each, are served from 7 until about 11pm. Spycher is located in the largest convention hall in the Bernese Oberland. Drinks run about 10F ($7.30).

Admission: 14F ($10.20).

WESTERN SALOON, in the Grand Hotel Victoria-Jungfrau, Höheweg 41. Tel. 22-12-38.

After touring the Jungfrau, you might get nostalgic for the Old West. This steakhouse, bar, and concert hall offers U.S. beef, fresh salads, and country-and-western acts from the United States and Britain. A full meal can easily cost 50F ($36.50) per person, although most visitors come here only to drink and dance. It's open every night from 8:30pm to 2am. Drinks run about 10F ($7.30).

Admission: Free.

EASY EXCURSIONS

By making the mountains of the Bernese Oberland accessible to train and cable car, Swiss engineers opened the way for visitors to this popular region to explore some of the most scenic and enjoyable spots in the country. There are many organized excursions, as adventurous as they are varied.

JUNGFRAUJOCH ✪ A trip to Jungfraujoch, at 11,333 feet, is the highlight of many visits to Switzerland. For more than a century it has been the highest railway station in Europe. It's also one of the most expensive: A second-class, round-trip tour costs 127.40F ($93.10) for adults. However, families can fill out a Family Card form, available at the railway station, which allows children 16 and under to ride free. Departures are usually daily at 8am from the east station in Interlaken; expect to return about 4pm. To check times, contact the sales office of Jungfrau Railways, Höheweg 37, CH-3800 Interlaken (tel. 036/22-52-52).

With luck, the weather and visibility will be ideal. You should always consult the tourist office in Interlaken before boarding the train. The trip is comfortable and safe, and packed with adventure. You first take the Wengernalp railway (WAB), a rack railway that opened in 1893. It takes you to Lauterbrunnen, at 2,612 feet, where you change to a train heading for the Kleine Scheidegg station, at 6,762 feet. Welcome to avalanche country. The view includes the Mönch, the Eiger Wall, and the Jungfrau, which was named for the white-clad Augustinian nuns of medieval Interlaken (*Jungfrau* means "virgin").

At Kleine Scheidegg you change to the highest rack railway in Europe, the Jungfraubahn. You have 6 miles to go; 4 of them will be going through a tunnel carved into the mountain between 1896 and 1912, under the direction of Adolf Guyer-Zeller. You stop twice, for about 5 minutes each time, at Eigerwand and Eismeer, where you can view the sea of ice from windows in the rock. The Eigerwand is at 9,400 feet and Eismeer is at 10,368 feet. When the train emerges from the tunnel, the daylight is momentarily blinding. Bring a pair of sunglasses to help your eyes adjust. Notorious among mountain climbers, the Eigernordwand, the "north wall" is very steep.

Once at the Jungfraujoch terminus, you may feel a little giddy until you get used to the air. You'll find much to do in this eerie world high up Jungfrau. But take it slow—your body metabolism will be affected and you may tire quickly.

Behind the post office is an elevator that takes you to a corridor leading to the famed ✪ **Eispalast (Ice Palace).** Here you'll be walking within what is called "eternal ice" in caverns hewn out of the slowest-moving section of the glacier. Cut 65 feet below the glacier's surface, they were begun in 1934 by a Swiss guide and subsequently enlarged and embellished with additional sculptures by others. Everything from wall to statue is made of ice, including full-size replicas of vintage automobiles and local chaplains.

After returning to the station, you can take the Sphinx Tunnel to another elevator. This one takes you up 356 feet to an observation deck called the **Sphinx Terraces,** overlooking the saddle between the Mönch and Jungfrau peaks. You can also see the Aletsch Glacier, a 14-mile river of ice—the longest in Europe. The snow melts into Lake Geneva and eventually flows into the Mediterranean.

Astronomical and meteorological research is conducted at a scientific station here. There is a research exhibition that explains weather conditions, and a video presentation.

There are several restaurants from which to choose. The traditional choice is **Jungfraujoch Glacier Restaurant. Top of Europe,** opened in 1987, offers five more restaurants. There is also a self-service cafeteria. As a final adventure, you can take a sleigh ride, pulled by stout huskies.

On your way back down the mountain, you return to Kleine Scheidegg station, but can vary your route by going through Grindelwald, which offers panoramic views of the treacherous north wall.

HARDER KULM   For a less ambitious excursion, set out from Interlaken East for this belvedere at 4,337 feet. The funicular ride takes 15 minutes and costs 16F ($11.70) round-trip. From the lookout, you can see Interlaken, the Bernese Alps, and the two lakes, Thun and Brienz, that give Interlaken its name. Departures are every half hour, daily, from May to mid-October. There is a mountain restaurant at Harder Kulm, with observation terraces. For details call 036/22-12-56; if there's no answer, try 036/22-52-52.

HEIMWEHFLUH   You can also take a funicular up to Heimwehfluh, at 2,215 feet, where you'll be rewarded with beautiful views of both lakes and of the classic trio of Jungfrau, Mönch, and Eiger. In addition to the lookout tower, there is a café and restaurant. The funicular station is about a 6-minute walk from the Interlaken West rail station at the southern end of Rugenparkstrasse. The ride takes about 5 minutes and costs 8F ($5.85) round-trip for adults, 4.40F ($3.30) for children. Departures are from May to mid-October, daily from 9:30am to 5:30pm.

LAKE TOURS   A fleet of ships with a total capacity of 6,720 passengers operates on **Lake Thun** daily from April to October. The lake is 11½ miles long and 2½ miles wide. A 4-hour voyage from Interlaken West to Beatenbucht, Spiez, Overhofen, Thun, and back costs 22F ($16.05). A shorter trip, Interlaken West to Beatenbucht, Spiez, and back, takes 2 hours and costs 15F ($10.95). Both trips are free with a Swiss Holiday Card.

Boat trips on **Lake Brienz** are also available daily from April to October. The lake is nearly 9 miles long and 1½ miles wide. There are five motor ships and one steamship, with a total capacity of 3,160 passengers. A 2½-hour voyage from Interlaken East to Iseltwald, Giessbach, Brienz, and back costs 17.50F ($12.80). A shorter trip (1¼ hr.), from Interlaken East to Iseltwald and back, costs 8F ($5.85). Both are free with a Holiday Card. For details, call 033/36-02-58.

ST. BEATUS CAVES   These caves are in the cliffs above Lake Thun, between Beatenbucht and Sundlauenen, to the west of Interlaken. According to legend, they were once a dragon's lair until Beatus, a 6th-century Irish missionary, slew the beast and set up residence here. The caves came to be known as Grottes de St-Béat in French and St.-Beatus-Höhlen in German. They can be reached by boat, or by bus or car along the cliff-bottom road, or on foot along the historic pilgrim's way.

The caves can be explored to a depth of 3,300 feet, along a path lit by electricity. There is a reproduction of a settlement made by prehistoric cave dwellers. The museum section also includes the cell of St. Beatus. Tours are available through the huge caverns and grottoes with striking stalactites and stalagmites. The caves are open from Palm Sunday to October, daily from 9:30am to 5:30pm. Tours depart every 30 minutes and cost 6F ($4.40) for adults and 2.50F ($1.85) for children. For details, call 036/41-16-43.

Just inside the cave entrance is a well-managed restaurant. You can have a meal or a snack inside the cozy dining area or outside on the cave terrace.

WILDERSWIL/SCHYNIGE PLATTE   Less than 2 miles south of Interlaken, Wilderswil stands on a plain between Lakes Brienz and Thun, at the foot of the Jungfrau Mountains. It is both a summer and a winter resort, and the starting point for many excursions. The resort has 16 levels of accommodations, ranging from hotels to guesthouses, but most tourists stay in Interlaken and visit Wilderswil to take the excursion to Schynige Platte. To get to Wilderswil, take a 6-minute train ride from the Interlaken East station. Switch to a cogwheel train for the harrowing, steep ascent to the Schynige Platte, at 6,454 feet. The rack railway, which opened in 1893, climbs the 4½-mile slope in less than an hour, with gradients of up to 25%. There are more than a dozen trips a day in season, from late May to mid-October, costing 38F ($27.75) round-trip.

There is an alpine garden in Schynige Platte, containing some 500 species of plants; admission is 2F ($1.45). From a nearby belvedere, visitors command a splendid view of the Eiger, Mönch, and Jungfrau. The Hotel Restaurant Schynige Platte offers good food and drink. For details, call 036/22-28-35.

LAKE THUN   ✪ Occupying an ancient terminal basin of a glacier, Lake Thun (Thunersee) was once connected to Lake Brienz (Brienzersee). It lies 17 miles south of Bern, to which it is connected by frequent rail service, which continues east to Interlaken. The Lutschine River deposited so much sediment at Interlaken that the one body of water eventually became two. Lake Thun, beloved by Brahms, is 13 miles long and 2 miles wide.

Because of its mild climate, Lake Thun is known as the "Riviera of the Bernese Oberland." Popular lake sports include waterskiing, yachting, and windsurfing. On shore there are excellent swimming pools (both indoor and outdoor), windsurfing schools, golf courses, tennis courts, horse stables, and caves.

The lake's major resort is Thun, a small city that was founded on an island where the Aare River flows out of Lake Thun. The city has since expanded onto the banks of the river to become the political and administrative center of the Bernese Oberland and the gateway to the Bernese mountains.

The most interesting part of the city is on the Aare's right bank. The busy main street, **Hauptgasse,** has walkways built above the arcaded shops. There's a 17th-century town hall on Rathausplatz, where you can climb a covered staircase up to the formidable **Schloss Thun (Castle Kyburg).** The castle is now a historical museum (tel. 033/23-20-01). It was built by the dukes of Zähringen at the end of the 12th century. Later it was the home of the counts of Kyburg, as well as the Bernese bailiffs. The massive residential tower has a large Knights' Hall, which contains a Gobelin tapestry from the time of Charles the Bold and a fine collection of halberds and other weapons. Other rooms have important archeological finds, an exhibit of military uniforms, period furniture, and toys. From the turrets there's a magnificent view of the surrounding area. The museum is open June through September, daily from 9am to 6pm; in April, May, and October, daily from 10am to 5pm. Admission is 4F ($2.90).

SPIEZ   Heading back east toward Interlaken along Route N8, you may have time for a stopover at the resort of Spiez, 6 miles east of Thun and about an equal distance from Interlaken. Frequent trains and buses connect both Interlaken and Thun to Spiez.

Dominated by its castle and vineyards, Spiez is an easily accessible resort at the foot of the Niesen, on the southern shore of the lake. The popular summer resort offers fishing, windsurfing, tennis, horseback riding, open-air theater performances, folklore shows, and many hiking paths. It also has a sailing school.

The **Castle of Spiez** (tel. 033/54-15-06), near the landing stage, offers a panoramic view over the lake and the Niesen. There is also a museum displaying relics from the former owners—the Minnesinger of Stretlingen and the Bernese Bubenberg and Erlach families. The medieval fortress was a rich man's castle in the 17th and 18th centuries; the furnishings and decor range from Romanesque to baroque. The museum is open from April to October, Tuesday through Sunday from 10am to 5pm. Admission is 3F ($2.20).

The town also has an 11th-century Romanesque church known as **Alte Kirche (Old Church).** The frescoes are worth a visit.

The major attraction in the area is the panoramic vista from the pyramid-shaped summit of **Mount Niesen,** at 7,615 feet. The view takes in the Jura, the Vosges massif in eastern France, the central Swiss peaks, the Bernese Oberland, and the Alps of the Vaud. The vista also includes Lake Thun and Lake Brienz. From the edge of Spiez, go 5 miles down the road through Mülehen, toward Simmental, to the funicular station. Take the funicular to the summit; the round-trip costs 26F ($19). There are frequent departures May to October, daily from 8am to 5pm. The ride to the summit takes about half an hour, so you should allow at least 2 hours to take in the splendor of the scenery. For information, call 033/76-11-12 or 033/76-11-13.

LAKE BRIENZ   Lake Brienz, directly east of Interlaken, is the smaller of the two Oberland lakes. It's about 9 miles long and up to 2 miles wide. Most Americans bypass the many holiday areas and charming resorts along its shores in favor of the more traditional resorts on Lake Thun. Many Europeans, on the other hand, prefer Lake Brienz.

The resort of Brienz is at the upper end of the lake, facing Giessbach Falls. The town is famous for its wood carvers, whose work can be found in souvenir shops throughout Switzerland. It's also known for its violin makers.

Brienz has frequent rail links with Interlaken. Trains run in both directions every hour. For information in Brienz about timetables, call 036/51-13-22.

The town's most popular excursion is a cogwheel railway trip to **Brienzer Rothorn,** where you'll get a magnificent vista of the Bernese Alps and Lake Brienz. The tour requires about 2 hours and takes you to an elevation of about 7,105 feet. Nine trips are made each day from June to October. A round-trip costs 52F ($37.95) per person.

The ✪ **Giessbach Falls** are accessible by funicular, which leaves from a platform across the lake. It can be reached by car or boat. The funicular costs 4.20F ($3.10) for adults and 2F ($1.45) for children 6 to 16. The boat to the funicular departs from the lakeshore wharf in the center of Brienz. Allow about 2 hours for the entire excursion.

For a glimpse of Switzerland's rural history, visit the ✪ **Swiss Open-Air**

Museum of Rural Dwellings and Lifestyle at Ballenberg, near Brienz. The museum is run by the Ballenberg Swiss Open-Air Museum Foundation, Direction CH-3855 Brienz (tel. 036/51-11-23). Seven scenic areas, comprising more than 2,000 acres, lie within the jurisdiction of this museum; they include clusters of typical old farm buildings, tiny settlements, and gardens as well as fields that Swiss farmers cultivate by using regional and time-tested methods. The various sections of the museum, which include both a nature park and the still alpine waters of Lake Wyssen, are interconnected with good roads. Most of the museum's acreage lies between the villages of Hofstetten and Brienzwiler, and various sections document architecture that is specific to different cantons and regions of Switzerland.

A tour of the museum will take about 3 hours. It's open daily in April, May, and October, from 10am to 5pm; June to September, from 9:30am to 5:30pm. Admission is 10F ($7.30) for adults and 5F ($3.65) for children. Guided tours are available by request, but reservations are necessary; there is a minimum charge of 60F ($43.80). During busy seasons, visitors can join groups of 15, with each participant paying 4F ($2.90).

For those driving to the museum, there is parking at the Hofstetten and Brienzwiler entrances. You can also take a train along the Interlaken–Meiringen–Lucerne line to the Brienz railroad station and transfer there to a bus to the museum. Or you can get off at the Brienzwiler station and take a forest path.

MEIRINGEN This resort lies about 8 miles from Brienz and can be easily visited on a day trip from Interlaken. Several trains stop at Interlaken's two railway stations every day, heading for Meiringen via about nine other villages along the way. Trip time between the two is about 50 minutes.

Strategically centered between three alpine passes (the Grimsel, the Brunig, and the Susten), this old town is a suitable base from which you can explore the eastern sections of the Bernese Oberland and the wild upper reaches of the Aare River. Classified as the major town in the Haslital district, and set above the waters of Lake Brienz, Meiringen is famous throughout Europe for meringue, a dessert that was supposedly invented here.

Rich in scenery and wildlife, the district attracts mountaineers, rock climbers, and hikers. The environs of the town contain more than 185 miles of marked hiking trails through unspoiled natural settings, with a complicated network of lifts to reach panoramic vantage points. Destinations for excursions include the Aare Gorge, the Rosenlaui glacier, and the Reichenbach Falls. The district also has a folklore museum, a crystal grotto, an antique water mill, and a pathway across a glacier. Almost everyone visits the parish church in the upper part of the village. Its crypt was built during the 11th century.

If you're in the mood for meringue, you can buy one or two at a local bakery. According to legend, the dessert was created when Napoleon visited the town and the local chef in charge of the welcoming banquet had a lot of leftover egg whites. Inspired, he created the puffy mounds and served them in a saucer brimming with sweet mountain cream, much to the general's delight.

The ✪ **Aare Gorge** is full of recesses, grottoes, precipices, and arches—all fashioned by the Aare's waters over centuries. The cleft is 1,500 yards long and 650 feet deep, carved in the Kirchet, a craggy barrier left over from the ice age. In some places, the towering rock walls of the gorge are so close together that only a few rays of sunshine can penetrate, just before noon. Considered a unique natural wonder in the Swiss Alps, the gorge can be reached by car from Meringen or by way of the Grimsel–Susten road along the Kirchet. Admission is 4F ($2.90) for adults and 2.50F ($1.85) for children. The gorge is open May to October, daily from 8am to 6pm.

If you're a fan of Sherlock Holmes, you'll enjoy an excursion to ✪ **Reichenbachfall,** where the rivers of the Rosenlaui Valley meet. The impressive beauty of the falls has lured many visitors, beginning with the British in the 19th century. One visitor, Conan Doyle, was so impressed with the place that he described it in *The Final Problem,* in which the villain, Dr. Moriarty, struggles with the detective to toss him into the falls. A Sherlock Holmes commemorative plaque is near the upper station of the funicular. The falls can be visited from mid-May to mid-September. Departures are every 10 minutes daily from 8am to noon and 1:10 to 6pm. The cost is 5F ($3.65). It's a 10-minute walk from Meiringen to the base of the funicular. If you're driving from Meiringen, take the road to Grimsel and turn right, toward Reichenbach Falls and Mervenklinik.

After you admire the cascade, you can hike through the river valley. The footpath through the **Rosenlaui Valley** is marked. After 90 minutes you'll arrive at the entrance to Rosenlaui Gorge. The surfaces of the sheer rock faces echo the sounds of the many small waterfalls within. You can walk from one end of this gorge to the other in about 30 minutes. A small hotel and a small seasonal restaurant are near the entrance. Most visitors turn around at the uppermost reaches of the gorge and make the 2-hour trek back to Reichenbach Falls to pick up the funicular back to Meiringen. The gorge can be visited May to October, daily from 8am to 4:30pm. The cost is 4F ($2.90) for adults and 2.50F ($1.85) for children.

---

2. MÜRREN

7 miles S of Lauterbrunnen, 4,485 feet above Stechelberg, 19 miles S of Interlaken

GETTING THERE   By Train   Take the mountain railway from the Interlaken East rail station via Lauterbrunnen and Grutschalp. The trip takes an hour from Interlaken and half an hour from Lauterbrunnen. The Lauterbrunnen–Mürren railway opened in 1891 and has two sections: the cog railway from Lauterbrunnen to Grutschalp and the narrow-gauge railway from Grutschalp to Mürren.

By Bus   A regular Postbus service goes from Lauterbrunnen to Stechelberg; the rest of the way you must go by cable car.

By Car   Mürren is not accessible to traffic. Drive as far as Stechelberg, the last town on the Lauterbrunnen Valley road. The cable car to Mürren costs 21F ($15.35) round-trip and takes about 10 minutes. Departures are every half hour.

ESSENTIALS   The **Mürren Tourist Information Bureau** is at the Sportzentrum (tel. 036/55-16-16), open Monday through Saturday from 9am to noon and 2 to 6pm, and on Sunday from 2 to 6pm. The **telephone area code** for Mürren is 036. There is no **street plan:** Follow clearly indicated directional signs to the various hotels and commercial establishments. The only street with a name is Bahnhofstrasse.

This village has a stunning location, high above the Lauterbrunnen Valley. At 5,414 feet, Mürren is the highest permanently inhabited village in the Bernese Oberland. It's an exciting excursion from Interlaken in the summer and a major ski resort in the winter. Downhill skiing was developed and the slalom invented here in the 1920s. Mürren is also the birthplace of modern alpine racing.

WHAT TO SEE & DO

There are 30 miles of prepared ski runs, including 16 downhills. The longest run measures 7½ miles. For cross-country skiers there's a 7½-mile track in the Lauterbrunnen Valley, 10 minutes by railway from Mürren.

The alpine **Sportzentrum (Sports Center)** (tel. 55-16-16), in the middle of Mürren, is one of the finest in the Bernese Oberland. The modern building has an indoor pool, a lounge, a snackbar, an outdoor skating rink, a tourist information office, and a children's playroom and toy library. There are facilities for playing squash, tennis, and curling, as well as a solarium, a sauna, and exercise classes. Hotel owners subsidize the operation, tacking the charges onto your hotel bill. Supplemental charges include 20F ($14.60) per hour for tennis, 12F ($8.75) per hour for squash, 10F ($7.30) per hour for use of the sauna, and 6F ($4.40) per hour for use of the solarium. The facility is usually open daily from 10am to noon and 2 to 6pm; it remains open until 9:30pm on Monday, Thursday, and Friday.

NEARBY ATTRACTIONS The famous ✪ **Mürren–Allmendhubel Cableway** leaves from the northwestern edge of Mürren. From the high destination there is a panoramic view of the Lauterbrunnen Valley as far as Wengen and Kleine Scheidegg. Between mid-June and late August the alpine meadows are covered with wildflowers. A hill walk in this region might be a highlight of your trip to Switzerland. The cable car operates daily throughout the year from 8am to 6pm. It costs 7.40F ($5.50) per person round-trip.

The most popular excursion from Mürren is a cable-car ride to the ✪ **Schilthorn,** famous for its 360° view. The panorama extends from the Jura to the Black Forest, including the Mönch, Jungfrau, and Eiger. The Schilthorn is also called "Piz Gloria," after the James Bond film *On Her Majesty's Secret Service* (Piz Gloria is the name of a revolving restaurant here). Parts of the movie were filmed at this dramatic location. The summit is the start of the world's longest downhill ski race. The cable car to Schilthorn leaves every 30 minutes during the summer. A round-trip costs 42F ($30.65) and takes 40 minutes. For details, call 23-14-44.

WHERE TO STAY

EXPENSIVE

HOTEL EIGER, Bahnhofstrasse, CH-3825 Mürren. Tel. 036/55-13-31. Fax 036/55-39-31. 44 rms (all with bath). TV TEL
$ Rates (including half board): 100F–170F ($73–$124.10) single; 210F–320F ($153.30–$233.55) double. AE, DC, MC, V. **Closed:** Mid-Sept to Dec and mid-Apr to June.
Founded in the 1920s and modernized many times since, this chalet is considered the best-established hotel in Mürren. It consists of two buildings, each with a large peaked roof, joined together by a low-lying passageway. The public rooms are warmly decorated, and many of the windows have spectacular views. The hotel is managed by Walter and Annelis Stähli-von Allmen. It's across the street from the terminus of the cable car from Lauterbrunnen.

Dining/Entertainment: The hotel has a fine restaurant and a popular après-ski bar.

Services: Laundry facilities, baby-sitting.

Facilities: Indoor heated swimming pool with a glassed-in view of the ice and snow outside, fitness room with a sauna.

MODERATE

HOTEL ALPENRUH, CH-3825 Mürren. Tel. 036/55-10-55. 26 rms (all with bath). MINIBAR TV TEL
$ **Rates** (including half board): 120F–145F ($87.60–$105.85) single; 220F–270F ($160.60–$197.05) double. AE, DC, MC, V.

Set in the most congested (yet charming) section of the village, the Alpenruh has an interior that is plusher than its chalet-style facade implies. The old building was meticulously upgraded in 1986 to be the town's premier hotel without sacrificing any of its small-scale charm. The rooms have pine paneling and a mix of antique and contemporary furniture. The hotel is owned by the company that operates the aerial cable cars to the Schilthorn's Piz Gloria.

HOTEL JUNGFRAU/JUNGFRAU LODGE, CH-3825 Mürren. Tel. 036/55-28-24. 46 rms (all with bath). TEL
$ **Rates** (including half board): 75F–170F ($54.75–$124.10) single; 130F–300F ($94.90–$218.95) double. AE, DC, MC, V.

This three-star, 19th-century building, a 3-minute walk from the Mürrenbahn, has stucco and brick walls, gables, and green shutters. A comfortable annex was constructed in 1965; both buildings have an inviting, modern decor with open fireplaces, clusters of armchairs, and a shared dining room. The bedrooms are sunny and appealing. Lunch is served on the terrace year-round; an après-ski bar is open until late at night. The hotel's sports center includes a swimming pool, a skating rink, and squash courts.

SPORTHOTEL EDELWEISS, CH-3825 Mürren. Tel. 036/55-26-12. Fax 036/55-42-02. 26 rms (all with bath). MINIBAR TEL
$ **Rates** (including half board): 115F–125F ($81.95–$91.25) single; 210F–230F ($153.30–$167.90) double. AE, DC, MC, V.

Swiss flags flutter from the balconies of this boxy hotel with red shutters and a flat roof. The sun terrace is built over an extremely steep dropoff. The rest of the hotel has a folksy, slightly kitschy decor, dating from 1927; the simple rooms are equipped with radios and other amenities. Mrs. Affentranger, the hostess, also offers an alpine dining room and a modern, attractive bar.

INEXPENSIVE

HOTEL BLUMENTAL, CH-3825 Mürren. Tel. 036/55-18-26. 20 rms (all with bath). MINIBAR
$ **Rates** (including half board): 80F–95F ($58.40–$69.35) per person per day, single or double occupancy. DC, V.

The facade of this family-run hotel has a masonry base and a weathered clapboard upper section. The rooms have wooden walls, contrasting bedcovers, and radios. The hotel's facilities include a squash court, a tennis court, and a swimming pool. The owners are the von Allmen family, who have innkeeper relatives all over the region.

HOTEL PALACE, CH-3825 Mürren. Tel. 036/55-24-24. Fax 036/55-24-17.
46 rms (all with bath). MINIBAR TV TEL
$ Rates (including half board): 125F–165F ($91.25–$120.45) per person per day,
single or double occupancy. AE, DC, MC, V.

Built earlier this century, the hotel has a black mansard roof and indented
loggias with wrought-iron balconies. There is a modern extension jutting off to
one side. A change of management in the early 1990s arranged the gradual
renovation and improvement of this property which had undergone several name
changes through the 1970s and 1980s. The hotel has a dance bar and a restaurant. A
passageway connects it with the adjacent sports center.

WHERE TO DINE

EXPENSIVE

EIGERSTÜBLI, in the Hotel Eiger, Bahnhofstrasse. Tel. 55-13-31.
  Cuisine: SWISS. **Reservations:** Recommended.
$ Prices: Appetizers 10F–20F ($7.30–$14.60); main courses 30F–45F ($21.90–
  $32.85); fixed-price dinner 36F–48F ($26.30–$35.05). AE, DC, MC, V.
  Open: Lunch daily 11:30am–2pm, dinner daily 6–10:30pm.

What is said to be the best food at the resort is served here in a festive
ambience. The Eigerstübli's cuisine includes fondues (both bourguignonne and
chinoise) and an international range of hearty specialties well suited to the
alpine heights and chill. All main dishes may be ordered with Rösti. Dessert specialties
include vodka sherbet and iced soufflé Grand Marnier.

MODERATE

HOTEL ALPENRUH. Tel. 55-10-55.
  Cuisine: CONTINENTAL. **Reservations:** Recommended in winter.
$ Prices: Appetizers 10F–18F ($7.30–$13.15); main courses 20F–35F ($14.60–
  $25.55). AE, DC, MC, V.
  Open: Lunch daily 12:30–2pm; dinner daily 6:30–9:30pm.
This small hotel contains one of the finest restaurants in Mürren, offering a large and
sophisticated menu to hotel residents and nonresidents. Both its dining rooms have an
attractive alpine theme and a wide terrace with a panoramic view of the surrounding
mountains.
    Appetizers include snails in herb butter and agnolotti flavored with basil. Typical
entrees are chicken breast Maryland and lamb cutlet Marie-Louise. The steaks are
delectable. Fish courses might include sole Colbert and salmon steak in a tarragon-
cream sauce. For dessert try fresh pineapple with a caramel mousse or a gratiné of
kiwi and oranges.

RESTAURANT IM GRUEBI, in the Hotel Jungfrau. Tel. 55-28-24.
  Cuisine: SWISS. **Reservations:** Recommended only in midwinter.
$ Prices: Appetizers 9F–18F ($6.55–$13.15); main courses 20F–36F ($14.60–
  $26.30). AE, DC, MC, V.
  Open: Lunch daily noon–2pm; dinner daily 7–10pm.
This popular restaurant has a sunny outdoor terrace on the lobby level of the Hotel
Jungfrau. The large hexagonal dining room has views of the mountains and ski slopes.
The chef specializes in flambé dishes, including peppersteak. Other specialties are
prepared only for two people, including chateaubriand, New York steak, rack of lamb

flavored with herbs, and veal filets with fruits in a cognac sauce. The classic fondue bourguignonne is also offered.

RESTAURANT SCHILTHORN, Piz Gloria. Tel. 55-21-41.
   Cuisine: SWISS. **Reservations:** Not needed. **Transportation:** The only access is via the Schilthorn cable car, which departs from the (relatively) low-lying town of Stechelberg and stops at three way stations, the most prominent of which is Mürren. The round-trip fare from Stechelberg is 71F ($51.82); the round-trip fare from Mürren is 45F ($32.85).
$ Prices: Appetizers 9F–16F ($6.55–$11.70); main courses 20F–35F ($14.60–$25.55); daily platters 17F–21F ($12.40–$15.35). AE, DC, MC, V.
   Open: Daily from the first cable car's arrival until the last car's afternoon departure. The first departure from Stechelberg is at 7:25am in the summer and at 7:55am in the winter. The cable car's last departure from Schilthorn is at 5:25pm in the summer and at 4:55pm in the winter.

★ The Schilthorn is one of the most dramatically located restaurants in Europe, with a setting so inhospitable, and an architecture so futuristic, that it has been used as the setting for one of the James Bond films. Designed like a big-windowed flying saucer and anchored solidly to the alpine bedrock, it was built at staggering expense in one of Switzerland's highest locations, the Schilthorn. Closed during blizzards, the restaurant has a terrace where newcomers should beware of becoming seriously sunburned by the rays of the high-altitude, unfiltered sunlight. You'll dine inside at long wooden tables, with a wraparound view that is spectacular. The menu includes hearty dishes suited to the climate, including Hungarian goulash, air-dried meat from the Grisons, and sirloin steak Café de Paris.

TAVERNE, in the Hotel Alpenruh. Tel. 55-10-55.
   Cuisine: SWISS. **Reservations:** Not needed.
$ Prices: Platters 14F–22F ($10.20–$16.05). AE, DC, MC, V.
   Open: Lunch daily 12:30–2pm; dinner daily 6:30–9:30pm.
Sheathed in pine—and filled with skiing enthusiasts, all of whom seem to have just stepped off the slopes—this unpretentious restaurant serves wholesome platters of food in generous portions. The menu lists three kinds of pizza and several kinds of fondue; steaming portions are laden with grilled pork cutlets or rumpsteak.

EVENING ENTERTAINMENT

In addition to the following choices, several mountain-chalet restaurants have fondue and raclette parties at the height of the winter ski season.

BLIEMLICHALLER, in the Hotel Blumental. Tel. 55-18-26.
   This rustic bar and disco is in the cellar of the Hotel Blumental. (The ceiling is carefully insulated so that the disco music doesn't rise to the upper floors.) The menu is limited to grilled entrecôtes and cutlets, but many clients come here after dinner primarily to drink and dance. The bar is open only in the wintertime, daily from 9pm to 2am. Light meals begin at 25F ($18.25); beer costs 6F ($4.40).

INFERNO-BAR, in the Hotel Palace. Tel. 55-24-24.
   Another popular nightclub, the Inferno offers music ranging from mild punk to rock 'n' roll and 1960s pop classics. Cheese platters and steaming bowls of goulash soup are served. Open Tuesday through Sunday from 8:30pm to 2:30am. Drinks run about 11F ($8.05).

TÄCHI-BAR, in the Hotel Eiger, Bahnhofstrasse. Tel. 55-13-31.
   Darkly paneled, rustic, convivial, and often rowdy, this is the most popular place

in Mürren for après-ski. It's usually overcrowded and can be a lot of fun, especially if you've spent the day hill climbing or skiing. Children are not allowed inside after 9pm. From a small stage, visiting bands perform in winter only, every day from 8:30pm to midnight. Drinks start at 8F ($5.85).

3. Wengen

16 miles S of Interlaken, 3 miles NE of Mürren

GETTING THERE   By Train   Take the train (frequent service) from Interlaken East to Lauterbrunnen. From there the journey to Wengen is by cog railway, a 15-minute trip.

By Bus   Take the postal bus from Interlaken, getting off at Lauterbrunnen for the final journey by cog railway to traffic-free Wengen.

By Car   From Interlaken, head south in the direction of Wilderswil, following the minor signposted road to Lauterbrunnen, where there are garages and open-air spaces for parking. After that, you'll have to go by cog railway to Wengen.

ESSENTIALS   The **Wengen Tourist Information Office** (tel. 036/55-14-14) is open Monday through Friday from 8am to noon and 2 to 6pm, and on Saturday from 8:30 to 11:30am and 4 to 6pm. The **telephone area code** for Wengen is 036. There are no **street names:** Hotels and other major establishments, such as restaurants, are signposted with directional signs, which make them relatively easy to find.

The Mönch, Jungfrau, and Eiger loom above this sunny resort, built on a sheltered terrace high above the Lauterbrunnen Valley, at about 4,160 feet. Wengen (pronounced *Ven*-ghen) is one of the chicer and better-equipped ski and mountain resorts in the Bernese Oberland. It has 30 hotels in all price categories, as well as 500 apartments and chalets for rent.

In the 1830s the International Lauberhorn Ski Race was established here. At that time Wengen was a farm community. The British were the first to popularize the resort after World War I. Today, parts of the area retain their rural charm. The main street, however, is filled with cafés, shops, and restaurants welcoming tourists. Robert Redford is a frequent visitor. No cars are allowed in Wengen, but the streets are still bustling with service vehicles and electric luggage carts.

WHAT TO SEE & DO

The **ski area** around Wengen is highly developed, with straight and serpentine ski trails carved into the sides of such sloping geological formations as Männlichen, Kleine Scheidegg, Lauberhorn, and Eigergletscher. Considered a triumph of alpine engineering, the town and its region contain three mountain railways, two aerial cableways, one gondola, five chair lifts, nine ski lifts, and three practice lifts. You'll also find here a branch of the Swiss ski school, more than 7 miles of trails for cross-country skiing, an indoor and outdoor skating rink, a curling hall, an indoor swimming pool, and a day nursery.

In the summer the district attracts hill climbers from all over Europe. Hiking trails are well maintained and carefully marked, with dozens of unusual detours to hidden lakes and panoramas.

NEARBY ATTRACTIONS   In the winter, skiers take the cableway to **Männlichen,** at 7,335 feet, which opens onto a panoramic vista of the treacherous

228 · THE BERNESE OBERLAND

Eiger. From here, there is no direct run back to Wengen; however, skiers can enjoy an uninterrupted ski trail stretching 4½ miles to Grindelwald.

From either Wengen or Grindelwald, many visitors take excursions up and down the Lauterbrunnen Valley. You can visit **Trümmelbach Falls,** which plunges in five powerful cascades through a gorge. You can take an elevator built through the rock to a series of galleries (bring a raincoat). The last stop is at a wall where the upper fall descends. The falls can be visited from April to October, daily from 8am to 6pm. Admission is 8F ($5.85) for adults and 3F ($2.40) for children 10 to 16. It takes about 45 minutes to reach the falls on foot. For information, call 036/55-32-12.

You might also want to visit the base of the **Staubbach Waterfall,** which plunges nearly 1,000 feet in a sheer drop over a rock wall in the valley above Lauterbrunnen. Lord Byron compared this waterfall to the "tail of the pale horse ridden by Death in the Apocalypse."

WHERE TO STAY

All the hotels in Wengen are mobbed in winter, so make reservations if you plan to arrive for skiing.

EXPENSIVE

HOTEL REGINA, CH-3823 Wengen. Tel. 036/55-15-12. Fax 036/55-15-74. 95 rms (all with bath). MINIBAR TV TEL
$ Rates (including half board): 106F–148F ($77.35–$108.05) single; 232F–276F ($169.35–$201.45) double. AE, DC, MC, V. **Closed:** Oct–Nov.
A time-honored hotel, the Regina stands near the cog railway station in an embellished Victorian elephant of a building with balconies and lots of charm. Guido Meyer has been known to arrange unusual concerts for his guests (once when I was there a group of high school students from Oklahoma gave a concert on the front lawn). One of the public rooms has a baronial carved-stone fireplace. The bedrooms are comfortable and cozy.
   Dining/Entertainment: The restaurant offers a fixed-price buffet of hot and cold appetizers, soups, main dishes, and desserts. You may also order à la carte. The attractive disco/bar features live bands.
   Services: Laundry service, baby-sitting.
   Facilities: Children's playroom, large garden, sun terrace.

PARKHOTEL BEAUSITE, CH-3823 Wengen. Tel. 036/56-51-61. Fax 036/55-30-10. 85 rms (all with bath). MINIBAR TV TEL
$ Rates (including half board): Winter, 200F–260F ($146–$189.75) single; 360F–430F ($262.75–$313.85) double. Summer, 160F–210F ($116.80–$153.30) single; 230F–370F ($167.90–$270.05) double. No credit cards.
This celebrity favorite is buttercup yellow, with vaguely Georgian styling. Located on a hill, it's considered the best hotel in Wengen. It was modernized in 1983 and has two additions. Most rooms are spacious and comfortable. Balconies offer views of the village and the surrounding mountains.
   Dining/Entertainment: The dining room becomes a social center in season. For breakfast, waiters in tuxedos will cook your eggs at your table. The five-course fixed-price dinners are the finest served in Wengen. The Rondo serves fondues and snacks.
   Services: Room service, laundry.
   Facilities: Heated indoor swimming pool, Finnish sauna.

HOTEL SILBERHORN, CH-3823 Wengen. Tel. 036/56-51-31. Fax 036/55-22-44. 75 rms (all with bath). MINIBAR TV TEL

$ Rates (including half board): Winter, 125F–160F ($91.25–$116.80) single; 230F–290F ($167.90–$211.65) double. Summer, 105F–135F ($76.65–$98.55) single; 180F–232F ($131.40–$169.35) double. AE, DC, MC, V.

Famous for its cluster of nightclubs, this hotel also offers comfortable modern rooms, many with wooden balconies and kitchenettes. The simple Victorian building near the cog rail station has several modern additions. Some of its accommodations are privately owned by absentee investors, and most of its two lowest floors are devoted to restaurants and clubs.

SUNSTAR HOTEL, CH-3823 Wengen. Tel. 036/56-51-11. Fax 036/55-32-72. 120 rms (all with bath). MINIBAR TV TEL

$ Rates (including half board): Winter, 143F–175F ($104.40–$127.75) single; 276F–340F ($201.45–$248.15) double. Summer, 114F–138F ($83.20–$100.75) single; 210F–260F ($153.30–$189.75) double. AE, DC, MC, V.

Margrit and Erich Leemann are the friendly hosts of this four-star hotel in the center of Wengen. It has a new addition and many balconies. An alpine design can be found on the wooden ceiling of one of the salons; this salon has leather-and-metal chairs, a fireplace, and stucco walls with rustic timbers. The rooms are well furnished and comfortable.

Dining/Entertainment: The dining room is high quality and the oval bar has a relaxed ambience.

Services: Laundry, wake-up calls.

Facilities: Indoor swimming pool, sauna, solarium.

VICTORIA-LAUBERHORN, CH-3823 Wengen. Tel. 036/56-51-51. Fax 036/55-33-77. 85 rms (all with bath). TV TEL

$ Rates (including half board): Winter, 127F–158F ($92.70–$115.32) single; 234F–292F ($170.80–$213.15) double. Summer, 104F–135F ($75.90–$98.55) single; 180F–234F ($131.40–$170.80) double. AE, DC, MC, V.

This venerable hotel with many gables is in the center of Wengen. It offers a pizzeria pub, a crêperie, a popular bar (the Parasol), and a busy outdoor café. The cozy rooms are decorated in a bewildering array of styles, ranging from modern to mountain. Amenities include a radio.

MODERATE

FALKEN HOTEL, CH-8323 Wengen. Tel. 036/56-51-21. Fax 036/55-33-39. 50 rms (40 with bath). MINIBAR TEL

$ Rates (including half board): 120F ($87.40) single without bath, 149F ($108.75) single with bath; 240F ($175.20) double without bath, 298F ($217.50) double with bath. AE, DC, MC, V.

The Falken's gabled roof and cream-colored facade date from 1895. Inside, much of the old-fashioned charm has been retained. The reception desk is in a lounge with Biedermeier sofas, Oriental rugs, and dated furniture. There is a bar in one corner. The elevator was installed in 1908, the first one in Wengen. Most rooms have phones, minibars, and balconies; in a chalet annex are 10 rooms without private baths. The hotel is a 5-minute uphill walk from the railroad station. The Cova family welcomes visitors, especially other families.

HOTEL EIGER, CH-3823 Wengen. Tel. 036/55-11-31. Fax 036/55-10-30. 46 rms (all with bath). TV TEL

$ Rates (including half board): Winter, 115F–149F ($83.95–$108.75) single;

230F–298F ($167.90–$217.50) double. Summer, 99F–120F ($72.25–$87.60) single; 198F–240F ($144.50–$175.20) double. AE, DC, MC, V.

⑤ Rustic timbers cover the walls and ceilings of this attractive hotel behind the cog rail station. Karl Fuchs and his family offer spacious, attractive rooms with balconies and radios. There is a modern dining room with views of the Jungfrau massif and the Lauterbrunnen Valley. The La Cabaña grillroom, however, is more inviting. I recommend the Arvenstube for après-ski.

INEXPENSIVE

HOTEL EDEN, CH-3823 Wengen. Tel. 036/55-16-34. Fax 036/55-39-50. 30 rms (6 with shower or bath). TEL
$ **Rates** (including half board): 85F ($62.05) single without bath, 95F ($69.35) single with bath; 170F ($124.10) double without bath, 190F ($138.70) double with bath. AE, DC, MC, V.

⑤ You'll find homelike comfort in this economy oasis. The symmetrical villa with red shutters is located among guesthouses and private chalets above the commercial center of town. Kerstin Bucher directs a cooperative staff. Meals are served in a simple, modern room with a few frivolous touches. There's a small TV lounge and a tiny Jägerstübli, where guests mix with locals over Swiss wine and specialties.

HOTEL HIRSCHEN, CH-3823 Wengen. Tel. 036/55-15-44. Fax 036/55-30-44. 12 rms (all with bath). TV TEL
$ **Rates** (including continental breakfast): 60F–80F ($43.80–$58.40) single; 120F–150F ($87.60–$109.50) double. DC, MC, V.
Simple, pleasant, and inexpensive, this family-run hotel lies above the town, with ski slopes passing a few steps from the front door. Accommodations are snug and comfortable. You'll recognize the hotel by its sheathing of ornate cedar shingles.

WHERE TO DINE

MODERATE

FALSENKELLER, in the Hotel Silberhorn. Tel. 56-51-31.
Cuisine: SWISS. **Reservations:** Recommended.
$ **Prices:** Appetizers 8F–18F ($5.85–$13.15); main courses 20F–35F ($14.60–$25.55). AE, DC, MC, V.
Open: Dec–Mar, dinner only, daily 5pm–1am.
The Hotel Silberhorn has a selection of restaurants and bars, but the Falsenkeller offers the finest food, in a medieval atmosphere with stone walls. The winter menu is sophisticated; continental dishes include many grills and fish. A typical meal might start with cream of snail soup, then follow with strips of beef filet in a beetroot sauce, veal kidneys simmered in chablis, or medallions of beef with vodka. For dessert, I recommend crêpes Suzette, parfait Grand Marnier, or the prune sherbet with prune liqueur.

RESTAURANT LA CABAÑA, in the Hotel Eiger. Tel. 55-11-31.
Cuisine: SWISS. **Reservations:** Recommended.
$ **Prices:** Appetizers 12F–18F ($8.75–$13.15); main courses 18F–32F ($13.15–$23.35); light lunch from 25F ($18.25). AE, DC, MC, V.
Open: Lunch daily 11am–2pm; dinner daily 6–9pm.

Rustic but glamorous, this pine-paneled restaurant is the most prestigious at the hotel. Cold game pie in a Cumberland sauce and smoked goose breast are two unusual hors d'oeuvres. There is also a big choice of salads. Specialties include a mixed grill Eiger, which is your choice of the finest cuts of meat. Some dishes are flambéed at your table. The rib roast of lamb is prepared according to an old Provence recipe dedicated to Cézanne. The menu also includes Swiss meals with Rösti. Children's plates are available.

INEXPENSIVE

HOTEL BERNERHOF RESTAURANT. Tel. 55-27-21.
   Cuisine: SWISS/ITALIAN. **Reservations:** Sometimes needed.
   $ Prices: Appetizers 6F–12F ($4.40–$8.75); main courses 8F–40F ($5.85–$29.20). AE, MC, V.
   Open: Daily 9am–11pm. **Closed:** Nov.
The Schweizers run this old family favorite with wine-red shutters. Near the entrance is a trout tank. There is also an alpine-themed bar, which fills up in the early evening with beer drinkers returning from the slopes. Hearty alpine food, including raclette and fondue, is served in the dining room. Several Italian dishes are featured. Trout is prepared in five different ways. The menu might also include perch with almonds, or pork and veal dishes with a mushroom-cream sauce.

HOTEL HIRSCHEN RESTAURANT. Tel. 55-15-44.
   Cuisine: SWISS. **Reservations:** Recommended.
   $ Prices: Appetizers 6F–18F ($4.40–$13.15); main courses 15F–28F ($10.95–$20.45); fixed-price meal from 28F ($20.45). DC, MC, V.
   Open: Lunch daily 11:30am–2pm; dinner daily 6:30–9:15pm. **Closed:** Apr 14–May 30 and Sept 20–Dec 15.

S This quiet retreat at the foot of the slopes has a true alpine flavor. The rear dining room is decorated with hunting trophies, pewter, and wine racks.
   Johannes Abplanalp and his family offer a dinner special called Galgenspiess—filet of beef, veal, and pork flambéed at your table. Other dishes include filet of breaded pork, rumpsteak Café de Paris, and fondue Bacchus, bourguignonne, or chinoise. A hearty lunch is Winzerrösti, consisting of country ham, cheese, and a fried egg with homemade Rösti.

RESTAURANT ARVENSTUBE, in the Hotel Eiger. Tel. 55-11-31.
   Cuisine: SWISS. **Reservations:** Not needed.
   $ Prices: Appetizers 8F–15F ($5.85–$10.95); main courses 20F–38F ($14.60–$27.75).
   Open: Lunch daily 11:30am–2pm; dinner daily 6:30–9pm; snacks daily 7am–midnight.
This local favorite has glowing pinewood panels and a polite crew wearing vests or dirndls. The menu might include smoked trout with horseradish, air-dried alpine beef, smoked breast of goose, Bernese-style beef with mushrooms, filet of fera (a lake fish), and veal steak Alfredo with morels. Fondues are also offered. The Valais-style braserade of beef is cooked at your table on a skewer above a small flame.

EVENING ENTERTAINMENT

Nightlife begins early—at sunset. Join just about everyone in watching the spectacular sunset over Wengen. Sometimes there's a raclette party at the Wengenalp, followed by night skiing by torchlight. This untamed perch is at 6,140 feet, below the glacial slopes of Jungfrau. Hotels offer most of the entertainment.

CARROUSEL, in the Hotel Regina. Tel. 55-15-12.

An active crowd is attracted by the unusual musicians who perform here. Guido Meyer brings bands in from Hungary, Holland, Britain, among other places. The club is part of the hotel—you'll have to negotiate a maze of hallways and stairs, passing through the large lobby. When you arrive, you'll find one of the hottest scenes in Wengen. There is a winter garden overlooking the village. Open year round Monday through Saturday from 9pm to 2:30am. Drinks run 10F to 16F ($7.30 to $11.70); beer, 6F to 8F ($4.40 to $5.85).

Admission: Free.

PICKEL BAR, in the Hotel Eiger. Tel. 55-11-31.

Many skiers seek out artfully rustic places for a drink—the Pickel Bar is a perfect example. The trapezoidal room has thick unfinished planks and stout timbers. It's illuminated by candlelight. The bar is open in the winter Tuesday through Sunday from 4pm to 2am. Beer costs 6F to 8F ($4.40 to $5.85).

HOTEL SILBERHORN. Tel. 56-51-31.

This hotel contains the densest concentration of nightlife opportunities in Wengen, conveniently located a few steps from the village's cog-railway station. Both the hotel and its facilities are closed from late April to May and from October 20 to early December, when business in the town slows to a virtual standstill.

In the hotel's basement is Wengen's most popular dance club, the **Tiffany Disco,** which is open summer and winter every day from 9:30pm to 2am. Admission is free, but a beer costs 11F ($8.05).

Popular and sudsy **La Strada,** despite its Italian name, serves Swiss specialties, such as fondues and raclettes, with foaming mugs of beer. A la carte meals cost 15F to 35F ($10.95 to $25.55) and are served daily from 11am to 11pm.

The hotel's most popular and uninhibited après-ski hangout is **Monika's Bar.** Rustically decorated, with a burning fireplace, it has loud recorded music and lots of bustle. It's open only in the winter, every day from 5pm to 2am. A mug of beer costs around 8F ($5.85).

Quiet moments are best appreciated in the **Silberhorn Bar,** near the reception area of the hotel's main floor. Open nightly in the winter from 6:30pm to midnight, it's restrained and formal, with a pianist. Long drinks cost 14F ($10.20) and more each.

AN EXCURSION TO KLEINE SCHEIDEGG

Perched on a treeless alpine tundra, this tiny village comprises little more than an isolated railway station, a handful of wood-sided buildings, and a network of hiking and skiing trails that meander through some of the most glorious countryside of Switzerland. Popular in both summer and winter, it sits on a plateau that connects the Grindelwald Valley with the Lauterbrunnen Valley. It's also one of the transfer points for the cog railway, which continues the ascent to the snowy heights of the Jungfraujoch. A one-way ticket between Interlaken and Kleine Scheidegg costs 35F ($25.55).

Because of its high altitude, there is usually snow at Kleine Scheidegg between mid-November and mid-May. The difference in altitude between Interlaken and Kleine Scheidegg is about 10,000 feet, so that the climate varies markedly between the two towns. There's a difference of only 4,500 feet between Scheidegg and the uninhabitable heights of Jungfraujoch.

In the summer, visitors spend most of their time hiking and climbing over the region's excellent and very safe trails. There is much to admire in these surroundings—alpine flora, ibex, chamois, marmots, and eagles. The resort is not accessible to traffic. Hiking trails can be reached by the Wengenalp and Jungfrau railways, the Wengen–Männlichen aerial cableway, and the Scheidegg–Lauberhorn chair lift. From your hotel room you may be able to watch high-altitude ascents and climbing parties. There is little to do here after dark, so expect to retire early after a day of exercise in the Alps.

WHERE TO STAY & DINE

SCHEIDEGG HOTELS, CH-3801 Kleine Scheidegg. Tel. 036/55-12-12.
  Fax 036/55-12-94. 90 rms (all with bath). TEL
$ Rates (including half board): 125F–160F ($91.25–$120.45) single; 225F–300F
  ($164.25–$218.95) double. DC, MC, V. **Closed:** Oct–Nov and May.
The two hotels, the Bellevue and the Désalpe, can be reached only by railroad. Clad in a weather-blackened sheathing of wooden planks, which contrast subtly with the rocks and lichens around them, the hotels are especially popular with skiers because of their easy access to the slopes. In the summer they offer plenty of hiking trails with spectacular views. Managed by Heidi von Almen and charging the same rates, the hotels are beautifully decorated with Oriental carpets, comfortable leather chairs, and fireplaces. Although their clientele tends to retire early for an early start in the great outdoors, they sometimes provide music at night in the bar.

---

4. GRINDELWALD

14 miles S of Interlaken, 120 miles SW of Zurich

GETTING THERE   By Train   The Bernese Oberland Railway (BOB) leaves from the Interlaken East station. The trip takes 35 minutes.

By Car   Take the Wilderswil road south from Interlaken and follow the signs all the way to Grindelwald.

ESSENTIALS   The **tourist office** is at Sportszentrum, Hauptstrasse, CH-3818 Grindelwald (tel. 036/53-12-13). The **telephone area code** is 036. The resort doesn't use **street names** or numbers; instead of street names, hotel direction signs are used to locate places.

If you're booked into a hotel or tourist home in Grindelwald, you may request a **pass** entitling you to many reductions, especially on mountain rides. Hotels will give you the pass.

The "glacier village" of Grindelwald is set against a backdrop of the Wetterhorn and the towering north face of the Eiger. It is both a winter and a summer resort.

Unlike Wengen and Mürren, it's the only major resort in the Jungfrau region that can be reached by car. Because of its accessibility, Grindelwald is often crowded with visitors, many of whom come just for the day.

WHAT TO SEE & DO

For details about any of the tours below, including seasonal changes, consult the tourist office.

GLACIER TOURS   The town maintains a sheltered observation gallery, adjacent to the base of the **Lower Grindelwald Glacier,** that offers a close look at the glacier's ravine. The half-mile gallery stretches past the deeply striated rocks, which include formations of colored marble worn smooth by the glacier's powers of erosion. The gallery is easy to reach on foot or by car. Bus service is available from Grindelwald for 10F ($7.30), and there's a parking lot, as well as a restaurant, nearby.

The **Blue Ice Grotto** is a nearby cave formed from the Upper Grindelwald Glacier. At midday the 150-foot-thick ice walls take on an eerie blue tinge. Local guides assure visitors that although the grotto—and the glacier that contains it—are moving slowly downhill, the visit is perfectly safe. The grotto is open from mid-June to mid-September. Tours, which include a bus transfer from Grindelwald, cost 15F ($10.95) per person.

HIKING AND MOUNTAIN CLIMBING   If you've come to Switzerland to see the Alps, Grindelwald and its surroundings offer dozens of challenging paths and mountain trails that are well marked and carefully maintained. Outdoor adventures range from an exhilarating ramble across the gentle incline of an alpine valley to a dangerous trek with ropes and pitons along the north face of Mount Eiger. The choice depends on your inclination and your skills. A map showing the region's paths and trails is available at the town's tourist office.

If you're adventurous enough to be tempted by peaks 13,000 feet high or higher, or if you'd like to learn the proper way to climb rocks and ice, contact **Bergsteigerzentrum,** CH-3818 Grindelwald (tel. 036/53-20-21).

Faulhorn, at 8,796 feet, has a historic vantage point from which you can view a panorama of untouched alpine beauty. There's also a mountain hotel that has been here for more than 150 years. It can be reached only by hiking from Bussalp (2¾ hr.), from First (2½ hr.), or from Schynige Platte (4 hr.).

A 30-minute ride on Europe's longest chair lift, via Oberhaus, will take you to **First Mountain,** at 7,113 feet. You can stop at the intermediate stations of Bort and Egg as you cross the lovely alpine meadows to the First Mountain terminal and sun terrace. You'll have many hiking possibilities into the neighboring Bussalp or Grosse Scheidegg area, returning by bus. An hour's brisk hike will take you to idyllic Lake Bachalp. Besides the 2½-hour trek to Faulhorn, you can make a trek on foot to the Schynige Platte in 6 hours. A round-trip chair-lift ride between Grindelwald and First costs 30F ($21.90). There is a large restaurant at First.

Grosse Scheidegg, at 6,434 feet, is a famous pass between the Grindelwald and Rosenlaui valleys. You can hike here in 3 hours from Grindelwald, or you can take a 40-minute bus ride from Grindelwald. This is a favorite climbing destination from the village of Wengen as well. My preference is usually to take a bus to Grosse Scheidegg and then begin my hill walking away from the village traffic and crowds. Round-trip bus passage from Grindelwald to Grosse Scheidegg is 22F ($16.05) per person.

If you want to climb in the upper regions of the Oberland, you might consider this **itinerary:** Take a bus from Grindelwald to Grosse Scheidegg. Walk for 2½ hours from Grosse Scheidegg to Schwartzwaldup. The peaks of First and Wetterhorn will loom on either side of you. After a panoramic respite in Schwartzwaldup, you can take a bus, which will retrace your steps, first to Grosse Scheidegg, then to Grindelwald. This excursion is possible only in the summer; the total bus fare is 28F ($20.45) per person.

Also only in the summer, a short aerial cable-car ride will take you to **Pfingstegg,** at 4,564 feet, from which you can hike to the Lower and Upper Grindelwald glaciers. The round-trip cost is 1F (75¢). A hike to **Baregg-Stieregg** (1 hr.) is highly recommended as a 1-day journey, as is the trek to **Banisegg** (2 hr.). You'll get a view of the Eismeer and the Fiescherwand, both worth the hike.

A popular half-day hike is to **Milchbach.** In about an hour you find yourself at the base of the Upper Grindelwald Glacier, with the Blue Ice Grotto nearby. You can take a bus back. The round-trip fare between Grindelwald and Pfinstegg is 11F ($8.05).

From Grindelwald-Grund you can also take Europe's longest gondola cableway to **Männlichen.** Along the way you'll have a panoromic view of all the peaks of the Jungfrau. The round-trip fare from Grindelwald-Grund to Männlichen is 36.60F ($26.75). Parking is available at Grindelwald-Grund.

From Grindelwald, it's also easy to visit **Kleine Scheidegg,** which is the departure point for the final ascent to the Jungfraujoch by train. A round trip on rack and pinion rail costs 30F ($21.90).

SPORTS   In addition to hiking and skiing, there are several other sports activities available:

Fishing   With a permit from the tourist office, you can fish in the Lutschine and the Bachalpsee.

Skating   Karl-Heinz Zitterbart runs a Swisskate Skating School for beginners to advanced skaters. For information on times and prices, contact Mr. Zitterbart at the Sportzentrum or by phone at the Hotel Schweizerhof (tel. 53-22-02). In the summer, the big ice hall at the Sports Center is open. Skating costs 4.50F ($3.30) for adults staying in Grindelwald, 6F ($4.40) for those staying elsewhere; 3F ($2.20) for children staying in Grindelwald, 4F ($2.90) otherwise.

Skiing   Set in a complicated network of hills and valleys, Grindelwald is the highest "skiable mountain" in the world. It has an altitude of 12,000 feet and a vertical drop of 5,010 feet. Grindelwald has 22 lifts, gondolas, and mountain railroads, providing access to the slopes. For "intermediate" training before making the long descent, Oberjoch, at 8,226 feet, is a good point.

Swimming   A heated outdoor swimming pool is open in Grindelwald from June to August. The Sports Center has an indoor pool and sauna, open daily. Adults staying in Grindelwald pay 6F ($4.40) to swim, 8F ($5.85) for those staying elsewhere; children staying in Grindelwald pay 4.50F ($3.30) to swim, 6F ($4.40) otherwise.

Tennis   Six sand courts are available through the tourist office at a cost of 18F ($13.15) per hour per court. The Regina, Spinne, and Sunstar hotels all have courts. The Sports Center has four hard indoor courts, which are available from late April to mid-June. Other indoor tennis facilities are available at Wilderswil and Interlaken all year.

WHERE TO STAY

VERY EXPENSIVE

GRAND HOTEL REGINA, CH-3818 Grindelwald. Tel. 036/54-54-55. Fax 036/53-47-17. 120 rms (all with bath). MINIBAR TV TEL

$ Rates: Off-season, 200F ($146) single; 320F ($233.55) double. Dec 21–Apr 1 and July 31–Sept 14, 240F ($175.20) single; 400F ($291.95) double. Half board 35F ($25.55) extra. No credit cards. **Closed:** Nov.

The architecture here is part rustic and part urban slick. The facade of the oldest part of the hotel has an imposing set of turrets with red-tile roofs. One of the salons has Victorian chairs clustered around bridge tables, with sculpture in wall niches. The collection of art includes etchings, gouaches, and oil paintings. The bedrooms, done in various styles, are comfortable. There is a steel-and-glass extension housing sports facilities.

Dining/Entertainment: Live bands perform at the hotel's disco. Both fixed-price and à la carte menus are presented in the hotel restaurant, and there is also a Grill Room, serving Swiss and international specialties. The hotel has a cocktail lounge, a pool bar, and a hotel bar.

Services: Laundry, room service.

Facilities: Indoor and outdoor swimming pool, sauna, tennis courts.

EXPENSIVE

BELVEDERE, CH-3818 Grindelwald. Tel. 036/54-54-34. Fax 036/53-41-20. 45 rms (all with bath), 6 suites. MINIBAR TV TEL

$ Rates (including buffet breakfast): 120F–150F ($87.60–$109.50) single; 190F–230F ($138.70–$167.90) double; 250F–330F ($182.50–$240.85) junior suite; 350F–720F ($255.45–$525.55) luxury suite. Half board 30F ($21.90) extra. AE, DC, MC, V. **Parking:** Free.

★ This four-star hotel once declined the offer of a higher rating from the Swiss government so that it could keep its prices within reason. It has the most spectacular view in Grindelwald. Parts of a Clint Eastwood movie were filmed here. Its luxurious public rooms include fireplaces and comfortable armchairs. The attractive bedrooms have balconies and such amenities as radios, room safes, and bathrobes. Twenty-two of the double rooms are classified as "luxury twins" or "junior suites." The hotel is a 5-minute walk from the center of the resort and is easily accessible to the mountain-railway systems. The hospitable owner, Urs Hauser, often goes skiing with his guests. His family has been running the hotel for three generations; their clients always mention the Hausers' personal attention.

Dining/Entertainment: The hotel's Restaurant Français is recommended separately (see "Where to Dine," below).

Services: Wake-up calls, massage.

Facilities: Indoor pool, Finnish sauna, bio-health sauna, sun studio, fitness room, children's game room.

HOSTELLERIE EIGER, CH-3818 Grindelwald. Tel. 036/53-21-21. Fax 036/53-21-21. 62 rms (all with bath). TV TEL

$ Rates: 110F–135F ($80.30–$98.55) single; 190F–250F ($138.70–$182.50) double. Half board 30F ($21.90) extra. AE, DC, MC, V.

This hotel appears from the outside like a collection of interconnected balconies, each on a different plane, angled toward the alpine sunshine, and built of contrasting shades of white stucco and natural wood. The interior is attractive, simple, and unpretentious, with lots of warmly tinted wood, hanging lamps, and contrasting lights. The Gepsi-Bar offers live music, recently released songs, and "evergreen" (mountain) tunes. The Heller family offers two bars and restaurants, including a steak house. The facilities include a sauna and a whirlpool.

MODERATE

HOTEL SPINNE, CH-3818 Grindelwald. Tel. 036/53-23-41. Fax 036/53-23-14. 48 rms (all with bath). TV TEL

$ Rates: 115F–140F ($83.95–$102.20) single; 205F–215F ($149.65–$156.95) double. Half board 35F ($25.55) extra. AE, DC, MC, V. **Closed:** Nov.

This well-insulated, modern hotel is better known for its restaurants and nightclubs than it is for its rooms. Nevertheless, its rooms are comfortable and well furnished. The five-story, flat-roofed hotel has dark bands encircling it both horizontally and vertically. Ranked four stars, it offers a sauna, a whirlpool, and at least three restaurants.

HOTEL SUNSTAR & ADLER, CH-3818 Grindelwald. Tel. 036/54-54-17.
Fax 036/53-31-70. 280 rms (all with bath). TV TEL
$ **Rates** (including continental breakfast): Summer, 95F–100F ($69.35–$73) single; 180F–220F ($131.40–$160.60) double. Winter, 110F–138F ($80.30–$100.75) single; 210F–260F ($153.30–$189.75) double. Half board 30F ($21.90) extra. AE, DC, MC, V.

Originally built as separate hotels, the Sunstar and the Adler were connected, renovated, and enlarged in 1983 and now offer some of the most comfortable and stylishly modern accommodations in Grindelwald, in an architectural style that harmonizes well with the tranquil location. There is a magnificent view of the surrounding mountains, the First and the Kleine Scheidegg. The decor includes Oriental carpets, wood furniture, and low-slung sofas, and a stone fireplace. There is a popular bar and tavern restaurant with rustic decor. The rest of the facilities include an indoor swimming pool, a sauna, and a solarium.

HOTEL KREUZ & POST, CH-3818 Grindelwald. Tel. 036/54-54-92. Fax 036/53-43-19. 45 rms (all with bath). MINIBAR TV TEL
$ **Rates** (including buffet breakfast): 105F–125F ($76.65–$91.25) single; 190F–250F ($138.70–$182.50) double. Half board 30F ($21.90) extra. No credit cards.
Parking: Free.

This angular, modern hotel is ideally located on the main square of town, across from the Sports Center. The Konzett family takes advantage of the location by setting up an outdoor café on the sidewalk in front. The interior is decorated in part with 18th-century antiques and engravings. The rooms are equipped with a radio; many have balconies. There is a sun terrace on the roof, with a magnificent view of the mountains; there is also an indoor pool.

PARKHOTEL SCHOENEGG, CH-3818 Grindelwald. Tel. 036/53-18-53.
Fax 036/53-47-66. 85 rms (all with bath). TEL
$ **Rates** (including continental breakfast): 120F–150F ($87.60–$109.50) single; 180F–260F ($131.40–$189.75) double. Half board 30F ($21.90) extra. AE, DC, MC, V. **Parking:** 8F ($5.85).

Established by the Stettler family in 1890, this hotel has a grandly expansive facade with tiers of wooden balconies, and public rooms accented with hewn stone and slabs of local wood. The bedrooms are cozy and comfortable. During the winter, the descendants of the original founders throw fondue parties for guests in their basement-level Gydis-Bar. (Opened in 1940, it is said to be one of the oldest bars in Grindelwald and a favorite of nostalgia buffs.) The hotel's dining room serves French cuisine.

Ask Tom and Christine Stettler to show you their kennels behind the swimming pool and service buildings: They breed award-winning Siberian huskies. The hotel also offers a swimming pool, a fitness room, and a sauna. Massage is available. Local ski runs terminate at the hotel; a ski lift to the ski school is close to the front door.

INEXPENSIVE

CENTRAL HOTEL WOLTER, CH-3818 Grindelwald. Tel. 036/53-22-33.
Fax 036/53-35-61. 52 rms (all with bath). TV TEL
$ **Rates** (including continental breakfast): 90F–112F ($65.70–$81.75) single; 158F–197F ($115.30–$143.80) double. Half board 28F ($20.45) extra. AE, DC, MC, V.

It's more modern and boxy than many other hotels in town, but its central location just a few steps from several more expensive hotels makes it attractive. On the ground floor there's a popular outdoor café, as well as a substantial restaurant. Upstairs is the reception area and a salon that resembles a room in a private home: It has armchairs, a few antiques, and a compact bar. The modern rooms are simply decorated. Unlike many other hotels in Grindelwald, this one remains open all year.

DERBY HOTEL, CH-3818 Grindelwald. Tel. 036/54-54-61. Fax 036/54-54-61. 70 rms (all with bath or shower). TV TEL
$ Rates: 90F–112F ($65.70–$81.75) single; 158F–197F ($115.30–$143.80) double. Half board 28F ($20.45) extra. AE, DC, MC, V.
Many modern twists have been given to this large adaptation of a mountain chalet, a centrally located three-star hotel on the site of the former Hôtel de la Gare. Peter and Christiane Märkle carry on the century-old family tradition. The present building dates from 1973. The roof has twin peaks and several irregularly shaped balconies. The pine-paneled rooms are brightly furnished.

The Derby offers some of the best restaurants and bars in town. I recommend the Föhrenstube (Pine Room); it's elegantly decorated, with a view of the Eiger. The Grosses Restaurant is big enough for a banquet; the Gaststube is an intimate place for a drink. The rustic Cava Bar, in the cellar, is one of the preferred rendezvous points for après-ski.

HOTEL HIRSCHEN, CH-3818 Grindelwald. Tel. 036/53-27-77. Fax 036/53-48-94. 28 rms (all with shower or bath). TEL
$ Rates (including continental breakfast): 70F–105F ($51.10–$76.65) single; 116F–170F ($84.65–$124.10) double. Half board 30F ($21.90) extra. MC, V.
In the three-star Hirschen, the Bleuer family offers one of the best values at the resort. The hotel, which has an attractive modern facade, is both comfortable and affordable. Its rooms come in a variety of styles and include such amenities as toilets and radios. The hotel has a respectable dining room, and a popular bowling alley in the cellar. It provides room service and laundry service.

SPORT JUNGFRAU, CH-3818 Grindelwald. Tel. 036/53-13-41. Fax 036/53-13-84. 47 rms (all with bath). A/C TEL
$ Rates (including buffet breakfast): 60F–85F ($43.80–$62.05) single; 100F–170F ($73–$124.10) double. Half board 30F ($21.90) extra. AE, DC, MC, V.
Located at the entrance to the village, this attractive, modernized chalet is 3 minutes from the train station. Its rooms are well furnished and comfortable (18 have TVs). The hotel has a bar, a dining room, and a lounge with a view of the north face of the magnificent Eiger. It also offers a terrace café in the front. Shops, entertainment, and a public pool are all nearby. The hotel is open year round.

WHERE TO DINE

EXPENSIVE

GRILL ROOM, in the Grand Hotel Regina. Tel. 54-54-55.
Cuisine: SWISS. **Reservations:** Recommended.
$ Prices: Appetizers 12F–18F ($8.75–$13.15); main courses 25F–45F ($18.25–$32.85). No credit cards.
Open: Dec–Apr, dinner only, daily 7–11pm.
One of the best restaurants in Grindelwald is an elegant version of a hunter's Stube, one floor below the hotel lobby. The decor includes hunting trophies. Separate menus detail meat and fish offerings. Typical dishes include poached eel with crayfish tails,

French snails, Russian caviar, steak tartare, scampi flambéed with Chivas Regal, and aiguillettes of veal in a saffron sauce. The service is formal and correct.

RESTAURANT FRANÇAIS, in the Hotel Belvedere. Tel. 54-54-34.
Cuisine: INTERNATIONAL. **Reservations:** Recommended.
$ **Prices:** Appetizers 10.50F–11.50F ($7.65–$8.40); main courses 23.50F–45F ($17.15–$32.85); menu du chef 79F ($57.65). AE, DC, MC, V.
Open: Dinner only, daily 7–9:30pm.

⭐ Many visitors agree that this is the best restaurant in Grindelwald. You might begin with a Burgundy snail stew in cream sauce or young Bornholm (Denmark) salmon served with noodles. Specialties for two include roast ribs of lamb with herbs from the hotel garden or whole filet of veal garnished with stuffed morels. If you're on your own, you might try the spicy beef Stroganoff, a dish from an original recipe created by Alexj Elkoff, onetime head chef of the Carlton Restaurant in Moscow. The owner, Urs Hauser, is always in the dining room during meal hours to aid and advice diners. Special buffets are also a feature of the restaurant.

ROTISSERIE, in the Hotel Spinne. Tel. 53-23-41.
Cuisine: SWISS. **Reservations:** Recommended.
$ **Prices:** Appetizers 12F–18F ($8.75–$13.15); main courses 19F–40F ($13.85–$29.20); menu dégustation 79F ($57.65); menu surprise 105F ($76.65). AE, DC, MC, V.
Open: Dinner only, daily 6:30–10:30pm.

The elegant alpine decor centers around a large window with a view of the mountains. In warm weather, tables are set out on the terrace dotted with flowers. Two fixed-price menus are offered. Appetizers include snails en cocotte, a terrine of foie gras with cognac, and good-tasting soups (my favorite is flavored with morels). The fish and meat dishes are usually delectable, including filets of sea bass, lobster, and salmon stuffed with leeks and tarragon. Elaborate desserts include sabayon with marsala and a "black and white" chocolate mousse. The most popular is the sorbet du jour. In the summer, the Garden Restaurant offers elaborate salad buffets and specialties from the grill.

MODERATE

RESTAURANT ALTE POST. Tel. 53-11-43.
Cuisine: SWISS. **Reservations:** Required.
$ **Prices:** Appetizers 9F–19F ($6.55–$13.85); main courses 21F–35F ($15.35–$25.55); fixed-price lunch 16F ($11.70). AE, MC, V.
Open: Lunch Thurs–Tues 11:30am–2pm; dinner Thurs–Tues 6:30–9pm.

Often fully booked at least a day in advance, this Swiss restaurant serves traditional specialties, often to local residents of Grindelwald, in a pine-paneled ambience with friendly service. Typical dishes include a terrine of morels, smoked filet of trout, asparagus with air-dried ham, filet steak with green peppers, scallop of veal Cordon Bleu, and lamb or pork cutlets.

RESTAURANT KREUZ & POST, in the Hotel Kreuz & Post. Tel. 54-54-92.
Cuisine: SWISS. **Reservations:** Not needed.
$ **Prices:** Appetizers 10F–15F ($7.30–$10.95); main courses 18F–25F ($13.15–$18.25); light lunch 22F ($16.05). No credit cards.
Open: Lunch daily 11:30am–1:30pm; dinner daily 6:30–9:30pm.

Explore this alpine restaurant before choosing a table. Tucked away in the corner is an attractive room, the Challi-Stube; the ceiling and paneling are especially well crafted. The menu is in English. Typical appetizers are smoked salmon and oxtail soup. For a main course, steak, pork, and fish are offered, including blue trout sautéed in butter. For a traditional Swiss dish, try sliced veal Zurich style with Rösti. The chef specializes in the two classic fondues, chinoise and bourguignonne, served for two.

STEAKHOUSE, in the Hostellerie Eiger. Tel. 53-21-21.
  Cuisine: SWISS. **Reservations:** Recommended.
  $ Prices: Appetizers 10F–15F ($7.30–$10.95); main courses 18F–35F ($13.15–$25.55). AE, DC, MC, V.
  Open: Dinner only, Sun–Thurs 5pm–midnight, Fri–Sat 5pm–1am. **Closed:** Mon in summer.
Located on the second floor of the hotel, this restaurant has stone walls, half-timbers, and farm antiques. There is a dark rustic bar, the Gepsi, near the entrance. The Steakhouse offers the best beefsteaks in town in a range of portions; some cuts are from the United States. Specialties include steak au poivre, chateaubriand, rack of lamb, julienne of veal with mushroom-cream sauce, and cheese crêpes, as well as a limited fish menu. Live music is presented from 8pm to midnight.

INEXPENSIVE

RESTAURANT SPORTZENTRUM. Tel. 53-33-66.
  Cuisine: SWISS. **Reservations:** Not needed.
  $ Prices: Appetizers 6F–10F ($4.40–$7.30); main courses 15F–23F ($10.95–$16.80). No credit cards.
  Open: Daily 8am–9:30pm.
The rustic, timbered dining room is in the modern Sports Center in the middle of the resort. Windows look out onto an indoor swimming pool and an enormous ice-hockey rink. The establishment opens early in the morning and serves snacks and drinks until late. The menu offers many Swiss specialties, including cheese fondue.

EVENING ENTERTAINMENT

After dark, Grindelwald is one of the liveliest towns in the Bernese Oberland. In addition to the following choices, there are get-together parties once a week at the outdoor ice rink.

CAVA BAR, in the Derby Hotel. Tel. 54-54-61.
  This popular bar, located in the cellar of the Derby Hotel, near the railway station, offers dance bands and a rustic decor. It's open in the winter, Monday through Friday from 6pm to 1:30am and on Saturday from 6pm to 2:30am. Mixed drinks run about 12F ($8.75); beer, 6F ($4.40).

CHALLI-BAR, in the Hotel Kreuz & Post. Tel. 54-54-92.
  This popular bar and disco resembles an alpine barnyard, with a timbered ceiling and plank siding. There is a prominent neon sign near the front of the hotel. Live musicians appear nightly. It's open daily from 8 to 11:30pm. Closed: Mid-April to mid-May. Beer costs 8F ($5.85).

ESPRESSO BAR, in the Hotel Spinne. Tel. 53-23-41.
  Cramped, hot, and crowded, this log-cabin bar nonetheless fills with skiers almost every evening. Despite its name, the most popular drink probably isn't espresso. The bar is a few steps from the main entrance to the hotel. Open daily from 11am to 1am. Beer costs 6F ($4.40).

GEPSI-BAR, in the Hostellerie Eiger. Tel. 53-21-31.
  One of the resort's most popular nightclubs is in the Hostellerie Eiger. Rustic and

cozy, the Gepsi-Bar is the place for live music. Drinks run about 12F ($8.75); beer, 8F ($5.85).

FONDUE-STÜBLI, in the Hotel Spinne. Tel. 53-23-41.

One of the many nightclubs in the Hotel Spinne, this rustic alpine restaurant offers music and dim lighting. Beer is served in big mugs. Raclette costs 15F ($10.95), and fondue bourguignonne is 35F ($25.55) for two people. Open winter Wednesday through Monday from 5pm until late. Drinks run 12F ($8.75).

HERBY'S BAR, in the Grand Hotel Regina. Tel. 54-54-55.

Located in the hotel lobby, this bar has comfortable sofas, Oriental carpets, and interesting paintings. Herbert Kuhn is one of the resort's most charming and sophisticated barmen. A piano player provides dance music. Diners from the hotel's Grill Room come here for a nightcap. Open daily from 7pm until 2am. Drinks cost about 14F ($10.20); beer, 5F ($3.65).

LE PLAZA CLUB, in the Hotel Sunstar and Adler. Tel. 53-42-40.

This popular disco and nightclub is accessible by way of a labyrinth of hallways and staircases. Open daily from 8pm to 3am. Drinks run 14F ($10.20), and beer costs 8F ($5.85).

Admission: Free, but there's a one-drink minimum.

SPIDER DISCO, in the Hotel Spinne. Tel. 53-23-41.

Beneath a ceiling covered with simulated stalactites and amid walls adorned with painted versions of spiders' webs, you can dance the night away. Open daily from 8:30pm to 1:30am. Drinks begin at 12F ($8.75).

Admission: Fri–Sat 6F ($4.40). Sun–Thurs free.

---

5. KANDERSTEG

16 miles S of Spiez, 27 miles SW of Interlaken

GETTING THERE   By Train   Kandersteg is at the northern terminus of the 9-mile-long Lötschberg Tunnel, which, ever since the beginning of World War I, has linked Bern with the Rhône Valley. The railroad that runs through the tunnel can transport cars. Trains leave every 30 minutes; no reservations are necessary. From Brig, it's possible to take the car through another tunnel into Italy. The resort is also served by the Berne–Lötschberg–Simplon railway.

By Car   From Interlaken, take N8 east to Spiez, where the Kandersteg road then heads south into the mountains.

ESSENTIALS   The **Kandersteg Tourist Office,** CH-3718 Kandersteg (tel. 033/75-12-34), is open Monday through Saturday from 8am to noon and 2 to 6pm. The **telephone area code** for Kandersteg is 033. In lieu of **street names,** directional signs are used. All guests who have a room in Kandersteg are given a **visitor's card,** entitling them to certain price reductions, including a discount on the town's network of chair lifts.

Lying between Grindelwald and Gstaad, Kandersteg is a popular resort at one of the southern points of the Bernese Oberland. It's a tranquil and lovely mountain village with rust- and orange-colored rooftops and green Swiss meadows. The summer-and-winter resort is spread over 2½ miles, so nothing is crowded. The village itself is at the foot of the Blumlisalp chain (12,000 feet) and provides access to six remote alpine hamlets.

Kandersteg developed as a resting point on the road to the Gemmi Pass, which long ago linked the Valais with the Bernese Oberland. The village still has many old farmhouses and a tiny church from the 16th century. It is proud of its traditions.

WHAT TO SEE & DO

In the summer, qualified riders in proper clothes can rent horses at the local riding school. There is an extensive network of level footpaths and strategically located benches around Kandersteg. These paths are open year round.

In the winter, the resort attracts cross-country skiers and downhill novices (top-speed skiers go elsewhere). It has a cable car, two chair lifts, and four ski tows; the National Nordic Ski Center offers a ski-jumping station. The 1½-mile cross-country ski trail is floodlit in the evening. Other facilities include an indoor and outdoor ice rink.

NEARBY ATTRACTIONS The most popular excursion from Kandersteg is to **Oeschinensee,** or Lake Oeschinen, high above the village. The lake is surrounded by snow-covered peaks of the Blumlisalp, towering 6,000 feet above the extremely clear water. You can walk to it from the Victoria Hotel or take a chair lift, costing 12F ($8.75), to the Oeschinen station and walk down from that point.

Another popular excursion is to **Klus Gorge.** Park your car at the cable station's lower platform at Stock. Walk 2 miles to the gorge, which was formed by the abrasive action of the Kander River. The rushing water creates a romantic, even primeval, setting. However, you must watch your step, as the path gets very slippery in places—the spray coats the stones and pebbles and has fostered a layer of moss. There is a tunnel over the gorge.

WHERE TO STAY & DINE

EXPENSIVE

ROYAL HOTEL BELLEVUE, CH-3718 Kandersteg. Tel. 033/75-12-12. Fax 033/75-13-33. 45 rms (all with bath). MINIBAR TV TEL
$ Rates (including continental breakfast): 200F–290F ($146–$211.65) single; 290F–600F ($211.65–$437.95) double. Half board 30F ($21.90) extra. DC, MC, V.

⭐ The four-story, brown-and-white facade of this hotel doesn't suggest the luxury that visitors find inside. Considered one of the finest hotels in Switzerland, it is listed both in *Relais & Châteaux* and in *The Leading Hotels of the World*. It has been owned by the Rikli family for three generations. The interior has flagstone floors covered with dozens of Oriental rugs, Louis XIII–style armchairs, a collection of antiques, and rococo lighting fixtures. Around the fireplaces are clusters of carved armchairs covered with gray brocades.

The expansive grounds include gardens, evergreens, and lawns. From the free-form swimming pool in the back garden there's a magnificent mountain vista. In the summer, hiking excursions are arranged; and guests can ride one of the many horses and bicycles. If you love horses, bring riding clothes and boots. The hotel also offers a 33-foot yacht suitable for six passengers and a motorboat for waterskiing. The lake is 20 minutes away. In the winter alpine skiing and cross-country skiing are available.

Dining/Entertainment: The Rôtisserie is the most glamorous restaurant in town, with French armchairs, crystal chandeliers, oak paneling, and handcrafted tapestries from the 16th century. It offers a fine light French cuisine. Guests are requested to wear dinner jackets or semiformal dresses for dinner. The Grill-Stübli is suitable for informal lunches. Only guests of this luxurious hotel are admitted to the restaurants and bar. Nonresidents are allowed by invitation only.

Services: Room service, laundry.

Facilities: Tennis court, indoor and outdoor swimming pool, sauna, riding stable, putting green, ice-skating rink.

MODERATE

HOTEL ADLER, CH-3718 Kandersteg. Tel. 033/75-11-22. Fax 033/75-19-61. 24 rms (all with bath). MINIBAR TV TEL

$ Rates (including continental breakfast): 75F–85F ($54.75–$62.05) single; 130F–140F ($94.90–$102.20) double. Half board 25F ($18.25) extra. AE, DC, MC, V.

An open fire crackling in the foyer sets the tone of this warm, cozy inn. A wood-sided chalet whose solid walls were originally built in 1906, it's set on the main street near the center of town. The fourth-generation owner, Andreas Fetzer, and his Finnish-born wife, Eija, offer comfortable bedrooms paneled in pinewood. All contain a radio, and a few have Jacuzzi-fitted bathtubs.

The Adler-Bar, which fills most of the ground floor, is one of the most popular après-ski hangouts in town. There is also a brasserie (the Adlerstube) as well as a relatively formal restaurant where full meals start at 40F ($29.20). In both places lunch is served daily from noon to 2:30pm and dinner is daily from 5:30 to 9:30pm; the brasserie offers a limited menu throughout the afternoon. Candlelight dinner, buffets, and fondue and raclette parties add to the fun of staying here. Facilities include a Finnish sauna.

HOTEL ALFA-SOLEIL, CH-3718 Kandersteg. Tel. 033/75-17-18. Fax 033/75-17-76. 37 rms (all with bath). TEL

$ Rates (including buffet breakfast): 70F–90F ($51.10–$65.70) single; 120F–180F ($87.60–$131.40) double. Half board 25F ($18.25) extra. AE, DC, MC, V.

Closed: Nov.

Built in several stages in the 1960s and 1970s, this popular spot is the first hotel many visitors see as they approach the resort. Peter and Agnes Seiler are avid skiers and offer comfortable rooms, many with a private balcony.

The Stella Restaurant is the perfect après-ski haven. The dining-room ceiling is made of saplings and century-old doors removed from a much older hotel. A collection of antique sleighs and wrought-iron implements is displayed in the upper galleries. The menu offers a variety of dishes suitable for most budgets, including pizza, pasta, large shrimp, filet of turbot, fresh cream of avocado soup, spaghetti carbonara, filet of pork with Roquefort, and an array of grilled meats. Main dishes start at 12F ($8.75), a four-course meal costs 30F ($21.90), and a seven-course menu dégustation runs 60F to 80F ($43.80 to $58.40). Lunch is served daily from 11:30am to 2pm; dinner, daily from 6:30 to 9:30pm.

HOTEL VICTORIA & RITTER, CH-3718 Kandersteg. Tel. 033/75-14-44. Fax 033/75-14-90. 84 rms (all with bath). TV TEL

$ Rates (including continental breakfast): 75F–95F ($54.75–$69.35) single; 140F–180F ($102.20–$131.40) double. Half board 25F ($18.25) extra. AE, DC, MC, V.

The original part of this hotel was built as a coaching inn in 1789 and named The Ritter (knight), after a local nobleman. In 1912 the Victoria, a larger and more opulent hotel, was added. Today the two hotels form a single architectural unit, and although much of the interior has been modernized, they still retain their original exterior detailing. The bedrooms are contemporary, with such amenities as a radio. The premises contain a kindergarten, a glass-enclosed swimming pool, and outdoor tennis courts. There is also a rustically paneled restaurant.

INEXPENSIVE

HOTEL ALPENBLICH, CH-3718 Kandersteg. Tel. 033/75-11-29. 12 rms (all with shower). TV TEL

$ Rates (including continental breakfast): 40F ($29.20) single; 80F ($58.40) double. AE, DC, MC, V. **Closed:** Oct and 4 weeks in Mar–Apr.

Built in 1902, this small chalet is in the center of town, a 5-minute walk from the train station. Register near the bar of the local popular brasserie, Oberlanderstube. The restaurant is open daily from 8am to midnight. Both the hotel and the restaurant are closed in October and four weeks between March and April. A la carte meals start at 22F ($16.05). The owner plays the clarinet, and his band performs on Friday night during the season.

EVENING ENTERTAINMENT

HIGH MOON DISCO, in the Hotel Alfa-Soleil. Tel. 75-17-18.
Located at the edge of town, a healthy hike from the center, this disco attracts many visitors with its octagonal dance floor, light show, and electronic dance music. It's open Tuesday through Sunday from 9pm to 2am. Beer costs 6F ($4.40); scotch, 12F ($8.75).
Admission: Free.

ADLER-BAR, in the Hotel Adler. Tel. 75-11-22.
This centrally located bar is crowded with skiers in the afternoon and evening. Located in a modern chalet, it has timbers and pine paneling. Piano music is played daily in winter. Open daily from 4pm to 1:30am; closed in November. Beer runs about 6F ($4.40).

---

6. GSTAAD

38 miles SW of Thun, 26 miles SE of Bulle

GETTING THERE By Train Gstaad is on the local train line connecting Interlaken with Montreux and several smaller towns in central-southwest Switzerland. About a dozen trains come into Gstaad every day from both of those cities, each of which is a railway junction with good connections to the rest of Switzerland. Travel time from Montreux can be as little as an hour and 20 minutes; from Interlaken, about 30 minutes, sometimes with a change of train at the hamlet of Zweisimmen.

By Bus Gstaad's only bus service connects the town railway station with a handful of high-altitude ski resorts in the Valais, most notably Les Diablerets.

By Car From Spiez, head southwest on Route 11; from Bulle, head south and then east on Route 11.

ESSENTIALS The **Gstaad Tourist Office,** CH-3780 Gstaad (tel. 030/4-71-41), is open Monday through Saturday from 8am to noon and 3 to 6pm. The **telephone area code** for Gstaad is 030. Some **streets** have names; others are placed outside street plans, but there are directional signs to follow to hotels and restaurants.

Against a backdrop of glaciers and mountain lakes, Gstaad is a haven for the rich and famous. Frequent visitors include King Juan Carlos II of Spain, Elizabeth Taylor, and Italian auto magnate Giovanni Agnelli. Film director Blake Edward and his wife, Julie Andrews, own a chalet nearby. Yet celebrities are usually treated simply as ordinary persons, except by first-time tourists.

Built at the junction of four quiet valleys near the southern tip of the Bernese Oberland, Gstaad was once only a place to change horses on the grueling voyage through the Bernese Oberland. As the railroad lines developed, it grew into a resort, beginning with the opening of the deluxe Alpina Grand Hotel, where wealthy Russian and Hungarian families came, together with their entourages of valets, nannies, and translators. In 1912, two years before the outbreak of World War I, a hotel that was to become one of the most legendary in Switzerland, The Palace, opened, promising the ultimate in luxury. In 1916, Le Rosey school (listed in the *Guinness Book of World Records* as "the most expensive prep school in the world") opened its doors, in the satellite town of Tolle. The school contributed to the fame of Gstaad, as prestigious visitors, including King Leopold of Belgium, came to see their children.

The town, the most chic in the Bernese Oberland, retains much of its turn-of-the-century charm. Some first-time visitors, however, say that the resort is a bore if you can't afford to stay at the Gstaad Palace or mingle with the stars in their private chalets. Yet the town has many moderately priced hotels, taverns, and guesthouses, with an allure of their own. Many of the bistros and cafés close from October to mid-December and from late April to mid-June.

WHAT TO SEE & DO

The resort is rich in entertainment and **sports facilities.** Many skiers stay in Gstaad and venture to one of the nearby ski resorts during the day. Cable cars take passengers to altitudes of 5,000 and 10,000 feet—at the higher altitude there's skiing even in the summer. Other facilities include tennis courts, heated indoor and outdoor swimming pools, and some 200 miles of hiking trails. The Gstaad International Tennis Tournament, held in July, is the most important tennis event in Switzerland.

Skiers setting off from Gstaad have access to 70 lifts, mountain railroads, and gondolas. The altitude of Gstaad's highest skiable mountain is 6,550 feet, with a vertical drop of 3,555 feet. Most beginner and intermediate runs are east of the village in Eggli, a ski area reached by cable car. Eggli has a sunny, southern exposure. Wispellan-Sanetch is favored for afternoon skiing, with lots of runs down to the village. At the summit is the Glacier des Diablerets, at a height of 9,900 feet. Wasserngrat, reached from the south side of the resort, is another skiing area. Advanced skiers prize Wasserngrat for its powder skiing on steep slopes.

The **Swiss Ski School** at Gstaad (tel. 030/4-18-65) has first-class teachers and qualified mountain and touring guides. Special classes for children are offered. Some 100 private instructors are available.

A full-day **ski pass** costs 40F ($29.20) per person. It's valid for all lifts in the Gstaad area. It includes passage on a bus departing from Gstaad for the base of the gondola platform at Reusch, the point where all the ski lifts begin.

Gstaad has several satellite resorts, which many visitors prefer. **Saanen** and **Schönried** are both summer-and-winter resorts, with excellent accommodations. Saanen, at 3,450 feet, is east of Gstaad; some of its wooden chalets date from the 1500s. In August the Menuhin Festival draws an international music-loving crowd. The resort can be reached easily by car or by the Montreux–Oberland railway; there's also a small airfield for visitors who fly in. Schönried, some 2½ miles northeast of

Gstaad, is appreciated because of its arguably better snowfall and accommodations, notably the Alpenrose Hotel.

Whichever resort you choose—Gstaad, Saanen, or Schönried—you'll be surrounded by dramatic glaciers and peaceful alpine pastures. This part of the country, called Saanenland, is considered the most beautiful part of Switzerland.

WHERE TO STAY

Gstaad is not known for its *in*expensive hotels. Prices soar in the winter. When business is slow, many of the hotels close; the dates of these closings can vary from year to year.

VERY EXPENSIVE

HOSTELLERIE ALPENROSE, Hauptstrasse, CH-3778 Schönried-Gstaad. Tel. 030/4-67-67. Fax 030/4-67-12. 21 rms (all with bath). MINIBAR TV TEL

$ **Rates** (including half board): 255F–290F ($186.10–$211.65) single; 400F–500F ($291.95–$364.95) double. DC, MC, V. **Closed:** 2 weeks in Nov, 2 weeks in May (dates vary).

For those who seek the charm of a small inn, this is the preferred choice in the area, the only *Relais & Châteaux* listing within 30 miles. Its soft-spoken owner, Monika von Siebenthal, is a memorable host, setting the fashionable tone of the chalet, which is famous for its restaurants. The pine-paneled rooms are exquisitely decorated with rustic furnishings. The bedrooms are comfortable and tastefully appointed.

Dining/Entertainment: Sammy's Bar & Bistro and its deluxe restaurant are described in "Where to Dine," below.

Services: Wake-up calls.

Facilities: Sunny terrace with alpine panorama.

HOTEL CHRISTIANA, Hauptstrasse, CH-3780 Gstaad. Tel. 030/4-51-21. Fax 030/4-71-09. 26 rms (all with bath). MINIBAR TV TEL

$ **Rates** (including half board): 210F–260F ($153.30–$189.75) single; 350F–430F ($255.45–$313.85) double. V.

This chalet is the smallest first-class hotel in Gstaad. The paneled interior has Oriental rugs and tasteful furniture. Some units are spectacular, especially one with white carpets and white upholstery. Nearly all units have a balcony.

Dining/Entertainment: The hotel has a first-class restaurant and a garden where meals are served.

Services: Room service, laundry.

Facilities: Outdoor swimming pool near the Palace Hotel.

HOTEL ERMITAGE-GOLF, Hauptstrasse, CH-3778 Schönried-Gstaad. Tel. 030/4-27-27. Fax 030-4-71-95. 71 rms (all with bath). MINIBAR TV TEL

$ **Rates** (including half board): 170F–235F ($124.10–$171.55) single; 480F–620F ($350.35–$452.55) double. AE, DC, MC, V. **Closed:** Early May and Nov.

Despite its name, this large hotel is not near the area's 9-hole golf course. In the winter it's a warm and cozy retreat; in the summer it's a pleasure chalet, as red geraniums bloom on its balconies and chaise longues are set up on its verdant lawns, so that guests can soak up the alpine sunshine. Heiner Lutz and Laurenz Schmid offer paneled bedrooms, each individually furnished for maximum comfort. Some have Oriental rugs.

Dining/Entertainment: The restaurants and bars are among the best in the resort, offering a wide price range. Le Gourmet restaurant is elegant and expensive. The Stübli is more economical. Other restaurants include Table d'Hôtes and Spycher. The bar, Downtown, is popular and fun.

Services: Laundry, room service.

Facilities: Heated indoor swimming pool, outdoor pool, Finnish sauna, biosauna, Turkish bath, Jacuzzi, solarium, bodybuilding room, massage treatments, tennis court.

PALACE HOTEL GSTAAD, CH-3780 Gstaad. Tel. 030/8-31-31. 150 rms (all with bath), 16 suites. MINIBAR TV TEL

$ Rates (including half board): 380F–540F ($277.35–$394.15) single; 660F–920F ($481.75–$671.50) double; from 1,200F ($875.90) suite. No credit cards.

Closed: Sept 21 to mid-Dec and late March to June 9.

⭐ This landmark hotel is on a wooded hill overlooking the center of Gstaad. Opened in 1912, the Palace has mock-fortified corner towers and a neomedieval facade. It is one of the most sought-after luxury hideaways in the world, attracting corporation heads, movie stars, and fashionable aristocrats. Owner and manager Ernst Scherz's motto is, "Every king is a client, and every client is a king." It's true—if you can afford it.

The nerve center of this chic citadel is an elegantly paneled main salon, with an eternal flame burning in the baronial stone fireplace. Radiating hallways lead to superb restaurants, bars, discos, sports facilities. The plush rooms are tastefully furnished and very distinguished.

Dining/Entertainment: Restaurants, bars, and a disco are offered. The pool is transformed into an extension of the disco when a platform is lowered on top of the water.

Services: Massage, hairdresser.

Facilities: Indoor swimming pool with underwater sound system, fitness center, sauna, solarium, ice rink.

EXPENSIVE

BELLEVUE GRAND HOTEL, Hauptstrasse, CH-3780 Gstaad. Tel. 030/8-31-71. Fax 030/4-21-36. 55 rms (all with bath). MINIBAR TV TEL

$ Rates (including half board): 195F–250F ($142.35–$182.50) single; 350F–450F ($255.45–$328.45) double. AE, DC, MC, V. **Closed:** Oct–Nov and Apr–May.
Superb hospitality, good food, excellent housekeeping, and lavish comfort have made this hotel a favorite. Gstaad's leading four-star hotel, it stands in a serene park with tall old trees. The rooms are spacious and well lit, with restful colors. Many have balconies. One of the elegant salons contains a fireplace.

Dining/Entertainment: The Grill Room and the Curling Restaurant offer many regional specialties, international favorites, and the cuisine of the Grisons. The hotel's gourmet restaurant is Chez Fritz. The piano bar is a focal point in the evening.

Services: Room service, laundry.

Facilities: Open-air heated swimming pool, indoor pool, curling hall, covered riding school, tennis courts.

GRAND HOTEL ALPINA, CH-3780 Gstaad. Tel. 030/4-57-25. Fax 030/4-11-53. 40 rms (all with bath). TV TEL

$ Rates (including half board): 140F–220F ($102.20–$160.60) single; 280F–440F ($204.35–$321.15) double. AE, DC, MC, V. **Closed:** Oct–Nov and Apr–May.
Set in a large park, this half-timbered Victorian building has a tile roof with many

gables and ridges, topped with a square turret. The interior is renovated and modern, with patterned carpets and deep armchairs. Few of the original embellishments remain, but the place is still warm, inviting, and restful. It's managed by the Burri family. The outstanding restaurant is known for its superb service.

HOTEL ARC-EN-CIEL, CH-3780 Gstaad. Tel. 030/8-31-91. Fax 030/4-33-36. 54 rms (all with bath). MINIBAR TV TEL

$ Rates (including breakfast): 70F–180F ($51.10–$131.40) single; 150F–330F ($109.50–$240.05) double. AE, DC, MC, V.

This tranquil alpine chalet is a 10-minute walk from the center of Gstaad, near cable cars and ski slopes. The rooms are attractively decorated and well lit, with wood planks and plaster walls. Most rooms open onto magnificent views. The Matti family are your hosts.

Dining/Entertainment: The hotel has a pizzeria, a cocktail bar, and two other restaurants. Swiss, French, and Italian meals are served.

Services: Room service, laundry.

Facilities: Two tennis courts, heated swimming pool, sunny terrace.

HOTEL BERNERHOF, CH-3780 Gstaad. Tel. 030/8-33-66. Fax 030/4-66-10. 46 rms (all with bath). MINIBAR TV TEL

$ Rates (including half board): Dec 15–Apr 6, 138F ($100.75) single; 252F ($183.95) double. July 6–Aug 17, 164F ($119.70) single; 304F ($221.90) double. AE, DC, MC, V.

Wood balconies extend across the front of this comfortable four-star hotel. Leonz Blunschi offers well-furnished rooms with hairdryers and radios. Facilities include a sauna, indoor swimming pool, and whirlpool. Children are catered to at the hotel, and many activities are planned for them. The restaurant is recommended in "Where to Dine," below. The Apero-Bar is a popular place for drinks.

HOTEL OLDEN, Hauptstrasse, CH-3780 Gstaad. Tel. 030/4-34-44. Fax 030/4-61-64. 15 rms (all with bath). MINIBAR TV TEL

$ Rates (including half board): Off-season, 110F–135F ($80.30–$98.55) single; 270F–350F ($197.05–$255.45) double. In season (part of the winter and July 6–Aug 17), 140F–180F ($102.20–$131.40) single; 270F–350F ($197.05–$255.45) double. AE, DC, MC, V. **Closed:** May. **Parking:** 8F ($5.85).

One of the most charming hotels in Gstaad, the Olden has a facade painted with regional floral designs and bits of folk wisdom. Embellishments are carved or painted into the stone lintels around many of the doors. The rooms are attractively furnished. Hedi Donizetti is the ruling "empress" of Gstaad. Celebrity guests are attracted to the restaurant, lodge, and bar. A summer terrace in front serves meals and drinks.

Services: Laundry, room service, baby-sitting.

Facilities: Garage, quiet garden, sun terrace.

STEIGENBERGER HOTEL, Auf der Halten, CH-3792 Saanen. Tel. 030/8-33-88; for reservations, 212/593-2988 in New York City, or toll free 800/223-5652 in the U.S., 800/882-4777 in New York State. 145 rms (all with bath). MINIBAR TV TEL

$ Rates (including half board): 240F–260F ($175.20–$189.75) single; 400F–440F ($291.95–$321.15) double. AE, DC, MC, V.

This cluster of wooden chalets blends well into the surrounding evergreen forests and mountains. It's located in Saanen, 1¼ miles from Gstaad, and guests enjoy panoramic vistas over the Saanen Valley and neighboring Gstaad.

The chalets have wide overhanging eaves and balconies. The interiors are carefully crafted; the lobby has a lounge and a fireplace. During the summer, geraniums adorn the balconies. The rooms have spruce and mountain pine paneling and traditional furniture. Amenities include radios.

Dining/Entertainment: Two restaurants are offered, one elegant and the other rustic. Hearty regional dishes and cuisine moderne specialties are served.

Services: Room service, laundry.

Facilities: Heated indoor pool, solarium, sauna.

MODERATE

HOTEL BOO, CH-3792 Saanen. Tel. 030/4-14-41. Fax 030/4-40-27. 22 rms (all with bath). MINIBAR TV TEL

$ Rates (including half board): 125F–145F ($91.25–$105.85) single; 210F–250F ($153.30–$182.50) double. MC, V.

This cozy chalet is located on the town's main street. It was built in 1891 but tastefully upgraded in 1962. There are rows of German verses stenciled on its wooden facade. Thomas Boo offers comfortable bedrooms with floral accents. All rooms have a radio, and some have a kitchenette and a private balcony. The most popular attraction is the pub.

POSTHOTEL RÖSSLI, Hauptstrasse, CH-3780 Gstaad. Tel. 030/4-34-12. Fax 030/4-61-90. 26 rms (all with shower or bath). TV TEL

$ Rates (including half board): 115F–135F ($83.95–$98.55) single; 210F–260F ($153.30–$189.75) double. DC, MC, V. **Closed:** May and Nov.

This authentic rustic chalet in the center of Gstaad has green shutters and the Bernese canton flag flying over the front door. It's well heated and furnished with modern conveniences. Reudi Widmer and his family offer paneled rooms. Locals mix with guests in the restaurant and Bierstube. A la carte meals start at 28F ($20.45).

INEXPENSIVE

HOTEL ALPHORN, CH-3780 Gstaad. Tel. 030/4-45-45. 21 rms (15 with bath). TEL

$ Rates (including half board): Off-season, 100F ($73) single without bath, 120F ($87.60) single with bath; 190F ($138.70) double without bath, 230F ($167.90) double with bath. Winter and July 6–Aug 17, 120F ($87.60) single without bath, 140F ($102.20) single with bath; 230F ($167.90) double without bath, 270F ($197.05) double with bath. AE, DC, MC, V.

Located at the base of the Wispile cable car, this intimate chalet is owned by the Mösching family. The hotel has an indoor pool and a ski shop. The rooms are comfortable and snug. The restaurant menu includes trout and cheese dishes, as well as a special dish made with fresh mushrooms.

WHERE TO DINE

Most visitors dine at their hotel, so there are few independent restaurants in Gstaad. The following choices are worth venturing out for.

VERY EXPENSIVE

GRILL ROOM, in the Palace Hotel. Tel. 8-31-31.
Cuisine: INTERNATIONAL. **Reservations:** Required.

$ Prices: Appetizers 15F–53F ($10.95–$38.70); main courses 42F–105F ($30.65–$76.65). No credit cards.

Open: Dinner only, daily 7:30–11pm. **Closed:** Sept 21 to mid-Dec and late Mar to June 9.

⭐ The hotel opens up to three different dining rooms, each elegantly paneled and boasting impeccable service. Some of the finest chefs in the Bernese Oberland create dishes for an exceptionally demanding clientele. Formal attire is essential—men without ties will be asked to dine in the Sans-Cravatte (see below).

For an appetizer, caviar and foie gras abound, but there are also superb hors d'oeuvres (which include beefsteak tartare) and delicate soups and consommés. Main courses are broken down into five major divisions: fish or shellfish, poultry, beef, veal, and lamb. This wide repertoire includes imaginative interpretations of old favorites. Most desserts are elaborate, but you can order a simple sorbet made with fresh fruits of the season.

RESTAURANT CHESERY, Lauenenstrasse. Tel. 4-24-51.
   Cuisine: INTERNATIONAL. **Reservations:** Required.
$ **Prices:** Appetizers 15F–55F ($10.95–$40.15); main courses 37F–98F ($27–$71.55); menu dégustation 120F ($87.60). AE, MC, V.
   Open: Daily 11:30am–11:30pm.

⭐ This is one of the 10 best restaurants in Switzerland. The floors are pink marble and the walls are polished pine. The menu changes daily, based on the freshest ingredients available. Typical dishes include a warm salad of red snapper, cassolette of flap mushrooms with a suprême of quail, filet of beef poached with grated horseradish, and a soufflé of white cheese with the essence of fresh seasonal fruits. Piano music is played from 9pm to 3am.

SANS-CRAVATTE, in the Palace Hotel. Tel. 8-31-31.
   Cuisine: INTERNATIONAL. **Reservations:** Required.
$ **Prices:** Appetizers 15F–55F ($10.95–$40.15); main courses 42F–105F ($30.65–$76.65). No credit cards.
   Open: Dinner only, daily 7:30–11:30pm. **Closed:** Sept 21 to mid-Dec and late March to June 9.

Don't assume that this is a budget restaurant just because the very formal staff doesn't require men to wear neckties. The tables are on a raised platform a few steps from the elegant main dining room of the Palace Hotel. There's a separate entrance so that sans-cravatte (tieless) diners can come in a sweater and not feel out of place. The menu is the same as that served in the Palace Hotel's Grill Room (see above).

EXPENSIVE

HOSTELLERIE ALPENROSE, Hauptstrasse, Schönried-Gstaad. Tel. 4-12-38.
   Cuisine: SWISS. **Reservations:** Recommended.
$ **Prices:** Appetizers 10F–53F ($7.30–$38.70); main courses 37F–98F ($27–$71.55); menu dégustation 140F ($102.20). DC, MC, V.
   Open: Winter, lunch daily noon–2pm; dinner daily 7–10pm. Summer, lunch Wed–Sun noon–2pm; dinner daily 7–10pm. **Closed:** 2 weeks in Nov and 2 weeks in May.

⭐ Superb gastronomy is offered at the Alpenrose. During the summer the paneled dining rooms are full of local residents and guests from the surrounding chalets. Monika von Siebenthal is your host; her father built the first ski lift in the region, in 1935. She has elevated a modest pension into a culinary citadel known throughout Switzerland for its superb cuisine.

The sophisticated menu changes every season; typical dishes include a traditional family recipe for slices of marinated saltwater salmon, various types of smoked fish with fresh baby vegetables, ravioli of Canadian lobster with spring vegetables, and a three-filet extravaganza, "Michel" (named after Mrs. von Siebenthal's talented young son, who trained as a chef in France). Other treats include medallions of hare with basil on a bed of eggplant and fresh peas, and Scottish lamb with lentils and pink peppercorn sauce. Sumptuous desserts include an apple sorbet with a champagne sabayon, and a pineapple crêpe with a ragoût of oranges. Consider having an after-dinner drink in the nightclub, Sammy's.

MODERATE

D'HALTE BEIZ, in the Steigenberger Hotel, Auf der Halten, Saanen. Tel. 8-33-88.
   Cuisine: SWISS. **Reservations:** Recommended.
   $ Prices: Appetizers 12F–22F ($8.75–$16.05); main courses 18F–35F ($13.15–$25.55). AE, DC, MC, V.
   Open: Daily 11:30am–11pm. **Closed:** Nov to mid-Dec.
This regional restaurant offers Swiss specialties in an atmosphere of rustic beams and colorful table settings. There is a view of the Rublihorn. In the winter there's a magnificent salad buffet. A typical meal includes local herb schnapps, Batzi, and Swiss cherry cake. For a main course, try a filet of fera (a fish from Lake Thun), chateaubriand, or carré d'agneau (lamb). This hotel also contains the more formal Sonnenhalte (see below).

FROMAGERIE, in the Palace Hotel. Tel. 8-31-31.
   Cuisine: SWISS. **Reservations:** Recommended.
   $ Prices: Appetizers 12F–25F ($8.75–$18.25); main courses 22F–42F ($16.05–$30.65). No credit cards.
   Open: Dinner only, daily 7–10:30pm. **Closed:** Sept 21 to mid-Dec and late Mar to June 9.
This is the only economical way to experience the most famous and prestigious hotel in the Bernese Oberland. The restaurant is a dignified version of an alpine raclette Stube, with pine-paneled walls and a simple menu. Most dishes include cheese. A salad buffet and pasta menu are also available. Jackets and ties are not required. The Fromagerie is below the lobby level.

OLDEN RESTAURANT, in the Hotel Olden, Hauptstrasse. Tel. 4-34-44.
   Cuisine: SWISS. **Reservations:** Recommended.
   $ Prices: Appetizers 10F–40F ($7.30–$29.20); main courses 25F–49F ($18.25–$35.75). AE, DC, MC, V.
   Open: Lunch daily noon–2pm; dinner daily 7:30–10pm.
The Olden Restaurant is more sophisticated and more expensive than La Pinte, also on the street level of this hotel. Meals are formally served in the pine-paneled dining room. The menu might include smoked salmon, fresh goose-liver terrine, shrimp bisque with green peppercorns, house-style tagliatelle, raclette, medallions of veal with a confit of lemon, and Scottish lamb.

RESTAURANT BERNERHOF, in the Hotel Bernerhof. Tel. 8-33-66.
   Cuisine: CONTINENTAL. **Reservations:** Recommended.
   $ Prices: Appetizers 12F–18F ($8.75–$13.15); main courses 18F–35F ($13.15–$25.55). AE, DC, MC, V.
   Open: Wed–Mon 7:30am–11:30pm. **Closed:** May and Oct–Nov.
This tavern-style restaurant serves many Italian specialties, such as seafood risotto,

excellent seafood soups, veal liver Venetian style, ravioli in a basil-flavored sauce, filet of beef in a mustard sauce, and some good pork dishes. The Hotel Bernerhof also offers the popular Stöckli Bar.

RESTAURANT CHLOSTERLI, Grund-Gstaad. Tel. 5-10-45.

Cuisine: SWISS. **Reservations:** Essential in winter.

$ **Prices:** Appetizers 8F–20F ($5.85–$14.60); main courses 18F–45F ($13.15–$32.85). AE, V.

Open: Lunch daily noon–3pm; dinner daily 7–11pm. **Closed:** May or June (it varies).

S This restaurant and disco complex south of Gstaad lies in the farming hamlet of Grund. The heavily timbered building was originally built as a barn in the 1600s. Today there are three cozy dining rooms. The menu includes soups, salads, medallions of veal with morels, grilled veal or beef steaks, house-style smoked trout, and flambéed mocha ice cream. Game is a seasonal feature.

RISTORANTE RIALTO, Hauptstrasse. Tel. 4-34-74.

Cuisine: ITALIAN. **Reservations:** Recommended.

$ **Prices:** Appetizers 14F–24F ($10.20–$17.50); main courses 28F–44F ($20.45–$32.10). AE, DC, MC, V.

Open: Lunch daily noon–2:30pm; dinner daily 7–10pm; light dishes, drinks, and salads Sun–Thurs 8:30am–midnight, Fri–Sat 8:30am–1am. **Closed:** Mon in May, June, Oct, and Nov.

One of the finest Italian restaurants in the Bernese Oberland, the Rialto lies in the heart of Gstaad. Proprietor Gianni Biggi uses the freshest ingredients, and his menu changes with the season. You might begin with a selection of antipasti, followed by the salmon carpaccio with a truffle-cream sauce or one of the pasta dishes, including pappardella. The risotto served with fresh asparagus and the chef's sole Caruso are both excellent. La Piccola Carta, a limited menu with such dishes as soups, pastas, salads, and one or two veal dishes, is offered from 2:30 to 6:30pm.

SONNEHALTE, in the Steigenberger Hotel, Auf der Halten, Saanen. Tel. 8-33-88.

Cuisine: CONTINENTAL. **Reservations:** Not needed.

$ **Prices:** Appetizers 12F–25F ($8.75–$18.25); main courses 18F–40F ($13.15–$29.20); fixed-price meal 50F ($36.50). AE, DC, MC, V.

Open: Breakfast daily 7–10:30am; dinner daily 7–9:30pm.

The Sonnenhalte offers cuisine moderne, regional, and continental dishes. Only the freshest ingredients are used. A sumptuous breakfast buffet is served daily from 7 to 10:30am. Nonresidents are welcome. There is a dinner buffet on Wednesday with live folk music, costing from 65F ($47.45) per person. The fixed-price menu is one of the best food values at the resort. There is a wide selection of Swiss and continental wines. This hotel also contains the less formal restaurant D'Halte Beiz.

LA GRANDE TERRASSE, in the Palace Hotel. Tel. 8-31-31.

Cuisine: SWISS. **Reservations:** Required.

$ **Prices:** Appetizers 12F–22F ($8.75–$16.05); main courses 22F–35F ($16.05–$25.55). No credit cards.

Open: Winter, lunch only, daily noon–3pm (on sunny days). Summer, lunch daily noon–3pm; dinner daily 7–11pm (depending on weather).

This restaurant has probably the largest covered terrace in Switzerland. At the flick of an electric switch, the dining area is either sheltered from the cold or exposed to the sun. The huge floor space is covered with white tiles in a classical Roman pattern, and adorned with potted pine trees and flowers. Elegant meals are served by white-jacketed employees from the same menu as that offered in the hotel's main dining room.

INEXPENSIVE

LA PINTE, in the Hotel Olden, Hauptstrasse. Tel. 4-34-44.
Cuisine: SWISS. **Reservations:** Not needed.
$ Prices: Appetizers 10F–15F ($7.30–$10.95); main courses 15F–25F ($10.95–$18.25). AE, DC, MC, V.
Open: Daily 11am–11pm.

Closest to the main entrance of the previously recommended hotel, La Pinte, distinguished by the floral patterns painted on its paneling, offers uncomplicated, hearty dishes, among them brochettes, grilled steaks, and Bündnerfleisch (air-dried beef), followed by kirsch-flavored tarts. It functions as both a restaurant and a bar, especially for the après-ski crowd. The more formal Olden Restaurant (see above) is in a secluded dining room to the rear.

EVENING ENTERTAINMENT

Gstaad has the most fashionable après-ski scene in the Bernese Oberland. Clubs quickly slip in and out of fashion, and sometimes out of sight. Visitors are sure to discover some newly opened piano bars and hot spots on their own. During the whole winter season, there are many gala evenings, ski balls, concerts, and cabarets sponsored by hotels and bars.

Wednesday is fondue party night in Gstaad. Skiers gather at a designated mountain restaurant such as the **Berghaus Eggli** (tel. 4-30-69) or the **Berghaus Wispile** (tel. 4-33-98). Participants take the ski lifts between 7 and 8pm and return around 10pm, skiing down by torchlight.

GREEN GO DISCO, in the Palace Hotel. Tel. 8-31-31.
At the most expensive disco in town, pinpricks of light illuminate a mysterious decor of orange, green, and black. A platform descends over the water of the adjacent indoor swimming pool for additional space to dance. Drinks run 24F ($17.50).
Admission: Winter, 40F ($29.20), including the first drink; summer, free.

DANCING DER STOLLEN, in the Steigenberger Hotel, Auf der Halten, Saanen. Tel. 8-33-88.
The Swiss metal sculptor Freddy Madorin designed this dimly lit disco at the base of a steep flight of stairs. The artist added his own sculptures and models, made from parts of mining locomotives and trucks. Top bands and singers appear here often. Open in season daily from 9:30pm to 3am. Drinks run 12F ($8.75).
Admission: Free.

HOSTELLERIE CHESERY, Lauenenstrasse. Tel. 4-24-51.
This piano bar and restaurant (see "Where to Dine," above) attracts a crowd of young people who enjoy dancing. Open daily from 9pm to 3am. Drinks cost around 14F ($10.20).

LA PINTE (Café Olden), in the Hotel Olden. Tel. 4-34-44.
Hedi and Fausto Donizetti purchased the Olden in the 1920s. Today it's one of the most popular places in town. Famous guests have included King Juan Carlos II of Spain and Liza Minnelli, who sang her version of "New York, New York." Hedi, who can be found in the rear bar, has glass bar mugs painted with larkspur and edelweiss for her favorite clients. Beer costs 5F ($3.65).

The Olden Hotel also has a disco, **La Cave,** in the basement. Bands perform in

the rustic surroundings and light meals are served. Open from December 20 to mid-March daily from 8pm to 3am. Beer costs 6F ($4.40).
Admission: Free.

THE PUB, in the Hotel Boo, Saanen. Tel. 4-14-41.

Residents of Gstaad travel to the neighboring hamlet of Saanen to enjoy this elegant pub run by Thomas Boo. The wood-trimmed room has a blazing fireplace and a curved wooden bar. You can order simple meals, such as soups, salads, grilled fish, and steaks, beginning at 30F ($21.90). Open Dec–Apr daily from 11am to 3am. Drinks run 12F ($8.75).

RESTAURANT CHLOSTERLI, Grund-Gstaad. Tel. 5-10-45.

This restaurant and disco is isolated amid fields and meadows about 3 miles south of Gstaad. The former barn is now a favorite nightclub of celebrities, including Tina Turner, Britain's Prince Charles, and Roger Moore, who has a favorite table in one of the semisecluded dining rooms. Ruedy Mullener is the owner. Dancing begins every night at 9:30pm and lasts until 2am. Closed from Easter to June, and November. Drinks cost about 12F ($8.75).
Admission: Free.

RIALTO BAR, in the Ristorante Rialto, Hauptstrasse. Tel. 4-34-74.

Connected to the previously recommended restaurant, this chic and beautifully decorated bar is also one of the town's most popular nightclubs. Some evenings, beginning around 8pm, live music is performed, perhaps by a country-western singer from Nashville. In addition to drinks, light meals are served. The establishment is open daily from 11am to between 12:30am and 1:30am, depending on the night of the week. It's closed only on Monday in May, June, October, and November. Champagne costs 14F ($10.20) a glass; light meals begin at 25F ($18.25).

SAMMY'S BAR/BISTRO, in the Hostellerie Alpenrose, Hauptstrasse, Schönreid. Tel. 4-12-38.

This basement nightclub is lighthearted and charming. The bar is named after the proprietor's dog and features a changing display of fine paintings (the place doubles as an art gallery). Live music is performed. The menu includes grillades, raclette, and veal in a mushroom-cream sauce, starting at 28F ($20.45). It's located about 2½ miles northeast of Gstaad in the alpine hamlet of Schönreid. Upstairs is a very grand restaurant (see "Where to Dine," above). Open in the winter from 7pm to 3am. Drinks cost 14F ($10.20).
Admission: Free.

CHAPTER 8

THE VALAIS

- **WHAT'S SPECIAL ABOUT THE VALAIS**
1. **VERBIER**
2. **SION**
3. **CRANS-MONTANA**
4. **ZERMATT & THE MATTERHORN**
5. **SAAS-FEE**
6. **BRIG & THE SIMPLON PASS**
7. **THE GRIMSEL PASS**

The Valais is the valley of the upper Rhône, a great river that springs from a glacier near the Furka Pass in southern Switzerland. The valley was called Vallis Poenina by the Romans, and the Germans refer to it as Wallis. Famous tourist attractions include the Matterhorn, the Great St. Bernard Pass, and Zermatt. The area offers excellent skiing as well as other winter sports. Zermatt and nearby towns are known for having one of the longest ski seasons in Switzerland.

The Valais is surrounded by the Alps, with more than 50 major mountain peaks, but the Matterhorn (14,701 ft) is the most majestic. The Valais has the largest glacier in Switzerland; several glaciers send tributaries to feed the Rhône, which flows west and north to Lake Geneva, then on through France to the Mediterranean. The Valais also contains about 5 square miles of lakes.

For centuries the Rhône Valley has been a major route through the Alps. The Celts used the Great St. Bernard Pass and Simplon Pass, and after them the Gauls held the territory for 500 years. Hannibal and Napoleon both passed through on their way to conquest. Today wide highways and tunnels provide a direct route to Italy. Many motorists still travel along the Great St. Bernard Pass (8,094 ft.) and the Simplon Pass (6,591 ft.).

Protected by mountains, the Valais enjoys a sunny, stable climate, comparable to that of Spain and France's Provence. The vineyards are second only to those of the Vaud, and the wine is known for its fruity bouquet and delicate flavor. Dairy farming is widespread. Raclette, the classic Swiss dish, is usually made of the rich, unskimmed milk from the Bagnes Valley, near the Great St. Bernard Pass. Outside towns you'll see many *mazots* or *raccards,* small grain-storage barns elevated on piles.

Most residents in the western part of the Valais, from Lake Geneva to Sierre, speak French, while those living to the east speak a German dialect. Many people speak both languages, as well as some English. Most residents of the Valais are Roman Catholic, and there are many churches, abbeys, and monasteries.

The Valais is an increasingly popular travel destination year round. The growth of resorts and recreation facilities has not disturbed the natural splendor of the alpine countryside, with its unique wildlife and natural tranquility.

SEEING THE VALAIS

There is daily air service between New York and Geneva. From Geneva, you can drive or take the train east into most of the resorts of the Valais. Where the train leaves off, a bus or cog railway stands ready to transport you the rest of your lofty way.

WHAT'S SPECIAL ABOUT THE VALAIS

Great Towns/Villages
☐ Sion, capital of the Valais, known for its springs and falls.
☐ Verbier, in Switzerland's southernmost Alps, one of Europe's premier ski resorts.
☐ Zermatt, at the foot of the Matterhorn, a world-class ski resort and a center of mountain climbing or viewing.

Natural Spectacles
☐ The Matterhorn, which towers 14,701 feet over Switzerland and Italy—its hooked and inclined pyramid is the grand challenge to all climbers.
☐ Gorgengrat, outside Zermatt, the highest open-air railway in Europe.

☐ Klein ("Little") Matterhorn, outside Zermatt, a towering peak reached by the highest aerial cableway in Europe.

Great Scenic Drives
☐ The Great St. Bernard Pass, the oldest and most famous of the alpine crossings.
☐ The Simplon Pass, at 6,578 feet, linking the Valais with Switzerland's Italian section, the Ticino; the pass was built by Napoleon's army.
☐ The Grimsel Pass, one of the great scenic roads of Switzerland, linking the Valais with the Bernese Oberland.

Museums
☐ The Alpine Museum, at Zermatt, housing relics of the first conquests of the Matterhorn.

The connecting rail and bus network in the Valais is extensive, so that it isn't necessary to rent a car. Roads reach all resorts except Zermatt and Saas-Fee, and mountain roads are all well graded. Horrifying bends are less common than they were in the past.

IF YOU HAVE A WEEK

Days 1 and 2: Explore Verbier and its surrounding attractions and drive to the Great St. Bernard Pass.
Day 3: Head east to Sion, the ancient capital of the Valais, for the night.
Days 4 and 5: Go to Zermatt for 2 nights. You'll spend these 2 days taking excursions to spots offering great views of the Matterhorn.
Day 6: While based in Brig, drive south over the Simplon Pass for a great scenic view.
Day 7: Head east of Brig and cross the famed Grimsel Pass into the Bernese Oberland.

---

1. VERBIER

80 miles E of Geneva, 25 miles N of Great St. Bernard Tunnel

GETTING THERE   By Train   From Martigny, take a train to Le Châble, where you can transfer to a postal bus or to the Le Châble–Verbier aerial cableway.

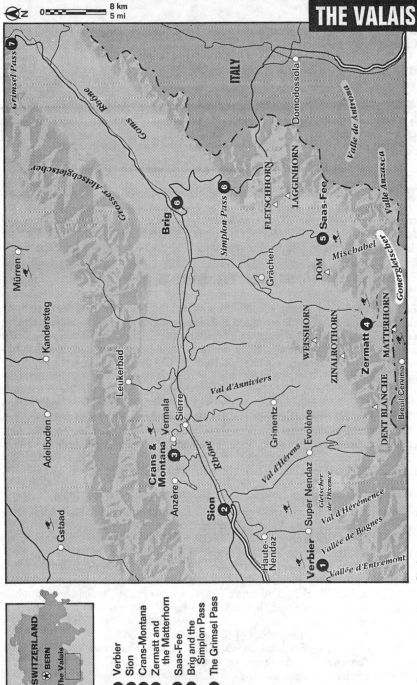

THE VALAIS

8 km
5 mi

ITALY

Grimsel Pass

Goms
Rhône

Grosser Aletschgletscher

Domodossola

Valle de Antrona

LÄGGINHORN

FLETSCHHORN

Simplon Pass

Saas-Fee

Valle Anzasca

Brig

Grächen

DOM

Mischabel

Gonergletscher

Mürren

WEISSHORN

ZINALROTHORN

Zermatt

MATTERHORN

Kandersteg

Leukerbad

Val d'Anniviers

DENT BLANCHE

Breuil-Cervinia

Adelboden

Vermala
Crans & Montana
Sierre

Grimentz

Rhône

Val d'Hérens

Evolène

Gstaad

Anzère

Sion

Super Nendaz
Gletscher
de Dixence

Val d'Hérémence

Haute-Nendaz

Verbier

Vallée de Bagnes

Vallée d'Entremont

Ski Areas

SWITZERLAND

★ BERN

The Valais

1 Verbier
2 Sion
3 Crans-Montana
4 Zermatt and
    the Matterhorn
5 Saas-Fee
6 Brig and the
    Simplon Pass
7 The Grimsel Pass

By Bus   In the winter there is direct bus service from Martigny to Verbier via Le Châble.

By Car   Take N9 as far as Martigny on the Great St. Bernard route. Turn left for Verbier at Sembrancher.

ESSENTIALS   The **Verbier Tourist Office** (tel. 026/31-62-22) is open Monday through Saturday from 8:30am to noon and 2 to 6:30pm. The **telephone area code** for Verbier is 026. Some areas have no **street names,** so some establishments are signposted.

Verbier is on a vast, sunny plateau in the Bagnes Valley in Switzerland's southernmost Alps. It looks toward the Combin and Mont Blanc Mountains, which are covered with snow year round, even when the town is bursting with leafy trees and flowers in their summer glory. At 5,000 feet, Verbier was a pastureland before developing into an outstanding sports center. The area is protected from the wind.

WHAT TO SEE & DO

Skiing tops the list of attractions. The area offers 190 miles of ski runs, serviced by 47 ski lifts, as well as by shuttle buses and an extensive search system, including avalanche dogs and regular patrols. Téléverbier, a company founded in 1950, oversees one of the biggest conveyance systems in all of Switzerland. A recent addition, a heavy-duty cable car between the region of La Chaux and the Col des Gentaines, is the largest lift in the country.

In cooperation with neighboring regions, visitors can use their Téléverbier passes on more than 86 additional lifts in the area known as Les 4 Vallées (valleys) and l'Entremont. This means that a single lift ticket can take skiers as high as 11,000 feet. The permit also authorizes cross-country skiing. Several circuits are possible. One goes from Verbier to Mont-Gelé, Mont-Fort, and La Chaux and then back to Verbier. Another circuit goes from Verbier to Tortin, Mont-Fort, and La Chaux. For information on skiing in the Téléverbier network, contact Téléverbier S.A., CP 326, CH-1936 Verbier (tel. 026/31-60-00).

Ski tours on the slopes of Mont-Gelé, Col de Chassoure, Vallon d'Arbi, and Col des Mines, as well as on other slopes, are not ski runs but high-mountain tours. Even in the summer, skiers should be accompanied by an experienced mountaineer.

The **Swiss Ski School** (tel. 31-68-25) has 140 instructors and offers group lessons daily from 9:30 to 11:45am, as well as private lessons.

The **Verbier Polysports Centre** (tel. 31-76-01) has greatly expanded the sports available in all seasons. Facilities include a covered swimming pool, 10 indoor curling lanes, an indoor ice rink, nine tennis courts, squash courts, saunas, whirlpools, a solarium, and a games area. The center also has a restaurant and an 18-hole golf course. The center is open daily from 9am to 9pm. A discount of 25% is available for guests of hotels that are members of the sports association.

Besides sports, Verbier abounds with alpine beauty. The **Haut Val de Bagnes Nature Reserve** has a rich variety of flora and fauna, including some rare species of plants. You might see alpine aquilegia, white gentian, yellow pond lily, edelweiss, and several kinds of orchids. Botanical walks are organized in the summer; inquire at the tourist office. There is a great view of the Bagnes Valley from the Combe des Violettes. In the distance, Mont-Pleureur can be seen, with Italy in the blue mist on the horizon.

WHERE TO STAY

There are some 28 hotels and other chalets and apartments in Verbier. Rates vary seasonally.

EXPENSIVE

HOTEL LES 4 VALLEES, rue de Médran, CH-1936 Verbier. Tel. 026/31-60-66. Fax 030/31-34-01. 20 rms (all with bath). MINIBAR TV TEL
$ Rates (including continental breakfast): Winter, 140F–190F ($102.20–$138.70) single; 210F–260F ($153.30–$189.75) double. Summer, 80F–110F ($58.40–$80.30) single; 140F–180F ($102.20–$131.40) double. AE, DC, MC, V. **Closed:** Oct and May–June. **Parking:** 10F ($7.30).
The hotel is near the main square and the Médran lift station. Each of its sunny rooms has pine paneling, plush carpeting, a radio, and a balcony.
   Dining/Entertainment: A copious breakfast buffet is served in a room with large windows and paneling. The hotel does not have a restaurant, but there is an elegant, civilized bar in the lobby.
   Services: Laundry, wake-up calls.
   Facilities: Sauna, free use of nearby indoor swimming pool, garage.

HOTEL ROSALP, rue de Médran, CH-1936 Verbier. Tel. 026/31-63-23. Fax 026/31-10-59. 22 rms (all with bath), 2 suites. A/C MINIBAR TV TEL
$ Rates (including continental breakfast): 170F–250F ($124.05–$182.50) single; 320F–350F ($233.55–$255.45) double; 750F ($547.45) suite for two. AE, DC, MC, V. **Closed:** May–June and Oct–Nov. **Parking:** 10F ($7.30).
⭐ Roger and Anita Pierroz built the Rosalp in 1945, and Anita's cooking brought early fame to the place. But their son, Roland, put it on the gastronomic map of Europe. Today, first-class rooms and refined cuisine are available at this four-star hotel listed in *Relais & Châteaux*. The suites are excellent, and the small public salon is a tranquil retreat. The rooms are decorated with flair and filled with modern comfort and amenities. Many have dark paneling, and some have a sun deck. The private baths are very luxurious. Suites for two contain two rooms, two baths, and a private salon.
   Dining/Entertainment: The hotel has the premier restaurant of the area, Pierroz, and also a more informal ground-floor restaurant, La Pinte. Its Bar l'Arlequin is a popular rendezvous point at night.
   Services: Laundry, room service, wake-up calls.
   Facilities: Fitness center, sauna, Jacuzzi, garage.

HOTEL VANESSA, place Centrale, CH-1936 Verbier. Tel. 026/31-61-41. Fax 026/31-14-08. 56 rms (all with bath). MINIBAR TV TEL
$ Rates (including half board): 255F–285F ($186.10–$208) single; 350F–390F ($255.50–$284.65) double. No credit cards. **Closed:** May and Oct–Nov. **Parking:** 10F ($7.30).
One of the biggest hotels in Verbier is also among the finest at the resort. Its rooms are comfortable and modern; most are like suites, with bright upholstery and balconies. This large modern chalet is right off place Centrale.
   Dining/Entertainment: The hotel has a restaurant and a piano bar.
   Services: Room service, baby-sitting, laundry.
   Facilities: Sauna, whirlpool, garage.

MODERATE

HOTEL CATOGNE, chemin de la Croix, CH-1936 Verbier. Tel. 026/31-65-05. Fax 026/31-52-05. 24 rms (all with bath). MINIBAR TV TEL
$ **Rates** (including half board): 110F–130F ($80.30–$94.90) single; 210F–260F ($153.30–$189.80) double. AE, MC, V.

This family hotel is about a 5-minute walk from the central square. The upper half looks like a chalet; the lower half consists of masonry and stucco, with big windows and a modern extension containing a restaurant and bar. The restaurant has rustic paneling and bright tablecloths and the bar is well stocked. Swiss specialties such as cheese fondue and raclette are served. Jean-Marc Corthay is the owner.

HOTEL GRAND COMBIN + GOLF, rue de Verbier, CH-1936 Verbier. Tel. 026/31-65-15. Fax 026/31-14-88. 36 rms (all with bath). MINIBAR TV TEL
$ **Rates** (including half board): 230F–300F ($167.90–$219) double. AE, DC, MC, V. **Closed:** May and Oct–Nov.

The rooms in this three-star chalet are equivalent to four-star accommodations in other towns. Opened in 1953, the hotel sits in isolated grandeur a short walk below the main square. The lobby has antique details. Many of the rooms, all doubles, contain Oriental carpets, pine paneling, and conservative furniture. Most have a radio, an original painting, and a private balcony. There is a sophisticated bar, Jacky's. Facilities include a sauna and a steam bath.

HOTEL LE MAZOT, chemin des Vernes, CH-1936 Verbier. Tel. 026/31-64-04. Fax 026/31-64-05. 48 rms (all with bath). MINIBAR TV TEL
$ **Rates** (including half board): 160F–210F ($116.80–$153.25) single; 250F–330F ($182.50–$240.90) double. AE, DC, MC, V. **Closed:** May–June and Oct–Nov.

This well-managed hotel is quietly isolated near the main town square. It consists of two modern chalets with a shared reception area. Serge Tacchini offers pleasant rooms with wall-to-wall carpeting, spacious closets, and radios; some units have a wide balcony facing southwest. There is a pleasant alpine dining room and bar.

HOTEL DE LA POSTE, rue de Médran, CH-1936 Verbier. Tel. 026/31-66-81. Fax 026/31-34-01. 64 rms (28 with bath). TV TEL
$ **Rates** (including half board): 86F ($62.75) single without bath, 139F ($101.45) single with bath; 172F ($125.55) double without bath, 300F ($219) double with bath. AE, DC, MC, V. **Closed:** May and Oct–Nov.

This red-shuttered chalet is on the main street near the central square. If you want a private bath, request lodgings in the chalet annex across the street, where the rooms have comfortable furniture and modern decor. The rooms in the main building have old-fashioned alpine accessories. I recommend the restaurant, on the ground level of the annex, A la Bonne Franquette. There's a restaurant and bar in the main building as well.

WHERE TO DINE

Verbier has several excellent restaurants, many serving traditional Swiss dishes and continental cuisine. Most of the best restaurants are connected with hotels.

EXPENSIVE

HOTEL VANESSA RESTAURANT, place Centrale. Tel. 31-61-41.

Cuisine: SWISS. **Reservations:** Recommended.

$ **Prices:** Appetizers 15F–25F ($10.95–$18.25); main courses 28F–45F ($20.45–$32.85); menu gastronomique 105F ($76.65). No credit cards.

Open: Lunch daily noon–2pm; dinner daily 7–10pm.

The modern dining room is a few steps from the hotel reception desk. The menu might include fresh oysters, salmon and turbot in puff pastry, pigeon with truffles, and rack of lamb. If you're looking for something simple and hearty, try the fondue chinoise.

RESTAURANT GASTRONOMIQUE PIERROZ, rue de Médran. Tel. 31-63-23.

Cuisine: FRENCH. **Reservations:** Required.

$ **Prices:** Appetizers 24F–38F ($17.50–$27.75); main courses 30F–40F ($21.90–$29.20). AE, DC, MC, V.

Open: Lunch daily noon–2pm; dinner daily 7–9:30pm. **Closed:** May–June and Oct–Nov.

The finest food in the Valais is served at this *Relais & Châteaux* selection. Roland Pierroz is one of the great chefs of Switzerland; gourmets drive across national borders to sample his light cuisine moderne and regional specialties. Seasonal dishes include oysters with caviar in puff pastry, turbot with crab, quail eggs, chicken with chervil, game dishes, and imaginative renderings of lobster and salmon.

The finest meal I ever had in Switzerland began with a fourrée of quail eggs and scallops tartare with caviar and bits of endive, followed with a langoustine couscous. Next appeared a delectable tortelloni Gorgonzola, reinforced with a plate of sea bass and sea urchins. But the pièce de résistance was a pigeon with truffles. The cheese trolley emerged with at least 35 selections, and it was followed by a crisp and tasty apple tart with ice cream that was celestial.

MODERATE

GRILL/BAR LA LUGE, rue de la Piscine. Tel. 31-31-43.

Cuisine: SWISS. **Reservations:** Recommended.

$ **Prices:** Main courses 25F–34F ($18.25–$24.80). AE, MC, V.

Open: Restaurant, winter only, dinner only, daily 7–10:30pm. Bar, daily 10am–midnight.

Many visitors get so caught up in the bar scene on this establishment's street level that they never descend the wooden staircase to the grill-restaurant in the basement. The plank-and-stucco dining room is very cozy and popular. Meat is grilled over an open flame; the menu includes veal steak, brochette of filet mignon, chateaubriand, entrecôte, julienne of filet La Luge, and a short list of rich desserts. No appetizers are served, although access to a plentiful salad bar is included in the price of the main course.

LA PINTE, in the Hôtel Rosalp, rue de Médran. Tel. 31-63-23.

Cuisine: SWISS. **Reservations:** Required.

$ **Prices:** Appetizers 10F–30F ($7.30–$21.90); main courses 24F–38F ($17.50–$27.75). AE, DC, MC, V.

Open: Lunch daily noon–2pm; dinner daily 7–9:30pm.

This is master chef Roland Pierroz's second, more reasonably priced restaurant, on the ground floor of the Hôtel Rosalp. The 19th-century paneling is decorated with painted flowers; in the back a snug room displays hunting trophies. The cuisine is superb, with simmered dishes and grills a specialty. A typical meal includes a tart made with leeks or Gruyère cheese. Meats, ranging from a brochette of lamb to tournedos, are grilled over an open fire. Several regional dishes are offered, including sausage with lentils. Specials change daily.

RESTAURANT A LA BONNE FRANQUETTE, in the Hôtel de la Poste, rue de Médran. Tel. 31-62-74.
   Cuisine: SWISS. **Reservations:** Recommended.
$ Prices: Appetizers 12F–22F ($8.75–$16.05); main courses 18F–32F ($13.15–$23.35); two-course fixed-price meal 32F ($23.35). AE, DC, MC, V.
   Open: Lunch daily 11:30am–2pm; dinner daily 6:30–10pm. **Closed:** May.
This brightly decorated tavern is on the street level of the hotel's annex. The menu includes raclette and fondue, four different spaghetti dishes, and julienne of veal braised with cream or with exotic mushrooms (bolets). Wine is sold by the carafe. The restaurant is an early-evening favorite of vacationing families.

RESTAURANT AU ROBINSON, place Centrale. Tel. 31-32-13.
   Cuisine: SWISS. **Reservations:** Recommended.
$ Prices: Appetizers 8F–15F ($5.85–$10.95); main courses 20F–35F ($14.60–$25.65). MC, V.
   Open: Lunch Mon–Sat noon–2pm; dinner Mon–Sat 7–10pm. **Closed:** Aug 20–Oct 1.
This stucco restaurant, hidden on the side of the main square, is a good place for lunch or drinks. The long wooden bar is especially popular after 9:30pm, when rock music is played. The menu includes three kinds of spaghetti, scallops of pork, roast chicken, grilled steaks, three varieties of fondue, filet Stroganoff, and a heaping platter of air-dried alpine beef with pickles and onions (assiette valaisanne). Established in the mid-1950s, the Robinson is one of the oldest restaurants in town.

AU VIEUX VERBIER, Gare de Médran. Tel. 31-16-68.
   Cuisine: SWISS. **Reservations:** Required for dinner.
$ Prices: Appetizers 12F–25F ($8.75–$18.25); main courses 30F–40F ($21.50–$29.20); lunch platters 15F–25F ($10.95–$18.25). AE, DC, MC, V.
   Open: Lunch daily 11:30am–3pm; dinner daily 6:30–10:30pm. **Closed:** Early May to mid-July; Mon in summer and fall.
One of the few restaurants in Verbier not affiliated with any hotel, the Old Verbier is set on a hillside a few paces from the beginning of the town's ski slopes. Its decor features brightly polished brassware, ceiling beams, and stone. The specialty of the house is pigs' feet in Madeira with Rösti. The menu also includes a heaping platter of sauerkraut garnished with local sausages and boiled ham, filet of sole in Pinot Noir, and suprême of duckling with red currants.

INEXPENSIVE

PIZZERIA FER A CHEVAL, rue de Médran. Tel. 31-36-69.
   Cuisine: SWISS/ITALIAN. **Reservations:** Recommended.
$ Prices: Appetizers 5F–9F ($3.65–$6.55); main courses 20F–32F ($14.60–$23.35); pizza 11F–15F ($8.05–$10.95). AE, DC, MC, V.
   Open: Daily 8am–midnight. **Closed:** Mid-May to June and Sept–Nov.
This usually crowded pizzeria is a short walk uphill from the main square. It has an outdoor terrace and a small, rustically decorated dining room with large windows and pinewood paneling. The menu includes nine different kinds of pizza, as well as lasagne, spaghetti, steaks, and several hearty Swiss dishes. A children's menu is available.

EVENING ENTERTAINMENT

Après-ski begins early in Verbier. In the late afternoon, skiers return from the slopes to have a glass of Dole, a red wine native to the region.

THE CLUB & MUSIC SCENE

FARM CLUB, route de Médran. Tel. 31-61-21.

Many local residents regard this as the best disco in town. A few weathered beams add to the modern decor. There are several fireplaces. January through March, arrive soon after the club opens; you'll need a reservation after 11pm on weekends. Open only in the winter, daily from 10pm to 3am. Drinks run 13F ($9.50).

Admission: 20F ($14.60), including one free drink.

TARA CLUB, rue des Creux. Tel. 31-35-15.

This popular disco has plank-covered walls and alpine details. The music is loud and hot. Open only in midwinter, daily from 10pm to 3am. Beer costs 10F ($7.30).

Admission: 15F ($10.95).

THE BAR SCENE

BAR L'ARLEQUIN, in the Hôtel Rosalp, rue de Médran. Tel. 31-63-23.

The most conservative, elegant, and comfortable bar in town serves the best drinks. The fireplace gives a warm glow. The visiting celebrity at Chez Corrine might be the king of Sweden or Roman Polanski or Diana Ross. Open daily from 5pm to 3am. Drinks cost about 13F ($9.50); beer, 6F ($4.40).

BAR NEW CLUB, rue de la Piscine. Tel. 31-22-67.

The best place for conversation is this comfortable, glossy version of a living room, with groups of couches. Steak sandwiches and croque monsieurs are the only items served. The club is warm and well lit. Open in the winter daily from 4pm to 1am; in the summer, only on Friday and Saturday from 4pm to 1am. Beer runs 8F ($5.85); drinks, about 13F ($9.50).

JACKY'S BAR (Chez Walter), in the Hôtel Grand Combin. Tel. 31-65-15.

Jacky's has a relaxed, adult atmosphere. The large paneled room has several comfortable couches. Open daily from 5pm to 2am. Drinks are about 13F ($9.50).

LE MILK BAR, place Centrale. Tel. 31-25-30.

An abundance of pastries are served at this family-run coffeehouse. Drinks include coffee, tea, mineral water, and hot chocolate—no alcohol is served. Chocolate chaumière, one of the specialties, comes in a two-handled ceramic bowl frothy with whipped cream. The best cakes in town are displayed in the center of the room on an open table. These include a Black Forest tart, banana cake, and rich chocolate cake. The menu also includes quiches and platters of air-dried alpine beef. Open daily from 8am to 7pm; closed May through June and September through November. Cake begins at 4F ($2.90) per slice, and hot chocolate runs 3.50F ($2.60).

NELSON PUB, in the Hôtel Eden, place Centrale. Tel. 31-31-51.

Its rows of small-paned bay windows are hard to miss as you come up the hill toward the main square of town. The large, elaborate interior has a Neo-Victorian style. In the winter the menu includes cheeseburgers, croque monsieurs, pizzas, and platters of air-dried alpine beef. The specialty, however, is beer, with more than 40 varieties in bottles and at least 3 on tap. Open daily from 4pm to 1am; closed May to mid-June and the first 2 weeks in November. Snacks start at 8F ($5.85); beer, 5F ($3.65).

EASY EXCURSIONS
GREAT ST. BERNARD PASS

Most winter motorists take the 4-mile Great St. Bernard Tunnel between Italy's Aosta Valley and the Valais instead of the road over the Great St. Bernard Pass. In the summer, however, many visitors make the pilgrimage over the pass. The road is usually open from mid-June to October; it's about an hour's drive from Martigny. If you're staying in Verbier and you'd like to visit the pass, you can drive east from Verbier along a winding road until you come to the village of Sembranchen. From there, E21 leads directly south to this historic pass (follow the signs). Travel time is about 1¼ hours.

St. Bernard dogs are beloved in Switzerland, even though they no longer roam the snowy passes with brandy in their casks. The dogs are still bred by monks at the Great St. Bernard Hospice. Before your arrival, make an appointment to visit the hospice by contacting **Hospice du Grand-St-Bernard,** Le Grand-St-Bernard, CH-1931 Bourg-St-Pierre (tel. 026/87-11-10). This famous hospice was founded in the mid-11th century to help travelers through the pass; it has a dog kennel and a history museum.

Where to Stay & Dine

AUBERGE DU VIEUX-MOULIN, CH-1946 Bourg-St-Pierre. Tel. 026/87-11-69. 30 rms (most with bath).
$ Rates: 41F–47F ($29.95–$34.30) single; 70F–80F ($51.10–$58.40) double. Half board 18F ($13.15) extra. No credit cards.
Part of a rocky hill was blasted away to make room for this small roadside inn in the hamlet of Bourg-St-Pierre. The rooms are streamlined and comfortable. The inn has a pleasant restaurant with large windows and paneling, as well as a gas station and a place to exchange currency.

2. SION

17¼ miles E of Martigny, 32¾ miles W of Visp

GETTING THERE By Train Sion lies on the major rail lines that connect Milan and Turin (via the Simplon Tunnel) with Geneva and Paris. Trains arrive from both directions every day.

By Car From Martigny head east, and from Visp go west, on E2.

ESSENTIALS The **telephone area code** for Sion is 027.

The capital of the Valais, Sion is known for its glorious springs and autumns and for its ancient status as a trading post on the trails leading between France and Italy.

Dating from Roman times, the town is dominated by the silhouettes of the castles of Valère and Tourbillon. Most of its population speaks French.

WHAT TO SEE & DO

The **Castle of Tourbillon** is perched on a steep rock on a hill overlooking the northern periphery of the town. It's the broodingly impressive ruin of a medieval stronghold built by a 13th-century bishop to defend Sion against the House of Savoy. Destroyed by a fire in 1788, it has never been rebuilt, but you can still make out the remains of a keep, watchtower, and chapel. There is a splendid view of the Rhône Valley from its base, which sits at an elevation of 2,149 feet.

Atop the town's other steep hill are the deeply weathered walls of a Gothic church, the **Collegiale de Valère,** whose foundations were probably built as a fortress by the ancient Romans. In much better shape than the previously mentioned castle, the three-aisle basilica dates from the 12th and 13th centuries. It contains splendid 17th-century choir stalls and what has been called "the oldest playable organ in the world," dating from the 14th century.

The **Valère Museum,** Château de Valère (tel. 21-69-22), is in the former residence of the cathedral chapter. It contains fine works of medieval religious art, ancient arms and armor, uniforms, Roman and Gothic chests, and interesting ethnological collections. The museum is open April through October, Tuesday through Sunday from 9am to noon and 2 to 6pm; November to March, Tuesday through Sunday from 9am to noon and 2 to 5pm. It's also open on Monday during July and August. Admission is 3F ($2.20) for adults and 1F (75¢) for children. From the parking lot it is a steep climb to the church.

Back in town, the **Hôtel de Ville** (Town Hall), rue du Grand-Pont, has beautiful 17th-century doors and columns. The Roman stones on the ground floor date from A.D. 377. On the main street of Sion, rue du Grand-Pont, is an **astronomical clock.**

Northeast of the Hôtel de Ville is the **Cathédrale de Notre-Dame-du-Glarier.** It was reconstructed in the 15th century, although the Romanesque belfry remains, dating from the 11th and 13th centuries. Inside, look for the triptych in gilded wood, called *The Tree of Jesse.*

A provincial governor built the **Supersaxo House** in 1505. Located at 7, rue de Conthey, the house is richly decorated and includes a room with a stunning rose ceiling. The house is open Monday through Saturday from 8am to noon and 2 to 6pm; closed holidays.

The **Cantonal Art Museum,** 15, place de la Majorie (tel. 21-69-11), was once a residence of the *major,* an episcopal authority. Today it's a fine arts museum, with special emphasis on local artists. The museum is open Tuesday through Sunday from 10am to noon and 2 to 6pm (to 5pm in winter). Admission is 3F ($2.20). To get there, take rue des Châteaux in the direction of the hilltop castles; the museum is on your left.

WHERE TO STAY

HOTEL DU RHONE, 10, rue du Scex, CH-1950 Sion. Tel. 027/23-11-88.
    Fax 027/23-11-88. 45 rms (all with bath). MINIBAR TV TEL
 $ Rates (including continental breakfast): 86F–98F ($62.75–$71.50) single; 130F–
    157F ($91.90–$114.60) double. AE, DC, MC, V.
This modern hotel allows you to escape the traffic congestion of the old city. However, the street-level café-restaurant is almost always overcrowded at lunch with

local office personnel and shop employees. The rooms are furnished with angular contemporary furniture; amenities include a radio.

HOTEL DU CASTEL, 38, rue du Scex, CH-1950 Sion. Tel. 027/22-91-71.
30 rms (all with shower). MINIBAR TV TEL
$ Rates (including continental breakfast): 80F ($58.40) single; 115F ($84.00) double. AE, DC, MC, V.
Modern and boxy, this three-star hotel is at the edge of the road to Simplon. The rooms have modern furniture, radios, and soundproof windows. Many have views of the jagged cliffs that support the medieval château.

WHERE TO DINE

CHEZ TCHETCHETT (Restaurant les Mayennets), 36, av. de Tourbillon. Tel. 22-18-98.
Cuisine: SWISS/ITALIAN. **Reservations:** Recommended.
$ Prices: Appetizers: 10F–17F ($7.30–$12.40); main courses 30F–45F ($21.90–$32.85); lunch plat du jour (brasserie only) 14F ($10.20).
Open: Restaurant, lunch Mon–Sat noon–2pm; dinner Mon–Sat 6:30–10pm. Café, Mon–Sat 7:30am–11pm. **Closed:** Sat in midsummer.
Set in a dignified corner building, this charming family-run restaurant contains both a popular French café and brasserie and a more formal and more upscale restaurant on the same floor. The restaurant serves a flavorful, old-fashioned cuisine, often using the daily shipments of fresh fish that arrive from Lausanne. The house specialties include bouillabaisse, marmite de poisson, and—in season—mussels marinara.

ENCLOS DE VALERE, 18, rue des Châteaux. Tel. 23-32-30.
Cuisine: FRENCH. **Reservations:** Recommended.
$ Prices: Appetizers 10F–24F ($7.30–$17.50); main courses 20F–35F ($14.60–$25.55); fixed-price meals 55F–75F ($40.15–$54.75). AE, DC, MC, V.
Open: Lunch daily 11:30am–2pm; dinner daily 6–10:30pm. **Closed:** Christmas to early Feb.
It's sometimes dangerous to drive a car up the steep and narrow street leading to this restaurant, but once you reach it, you'll find one of the most charming restaurants in Sion. Located near the edge of the gardens that surround the château, the restaurant is small and intimate, with an outdoor dining area. The dining room has a regional decor, with flagstone floors and a beamed ceiling. The menu changes monthly, but might include lamb with garlic and thyme, sea bass with mustard and red cabbage, and veal kidneys with saffron.

CAVES DE TOUTS-VENTS, 16, rue des Châteaux. Tel. 22-46-84.
Cuisine: VALAISIAN. **Reservations:** Recommended.
$ Prices: Appetizers: 12F–16F ($8.75–$11.70); main courses 23F–46F ($16.80–$33.60); raclette 24F ($17.50) per person; fondue 17F ($12.40) per person. No credit cards.
Open: Restaurant, dinner only, daily 7–10:30pm. Café and bar, Tues–Sun 5:30pm–midnight.
It occupies several levels of a 13th-century cellar, whose vaultings were originally built to store wine. You descend a steep flight of stairs to reach the first room of the cellars, much of which is devoted to a well-stocked bar. Claustrophobes might elect to go no farther. The lack of windows, the ancient stones, the flickering candles, and the effect

of the wine work together to make the room strangely cozy. The café's specialties include tagliatelle with salmon, mushrooms in puff pastry, calves' liver with shallots, and, of course, fondue.

3. CRANS-MONTANA

9 miles N of Sierre, 13 miles E of Sion, 99 miles E of Geneva

GETTING THERE   By Train   From Geneva, take a direct train to Sierre; at Sierre, change to a funicular or bus to Crans-Montana.

By Bus   A postal bus from Sion makes the run up the mountain to Crans-Montana. There are frequent bus connections between Sierre and Crans-Montana.

By Car   The resorts are accessible by good roads from Sion or the market town of Sierre. From Sion, take E2 east to Sierre; from there, follow the signs up the winding mountain road until you reach Crans-Montana.

By Funicular   You can take a funicular from Sierre. Telephone 55-15-11 for departure times.

ESSENTIALS   The **Tourist Information Office** is at Immeuble Scandia, Crans-sur-Sierre (tel. 027/41-21-32); it's open Monday through Saturday from 8:30am to noon and 2 to 6:30pm. The **telephone area code** for Crans-Montana and the surrounding region is 027. Not all thoroughfares have **street names;** to find establishments that lie off the street plans you should look for directional signs pointing the way.

Crans and Montana-Vermala, at 4,985 feet, are twin ski resorts; both are modern and fashionable. Set on a handsome plateau where the air is said to be "lighter than champagne," they enjoy excellent snowfall and views as far as the valley of the Rhône. Crans, whose hotel construction began in 1912, is composed for the most part of colonies of apartments and hotels, many in the half-timbered mountain style. Montana, clustered around the shores of Lac Grenon, is the older section, begun in 1892. Connected to them both, at a slightly lower altitude, is Aminona, still an infant resort but rising rapidly.

WHAT TO SEE & DO

Neither resort limits its allure to wintertime diversions. During the summer Montana is a health resort and Crans is a golf center, with the 18-hole Plan-Bramois course and the 9-hole Xires course. The Swiss Open, held at Crans, draws top golfers from all over the world. Tennis, hiking, and mountain climbing are the main summer sports at Crans-Montana; others include horseback riding, hiking, and fishing. Winter sports include skating, ski-bobbing, and ice-hockey matches. Skiing is available year round.

NEARBY ATTRACTIONS   There's a spectacular ascent to **Point Plaine-Morte,** at nearly 10,000 feet; even at such a great height there are still runs suitable for novice skiers. To get there, take the gondola from Montana-Barzettes to the east of Montana, stopping at Les Violettes first. There's a restaurant at Plaine-Morte.

Cry d'Err, at 7,430 feet, has a large restaurant and a sunbathing terrace. To get there, take a gondola from Montana or Crans.

The **Piste Nationale** is known for its steep, narrow runs, which attract many skiers. Mount Tubang, with its more challenging runs, is another slope only for the advanced skier.

WHERE TO STAY

IN CRANS

Expensive

HOTEL ALPINA & SAVOY, route touristique de Crans, CH-3963 Crans. Tel. 027/41-21-42. Fax 027/41-61-75. 75 rms (all with bath). MINIBAR TV TEL
$ Rates (including continental breakfast): 169F–220F ($123.35–$160.60) single; 247F–305F ($180.30–$222.60) double. Half board 37F ($27) extra. AE, DC, MC, V.

The oldest hotel in Crans was built in 1912. Owned by three generations of the Mudrey family, it has been frequently modernized and expanded; it remains consciously unfashionable but venerable. The hotel has a restaurant with large windows, a pleasant bar, and an outdoor sun terrace. Facilities include a pool area and saunas.

HOTEL DU GOLF ET DES SPORTS, CH-3963 Crans. Tel. 027/41-42-42. Fax 027/41-97-58. 98 rms (all with bath). MINIBAR TV TEL
$ Rates (including continental breakfast): Winter, 325F–420F ($237.20–$306.55) single; 431F–560F ($314.60–$408.75) double. Summer, 130F–165F ($94.90–$120.45); 240F–305F ($175.20–$222.60) double. Half board 55F ($40.15) extra. AE, DC, MC, V.

This attractively designed, five-star hotel is located near a lake and golf course. The salons are very elegant, with reproductions of antique chairs and with fireplaces. Some of the rooms are renovated, while others retain their old decor; all have balconies and radios. This is one of the few large hotels in town that remain open all year.

Dining/Entertainment: The hotel has a bar and a restaurant, which serves both Swiss and continental recipes.
Services: Room service, baby-sitting.
Facilities: Spa, diet center.

Moderate

HOTEL DE L'ETRIER, CH-3963 Crans. Tel. 027/40-11-81. Fax 027/40-11-81. 176 rms (all with bath). MINIBAR TV TEL
$ Rates (including continental breakfast): 100F–147F ($73–$107.30) single; 189F–241F ($137.95–$175.90) double. Half board 37F ($27) extra. AE, DC, MC, V. **Parking:** 15F ($10.95).

Two modern buildings with steep roofs are set at slightly different angles for a dramatic effect, especially at night when light filters through the colored curtains, giving the windows the appearance of stained glass. The interior is comfortable, modern, and attractive, with abstract murals and shaggy rugs. The rooms are well furnished, with large windows, colored curtains, and prominent balconies. Lawn chairs are set up in a 7½-acre park out front.

Dining/Entertainment: The hotel's two restaurants serve a typically Swiss and continental cuisine. Two bars are popular with the après-ski crowd, and live entertainment is provided in the winter.

Services: Laundry, baby-sitting, hairdressing salon, massage.

Facilities: Heated, partially covered swimming pool, outdoor swimming pool, sauna, solarium.

Inexpensive

HOTEL DES MELEZES, CH-3963 Crans. Tel. 027/43-18-12. Fax 027/43-16-08. 25 rms (all with bath). MINIBAR TV TEL
$ **Rates** (including continental breakfast): 65F–85F ($47.45–$62.05) single; 120F–160F ($87.60–$116.80) double. Half board 30F ($21.90) extra. AE, DC, MC, V.
Closed: May and Oct–Nov.

Relative isolation can be found here, about a half mile from the town's commercial district in a forest of pines that the French call *mélèzes*. This hotel has one of the most appealing sun terraces and greenhouse dining rooms in town: You can watch skiers finish their run at the nearby slope. There is also a popular bar. Henri and Marie-Louise Lamòn offer rooms with balconies and radios. Breakfast is served outdoors in the summer, near the 7th hole of an 18-hole golf course.

HOTEL PENSION CENTRALE, route touristique de Crans, CH-3963 Crans. Tel. 027/41-37-67. 36 rms (22 with bath). TEL
$ **Rates** (including continental breakfast): 50F ($36.50) single without bath, 64F ($46.70) single with bath; 85F ($62.05) double without bath, 109F ($79.55) double with bath. Half board 22F ($16.05) extra. AE, DC, MC, V.

Miss Hürlimann and Mr. Funkenberg, your hosts, manage this centrally located stone boarding house with shutters and offer personalized service. There is a restaurant on the ground floor. The renovated rooms have radios.

IN MONTANA

LES HAUTS DE CRANS, CH-3962 Montana. Tel. 027/41-55-53. Fax 027/41-97-67. 36 rms (all with bath). MINIBAR TV TEL
$ **Rates** (including continental breakfast): 230F–300F ($167.90–$218.95) single; 392F–510F ($286.10–$372.25) double. Half board 40F ($29.20) extra. AE, DC, MC, V. **Closed:** May and Oct–Nov. **Parking:** Available.

The most dramatic and probably the most isolated lodgings in Montana are located at the top of a road that winds through the forest above the town. Part of a complex that includes privately owned chalets and condominiums, this four-star hotel offers comfortable rooms with balconies. A few steps from the hotel is the meeting point of several forested walkways, ideal for cross-country skiing or summertime hikes. The hotel contains both a restaurant and a grill room, a bar, an indoor swimming pool with sauna, tennis courts, and a solidly buttressed underground garage chiseled into the sloping hillside below the hotel.

HOTEL CRANS-AMBASSADOR, CH-3962 Montana. Tel. 027/41-52-22. Fax 027/41-91-55. 70 rms (all with bath). 20 apartments. MINIBAR TV TEL

$ Rates (including continental breakfast): 197F–255F ($143.80–$186.10) single; 335F–435F ($244.50–$317.50) double; 610F ($445.25) apartment. Half board 35F ($25.55) extra. AE, DC, MC, V. **Closed:** May and Oct–Nov.

★ This stylish, dramatic hotel with a roof that resembles three alpine peaks is high above the town. In the lobby you can sit in comfort and admire the rugged, snowy mountains. Philodendron trails over the wooden beams. In the summer guests enjoy an outdoor terrace with flowers. The rooms are conservatively modern, with a balcony or terrace; the amenities include a radio.

Dining/Entertainment: There is a bar near the lobby. The hotel restaurant serves Swiss and continental specialties.

Services: Room service, baby-sitting.

Facilities: Outdoor pool.

HOTEL ST-GEORGES, CH-3962 Montana. Tel. 027/41-24-14. Fax 027/41-58-96. 65 rms (all with bath). TV TEL

$ Rates (including continental breakfast): 119F–155F ($86.85–$113.15) single; 203F–264F ($148.15–$192.70) double. Half board 37F ($27) extra. AE, DC, MC, V. **Closed:** Nov.

This resort-style hotel has a rock garden, a swimming pool, and white balconies in front. Its rooms are well decorated with traditional furniture, and its interior is full of intimate corners and conversational groupings. Roland Grunder-Fischer is the capable manager.

HOTEL DE LA FORET, CH-3962 Montana. Tel. 027/40-21-31. Fax 027/41-31-20. 118 rms (all with bath). TV TEL

$ Rates (including continental breakfast): Feb–Mar, 71F–92F ($51.80–$67.15) single; 121F–151F ($88.30–$110.20) double. July–Aug, 94F–118F ($68.60–$86.15) single; 160F–201F ($116.80–$146.70) double. Half board 30F ($21.90) extra. AE, DC, MC, V.

This establishment consists of three buildings—the main hotel, an annex, and a big-windowed sports center, whose star attraction is an indoor swimming pool with sweeping panoramic views. Skiers appreciate the hotel's proximity to the slopes—only 200 yards from the cable car of Les Violettes–Plaine Morte. Alain and Serge Morard throw weekly raclette parties for their guests. A large dining room serves well-prepared meals, and dancing is encouraged in the piano bar.

WHERE TO DINE
EXPENSIVE

LE PAVILLON (Chez Micha), Montana. Tel. 41-24-69.
Cuisine: SWISS. **Reservations:** Recommended.

$ Prices: Appetizers 14F–20F ($10.20–$14.60); main courses 30F–42F ($21.90–$30.65); fixed-price meals 20F–35F ($14.60–$25.55). DC, MC, V.

Open: Lunch daily noon–2pm; dinner daily 7–10pm; drinks and snacks daily 9:30am–midnight.

It has a desirable lakeside frontage, a verdant setting, and an expansive terrace that make it popular in both winter and summer. You can drop in for snacks and drinks at any time; at mealtime, the chef presents a cuisine du marché, based on fresh ingredients from the marketplace. The grande carte de poissons (seafood menu) includes oysters Rockefeller. Other dishes are carpaccio, tagliatelle with a truffle-cream sauce, and filet goulash.

RESTAURANT DE LA COTE, Corin-sur-Sierre. Tel. 55-13-51.

Cuisine: FRENCH. **Reservations:** Recommended.

$ Prices: Appetizers 25F–35F ($18.25–$25.55); main courses 30F–40F ($21.90–$29.20); fixed-price meals 55F ($40.15) at lunch, 80F–110F ($58.40–$80.30) at dinner. MC, V.

Open: Lunch Wed–Sun 11:30am–2pm; dinner Wed–Sun 7–9pm. **Closed:** May 20–June 20.

⭐ Monsieur and Madame Georges Berguet-Vieusart are indisputably the gastronomic stars of the region, in spite of their location almost 2 miles from Sierre and 7½ miles from Montana (you'll have to drive or take a taxi). Their restaurant, set behind a modest facade, has a comfortably appointed interior and a panoramic view over the vineyards and valleys of the region below. The menu might include sea bass grilled with fennel and oysters gratiné with champagne, as well as an array of delectable desserts. The fixed-price lunch is one of the best values in town for high-quality food.

ROTISSERIE DE LA REINE, Crans. Tel. 41-18-25.

Cuisine: FRENCH/SEAFOOD. **Reservations:** Recommended, especially in high season (Feb–Mar).

$ Prices: Appetizers 10F–25F ($7.30–$18.25); main courses 35F–65F ($25.55–$47.45); fixed-price meals 65F–120F ($47.45–$87.60). AE, DC, MC, V.

Open: Lunch daily noon–2pm; dinner daily 7–10pm. **Closed:** Most of May and Nov.

Set in a modern building, this restaurant specializes in French-inspired seafood (the ingredients are frequently imported fresh from the wholesale markets of Paris). Bernard Leonard specializes in fresh preparations of fish, offering such dishes as bouillabaisse and salmon en papillote.

LE CERVIN/LA BERGERIE, quartier Vermala, Crans. Tel. 41-21-80.

Cuisine: SWISS/FRENCH. **Reservations:** Required in the evening.

$ Prices: Le Cervin, appetizers 12F–20F ($8.75–$14.60); main courses 30F–45F ($21.90–$32.85); fixed-price menu dégustation 95F ($69.35). La Bergerie, prices are about 40% lower.

Open: Daily 10am–3pm and 6pm–1am **Closed:** May to mid-June.

Set in a meadow above the resort, this red-shuttered and barnlike restaurant contains two different sections, both of which are rustically decorated. The more formal is Le Cervin, where the Swiss and French specialties include salmon steak with fresh mushrooms, tournedos with onions, and salads studded with quail eggs and foie gras. In the establishment's cellar is the snug Bergerie, where an all-Swiss menu features an array of raclettes, fondues, and brochettes.

ROTISSERIE DE LA CHANNE VALAISANNE, rue Centrale, Crans. Tel. 41-12-58.

Cuisine: SWISS. **Reservations:** Required.

$ Prices: Appetizers 15F–22F ($10.95–$16.05); main courses 18F–32F ($13.15–$23.35). AE, DC, MC, V.

Open: Tues–Sun 8:30am–midnight. **Closed:** Mid-May to mid-June and Nov.

What is reported to be the best meat in the region is served at this restaurant in Crans. The bar is so *gemütlich* that many guests ask to wait a while before going to their table. Appetizers include homemade pâté in puff pastry and a plate of air-dried alpine beef. For a main course, try the côte de Charolais, chateaubriand, spit-roasted lamb or chicken, or two kinds of fondue. The blue trout is very appealing. The wine list features the local wine Fendant.

LA TRAPPE, in the Hôtel Cisalpin, Montana. Tel. 41-24-25.

Cuisine: SWISS. **Reservations:** Recommended.
$ Prices: Appetizers 12F–18F ($8.75–$13.15); main courses 18F–32F ($13.15–$23.35). DC, MC.
Open: Lunch daily 11am–3pm; dinner daily 5–10pm. **Closed:** Late Apr to early June.

This old-world tavern on the outskirts of town serves the specialties of the Valais. It's decorated with heavy beams, copper pots, and antique accessories, and it has a fireplace. The large menu features grilled meat and other favorites, such as frogs' legs, crêpes valaisanne, escargots bourguignons, and lamb provençal. Fondue Bacchus (with white wine) and raclette are often served.

INEXPENSIVE

AUBERGE DE LA DILIGENCE, quartier La Combaz, Montana. Tel. 41-13-28.
Cuisine: VALAISIAN/LEBANESE. **Reservations:** Recommended in the evening.
$ Prices: Appetizers: 7F–15F ($5.10–$10.95); main courses 20F–35F ($14.60–$25.55). Fixed-price lunch 15F ($10.95). AE, DC, MC, V.
Open: Restaurant, lunch 11:45am–1:45pm; dinner 6:30–9:30pm. Café, daily 8am–midnight.

This relatively inexpensive alpine tavern is set on the highway beside the road leading in from Sierre. It specializes in flavorful combinations of cuisine from both the Valais and faraway Lebanon, whose spices and succulent flavors are much appreciated in the cold alpine air. The outdoor terrace is popular on fine days in both winter and summer, and there's ample parking nearby. Offered are such dishes as raclettes and fondues, grilled fish and steaks, well-spiced kebabs of chicken and lamb, and a succulent platter of Lebanese appetizers.

EVENING ENTERTAINMENT

Many visitors spend their evenings in one of the local restaurants, enjoying the food, the alpine setting, and the vine-inspired conviviality. Later, they repair to the lively hotel bars.

THE CLUB & MUSIC SCENE

CLUB GYPSY, at the Rôtisserie de la Reine, Crans. Tel. 41-23-73.
An energetic young crowd is attracted to this club at the Rôtisserie de la Reine. The club is downstairs from the Rôtisserie bar. Closed in May and Nov. Drinks run about 16F ($11.70).
Admission: Free.

CRANS-AMBASSADOR, in the Hôtel Crans Ambassador, Montana. Tel. 41-52-22.
This club, directly north of Lac Grenon, has an attractive decor, good music, and a grand buffet. The crowd is generally chic. Drinks cost 13F ($9.50).
Admission: Free.

JACK AND LUCY, in the center of Crans. Tel. 41-65-65.

This sporty disco is warmly decorated and very chic. It's a favorite spot with German- as well as French-speaking skiers. Open in the winter only, daily from 9pm to 4am. Drinks cost about 15F ($10.95).

Admission: 20F ($14.60).

THE BAR SCENE

HOTEL DE LA FORET, Montana. Tel. 40-21-31.

Raclette evenings with musical entertainment are occasionally offered. There is also a pleasant piano bar. To reach the club, head for the cable car of Les Violettes–Plaine-Morte. Drinks run 13F ($9.50).

LOBBY BAR, in the Hôtel du Golf et des Sports, Crans. Tel. 41-42-42.

This elegant bar has Louis Philippe–style furniture. It's quiet in the afternoon; musical entertainment is presented January through March, daily from 6:30pm to very late. It lies directly south of Lac Long. Drinks will cost you about 13F ($9.50).

BAR LE MEMPHIS, Bâtiment Prado, Crans. Tel. 41-24-30.

Associated with one of the Crans restaurants, Les Jardins de Memphis, this bar is considered to be one of the town's most interesting destinations for après-ski. Popular during the day as a café, it comes truly alive after dusk, when piano music filters out onto a terrace. Open daily from 9am to 1am. Depending on the time of day, mixed drinks range from 10F to 15F ($7.30 to $10.95).

4. ZERMATT & THE MATTERHORN

41 miles SE of Sierre, 30 miles SW of Brig, 151 miles E of Geneva

GETTING THERE   By Train   Take a train to Visp or Brig, where you can transfer to a narrow-gauge train to Zermatt. It's about a 4-hour trip from Geneva.

By Bus   Buses run from Visp and Brig to Täsch, which is the departure point for the cog railway that ascends frequently to Zermatt.

By Car   Drive to Täsch, 3 miles from Zermatt, and park your car in an open lot or a garage. A rail shuttle takes you to the resort for 10F ($7.30) per person round-trip.

Zermatt, 5,315 feet above sea level, is a small village at the base of the **Matterhorn.** It made its debut as a hiking and hill-climbing resort more than 150 years ago, when it was discovered by English tourists. World attention was turned on the Matterhorn in the 1860s, when Edward Whymper, the English explorer and mountaineer, made a series of attempts to ascend it. Approaching the Matterhorn from the Italian side, he tried six times to climb it and failed. Then, on July 14, 1865, after changing his strategy and approaching the mountain from the Swiss side (using Zermatt as his departure point), he succeeded and—accompanied by two of his guides—became the first person to reach the summit of the Matterhorn. In the process, however, four climbers in his team had fallen to their deaths.

Three days later an Italian guide, Jean-Antoine Carrel, spurred on by the acclaim of Whymper's feat, successfully made the climb from the Italian side. Since then, the Matterhorn (known as Mont Cervin to the French-speaking Swiss) still lures mountain climbers, although only a few of them attempt to reach its summit. Two of the most memorable hikes are the climb up to the **Mettelhorn** (11,000 ft.) and the hike up to the **Matterhorn Hut,** a few thousand feet below the wind-blasted cliffs that surround the summit.

Zermatt is a world-renowned international resort, with many luxurious accommodations and dozens of fashionable boutiques. You can walk from one end of the town to the other in about 15 minutes. In the peak season it's mobbed with hundreds of tourists.

Because more snow falls on Zermatt than at many other winter resorts in Europe, high-altitude skiing (especially at the Théodul Pass) continues at Zermatt throughout the spring and early summer. As for winter skiing, participants can choose between wide, gentle slopes or difficult runs meant to be attempted only by world-class champion skiers. Zermatt's ski school (tel. 67-24-51) offers certified instruction and mountain guides.

ORIENTATION

INFORMATION The **Zermatt Tourist Office** is on Bahnhofplatz (tel. 028/66-11-81).

TOWN LAYOUT Only a few of Zermatt's streets, notably Bahnhofstrasse, have names; most do not. To find your way around you can rely on the dozens of signposts pointing the way to the various hotels and restaurants at the resort.

GETTING AROUND

Except for construction trucks, vehicles with internal-combustion engines (like cars) are not allowed on the streets of Zermatt. Most visitors walk everywhere. There are, however, a battalion of battery-operated vehicles that run quickly and silently along the town's streets, hauling baggage, passengers, and supplies from the cog-railway station to various points around town. There are also horse-drawn carriages, and one of the best networks of alpine cable cars, gondolas, and cog railways in Switzerland—36 of them operating in the winter and 21 in the summer.

FAST FACTS

Area Code The telephone area code for Zermatt is 028.

Baby-sitting If you need a baby-sitter, call **Kindergarten-Pumbuckel** (tel. 67-45-35).

Drugstore For over-the-counter medications and prescriptions, go to **Pharmacie International Zermatt** (tel. 67-34-84).

Emergency The **Swissair Rescue Service** (tel. 47-47-47) helps skiers and others in distress. It operates 24 hours daily.

Police If you need help, call the community police (tel. 67-38-22) or the district police (tel. 67-21-97).

Post Office It's open Monday through Friday from 7:30am to noon and 1:45 to 6:30pm, and on Saturday from 7:30 to 11am.

Religious Services Religious services are conducted at the Roman Catholic church and at the Anglican church of St. Peter's. For details, call the tourist office.

Telephone/Telegram/Telex/Fax The telephone and telegraph office (tel. 67-41-94) is between the post office and the Alpine Museum. There are 18 phone booths, one of which contains a telex and fax machine for public use. Another can be used by handicapped callers. The office is open December to mid-April and mid-June to September, Monday through Saturday from 8am to 9pm and on Sunday and holidays from 9am to noon and 5 to 9pm; the rest of the year, Monday through Friday from 8am to noon and 1:45 to 7pm, and on Saturday from 9am to noon and 1:45 to 5pm (closed holidays).

WHAT TO SEE & DO

IN TOWN There are many diversions in Zermatt, including a popular **curling center,** with eight rinks, each equipped with precision-crafted curling stones. There are also two natural **ice-skating rinks,** unusual shops, and a variety of bars and restaurants.

You might also pay a visit to the **Alpine Museum** (tel. 67-41-00), which details Whymper's race to climb the Matterhorn. Exhibits include climbing equipment, relief models of the great mountain, and artifacts discovered near Zermatt from prehistoric and Roman times. The museum is open July through September, daily from 10am to noon and 4 to 6pm; December through June, daily from 4:30 to 6:30pm. Admission costs 3F ($2.20).

SKIING AND HIKING ✪ The ski and hiking areas of Zermatt are divided between the Gornergrat, the Blauherd–Unter Rothorn, and the Schwarzsee-Théodul regions.

Gornergrat Gornergrat is perched at a lofty altitude of 10,170 feet. To get there you take a cog-wheel train (the highest open-air railway in Europe) to its terminus. On the way you'll stop at **Riffelberg,** which offers a spectacular view of both the Matterhorn and another famous peak, Mount Rosa. The train ride from Zermatt to Riffelberg costs 31F ($22.65) round-trip, while the complete ride from Zermatt to Gornergrat costs 45F ($32.85) round-trip. At **Gornergrat,** an observatory looks out on the bleak expanses of the Gorner glacier and over the heights of the Dom, which, at nearly 15,000 feet, is the highest mountain lying entirely within Switzerland.

At Gornergrat you can take a cable car to other elevations. A two-stage cable car reaches a point near the top of the **Stockhorn,** at 11,180 feet; the cost is an additional 16F ($11.70) round-trip from Gornergrat. Another cable car, going downhill, takes you to the calm waters of the **Schwartzsee** (Black Lake), at 8,480 feet. There the Schwartzseehotel offers magnificent vistas and the possibility of lunch or a drink on its terrace. The round-trip excursion from Gornergrat to the Schwartzsee costs an additional 20.60F ($15.05).

Blauherd–Unter Rothorn To get to Blauherd–Unter Rothorn, take a cog railway through a very long tunnel from Zermatt to the alpine meadows of Sunegga and then transfer to a cable car. After changing cable cars at Blauherd (which in its own right offers many hiking and skiing options), you'll continue by cable car to the flat, rocky summit of the Unter Rothorn, where possibilities for alpine rambles or ski descents abound.

Schwarzsee-Théodul To reach Zermatt's third major ski area, take a cable car from Zermatt to **Furi-Schweigmatten** (usually abbreviated to Furi). There, you'll find a variety of cross-country skiing and hiking trails, and downhill skiing even in midsummer across the Théodul Pass and the border into Italy. In the winter you can continue downhill on skis to the charming Italian ski resort of Breuil-Cervinia for lunch, on the opposite side of the Matterhorn from Zermatt.

If you decide to continue your excursion from Furi, however, you can go from here to the Schwartzsee or you can embark upon one of the most thrilling cable-car rides in the world, the highest in Europe, to the ○ **Klein Matterhorn.** To reach the "Little Matterhorn" from Furi, you must take two additional cable cars (the first of which will transfer at an alpine junction named Trockenersteg) before reaching an elevator that will carry you up to one of the highest mountain terraces in the world (12,533 ft.). If the sky is clear, you'll be able to see both the French and the Italian Alps and breathe a rarified air usually reserved for the hardiest of alpine climbers. The excursion to Klein Matterhorn from Zermatt costs 42F ($30.65) round-trip.

A HELICOPTER TOUR Finally, if it's a clear day, consider a helicopter ride around the "pyramid" formed by the summit of the Matterhorn and over some of the nearby glaciers. The rides cost 140F ($102.20) per person, last about 20 minutes, and require a minimum of four passengers. They are operated by **Air Zermatt** from the town's heliport (tel. 67-34-87), outside the village.

Schedules for the helicopter rides and for the various cable-car and train rides from Zermatt are available at the tourist office and also at most hotels.

WHERE TO STAY

Zermatt has something for most purses. It contains about 100 hotels and guesthouses, plus a growing array of private apartments and condominiums. Some hotels make arrangements to meet clients at the cog-railway station if you inform them in advance of your arrival.

EXPENSIVE

ALEX SCHLOSSHOTEL TENNE, CH-3920 Zermatt. Tel. 028/67-18-01.
Fax 028/67-18-03. 35 rms (all with bath), 9 suites. TV TEL
$ Rates (including half board): 182F–237F ($132.85–$173) single; 364F–380F ($265.70–$277.35) double; from 440F ($321.15) suite. MC, V.

⭐ Its chiseled stonework and baroque-style step roofs, coupled with the art nouveau decor of its bedrooms and public rooms, make this hotel a welcome change from the many chalet-style hotels that surround it. Each of its suites contains a whirlpool bath and a separate sitting room with a fireplace.

Dining/Entertainment: The hotel has a restaurant and one of the most attractive nightclubs in Zermatt, the Bar Tenne, whose decor is an imaginative mixture of medieval and art nouveau styles.

Services: Room service

Facilities: Sauna, swimming pool, free use of the solarium at the nearby Hotel Alex.

GRAND HOTEL ZERMATTERHOF, Bahnhofstrasse, CH-3920 Zermatt. Tel. 028/66-11-00. Fax 028/67-48-42. 61 rms (all with bath), 32 suites. MINIBAR TV TEL
$ Rates (including half board): Winter, 208F–270F ($151.80–$197.05) single; 416F–540F ($303.65–$394.15) double. Summer, 165F–215F ($120.45–$156.95) single; 330F–430F ($240.85–$313.85) double; from 650F ($474.45) suite. AE, DC, MC, V. **Closed:** Nov.
This white-walled, Regency-style hotel pointedly refuses to imitate a chalet. Rated five

stars by the Swiss government, it's as plush (in an understated way) and comfortable as anything else in town. The bedrooms are paneled and well upholstered, with vivid colors and at least one handmade carpet.

Dining/Entertainment: The intimate bar has bronze-colored details, and the grill, Prato Borni, has French provincial chairs with cane backs. There is dancing to live music in the winter.

Services: Massages, room service, baby-sitting.

Facilities: Exercise room and a beautifully illuminated swimming pool; tennis court, sauna, large garden, solarium, fitness center.

HOTEL ALEX, CH-3920 Zermatt. Tel. 028/67-17-26. Fax 028/67-19-43. 50 rms (all with bath), 20 suites. TV TEL

$ Rates (including half board): 182F–237F ($132.85–$173) single; 364F–474F ($265.70–$345.95) double; from 760F ($554.70) suite. MC, V. **Closed:** Nov.

This hotel contains some of the most amusing interior architectural features in Zermatt. The public rooms, with flagstone floors and elegant paneling, have amusingly grotesque statues of demigods; one figure above a fireplace stirs a cauldron with a trident. The hotel has a free-form swimming pool below a half-timbered ceiling with a round lunette window on top. Alex and Gisela Perren offer many rooms with good views of the mountains.

Dining/Entertainment: The stools in the dance bar are carved to resemble ibex torsos, with cowhide seats. The restaurant serves a six-course gourmet dinner nightly.

Services: Room service, laundry, massages.

Facilities: Swimming pool, fitness rooms, squash courts, tennis courts (including one inside), saunas (private and community).

HOTEL GARNI SIMI, CH-3920 Zermatt. Tel. 028/67-46-56. Fax 028/67-48-61. 24 rms (all with bath). MINIBAR TV TEL

$ Rates (including continental breakfast): Winter, 90F–117F ($65.70–$85.40) single; 180F–234F ($131.40–$170.80) double. Summer, 69F–90F ($50.35–$65.70) single; 138F–180F ($100.75–$131.40). double. AE, MC, V.

A block from the main street, this four-star hotel has a stylish lobby and comfortable rooms; the rooms have modern alpine furniture. The hotel is named after the owner, Simon Biner. There is a breakfast room and an interesting disco bar, the Dancing Bar (Dancing Delphine). An Italian restaurant is connected to the hotel.

HOTEL MIRABEAU, CH-3920 Zermatt. Tel. 028/67-17-72. Fax 028/67-13-34. 44 rms (all with bath). MINIBAR TV TEL

$ Rates (including half board): Off-season, 118F–153F ($86.15–$116.80) single; 236F–306F ($172.25–$223.35) double. Dec 23–mid-Apr, 154F–200F ($112.40–$146) single; 308F–400F ($224.80–$291.95) double. AE, DC, MC, V.

This modern chalet has many balconies and traditional touches, such as stone detailing, ceiling beams, and a fireplace. The Julen family offers attractively furnished rooms. The terrace opens onto a view of the Matterhorn. Children are especially welcome—cots and early dinners are available.

Dining/Entertainment: You can enjoy drinks on the terrace while taking in a view of the Matterhorn. The excellent restaurant, Beau d'Or, offers Swiss and continental specialties. There is a piano bar.

Services: Laundry, room service.

Facilities: Fitness room, sauna, and heated indoor swimming pool; tennis court.

HOTEL MONTE ROSA, CH-3920 Zermatt. Tel. 028/66-11-31. Fax 028/67-11-60. 49 rms (all with bath). MINIBAR TV TEL

$ Rates (including half board): 154F–200F ($112.40–$146) single; 308F–400F ($224.80–$291.95) double. AE, DC, MC, V. **Closed:** Nov and May.

⭐ Edward Whymper, the Englishman who conquered the Matterhorn, recommended this as the best hotel in Zermatt in the 1860s. Located on the main street, the Monte Rosa has stone posts and lintels around its windows and red shutters. It was built in 1853. The lounges have parquet floors, thick rugs, and crackling fireplaces; the antique armchairs are beautifully upholstered in stripes and patterns. The pleasant bedrooms are among the most comfortable in Zermatt. This hotel is part of the Seiler chain.

Dining/Entertainment: The dining room, serving Swiss and continental specialties, is in the Belle Epoque style. The Montrose bar is a lively rendezvous place.

Services: Room service, baby-sitting.

Facilities: Use of the swimming pool at the Mont Cervin Hotel.

HOTEL SCHWEIZERHOF, Bahnhofstrasse, CH-3920 Zermatt. Tel. 028/ 66-11-55. Fax 028/67-31-21. 103 rms (all with bath), 14 suites. MINIBAR TEL
$ Rates (including half board): 182F–237F ($132.85–$172.95) single; 364F–474F ($265.70–$345.95) double; from 500F ($364.95) suite. **Closed:** First 3 weeks in May and Oct 15–Dec.

Located on the resort's main street, this chalet has shops on its ground floor and a spacious, carpeted lobby with comfortable modern chairs and a fireplace. Most of the sunny rooms have carved blond-wood furniture. More than half the rooms contain TV. The hotel is part of the Seiler chain. The management is conscientious.

Dining/Entertainment: One elegant restaurant features Italian specialties, raclette, and fondue; another specializes in Swiss cheese dishes; and a third offers Swiss regional specialties. Typical Swiss music is presented in the hotel's beer hall, Schwyzerstübli. There is a popular bar and disco.

Services: Laundry, baby-sitting, room service.

Facilities: Fitness club, swimming pool.

HOTEL WALLISERHOF, Bahnhofstrasse, CH-3920 Zermatt. Tel. 028/ 67-11-74. Fax 028/67-55-31. 40 rms (all with bath). MINIBAR TV TEL
$ Rates (including half board): Winter, 154F–200F ($112.40–$146) single; 308F–400F ($224.80–$291.95) double. Summer, 118F–153F ($86.15–$111.70) single; 236F–306F ($172.25–$223.35) double. AE, DC, MC, V.

The hotel stands in the center of town in a red-shuttered and balconied building that was originally a Valaisian farmhouse. Inside, you'll find stone fireplaces, thick walls, masonry columns, and flagstone floors. The carpeted bedrooms have wooden furniture. The hotel has a popular streetside café and a restaurant.

SEILER HOTEL NICOLETTA, CH-3920 Zermatt. Tel. 028/66-11-51. Fax 028/67-52-15. 62 rms (all with bath). MINIBAR TV TEL
$ Rates (including half board): 123F–220F ($89.80–$160.60) single; 206F–400F ($150.35–$291.95) double. AE, DC, MC, V.

The Nicoletta was built in 1970 and renovated in the late 1980s. Its chalet-inspired facade is accented with a series of op-art designs in muted colors set between the windows. Owned by the respected Seiler chain, it has a lobby whose focal point is a dramatic fireplace, around which the hotel's activities seem to revolve. The comfortably furnished bedrooms contain a radio, a VCR, and a hairdryer.

Dining/Entertainment: The hotel has a well-managed restaurant and a piano bar.

Services: Massage.
Facilities: Swimming pool, three saunas, solarium.

SEILER MONT CERVIN, Bahnhofstrasse, CH-3920 Zermatt. Tel. 028/ 66-11-22, or toll free 800/223-6800 in North America. Fax 028/67-28-78. 132 rms (all with bath). MINIBAR TV TEL
$ Rates (including half board): Winter, 208F–270F ($151.80–$197.05) single; 416F–540F ($303.65–$394.15) double. Summer, 165F–215F ($120.45–$156.95) single; 330F–430F ($240.85–$313.85) double. AE, DC, MC, V.
Closed: Nov and May.

⭐ This has been one of Zermatt's leading hotels since it was established more than 130 years ago. The rooms are sunny and spacious, with fine craftsmanship.
You and your bags will be picked up at the hotel by a horse-drawn sleigh in the winter or by an old-fashioned horse-drawn carriage in the summer. This hotel is part of the Seiler chain.
Dining/Entertainment: The top-notch bar and restaurant offers food, drink, and live music.
Services: Massage, room service, laundry.
Facilities: One of the town's best swimming pools, sauna, kindergarten.

MODERATE

HOTEL ANTIKA, CH-3920 Zermatt. Tel. 028/67-21-50. Fax 028/67-57-83. 23 rms (all with bath). TV TEL
$ Rates (including continental breakfast): Winter, 75F–97F ($54.75–$70.80) single; 150F–194F ($109.50–$141.60) double. Summer, 61F–80F ($44.50–$58.40) single; 122F–160F ($89.05–$116.80) double. MC, V.

Ⓢ Set behind an attractive facade, each of the bedrooms of this hotel opens onto its own covered loggia with flower boxes and wooden trim. The interior is accented with Oriental carpets and a partial sheathing of weathered planks. Facilities include a Jacuzzi lined with smooth-sided river rocks, a whirlpool, a sauna, and a solarium. A large garden behind the hotel is suitable for a quiet contemplation of the Matterhorn. The hotel's Stockhorn restaurant, set a short distance away, offers good food in a rustic setting. Room service is available.

HOTEL BUTTERFLY, CH-3920 Zermatt. Tel. 028/67-37-21. Fax 028/67-59-06. 62 rms (all with shower or bath).
$ Rates (including half board): Winter, 120F–156F ($87.60–$113.85) single; 240F–312F ($175.20–$227.85) double. Summer, 95F–123F ($69.35–$89.80) single; 190F–246F ($138.70–$179.55) double. AE, DC, MC, V. **Closed:** Nov.
This Best Western hotel has a peaked roof, large windows, and flower boxes. The Alps loom in the distance. The interior is warm and rustic, with arched windows, Oriental rugs, and knotty-pine furniture. Gunda Woischnig offers rooms with toilets and balconies facing south. Amenities include radios, and, if you request, TVs. A well-stocked bar serves as an intimate rendezvous point for hotel guests and their friends. A buffet breakfast is served. Facilities include a sauna, whirlpool, solarium, and fitness center.

HOTEL CARINA, CH-3920 Zermatt. Tel. 028/67-17-67. 28 rms (all with shower or bath). TV TEL
$ Rates (including half board): 120F–156F ($87.60–$113.85) single; 240F–312F ($175.20–$227.75) double. AE, DC, MC, V.

The Carina's outside is similar to that of dozens of other hotels in Zermatt, but inside you'll find wood paneling, stenciled plaster, and a *gemütlich* ambience that is heightened by a blazing fireplace. The bedrooms are comfortably furnished. The Fritz Biner family offer guests free use of the swimming pool at a nearby hotel.

HOTEL DARIOLI, Bahnhofstrasse, CH-3920 Zermatt. Tel. 028/67-27-48. 28 rms (15 with bath). TV TEL

$ Rates (including continental breakfast): 74F ($54) single without bath, 97F ($70.80) single with bath; 148F ($108.05) double without bath, 194F ($141.60) double with bath. AE, DC, MC, V.

This five-story balconied hotel is on the main street near the train station. The sunny reception area is upstairs. The hotel has a blue-and-white ceramic stove, Oriental rugs, and an attractive wooden bar. The Darioli family offer comfortable rooms with regional furniture, usually painted in vivid colors with stenciled floral patterns.

HOTEL EXCELSIOR, CH-3920 Zermatt. Tel. 028/67-30-17. Fax 028/67-16-25. 32 rms (all with bath). MINIBAR TV TEL

$ Rates (including half board): 120F–156F ($87.60–$113.85) single; 240F–312F ($175.20–$227.75) double. AE, DC, MC, V. **Closed:** 3 weeks in May.

Weathered wood trim makes this concrete building look like a modern chalet. It's across the river from the commercial center of town. The rooms have balconies, many of them with a view of the Matterhorn. Amenities include a radio. There are two bars and an attractive restaurant, La Ferme, on the lobby level.

HOTEL POST, Bahnhofstrasse, CH-3920 Zermatt. Tel. 028/67-19-33. Fax 028/67-41-14. 21 rms (all with bath), 2 suites. TEL

$ Rates (including continental breakfast): 70F–120F ($51.10–$87.60) single; 110F–200F ($80.30–$146) double; 220F–280F ($160.60–$204.35) suite. AE, DC, MC, V.

Built in 1903 and overhauled in the 1950s when American-born Karl Iversson and his family acquired it, this establishment is better known for its sprawling restaurant and nightlife facilities than for its bedrooms. The bedrooms have unusual floor plans, charmingly mismatched pieces of antique furniture, modern plumbing, and an ambience best described as "raffish." A minimum of 7 days' overnight is required during midwinter.

HOTEL RESTAURANT ORION, CH-3920 Zermatt. Tel. 028/67-16-67. 26 rms (all with bath). TV TEL

$ Rates (including half board): 106F–138F ($77.35–$100.75) single; 212F–276F ($154.75–$201.45) double. AE, DC, MC, V. **Closed:** Nov.

The Orion's traditional facade has a sloping roof and bands of weathered shingles and white stucco. The modern, yet rustic, interior includes heavy timbers and skylights. The pleasant dining room has colorful tablecloths. The rooms are comfortable.

HOTEL RIFFELBERG, CH-3920 Zermatt-Umgebung. Tel. 028/67-22-16. Fax 028/67-39-94. 45 rms (all with bath). TEL

$ Rates (including half board): 120F–156F ($87.60–$113.85) single; 240F–312F ($175.20–$227.75) double. AE, DC, MC, V.

This hotel was built in 1853 by a local clergyman in a dramatically desolate area just below the Matterhorn. Purchased by the city of Zermatt in 1862, it has served ever since as a hotel and restaurant, with the kind of view that people come from miles around to see. An ibex colony is said to live close to the nearby Riffelsee. The area gets 8 full hours of sunlight in December and even more in midsummer. Though the interior was recently renovated, the Riffelberg retains its rustic alpine decor. The hotel is within skiing distance of the Gornergrat cableway.

HOTEL ROMANTICA, Bahnhofstrasse, CH-3920 Zermatt. Tel. 028/67-15-05. Fax 028/67-15-05. 14 rms (all with bath). TEL

$ **Rates** (including continental breakfast): 75F–97F ($54.75–$70.80) single; 150F–194F ($109.50–$141.60) double. AE, DC, V.

If you don't want to walk up the main street to this hotel (10 minutes from the rail station), call owner Yvonne Cremonini and request to be picked up in an electric cart. Built in 1962 in a much older style, the building has a flagstone roof. The rooms are small but efficient. In the summer one of the loveliest gardens in Zermatt blooms on either side of the flagstone path leading up to the hotel. Two small log cabins near the front door have been converted from grain storehouses to rustic guesthouses. Baby-sitting, room service, and laundry facilities are provided.

ROMANTIK HOTEL JULEN, CH-3920 Zermatt. Tel. 028/67-24-81. Fax 028/67-14-81. 34 rms (all with bath). MINIBAR TV TEL

$ **Rates** (including half board): 120F–156F ($87.60–$113.85) single; 240F–312F ($175.20–$227.75) double. AE, DC, MC, V.

Across the river from Zermatt's historic cemetery, this attractive hotel has weathered balconies with a view of the Matterhorn. The Julen family offer good meals in the dining room, which has an ornate wooden ceiling and beautifully paneled walls. The bedrooms are furnished in a modern chalet style. The hotel has a restaurant, Schaferstube, and an indoor swimming pool is about 50 yards away.

INEXPENSIVE

HOTEL ALPHUBEL, CH-3920 Zermatt. Tel. 028/67-30-03. 50 rms (all with bath). TV TEL

$ **Rates** (including half board): 80F–103F ($58.40–$75.20) single; 160F–204F ($116.80–$148.90) double. AE, MC, V.

Near the train station, this large chalet has a solid stone foundation and curved stairs leading to the entrance. The Julen family named it after a local mountaintop. The rooms are in a functional modern style. The restaurant serves a good, moderately priced cuisine. Facilities include a sauna.

HOTEL TOURING, CH-3920 Zermatt. Tel. 028/67-11-17. Fax 028/67-46-01. 28 rms (15 with bath). TEL

$ **Rates** (including half board): 87F ($63.50) single without bath, 103F ($75.20) single with bath; 174F ($127) double without bath, 206F ($150.35) double with bath. No credit cards. **Closed:** Nov.

Ski racks are set up outside the front door of this pleasant chalet with green shutters and wooden walls. Many rooms have private balconies with a view of the Matterhorn. Wendelin Julen and his family are the owners.

WHERE TO DINE

You'll want to sample the fondue and raclette at various places, not to mention rack of lamb grilled over a larchwood fire.

ALEX GRILL, in the Hotel Alex. Tel. 67-17-26.
Cuisine: SWISS. **Reservations:** Recommended.

$ **Prices:** Appetizers 12F–22F ($8.75–$16.05); main courses 34F–70F ($24.80–$51.10). MC, V.
Open: Dinner only, daily 7–10pm. **Closed:** May and Nov.

This stylish basement restaurant has alpine decor: carved paneling, leaded windows, flagstone floors, sky-blue upholstery, and rich accessories. As an appetizer, try a platter of three kinds of smoked fish or fresh Atlantic oysters. The main courses include grilled lobster, grilled salmon scallop, and giant shrimp with a chive-flavored cream sauce. The meat dishes include veal kidneys in a mustard sauce, grilled rack of lamb, filet of beef with bordelaise sauce, and a variety of game in season.

ALEX SCHLOSSHOTEL TENNE. Tel. 67-18-01.

Cuisine: SWISS. **Reservations:** Required in winter.

$ Prices: Appetizers 12F–22F ($8.75–$16.05); main courses 22F–45F ($16.05–$32.85). MC, V.

Open: Off-season, dinner only, daily 7–10:30pm. Dec 23–mid-Apr, lunch daily noon–2pm; dinner 7–10:30pm.

⭐ On the lobby level of the hotel, this restaurant is designed in a duplex that includes an upper wraparound gallery and a ceiling fresco covered with a representation of the zodiac. The menu items include lobster-cream soup, chipped pike with saffron sauce and vegetables, an array of fresh shellfish kept fresh in aquariums, sweetbreads and veal kidneys, woodcock braised in tarragon, and duckling breast in an Armagnac-flavored sauce. For dessert, you might be tempted with a soufflé of white cheese covered with essence of apricots.

LA FERME, in the Hotel Excelsior. Tel. 67-30-17.

Cuisine: SWISS. **Reservations:** Recommended.

$ Prices: Appetizers 12F–18F ($8.75–$13.15); main courses 22F–38F ($16.05–$27.75); fixed-price menu 45F ($32.85). AE, DC, MC, V.

Open: Dinner only, daily 6:30–11pm. **Closed:** Early May to mid-June and early Oct to mid-Nov.

Downstairs from the hotel reception area, this large restaurant has knotty-pine paneling, plants, and racks of wine. The *menu du patron* (proprietor's menu) might include cream of zucchini soup, a salad with quail breasts, and filet goulash Stroganoff. Many of the specialties—including veal steak with morels and flambéed filet Medici—are prepared only for two people. Lunch is served only during blizzards, when the ski lifts are closed.

LE MAZOT. Tel. 67-27-77.

Cuisine: SWISS. **Reservations:** Recommended.

$ Prices: Appetizers 12F–20F ($8.75–$14.60); main courses 30F–45F ($21.90–$32.85); fixed-price meals 45F–60F ($32.85–$43.80). AE, MC, V.

Open: Daily 4pm–midnight; meals served 6:30–11pm. **Closed:** June and Nov.

In a dining room overlooking the town's river, amid pinewood paneling, rustic accessories, and an open grill, you can enjoy some of the best food in town. Owned by Roger Muther, Le Mazot specializes in a delectable array of lamb dishes; in a hot-and-cold salad garnished with filets of rabbit, garlic, and mushrooms; and in scampi flavored with ginger sauce.

RESTAURANT SEILERHAUS, Bahnhofstrasse. Tel. 66-11-21.

Cuisine: SWISS. **Reservations:** Required.

$ Prices: Appetizers 15F–22F ($10.95–$16.05); main courses 25F–32F ($18.25–$23.35); fixed-price meal 85F–90F ($62.05–$65.70). AE, DC, MC, V.

Open: Lunch daily 11:45am–2pm; dinner daily 7–10pm.

This fine restaurant has hanging, red-tinted lamps that vibrate musically when you touch them. Upstairs is a long room with stone walls, a fireplace, and large windows overlooking an outdoor terrace. As an appetizer, try dandelion salad with poached egg or fresh asparagus with a mousseline sauce in season. The main courses include salmon trout with braised chicory and stewed onions, braised leg of duck with new vegetables, and regional dishes such as leek-and-potato stew with smoked sausages.

RESTAURANT WALLISERHOF, in the Hotel Walliserhof, Bahnhofstrasse. Tel. 67-11-74.

Cuisine: SWISS. **Reservations:** Recommended.

$ **Prices:** Appetizers 12F–25F ($8.75–$18.25); main courses 22F–40F ($16.05–$29.20); fixed-price meal 38F ($27.75). AE, DC, MC, V.

Open: Lunch daily noon–2pm; dinner daily 7–9:30pm.

This hotel restaurant has a particularly elegant selection of hors d'oeuvres, including goose liver and caviar. Specialties include fondue bourguignonne or chinoise, ribs of lamb with herbs, double veal cutlet with noodles Alfredo, and brook trout.

MODERATE

ARVENSTUBE, in the Hotel Pollux, Bahnhofstrasse. Tel. 67-19-46.

Cuisine: SWISS. **Reservations:** Recommended.

$ **Prices:** Appetizers 10F–18F ($7.30–$13.15); main courses 18F–32F ($13.15–$23.35). AE, DC, MC, V.

Open: Lunch daily noon–2pm; dinner daily 6–9:30pm.

A tempting variety of international dishes is served in a beautifully paneled dining room with a corner bar. As an appetizer, try the assiette valaisanne, a plate of air-dried meats from the Grisons. Other specialties include riz Casimir (a curry dish), tournedos in a savory-mustard sauce, and sliced veal in a mushroom-cream sauce. These dishes are often served with Rösti. Trout with almonds is another favorite. Upstairs is a less formal tavern, Pinte Valaisanne, offering the same menu.

ENZO'S HITTA, Findeln. Tel. 67-25-88.

Cuisine: SWISS/ITALIAN. **Reservations:** Required. **Directions:** Take the Sunnegga chair lift to first stop, then hike across the fields; leave your skis in the snow and head down steep, winding pathway, passing plastic palm trees.

$ **Prices:** Appetizers 9F–17F ($6.55–$12.40); main courses 19F–32F ($13.85–$23.35); light lunch 25F ($18.25). AE, MC, V.

Open: Daily 10am–5pm.

Enzo's Hitta is reputedly the best mountain restaurant near Zermatt. It's in the small hamlet of Findeln, on a steep mountainside, but despite its remote location, the Hitta is very popular. It has a sun terrace and a roof terrace facing the spectacular Matterhorn. Enzo, the chef and owner, is Swiss-Italian. Specialties include carpaccio, spinach salad, grilled meats, and excellent pasta dishes. Try the Eskimo spaghetti, made with smoked salmon.

LE GITAN, in the Hotel Darioli, Bahnhofstrasse. Tel. 67-10-98.

Cuisine: SWISS. **Reservations:** Required in winter.

$ **Prices:** Appetizers 4.50F–19.50F ($3.30–$14.25); main courses 23F–36.50F ($16.80–$26.65). MC, V.

Open: Lunch daily noon–1:45pm; dinner daily 6:30–10pm. **Closed:** Nov.

This rustic grillroom with an antique fireplace has candlelit tables and good service. Beef fondue and grilled meat are the specialties; shrimp is also offered. Appetizers include a savory tomato soup spiked with gin.

GRILLROOM STOCKHORN. Tel. 67-17-47.

Cuisine: SWISS. **Reservations:** Required.

$ **Prices:** Appetizers 5F–15F ($3.65–$10.95); main courses 25F–32F ($18.25–$23.35). AE, MC, V.

Open: Lunch daily noon–1:30pm; dinner daily 6:30–11pm.

A fireplace extends into the dining room of this elegant chalet owned by Emil Julen. The decor includes an alpine wedding chest and regional chairs, as well as travertine floors, heavy beams, and stained stucco walls. Specialties include raclette, piccata with spaghetti, fondue bourguignonne, and grilled meats. There is also a bar.

OTTO FURRER STUBE, Bahnhofstrasse. Tel. 63-35-20.

Cuisine: SWISS. **Reservations:** Not needed.

$ **Prices:** Appetizers 8F–15F ($5.85–$10.95); main courses 22F–32F ($16.05–$23.35). AE, DC, MC, V.

Open: Dinner only, daily 6–11pm. **Closed:** Apr 25–June.

Named after a famous 1930s skier and mountain guide, this cellar restaurant features a country-inspired *cuisine grandmère*. The hearty food includes cassoulet from Toulouse and gigot d'agneau (lamb) with garlic. The dining room is lined with 19th-century engravings of the Matterhorn and other alpine memorabilia. The waitresses wear regional clothing.

RISTORANTE DA MARIO, in the Hotel Schweizerhof, Bahnhofstrasse. Tel. 66-11-55.

Cuisine: SWISS/ITALIAN. **Reservations:** Recommended.

$ **Prices:** Appetizers 12F–22F ($8.75–$16.05); main courses 23F–38F ($16.80–$27.75). AE, MC.

Open: Dinner only, daily 6:30–10:30pm.

This stylish trattoria has a good reputation for imaginative cooking and traditional Italian dishes. The dining room is decorated with wood and brass, and piano music is played. Antipasti include chicken-stuffed ravioli and risotto with porcini. A local favorite is pasta e fagiolo, followed by homemade pasta. The few seafood dishes might include scallops with small vegetables. A variety of meat is served, from saltimbocca to veal liver Venetian style. For a treat, try the tenderloin steak with goose liver and a red-wine sauce. You can order classic desserts such as cassata with pistachio sauce or a more exotic iced-apricot mousse.

SCHAFERSTUBE, in the Romantik Hotel Julen. Tel. 67-24-81.

Cuisine: SWISS. **Reservations:** Required.

$ **Prices:** Appetizers 10F–15F ($7.30–$10.95); main courses 18F–30F ($13.15–$21.90); cheese fondues 18F ($13.15) per person; raclette 8F ($5.85) per person; fixed-price meals 32F ($23.35). AE, DC, MC, V.

Open: Dinner only, daily 6–9pm.

This moderately priced restaurant offers atmospheric dining amid plank-covered walls, heavy beams, flickering candles, and leaded-glass windows. The specialty is lamb, served in a variety of styles. You can also order grilled veal and beef dishes, traditionally prepared. The restaurant is part of the Romantik Hotel Julen but has its own separate entrance.

BUDGET

SPAGHETTI FACTORY, in the Hotel Post, Bahnhofstrasse. Tel. 67-19-32.

Cuisine: ITALIAN. **Reservations:** Required.

$ **Prices:** Appetizers 9F–20F ($6.55–$14.60); main courses 20F–32F ($14.60–$23.35). AE, DC, MC, V.

Open: Dinner only, daily 7pm–midnight.

This Italian tavern is one of the most popular restaurants in Zermatt. A typical meal begins with a tomato-and-mozzarella salad, followed by carpaccio or Parma ham.

Pasta dishes include spaghetti, linguini, fettuccine, and lasagne verdi. You can also order a risotto with three mushrooms, grilled scampi, or beefsteak pizzaiola. The restaurant sits on a balcony overlooking the dance floor of the disco Le Village.

EVENING ENTERTAINMENT

Zermatt is known for its après-ski activities, which include tea dances, restaurants, bars, nightclubs, and discos. It has more nightclubs than any other resort in the Valais.

AN ENTERTAINMENT COMPLEX

The **Hotel Post** (tel. 67-19-32), where everybody shows up after recovering from Elsie's Irish coffee, has a virtual monopoly on nightlife in Zermatt. The owner, Karl Ivarsson, an American, has gradually expanded it into one of the most complete entertainment complexes in Zermatt, with many restaurants and nightspots under one roof. Photographs of former guests, including athletes and models, are displayed under glass at the reception desk. On the way to the restaurant, in the basement, you'll pass a series of murals telling the story of a lonely tourist looking for love in Zermatt.

The **Brown Cow,** on the street level, is a rustic room with 19th-century farm implements hanging from the ceiling. Drinks and snacks are served at the "Cow," and there is a jukebox. The menu includes hamburgers, goulash soup, Beach Bun sandwiches, and salads. Light meals start at 18F ($13.15). It's open daily from 8am to midnight.

Beyond the reception desk, the **Pink Elephant** is an exclusive, art nouveau bar. It has Edwardian palms, leather couches, candles, and bentwood chairs. It's a favorite with David Bowie and John Lord (Deep Purple), both of whom have performed here. A stainless-steel dance floor is surrounded by marble tables. Drinks cost 9F ($6.55) during happy hour (every night from 6 to 10pm), and 16F ($11.70) after 10pm until the bar's 2am closing.

Le Village is the most interesting disco in Zermatt. Built in a 19th-century alpine barn still supported by its original weathered beams, it's fun, crowded, and noisy. The disco opens every night at 8:30pm and shows old movies (many of them with skiing themes) against a foldaway screen until the music begins about an hour later. Closing time is 2am. Admission, use of the cloakroom, and your first drink cost 13F ($9.50). The entrance price for Le Village will gain your admission to an even rowdier hangout, the **Broken Ski Bar,** located in the complex's basement, where the most hardened ski bums listen to hard rock music at very high volumes, drink heavily, and generally raise hell. Once you've gained admission, a beer costs around 9F ($6.55). The Broken Ski Bar is open daily from 5pm to 3am.

THE CLUB & MUSIC SCENE

CASTLE CLUB. Tel. 67-22-98.

A great place to watch people, this white-walled, rustic club has two levels. There are low couches upstairs, overlooking the dance floor. Most visitors are under 25. Open in the winter only, daily from 9pm to 3am. Beer costs 8F ($5.85).

Admission: Free.

DANCING SIMI, in the Hotel Simi. Tel. 67-46-56.

This large alpine room has paneling, a comfortable bar, and a dance floor devoted to the presentations of Swiss folkloric music. Open only in high season (December 23 to mid-April and July to August), daily from 9pm to 2am. Beer runs 8F ($5.85).

Admission: Free.

HOTEL POLLUX DISCO, Bahnhofstrasse. Tel. 67-19-46.

This glossy, modern disco is very crowded in the winter. It attracts local service personnel, ski instructors, and tourists. The dance floor is surrounded by little tables. Open in the winter only, daily from 9pm to 2am. Drinks run about 13F ($9.50).

Admission: Free.

THE BAR SCENE

THE BAR/THE KEGELSTUBE, in the Hotel Bristol. Tel. 67-24-98.

Have dinner at the small tables or drink at the long wooden bar and listen to live music. **The Bar** also has a dance floor, a fireplace, and a view of the attached restaurant, which is separated from it by stucco arches. It's open daily from noon to 2am, but it doesn't get busy until after dark. Dancing starts at 9pm.

Located in the basement, the pleasantly unpretentious **Kegelstube** (Bowling Alley Bar) is the only place in town to bowl. Make reservations a day in advance to use one of the two bowling lanes. Stop in for a beer-and-Wurst salad at one of the dimly lit and battered tables. Bowling costs 13F ($9.50) per hour. The bar is open Monday through Saturday from 4:30pm to midnight. Drinks cost 13F ($9.50); full meals begin at 45F ($32.85).

BAR TENNE, in the Alex Schlosshotel Tenne. Tel. 67-18-01.

For a change from the traditional chalet, try this art nouveau bar with turn-of-the-century silver sconces and rough stone walls. Four stone columns support a beamed truss above a circular dance floor. The bar looks like an ambulatory in a monastery; the DJ booth might have been a church pulpit. There are comfortable sofas and chairs scattered around the dance floor. Music is played daily from 8pm to midnight or 2am. Drinks cost about 13F ($9.50).

ELSIE'S PLACE, Kirchplatz. Tel. 67-24-31.

This small house, dating from 1879, packs a large crowd around 6pm. Skiers show up for hot chocolate or Elsie's famous Irish coffee (5F or $3.65). The house is on the main street, near the Zermatterhof Hotel. During the day the menu includes ham and eggs, hot dogs, and even escargots. Caviar and oysters (a luxury in this area) are also served. Open in the winter daily from 3pm to midnight and in the summer daily from 10am to midnight. Light meals begin at 22F ($16.05).

EX-BAR/LUNA BAR, in the Hotel Excelsior. Tel. 67-30-17.

These twin bars are near the lobby of the Hotel Excelsior. The rustic Ex-Bar is more rowdy and less expensive. It serves drinks, cheeseburgers, steaks, and snacks, while recorded pop music is played in the background. The Luna Bar is quieter, shielded from the noise by thick doors. Open daily from 9pm to midnight. Drinks run about 13F ($9.50).

GRILL RESTAURANT SPYCHER AND SCOTCH CORNER BAR. Tel. 967-11-41.

This half-timbered restaurant has a large, weathered bar against one wall. It's a popular place for après-ski drinks, including Swiss coffee, café normand, and French coffee. The restaurant is connected to the Hotel Aristella. Excellent meals are served and the wine selection is superb. The grill restaurant is open daily from 11:30am to 1:30pm and 6:30 to 9:30pm (closed Nov). Coffee costs 9F ($6.55); meals start at 30F ($21.90).

MATTERHORNSTUBE, in the Hotel Mont Cervin. Tel. 66-11-22.

This large alpine room has wooden tables and a wooden ceiling, two bars, and lots of space. It's in one of the most glamorous hotels in the village. Most visitors are over 30. Open daily from 9pm to 2am (closed Mon in the summer). Drinks go for 13F ($9.50).

PAPPARLA PUB. Tel. 67-40-40.

This Neo-Victorian pub has windows with many panes and a wide sun terrace in the front. The interior has wood paneling that curves around the building somewhat like the hull of a boat. International beers are served. The pub has a dart board, a pool table, and a jukebox that plays rock music. The menu includes cheeseburgers, pork chop platters, fish and chips, and steaks. Open daily from 11am to midnight. Beer costs 6F ($4.40); drinks, 13F ($9.50); snacks, 9F ($6.55).

WHYMPERSTUBE, in the Hotel Monte Rosa. Tel. 67-19-22.

Located in the cellar of the Monte Rosa, the bar has antique planks, battered tables, and a warm, intimate ambience. Mountain snacks include raclette, hot sausages with potato salad, platters of air-dried alpine beef, and Wiener Schnitzel. Full meals are also available, beginning at 30F ($21.90). Open daily from 6pm to midnight.

5. SAAS-FEE

18 miles S of Visp, 36 miles SE of Sierre

GETTING THERE By Train Saas-Fee is not connected to the rest of Switzerland's rail lines. The nearest railway station is at Stalden, a 40-minute bus ride to the north.

By Bus Between 6:15am and 5:15pm, a bus departs every 30 minutes from Brig, passing through both Visp and Stalden on its way to Saas-Fee. After 5:15pm buses run until around 7:15pm every hour. Travel time from Brig is about 65 minutes.

By Car The road to Saas-Fee south from Visp (follow the signs) is steep and narrow. If winter road conditions are poor, police require chains on car wheels. No motor vehicles are permitted within Saas-Fee; park in one of the large garages outside the village.

ESSENTIALS The **Saas-Fee Tourist Office** (tel. 028/57-14-57) is open Monday through Saturday from 8:30am to noon and 2 to 6pm. The **telephone area code** for Saas Fee is 028. In lieu of **street names** and numbers, follow directional signs to the town's hotels and restaurants.

The 13th-century village of Saas-Fee (*sauce*-fay) has been called a "pearl of the Alps" and a "glacier village." The grass-covered plateau on which the village sits is surrounded by 13 mountains, each of which is noteworthy for towering more than 13,000 feet. There is a spectacular view of the Dom and the mammoth **Feegletscher** (Fee Glacier). The tilted pyramid of the Matterhorn, however, is not visible.

The resort is famous for the "highwire" mountain trails along the western and eastern escarpments of the Saas Valley. Saas-Fee is the end of the famous High Route from Verbier through the Alps. In the outlying areas, many residents wear traditional garb. Cows are another common sight. Motor vehicles are prohibited within the resort.

WHAT TO SEE & DO

Saas-Fee has two aerial cableways, three multicabin cableways, two chair lifts, and 15 ski lifts. There are 32 miles of ski runs and 175 miles of footpaths, including the **Gemsweg** ("chamois track") from Hannig to Plattjen and the geological mountain high-level trail from Felskinn to the Britannia Hut. Other facilities include 11 tennis courts, two ice rinks, and a swimming pool at the entrance of the village.

Skiing tours and **climbing expeditions** are offered by the mountaineering school from April to October.

NEARBY ATTRACTIONS You can take a gondola cable lift to **Plattjen,** enjoying a panoramic view of the Saas Valley and the artificial lake of Mattmark. If you go in the spring, you'll see many alpine flowers and, if you're lucky, a chamois.

Summer skiers can take the Felskinn aerial cableway to **Egginer-Felskinn.** Two or three ski lifts are open year round, but summer hours are limited—from 8:30am to 1:30pm daily. In warm weather the snow usually gets mushy in the afternoon.

The Spielboden gondola ski lift and the Längfluh aerial cableway take you to **Längfluh,** an oasis in the middle of the Fee Glacier. This is the starting point for the classic mountain tour and the grand glacier tour to the Britannia Hut and to Mattmark.

Another gondola cableway goes to **Hannig.** You arrive at a balcony overlooking the Saas Valley, with a scenic alpine view all around you. There are many walking tours in this pristine area. It's also the starting point for a trip to the **Mischabel Hut** and many alpine tours in the Mischabel massif. This is your best chance to spot a chamois or ibex.

The tourist office will supply all the details about tours and sports activities in the area.

WHERE TO STAY

EXPENSIVE

HOTEL BEAU-SITE, CH-3906 Saas-Fee. Tel. 028/57-11-22. 72 rms (all with bath). MINIBAR TV TEL

$ Rates (including half board): 156F ($113.85) single; 260F–280F ($189.75–$204.35) double. AE, DC, MC, V.

This large brown-and-white building has many balconies and is located in the center of the village. Built in 1893, the hotel was expanded and modernized in 1957, but much of the original masonry, timber, and paneling remain. The rooms are comfortable and well furnished. A large breakfast buffet is served and five-course dinners are available. Facilities include a swimming pool.

GRAND HOTEL SAAS-FEE, CH-3906 Saas-Fee. Tel. 028/57-10-01. Fax 028/57-20-85. 88 rms (all with bath). MINIBAR TV TEL

$ Rates (including half board): 150F–165F ($109.50–$120.45) single; 260F–310F ($189.75–$226.25) double. AE, DC, MC, V. **Closed:** May and Oct–Nov.

✪ This elegant hotel in the center of the village resembles three streamlined and interconnected chalets, layered with balconies on the south side. The decor includes beamed ceilings and several 19th-century antiques. Most of the comfortable rooms have pine paneling and are decorated in monochromatic earth tones. Ursula and Hans Hess-Zurbriggen are the English-speaking hosts.

Dining/Entertainment: There is a restaurant, a popular bar, and a disco called Sans Souci.

Services: Baby-sitting, room service.

Facilities: Sauna, whirlpool.

MODERATE

HOTEL ALLALIN, CH-3906 Saas-Fee. Tel. 028/57-18-15. Fax 028/57-31-15. 40 rms (all with bath). TV TEL
$ Rates (including half board): 133F ($97.10) single; 246F ($179.55) double. AE, DC, MC, V. **Closed:** May and Oct–Nov.
This modern three-star hotel has a warm ambience, created by the old timber and hand-carved furniture and the hospitality of the three Zurbriggen brothers. The rooms contain a sitting area and a balcony, with views of the mountains and glaciers. Facilities include a Jacuzzi and sauna. There is laundry and room service. The restaurant offers a varied cuisine; there's also a bar.

HOTEL BRITANNIA, CH-3906 Saas-Fee. Tel. 028/57-16-16. 32 rms (all with bath). TV TEL
$ Rates (including half board): 82F–93F ($59.85–$67.90) single; 164F–192F ($119.70–$140.15) double. AE, DC, MC, V.
Situated on a hill in the center of the village, this six-story chalet offers especially good views of the mountains. Most of the rooms have balconies, with eastern or southern exposure. The rooms have brightly colored furniture. There is a concrete extension on the back.

HOTEL BURGENER, CH-3906 Saas-Fee. Tel. 028/57-15-22. Fax 028/57-28-88. 17 rms (all with bath). TV TEL
$ Rates (including half board): 82F–106F ($59.85–$77.35) single; 164F–212F ($119.70–$154.75) double. AE, DC, MC, V. **Closed:** Nov.
Ⓢ This chalet with yellow trim is near the ski lifts. Rustic, even by alpine standards, it's owned by the Burgener family. Its rooms are snug and comfortable. Some units have TV. Next door, Ski-Hütte is a popular terrace restaurant.

HOTEL DES ALPES, CH-3906 Saas-Fee. Tel. 028/57-15-95. 45 rms (32 with bath). TEL
$ Rates (including continental breakfast): 55F ($40.15) single without bath, 62F ($45.25) single with bath; 104F ($75.90) double without bath, 120F ($87.60) double with bath. AE, DC, MC, V.
This is a rambling, chalet-inspired hotel composed of a pair of wings sheathed, respectively, in weathered wood and white-painted stucco. Alpine balconies surround the construction on several tiers. The decor inside is informal, with the kind of sturdy furniture that many generations of visitors have found difficult to demolish. The hotel is not particularly stylish, but the bedrooms are comfortable. The Zurbriggen family are conscientious hosts. Only breakfast is served.

WHERE TO DINE

WALDHOTEL FLETSCHORN. Tel. 57-21-31.
Cuisine: SWISS. **Reservations:** Required.
$ **Prices:** Appetizers 15F–22F ($10.95–$16.05); main courses 25F–38F ($18.25–$27.75); fixed-price meal 85F–110F ($62.05–$80.30). AE, DC, MC, V.
Open: Daily 7am–midnight. **Closed:** Late April to mid-June and mid-Oct to mid-Dec.

The best food at the resort is served at this handsome chalet north of the center of Saas-Fee, on the road to Wildi. Most diners walk here; the trip will take about 20 minutes on a well-marked footpath and improve your appetite in the process. Irma and Jorge Dütsch-Grandjean are the finest chefs in the region. Appetizers include cream of snail soup, frogs' legs in puff pastry, and fresh duck liver with endive prepared in the style of cuisine moderne. For a main course, I recommend filet of red snapper grilled with walnuts, marinated rack of lamb, escalope of salmon à la crème de ciboulette, or flambéed beef. Consommé of quail is a seasonal dish. Regional dishes include veal.

EVENING ENTERTAINMENT

BEAU SITE, in the Hotel Beau Site. Tel. 57-11-22.
If you like a cozy bar on a cold winter's night, visit the rustic bar in this four-star hotel. The crowd is fun and convivial. In the winter there is sometimes live music. Drinks cost about 13F ($9.50).

SANS-SOUCI, in the Grand Hotel. Tel. 57-10-01.
A favorite place after dark features live entertainment and dance music. This rustic tavern, in a four-star hotel, packs in as many as 300 clients on a busy night. Call the hotel for details. Drinks run 13F ($9.50).

---

6. BRIG & THE SIMPLON PASS

119 miles E of Geneva, 119 miles S of Zurich

GETTING THERE   By Train   Trains arrive in Brig every hour during the day from Bern, Geneva, and Lausanne on their way to Italy.

By Bus   During the day, frequent buses arrive from Visp in the west and from a handful of mountain hamlets in the northeast.

By Car   To reach Brig, take E2 from Montreux on Lake Geneva, going via Sierre.

ESSENTIALS   The **Brig Tourist Information Office** is on Marktplatz (tel. 028/23-19-01); its hours are Monday through Friday from 8:30am to noon and 2 to 6pm, and on Saturday from 8:30am to noon. The **telephone area code** for Brig and the Simplon area is 028.

Since the Middle Ages, Brig has been a strategic stopover for international visitors. Located south of the Rhône River, this capital of the Upper Valais region is the starting point of the historic road over the Simplon Pass. Traveled by merchants for centuries, and improved and enlarged by Napoleon for his anticipated conquests of Italy, the road is still the shortest above-ground route between the Valais and the Ticino. In fair weather, the barren heights of the pass offer one of the most stunning views in Europe. Because of the route's many tricky curves and steep drop-offs at many points, motorists should take special caution. After snowfalls in the winter, the pass is closed; at such times, cars can be carried by rail through the rock-ringed confines of the Simplon Tunnel.

Measuring 12 miles in length, the ○ **Simplon Tunnel** is the longest in the world. Work began on the first of its twin tunnels at the turn of the century. Today a double tunnel ferries huge numbers of cars and trucks on one of the most important north-south traffic arteries of Europe. Unlike other famous tunnels of Switzerland, the Simplon Tunnel was designed only for railway travel. Cars, trucks, and buses are driven onto the flatbeds of railway cars and then are hauled by locomotives the length of the pass. Brig is the northern terminus of the tunnel. One-way passage through the tunnel between Brig and Iselle, across the border in Italy, costs 24F ($17.50).

Northwest of Brig, another famous tunnel, the **Lötschberg Tunnel** (whose northern and southern termini are Kandersteg and Goppenstein, respectively) connects Brig to the Bernese Oberland and Bern and from there to the rest of Northern Europe. Trains leave Brig in both directions every hour until 8pm.

WHAT TO SEE & DO

In its heyday, **Stockalperschloss (Stockalper's Castle),** on the road to the Simplon Pass (tel. 23-38-18), was the largest private residence in Switzerland. It was built between 1658 and 1678 by Kasper von Stockalper, who grew rich from his control of traffic over the Simplon Pass. Although he was eventually driven from his home by irate citizens of the Valais, he eventually returned from exile to die here, perhaps with memories of when he'd been welcomed into some of the royal courts of Europe. The manor was designed with four floors and a monumental gateway. The three towers with their bulbous onion-shaped domes each symbolize one of the Wise Men. The city of Brig has owned the manor since 1948 and now maintains it as a museum and as an administrative headquarters for the city's government. Guided tours are conducted May through October, Tuesday through Sunday from 9 to 11am and 2 to 5pm. Admission is 4F ($2.90).

WHERE TO STAY

HOTEL RESTAURANT VICTORIA, Bahnhofstrasse 2, CH-3900 Brig. Tel. 028/23-15-03. Fax 028/24-21-69. 40 rms (all with bath). MINIBAR TV TEL
$ Rates (including continental breakfast): 90F–105F ($65.70–$76.65) single; 150F–160F ($109.50–$116.80) double. AE, DC, MC, V.

Because of its location opposite the railroad station, this is a convenient stopping point if you've missed the last train to Kandersteg or to Italy. Built in the 19th century, with a modern extension added on later, the hotel has comfortably furnished bedrooms with modern furniture. Its French restaurant serves a first-class cuisine, with many specialties of the Valais along with some international dishes. There is also a snack bar, as well as a large terrace. Laundry facilities are provided, as is room service.

SCHLOSSHOTEL GARNI, route Simplon Pass, CH-3900 Brig. Tel. 028/ 23-64-55. Fax 028/23-95-36. 36 rms (all with bath). TV TEL

$ Rates (including continental breakfast): 77F–100F ($56.20–$73) single; 120F– 155F ($87.60–$113.15) double. AE, DC, MC, V.

Travelers heading for the Simplon Pass often stay at this modern hotel at the foot of the château. The facade resembles a medieval fortress. The rooms are clean and comfortable. There is a playground out front. Breakfast is the only meal served.

WHERE TO DINE

RESTAURANT CHANNA, Furkastrasse 5. Tel. 23-65-56.
   Cuisine: SWISS. **Reservations:** Not needed.
$ Prices: Fixed-price meal 35F ($25.55). AE, DC, MC, V.
   Open: Lunch daily noon–2pm; dinner daily 6–9pm.
In warm weather, Peter Walch invites guests to dine on the terrace decorated with flowers. Specialties include green-pepper filet steak Madagascar, frogs' legs in the style of Provence, and veal kidneys flambé.

SCHLOSSKELLER, Alte Simplonstrasse 26. Tel. 23-33-52.
   Cuisine: SWISS. **Reservations:** Recommended.
$ Prices: Appetizers 10F–18F ($7.30–$13.15); main courses 20F–30F ($14.60– $21.90); fixed-price meal 28F ($20.45). AE, DC, MC, V.
   Open: Tues–Sun 8am–11pm. **Closed:** 3 weeks in Jan.

Filling meals are served in this historic building in the center of town. A typical meal includes a plate of air-dried alpine beef, followed by filets of fera with wild rice or filet of pork madeleine.

---

7. THE GRIMSEL PASS

From Innertkirchen to Gletsch, 19 miles

GETTING THERE   By Car   From Brig, continue east along Route 19 until you reach the pass; you approach the southern route to the pass via the hamlet of Gletsch. You can also drive down from the Bernese Oberland, beginning your approach to the pass at Innertkirchen.

ESSENTIALS   The **telephone area code** is 036. The **information office** is at Oberwald (tel. 036/53-12-12).

One of the great scenic roads of Switzerland, the Grimsel Pass runs along the border between the cantons of Bern and Valais. Travel through the pass if you're heading from the Valais back to the Bernese Oberland.

WHAT TO SEE & DO

One of the best views is of the **Gries Glacier** (also called the Lake of the Dead), a memorial to the soldiers killed in the battles between the French and the Austrians in 1799. You may also want to see the snowy summit of the **Galenstock,** as well as the **Furka Pass,** which heads toward Andermatt on the way to Lucerne and the heart of Switzerland.

In the vicinity of Gletsch, on the road to the Furka Pass, you can stop at the

Belvedere Hotel for a scenic vista and refreshment. From the hotel you can see the celebrated **Rhône Glacier,** where the Swiss have carved an ice grotto. The vista of the Bernese Alps and the Valais Alps is stunning.

WHERE TO STAY

HOTEL GRIMSELBLICK, CH-3861 Grimsel-Passhöhe. Tel. 036/73-11-26. Fax 036/67-45-60. 26 rms (18 with bath).

$ **Rates** (including continental breakfast): 43F ($31.40) single without bath, 55F ($40.15) single with bath; 75F ($54.75) double without bath, 94F ($68.60) double with bath. Half board 20F ($14.60) extra. AE, DC, MC, V. **Closed:** Nov–May.

Across the road from the still waters of Lake Grimselsee, this hotel is white with red shutters. The Gemmet family has an interest in rock crystal and offers simple but comfortable rooms. Parking is available.

CHAPTER 9

LAUSANNE &
LAKE GENEVA

- **WHAT'S SPECIAL ABOUT LAUSANNE & LAKE GENEVA**
1. **LAUSANNE**
2. **MORGES**
3. **NYON**
4. **VEVEY**
5. **MONTREUX**

For decades tourists have sought the scenic wonders of Lake Geneva (Lac Léman) in the southwestern corner of Switzerland. Native son Jean-Jacques Rousseau popularized the lake among the Romantics, and Lord Byron and Shelley both made pilgrimages here.

Formed by the Rhône, Lac Léman is the largest lake in central Europe. It consists of a Grand Lac to the east and a Petit Lac to the west, near Geneva (for a description of Geneva and its environs, see Chapter 10). The lake covers 225 square miles; more than half belongs to Switzerland, the rest to France. The French own most of the southern shore, except for Geneva in the west and the Valais in the east; the Swiss hold the entire northern shore, which forms a large arc. The water is limpid blue, except where the muddy Rhône empties into it.

Famous people who have chosen to live on the lake's shores include historian Edward Gibbon; writers Honoré de Balzac, George Eliot, and André Gide; composers Richard Wagner and Franz Liszt; aviator Charles Lindbergh; and more recently, actors Charlie Chaplin, Yul Brynner, Audrey Hepburn, James Mason, Noël Coward, William Holden, David Niven, and Sophia Loren (many of whom went there for tax reasons).

Since 1823 the most popular way to tour the lake has been by steamer. Nearly all the cities, hamlets, and towns along the lake have schedules posted at the landing quays, and service is usually from Easter to October. If possible, though, tour by car or bus so that you can stop and visit the sights along the way. Railways also run along both shores. Our exploration will begin with Lausanne.

SEEING LAUSANNE & LAKE GENEVA

For many visitors, the gateway to both Lausanne and Lake Geneva is Geneva, because of its international airport. From Geneva, it's easy to reach all the major resorts along the lake, including Lausanne (Ouchy), Montreux, Nyon, and Vevey. You can go either by lake steamer or by rail (which is more efficient than bus connections). It's even better to rent a car in Geneva and drive along the lake.

IF YOU HAVE 4 DAYS

Days 1 and 2: Spend as much time as you can in Lausanne to visit its lake resort, Ouchy, and its Old Town.

Day 3: Head for an overnight stopover in Montreux to see the Château of Chillon. En route to Montreux, pay a morning visit to Vevey.

WHAT'S SPECIAL ABOUT LAUSANNE & LAKE GENEVA

Great Towns/Villages

☐ Lausanne, a cosmopolitan city on Lake Geneva, rising in tiers from the lake.

☐ Vevey, haunt of international celebrities, including the late Charles Chaplin.

☐ Montreux, the major resort on the Vaud Riviera, an Edwardian-looking town with a French accent.

Natural Attractions

☐ The Lavaux Corniche, or Corniche Vaudoise, a lakeside strip filled with villages, such as Chexbres, called the "balcony of Lake Geneva."

Religious Shrines

☐ The Cathedral of Lausanne, one of the finest medieval churches in Switzerland, begun in 1175.

Ancient Monuments

☐ The Roman villa of Pully, outside Lausanne, discovered in 1921, with the most important 1st-century mural north of the Alps.

Historic Castles

☐ Château of Chillon, outside Montreux, immortalized by Lord Byron in *The Prisoner of Chillon*.

☐ Castle of Nyon, at Nyon, an impressive stronghold of the counts of Savoy from the 13th century.

Day 4: Head northwest once again, by passing Lausanne this time, to visit some famous old towns west of the city, including Morges and Nyon. Stay overnight in Nyon or drive on to Geneva for the night.

---

1. LAUSANNE

38 miles NE of Geneva, 134 miles SW of Zurich

GETTING THERE By Plane Lausanne doesn't have an airport, so most visitors fly to Cointrin Airport in Geneva and then travel on to Lausanne.

By Train The train from Geneva leaves for Lausanne every 20 minutes and the trip takes 45 minutes.

By Lake Steamer Between late May and late September, a lake steamer cruises several times a day in both directions between Geneva and Saint-Gingolph. Lausanne, Vevey, Montreux, and Nyon are some of the cities serviced by this boat. Sailing time from Geneva is about 3½ hours.

By Car Lausanne is connected by motorway (E4) to Geneva. The Great Saint Bernard road tunnel is 70 miles to the southeast, reached along E2, which becomes E21 during its final approach.

Lausanne, whose 127,000 inhabitants make it the second-largest city on Lake Geneva and the fifth-largest city in Switzerland, is built on three hills overlooking the lake, called Lac Léman by the city's inhabitants. The upper and lower towns are connected by a small metro (subway).

Lausanne has been inhabited since the Stone Age. It was the ancient Roman town of Lousanna. In 1803 the canton of Vaud, of which Lausanne is the capital, became the 19th to join the Confederation.

For centuries Lausanne has been a favorite spot for exiles and expatriates, attracting, among others, deposed monarchs. Lausanne flourished particularly in the Age of Enlightenment, when it was associated with Rousseau and Voltaire, two of the leading writers in the 18th century. Even today the city is cited by many French-speaking Swiss as the place they would most like to live in, as it continues to exercise a potent attraction because of its low-key elegance and sense of grace.

ORIENTATION

ARRIVING   Most people arrive at the **Gare CFF** (Chemins de fer fédéraux), the Lausanne train station, at place de la Gare (tel. 342-11-11). Many hotels are located near the station; if yours isn't and you have heavy luggage, you'll find a line of taxis outside. If you're traveling light, a shuttle-bus service operates between the railroad station and the town center Monday through Saturday from 6:30am to 8:30pm; tickets cost 1F (75¢) and a book of 10 tickets is 8F ($5.85). For other public transportation, see "Getting Around," below.

INFORMATION   The major **Lausanne tourist office** is at 2, avenue de Rhodanie (tel. 617-73-21). There's also a tourist office in the main hall of the railroad station, place de la Gare.

CITY LAYOUT   Lausanne is spread out along the shore of Lake Geneva, surrounded by suburbs. Only two sections attract most visitors: the **Upper Town (Haute Ville),** which is the old part of the city, and the **Lower Town** (Basse Ville), or **Ouchy;** the two sections are connected by a small subway (métro).

   The Cité (Old Town)   Lausanne's old town still evokes the Middle Ages, as a nightwatchman calls the hours from 10pm to 2am from the top of the cathedral's belfry. A visit to the old town takes about 2 hours and is best done on foot. This area is north of the railroad station; you reach it by going along rue du Petit-Chêne. The focal point of the Cité, and the shopping and business heart of Lausanne, is **place Saint-François.** The Church of St. François, from the 13th century, is all that remains of an old Franciscan friary. Today the square is filled with office blocks and the main post office; regrettably, La Grotte, the villa with the terrace on which Edward Gibbon completed *The History of the Decline and Fall of the Roman Empire* in 1787, was torn down in 1896 to make room for the post office. While vehicles are permitted south of the church, the area to the north is reserved for pedestrians; it has more than 1¼ miles of streets, including **rue de Bourg,** northeast of the church, the best street for shopping. Rue de Bourg leads to the large, bustling **rue Caroline,** which winds north to **Pont Bessières,** one of the three bridges erected at the turn of the century to connect the three hills on which Lausanne was built. From the bridge, you will see the Cité (the old town) on your right, with the 13th-century **cathedral of Lausanne,** opening onto place de la Cathédrale. From the square, rue Cité de Vant goes north to the 14th-century Château Saint-Marie, on place du Château—once the home of bishops and now containing the offices of the canton administration.

   From here, **avenue de l'Université** leads to **place de la Riponne,** with the Palais de Rumine on its east side. From the square, rue Madeleine continues south to place de la Palud. From place de la Riponne, rue Pierre-Viret leads to the **Escaliers**

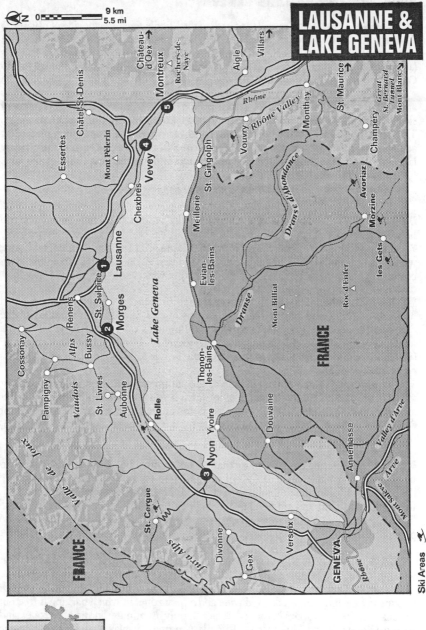

LAUSANNE & LAKE GENEVA

Château-
d'Oex
Rochers-de-
Naye
Montreux
Aigle
Villars ↑
St. Maurice ↑
5
Vouvry
Rhône
Rhône Valley
Monthey
St. Maurice
*Great
St. Bernard
Tunnel*
Champéry
Mont Blanc ↗
Châtel-St-Denis
Mont Pèlerin △
4 Vevey
Essertes
Chexbres
Avoriaz
Morzine
Veytaux
Drans d'Abondance
Lausanne
Meillerie
St. Gingolph
les Gets
1
St. Sulpice
Renens
Evian-
les-Bains
Lake Geneva
Roc d'Enfer △
Cossonay
Alps
Bussy
2 Morges
Dranse
Mont Billiat △
FRANCE
Pampigny
Vaudois
St. Livres
Aubonne
Rolle
Thonon-
les-Bains
Douvaine
Valley d'Arve
Nyon Yvoire
3
Annemasse
Vallée de Joux
St. Cergue
Versoix
Arve
FRANCE
Divonne
Gex
GENEVA
Jura Alps
Mont Salève
Rhône

Ski Areas 🎿

N
0 ▭▭▭ 9 km
5.5 mi

SWITZERLAND
★ **BERN**
Lausanne &
Lake Geneva

1 Lausanne
2 Morges
3 Nyon
4 Vevey
5 Montreux

du Marché, a covered stairway dating back to the Middle Ages. On the side of place de la Palud stands the 17th-century Hôtel de Ville (Town Hall).

South of place de la Palud is **rue du Pont,** which soon becomes rue Saint-François (after crossing rue Centrale). Nearby, at **place du Flon,** you can take the subway to Ouchy.

Ouchy Ouchy, once a sleepy fishing hamlet, is now the port and hotel resort area of Lausanne, opening onto Lake Geneva. The lakefront of Lausanne consists of shady quays and tropical plants, spread across a lakefront district of about half a mile. The Château d'Ouchy stands on **place de la Navigation;** from there, place Port adjoins immediately on the east. The **Quai de Belgique** and **Quai d'Ouchy** are lakefront promenades planted with greenery and offering the best views of the lake.

GETTING AROUND

BY SUBWAY To avoid the slow pace of the city's trams, take the subway. The trip between the heart of the old town and Ouchy takes 6 minutes. Departures are every 7½ minutes Monday through Friday from 6:15am to 11:45pm. During off-hours, weekends, and holidays, trains run every 15 minutes. A one-way ride from the town center to Ouchy costs 2F ($1.45); a book of 10 tickets is sold for 15F ($10.95).

BY BUS/TRAM The TL (Lausanne Public Transport Company) has a good network of trams and buses. The tram or bus fare is 2F ($1.45), regardless of the distance, for a single trip completed within 60 minutes on Lines 1 to 19 of the TL urban network and on the Lausanne–Ouchy métro. A book of 10 tickets costs 15F ($10.95). For short trips of up to four stops the fare is 1F (70¢); a book of 10 tickets costs 8.50F ($6.20).

You purchase or stamp your tickets at the automatic machines installed at most stops, or ask the driver. (A surcharge is collected if you get your ticket from the driver at a stop that has a machine.) A 1-day ticket for unlimited rides costs 5F ($3.65) for adults, 2.50F ($1.85) for children. The ticket for 3 consecutive days costs 12F ($8.75) for adults, 6F ($4.40) for children.

BY TAXI Lausanne contains more than 40 taxi stands, but if any stand happens to be empty, you can telephone 311-20-01 or 653-13-13 for a cab. The meter starts at 5F ($3.65); each 1 kilometer (.62 miles) traveled adds 2F ($1.45) in town (2.50F, or $1.85, from 10pm to 6am and on Sunday and holidays) and 3F ($2.20) outside the town limits. The first 22 pounds of luggage is free, with 1F (75¢) charged for every 66 pounds thereafter.

BY CAR If you drive to Lausanne or rent a car while there, you should know that wearing seatbelts is required, and that children under 12 are not allowed to ride in the front seat. In Lausanne, there are four types of parking zones: a white zone, in which parking is free and unlimited; a red zone and a blue zone, in which parking is free but variously limited (15 hours in the red zone and only 90 minutes in the blue zone); and a fourth zone with parking meters. To park, you must display a parking disk on the dashboard of your car; parking disks are free and can be obtained at police stations and automobile clubs.

BY BICYCLE You can rent bicycles at the baggage-forwarding counter of the railroad station (tel. 342-21-62). It's open Monday through Friday from 6:30am to 8:50pm and on Saturday and Sunday from 6:40am to 6:40pm.

BY BOAT   To rent boats or *pédalos* (pedal boats), try the ports at Ouchy and Parc Bourget at Vidy.

ON FOOT   This is the only way to see the old town effectively. Afterward, you can take the subway to Ouchy and resume your walk along the lakefront quays.

FAST FACTS

This is a quick reference guide to Lausanne. For more information, see "Fast Facts: Switzerland," in Chapter 2.

Area code   The telephone area code for Lausanne is 021.

Drugstores   The local newspapers publish lists of pharmacies.

Lost Property   The lost-property office is at 6, rue Saint-Laurent (tel. 319-60-58), open Monday through Friday from 7:30 to 11:45am and 1 to 5pm, and on Saturday from 7:30 to 11:30am.

Dentist/Doctor   For 24-hour medical and dental service, call the doctors' exchange at 652-99-32.

Post Office   The main office is at avenue de la Gare and place Saint-François (tel. 344-01-11). It's open Monday through Friday from 7:30am to noon and 1:30 to 6:30pm, and on Saturday from 7:30 to 11am. Telegrams and faxes can be sent from the telegraph office, place de la Gare and place Saint-François.

WHAT TO SEE

The **Cathedral of Lausanne,** place de la Cathédrale, is the focal point of the Cité and one of the finest medieval churches in Switzerland. North of the cathedral, at the end of the Cité, is the **Château Saint-Marie.** It was built of brick and stone in the 14th and early 15th centuries. Powerful bishops lived here until they were replaced by the Bernese bailiffs, who turned Lausanne into a virtual colony of Bern. Today the château is used for administrative offices of the canton.

In the center of town is **place de la Palud.** Located on the square is the Hôtel de Ville (Town Hall), which has a 17th-century Renaissance facade; it was completely restored in the late 1970s. Today it's the headquarters of the Communal Council. Guided tours are conducted Monday through Friday; call 43-22-55 to make an appointment. Also on the square is the **Fountain of Justice,** dating from 1726. A clock with animated historical scenes presents a drama daily every hour on the hour from 9am to 7pm. A traditional market is held here every Wednesday and Saturday. To visit the cathedral, take the **Escaliers du Marché,** a covered flight of medieval stairs on one side of the square.

North of place de la Palud is **place de la Riponne,** where you can visit the Italianate **Palais de Rumine,** built in 1906. It contains several museums, a university founded in 1537, and the university and cantonal library (with some 700,000 volumes).

On the east side of town, **Mon Repos Park** contains landscaped gardens and the **Empire Villa,** where Voltaire performed his work *Zaïre* for a group of friends. The **Tribunal Fédéral** is in the northern area of the park; it was constructed in the 1920s and today houses Switzerland's highest court.

To the north, the **Signal de Sauvabelin** (known popularly as *le signal*) rises above the town. At 2,125 feet, it has a restaurant and a belvedere opening onto Lake Geneva, with the Fribourg Alps in the distance. It's a 20-minute hike from town.

Ouchy is the lakeside resort and bustling port of Lausanne. Its tree-shaded quays have flower gardens that are nearly a half mile long. The small harbor contains a 700-boat marina, and the Savoy Alps are visible on the opposite shore. The **Château d'Ouchy** is now a hotel and restaurant. The Allies, Greece, and Turkey signed a peace treaty here in 1923. The 13th-century keep is still standing. In the Hôtel d'Angleterre (formerly the Auberge de l'Ancre), there's a plaque commemorating the stay of Lord Byron, who wrote *The Prisoner of Chillon* here. In the Beau-Rivage, the Treaty of Lausanne was ratified in 1923; it settled the final reparations disputes after World War I.

THE SIGHTS

CATHEDRAL OF LAUSANNE, place de la Cathédrale. Tel. 44-72-85.

One of the most beautiful Gothic structures in Europe, the cathedral stands 500 feet above Lake Geneva. Construction began in 1175; in 1275 the church was consecrated by Pope Gregory X. While in Lausanne, the pope met Rudolph of Hapsburg, emperor of Germany and of the Holy Roman Empire. The doors and facade of the cathedral are luxuriously ornamented with sculptures and bas-reliefs. The architect Eugène Viollet-le-Duc began a restoration of the cathedral in the 19th century—it's still going on! The interior is relatively austere except for some 13th-century choir stalls; the beautiful rose window also dates from the 13th century. The cathedral has two towers; you can climb 225-odd steps to the observation deck of one of the towers.

Admission: Cathedral, free; tower, 2F ($1.45).

Open: Apr–Sept, Mon–Fri 7am–7pm, Sat 8am–7pm, Sun 2–7pm; Oct–Mar, Mon–Fri 7am–5:30pm, Sat 8am–5:30pm, Sun 2–5:30pm. Visits not permitted Sun morning during services. **Bus:** 7 or 16.

ANCIEN-EVECHE, 4, place de la Cathédrale. Tel. 312-13-68.

A bishop's palace until the early 15th century, the Ancien-Evêché has a 13th-century fortified tower and a collection of icons as well as historical studies of Old Lausanne. You can see a 250-square-foot scale model depicting the old city as it was in the 17th century.

Admission: 4F ($2.90).

Open: Mid-March to mid-Sept, Tues–Sun 10am–6pm. **Closed:** Mid-Sept to mid-Mar. **Bus:** 7 or 16.

MUSEE CANTONAL DES BEAUX-ARTS [Cantonal Museum of Fine Arts], 6, place de la Riponne. Tel. 312-83-32.

The chief city museum is devoted to the works of 19th-century artists who painted in western Switzerland, but it also has an impressive collection of French paintings, including works by Degas, Renoir, Bonnard, Matisse, and Utrillo. This complex also houses the Geological Museum, the Museum of Paleontology, the Archeological and Historical Museum, and the Zoological Museum.

Admission: Permanent collection, free; temporary exhibitions 3F–5F ($2.20–$3.65).

Open: Tues–Wed 11am–6pm, Thurs 11am–8pm, Fri–Sun 11am–5pm. **Bus:** 16.

CHATEAU DE BEAULIEU AND MUSEE DE L'ART BRUT [Museum of the Maladjusted], 11, av. des Bergières. Tel. 37-54-35.

Located on the northwestern side of town, the château dates from 1756. In the

west wing is a museum containing a curious mélange of artworks collected by the famous painter Jean Dubuffet. The paintings and sculptures are the work of prisoners, the mentally ill, and the criminally insane.
Admission: 5F ($3.65).
Open: Museum, Tues–Sun 2–6pm. **Bus:** 16.

PULLY ROMAN VILLA MUSEUM, place du Prieure. Tel. 28-33-04.

First discovered in 1921, this Roman villa has been restored and is open to the public. It has a double apse and a 215-square-foot fresco—the most important 1st-century mural north of the Alps. The museum shows a reconstruction of the ruins and a display of the artifacts found during excavation.
Admission: Free.
Open: Apr to late Oct, Tues–Sun 2–5pm; late Oct to Mar, Sat–Sun 2–5pm. **Bus:** 4.

MUSEE D'ART CONTEMPORAIN FONDATION ASHER-EDELMAN, 85 av. du Général-Guisan. Tel. 312-48-49.

This museum is located in the village of Pully, on the shore of Lake Geneva. It is the only contemporary art museum in French-speaking Switzerland. With some 500 pieces of art, its main focus is on American art since 1945, with two to four shows per year. The facilities include a library (visited by appointment only), a café, a bookstore, and a gift shop.
Admission: 12F ($8.75).
Open: Sat–Thurs 10am–6pm, Fri 10am–8pm. **Bus:** 8 to the Verney stop.

AN ORGANIZED TOUR

The best way to get acquainted with the city is to take the Lausanne City Tour in summer. The tour includes a visit to the old city and a drive through the surrounding vineyards. The tour departs on Tuesday, Wednesday, Friday, and Sunday at 10am from the front of the tourist office at 2, avenue de Rhodanie (tel. 617-73-21). It lasts 3 hours. Tickets cost 30F ($21.90) for adults and 15F ($10.95) for children, and can be purchased at major hotels as well as at the tourist office at the main train station. I recommend that you call the tourist office to make a reservation.

SPORTS & RECREATION

Lausanne is the home of the International Olympic Committee. The city offers first-rate sports facilities, as well as lake sports including swimming, rowing, yachting, waterskiing, and windsurfing. Summer sports include tennis, golf, bicycling, horseback riding, and hiking. For more information, call the **Service des Sports** of the commune of Lausanne (tel. 43-42-91).

Curling Five curling areas are available at **Winter Ouchy Curling** link, La Nautique building, Ouchy (tel. 617-60-31). The rink is open from mid-September to March.

Golf There is an 18-hole golf course at En Marin (tel. 784-13-16), above Lausanne at 2,800 feet. It's open from April to November.

Horseback Riding **Chalet-à-Globet Equestrian Centre** (tel. 784-14-34) has a jumping paddock and other facilities.

Skating In the winter you can skate at the **Montchiosi open-air rink**, 30, avenue de Servan (tel. 26-10-62), and **La Pontaise open-air rink,** 11, Plaines-du-Loup (tel. 36-81-63). Both are open from October to March. **Intercommunal Ice-Skating Center,** at Malley, 14, chemin du Viaduc (tel. 24-21-22), has one indoor and two outdoor rinks. It's open from October to mid-March.

Skiing The **Swiss Ski School of Lausanne** offers floodlit cross-country ski tracks at Chalet-à-Gobet above Lausanne. It's open daily from 9am until 10pm. There is a small ski lift for children open on Wednesday afternoon, Saturday, and Sunday. To schedule a lesson in alpine skiing or cross-country skiing, call 26-55-65.

In the summer, you can ski on the glacier of Les Diablerets (9,840 ft.), 38 miles southeast of Lausanne.

Swimming The indoor pool at **Mon Repos** 4, avenue du Tribunal-Fédéral (tel. 23-45-66), is open from mid-August to mid-July, but the lawn solarium is open year round. **Bellerive Beach and Pool,** 23, avenue de Rhodanie (tel. 617-81-31), and **Montchoisi Pool,** 30, avenue du Servan (tel. 26-10-62), are open from May to September. There's a free public beach at Vidy, **La Voile d'Or beach** (tel. 617-80-11).

Tennis The **Lausanne Tennis Association** has six indoor hard courts at Vidy at the Clubhouse Stade-Lausanne (tel. 691-99-91). The **Montchoisi Tennis Club,** 15, avenue de l'Elysée (tel. 26-36-25), offers six hard courts and two with "greenset" synthetic surfaces, open from April to mid-November.

Waterskiing Skiers are attracted to the stretch of water at the Ouchy promenade (near the Tour Haldimand). For weather information, call 28-94-91.

WHERE TO STAY

The luxury and elegance of the top hotels in Lausanne have made the city a favorite destination of the wealthy. In the summer space is tight, so try to get a reservation. Many of the better hotels are also booked solid by visitors attending trade fairs and conventions. (The International Tourism Fair is in March.) The tourist office can help you find a hotel. If you want to stay directly on the lake, I recommend a hotel in Ouchy.

VERY EXPENSIVE

BEAU-RIVAGE PALACE, 18, place du Général-Guisan, CH-1006 Lausanne-Ouchy. Tel. 021/617-17-17. Fax 021/617-78-78. 204 rms, 12 suites. MINIBAR TV TEL **Métro:** Ouchy

$ Rates: 205F–300F ($149.65–$219.00) single; 295F–420F ($215.30–$306.55) double; 510F ($394.15) junior suite for two. AE, DC, MC, V.

One of the leading hotels in the world, the Beau-Rivage is surrounded by 10 acres of the most exquisitely maintained gardens in Lausanne, with cedars, begonias, and sculptures. Built in 1908, the huge, elaborately detailed building has a mansard roof, tall French windows, and miles of wrought-iron balconies. The rotunda is a mammoth rococo room with columns, statues of heroic deities, and a series of illuminations worthy of Vienna at its peak. The hotel is the last bastion of formal Europe and attracts both aristocrats and *la grande bourgeoisie* from throughout Europe (so dress appropriately).

Accommodations are beautifully furnished and decorated. Amenities include a radio and refrigerator; some rooms have a safety-deposit box. About half the rooms have a private terrace or balcony. Eight suites and junior suites have a Jacuzzi.

Dining/Entertainment: One of the hotel's restaurants, La Terrasse-Rotonde, offers a panoramic view of the lake and mountains; it's open all day. The Café Beau-Rivage is a Parisian-style brasserie under the hotel arcades facing the quay, offering regional dishes and seasonal specialties. There are also several bars, including Le Bar Anglais, with a piano player, and the Café Beau-Rivage Bar, with musical entertainment. The hotel's nightclub consists of both a music bar and a disco.

Services: Room service, laundry service, baby-sitting.

Facilities: Indoor and outdoor pools, tennis courts, jogging path, sporting club.

LAUSANNE PALACE, 7-9, Grand-Chêne, CH-1002 Lausanne. Tel. 021/ 20-37-11, or toll free 800/637-94-77 in North America. Fax 021/23-25-71. 163 rms, 13 suites. MINIBAR TV TEL **Bus:** 7 or 16.

$ **Rates:** 200F–270F ($146–$197.05) single; 250F–380F ($182.50–$277.36) double; from 600F ($437.95) suite. Breakfast 18F ($13.15) extra. AE, DC, MC, V. **Parking:** 25F ($18.25).

⭐ The "Palace" is as grand and elegant a hotel as you'll find anywhere in Europe. The columns, plaster details, and marble floors date from the 19th century; the public rooms are decorated with tapestries, crystal chandeliers, and gilded rococo furniture. The hotel, in the center of Lausanne, offers a good view of the mountains and the lake.

Dining/Entertainment: There is a bar with richly oiled woodwork. The hotel restaurant serves Swiss and French dishes.

Services: Limousine service, room service, laundry service.

Facilities: Health club, business center, private garden.

EXPENSIVE

HOTEL DE LA PAIX, 5, av. Benjamin-Constant, CH-1002 Lausanne. Tel. 021/20-71-71. Fax 021/23-02-07. 188 rms (all with bath). TV TEL **Bus:** 18, 19, or 27.

$ **Rates** (including continental breakfast): 145F–185F ($105.85–$135.05) single; 200F–280F ($146–$204.35) double. AE, DC, MC, V.

This large, 19th-century hotel has rows of elaborate balconies and loggias, many with wrought-iron details. On the south side, awnings provide shade in the summer. Many of the rooms overlook the lake. The hotel has a restaurant and bar.

HOTEL LA RESIDENCE, 15, place du Port, CH-1006 Lausanne-Ouchy. Tel. 021/617-77-11. Fax 021/617-06-67. 82 rms (all with bath). MINIBAR TV TEL **Métro:** Ouchy.

$ **Rates** (including continental breakfast): 145F–185F ($105.85–$135.05) single; 200F–280F ($146–$204.35) double. AE, DC, MC, V.

This lakefront hotel consists of several Regency buildings separated by flowered walkways. The lobby has a floor made of black and white, diamond-shaped slabs of stone, a massive fireplace, and a beamed ceiling. This building was once an annex of the neighboring Beau-Rivage, and before that it was an offshoot of the town hall. Two of the other buildings were once private villas.

LE CHATEAU D'OUCHY, 2, place du Port, CH-1006 Lausanne-Ouchy. Tel. 021/26-74-51. Fax 021/617-51-37. 43 rms (all with bath). MINIBAR TV TEL **Métro:** Ouchy.

$ **Rates** (including continental breakfast): 120F–160F ($87.60–$116.80) single; 170F–380F ($124.10–$277.35) double. AE, DC, MC, V.

This hotel offers a complete retrospective of pre-20th-century architecture. A fortified tower with a black- and red-tile roof is surrounded by wings, dungeons, Renaissance-style gables, and Romanesque arches—all marvelously crafted from gray stone. The oldest parts date from the 12th century, and the renovated bedrooms include Louis XIII–style furniture. The public rooms are also impressive.

Dining/Entertainment: The nightclub is one of the most popular in town. Guests can dine in the hotel's French restaurant, Swiss tavern, or grillroom.

Services: Laundry service, baby-sitting, room service, car-rental service (at reception).

Facilities: Snack terrace on the lake seating 200, garden, public swimming pool near the hotel.

ROYAL SAVOY, 40, av. d'Ouchy, CH-1000 Lausanne. Tel. 021/26-42-01.
Fax 021/26-46-95. 168 rms (all with bath). MINIBAR TV TEL **Métro:** Ouchy

$ **Rates** (including continental breakfast): 150F–200F ($109.50–$146) single; 220F–280F ($160.60–$204.40) double. Half board 40F ($29.20) extra. AE, DC, MC, V.

The former residence of the Spanish royal family, the hotel is in a park with towering trees. The château has a mansard roof, turrets with round pointed roofs, and gracefully arched windows with balconies. The spacious rooms have Oriental rugs and reproductions of antiques.

Dining/Entertainment: There are several restaurants and a bar—all with good service and elegant decor. The Savoy Restaurant offers traditional, gourmet food. The Jardin d'Hiver offers seasonal specialties in a garden setting.

Services: Room service, baby-sitting, laundry.

Facilities: Swimming pool.

MODERATE

HOTEL AGORA, 9, av. Rond-Point, CH-1006 Lausanne. Tel. 021/617-12-11. Fax 021/26-26-05. 158 rms (all with bath) A/C MINIBAR TV TEL **Bus:** 1, 3, or 5.

$ **Rates** (including buffet breakfast): 130F–180F ($94.90–$131.40) single; 190F–260F ($138.70–$189.75) double. AE, DC, MC, V. **Parking:** Free.

Set only 300 yards from the railroad station, this is a four-star hotel that opened in 1986 after a total renovation of an older hotel set on the site. Bedrooms are comfortable and contain modern furniture; amenities include satellite TV reception, hairdryer, radio, soundproof windows, and a safe (if you request one).

Dining/Entertainment: The luxury restaurant serves French cuisine, and the hotel has a bar.

Services: Room service, baby-sitting.

Facilities: Meeting rooms.

HOTEL ALPHA, 34, Petit-Chêne, CH-1003 Lausanne. Tel. 021/23-01-31. Fax 021/23-01-45. 220 rms (all with bath). A/C MINIBAR TV TEL

$ **Rates** (including buffet breakfast): 130F–180F ($94.90–$131.40) single; 190F–260F ($138.70–$189.75) double. AE, DC, MC, V.

This hotel belongs to the Fassbind chain, which also operates hotels in Geneva and Lugano. The hotel in Lausanne, just 200 yards from the train station, was opened in 1970 and was renovated in 1984. The rooms have soundproof windows, hairdryers, videos, and radios, and the hotel has a fire-prevention system. It also has a good restaurant and bar.

HOTEL CARLTON, 4, av. de Cour, CH-1000 Lausanne. Tel. 021/26-32-35. Fax 021/26-34-30. 50 rms (all with bath). MINIBAR TV TEL **Bus:** 5.

$ **Rates** (including buffet breakfast): 130F–175F ($94.90–$127.25) single; 190F–260F ($138.70–$189.75) double. Half board 40F ($29.20) extra. AE, DC, MC, V.

In the summer, awnings decorate the arched windows of this white Mediterranean-style villa with a red-tile roof, located in a park near the lake. André Chollet is the manager. The garden restaurant is popular in the summer and offers quality cuisine. Snacks are served in the Carlton's bar and cafeteria.

CONTINENTAL HOTEL, 2, place de la Gare, CH-1001 Lausanne. Tel. 021/20-15-51. Fax 021/23-76-79. 162 rms (all with bath). MINIBAR TV TEL **Bus:** 1, 3, or 5.
$ **Rates** (including continental breakfast): 120F–170F ($87.60–$124.05) single; 170F–250F ($124.05–$182.50) double. AE, DC, MC, V.
This glass-and-concrete hotel is located downtown, near the train station. The glossy lobby has a black trim and metal ceiling. The rooms are equipped with radios and other amenities.

The formal restaurant, Le Beaujolais, is one of the finest rôtisseries in the city and specializes in rack of lamb with Provençal herbs, lobster in season, salmon trout with sorrel, bouillabaisse Marseilles style, and sea bass flambé with fennel. A la carte meals begin at 75F ($54.75). The restaurant is open daily from 11:30am to 3pm and 6:30pm to midnight.

HOTEL DE LA NAVIGATION, place Navigation, CH-1006 Lausanne-Ouchy. Tel. 021/26-20-41. Fax 021/26-70-80. 38 rms (all with bath). MINIBAR TV TEL **Métro:** Ouchy.
$ **Rates** (including continental breakfast): 120F–170F ($87.60–$124.10) single; 170F–220F ($124.10–$160.60) double. AE, DC, MC, V.
Crowds of local residents enjoy the view of the sailboat port from the covered terrace of this gray hotel with a flat roof. The interior is attractively lit and furnished. The comfortably furnished bedrooms include a radio and other amenities (all with bath).

INEXPENSIVE

HOTEL ALAGARE, 14, rue du Simplon, CH-1006 Lausanne. Tel. 021/617-92-52. Fax 021/617-92-55. 79 rms (all with shower or bath). TV TEL **Bus:** 1, 3, or 5.
$ **Rates** (including continental breakfast): 95F–140F ($69.35–$102.20) single; 140F–210F ($102.20–$153.30) double. Children under 14 stay free with their parents. AE, DC, MC, V.
Ⓢ In the summer flowers bloom in the window boxes of this three-star stucco hotel a block from the train station. The interior has pine paneling stained in several different tones. There is a rustic restaurant, where local residents go for raclette and specialties of the Vaud.

HOTEL AULAC, 4, place de la Navigation, CH-1006 Lausanne-Ouchy. Tel. 021/617-14-51. Fax 021/617-11-30. 149 rms (all with bath). A/C MINIBAR TV TEL **Métro:** Ouchy
$ **Rates** (including continental breakfast): 100F–140F ($73–$102.20) single; 140F–200F ($102.20–$146) double. No credit cards.
This lakefront hotel has a baroque yellow facade with white trim and a three-story Renaissance porch flanked by two elaborate columns. The mansard roof is inlaid with tiles in a geometric design and topped with a tall Victorian clock tower. Sailboats bob in the lake nearby. The rooms are well maintained, simply furnished, and spacious.

HOTEL CITY, 5, rue Caroline, CH-1007 Lausanne. Tel. 021/20-21-41. Fax 021/20-21-49. 92 rms (all with shower or bath). MINIBAR TV TEL **Bus:** 7 or 16.
$ **Rates** (including buffet breakfast): 90F–135F ($65.70–$98.55) single; 140F–200F ($102.20–$146) double. AE, DC, MC, V.

For comfort with few frills, try this centrally located hotel just outside the old town. It's near the indoor swimming pool and parking lot of Mon Repos. The rooms are soundproof and include videos in four languages as well as radios. The hotel has a fire-prevention system.

HOTEL CRYSTAL, 5, rue Chaucrau, CH-1003 Lausanne. Tel. 021/20-28-31. Fax 021/20-04-46. 40 rms (all with bath). TV TEL **Bus:** 7 or 16.

$ Rates (including continental breakfast): 95F–140F ($69.35–$102.20) single; 140F–210F ($102.20–$153.30) double. AE, DC, MC, V.

This downtown hotel curves along a pedestrian walkway lined with shops. The public rooms resemble a private home. The Fiora family offers pleasantly furnished rooms with a radio and other amenities. The bar is open 24 hours.

HOTEL D'ANGLETERRE, 9, place du Port, CH-1006 Lausanne-Ouchy. Tel. 021/26-41-45. Fax 021/26-80-75. 38 rms (24 with bath). TV TEL **Métro:** Ouchy.

$ Rates (including continental breakfast): 65F ($47.45) single without bath, 110F ($80.30) single with bath; 100F ($73) double without bath, 155F ($113.15) double with bath. AE, DC, MC, V.

This four-story, 19th-century hotel is directly on the lake, and its view extends across the water to the mountains on the other side. The pleasantly furnished rooms are clean and comfortable; the cheapest units have sinks and no bath. There is a café on the ground floor.

HOTEL ELITE, 1, av. Sainte-Luce, CH-1003 Lausanne. Tel. 021/20-23-61. Fax 021/20-39-63. 42 rms (all with shower or bath). TEL **Bus:** 1, 3, or 5.

$ Rates (including continental breakfast): 95F–140F ($69.35–$102.20) single; 140F–210F ($102.20–$153.28) double. AE, DC, MC, V.

The large illuminated sign on the front lawn obscures the neoclassical details of this white five-story hotel with balconies and a flat roof. M. Zufferey offers comfortable rooms.

HOTEL JAN, 8, av. de Beaulieu, CH-1004 Lausanne. Tel. 021/36-11-61. Fax 021/36-69-25. 92 rms (all with bath). TV TEL **Bus:** 15.

$ Rates (including continental breakfast): 100F–150F ($73–$109.50) single; 160F–220F ($116.80–$160.60) double. AE, DC, MC, V.

This massive, concrete-and-glass hotel is slightly west of center, near the Palais de Beaulieu, where international congresses and sports events take place. The rooms are spacious and clean, with comfortable, slightly dated furniture. The hotel offers a restaurant and bar.

WHERE TO DINE

Lausanne offers a large range of restaurants, where you can find the specialties of Switzerland and the Vaud, as well as those of France, Greece, Italy, and China. Typical Swiss food is served in the old town.

Try the Geneva lake fish, omble chevalier. Trout and perch from the lake are also popular; in autumn many restaurants feature game dishes.

VERY EXPENSIVE

GIRARDET, in the Hôtel de Ville, 1, rue d'Yverdon, Crissier. Tel. 634-05-05.

Cuisine: SWISS. **Reservations:** Required 3 months in advance; 2 weeks in advance for lunch Mon–Fri; 2 months in advance for lunch Sat.

$ Prices: Appetizers 25F–52F ($18.25–$37.95); main courses 28F–98F ($20.45–

$71.55); fixed-price meals from 150F ($109.50). No credit cards.
Open: Lunch Tues–Sat noon–2pm; dinner Tues–Sat 7pm–midnight. **Closed:** 3 weeks in July or Aug and 3 weeks in Dec or Jan.

★ Some critics say that Alfred Girardet (often known as Frédy) is the world's greatest chef. Certainly he's on every serious gourmet's gastronomic tour of Europe. His restaurant is located in a modest building erected in 1929 as the Crissier town hall, near Lausanne. Many devotees regularly travel the 38 miles from Geneva.

Assisted by a brigade of talented sous-chefs, Girardet prepares a delectable cuisine moderne, some of which is inspired by recipes from his grandmother's favorite collection. Only fresh ingredients are used—shipments of fresh fish arrive daily; the menu changes with the season. Specialties include a ragoût of fresh quail with young vegetables, crayfish in caviar butter, and "wild" salmon steak with small turnips and a perfect chervil sauce. For dessert, try passion fruit soufflé or one of the spectacular ice creams.

EXPENSIVE

LA GRAPPE D'OR, 3, rue Cheneau-de-Bourg. Tel. 23-07-60.
  Cuisine: SWISS. **Reservations:** Required. **Bus:** 7 or 16.
$ **Prices:** Appetizers 15F–22F ($10.95–$16.95); main courses 22F–42F ($16.05–$30.65); fixed-price meals 55F ($40.15) at lunch, 89F–125F ($64.95–$91.25) at dinner. AE, MC, V.
  Open: Lunch Mon–Fri noon–2:15pm; dinner Mon–Sat 7–10pm.
Excellent food is served in the luxurious atmosphere of this rôtisserie, a favorite among wealthy locals. The seafood menu includes scampi, red mullet, sea bass, and fennel. You can also order excellent meat dishes and roebuck in season. The restaurant is set in the heart of the old city.

RESTAURANT L'AGORA, in the Hôtel Agora, 9 av. du Rond-Point. Tel. 617-12-11.
  Cuisine: SWISS/FRENCH. **Reservations:** Required. **Bus:** 1, 3, or 5.
$ **Prices:** Appetizers 18F–30F ($13.15–$21.90); main courses 32F–45F ($23.35–$32.85); fixed-price meals 55F–120F ($40.15–$87.60). AE, DC, MC, V.
  Open: Lunch Mon–Fri noon–2pm; dinner Mon–Sat 7–11pm. **Closed:** Mid-July to mid-Aug.

★ The proprietor, Georges Fassbind, and his chef, Pascal Santailler—a student of famous French chef Georges Bardet—prepare specialties of France and the Vaud at this restaurant, one of the best in Lausanne. Specialties include terrine of goose liver, halibut with curry sauce, baked lobster with a concentrated essence of vintage wine, and Bresse chicken with a cabbage and mushroom-cream sauce. For dessert, try the fresh figs with vanilla ice cream. A fixed-price menu du marché includes an *amuse bouche* and four courses.

RESTAURANT SAN MARINO, 20 av. de la Gare. Tel. 312-93-69.
  Cuisine: TUSCAN. **Reservations:** Required. **Bus:** 1, 3, or 5.
$ **Prices:** Appetizers 15F–22F ($10.95–$16.05); main courses 22F–38F ($16.05–$27.75); fixed-price meals 55F–80F ($40.15–$58.40). AE, MC.
  Open: Lunch Mon–Fri 11:30am–2:15pm; dinner Sun–Fri 6:30–10:15pm. **Closed:** Last 2 weeks of July.
What is said to be the finest and most formal Italian restaurant in the city has an elegant Venetian decor and an experienced team of chefs and attendants. Dishes are made with fresh ingredients and are presented with flair. An unusual version of saltimbocca is made with seawolf and baby zucchini instead of veal and ham. Other

dishes, many derived from Tuscany, include braised quail with artichokes, a saffron-laden mélange of shellfish, and filet of poultry on a bed of braised leeks.

MODERATE

CAFE BEAU-RIVAGE, in the Beau-Rivage Palace, 18, place du Général-Guisan, Ouchy. Tel. 26-96-57.
  Cuisine: SWISS. **Reservations:** Recommended. **Métro:** Ouchy.
$ **Prices:** Appetizers 12F–20F ($8.75–$14.60); main courses 22F–35F ($16.05–$25.55). AE, DC, MC, V.
  Open: Daily 9am–1am; hot food served 11:45am–11:45pm.

Although its prices are within the median range, its grandeur and elegance help it to compete with the style of some of the most expensive restaurants in the city. The restaurant is in a lakeside pavilion. The dining room resembles a café in Paris, with mirrors, pillars, and bay windows. There's a flowery terrace. Typical dishes, made only with fresh ingredients, include steak tartare, marmite de pecheur, fricassée of chicken flavored with vinegar and tarragon, and tagliatelle with seafood. Sumptuous desserts can be ordered from the trolley. After 7:30pm the place becomes an enjoyable piano bar (see "Evening Entertainment," below).

CHURRASCO, 51, rue de Bourg. Tel. 23-14-23.
  Cuisine: ARGENTINIAN. **Reservations:** Recommended. **Bus:** 18, 19, or 27.
$ **Prices:** Appetizers 8F–18F ($5.85–$13.15); main courses 18F–40F ($13.15–$29.20). AE, DC, MC, V.
  Open: Daily 11:30am–11:30pm.

This Argentinian steakhouse is part of a chain that has opened branches in many different Swiss cities. The decor is South American and rustic, and waiters are dressed as gauchos. The menu includes sangría, gazpacho, and beefsteak grilled on a wood fire. You can select rumpsteak, entrecôte, or filet. For dessert, try tequila sherbet.

IL GROTTINO, 4, Grand-Chêne. Tel. 22-76-58.
  Cuisine: SWISS. **Reservations:** Not needed. **Bus:** 7 or 16.
$ **Prices:** Appetizers 4F–13F ($2.90–$9.50); main courses 21F–33F ($15.35–$24.10); pizza 10F–12F ($7.30–$8.75). No credit cards.
  Open: Lunch Mon–Fri 11:30am–2pm, Sat 11:30am–3pm; dinner Mon–Fri 6–10:30pm; bar open until midnight.

This pizzeria serves veal, fish, and beef dishes as well as pizza and pastas. For dessert, try the ice cream or one of the fruit dishes. The adjacent bar is called l'Escalier.

LA VOILE D'OR, 9, av. de Jacques-Delacroze, at Lausanne-Vidy. Tel. 617-80-11.
  Cuisine: SWISS. **Reservations:** Required.
$ **Prices:** Appetizers 15F–22F ($10.95–$16.05); main courses 18F–35F ($13.15–$25.55); fixed-price meals 40F–50F ($29.20–$36.50). DC, MC, V.
  Open: Lunch daily 11:30am–2pm; dinner daily 7–10pm.

The lakeside park surrounding this popular restaurant evokes scenes of the French Riviera. Park your car and follow the signs on foot for a few hundred feet through a forest of conifers. The place is especially busy on summer weekends, when many people come just for drinks. Specialties include entrecôte bordelaise, filets of perch from the lake, and wild game in season. After 11pm there's dancing on the terrace from May to September.

LE MANDARIN, 7, av. du Théâtre. Tel. 23-74-84.
  Cuisine: CHINESE. **Reservations:** Not needed. **Bus:** 7 or 16.

$ Prices: Appetizers 12F–20F ($8.75–$14.60); main courses 15F–32F ($10.95–$23.35); Canton menu 35F ($25.55); Shanghai menu 45F ($32.85); Beijing menu 55F ($40.15). DC, MC, V.
Open: Lunch Mon–Sat noon–2pm; dinner Mon–Sat 7–10pm.

One of the finest Chinese restaurants in Lausanne is located adjacent to place Saint-François under a market arcade. It offers dishes from the cuisines of both Canton and Beijing. Specialties include sautéed chicken with black mushrooms, beef Shanghai style, Mongolian shrimp, and sautéed fish with hot sauce. The "Emperor's Wedding" is an interesting noodle dish.

MANUEL, 5, place St-François. Tel. 23-17-64.
   Cuisine: SWISS/FRENCH. **Reservations:** Not needed. **Bus:** 7 or 16.
$ Prices: Appetizers 10F–25F ($7.30–$18.25); main courses 30F–42F ($21.90–$30.65); fixed-price meals 23F–27F ($16.80–$19.70). AE, DC, MC, V.
   Open: Mon–Sat 7:30am–7pm.

Located in an ornate building adjacent to the cathedral, this is one of the most famous pastry shops, tearooms, and daytime restaurants of Lausanne. An ultramodern pâtisserie sells take-away cakes, tarts, and chocolates on street level. Upstairs, in a fashionably decorated Louis XV–style tearoom, you can order light meals. These might include an array of fresh fish, tortellini with smoked salmon, cassolette of crayfish with herbs, or thinly sliced dried meat of the Grisons. An open-air terrace on the third floor offers additional warm-weather seating and a view of the square below.

INEXPENSIVE

BUFFET DE LA GARE CFF, 11, place de la Gare. Tel. 20-78-01.
   Cuisine: SWISS/FRENCH. **Reservations:** Recommended in the restaurant only. **Bus:** 1, 3, or 5.
$ Prices: Restaurant, appetizers 8F–24F ($5.85–$17.50); main dishes 30F–38F ($21.90–$27.75); fixed-price meals 27F ($19.70). Brasserie, appetizers 8F–17F ($5.85–$12.40); main dishes 20F–28F ($14.60–$20.45); plat du jour 19F ($13.85).
   Open: Restaurant, daily 6am–midnight; brasserie, daily 5am–1am.

The brasserie is larger and more bustling. The restaurant offers a secluded series of cubbyholes and nooks and more upscale service. Dishes available at both include vol-au-vent in the style of Toulouse, filets of sole "Uncle Charles," poached turbot in hollandaise sauce, and mignons of pork in cream sauce.

CAFE DU JORAT, 1, place de l'Ours. Tel. 20-22-61.
   Cuisine: SWISS. **Reservations:** Not needed. **Bus:** 7.
$ Prices: Appetizers 8F–12F ($5.85–$8.75); main courses 22F–35F ($16.05–$25.55); fondue 16F ($11.70) per person; fixed-price lunch 13F–16F ($9.50–$11.70). AE, DC, MC, V.
   Open: Mon–Sat 7am–midnight.

This local hangout is at a busy intersection in an obscure part of the city. It is nevertheless well known for its flavorful and unpretentious food. Six cheese and three meat fondues are offered, including fondue vigneronne (with red meat and bouillon made from red wine), fondue aux bolets (with meat and flap mushrooms), and fondue valaisanne (made with three different cheeses). The staff is polite, and the place has an honest, wholesome atmosphere.

PINTE BESSON, 4, rue d'Ale. Tel. 312-72-27.
   Cuisine: SWISS. **Reservations:** Not needed. **Bus:** 7 or 16.

$ Prices: Appetizers 8F–12F ($5.85–$8.75); main courses 14F–18F ($10.20–$13.15). No credit cards.
Open: Lunch Mon–Sat noon–2pm; dinner Mon–Fri 7–10:30pm; light meals Mon–Fri 7:30am–midnight, Sat 7:30am–7pm.

⑤ This tiny restaurant is only about 20 by 40 feet and has a smoke-stained vault of hand-chiseled masonry dating from 1780. It is celebrated in Lausanne for its fondues, but it also serves croûtes with fresh mushrooms or sausages, as well as dried alpine beef and, occasionally, horsesteak. There are sidewalk tables in the summer, and benches are placed outside in the sunshine.

SHOPPING

Lausanne offers the possibility of several interesting shopping adventures. Many first-class stores are found along rue St-François and rue de Bourg. In the center of town, several squares and shopping streets are for pedestrians only. Among the best buys are watches and jewelry, clothes, and leather goods. There are also the traditional Swiss souvenirs and chocolates.

ANTIQUES

LA VIEILLE FONTAINE ANTIQUITES, 9-13, rue Cheneau-de-Bourg. Tel. 23-47-87.
French furniture and art from the 18th century, Oriental sculpture, and Chinese and Japanese art are sold in a building with beautifully hand-painted beams and Oriental rugs. The showrooms are crowded, so be careful as you walk among these treasures.

BOOKS

PAYOT, 4, place Pepinet. Tel. 20-33-31.
The biggest (and some say the best) bookstore in Lausanne sells many English-language titles.

CRYSTAL

PAVILLON CHRISTOFLE, 10, rue de Bourg. Tel. 20-60-50.
This is the major outlet of Christofle crystal in the Lausanne region. The showroom's glass shelves are loaded with glittering objects. Open Tuesday through Saturday, and Monday in the afternoon.

FABRIC

LEINENWEBEREI LANGENTHAL, 8, rue de Bourg. Tel. 23-44-02.
Madame Lutz sells Swiss embroideries, Langenthal table linens, napkins, and crocheted potholders. The store also sells satin sheets and lace from St. Gallen.

INTERNATIONAL GOODS

MAGASIN CARDAS, 10, rue de Bourg. Tel. 312-55-60.

This unusual store has crosscut tree trunks inset in the white gravel floor, and skylights. Merchandise from 15 countries includes ceramics, sculpture, and textiles, many of them from Asia. There is a small café in the courtyard beside a modern fountain.

JEWELRY

BUCHERER, 5, place St-François. Tel. 20-63-54.
This is the biggest jeweler in Lausanne and has a well-established international reputation.

LEATHER

KOBA CUIR, 12, rue de la Madeleine. Tel. 23-89-80.
Leather goods from France, Germany, and Spain, as well as from Switzerland itself, are sold at Koba Cuir, one of the finest leather specialists in Lausanne. Merchandise includes shoes, pants, vests, coats, trinkets, and hats.

MEDICINE

PHARMACIE BULLET, 30, rue de Bourg. Tel. 22-86-82.
This centrally located pharmacy can suggest over-the-counter Swiss substitutes for American medications.

MEN'S FASHION

NELSON BOUTIQUE, Galerie St-François. Tel. 312-21-24.
The best place for men's fashion in Lausanne has stylish and traditional clothes, along with shoes, luggage, suits, and sportswear.

TOBACCO

TABACS-CIGARES BESSON, 22, rue de Bourg. Tel. 312-67-88.
One of the leading tobacco shops in Lausanne, this has a special climate-controlled room for the storage of the best cigars, many of which come from Cuba. Other merchandise includes Davidoff cigars, meerschaum pipes, and a variety of tobacco. The staff will mail certain goods back to North America for a small fee.

EVENING ENTERTAINMENT

Lausanne ranks with Geneva as the focal point of cultural life in French-speaking Switzerland. Orchestras, famous soloists, and theater and ballet troupes from all over the world perform here. The tourist office can give you information on what's currently available.

THE PERFORMING ARTS

BEAULIEU THEATRE, 10, av. des Bergières. Tel. 643-21-11.

This is one of the most prestigious places in Lausanne for concerts, operas, and ballet.

Prices: Tickets, 21F ($15.35).

THEATRE MUNCIPAL DE LAUSANNE, 12, av. du Théâtre. Tel. 312-64-33.

A distinguished program of opera, ballets, and concerts is performed here.

Prices: Tickets, 22F ($16.05).

LES FAUX-NEZ THEATER, 5, rue de Bourg. Tel. 312-31-73.

Fully appreciated only by French-speaking theater lovers, this is a *boîte des chansons,* where the wit, wine, and song flow freely, sometimes with political connotations. It is well known for its comedy and music. It's open Tuesday through Saturday from 8:15pm to 1 or 2am.

Prices: Tickets, 22F ($16.05).

THE CLUB & MUSIC SCENE

LA GRIFFE, in the Continental Hôtel, 2, place de la Gare. Tel. 311-02-62.

The most popular dance club in town, across from the railway station, La Griffe has a modern decor and alternately features live bands and disco music. People come to hear the jazz groups, which are imported from as far away as America. Open Tuesday through Sunday from 9:30pm to 4am. Beer costs 20F ($14.60).

Admission: Free.

LA CRAVACHE, 7, rue du Grand-Chêne. Tel. 312-88-10.

One of Lausanne's most inviting watering holes, La Cravache is next to the Lausanne Palace and is set much like an English pub, behind a wall of small-paned bull's-eye glass. Lausanne yuppies mingle with the pillars of the community, while occasionally a politician or a stripper from a nearby club strolls in. It's all very cosmopolitan. Open on Monday from 7am to 8pm, Tuesday through Thursday from 7am to 1am, on Friday from 7am to 2am, and on Saturday from 5pm to 2am. Drinks run 18F ($13.15).

Admission: Free.

DANCING-BAR, in the Château d'Ouchy, place du Port, Ouchy. Tel. 26-74-51.

Located in a famous hotel (see "Where to Stay," above), this nightclub has stone-rimmed windows with a view of the lake and the café below. The large, wood-paneled room has an arched ceiling with festive red and blue lights; there is a wall mural of the masked courtiers of Mozart's day. The establishment draws an older crowd, who come to drink and dance to popular music. Open Tuesday through Sunday from 9:30pm to 2am. Drinks range from 21F to 26F ($15.35 to $19) and a beer will cost 15F to 17F ($10.95 to $12.40).

Admission: Free.

LE PADDOCK, in the Hôtel Victoria, 46, av. de la Gare. Tel. 20-57-75.

This popular disco is lined with mirrors. The DJ plays requests as well as recently released music from New York and Paris. Open Tuesday through Sunday from 9:30pm to 4am. Drinks begin at 15F ($10.95).

Admission: Sun and Tues–Thurs free, Fri–Sat 5F ($3.65).

THE BAR SCENE

BAR DU RELAIS, in the Lausanne Palace, 7-9, rue du Grand-Chêne. Tel. 20-37-11.

Large, opulent, and dignified, this prestigious and rather formal bar is lined with red velvet and some neo-impressionist paintings. Its allure is a lot like that of a grand London hotel. Open daily from 11:30am to 1pm. Whisky costs 18F ($13.15).

CAFE BEAU-RIVAGE, in the Beau-Rivage Palace, 18, place du Général-Guisan, Ouchy. Tel. 617-17-17.

This previously recommended restaurant includes a fashionable piano bar, which opens at 7:30pm. Drinks run 18F ($13.15); beer, 8F ($5.85).

---

2. MORGES

7 miles W of Lausanne, 16 miles E of Geneva

GETTING THERE   By Train   Trains run almost every 30 minutes throughout the day between Geneva and Lausanne, and most of them stop at Morges along the way.

By Bus   Bus no. 27 runs from Lausanne to Morges.

By Car   From Lausanne, head west toward Geneva along N1.

By Lake Steamer   Between late May and September, several lake steamers stop at Morges every day on their way between Geneva and Lausanne; depending on their schedule, some require a boat change at Yvoire.

ESSENTIALS   The **Morges Tourist Information Office** is at 80, Grand'Rue (tel. 021/801-31-33), and it is open Monday through Saturday from 9:30am to noon and 2 to 6:30pm. The **telephone area code** for Morges is 021.

Set against a backdrop of the Savoy Alps, the small town of Morges, on Lac Léman, is headquarters for the region's vineyards. Its port was built on an ancient site inhabited by prehistoric lake dwellers. Today the town is a favorite stop for a chic set of international yachters.

WHAT TO SEE & DO

Duke Amadeus of Savoy built the **Castle of Morges** in 1286 to defend himself against the bishopric of Lausanne. The imposing bastion, which originally had a moat, was the residence of a Bernese bailiff from 1536 to 1798. It eventually passed to the canton of Vaud, which used it as an arsenal. Today it contains the **Vaud Military Museum** (tel. 801-26-16). The weapons and uniforms on display date from the late 18th century to modern times. The museum is open from February to mid-December, Monday through Friday from 10am to noon and 1:30 to 5pm, and on Saturday, Sunday, and holidays from 1:30 to 5pm. Admission is 5F ($3.65).

At least as interesting as the military museum is the **Alexis Forel Museum,** a museum of dolls and toys, at 54, Grand' Rue (tel. 801-26-47). The old patrician house once belonged to a local engraver; exhibits document the history and variety of dolls and toys. The museum is open Tuesday through Sunday from 2 to 5pm; admission is 5F ($3.65) for adults, free for children.

WHERE TO DINE

FLEUR DU LAC, 70, route de Lausanne. Tel. 802-43-11.
    Cuisine: SWISS. **Reservations:** Required. **Bus:** 27 from Lausanne.

$ Prices: Appetizers 10F–24F ($7.30–$17.50); main courses 37F–44F ($27–$32.10); fixed-price meals 44F–102F ($32.10–$74.45). AE, DC, MC, V.
Open: Daily noon–11pm.

Many residents of Geneva make weekend excursions to taste the unusual food served at this beautiful restaurant on the quay beside the lake. Famous specialties include Lake Geneva perch and imported seafood. The menu, which changes with the season, also includes cuisine moderne dishes, such as grilled turbot in champagne sauce or crayfish with smoked salmon. More than 250 domestic and foreign wines are available. There is an outdoor terrace facing the lake. A small "bistro" offers delicious specialties of the day costing 16F ($11.70) and up. The bus from Lausanne stops in front of the hotel.

---

3. NYON

14 miles E of Geneva, 24 miles W of Lausanne

GETTING THERE   By Train   Nyon lies directly on the rail lines that connect Geneva with Lausanne. Trains depart from both of the larger cities for Nyon every 30 minutes throughout the day.

By Bus   Nyon is connected by bus to a handful of other French-speaking towns to its northwest, few of which have railway junctions of their own. There are also bus connections from Nyon's railway station to Geneva several times throughout the day. Despite these buses, most travelers arrive in Nyon by train.

By Car   Drive west from Lausanne, or east from Geneva, along N1.

By Lake Steamer   The handful of lake steamers that travel in summer (May to September) between Geneva and Lausanne stop briefly in Nyon. Trip time by boat from Lausanne to Nyon is 2½ hours.

ESSENTIALS   The **Nyon Tourist Information Office** is at 7, avenue Viollier (tel. 022/61-61-61), open Monday through Friday from 8:30am to noon and 2 to 6pm. The **telephone area code** for Nyon is 022.

Unhurried and peaceful, Nyon has been popular as a lakefront resort since the Victorian era; masses of flowers decorate its waterfront quays. In Roman times, Julius Caesar used the settlement here as a military outpost for his soldiers. Between 1781 and 1813, Nyon was famous for its delicate, almost translucent porcelain.

WHAT TO SEE & DO

A ticket for 5F ($3.65) entitles you to visit the following three museums.

HISTORICAL AND PORCELAIN MUSEUM, Castle of Nyon, place du Château. Tel. 61-38-81.
     The Castle of Nyon, originally built in the 13th century, was almost completely redesigned between the 16th and 18th centuries. It contains a porcelain museum on its first floor. The rest of the building is used by the city of Nyon as a district court and

town council headquarters. From the castle's belvedere there's a sweeping view of the lake and the Alps, with Mont Blanc and the French coastline rising in the background.

Admission: See above.

Open: Daily 9–11am and 2–6pm. **Closed:** Nov–Mar.

LAKE OF GENEVA MUSEUM, 8, quai Louis-Bonnard. Tel. 61-09-49.

This museum is devoted exclusively to the geography, history, marine culture, and sociology of Lake Geneva. It also contains an aquarium.

Admission: See above.

Open: Mar–Oct, daily 9–11am and 2–6pm; Nov–Mar, Tues–Sun 2–5pm.

ROMAN BASILICA AND MUSEUM, rue Maupertuis. Tel. 61-75-91.

It displays specimens of Roman architecture, as well as Roman statuary, inscriptions, mosaics, crafts, amphorae, glasswork, and coins. The basilica was a public building for justice and commerce, standing at one end of the forum of the Roman colony (Colonia Julia Equestris).

Admission: See above.

Open: Mar–Oct, daily 9–11am and 2–6pm; Nov–Mar, Tues–Sun 2–5pm.

WHERE TO STAY

HOTEL BEAU-RIVAGE, 49, rue de Rive, CH-1260 Nyon. Tel. 022/61-32-31. Fax 022/62-09-63. 50 rms (all with bath). MINIBAR TV TEL

$ Rates (including continental breakfast): 110F–160F ($80.30–$116.80) single; 160F–260F ($116.80–$189.75) double. AE, DC, MC, V. **Parking:** 15F ($10.95) per day.

Cozy and old-fashioned, this hotel, 7 minutes from the railroad station, was built directly on the quays in the heart of the old town. Sweeping views of the lake are available from any of the hotel's many balconies. The public rooms have been tastefully modernized in a summertime motif, which includes a series of brightly colored modern paintings. The hotel's beautiful restaurant, Le Veranda, overlooks the lake. Both French and Italian dishes are served.

WHERE TO DINE

LE LEMAN, 28, rue de Rive. Tel. 61-22-41.

Cuisine: SEAFOOD. **Reservations:** Required.

$ Prices: Appetizers 15F–25F ($10.95–$18.25); main courses 22F–45F ($16.05–$32.85); fixed-price dinner 65F ($47.45). AE, DC, MC, V.

Open: Lunch Tues–Sun noon–2pm; dinner Tues–Sat 7–10pm.

This seafood restaurant overlooking a jetty is the best place to dine along the lake. The comfortable dining room is decorated with a changing exhibit of paintings by local artists. The owners offer many specialties, including foie gras in a terrine or sautéed, a small but succulent portion of filet of perch served as an appetizer, lobster ragoût with endive, cream of lobster soup with herbettes (baby herbs), sweetbreads roasted with exotic mushrooms, roast guinea fowl with lentils, roast pigeon from the Haut-Anjou (a region of France), and filet mignon of lamb.

ROTISSERIE DU XVI SIECLE, place du Marché, CH-1260 Nyon. Tel. 022/61-24-41.

Cuisine: SWISS. **Reservations:** Required.
$ Prices: Appetizers 13F–30F ($9.50–$21.90); main dishes 20F–35F ($14.60–$25.55); fixed-price meals 30F–50F ($21.90–$36.50). AE, DC, MC, V.
Open: Lunch daily 10am–2pm; dinner daily 5pm–1am.

The building that gives this establishment its name was built during the 16th century on ancient Roman foundations. Today its comfortable stone-walled interior has touches of red and furniture in the 19th-century style of Louis Philippe. There is also a comfortable bar. The cuisine includes such dishes as filets of perch sautéed with almonds, filet of veal with sage sauce, and an array of grilled meats.

The hostellerie also offers 14 pleasantly furnished bedrooms, each with a private bath. With breakfast included, singles cost 80F ($58.40); doubles, 100F ($73).

THE LAVAUX CORNICHE

The Lavaux Corniche, known in French as the Corniche Vaudoise, is one of the most famous wine-producing regions of Switzerland—a beautiful region of rolling hills and vineyards. Many wealthy individuals have chosen to retire here.

The first stopover, **Pully,** is an ancient Roman citadel now inside the municipal limits of Lausanne. Next you'll pass through **Corsier,** a vintner's village with a 12th-century church; here, Charlie Chaplin was buried in 1977. **Cully,** 5 miles east of Lausanne, is the heart of the Lavaux Corniche's wine fields. Located at the side of a small bay, it offers ample opportunities to swim, fish, and boat.

If you have time, turn right off the Corniche and head toward the lake. This will take you through fertile vineyards to the small summer resort of **Chexbres,** which, because of its position on the steep lakeside slopes, is known to some holiday-makers as the "balcony of Lac Léman." From here you can stroll through the nearby vineyards and forests. The nearby hamlet of **Dézaley** produces a light white wine that has been traditionally favored by the residents of Geneva.

WHERE TO STAY & DINE

HOTEL DU SIGNAL, Puidoux Gare, CH-1604 Chexbres. Tel. 021/946-25-25. Fax 021/946-20-15. 82 rms (all with bath). MINIBAR TV TEL **Transportation:** CFF-Puidoux train from Lausanne.
$ Rates (including continental breakfast): 80F–140F ($58.40–$102.20) single; 138F–198F ($100.75–$144.45) double, 196F–250F ($143.05–$182.50) deluxe double. MC, V.

This four-star château, with several modern extensions, is situated in a 60-acre wooded park by the lake. The public rooms contain modern and Victorian furniture, as well as a few Oriental rugs. Large windows offer a panoramic view over Lake Geneva and the rolling hills of the Vaud. The Gunten family offers streamlined, comfortable rooms, which vary in size and amenities. Good food is served in the French restaurant as well as on the terrace. Meals begin at 35F ($25.55). Facilities include a 30-yard indoor swimming pool and a tennis court.

---

4. VEVEY

11 miles E of Lausanne, 4 miles NW of Montreux

GETTING THERE By Train Vevey lies on the major rail link between Lausanne and (via the Simplon Tunnel) the great cities of northern Italy. Dozens of trains stop here every day. Trip time from Lausanne is 25 minutes.

By Car From Lausanne, head south along Route N9; from Montreux, drive northwest on Route N9.

By Lake Steamer Throughout the year, about a half dozen lake steamers transit the length of Lake Geneva, stopping at Lausanne, Vevey, Geneva, and several other cities along the way. Travel time to Vevey from Geneva is almost 5 hours; from Lausanne, about 1 hour.

ESSENTIALS The **Vevey Tourist Office,** place de la Gare (tel. 021/921-48-25), is open June to September, Monday through Friday from 8:30am to 9pm. The **telephone area code** for Vevey is 021.

SPECIAL EVENTS About every 25 years Vevey stages the **Fêtes des Vignerons,** a winegrowers' carnival in honor of Bacchus, the god of wine. The first celebration was in 1673; the last was in 1977.

Home of Nestlé chocolate, the resort of Vevey has been popular with British visitors since the 19th century. It is at the foot of Mount Pélerin, to which an excursion can be made. The town, dating from Roman times, was built at the mouth of the Veveyse River and is the center of the Lavaux vineyards. In the Middle Ages it was known as an important trading post on the route from Piedmont, in Italy, to Burgundy, in France. It has long been accustomed to receiving and entertaining visitors.

Rousseau's descriptions of his "sentimental rambles" in the lake district lured the first Romantic tourists. In time, English and Russian aristocrats selected the sheltered Swiss Riviera for long winter sojourns. Famous exiles to the area have included the English regicide Edmund Ludlow, the French painter Gustave Courbet, and the Polish pianist Ignace Paderewski and novelist Henryk Sienkiewicz.

WHAT TO SEE & DO

IN TOWN

Begin by exploring the **Grand-Place,** a mammoth market plaza facing Lac Léman. The corn exchange on the north dates from the early 19th century. In 1730, Rousseau lodged at the Auberge de la Clef, near the Théâtre. As you walk in this area and along the quay, you'll enjoy the views of the Savoy Alps.

The **Church of St. Martin,** dating from the 10th century, is on a belvedere overlooking the resort. It has a large rectangular tower with four turrets; there is a good view of Vevey from the tower.

A statue by John Doubleday on the new **Square Chaplin, Quai Perdonnet,** commemorates the town's most illustrious former resident, Charlie Chaplin. Chaplin moved here from the United States, together with his young wife, Oona O'Neill, in 1952, in part to escape accusations of Communist sympathies. Except for brief interludes, he remained in Vevey until his death, in 1977. The life-size statue erected to him is that of the little tramp in baggy pants—the character Chaplin made famous—gazing out at his favorite view of Lake Geneva and the Alps in the distance.

Chaplin actually lived in the little village of **Corsier,** above Vevey, which dates at least from the 2nd century. Its church is thought to have been established by the abbey of St. Maurice. In it you can see some 15th-century paintings. Villagers dedicated a park to their famous resident. The comedian is buried in the cemetery right below the village. Bus no. 11 or 12 goes from Vevey to Corsier.

JENISCH MUSEUM. 2, ave. de la Gare. Tel. 021/921-29-50.

This art gallery has some fine works by Courbet, as well as by local modern Swiss painters.

Admission: Free.

Open: May–Oct, Mon 10am–noon and 2–5pm, Tues–Fri 10am–noon and 2–4pm; Nov–Apr, Tues–Sat 2–4pm, Sun and hols 11am–noon and 2–4pm.

MUSEE DU VIEUX-VEVEY, 43, rue d'Italie. Tel. 921-07-22.

This château has two museums: the **Musée Historique du Vieux-Vevey** and the **Musée de la Confrerie des Vignerons** (Winemakers Museum). If you missed the Bacchus festival, you'll see many of the costumes displayed here. Other exhibits include 18th-century antiques and mementos of the vinters, wrought-iron work, arms, pewter, and tools. Paintings by local artists are also displayed, as well as artifacts excavated from the area around Vevey.

Admission: 4F ($2.90) for both museums.

Open: Tues–Sat 10:30am–noon and 2–5:30pm, Sun 11am–noon and 2–5pm. **Closed:** Nov–Feb.

NEARBY

The most important excursion in the area is to **Mount Pélerin,** 15 miles away. You can drive by way of Corsier or go by funicular by way of Corseaux. As you ascend, you'll see a panoramic sweep of Lake Geneva, the Savoy Alps, and the valley of the Rhône.

WHERE TO STAY

HOTEL LES TROIS COURONNES, 49, rue d'Italie, CH-1800 Vevey. Tel. 021/921-30-05. Fax 021/922-72-80. 88 rms (all with bath). MINIBAR TV TEL **Bus:** 1 or 2.

$ Rates (including continental breakfast): 150F–225F ($109.50–$164.25) single; 260F–390F ($189.75–$284.65) double. Half board 50F ($36.50) extra. AE, DC, MC, V.

⭐ This leading hotel is famous as the setting of Henry James's first important work, *Daisy Miller;* the film version, by director Peter Bogdanovich, was also made here. It's located in the center of town, in a white-stucco and gray-stone building with noble details. The lobby has an elegant gallery with white balustrades overlooking the carpeted lobby three floors below. The rooms are redecorated and retain their 19th-century charm. The more expensive rooms have attractive antiques. The hotel has a first-class restaurant, serving French and Swiss specialties.

HOTEL DU LAC, 1, rue d'Italie, CH-1800 Vevey. Tel. 021/921-10-41. Fax 021/921-75-08. 53 rms (all with bath). MINIBAR TV TEL **Bus:** 1 or 2.

$ Rates (including continental breakfast): 130F–195F ($94.90–$142.35) single; 190F–285F ($138.70–$208) double. Half board 35F ($25.55) extra. AE, DC, MC, V.

This well-established hotel, affiliated with Vevey's more expensive Hôtel Les Trois Couronnes, is popular because of its lakeside view. It has a swimming pool, as well as a flower-studded lakeside terrace. Appropriate for a relaxing holiday beside the lake, the hotel is patronized by foreign, especially British, visitors. The rooms are pleasantly furnished and comfortable.

Dining/Entertainment: The hotel restaurant enjoys an excellent reputation for its Swiss and French specialties.

Service: Laundry.

Facilities: Swimming pool, tennis courts, health club.

HOTEL DE FAMILLE, 20, rue des Communaux, CH-1800 Vevey. Tel. 021/921-39-31. Fax 021/921-43-47. 62 rms (all with bath). TEL **Bus:** 1 or 2.
$ Rates (including buffet breakfast): 55F–85F ($40.15–$62.05) single; 100F–150F ($73–$109.50) double. Children under 6 stay with parents at a 50% discount; children 6–12, at a 30% discount. AE, DC, MC, V.

Near the railroad station and at the center of the commercial district, this 19th-century resort has a modern interior and clean and comfortable rooms, half of which contain TV. La Veranda is a restaurant and tearoom, where meals are served from 11am to 9:30pm. There is a small indoor swimming pool, as well as a rooftop terrace with chaise longues and card tables.

WHERE TO DINE

EXPENSIVE

DU RAISIN, 3, place du Marché. Tel. 921-10-28.
Cuisine: SWISS. **Reservations:** Required. **Bus:** 1 or 2.
$ Prices: Appetizers 15F–22F ($10.95–$16.05); main courses 22F–42F ($16.05–$30.65); menu dégustation 95F ($69.35). AE, DC, MC, V.
Open: Lunch Tues–Sun noon–2pm; dinner Tues–Sat 7–9:30pm.

Du Raisin has won several culinary awards. Located at the edge of Vevey's sprawling open-air market, it contains two floors of well-appointed comfort. On the street level is a cozy brasserie serving simple food at reasonable prices. The culinary skill of the place is evident in the upstairs restaurant, where chef Philippe Corsaletti prepares sophisticated dishes, served by his wife, Catherine. The menu might include a salad of sweetbreads with an essence of eggplant, gratiné of curried lobster with baby vegetables and homemade pasta, and roast monkfish with rosemary. For dessert, try one of the three types of chocolate mousse served with mint sauce.

TAVERNE DU CHATEAU, 43, rue d'Italie. Tel. 921-12-10.
Cuisine: SWISS. **Reservations:** Required. **Bus:** 1 or 2.
$ Prices: Appetizers 12F–22F ($8.75–$16.05); main courses 18F–40F ($13.15–$29.20); fixed-price meals 58F ($42.35) and 72F ($52.55). AE, MC, V.
Open: Lunch daily noon–1:45pm; dinner Mon–Sat 7–9:45pm. **Closed:** Mon in winter.

Built in 1681, this large stucco building resembles a farmer's grange, with a large carved beam extending out over one of the top-floor windows. A pulley was probably attached to the beam to transport supplies to the upper floors. Over the pavement hangs a wrought-iron and gilt sign with a picture of a horse and two men fighting. The menu might include filet of beef in a morel sauce, roebuck with pears and red wine, and smoked salmon. For dessert, try a lemon soufflé.

MODERATE

LA TERRASSE, 2, rue Chenevières. Tel. 944-33-96.
Cuisine: SWISS. **Reservations:** Recommended. **Bus:** 1 or 2.
$ Prices: Appetizers 12F–18F ($8.75–$13.15); main courses 20F–32F ($14.60–$23.35); fixed-price meals 30F ($21.90). AE, DC, MC, V.
Open: Lunch daily 11am–2pm; dinner daily 6–9:30pm; snacks and drinks served daily 9am–midnight.

Located in the center of town, this restaurant is across from the Hôtel du Lac, near the Church of Notre-Dame. There is a terrace with flowers, which is covered and heated in inclement weather. The menu features filet of fried perch, sole with almonds served with fine herbs, and filet of beef with morels. A raclette special is offered on Friday nights in summer.

INEXPENSIVE

BRASSERIE FELDSCHLÖSSCHEN, 45, rue du Simplon. Tel. 921-31-67.
  Cuisine: SWISS. **Reservations:** Not needed. **Bus:** 1 or 2.
$ Prices: Appetizers 7F–12F ($5.10–$8.75); main courses 15F–35F ($10.95–$25.55); fixed-price meals from 26F ($19); large beer 2.50F ($1.85). AE, DC, MC, V.
  Open: Daily 7am–midnight; hot food served 11am–midnight.
Named after a popular beer, this working-class brasserie is on a busy commercial street in downtown Vevey. A picture-view window overlooks a garden with geraniums and a fountain. The dining room has a nickel-plated serving area and a large mural of medieval maps of Vevey. The menu might include peppersteak, Indian rice, or two types of spaghetti, along with good hams, sausages, and a variety of hors d'oeuvres.

LA PINTE DE L'HOTEL DE VILLE, 17, rue de l'Hôtel de Ville. Tel. 922-63-43.
  Cuisine: SWISS. **Reservations:** Recommended. **Bus:** 1.
$ Prices: 10F–25F ($7.30–$18.25); main courses 20F–32F ($14.60–$23.35); lunchtime platters 13F ($9.50). V.
  Open: Lunch Mon–Sat 11:30am–2pm; dinner Mon–Sat 6–11pm; café snacks Mon–Sat 7am–midnight.
Pinte is old French for "bistro." The landmark café overlooks the trees and cobblestones of an old square, and outside tables are available in fair weather. The food is simple but good. Appetizers include assiette valaisanne (air-dried beef); typical main courses are steak maison, steak with mushroom sauce, and horsesteak. Three kinds of fondue are offered, as are sandwiches.

WHITE HORSE PUB, 33, rue du Simplon. Tel. 921-02-34.
  Cuisine: INTERNATIONAL. **Reservations:** Not needed. **Bus:** 1 or 2.
$ Prices: Plat du jour (lunch only) 13F ($9.50); hamburgers, pastas, french fries, ice creams 6F–14F ($4.40–$10.20). AE, MC, V.
  Open: Mon–Sat 7am–midnight, Sun 4pm–midnight.
This is a popular tavern, with smoky paneling, comfortable Jacobean chairs, pink lampshades, a young clientele, and an amplified radio station playing recently released music. Many office workers stop here at lunchtime for a plat du jour; at night, snack food and drinks are the most popular offering. Whisky costs 7F ($5.10) and up, and a mug of beer runs 3.50F ($2.55).

---

5. MONTREUX

2 miles E of Vevey, 15 miles E of Lausanne, 62 miles E of Geneva

GETTING THERE **By Train** Montreux is on the rail lines linking Geneva and Lausanne with the Simplon Tunnel and the major cities of northern Italy. Dozens of trains stop at Montreux every day from both directions. Secondary rail lines connect the town to the ski resorts of the Bernese Oberland, in the northeast.

By Car Montreux sits amid a network of superhighways linking Germany, France, and Italy with Switzerland. From Lausanne, head southeast along Route N9.

By Lake Steamer Montreux is one of the stops on the east-west steamer route between Geneva and Lausanne, throughout the year across Lake Geneva. Travel time from Lausanne or Geneva is about 70 minutes.

ESSENTIALS The **Montreux Tourist Information Office,** place du Débarcadère (tel. 021/963-12-12), is open Monday through Saturday from 9am to 6pm and on Sunday from 9am to noon. The **telephone area code** for Montreux is 021.

SPECIAL EVENTS The **Festival de Jazz** begins the first Friday in July. Billed as a musical extravaganza, with some of the most lavish publicity in Switzerland, it usually lasts 2½ weeks and draws aficionados from around the world. Tickets range from 38F to 100F ($27.75 to $73), depending on the event. For more information, write to Festival de Jazz, Case Postale 97, CH-1820 Montreux. At the end of every summer, the city sponsors a classical-music festival. For information, write to **Festival de Musique,** Case Postale 162, CH-1820 Montreux. Remember that during these music festivals it's very difficult to get a hotel room in Montreux without reservations many months in advance.

Built on a curve of the great bay of Lac Léman, the chief resort of the Swiss Riviera, Montreux, rises in the shape of an amphitheater from the shores of the lake. Known as an Edwardian town with a distinct French accent, it has been a refuge for expatriates, among whom in recent times was novelist Vladimir Nabokov. Known for its balmy climate, it sports a profusion of Mediterranean vegetation, which grows lushly in the town's many lakeside parks. The mountains at the town's back protect it from the winds of winter, allowing fruit trees, cypresses, magnolias, bay trees, almonds, and even palms to flourish.

The city has expanded greatly from its original 19th-century core, incorporating several former villages along the shoreline. One of these, Clarens, was used by Rousseau as the setting for his epistolary novel *La Nouvelle Héloïse.* The resort is said to have enjoyed its heyday in the years just before World War I, when it had only 85 hotel beds. It hosted such distinguished visitors as Tolstoy, Flaubert, Dostoyevsky, and Ruskin. In recent times the town has revived, and today about three-fourths of the resort's 20,000 inhabitants are engaged in some touristic capacity or another.

Though the resort is favored year round, it is most densely crowded in summertime, when traffic clogs most of the city's streets and highways.

WHAT TO SEE & DO

Explore the old houses and crooked streets of Old Montreux. Later, stroll along the quayside promenade by the lake.

The most impressive castle in Switzerland, the **✪ Château of Chillon** (tel. 963-39-11), is on the lake 2 miles south of Montreux, reached by tram no. 1. Most of the castle dates from the 13th century, but its oldest section is thought to be 1,000 years old. The castle was built by Peter II of Savoy and is one of the best-preserved medieval castles of Europe. So-called sorcerers were tried and tortured here. The most famous prisoner, François Bonivard, was described by Byron in *The Prisoner of Chillon.* Bonivard was the prior of St. Victori in Geneva, and when he supported the Reformation in 1532, the Catholic duke of Savoy chained him in the dungeon until 1536, when he was released by the Bernese.

The château is open April through June and in September, daily from 9am to 6:30pm; in July and August, daily from 9am to 7pm; November through February, daily from 10am to 12:45pm and 1:30 to 4:45pm; in March, daily from 10am to 12:45pm and 1:30 to 5:30pm; and in October, daily from 10am to 5:30pm. The last tickets are sold 45 minutes before closing. Admission is 4.50F ($3.30) for adults and 2F ($1.45) for children.

Villeneuve, the little port town at the end of the lake, is where Lord Byron wrote *The Prisoner of Chillon* in 1816. Mahatma Gandhi visited Romain Rolland when the French novelist and pacifist lived here. The town and the surrounding countryside have been painted by many artists, including Oskar Kokoschka, who lived here. Villeneuve is a short walk from the Château of Chillon.

WHERE TO STAY

Many of the leading hotels of Montreux have greatly improved in recent years. Unfortunately, the less expensive hotels have been neglected; good budget accommodations are lacking.

EXPENSIVE

GRAND HOTEL EXCELSIOR, 21, rue Bon-Port, CH-1820 Montreux. Tel. 021/963-32-31. Fax 021/963-77-95. 76 rms (all with bath). MINIBAR TV TEL **Bus:** 1.
$ **Rates** (including breakfast): 180F–240F ($131.40–$175.20) single; 300F–360F ($218.95–$262.75) double. Half board 40F ($29.20) extra. AE, DC, MC, V.
A renowned Montreux landmark, this five-star lakeside hotel offers quiet opulence and discreet personal service. The elegant marble foyer has Venetian sedan chairs, marquetry, and Queen Anne antiques. The charm of this hotel is enhanced by oil paintings and baroque sculpture. Rooms are spacious and all have lakefront balconies.

Dining/Entertainment: Superb French cuisine is served at Le Yaka, an elegant grillroom, and La Terrasse, a more formal restaurant. Le Snack Piscine, by the swimming pool, serves light meals.

Services: Hairdresser, beauty salon, massage parlor, and beauty, slimming, and fitness programs.

Facilities: 82½-foot indoor swimming pool, sauna, gym.

HYATT CONTINENTAL, 97, Grand'Rue, CH-1820 Montreux. Tel. 021/963-51-31, or toll free 800/228-9000 in North America. Fax 021/963-56-37. 143 rms (all with bath), 20 suites. A/C MINIBAR TV TEL **Bus:** 1.
$ **Rates:** 170F–310F ($124.10–$226.25) single; 220F–370F ($160.60–$270.05) double; from 550F ($401.45) suite. Breakfast 18F ($13.15) extra. AE, DC, MC, V.
Parking: 25F ($18.25).

This lakeside hotel, on a beautifully maintained promenade, is decorated with elegant materials and unusual lighting. Rooms face the lake and are among the most luxurious and beautifully kept at the resort.

Dining/Entertainment: A creative French cuisine is served in the Gourmet Restaurant, which features a fixed-price menu for 90F ($65.70). There is also a beautifully decorated coffee shop called Romance, which serves a changing menu based on fresh ingredients. On the Garden Terrace, in the summer you can enjoy fresh fish from Lake Geneva, grilled steaks, and a salad buffet. Musical entertainment is presented once or twice a week. The piano bar on the ground floor is comfortable and decorated in subtle colors.

Services: Hall porter, laundry and dry cleaning, room service.

Facilities: Heated indoor pool, sauna, underground parking, car-rental office, fitness center.

LE MONTREUX PALACE, 100, Grand'Rue, CH-1820 Montreux. Tel. 021/963-53-73. Fax 021/963-73-23. 460 rms (all with bath) MINIBAR TV TEL **Bus:** 1.

$ **Rates** (including continental breakfast): 290F–320F ($211.65–$233.55) single; 430F–480F ($313.85–$350.35) double. AE, DC, V. **Parking:** 25F ($18.25).

⭐ Facing the lake, this opulent 19th-century palace has embellished ceilings, parquet floors, and crystal chandeliers. Once a favorite of Russian tsars, it later attracted Nabokov—the author of *Lolita,* among other works—who used to spend his summers here. Renovations have preserved the original style. One room has an arched ceiling with an art nouveau stained-glass skylight and statues of cupids and demigods. Each of the comfortably old-fashioned bedrooms—many quite spacious—has French doors and a balcony.

Dining/Entertainment: Guests dine on an international menu in sumptuous splendor. For connoisseurs, I recommend the menu dégustation, based on fresh ingredients; it costs 79F ($57.65). A buffet lunch is offered at the Garden Restaurant by the lake. There is also a bar as well as a snack bar.

Services: Room service, laundry and dry cleaning service, baby-sitting.

Facilities: Use of an 18-hole golf course, tennis courts, swimming pool, garage.

MODERATE

HOTEL EDEN AU LAC, 11, rue du Théâtre, CH-1820 Montreux. Tel. 021/963-55-51. 105 rms (all with bath), 6 suites. MINIBAR TV TEL **Bus:** 1.

$ **Rates** (including continental breakfast): 180F–220F ($131.40–$160.60) single; 230F–270F ($167.90–$197.05) double; 280F–520F ($204.35–$379.55) junior or senior suite for two. AE, DC, MC, V.

⭐ The lingering nostalgia and beautiful restoration of this hotel evoke scenes from the movie *Death in Venice.* It's a favorite hotel in Montreux, and it's less expensive than the palaces. Situated on the lakeside promenade, it has a grand 19th-century style and a facade that resembles an art nouveau wedding cake. The pink-and-white neobaroque Gatsby Bar has stained-glass windows. There is a garden terrace with magnolias and clipped chestnuts. Bernard and Nicole Tschopp offer well-appointed rooms, many of which are spacious. The junior and senior suites are among the most opulent in Montreux. Dining facilities include "Le 1900," a Belle Epoque dining room; La Terrasse, a more upscale restaurant catering to a clientele of gourmets; and the Garden Restaurant, directly on the lakefront, serving daytime buffets.

EUROTEL RIVIERA, 81, Grand' Rue, CH-1820 Montreux. Tel. 021/963-49-51. Fax 021/963-53-92. 175 rms (all with bath). MINIBAR TV TEL **Bus:** 1.

$ **Rates** (including buffet breakfast): 100F–170F ($73–$124.10) single; 150F–250F ($109.50 $182.50) double. AE, DC, MC, V. **Parking:** 25F ($18.25).

Efficient and modern, this silvery high-rise sits on a parcel of lakefront property beside the main road leading into Montreux. The rooms are modern and comfortable, with wood-and-leather foyers and, in most cases, a balcony with a view of the lake. Waterskiing and sailing are provided several times a week.

Dining/Entertainment: Two restaurants are offered, including a specialty room, Bel Horizon, for international gourmet food, and the Matara, a grill and restaurant at the lake promenade. There is also a piano bar.

Services: Hairdresser, room service, baby-sitting, laundry.

Facilities: Covered garage, solarium, sauna, car-rental office.

GRAND HOTEL SUISSE MAJESTIC, 43, av. des Alps, CH-1820

Montreaux. Tel. 021/963-51-81. Fax 021/963-35-06. 225 rms (all with bath). MINIBAR TV TEL **Bus:** 1.

$ Rates (including continental breakfast): 150F–190F ($109.50–$138.70) single; 200F–270F ($146–$197.05) double. AE, DC, MC, V.

This opulent, 19th-century landmark is in the center of Montreux, beside the lake. Take one of the three elevators past the trompe-l'oeil murals to the art nouveau lobby on the top floor. From there you'll have access to a terrace with classical statuary and a panoramic view. Comfort and subdued elegance are the keys to the success of this hotel. Most rooms have an updated Belle Epoque decor. The Restaurant Français is well worth a visit. Specialties include poached fresh salmon, chaudrée of seafood flavored with saffron, and entrecôte with three peppers. Dishes are sometimes flambéed at your table. The fixed-price menu costs 45F ($32.85). There is an adjacent coffee shop, as well as a cocktail bar, the Majestic.

WHERE TO DINE

VERY EXPENSIVE

LE PONT DE BRENT, in Brent. Tel. 964-52-30.
Cuisine: SWISS. **Reservations:** Required.
$ Prices: Appetizers 18F–25F ($13.15–$18.25); main courses 28F–48F ($20.45–$35.05); fixed-price meals 105F ($76.65); "menu surprise" 125F ($91.25). V.
Open: Lunch Tues–Sun noon–2pm; dinner Tues–Sat 7–9:30pm.

Delicacies wrapped in a puff pastry are served at this renovated town house in Brent, a small village 2 miles northwest of Montreux. Gérald Rabaey, the owner and chef, changes the menus seasonally. The soups are exceptional, including one made with leeks and mussels. Fish dishes include filet de loup (sea bass) with Pinot Noir and rabbit in a mustard sauce or roast pigeon with cabbage.

EXPENSIVE

LA VIEILLE FERME, in Montreux-Chailly. Tel. 964-65-65.
Cuisine: SWISS/INTERNATIONAL. **Reservations:** Required.
$ Prices: Appetizers 15F–20F ($10.95–$14.60); main courses 20F–49F ($14.60–$35.75); fixed-price meals from 78F ($56.95). AE, DC, MC, V.
Open: Lunch Wed–Sun noon–1:45pm; dinner Wed–Sun 7–10pm. **Closed:** July.

This old and rustic stone-walled house is in the village of Chailly, 2½ miles north of Montreux. Accompanying your meal will be traditional music from the region, which is performed almost every night. Monsieur Mabillard offers such specialties as boneless quail, veal, salmon, and a superb homemade terrine. The menu also includes gratiné of shrimp or grilled beef. The arrival of large tour groups may interrupt your intimate dinner.

LE YAKA, in the Grand Hotel Excelsior, 21, rue Bon-Port. Tel. 963-32-31.
Cuisine: FRENCH. **Reservations:** Required. **Bus:** 1.
$ Prices: Appetizers 14F–22F ($10.20–$16.05); main courses 25F–40F ($18.25–$29.20); fixed-price meals ($32.85). AE, DC, MC, V.
Open: Lunch daily 11am–2pm; dinner daily 7–9:30pm.

One of the best French restaurants at the resort is in this five-star hotel; the entrance to the restaurant is through the marble lobby. The maître d' grandly shows you to your seat in a dining room decorated with a nautical theme. The menu includes trout meunière, veal kidneys in a whisky sauce, and steak tartare. For an appetizer, try one of the refreshing, well-seasoned soups. Desserts are classic.

MODERATE

RESTAURANT CHINOIS WING WAH, 42, Grand'Rue. Tel. 963-34-47.
   Cuisine: CANTONESE. **Reservations:** Required. **Bus:** 1.
$ Prices: Appetizers 12F–18F ($8.75–$13.15); main courses 18F–40F ($13.15–$29.20). AE, DC, MC, V.
   Open: Lunch daily 11:30am–2:30pm; dinner daily 6–10:30pm.
Hearty portions of well-prepared Chinese food attract many families to this scarlet-and-gold dining room. The owner, originally from Hong Kong, prepares such specialties as lacquered duck, twice-grilled beef, diced chicken with hot peppers, and curried shrimp.

EVENING ENTERTAINMENT

THE CASINO, rue du Théâtre. Tel. 963-53-31.
   Most of the town's nightlife takes place in the casino, in the center of town. Since the limit of any official wager in Switzerland is 5F ($3.65), the casino is more a place of entertainment than a gambling hall. Yes, there are green-baize tables and spinning wheels, but the main focus is on the cabaret, disco, restaurant, four bars, music hall, and movie theater. For easy parking (a rarity in Montreux), there's a garage with coin-operated meters in the basement.
   The **cabaret** is positioned at the end of a long red staircase with a short tunnel at the end. This club has everything, from strip acts to clowns. It's open Monday through Saturday from 10pm to 4am. Admission is free and drinks cost 15F ($10.95).
   Platinum is the American-style disco on the main floor. It has comfortable banquettes and lots of chrome; recently released electronic music is played. Admission is 6F ($4.40) on Friday and 8F ($5.85) on Saturday (other days free). Drinks cost 13F ($9.50). The disco opens at 9:30pm.
   On the same floor is a **piano bar,** Bar du Festival, where videos of the most recent Montreux Jazz Festival are shown. There also is a 3,000-seat **concert hall.**
   The latest attraction is the **Western Saloon,** with live country music and large platters of steaks. It's open Tuesday through Sunday from 9pm until late. The **restaurant** has upholstered bentwood chairs and a panoramic view of the lake.

HARRY'S NEW YORK BAR, in Le Montreux Palace, 100, Grand'Rue. Tel. 963-53-73.
   There's a Harry's Bar in just about every city these days, but this particular example—managed by one of the grandest hotels in Montreux—won't remind you of any of them. Once the home of an automobile showroom, it underwent an elegant transformation with the installation of rich paneling and touches of brass and leather. The bartenders—a well-trained crew hailing from almost everywhere except Switzerland—mix cocktails the old-fashioned way (shaken, not stirred). Most clients come only to drink; but if you're hungry, you can order light and elegant meals, composed of grills, salads, sandwiches, and such platters as beluga caviar and lobster thermidor. Open Monday through Friday from 5pm to 1am, and on Saturday and Sunday from 5pm to 2am. Light meals begin at 45F ($29.20); drinks run 13F ($9.50).

HAZYLAND DISCO, 100, Grand'Rue. Tel. 963-56-46.
   Located on a busy street opposite the Palace, this disco has large, art nouveau windows with fanciful wrought-iron details. Live acts are presented frequently. There is also a bar on the right side, near the entrance. Most patrons are under 25. The last time I was there, a Michael Jackson look-alike sang under a red strobe light. Open daily from 9:30pm to 4am. Drinks run 15F ($10.95); beer costs 13F ($9.50).
   Admission: Sun–Thurs free, Fri–Sat 10F ($7.30).

PIANO BAR, in the Hyatt Continental, 97, Grand'Rue. Tel. 963-51-31.

Rock musicians who come to Montreux for the annual music festival are attracted to this bar one floor below the lobby of the previously recommended Hyatt hotel. It is stylish and modern, with pink granite, black lacquer, and comfortable settees. Large windows overlook the lake. The bartender might know what your favorite rock star likes to drink. Margaritas are popular. Open Sunday through Thursday from 6pm to midnight and on Friday and Saturday from 6pm to 2am. Drinks run 13F ($9.50).

AN EXCURSION TO ROCHERS-DE-NAYE

Traveling to Rochers-de-Naye (6,700 ft.) by cogwheel train is the most popular excursion along Lake Geneva. Along the way you'll see many spectacular alpine vistas. Rochers-de-Naye is the last stop on the train and is inaccessible to motor vehicles. There is no hotel, but cots are available in a dormitory used by campers and school groups.

The train leaves from the Montreux railroad station seven times a day in season, with the last departure at 4pm. The trip takes 50 minutes and round-trip costs 41F ($29.95) per person. Check with the tourist office for departure times.

The train passes **Glion,** a little resort on a rocky crag. Farther on, **Caux** (3,600 ft.) is on a natural balcony overhanging the blue bowl of the lake. The peak of Rochers-de-Naye is high in the Vaudois Alps. In the distance you can see the Savoy Alps, including Mont Blanc, and the Jura Alps. Skiing is possible between December and April. There's a ski lift, a Swiss ski school, and a hotel.

WHERE TO STAY

HOTEL VICTORIA, CH-1823 Glion-sur-Montreux. Tel. 021/963-31-31.
Fax 021/963-31-31. 57 rms (all with bath), 3 suites. TV TEL
$ Rates (including continental breakfast): 150F–180F ($109.50–$131.40) single; 220F–270F ($160.60–$197.05) double; from 500F ($364.95) suite. AE, DC, MC, V. **Parking:** 10F ($7.30).

Dozens of charming Victorian features make this hotel special, including art nouveau plaster friezes, ornate fireplaces, and an Edwardian glass-enclosed terrace with plants and wicker chairs. This grand hotel, built in 1886, is in a hillside village high above Montreux. Toni Mittermair offers rooms with antique furniture and large windows; most have a turn-of-the-century oil painting and a private terrace. Many of the furnishings were collected by the former owner, an antiques dealer from Geneva.

Dining/Entertainment: The menu is written on an elaborate scroll and features French dishes. Specialties include grilled veal kidneys in a dijonnaise sauce with a gratiné of zucchini, braised pork with Madeira, and a wide selection of grills served with creamy gratiné Dauphine. There is a limited but well-chosen selection of fish. Special seasonal dishes are made from only the freshest produce. Meals cost 55F to 75F ($40.15 to $54.75). The restaurant is open daily from noon to 2pm and 7 to 9pm.

Services: Room service, laundry services.

Facilities: Locked garage, open-air swimming pool, tennis.

WHERE TO DINE

RESTAURANT PLEIN ROC, Rochers-de-Naye. Tel. 963-74-11.
Cuisine: SWISS. **Reservations:** Required.
$ Prices: Appetizers 7F–20F ($5.10–$14.60); main courses 18F–31F ($13.15–$22.65). MC, V.

Open: Summer, daily 10am–8pm; winter, daily 10am–5pm.

Local engineers won praise in 1985 for successfully drilling a 750-foot tunnel to provide access to this restaurant, which is considered the highest dining room in the Vaud. The dining area has a sweeping view of Lac Léman and Lausanne. The menu includes meat fondues, veal escalope Gruyèrienne, and entrecôte with herb butter. Snacks and drinks are served throughout the afternoon. If you stay for dinner, plan to finish in time to catch the last train down the mountain—it departs at 8pm in the summer and 5pm in the winter. To get to the restaurant from the train station, bypass the self-service snack bar near the train platform and follow the tunnel to the end.

GENEVA

Geneva is located in the Rhône Valley at the southwestern corner of Lake Geneva (or Lac Léman, in French), between the Jura Mountains and the Alps. It is the capital of the canton of Geneva, the second-smallest canton in the Swiss confederation.

Switzerland's second-largest city has an idyllic setting on one of the biggest alpine lakes and within view of the glorious pinnacle of Mont Blanc. Filled with parks and promenades, the city becomes a virtual garden in summer. Not surprisingly, it's also considered one of the healthiest cities in the world because the prevailing north wind blows away any pollution.

Geneva is surrounded by French territory, connected to Switzerland only by the lake and a narrow corridor. The city's French influence is apparent in its mansard roofs, iron balconies, sidewalk cafés, and French signs.

A BIT OF HISTORY

Geneva's roots go back to prehistoric times. Over the centuries it has been a Gallic town, a Roman city, a Burgundian capital, and an episcopal principality. The city was occupied by the Romans for 500 years; Caesar had the bridge over the Rhône destroyed. By the end of the 11th century, Geneva was ruled by bishop-princes, who more or less engaged the House of Savoy in battles that continued for almost 200 years.

Annexed by France in 1798, during the French Revolution, Geneva remained unwillingly under French control until the collapse of Napoleon in 1814. It was admitted into the Swiss Confederation as the capital of its own canton in 1815.

Geneva rejected its Catholic heritage and officially embraced the Protestant faith in 1536. The strict reformist movement was introduced by Guillaume Farel and brought to the height of its power by a Frenchman named John Calvin. One of the strictest Puritans in European history, Calvin ranted against theaters and dancing, and even against wine and

WHAT'S SPECIAL ABOUT GENEVA

City Spectacles

☐ Jet d'Eau, a huge fountain spouting water 425 feet into the air over Lake Geneva, the virtual symbol of the city.

☐ Flower Clock, in the Jardin Anglais, with 6,300 flowers filling an area 50 feet in circumference—and keeping accurate time!

Monuments

☐ Monument de la Réformation, commemorating one of the city's most important historical events—the Protestant Reformation, as advocated by John Calvin.

Religious Shrines

☐ Cathédrale de St-Pierre, in the old town, dating from the 12th century but a Protestant church since 1536, with a superb panoramic view from its north tower.

Museums

☐ Musée d'Art et d'Histoire, Geneva's largest museum, a repository of art and antiquities, from mummies to medieval arms and armor.

☐ Red Cross Museum, documenting the history of the Red Cross from its founding in Geneva in 1863 to the present day.

Events and Festivals

☐ Fêtes de Genève, first week of August, marked by riotious celebrations and free concerts.

☐ L'Escalade, in early December, when period costumes and torchlight marches celebrate a victory back in 1602.

---

food if they were consumed for enjoyment rather than simply to sustain life. Calvin is probably the most memorable figure to come out of Geneva. Stern, forbidding, and bigoted, he made the city legendary for the strictness of its moral codes. Under his guidance Geneva was called the "Rome of the Protestants" and soon received a flood of Protestant refugees from France, Germany, Italy, and England.

The new energies released by this influx of ideas and workers transformed Geneva into one of the most prosperous and best-educated cities of the world. By the 18th century, Geneva had become one of the intellectual centers of Europe. Rousseau was born here in 1712, and Voltaire, Byron, Goethe, Victor Hugo, François Chateaubriand, and countless other literary figures spent time in the city as well.

Geneva is such an international city that the French statesman Talleyrand is reputed to have said that there are five continents: Europe, America, Asia, Africa, and Geneva. In some respects Geneva is the epitome of Swiss neutrality. In 1863 Henri Dunant encouraged the signing of the Geneva Convention, which led to the eventual creation of the Red Cross. In 1920, U.S. President Woodrow Wilson proposed that the newly formed League of Nations be headquartered in Geneva (in the Hôtel Nation), where it remained until 1946. Today Geneva is the European headquarters of the United Nations.

Geneva is also a financial and industrial center. The city has 1,000 banks, and watchmaking, insurance, and technological companies are located along the Arve and Rhône rivers.

1. ORIENTATION

ARRIVING

BY PLANE The **Geneva-Cointrin Airport** (tel. 717-71-11), though busy with the comings and goings of tourists and employees of or visitors to the city's many international organizations, is quite compact and easily negotiated. To get into downtown Geneva, there's a train station in the basement of the air terminal with trains leaving about every 5 minutes from 5:30am to 12:20am for the 6-minute trip; the one-way fare is 6F ($4.40) in first class and 4F ($2.90) in second class. A taxi into town will cost 25F to 28F ($18.25 to $20.45), or you can take bus no. 10 for 1.50F ($1.10).

BY TRAIN Geneva's CFF (Chemins de fer fédéraux) train station downtown is **Gare Cornavin,** place Cornavin (tel. 731-64-50). The main tourist office is nearby on place Cornavin.
  Note: When the Lausanne–Geneva railroad line was extended to Cointrin Airport, a second "main" railroad station was built there, with both long-distance and intercity trains. To avoid having to make the trip back downtown from the airport, be sure you get off the train at the Cornavin station.

BY CAR From Lausanne, head southwest on Route N1 to the very "end of southwestern Switzerland."

BY LAKE STEAMER From late May to late September there are frequent daily arrivals by Swiss lake steamer from Montreux, Vevey, and Lausanne (you can use your Eurailpass for the trip). If you're staying in the Left Bank (Old Town), get off at the Jardin Anglais stop in Geneva; Mont Blanc and Pâquis are the two Right Bank stops.

TOURIST INFORMATION

Geneva's tourist office, the **Office du Tourisme de Genève,** is located on place Cornavin (tel. 022/738-52-00), near the downtown CFF railroad station, Gare Cornavin. The staff provides helpful information about the city, and can also arrange hotel reservations (both in Geneva and throughout Switzerland), car and motorcycle rentals, excursion bookings, and an audio-guided visit to the old town. The tourist office is open July to September, daily from 8am to 10pm; the rest of the year, Monday through Friday from 8:30am to 8pm, on Saturday from 9am to 6pm, and on Sunday from 4 to 8pm.

CITY LAYOUT

Geneva is a perfect city to explore on foot. It is divided by Lake Geneva (Lac Léman) and the Rhône River into two sections: the Right Bank and the Left Bank.

Rive Gauche (Left Bank) This compact and colorful area is the oldest section of the city. Here you'll find Old Town, some major shopping streets, the famous Flower Clock, the university, and several important museums.
  Grand'Rue is the well-preserved main street of Old Town. It's flanked by many houses dating from the 15th and 18th centuries. The street winds uphill from the Ponts de l'Ile; at place Bel-Air it becomes rue de la Cité, then Grand'Rue, and finally

rue Hôtel-de-Ville. Eventually it reaches **place du Bourg-de-Four**—one of the most charming squares of Geneva (Rousseau was born in a simple house at no. 40).

South of this street is the **promenade des Bastions,** a green-belt area with a monument to the Reformation; it overlooks the Arve River. Directly to the west, in the northern corner of the promenade des Bastions is **place Neuve,** which is considered the finest square in Geneva.

From place Neuve, you can take **rue de la Corraterie,** which was once surrounded by the city wall, to the Rhône and the **pont de l'Ile.** On this bridge is the Tour de l'Ile, what's left of the 13th-century bishops' castle.

On the shore of Lake Geneva is the **Jardin Anglais** (English Garden) with its Flower Clock and, farther out, the **Parc La Grange** and the nearby **Parc des Eaux-Vives.**

Rive Droite [Right Bank]   You can cross to the other side of the Rhône on any of several bridges, including pont du Mont-Blanc, pont de la Machine, pont des Bergues, and ponts de l'Ile. The Right Bank is home to Gare Cornavin, the major international organizations, and several attractive parks.

Place St-Gervais is in the St-Gervais district; since the 18th century this has been an area for jewelers and watchmakers.

Along the northern shore of the Lake Geneva is **quai du Président-Wilson,** named for the U.S. president who helped found the League of Nations.

The Right Bank is surrounded by parks, from the tree-shaded promenades along the Rhône to the **Parc de la Perle du Lac, Parc Barton,** and **Parc Mon-Repos** on the outskirts.

FINDING AN ADDRESS   In a system developed during the Middle Ages, all Swiss cities, including Geneva, begin their street-numbering system with the lowest numbers closest to the old center of town. The numbers increase the farther out from Old Town you go. Even numbers are on one side of a street; odd numbers are on the other side.

MAPS   The tourist office (see above) presents visitors with a detailed and easy-to-follow map of Geneva.

NEIGHBORHOODS IN BRIEF

Rues Basses   Rues Basses (translated either as "low streets" or figuratively as "lower town") is found between Old Town and the south bank of the Rhône. It is the major commercial and shopping district of Geneva. Its major street is rue du Rhône, although rue de la Confédération and rue du Marché are also important arteries.

Old Town, or Vieille Ville, at an altitude of 1,326 feet, is the most history-rich section of Geneva. This is Left Bank Geneva, with its narrow streets, flower-bedecked fountains, and architectural blends of Gothic, Renaissance, and 18th-century features. The twin towers of the Cathedral of St. Pierre dominate Old Town, whose geographical and spiritual center is place du Bourg-de-Four.

The Promenades of Geneva   These streets almost constitute a "neighborhood" in themselves. This section of quays along both Lake Geneva and the Rhône is best experienced by walking. One of the most scenic walks is from the Parc des Eaux-Vives on the Left Bank to the Parc de Mon-Repos on the Right Bank. Along the way you'll have a clear view of Geneva's most famous and visible monument, the

Jet d'Eau. Set a few inches above the surface of the lake, this is a powerful fountain spurting a plume of shimmering water more than 425 feet into the air.

2. GETTING AROUND

Walking is the cheapest, most practical form of transportation in Geneva. It is also the most advantageous, from a tourist's point of view. For the city's quaint old town, charming, tree-shaded promenades along the lake, and many chic shops can be enjoyed best if you walk leisurely about Geneva, savoring not only the scenes offered up to you but, equally important, the measured tempo of life that makes this city particularly attractive to the foreign visitor accustomed to a faster pace.

Nevertheless, if rapidity of movement is the object, you may avail yourself of the public transportation system, which is reasonably priced and as dependable as a Swiss watch.

BY PUBLIC BUS & TRAM   For the most part, all of Geneva's transportation lines begin at place Cornavin, in front of the main railroad station. From here, you can take bus F to the Palais des Nations.

No tickets are sold or validated on Geneva's buses and trams. Every financial transaction must take place at one of the coin-operated vending machines placed at each stop. The **three basic types of tickets** provide for:
1. Free transportation for 1 hour, with as many changes as you wish, on any vehicle, at a cost of 1.50F ($1.10).
2. A trip limited to three stops without changing vehicles, at a cost of .90F (75¢).
3. Rides for 1 hour only, for children 6 to 12 as well as for seniors (women over 62 and men over 65), at a cost of .80F (65¢).

If you plan to use the system frequently, you can save a small amount of money by purchasing multifare tickets at the agents whose addresses are listed on the stop posts. These tickets must be validated at the vending machine before entering the vehicle. The tickets cost 8F ($5.85), 5.50F ($4), and 4.50F ($3.30), respectively. Children under 6 ride free, with a limit of two children per adult.

The Réseau de Campagne lines in the Geneva public transport system extend far into the countryside. Tickets for long distances are sold by the conductor.

Most tourists will be interested in the **day tickets** good on any line, costing 6F ($4.40) for adults and 3F ($2.20) for children for 1 day, 11F ($8.05) for adults and 5.50F ($4) for children for 2 days, and 14F ($10.20) for adults and 7F ($5.10) for children for 3 days. These tickets may be purchased at the agents whose addresses are listed on each of the stop posts, and must be validated at the machine at the stop before you enter the vehicle. Special **commuter cards,** good on any line and transferable, may be purchased at the agents at a cost of 45F ($32.85) for a period of 1 calendar month.

For more information, call 21-25-09.

BY TAXI   Cab fares start at 5F ($3.65), plus 2.50F ($1.85) additional for each kilometer (.62 miles) in the city and 3.50F ($2.55) in the countryside. The fare from the airport is about 25F to 28F ($18.25 to $20.45). No tipping is required. For a taxi, call 141.

BY CAR   Driving is not recommended because parking is too difficult and the many one-way streets make navigation complicated. However, should you wish to rent a car and tour Lake Geneva, you'll find many car-rental companies represented at the airport or in the center of the city. Major offices include **Avis,** 44, rue de Lausanne (tel. 731-90-00); **Budget Rent-a-Car,** 37, rue de Lausanne (tel. 732-52-52), and **Hertz,** 60, rue de Berne (tel. 731-12-00).

BY BICYCLE Touring the city by bicycle isn't practical because of the steep cobblestone streets and general congestion. However, you might want to consider renting a bike for touring the countryside around Geneva.

A major outlet for this type of rental is **Horizon Motos,** 22, rue des Pâquis (tel. 731-23-39), which offers mopeds and mountain bicycles for 20F ($14.60) per day. Motorcycles can also be rented, beginning at 25F ($18.25) per day.

ON FOOT This is the ideal way to see Geneva, especially the old city—in fact, the only way to really explore it. The quays of Geneva and Old Town can easily be explored on foot, but you'll need to rely on public transportation when visiting attractions farther out.

 GENEVA

American Express The American Express office at 7, rue du Mont-Blanc (tel. 022/733-32-65), is open Monday through Friday from 8:30am to 5:30pm and on Saturday from 9am to noon.

Area Code The telephone area code for Geneva is 022.

Baby-sitters A list of agencies offering this service is available at the tourist office. Hotels will also secure an English-speaking baby-sitter for you, or you can call **Service de Placement de l'Université,** 4, rue de Candolle (tel. 29-39-70). Call this office before 11am if you want a sitter that night.

Bookstore One of the largest in Geneva is the well-respected **Payot,** 6, rue Grénus (tel. 731-89-50), with a good selection of books in French, German, and English.

Business Hours Most **banks** are open Monday through Friday from 8:30am to 4:30pm (until 5:30pm on Wednesday). Most **offices** are open Monday through Friday from 8am to noon and 2 to 6pm, although this can vary. It's always best to call first.

Car Rentals See Section 2, "Getting Around," in this chapter.

Climate See Section 2, "When to Go," in Chapter 2.

Consulates If you lose your passport or have other business with your home government, go to your nation's consulate: **United States,** 1-3, avenue de la Paix (tel. 022/733-55-37); **Australia,** 56, rue Moillebeau (tel. 734-62-00); **Canada,** 11, chemin du Pré-de-la-Bichette (tel. 733-90-00); **New Zealand,** 28, chemin du Petit-Saconnex (tel. 734-95-30); the **United Kingdom,** 37-39, rue de Vermont (tel. 734-38-00).

Currency See Section 1, "Information, Documents & Money," in Chapter 2.

Currency Exchange The money exchange at **Gare Cornavin,** place Cornavin (tel. 715-23-89), is open daily from 6am to 9:45pm. For other financial transactions, the **Société de Banque Suisse (Swiss Bank Corporation)** is at 2, rue de la Confédération (tel. 22-41-11).

Dentist English-speaking dentists are available at one of the *cliniques dentaires* at 5, chemin Malombré (tel. 46-64-44), daily from 7:30am to 8pm.

Doctor In a **medical emergency,** call 20-25-11; or arrange an appointment with an English-speaking doctor at the **Hôpital Cantonal,** 24, rue Micheli-du-Crest (tel. 46-92-11).

Drugstores One of the world's biggest drugstores, **Pharmacie Principale,** Confédération-Centre, rue de la Confédération (tel. 21-31-30), offers everything from medicine to clothing, perfumes, optical equipment, cameras, and photo supplies. It's open on Monday from 1 to 6:45pm, Tuesday through Friday from 8:15am to 6:45pm, and on Saturday from 8:15am to 5pm. The **Pharmacie de Saint-Gervais,** 1 Tour-de-l'Ile (tel. 21-30-05), is located next door to the main tourist office, and is open Monday through Friday from 8:30am to 12:30pm and 1:30 to 6:30pm.

Emergencies In an emergency, dial 117 for the **police** or an **ambulance.** Dial 118 to report a **fire.**

Eyeglasses For your eyeglass needs, you can go to **Pharmacie Principale,** Confédération-Centre, rue de la Confédération (tel. 21-31-30). It's on the second floor.

Hairdressers/Barbers One of the best places to get your hair done—for both *dames* and *messieurs*—is **Coiffure Sofia,** 26, boulevard Helvétique (tel. 735-84-40), open Tuesday through Saturday from 8am to 7pm; closed Monday afternoon.

Holidays See Section 2, "When to Go," in Chapter 2.

Hospitals You can go to the **Hôpital Cantonal,** 24, rue Micheli-du-Crest (tel. 46-92-11).

Information See "Tourist Information" in Section 1, "Orientation," above.

Laundry If you need a self-service laundry, try **Lavandière,** 8, rue Lyon (tel. 45-36-01), in back of Gare Cornavin, the railroad station.

Library The **American Library,** at 3, rue de Monthoux (tel. 732-80-97), has a subscription service open to those looking for a wide variety of the latest books in English. A subscription must be for at least a month.

Lost Property Go to the **Bureau cantonal des objets trouvés,** 7, rue des Glacis-de-Rive (tel. 787-60-00), open Monday through Thursday from 8am to noon and 1 to 4:30pm, and on Friday from 8am to noon and 1 to 4pm.

Luggage Storage/Lockers Luggage can be stored and lockers rented at the main railroad station, Gare Cornavin, place Cornavin (tel. 715-21-11).

Newspapers/Magazines Newspapers in Geneva are printed in French, but the latest copies of the *International Herald Tribune* are available at most newsstands and in large hotel newsstand kiosks. These same places usually carry the latest issues of the European editions of *Newsweek* and *Time.* The English-language *Geneva News and International Report* is published bimonthly, with a good section on various entertainment possibilities offered in Geneva.

Photographic Needs Camera stores are found throughout the central city. Otherwise, patronize **Photo Hall,** 5, rue de la Confédération (tel. 28-12-60).

Police In an emergency, call 117.

Post Office The post office at Gare Cornavin, 16, rue des Gares (tel. 739-24-51), is open Monday though Saturday from 6am to 9pm, and on Sunday from 9am to 12:30pm and 3 to 10pm.

Radio Radio Pays de Gex plays the American top 10 songs in Geneva with comment and introduction by an American DJ. This program is on daily from 8 to 9am and on Saturday at 8:30pm.

Religious Services Protestant services in English are conducted at **Church of Scotland,** Auditoire de Calvin, 1, place de la Taconnerie (tel. 798-29-09). There's an American church, **Emmanuel Episcopal,** at 3, rue de

Monthoux (tel. 732-80-78). **Roman Catholic** services (in French only) are conducted at the Basilique de Notre-Dame, place Cornavin (tel. 731-31-57). Jewish services are at **Rite Ashkenaze Synagogue,** place de la Synagogue (tel. 20-46-86).

Rest Rooms You'll find public facilities at all rail and air terminals and on main squares. Otherwise, you can patronize those in cafés and other commercial establishments such as department stores.

Safety Geneva is one of the safest cities in the world, but that doesn't mean you shouldn't take the usual precautions when traveling anywhere. Protect your valuables. Car thefts have been on the rise. Of course, high-class prostitutes and confidence swindlers proliferate in Geneva to prey on the well-heeled.

Shoe Repairs An outlet of **Mr. Minit** is located in the Metro-Shopping arcade, 30, rue du Mont-Blanc (tel. 732-42-59). Most repairs can be performed while you wait.

Taxes There is no special city tax, other than the 6.2% Value-Added Tax (VAT) attached to all goods and services throughout Switzerland.

Taxis See Section 2, "Getting Around," in this chapter.

Telegrams/Telex/Fax A big long-distance phone center is at the main train station, Gare Cornavin, place Cornavin, and it's open 24 hours a day. It's much cheaper to make your long-distance calls here than at your hotel—some Geneva hotels add a 40% surcharge to long-distance calls. Telegrams and faxes can be sent at the main post office at 18, rue du Mont-Blanc (tel. 739-21-11), two blocks from the train station.

Television TV broadcasts are in three languages: French, German, and Italian. Sometimes films are shown in their original language, such as English. Many of the big hotels have the English-language Sky Channel or CNN.

Tipping Most restaurants and hotels, even taxis, add a service charge of 10% to 15% to your bill, so no further tipping is necessary unless you want to reward someone for a special service.

Transit Information Call 731-64-50 for rail information, or the airport at 717-71-11. For bus information, call 732-02-30.

Useful Telephone Numbers For general information, call 111; for the time, 160; for the weather, 162.

Yellow Pages They are in French and a basic knowledge of that language is needed to use them successfully.

3. ACCOMMODATIONS

Consistent with its status as a world-class city, Geneva has lots of hotels, many of which are either clustered around the main railway terminal or (usually the more expensive ones) stretched along the lakefront. Because Geneva hosts many international conferences and conventions, many of its hotels are often booked many months in advance. While it contains dozens of expensive hotels in all different architectural styles (from the antique to the super-modern), it does not have very many intimate, family-run inns.

Hotels listed here as "Very Expensive" offer double rooms for 350F ($255.45) and

SWITZERLAND
★ BERN
Geneva

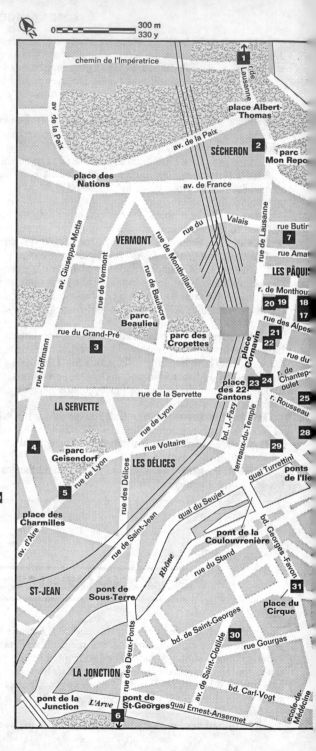

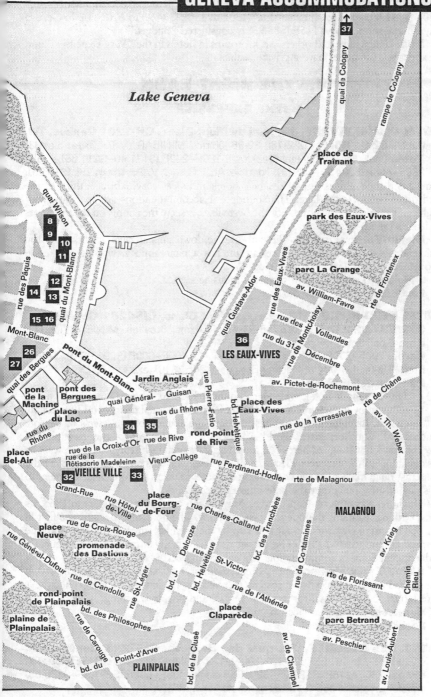

GENEVA ACCOMMODATIONS

Lake Geneva

place de Traînant

park des Eaux-Vives

parc La Grange

quai Wilson

8
9
10
11
12
14
13
15 16

rue des Pâquis

quai du Mont-Blanc

Mont-Blanc

26
27

quai des Bergues

pont du Mont-Blanc

pont de la Machine

pont des Bergues

place du Lac

quai Général- Guisan

Jardin Anglais

quai Gustave-Ador

rue des Eaux-Vives

av. William-Favre

rue des Montchoisy

rue du 31 Vollandes

Décembre

LES EAUX-VIVES

36

rte de Frontenex

rampe de Cologny

quai de Cologny

37

av. Pictet-de-Rochemont

rue Pierre-Fatio

place des Eaux-Vives

bd. Helvétique

rue du Rhône

34 35

rue de Rive

rond-point de Rive

rue de la Croix-d'Or

rue de la Rôtisserie Madeleine

Vieux-Collège

rue Ferdinand-Hodler

rte de Malagnou

place Bel-Air

rue du Rhône

32 VIEILLE VILLE 33

Grand-Rue

rue Hôtel- de-Ville

place du Bourg- de-Four

rue Charles-Galland

bd. des Tranchées

MALAGNOU

rue de la Terrassière

rte de Chêne

av. Th. Weber

place Neuve

rue de Croix-Rouge

rue Général-Dufour

promenade des Bastions

rue de Candolle

Dalcroze

rue St-Léger

bd. J-

rue Helvétique

St-Victor

rue de l'Athénée

rue de Contamines

rte de Florissant

av. Krieg

Chemin Rieu

rond-point de Plainpalais

bd. des Philosophes

rue de Carouge

bd. de la Clusé

place Claparède

av. de Champel

parc Betrand

av. Peschier

av. Louis-Aubert

plaine de Plainpalais

bd. du Point-d'Arve

PLAINPALAIS

beyond; "Expensive," between 190F and 260F ($138.70 and $189.75); "Moderate," 180F ($131.40) and up; "Inexpensive," 130F to 150F ($94.90 to $109.50). In Geneva any double room below 115F ($83.95) is considered "Budget."

Note: Unless indicated otherwise, all rooms in hotels in the "Very Expensive" and "Expensive" categories have a private bath.

ON THE RIGHT BANK
VERY EXPENSIVE

HOTEL D'ANGLETERRE, 17, quai du Mont-Blanc, CH-1201 Genève. Tel. 022/732-81-80. Fax 022/738-62-86. 66 rms. MINIBAR TV TEL **Bus:** 6 or 33.

$ Rates (including continental breakfast): 180F–290F ($131.40–$211.65) single; 280F–400F ($204.35–$291.95) double. AE, DC, MC, V. **Parking:** 25F ($18.25).
Grand and solid, this is one of the best hotels in its category. About a third of the bedrooms overlook the lake. The soundproof accommodations are spacious, with high ceilings and fine furniture. For the best views, reserve the rooms on the top floors at least a month in advance.

Dining/Entertainment: The club lounge downstairs attracts visitors from the financial district, and the hotel restaurant has a panoramic view of the lakeside promenade.

Services: Laundry, room service, limousine service.

Facilities: Garage, tour desk.

HOTEL BEAU-RIVAGE, 13, quai du Mont-Blanc, CH-1201 Genève. Tel. 022/731-02-21. Fax 022/738-98-47. 104 rms, 6 suites. MINIBAR TV TEL **Bus:** 6 or 33.

$ Rates: 290F–330F ($211.65–$240.85) single; 400F–600F ($291.95–$437.95); from 1,500F ($1,094.85) suite. Breakfast 26F ($19) extra. AE, DC, MC, V. **Parking:** 25F ($18.25).

This landmark hotel, which has counted Richard Wagner among its guests, receives my highest recommendation for its traditional charm and impeccable service. Its colorful history has included the auction of the jewels of the late Duchess of Windsor; after World War I, the treaty creating the Republic of Czechoslovakia was signed here. The most tragic event in its history, however, was the assassination of the Empress Elisabeth of Austria, who was stabbed in 1898 by the anarchist Luigi Lucheni as she was leaving the hotel to take a trip on a lake steamer. To this day, history buffs rent the pale blue Empress Suite.

The hotel was built by Jean-Jacques Mayer, who came from Stuttgart in 1865. Its most striking feature is the open, five-story lobby. The hotel also became the first in Europe to install elevators. Today it is run by the founder's great-grandson, with the help of an enthusiastic staff. The rooms are individually furnished and frequently redecorated. Some accommodations are air-conditioned.

Dining/Entertainment: The hotel restaurant, Le Chat-Botté (Puss in Boots), is considered one of the top five in the city (see Section 4, "Dining," below). The hotel's café terrace is also known for its good service and people-watching.

Services: Laundry service, room service.

Facilities: Garage.

HOTEL DES BERGUES, 33, quai des Bergues, CH-1211 Genève. Tel. 022/731-50-50. Fax 022/732-19-89. 123 rms. A/C MINIBAR TV TEL **Bus:** 7.

$ Rates: 260F–315F ($189.75–$229.90) single; 400F–530F ($291.95–$386.85) double. Breakfast 25F ($18.25) extra. AE, DC, MC, V.

This elegant, four-story hotel—designated a historic monument by the Swiss—once catered to the monarchs of Europe. Today it is a favorite with the international business community, diplomats, and members of European society. It has long been ranked by *Institutional Investor* as one of the world's top hotels. The hotel's impressive guest list has included Jean Cocteau, the duke of Edinburgh, the queen of Spain, Edward VIII, the queen of Hawaii, and Emperor Franz Joseph and Empress Elizabeth ("Sissi") of Austria. Grandly memorable from its centrally located position at the edge of the Rhône, the hotel also hosted many meetings of the League of Nations. During World War II it was known as the "hotel of the Allies," because it played host to so many Allied leaders.

The hotel and its efficient 150-person staff are well directed by Reto Grass. Public rooms are lavish. The bedrooms have Directoire and Louis Philippe furnishings, along with many other amenities.

Dining/Entertainment: Its two restaurants and bar are highly recommended (see Section 4, "Dining," below).

Services: Room service, laundry.

Facilities: Electronically sophisticated 19th-century conference rooms.

HOTEL BRISTOL, 10, rue du Mont-Blanc, CH-1201 Genève. Tel. 022/ 732-38-00. Fax 022/738-90-39. 94 rms, 5 suites. MINIBAR TV TEL **Bus:** 1, 6, 8, 9, or 23.

$ Rates: 225F–270F ($164.25–$197.05) single; 285F–330F ($208–$240.85) double; from 440F ($321.15) suite. Breakfast 16F ($11.70) extra. AE, DC, MC, V.

This 130-year-old hotel is one of the most respected and sought-after establishments in Geneva, set in a public park not far from the central Mont Blanc bridge. The public rooms are elegant and sedate, and the bedrooms have soundproof windows, clear colors, and the kinds of antiques you'd expect in a private manor house. A few have air conditioning.

Dining/Entertainment: The Bar Anglais is popular with Geneva's business-lunch crowd; at night it becomes a piano bar. The restaurant serves a French cuisine based on seasonal ingredients.

Services: Room service, baby-sitting, massages.

Facilities: Health club, sauna, solarium.

HOTEL DE LA PAIX, 11, quai du Mont-Blanc, CH-1201 Genève. Tel. 022/732-61-50. Fax 022/738-87-94. 100 rms, 14 suites. MINIBAR TV TEL **Bus:** 6 or 33.

$ Rates: 280F ($204.35) single; 350F–460F ($255.45–$335.75) double; from 500F ($364.95) suite. Breakfast 25F ($18.25). AE, DC, MC, V.

This 18th-century hotel, directly on the lake, attracted the princes and diplomats of yesterday and welcomes their descendants today. Royalty from Liechtenstein, Monaco, and the Netherlands, as well as international dignitaries and celebrities, such as guitarist Andrès Segovia, have stayed here. Designed by an Italian architect and built of stone from Meillerie, the building belonged to the kingdom of Sardinia for a long time. The main salon is a double-tiered arched extravaganza, with marble columns, elaborate Corinthian capitals, and a balustraded loggia overlooking a massive crystal chandelier. The accommodations have modern baths and deluxe amenities; nearly half are air-conditioned. This hotel is listed in *Leading Hotels of the World*.

HOTEL PRESIDENT, 47, quai du Président-Wilson, CH-1211 Genève. Tel. 022/731-10-00. Fax 022/731-22-06. 180 rms, 27 suites. A/C MINIBAR TV TEL **Bus:** 1.

$ Rates: 225F–280F ($164.25–$204.35) single; 325F–375F ($237.20–$273.70) double; from 500F ($364.95) suite. Breakfast 25F ($18.25) extra. AE, DC, MC, V.

Located across a busy boulevard from the lakefront, a 5-minute drive (or a brisk walk) from the center of town, this modern hotel is sometimes mistaken for the diplomatic headquarters of some international agency. The public rooms are opulently decorated, with velvet-covered walls, floors that resemble lapis lazuli, and a scattering of valuable antiques. One of the galleries displays the hotel's collection of Gobelin tapestries. The impeccable service is directed by Jacques Favre, for the Swissotel chain. The bedrooms are beautifully furnished with antiques and elegant upholstery, and always provide two beds regardless of occupancy. Each contains floor-to-ceiling windows overlooking the lake.

Dining/Entertainment: The hotel's restaurant is the famous Nuances, with a French and traditional cuisine. There is also a piano bar.

Services: Hairdresser, beauty salon, room service, baby-sitting.

Facilities: Fitness club next door.

HOTEL DU RHONE, 1, quai Turrettini, CH-1211 Genève. Tel. 022/731-98-31. Fax 022/732-45-58. 222 rms, 8 suites. A/C MINIBAR TV TEL

$ Rates: 255F ($186.10) single; 385F ($281) double; from 560F ($408.75) suite. Breakfast 25F ($18.25) extra. AE, DC, MC, V. **Parking:** 25F ($18.25).

Built in 1950, this hotel has remained up-to-date with the amenities and service provided by most of Geneva's other deluxe hotels. Located behind a bank of trees along the edge of the Rhône, it belongs to the Rafael Group of Hoteliers and is listed in *Leading Hotels of the World*. Public rooms display tapestries by contemporary artists. The rooms are all decorated with patterned wall-to-wall carpeting, natural colors, and classically elegant furniture.

Dining/Entertainment: The bar and one of the two restaurants have a terrace.

Services: Room service, baby-sitting, laundry.

Facilities: A subterranean parking garage accommodates 120 cars.

NOGA HILTON INTERNATIONAL, 19, quai du Mont-Blanc, CH-1211 Genève. Tel. 022/731-98-11, or toll free 800/445-8667 in North America. 367 rms, 46 suites. A/C MINIBAR TV TEL **Bus:** 1.

$ Rates: 315F ($229.90) single; 415F ($302.90) double; from 525F ($383.20) suite. Breakfast buffet 27F ($19.70) extra. AE, DC, MC, V. **Parking:** 25F ($18.25).

Located at the edge of the lake, this is the largest deluxe hotel in Switzerland, and one of the best in the Hilton chain. All the rooms are custom designed, with beautiful wood, fabrics, artwork, and an array of hi-tech amenities. Some have panoramic lake views. The general manager is Eric Kuhne, a Swiss-born hotelier and native of Geneva, who supervises an international staff of 450 people.

Dining/Entertainment: The hotel has a gourmet restaurant, Le Cygne, one of the best in Geneva, and an elegant Oriental restaurant, Le Tse-Yang (see Section 4, "Dining," below). In addition, La Grignotière has a casual atmosphere, good food, and a terrace with a lake view. Le Bistroquai offers a selection of Swiss ice creams, sandwiches, and salads. Drinks are served in the intimate Bar du Cygne as well as the Lobby Bar, which is open all day long. The hotel's disco is the Blue Chip.

Services: Room service, dry cleaning and laundry, baby-sitting, hairdresser, barber.

Facilities: Gym with solarium cabins, saunas, massage area, indoor heated swimming pool; tunnel across to the lake shore for joggers; games room which limits the stakes to 5F ($3.65) according to Swiss law; underground parking garage.

LE RICHEMOND, Jardin Brunswick, CH-1211 Genève. Tel. 022/731-14-00. Fax 022/731-67-09. 69 rms. A/C MINIBAR TV TEL **Bus:** 1 or 9.

$ Rates: 325F–455F ($237.20–$332.10) single; 545F–580F ($397.80–$423.35) double. Breakfast 25F ($18.25) extra. AE, DC, MC, V. **Parking:** 25F ($18.25).

⭐ Le Richemond, which counts some of the world's most prominent people among its guests, is the greatest hotel in Geneva. Erected in 1875, the neoclassical, travertine building has wrought-iron balustrades and is situated near the lake, across from a small park. In the 19th century it was an unpretentious guesthouse. The hotel has been transformed under the direction of Jean Armleder, who is one of the best hoteliers in Switzerland and whose family opened the hotel. Its public rooms look like a museum, with dozens of valuable engravings and an array of furniture dating from the days of Louis XIII.

Dining/Entertainment: The hotel restaurant, Gentilhomme, is considered by many to be the finest dining establishment in Geneva (see Section 4, "Dining," below). Le Jardin is the most fashionable café in the city.

Services: Personalized excursions in luxury cars, valet parking, beauty salon, 24-hour room service.

Facilities: Garage.

EXPENSIVE

HOTEL AMBASSADOR, 21, quai des Bergues, CH-1201 Genève. Tel. 022/731-72-00. Fax 022/738-90-80. 92 rms. MINIBAR TV TEL **Bus:** 7.

$ Rates: 130F–170F ($94.90–$124.10) single; 190F–260F ($138.70–$189.75) double. Breakfast 15F ($10.95) extra. AE, DC, MC, V. **Parking:** 25F ($18.25).

Built in 1966, this hotel is located on a well-known part of the lake. The restrained facade has neoclassical detailing. The rooms, though small, are decorated in light colors with traditional furnishings, radio, and refrigerator.

Dining/Entertainment: There is a pleasant summer café and a French-Swiss restaurant.

Services: Room service, laundry.

Facilities: Garage.

HOTEL DE BERNE, 26, rue de Berne, CH-1201 Genève. Tel. 022/731-60-00. Fax 022/731-11-73. 84 rms. A/C MINIBAR TV TEL **Bus:** 6 or 33.

$ Rates (including continental breakfast): 140F–180F ($102.20–$131.40) single; 170F–220F ($124.10–$160.60) double. AE, DC, MC, V.

This centrally located, modern hotel has maroon stripes across its boxy facade. The lobby has a high ceiling, with wood columns and carpeting. The soundproof bedrooms are decorated in muted tones with comfortable furnishings as well as a radio and other amenities. A restaurant and bar are on the premises.

HOTEL CALIFORNIA, 1, rue Govray, CH-1200 Genève. Tel. 022/731-55-50. Fax 022/731-55-56. 69 rms. 9 suites. MINIBAR TV TEL **Bus:** 6 or 33.

$ Rates (including continental breakfast): 125F–165F ($91.25–$120.45) single; 185F–225F ($135.05–$164.25) double; from 550F ($401.45) suite. AE, DC, MC, V.

This six-story, aluminum-and-glass building is only a block from the lake, behind quai du Mont-Blanc. As its name implies, the hotel is colorful, functional, and modern. The bedrooms have cosmetic bars, hairdryers, and radios, among other amenities. There's one entire floor of single and double suites with kitchenettes. The hotel has no restaurant, but you can get a drink in the rooftop bar until dawn.

HOTEL CORNAVIN, place Cornavin, 33, bd. James-Fazy, CH-1211

Genève. **Tel. 022/732-21-00.** Fax 022/732-88-43. 125 rms. MINIBAR TV
TEL **Bus:** 6 or 33.
$ Rates (including continental breakfast): 125F–190F ($91.25–$138.70) single;
180F–260F ($131.40–$189.75) double. AE, DC, MC, V.

Just 50 yards from the train station, this simple but attractively renovated hotel is on a
busy thoroughfare in Geneva's business district. It has a gray-and-white marble lobby
and bright-colored, carpeted bedrooms. The rooms are soundproofed against the
traffic noises; 46 units are air-conditioned. Only breakfast is served.

HOTEL REX, 44, av. Wendt, CH-1203 Genève. Tel. 022/45-71-50. Fax
022/44-04-20. 74 rms, 15 suites. A/C MINIBAR TV TEL **Bus:** 3, 10, 15, or 33.
$ Rates (including buffet breakfast): 170F ($124.10) single; 280F ($204.35) double;
from 550F ($401.45) suite. AE, DC, MC, V.

The Hotel Rex is 5 minutes away from the airport and a few blocks away from the
train station and the lake. The rooms are tastefully furnished, with leather armchairs
and modern bathrooms. The hotel also has a drawing room and a reading room.

Dining/Entertainment: There is an English bar. La Régent is one of the best
French restaurants in Geneva. In the summer, guests enjoy dining in the garden.

 FROMMER'S COOL FOR KIDS

HOTELS

Hôtel d'Angleterre (see p. 338) A grand old hotel overlooking Lake
Geneva, this excellent choice supplies baby cots for free and lets children under
12 stay free in their parents' room.

Hôtel Bernina (see p. 344) This six-story building at the railroad station
rents many rooms with three beds (either with or without a shower) for families
on a budget.

Hôtel Le Grenil (see p. 346) Another good choice for value-conscious
family travelers, Le Grenil offers five family rooms with shower (each unit
containing four beds).

**LE WARWICK, 14, rue de Lausanne, CH-1201 Genève. Tel. 022/731-62-
50.** Fax 022/738-99-35. 169 rms. A/C MINIBAR TV TEL **Bus:** 6 or 33.
$ Rates: 190F–285F ($138.70–$208) single; 260F–390F ($189.75–$284.65)
double. Breakfast 22F ($16.05) extra. AE, DC, MC, V.

This contemporary hotel is located across from the train station. The abstractly
modern lobby contains sweeping staircases, loggias, balconies, marble floors, and
Oriental rugs. The refurbished, soundproof bedrooms are sunny, boldly patterned,
and comfortable.

Dining/Entertainment: The hotel has restaurants and a piano bar.
Services: Room service, laundry.
Facilities: Gift shop, sauna.

MODERATE

HOTEL CARLTON, 22, rue Amat, CH-1202 Genève. Tel. 022/731-68-50.
Fax 022/732-82-47. 123 rms (all with bath). TV TEL **Bus:** 6 or 33.

$ Rates (including breakfast): 125F–185F ($91.25–$135.05) single; 180F–270F ($131.40–$197.05) double. AE, DC, MC, V.

This hotel lies about seven city blocks east of the railroad station and 300 yards from the waterfront views of quai du Président-Wilson. The facade combines weathered vertical slats and smooth stones decoratively cemented into rectangular patterns beneath the modern windows. The public areas are warmly decorated in monochromatic tones of brown and beige. The bedrooms are comfortably furnished with modern styling.

HOTEL EDELWEISS, 2, place de la Navigation, CH-1201 Genève. Tel. 022/731-36-58. Fax 022/738-85-33. 62 rms (all with bath). TV TEL **Bus:** 6 or 33.

$ Rates (including continental breakfast): 135F ($98.55) single; 180F ($131.40) double. AE, DC, MC, V.

This green-and-white, eight-story hotel towers above its neighbors near quai du Président-Wilson. Inside, it has a rustic decor that contrasts with its modern exterior. The bedrooms are cozy and furnished with pinewood furniture crafted in a country-Swiss style.

HOTEL GRAND-PRE, 35, rue du Grand-Pré, CH-1202 Genève. Tel. 022/733-91-50. Fax 022/734-76-91. 80 rms (all with bath). TV TEL **Bus:** 3 or 33.

$ Rates (including continental breakfast): 140F–165F ($102.20–$120.45) single; 195F–215F ($142.35–$156.95) double. AE, DC, MC, V.

Located on the way to the airport, this modern hotel is convenient and friendly. The rooms are well decorated and well maintained; each contains a radio and refrigerator. Special terms are available for families and for long stays. Other than a room for breakfast, there is no restaurant.

HOTEL DU MIDI, 4, place Chevelu, CH-1211 Genève. Tel. 022/731-78-00. Fax 022/731-00-20. 85 rms (all with bath). A/C TV TEL **Bus:** 7.

$ Rates (including continental breakfast): 140F–165F ($102.20–$120.45) single; 195F–215F ($142.35–$156.95) double. AE, DC, MC, V.

Ideally situated on a tree-lined square near the center of Geneva, the angular modernity of this salmon-colored, eight-story hotel reminds most visitors of an apartment building. The windows are double-glazed to keep out the noise of the city's traffic, and there's wall-to-wall carpeting in every room. The bedrooms contain such accessories as warming racks for towels, small refrigerators, and safes. The hotel has a brasserie, a tavern, and a sidewalk café overlooking the antique fountain in place Chevelu.

HOTEL MON-REPOS, 131, rue de Lausanne, CH-1202 Genève. Tel. 022/732-80-10. Fax 022/732-85-95. 155 rms (all with bath). TV TEL **Bus:** 23.

$ Rates (including continental breakfast): 120F–150F ($87.60–$109.50) single; 150F–180F ($109.50–$131.40) double. AE, DC, MC, V.

Located on the Right Bank of Lake Geneva, this hotel offers lakeside rooms with views of a verdant lawn and Mont Blanc in the distance. The sandstone, corner hotel has recessed balconies and elegantly detailed windows. All the comfortable bedrooms have a radio. The hotel is owned by the Keller family.

HOTEL TOURING-BALANCE, 13, place Longemalle, CH-1204 Genève. Tel. 022/28-71-22. Fax 022/28-51-41. 82 rms (all with bath). TV TEL **Bus:** 6 or 33.

$ Rates (including continental breakfast): 130F–150F ($94.90–$109.50) single; 180F–200F ($131.40–$146) double. AE, DC, MC, V.

This hotel, set two blocks east of the lake and just off the street that runs into pont du Mont-Blanc, was created by the architectural union of two 19th-century properties, the Hôtel Touring and the Hôtel Balance. It enjoys a loyal clientele. Its brightly colored interior combines some of the original decorative details with modern paintings and accessories. The hotel has a restaurant.

INEXPENSIVE

HOTEL BERNINA, 22, place Cornavin, CH-1211 Genève. Tel. 022/731-49-50. Fax 022/732-73-59. 80 rms (68 with bath). TV TEL **Bus:** 6 or 33.

$ Rates (including continental breakfast): 60F ($43.80) single without bath, 95F ($69.35) single with bath; 95F ($69.35) double without bath, 130F ($94.90) double with bath; 130F ($94.90) triple without bath, 180F ($131.40) triple with bath. AE, MC, V.

This six-story hotel occupies an old-fashioned building with iron balustrades and neoclassical detailing. The simply furnished bedrooms have more space than you might have expected, closets, and double glazing to keep out the noise of traffic.

HOTEL EXCELSIOR, 34, rue Rousseau, CH-1201 Genève. Tel. 022/732-09-45. Fax 022/738-4369. 54 rms (all with bath). MINIBAR TV TEL **Bus:** 3 or 33.

$ Rates (including continental breakfast): 95F–120F ($69.35–$87.60) single; 140F–150F ($102.20–$109.50) double. AE, DC, MC, V.

This hotel is situated only 200 yards from the train station. It has a sidewalk café as well as a French-Swiss restaurant, La Brocherie. The rooms are comfortable and brightly decorated, with modern plumbing. Laundry service is available for clients staying more than 1 night.

HOTEL INTERNATIONAL & TERMINUS, 20, rue des Alpes, CH-1201 Genève. Tel. 022/732-80-95. Fax 022/732-18-43. 67 rms (52 with bath). TV TEL **Bus:** 6 or 33.

$ Rates (including continental breakfast): 65F ($47.45) single without bath, 110F ($80.30) single with bath; 95F ($69.35) double without bath, 148F ($108.05) double with bath. AE, DC, MC, V.

This hotel, run by the Cottier family, is about a 10-minute walk to the railroad station and the lake. The rooms all have a radio and a sink; some are not equipped with a bath. The public rooms are decorated with reproduction Louis XIII chairs and Oriental rugs. Plats du jour in the attached restaurant start at a reasonable 10.50F ($7.65).

HOTEL MODERNE, 1, rue de Berne, CH-1211 Genève. Tel. 022/732-81-00. Fax 022/738-26-58. 55 rms (all with bath). TV TEL **Bus:** 6 or 33.

$ Rates (including continental breakfast): 90F–100F ($65.70–$73) single; 120F–140F ($87.60–$102.20) double. AE, DC, MC, V.

Near the railroad station and the lake, this is a seven-story rectangle painted white, with a low-lying, glassed-in extension containing the breakfast room. The public rooms are very modern, with Nordic furniture and abstract angles and curves. The bedrooms are predictably furnished, clean, modern, and sunny. Baby-sitting, room service, and laundry facilities are available. The hotel's restaurant serves only breakfast.

BUDGET

HOTEL LE CLOS VOLTAIRE, 49, rue de Lyon, CH-1203 Genève. Tel. 022/744-70-14. 41 rms (16 with bath or shower, 25 with sink). **Bus:** 3 or 33.
$ Rates (including continental breakfast): 60F ($43.80) single without bath, 85F ($62.05) single with bath; 105F ($76.65) double without bath, 135F ($98.55) double with bath. AE, DC, MC, V.

This hotel, a suitable choice in the budget category, is named after the famed French writer who used to live nearby. Set in a tranquil, suburban park, this vine-covered house inside a walled garden is on the main road to Lyon. It's ideal if you have a car, and is only about a 5-minute walk from the train station. It has a garden and parking spaces. Four of the rooms have kitchens.

HOTEL LIDO, 8, rue Chantepoulet, CH-1201 Genève. Tel. 022/731-55-30. Fax 022/731-65-01. 32 rms (all with bath). TEL **Bus:** 6 or 33.
$ Rates: 65F ($47.45) single; 115F ($83.95) double. AE, DC, MC, V.
Located two blocks from the railroad station, this hotel offers sunny, comfortable, soundproof rooms with city views. The rooms are simply furnished in a functional modern style. The Rossier family offers personalized service.

HOTEL WINDSOR, 31, rue de Berne, CH-1201 Genève. Tel. 022/731-71-30. Fax 022/731-93-25. 64 rms (all with bath). TV TEL **Bus:** 6 or 31.
$ Rates (including continental breakfast): 100F ($73) single; 115F–135F ($83.95–$98.55) double. AE, DC, MC, V.
This hotel is four blocks from quai du Président-Wilson and three blocks from the train station. The rooms are small and a little dated, but not bad for the price. Each room has a radio. The lobby is designed around a large masonry fireplace and is decorated in shades of blue and red.

ON THE LEFT BANK

VERY EXPENSIVE

HOTEL DE LA CIGOGNE, 17, place Longemalle, CH-1204 Genève. Tel. 022/21-42-42. Fax 022/21-40-65. 50 rms. A/C MINIBAR TV TEL **Bus:** 2 or 12.
$ Rates (including continental breakfast): 250F ($182.50) single; 435F ($317.50) double. AE, DC, MC, V.
This is a deluxe hotel that was rebuilt after years of dilapidation. Combined with an adjoining building, the old hotel and its mate have the carefully renovated facades of the original 18th- and 19th-century structures. With three sheltered courtyards overlooking a flowering plaza, this is one of the quietest hotels in Geneva. The bedrooms contain handmade mattresses, luxurious bathrooms, radios, safes, and bed linens embroidered with the hotel's coat of arms. Director Richard Bischoff is assisted by an attentive staff.

Dining/Entertainment: The hotel restaurant serves classic cuisine in an artfully designed setting.
Services: Room service, laundry.
Facilities: Three different courtyards.

EXPENSIVE

HOTEL LES ARMURES, 1, rue des Puits-St-Pierre, CH-1204 Genève. Tel. 022/28-91-72. Fax 022/28-98-46. 28 rms. A/C MINIBAR TV TEL **Bus:** 3 or 33.
$ Rates (including continental breakfast): 215F–255F ($156.95–$186.10) single; 330F–430F ($240.85–$313.85) double. AE, DC, MC, V.

★ This hotel, located in the center of the old town, is one of the most charming in Geneva. The 17th-century building had been used as a printing factory until 1981. The restored public rooms reveal the original painted ceiling beams and an old blue-and-gray fresco. Today the lobby has Oriental rugs, modern sculpture, and a suit of armor. Parking might be a problem, as the hotel is in a maze of one-way streets. All the handsomely furnished bedrooms have a radio and a VCR. The hotel is housed in the same building as the oldest café in Geneva (see Section 4, "Dining," below).

INEXPENSIVE

HOTEL LE CHANDELIER, 23, Grand'Rue, CH-1204 Genève. Tel. 022/21-56-88. Fax 022/28-74-90. 24 rms (all with bath or shower). TV TEL **Bus:** 12

$ Rates (including continental breakfast): 80F–140F ($58.40–$102.20) single; 120F–170F ($87.60–$124.10) double. AE, DC, M, MC, V.

Considered one of the city's special hotels, this 14th-century inn is located in the heart of the old city, on a cobblestone street that's closed to traffic every night between 11pm and 6am. The carefully renovated rooms are spacious, and each contains a radio. My favorite rooms, with shopping ceilings and gabled windows, are on the top floor. There are a dozen studios with kitchens, for longer visits.

BUDGET

HOTEL BEAU-SITE, 3, place du Cirque, CH-1204 Genève. Tel. 022/28-10-08. Fax 022/29-23-64. 25 rms (18 with bath). **Bus:** 1 from the train station.

$ Rates (including continental breakfast): 53F ($38.70) single without bath, 58F ($42.35) single with bath; 73F ($53.30) double without bath, 78F ($56.95) double with bath. MC, V.

This hotel near the university offers simple, well-kept bedrooms. The English-speaking management recently renovated it. Nonworking marble fireplaces are in some of the bedrooms, while the dining room, serving breakfast only, is decorated with a heavily carved sideboard. The hotel has an elevator.

HOTEL DU LAC, 15, rue des Eaux-Vives, CH-1207 Genève. Tel. 022/735-45-80. 26 rms (none with bath). TEL **Bus:** 6 or 9 from the train station to place des Eaux-Vives (fifth stop).

$ Rates (including continental breakfast): 47F–54F ($34.30–$39.40) single; 73F ($53.30) double; 100F ($73) triple. No credit cards.

⑤ This small, budget hotel is on the Left Bank in the old city, occupying the sixth and seventh floors of an apartment building. The Swiss-Italian managers do not pretend to offer luxury service, but they make up for it with their hospitality and their ability to speak English. The rooms are simple, immaculate, and comfortably furnished; all have a radio and a balcony. Showers are in the hall.

HOTEL LE GRENIL, 7, av. de Sainte-Clothilde, CH-1205 Genève. Tel. 022/28-30-55. 48 rms (40 with shower). MINIBAR TEL **Bus:** 1, 10, or 44.

$ Rates (including continental breakfast): 70F ($51.10) single without shower, 100F ($73) single with shower; 90F ($65.70) double without shower, 120F ($87.60) double with shower; 140F ($102.20) triple with shower; 160F ($116.80) quad with shower. AE, DC, MC, V.

S This hotel, which is affiliated with the YMCA, is only a short distance from the center of town and is said to be one of the best values in Geneva. Not far from rue des Deux Ponts, the modern, simply decorated hotel is between the junction of the Rhône and the Arve rivers. The rooms are small but sunny. The director, Harry von Dongen, has complete facilities for conferences and for handicapped patrons. The hotel has a restaurant and a snack bar.

AT BELLEVUE

HOTEL LA RESERVE, 301, route de Lausanne, CH-1293 Bellevue-Genève. Tel. 022/774-17-41. Fax 022/774-25-71. 115 rms (all with bath), 9 suites. MINIBAR TEL TV
$ Rates: 250F–360F ($182.50–$262.75) single; 360F–450F ($262.75–$328.45) double; from 700F ($510.95) suite. Breakfast 25F ($18.25) extra. AE, DC, MC, V. **Parking:** Free.

★ Classified as an architectural landmark of significant importance, this deluxe, conservative establishment is surrounded by 8 acres of gardens that explode into bloom every spring with thousands of tulips. Because of its beauty, the exquisite taste of its public and private rooms, and its location off the road to Lausanne, within a 12-minute drive of both the city center and the airport, La Réserve draws a high percentage of repeat business. This is a hotel of great style and charm.

Dining/Entertainment: The Chinese restaurant, Tse-Fung, has the best Oriental food in Geneva; the French food in the main dining room costs 100F to 150F ($73 to $109.50) for a full meal. There are also Italian and Japanese restaurants. Buffet lunches are also available by the pool in the summer.

Services: Massages, laundry, room service.

Facilities: Outdoor pool, lakeside terrace, four tennis courts, private pier with boat rental, health center.

AT PETIT-LANCY

HOTELLERIE DE LA VENDEE, 28, chemin de la Vendée, CH-1213 Genève–Petit-Lancy. Tel. 022/792-04-11. Fax 022/792-05-46. 34 rms (all with bath). A/C MINIBAR TV TEL **Bus:** 2, 10, or 22.
$ Rates (including continental breakfast): 165F ($120.45) single; 215F ($156.95) double. AE, DC, MC, V.

Located 3 miles southwest of the center of Geneva, this modern hotel has the ambience of a country inn. Its public rooms have a cozy and rustic decor. The bedrooms, on the other hand, have been renovated and decorated in a comfortably modern style. The Righetto family runs the hotel, as well as its bar and restaurant (see Section 4, "Dining," below).

AT VESENAZ

HOTEL LA TOURELLE, 26, route d'Hermance, CH-1222 Vésenaz-Genève. Tel. 022/752-16-28. Fax 022/752-54-93. 22 rms (all with bath or shower). TEL **Bus:** E.
$ Rates (including continental breakfast): 100F–110F ($73–$80.30) single; 130F–160F ($94.90–$116.80) double. DC, MC, V. **Parking:** Free.

Located in the exclusive suburb of Vésenaz, northeast of Geneva, this hotel, once a private villa, is a 12-minute car or bus ride from town. It offers attractive and comfortable rooms, many with views of the lake beyond the well-maintained grounds. Alice and Roland Klinger are the owners. Baby-sitting, room service, and laundry facilities are provided. Only breakfast is served.

4. DINING

Geneva is one of the gastronomic centers of Europe, with a decidedly French influence. Calvin notwithstanding, the Genevese today practice fine eating with consummate flair and style. Meals are frequently long, drawn-out affairs.

Naturally, Geneva serves all the typically Swiss dishes, such as filets of perch from Lake Geneva and fricassee of pork. In season, many of its restaurants offer cardoon, which is similar to an artichoke and is usually served au gratiné. By all means try the Genevese sausage, longeole. Omble chevalier comes from Lac Léman and is like a grayling, although some compare it to salmon. Unfortunately, this fish has been harvested so much that it's now endangered.

Cheese is also an important part of the Genevese table, including such Swiss cheeses as tomme and Gruyère, plus, in season, vacherin from the Joux Valley. Naturally, everything will taste better with Perlan (white wine) and Gamay (red wine) from Geneva's own vineyards.

Now, the bad news: Geneva's restaurants are among the most expensive in Europe. Restaurants I've categorized as "Very Expensive" charge $65 and up for dinner for one, without drinks; "Expensive," around $50; "Moderate," around $35. Any dinner under $25 is considered "Inexpensive" in Geneva.

ON THE RIGHT BANK

VERY EXPENSIVE

LE CHAT-BOTTE, in the Hôtel Beau-Rivage, 13, quai du Mont-Blanc. Tel. 731-65-32.
   Cuisine: FRENCH. **Reservations:** Required. **Bus:** 6 or 33.
$ **Prices:** Appetizers 22F–54F ($16.05–$40.85); main courses 30F–65F ($21.90–$47.45); fixed-price dinner 120F ($87.60). AE, DC, MC, V.
   Open: Lunch Mon–Fri noon–2:15pm; dinner Mon–Fri 7–10:15pm. **Closed:** 15 days at Christmas and Easter.

This elegant restaurant, decorated with tapestries and sculpture, serves some of the best food in Geneva. The meals are expensive but worth the price. The cuisine, although inspired by French classics, is definitely contemporary. The large selection includes filets of fresh red mullet vinaigrette, cutlets of fresh salmon pan-fried with spices, and breast of chicken stuffed with vegetables.

LE CYGNE, in the Noga Hilton International, 19, quai du Mont-Blanc. Tel. 731-98-11.
   Cuisine: FRENCH. **Reservations:** Required. **Bus:** 1.
$ **Prices:** Appetizers 21F–56F ($15.35–$40.85); main courses 28F–63F ($20.45–$46); business lunch 56F ($40.85); fixed-priced dinner 120F–140F ($87.60–$102.20). AE, DC, MC, V.
   Open: Lunch daily noon–2:30pm; dinner daily 7–10:30pm.

This restaurant is considered the best in Geneva. It offers a refined cuisine, with impeccable service. Plushly comfortable, Le Cygne is a showcase for the culinary skills of its young chef, Alain Soulard. The menu changes seasonally and may offer such choices as vegetable foie-gras soup, smoked scallops marinated in caviar and seaweed, filet of sole, and veal with tarragon. Of course, the roast salmon and smoked sea bass remain forever popular. To finish your meal, there are some half dozen dessert carts.

EXPENSIVE

LA MERE ROYAUME, 9, rue des Corps-Saints. Tel. 732-70-08.
 Cuisine: SWISS. **Reservations:** Required. **Bus:** 7.
 $ Prices: Brasserie, fixed-price meals 38F ($27.75) and 46F ($33.60). Restaurant, fixed-price meals 52F ($37.95) at lunch, 80F–110F ($58.40–$80.30) at dinner. AE, DC, MC, V.
 Open: Lunch Mon–Fri noon–2pm; dinner Mon–Sat 7–10pm.

This wood-paneled restaurant is named after a heroine who, in 1602, poured boiling stew over a soldier's head and then cracked his skull with the kettle. With an antecedent like that, you'd expect some of the heartiest fare in Geneva, but instead the kitchen offers delicately cooked French specialties, such as the omble chevalier from Lake Geneva, and a version of trout that has been pronounced "divine." Less expensive meals are served in the informal brasserie.

TSE-FUNG, in the Hôtel La Réserve, 301, route de Lausanne. Tel. 774-17-41.
 Cuisine: CHINESE. **Reservations:** Required.
 $ Prices: Appetizers 10F–40F ($7.30–$29.20); main courses 35F–80F ($25.55–$58.40); fixed-price meals 75F–95F ($54.75–$69.35). AE, DC, MC, V.
 Open: Lunch daily noon–2pm; dinner daily 7–10pm.

Tse-Fung is one of the best Chinese restaurants in Switzerland. The specialties are Pekinese, including marmite mongole, lacquered duck, and steamed fish with Chinese mushrooms. The restaurant is off the road to Lausanne at the Hôtel La Réserve (see Section 3, "Accommodations," above) and has a lovely terrace by the swimming pool. There is also a bar, as well as private parking.

TSE-YANG, in the Noga Hilton, 19, quai du Mont-Blanc. Tel. 732-50-81.
 Cuisine: CHINESE. **Reservations:** Required. **Bus:** 1.
 $ Prices: Appetizers 15F–24F ($10.95–$17.50); main courses 22F–36F ($16.05–$26.30). AE, DC, MC, V.
 Open: Lunch daily noon–2:30pm; dinner daily 7:30–10:45pm.

This is another one of the finest Chinese restaurants in Switzerland, conveniently located on the quays of the Rhône, a short walk from the center of town. The main dishes include a filet of beef in lobster sauce, breast of chicken in lime sauce, and prawns in black-bean sauce. The more expensive dishes include lacquered duck Peking style and a delectable Szechuan lobster.

MODERATE

CHEZ JACKY, 9-11, rue Necker. Tel. 732-86-80.
 Cuisine: SWISS. **Reservations:** Required. **Bus:** 5, 10, or 44.
 $ Prices: Appetizers 12F–20F ($8.75–$14.60); main courses 29F–33F ($21.15–$24.10); fixed-price meals 45F ($32.85); menu dégustation 69F ($50.35). MC, V.
 Open: Lunch Mon–Fri 11:15am–3pm; dinner Mon–Fri 7–10pm. **Closed:** 1st week of Jan, 3 weeks in Aug.

This French provincial bistro should be better known, although it already attracts everyone from grandmothers to young skiers en route to Verbier. It's the domain of Jacky Gruber, an exceptional chef from Valais. There is a

SWITZERLAND

★ BERN

Geneva

Aïoli, L' 24
Amphitryon, L' 7
Arlequin, L' 16
Armures, Les 18
Béarn, Le 10
Brasserie Lipp 12
Café du Centre 14
Chat Botté Le 5
Chez Jacky 9
Coupole, la 23
Curling, Le 28
Cygne, Le 3
Edelweiss 4
Francis, Le 22
Gentilhomme, Le 6
Louisiane, La 13
Lyrique, Le 11
Mère Royaume, la 8
Olivier de Provence, A l' 26
Palais de Justice,
    Restaurant du 20
Papon, Le 19
Parc des Eaux-Vives,
    Restaurant du 25
Pavillon, Le 7
Perle du Lac, La 2
Pied de Cochon, Au 21
Relais de l'Entrecôte 15
Taverne de la Madeleine 17
Tse-Fung 1
Tse-Yang 3
Vendée, Hostellerie de la 27

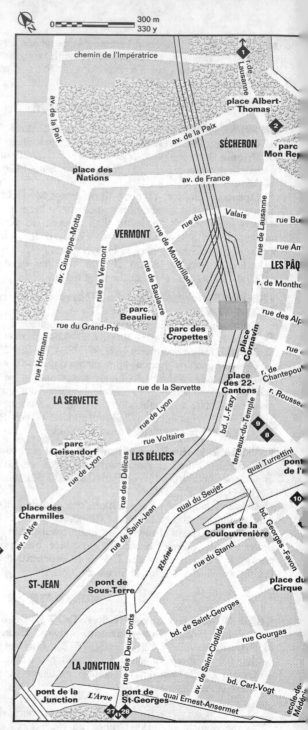

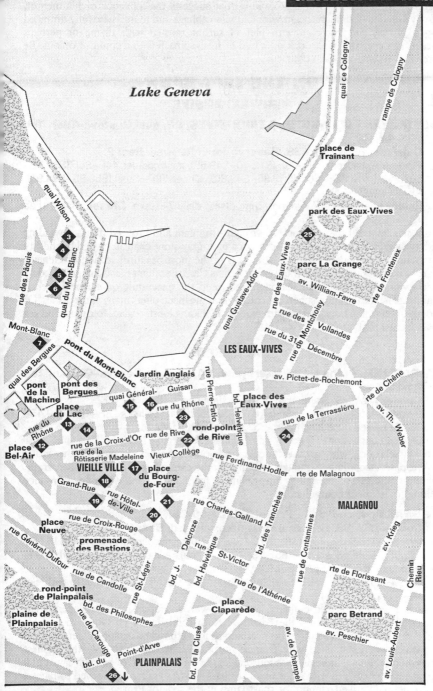

Lake Geneva

quai ce Cologny

rampe de Cologny

place de
Traînant

park des Eaux-Vives

25

parc La Grange

rte de Frontenex

quai Wilson

rue des Pâquis

3

4

quai du Mont-Blanc

5

6

av. William-Favre

rue des Eaux-Vives

rue des

rue de Montchoisy

Vollandes

Mont-Blanc

7

rue du 31 Décembre

LES EAUX-VIVES

pont du Mont-Blanc

quai des Bergues

Jardin Anglais

av. Pictet-de-Rochemont

rte de Chêne

pont
de la
Machine

pont des
Bergues

quai Général- Guisan

rue Pierre-Fatio

place des
Eaux-Vives

bd. Helvétique

av. Th. Weber

place
du Lac

15

16

rue du Rhône

rue de la Terrasslère

13

rue du
Rhône

23

rond-point
de Rive

14

rue de Rive

22

24

12

rue de la Croix-d'Or

place
Bel-Air

rue de la
Rôtisserie Madeleine

Vieux-Collège

rue Ferdinand-Hodler

rte de Malagnou

VIEILLE VILLE

17

place
du Bourg-
de-Four

Grand-Rue

18

19

rue Hôtel-
de-Ville

21

rue Charles-Galland

bd. des Tranchées

MALAGNOU

place
Neuve

rue de Croix-Rouge

20

Dalcroze

rue de Contamines

av. Krieg

promenade
des Bastions

rue Général-Dufour

rue de Candolle

rue St-Léger

bd. J.-

bd. Helvétique

St-Victor

rte de Florissant

Chemin
Rieu

rond-point
de Plainpalais

bd. des Philosophes

rue de Carouge

rue de l'Athénée

place
Claparède

parc Betrand

av. Louis-Aubert

plaine de
Plainpalais

bd. de la Cluse

av. de Champel

av. Peschier

Point-d'Arve

bd. du

PLAINPALAIS

26 ↓

subtlety in Monsieur Gruber's cooking that suggests the influence of his mentor, Frédy Giradet. You might begin with Chinese cabbage and mussels, artfully arranged on a platter, and continue with filet of turbot roasted with thyme or perhaps beautifully prepared pink duck on a bed of fresh spinach with a confit of onions. Be prepared to wait for each course.

ON THE LEFT BANK
VERY EXPENSIVE

RESTAURANT DU PARC DES EAUX-VIVES, 82, quai Gustave-Ador. Tel. 735-41-40.
   Cuisine: FRENCH/SWISS. **Reservations:** Required. **Bus:** 2.
$ **Prices:** Appetizers 17F–68F ($12.40–$49.65); main courses 44F–86F ($32.10–$62.75); lunch 45F–60F ($32.85–$43.80); dinner 78F–130F ($56.95–$94.90). AE, DC, MC, V.
   Open: Lunch Tues–Sun noon–2pm; dinner daily 7–10pm. **Closed:** Jan 1–Feb 15.
To reach it, you'll pass through a wrought-iron gate and proceed along a winding driveway that leads to the dining room of a pink-gray-stone château owned by the city of Geneva. By almost everyone's vote, it is in the most beautiful section of Geneva, part of which is reserved for the Geneva Tennis Club. Excellent meals are prepared by chefs who adjust the menu seasonally but tend to concentrate on classical French cuisine. The local trout is superb; in the autumn the menu offers many game dishes. Of course, everything tastes better with truffles, including lobster salad, foie gras, and sea bass flambé with fennel.

EXPENSIVE

L'ARLEQUIN, in the Hôtel Métropole, 34, quai du Général-Guisan. Tel. 21-13-44.
   Cuisine: SWISS. **Reservations:** Recommended. **Bus:** 2 or 22.
$ **Prices:** Appetizers 22F–35F ($16.05–$25.55); main courses 28F–48F ($20.45–$35.05); fixed-price lunch 52F ($37.95). AE, DC, MC, V.
   Open: Lunch Mon–Fri noon–1pm; dinner Mon–Fri 7–10pm.
The large room, with a classic decor and lots of flowers, is part of the Hôtel Métropole. According to the day's shopping, the chef offers omble chevalier, trout, sea bass, and turbot, as well as mousseline of frogs' legs with a warm crayfish sauce and côte de boeuf bourguignon.

LE BEARN, 4, quai de la Poste. Tel. 21-00-28.
   Cuisine: SWISS. **Reservations:** Recommended. **Bus:** 2 or 22.
$ **Prices:** Appetizers 18F–38F ($13.15–$27.75); main courses 22F–48F ($16.05–$35.05); fixed-price lunch 65F ($47.45); menu tradition 110F ($80.30); menu surprise 135F ($98.55). AE, MC, V.
   Open: Lunch Mon–Fri noon–2pm; dinner Mon–Sat 7:15–10pm. **Closed:** Sat May–Sept.
This is a well-established culinary landmark, with an impressive list of clients that includes the Aga Khan and the Baron de Rothschild. Jean-Paul Goddard and his excellent staff have created the best restaurant in the business center of Geneva. The renovated interior is filled with Empire furniture. The chefs use only the freshest ingredients. You might begin with lobster vichyssoise with grains of Sevruga caviar or a feuillantine of crayfish with a tartare of sea bass and fresh salmon, followed by pigeon suprême, wild grilled salmon, or roast lamb in the style of Provence.

MODERATE

BRASSERIE LIPP, Confédération-Centre, 8, rue de la Confédération. Tel. 29-31-22.
   Cuisine: SWISS. **Reservations:** Recommended. **Bus:** 12.
$ **Prices:** Appetizers 11F–14.50F ($8.05–$10.60); main courses 10F–42F ($7.30–$30.65). AE, DC, MC, V.
   Open: Daily 7am–2am.
This bustling restaurant is named after the famous Parisian brasserie, and when you enter, especially at lunch, you'll think you've been transported to Paris. Waiters in black jackets with long white aprons rush about with platters of food to feed the hungry. The impossibly long menu contains a sampling of the French repertoire of bistro dishes. The restaurant is on the top floor of a modern shopping complex. Tables are placed outside in the summer.
   Like its Parisian namesake, the Geneva Lipp specializes in several versions of charcuterie. You can also order three kinds of pot-au-feu and such classic dishes as a Toulousain cassoulet with confit de canard (duckling). The fresh oysters are among the best in the city.

CAFE DU CENTRE, 5, place du Molard. Tel. 21-85-86.
   Cuisine: SWISS. **Reservations:** Recommended. **Bus:** 12.
$ **Prices:** Appetizers 10F–18F ($7.30–$13.15); main courses 15F–32F ($10.95–$23.35); simple menu from 24F ($17.50); fisherman's menu 35F ($25.55); vegetarian menu 22F ($16.05). AE, DC, MC, V.
   Open: Restaurant, lunch daily 11:30am–2:30pm; dinner Sun–Thurs 6pm–1:30am, Fri–Sat 6pm–2am. Brasserie, 11:30am–2am.
The square where this establishment is located is separated from the busy quays by a clock tower of chiseled stone. It has many flower stalls and café tables in the summer. The old-fashioned brasserie has a more expensive upstairs room, which is decorated with 17th-century stained glass. But most of the business takes place outdoors in the summer or on the café level, which opens onto the square. A thick English-language menu offers more than 120 food items. Fish is usually good here, including fera (a white lake fish), sole, dorade, and trout. The chef is known for his fine cuts of beef, such as the delectable onglet. The brasserie and café serve morning coffee and croissants from 6am.

 FROMMER'S COOL FOR KIDS

RESTAURANTS

Le Papon (see p. 357) At one of Geneva's oldest restaurants, kids delight in the house specialty, a crêpe filled with Gruyère or with ham and cheese. The rich pastries also please them.

Les Armures (see p. 357) Some Swiss children make an entire meal out of the Rösti, or Swiss-style hash brown potatoes, served here. Pastas and hamburgers round out the menu.

La Louisiane (see p. 359) Sandwiches, pastas, or freshly made salads please most kids, or else they go for one of the omelets named after various movie stars.

LA COUPOLE, 116, rue du Rhône. Tel. 735-65-44.
   Cuisine: SWISS. **Reservations:** Not needed. **Bus:** 2 or 22.
$ **Prices:** Appetizers 8F–22F ($5.85–$16.05); main courses 18F–32F ($13.15–$23.35); fixed-price meal from 26F ($19). MC, V.
   Open: Daily 7am–1am.

This is a true brasserie—far more elegant than its Parisian namesake. The place is more popular at noon, especially with businesspeople, than it is at night. There's a pink-and-red piano bar to the left as you enter and a green-and-black English bar to the right. Fanciful and fun, it is dotted with grandfather clocks, a bronze *Venus*, Edwardian palms, and comfortable banquettes. The menu is limited but sophisticated; the cuisine du marché is a delight.

LE FRANCIS, 8, bd. Helvétique. Tel. 46-32-52.
   Cuisine: FRENCH/INTERNATIONAL. **Reservations:** Recommended. **Bus:** 12.
$ **Prices:** Appetizers 12F–40F ($8.75–$29.20); main courses 28F–55F ($20.45–$40.15). AE, DC, MC, V.
   Open: Lunch daily 12:30–2:30pm; dinner daily 8pm–2am.

Le Francis is currently one of the most fashionable spots in Geneva. The well-known restaurant offers such appetizers as mussel soup with anise or a gratiné of leeks with a fondue of tomatoes. For a main course, you might be tempted by a fricassee of sweetbreads, a sauté of veal and beef with a fricassee of artichokes, sea bass gros sel, or a panaché of John Dory with salmon and green cabbage cooked in sauterne.

Le tout Genève also is likely to patronize the piano bar in the evening until 1 or 2am. A scotch costs 14F ($10.20).

INEXPENSIVE

L'AIOLI, 6, rue Adrien-Lachenal. Tel. 736-79-71.
   Cuisine: SWISS. **Reservations:** Not needed. **Bus:** 1 or 6.
$ **Prices:** Appetizers 6F–16F ($4.40–$11.70); main courses 15.50F–32F ($11.30–$23.35); three-course lunch 28F ($20.45); fixed-price dinner 62F ($45.25). AE, DC, MC, V.
   Open: Lunch Mon–Sat, noon–3pm; Dinner Mon–Sat 7–10:30pm.

Named after the famous garlic sauce of Provence, this popular neighborhood restaurant stands opposite Le Corbusier's Maison de Verre. Considered something of a local secret, it offers a personalized service and some of the finest provençal cooking in town. Marius Anthoine, the owner, hails from the Valais. An evening meal includes an appetizer, first plate, main dish, cheese, dessert, coffee, and wine (you can spend more by ordering à la carte). Among featured dishes are lamb gigot and frogs' legs provençal. Monsieur Anthoine also makes a delectable pot-au-feu as well as scampi. Look for the daily specials.

AU PIED DE COCHON, 4, place du Bourg-de-Four. Tel. 20-47-97.
   Cuisine: LYONNAIS/SWISS. **Reservations:** Recommended. **Bus:** 2 or 22. **Tram:** 12.
$ **Prices:** Appetizers 8F–25F ($5.85–$18.25); main courses 20F–36F ($14.60–$26.30); meals from 30F ($21.90). AE, DC, MC, V.
   Open: Lunch daily noon–2:30pm; dinner daily 6:30–11:30pm.

Named after a restaurant at Les Halles, in Paris, this is the best place to go in Geneva for hearty Lyonnaise fare. It is popular with young people. The setting is fin-de-siècle. Most of the meat and poultry dishes, especially the pork, are excellent.

RESTAURANT DU PALAIS DE JUSTICE, 8, place du Bourg-de-Four. Tel. 20-42-54.

Cuisine: SWISS. **Reservations:** Not needed. **Bus:** 2 or 22.

$ **Prices:** Appetizers 8F–12F ($5.85–$8.75); main courses 14.50F–18.50F ($10.60–$13.50). AE, MC, V.

Open: Lunch daily noon–1:30pm; dinner daily 6:30–11:15pm. **Closed:** Sun June–Aug.

A simple little place with lots of atmosphere, this restaurant is in the old town on a colorful square, across from the Palais de Justice. The building actually contains three different places to eat, with a separate menu for each. The most formal and expensive restaurant, one flight above street level, offers such well-prepared meals as terrine maison and a savory array of beef dishes. La Taverne, in the basement, serves six different kinds of pizza, ranging in price from 12F to 14F ($9.50 to $10.20), and three kinds of fondue, starting at 18.50F ($13.50). The ground-floor Restaurant du Rez-de-Chaussée serves basically the same dishes as La Taverne. It is open daily from 9am to midnight. The Taverne and the expensively priced restaurant keep the same hours as the restaurant.

LE LYRIQUE, 12, bd. du Théâtre. Tel. 28-00-95.

Cuisine: SWISS. **Reservations:** Recommended. **Bus:** 2 or 22.

$ **Prices:** Appetizers 12F–18F ($8.75–$13.15); main courses 18F–25F ($13.15–$18.25); fixed-price meals 38F ($27.75). AE, DC, MC, V.

Open: Lunch Mon–Fri noon–3pm; dinner Mon–Fri 6:30–10:30pm.

Le Lyrique contains both a formal restaurant and a brasserie. With its turn-of-the-century decor, it has been attracting theatergoers for years. The brasserie, which has a terrace, is open all day but serves hot meals only during the hours mentioned above. It may remain open to midnight, depending on whether there is a performance at the theater nearby. In the brasserie, a plat du jour goes for 16F ($11.70). The menu might include chicken suprême with leeks, succulent steaks, or grilled sole. In the restaurant, you can order omble chevalier (the famous lake fish of Geneva), served poached, or turbot stuffed with red peppers. Filet of lamb with baby onions is also a popular item. For dessert, try a pear gratiné with sabayon.

RELAIS DE L'ENTRECOTE, 49, rue du Rhône. Tel. 28-05-01.

Cuisine: FRENCH. **Reservations:** Not accepted. **Bus:** 6 or 8. **Tram:** 12.

Open: Lunch daily noon–2:30pm; dinner daily 7–11pm.

Prices: Entrecôtes 35F ($25.25); desserts from 12F ($8.75) and up.

The gimmick here is that the kitchen serves only entrecôte, accompanied by french-fried (or steamed) potatoes, herb-flavored butter, and a crisp fresh salad with walnuts. The bistro, on the fashionable shopping street, resembles a 19th-century Parisian restaurant, with brass rails and lots of paneling. Desserts tend to be elaborate and cost extra. In fact, the creativity of the kitchen really comes out in its desserts, which are likely to include a tulipe of fresh peaches and apricots or a hot apple tart with honey ice cream.

TAVERNE DE LA MADELEINE, 20, rue Toutes-Ames. Tel. 28-40-32.

Cuisine: SWISS. **Reservations:** Recommended. **Bus:** 2 or 22.

$ Prices: Appetizers 8F–10F ($5.85–$7.30); main courses 15F–20F ($10.95–$14.60). No credit cards.

Open: Summer, Mon–Sat 11:45am–9:45pm; winter, Mon–Sat 11:45am–8pm.

This very good restaurant, one of the oldest in Geneva, is set against the old city wall beside the Eglise de la Madeleine. If you are having difficulty finding the address, just circle the church and the old three-story house will be on the corner of rue des Barrières. Inside are bistro tables, red café chairs, and a brusquely efficient staff catering to the lunchtime business crowd. The establishment is operated by a philanthropic organization that forbids the consumption of alcohol (alcohol-free beer is available). You can order a variety of well-prepared dishes. Specials include four types of pasta, vegetarian sandwiches, and such hearty fare as a big plate of osso bucco with pommes frites. An escalope of turkey with potatoes and salad is regularly featured. The kitchen also prides itself on its filet of lake perch prepared meunière style or Vevey style with exotic mushrooms.

AT PETIT-LANCY

HOSTELLERIE DE LA VENDEE, 28, chemin de la Vendée, Petit-Lancy. Tel. 792-04-11.

Cuisine: SWISS. **Reservations:** Required. **Bus:** 2, 10, or 22.

$ Prices: Appetizers 15F–22F ($10.95–$16.05); main courses 24F–38F ($17.50–$27.75); fixed-price meals 50F ($37.20) at lunch, at dinner 75F–110F ($54.75–$80.30). AE, DC, MC, V.

Open: Lunch Mon–Fri noon–2pm; dinner Mon–Sat 7–10pm. **Closed:** Long Christmas holiday.

Located at Petit-Lancy, at the edge of Geneva, this chic restaurant is known for its seasonal specialties. It is run by the Righetto brothers. You'll enjoy the variety of foie gras dishes prepared by the chef. Try also his filet of sea bass or his duckling with peaches. Dessert might be a soufflé Grand Marnier. There is a terrace for summer dining.

LE CURLING, 9bis, chemin du Fief-du-Chapitre, Petit-Lancy. Tel. 793-62-44.

Cuisine: CONTINENTAL. **Reservations:** Required. **Bus:** 2, 10, or 22.

$ Prices: Appetizers 15F–22F ($10.95–$16.05); main courses 24F–38F ($17.50–$27.75); fixed-price meals 32F ($23.35), 38F ($27.75), and 45F ($32.85); menu gastronomique 72F ($52.55). AE, DC, MC, V.

Open: Mon–Sat 9am–midnight.

Located in the suburb of Petit-Lancy, in a building set at the edge of the neighborhood's curling rink, this restaurant is prefaced with an informal brasserie and café. Unpretentious and known for accommodating a wide range of clients, it's maintained by chef Acelsino Veiras and his wife, Monique, who offer a delicious medley of Galician and continental cuisine. The zarzuela of fish and any of their three different versions of royal paella are noteworthy.

AT CAROUGE

A L'OLIVIER DE PROVENCE, 13, rue Jacques-Dalphin, Carouge. Tel. 42-04-50.

Cuisine: FRENCH. **Reservations:** Required. **Transportation:** Car or taxi.

$ Prices: Appetizers 14F–24F ($10.20–$17.50); main courses 25F–38F ($18.25–$27.75); fixed-price meals 65F–95F ($47.45–$69.35). AE, DC, MC, V.
Open: Lunch Mon–Sat noon–2pm; dinner Mon–Sat 7–9:45pm.

Set in the satellite city of Carouge, about 3 miles south of Geneva, this Provençal restaurant offers some of the best dining on the city's perimeter. Though open throughout the year, it's especially popular in warm weather, when patrons can dine on its lovely, tree-shaded terrace. The savory dishes include flambéed versions of loup de mer (sea bass), tournedos, entrecôtes, and fresh salmon with sorrel.

SPECIALTY DINING

LOCAL FAVORITES

LE PAPON, 1, rue Henri-Fazy. Tel. 29-54-28.
  Cuisine: SWISS. **Reservations:** Recommended. **Bus:** 12.
$ Prices: Appetizers 12F–15F ($8.75–$10.95); main courses 16F–28F ($11.70–$20.45); fixed-price lunch 18F ($13.15). AE, MC, V.
  Open: Lunch daily noon–2pm; dinner daily 7–10:30pm.

This establishment, one of the oldest in Geneva, is near Tour Baudet, in the vicinity of the Hôtel de Ville in the old town. Now a restaurant, crêperie, and tearoom, Le Papon has been entertaining under its vaulted ceilings since the 17th century. In the summer, cold food is available all afternoon, but hot meals are served only during the hours mentioned above. You can also come here for coffee and rich pastries. The house specialty is a sort of crêpe called galette au sarrazin, served seven different ways, often filled with Gruyère, ham and cheese, or fish. You can also order more substantial fare, including fish soup with rouille, squid, a brochette of scampi, entrecôte, and pork kidneys in a Dijon mustard sauce with Rösti.

LES ARMURES, 1, rue des Puits-St-Pierre. Tel. 28-34-42.
  Cuisine: SWISS. **Reservations:** Not needed.
$ Prices: Appetizers 8F–12F ($5.85–$8.75); main courses 18F–32F ($13.15–$23.35). AE, DC, MC, V.
  Open: Mon–Sat 8am–1am.

This rustic stone building, the oldest café in Geneva, is located on a cobblestone street, across from a medieval arsenal in one of the most colorful neighborhoods of the old town. The establishment's three different fondues are considered the best in Geneva. Many customers make a meal out of Rösti. Other specialties include raclette and several pizza and pasta dishes. The sauerkraut garni is also a savory meal.

HOTEL DINING

LE GENTILHOMME, in the Hôtel Richemond, Jardin Brunswick. Tel. 731-14-00.
  Cuisine: FRENCH/SWISS/ITALIAN. **Reservations:** Required. **Bus:** 1 or 9.
$ Prices: Appetizers 7F–48F ($5.10–$35.05); main courses 21F–59F ($15.35–$43.05). AE, DC, MC, V.
  Open: Lunch Sun–Fri 11:30am–2:30pm; dinner daily 7pm–midnight.

Le Gentilhomme is one of Geneva's most glamorous restaurants, where well-dressed patrons enjoy Périgord truffles (served in a salt crust) and lobster flown in from Brittany. Gourmet meals are served in a 19th-century setting of crimson silk and crystal. Specialties prepared by chef Silvio Bianchi include grilled sea bass with fresh garden herbs, seafood and champagne risotto, and smoked salmon and caviar in a rolled pancake. The restaurant also offers a choice of caviar. The menu varies because the cuisine du marché is based on only the freshest of ingredients.

LE PAVILLON, in the Hôtel des Bergues, 33, quai des Bergues. Tel. 731-50-50.
    Cuisine: FRENCH. **Reservations:** Required. **Bus:** 7.
$ **Prices:** Appetizers 12F–18F ($8.75–$13.15); main courses 22F–38F ($16.05–$27.75). AE, DC, MC, V.
    Open: Daily 7am–11pm.

Sophisticated and elegant, this is the less formal of the two restaurants in the Hôtel des Bergues. Large windows overlook the Rhône and the traffic, but inside all is serene. This fine restaurant, which is referred to as the hotel's "coffeehouse," serves breakfast, lunch, and dinner, as well as snacks and afternoon tea. Directed by the chef of the hotel's more upscale restaurant, L'Amphitryon, Le Pavillon serves outstanding classic and cuisine moderne dishes, including a homemade foie gras. You might begin with a seafood soup and go on to a pot-au-feu of fish, the rosemary-flavored roast chicken, or the veal piccata with mushrooms. The desserts are lavish.

RESTAURANT L'AMPHITRYON, in the Hôtel des Bergues, 33, quai des Bergues. Tel. 731-50-00.
    Cuisine: SWISS. **Reservations:** Required. **Bus:** 7.
$ **Prices:** Appetizers 22F–30F ($16.05–$21.90); main courses 30F–65F ($21.90–$47.45). AE, DC, MC, V.
    Open: Lunch Mon–Fri noon–3pm; dinner Mon–Fri 7–11pm.

Housed in one of Geneva's most prestigious hotels, this restaurant offers classic and modern cuisine, along with impeccable service and an elegant Louis Philippe decor. The restaurant's name was adopted from a perfect host (Amphitryon) depicted by Molière in one of his plays. It can be difficult to select just one of the tempting offerings: pigeon of Bresse served in a mold blended with Armagnac, marinated crab claws with soya beans and pink grapefruit quarters, artichoke hearts with spinach leaves seasoned with shallots, and a delectable shellfish ravioli in a crayfish sauce flavored with basil. Even the soups are unique: cream of chicken soup with frogs' legs or a clear duck soup with beet juice and sour cream. Main courses vary seasonally, but you might be offered a delicious steamed sea bass with leeks and truffles or medallions of lobster with quail eggs and spinach flan. You may also try the flambéed meats prepared at your table.

DINING WITH A VIEW

LA PERLE DU LAC, 128, rue de Lausanne. Tel. 731-79-35.
    Cuisine: SWISS. **Reservations:** Required. **Bus:** 4 or 44.
$ **Prices:** Appetizers 24F–45F ($17.50–$32.85); main courses 62F–95F ($45.25–$69.35); fixed-price meals 55F ($40.15) at lunch, 95F ($69.35) at dinner. AE, DC, MC, V.
    Open: Lunch Tues–Sun noon–2pm; dinner Tues–Sun 7–10pm. **Closed:** Dec 22–Jan 23.

Situated in a single-story pavilion owned by the city and managed by André Hauri, this is the only restaurant in Geneva that is not separated from the waters of the lake by a stream of traffic. It is set beneath the venerable trees of Mon Repos Park, not far from the United Nations complex. Although the candlelit interior is lovely, you might want to reserve a table on the outdoor terrace in warm weather. A talented French chef prepares a marvelous fricassée of frogs' legs. Other specialties include omble chevalier (if available), sea bass with a mint sabayon, and filet mignon of veal with mushroom mousse and basil. The sorbets (ask for a mixture) are superb.

AFTERNOON TEA/SANDWICHES

LA LOUISIANE, 21, rue du Rhône. Tel. 28-29-25.
   Cuisine: SWISS/INTERNATIONAL. **Reservations:** Required for lunch. **Bus:** 2, 6, 7, or 10.
   $ Prices: Appetizers 4.20F–15F ($3.10–$10.95); main courses 15F–30F ($10.95–$21.90). No credit cards.
   Open: Mon–Sat 7:30am–11pm.
This tearoom serves pastries, small sandwiches, and light meals to a Swiss version of a crowd you might find in New York's Greenwich Village. It has bamboo and wicker chairs and lots of plants. Caviar blinis are the most expensive item on the menu, followed by an assortment of pâtés, smoked salmon, morels, and crabmeat. An imaginative list of omelets and homemade pasta is also offered. Salads are varied and come in generous portions. All items are named after 20th-century celebrities. A James Dean omelet is made with truffles and a Laurel and Hardy omelet is made with smoked salmon.

LATE-NIGHT DINING

EDELWEISS, in the Hôtel Edelweiss, 2, place de la Navigation. Tel. 731-36-58.
   Cuisine: SWISS. **Reservations:** Not needed. **Bus:** 6 or 33.
   $ Prices: Appetizers 10F–18F ($7.30–$13.15); main courses 15F–30F ($10.95–$21.90). AE, DC, MC, V.
   Open: Dinner only, daily 7pm–midnight.
This restaurant has a rustic wood interior enlivened by geraniums and the flags of the various Swiss cantons. Here you can dine on Swiss specialties, such as fondue, listen to folk music, and even dance—all for a relatively moderate price. It's economical when you consider that you get both food and entertainment.

PICNIC FARE & WHERE TO EAT IT

On a sunny day, the people of Geneva often like to secure the makings of a picnic and go on an excursion, on the French or Swiss side of Lake Geneva or to the nearby mountains. At the **Halle de Rive,** place du Rive, on the Left Bank, is a sprawling market that stretches for an entire block. There you can find all sorts of delectable prepared food. The best times to go are market days on Wednesday and Saturday morning, when locals from the surrounding hills come into town to display their produce. Some fresh fruit and a bottle of Vaudoise wine are all you'll need for a picnic.

   You can enjoy the fare in any of Geneva's parks. One of the most idyllic places for a picnic is slightly north of the center, where three parks adjoin: **Parc Villa-Barton, La Perle du Lac,** and **Parc Mon-Repos.** All these green belts open onto Lake Geneva and a view of its famous fountain.

RESTAURANTS BY CUISINE

Cuisines and Restaurants	Rating*
CHINESE	
Tse-Fung (*page 349*)	E
Tse-Yang (*page 349*)	E
CONTINENTAL	
Le Curling (*page 356*)	M
FRENCH	
A l'Olivier de Provence (*page 356*)	E
Le Chat-Botté (*page 348*)	VE
Le Cygne (*page 348*)	VE
Le Francis (*page 354*)	M
Le Gentilhomme (*page 357*)	VE
Le Pavillon (*page 358*)	M
Relais de l'Entrecôte (*page 355*)	I
Restaurant du Parc des Eaux-Vives (*page 352*)	VE
INTERNATIONAL	
Le Francis (*page 354*)	M
La Louisiane (*page 359*)	M
ITALIAN	
Le Gentilhomme (*page 357*)	VE
LYONNAIS	
Au Pied de Cochon (*page 354*)	I
SWISS	
L'Aïoli (*page 354*)	I
L'Arlequin (*page 352*)	E
Les Armures (*page 357*)	M
Au Pied de Cochon (*page 354*)	I
Le Béarn (*page 352*)	E
Brasserie Lipp (*page 353*)	M
Café du Centre (*page 353*)	M
Chez Jacky (*page 349*)	M
La Coupole (*page 354*)	M
Edelweiss (*page 359*)	M
Le Gentilhomme (*page 357*)	VE
Hostellerie de la Vendée (*page 356*)	M
La Louisiane (*page 359*)	M
Le Lyrique (*page 355*)	I
La Mère-Royaume (*page 349*)	E
Le Papon (*page 357*)	M
La Perle du Lac (*page 358*)	VE
Restaurant du Palais de Justice (*page 355*)	I
Restaurant du Parc des Eaux-Vives (*page 352*)	VE
Restaurant L'Amphitryon (*page 358*)	VE
Taverne de la Madeleine (*page 355*)	I

*VE = Very Expensive; E = Expensive; M = Moderate;
I = Inexpensive; B = Budget.

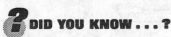

? DID YOU KNOW . . . ?

- Geneva didn't enter the Helvetic Confederation until as late as 1815.
- Jean-Jacques Rousseau was born in Geneva in 1712, and his archrival, Voltaire, lived there from 1755 to 1759.
- During the Dark Ages, the kings of Burgundy made Geneva their capital.
- John Calvin, the reformer, settled in Geneva in 1536, turning it into the "Rome of the Protestants."
- Napoleon slept in the old town on May 9, 1800, and Geneva remained part of France until December 31, 1813.
- Geneva's annual Escalade celebration still commemorates a victory over the Duke of Savoy's troops in 1602.
- Villa Montalegre in Cologny, outside Geneva, was the birthplace of the horror story *Frankenstein*.

5. ATTRACTIONS

You can see most of Geneva on foot. The best way to familiarize yourself with the city, however, is by taking a walking tour, which covers all the major sites.

SIGHTSEEING STRATEGIES

IF YOU HAVE 1 DAY Begin the morning by viewing the spectacular water fountain, the Jet d'Eau, and the Flower Clock in the Jardin Anglais. Then take a cruise of Lake Geneva on a steamer. Return in the early afternoon and explore the Left Bank's Old Town, having dinner at a restaurant on place du Bourg-de-Four.

IF YOU HAVE 2 DAYS Spend the first day as above. On the second day, visit some of the most important museums of Geneva, each completely different. It'll take a full day of sightseeing to absorb the most important: the Musée d'Art et d'Histoire, the Musée International de la Croix-Rouge et du Croissant-Rouge (Red Cross Museum), and the Palais des Nations.

IF YOU HAVE 3 DAYS Spend the first 2 days as above. On your third day, take the walking tour of Geneva (see below) in the morning, and in the afternoon go on one of the organized excursions to the Alps, including Mont Blanc, for a spectacular view.

IF YOU HAVE 5 DAYS Spend the first 3 days as outlined above. By now, you are an old hand at finding your way around Geneva, and you can use your last days for excursions. While still based in Geneva, take a lake steamer to Lausanne. You'll have time to explore its old town and walk its lakeside quays at Ouchy before returning to Geneva in the evening. On the fifth day, take another lake steamer, this time to Montreux; after visiting this lakeside resort, take a trip outside the town to see the famous Château de Chillon, immortalized by Lord Byron.

THE TOP ATTRACTIONS

In addition to the three museums discussed below, Geneva's other top attractions—all must-see sights—are the **Jet d'Eau,** the famous fountain that has virtually become the city's symbol; the **Flower Clock,** in the Jardin Anglais; and **Old Town,** the oldest part of the city. All of these sights, and more, are detailed in the Walking Tour, below.

SWITZERLAND
★ BERN
Geneva ◉

GENEVA ATTRACTIONS

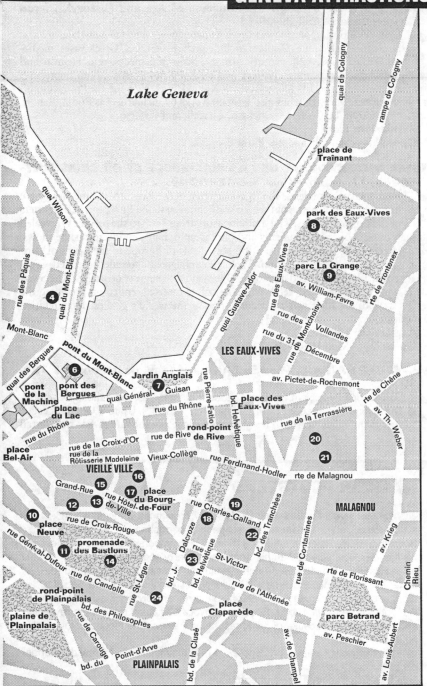

Lake Geneva

quai de Cologny

rampe de Cologny

place de Traînant

park des Eaux-Vives
8

quai Wilson

rue des Pâquis

parc La Grange
9

av. William-Favre

rte de Frontenex

quai du Mont-Blanc

4

rue des Eaux-Vives

rue des Vollandes

rue du Montchoisy

Mont-Blanc

LES EAUX-VIVES

rue du 31 Décembre

pont du Mont-Blanc

quai des Bergues

6

Jardin Anglais
7

quai Général-Guisan

av. Pictet-de-Rochemont

rte de Chêne

pont des Bergues

pont de la Machine

place du Lac

quai Gustave-Ador

rue Pierre-Fatio

place des Eaux-Vives

bd. Helvétique

av. Th. Weber

rue du Rhône

rue de la Terrassière

place Bel-Air

rue du Rhône

rond-point de Rive

rue de Rive

20

rue de la Croix-d'Or

rue de la Rôtisserie Madeleine

Vieux-Collège

rue Ferdinand-Hodler

21

rte de Malagnou

VIEILLE VILLE

Grand-Rue **15**

16

17 place du Bourg-de-Four

rue Charles-Galland

MALAGNOU

12 **13**

rue Hôtel-de-Ville

19

av. Krieg

10

place Neuve

rue de Croix-Rouge

18

rue Général-Dufour

11

promenade des Bastions

14

22

St-Victor

bd. des Tranchées

rue de Contamines

rte de Florissant

rue de Candolle

rue St-Léger

Dalcroze

rue Helvétique

23

bd. J.-

bd. Helvétique

rue de l'Athénée

av. de Champel

parc Betrand

rond-point de Plainpalais

24

bd. des Philosophes

place Claparède

av. Peschier

Chemin Rieu

plaine de Plainpalais

rue de Carouge

bd. de la Cluse

av. Louis-Aubert

bd. du Point-d'Arve

PLAINPALAIS

MUSEE D'ART ET D'HISTOIRE (Museum of Art and History), 2, rue Charles-Galland. Tel. 29-00-11.

 Geneva's most important museum is between boulevard Jacques-Dalcroze and boulevard Helvétique. Displays include prehistoric relics, Greek vases, medieval stained glass, 12th-century armory, Swiss timepieces, and Flemish and Italian paintings. The Etruscan pottery and medieval furniture are both impressive. You should also see the 1444 altarpiece by Konrad Witz, showing the "miraculous" draught of fishes. Many galleries also contain works by such artists as Rodin, Renoir, Hodler, Vallotton, Le Corbusier, Picasso, Chagall, and Pissarro.

Admission: Free.

Open: Tues–Sun 10am–5pm. **Bus:** 3 or 33.

MUSEE INTERNATIONAL DE LA CROIX-ROUGE ET DU CROISSANT-ROUGE, 17, av. de la Paix. Tel. 734-52-48.

Here you can experience the legendary past of the Red Cross in the city where it started, lying across from the visitors' entrance to the European headquarters of the United Nations. The dramatic story from 1863 to the present is revealed through displays of rare documents and photographs, films, multiscreen slide shows, and cycloramas. You are taken from the battlefields of Europe to the plains of Africa to see the Red Cross in action. When Henry Dunant founded the Red Cross in Geneva in 1863, he needed a recognizable symbol to suggest neutrality. The Swiss flag (a white cross on a red field), with the colors reversed, ended up providing the perfect symbol for what was to become one of the world's greatest humanitarian movements.

Admission: 10F ($7.30).

Open: Wed–Mon 10am–5pm. **Bus:** 8 or F.

PALAIS DES NATIONS, Parc de l'Ariana, 14, av. de la Paix. Tel. 734-60-11.

Surrounded by ancient trees and modern monuments, the buildings comprise the second-largest complex in Europe after Versailles. Up to 1936, the League met at the Palais Wilson. That year the League's headquarters was transferred

---

IN THEIR FOOTSTEPS

Jean-Jacques Rousseau (1712–78) Through his writings, which advocated a "return to nature" to escape the "corruption" of civilization, Rousseau exerted a great influence over his contemporaries. He spent most of his life in France, where, with his doctrine of liberty and equality for all, he helped pave the way for the French Revolution. Rousseau is considered the father of the romantic movement. His principal literary work is *The Social Contract*, a political treatise. He also wrote a remarkably frank account of his life, aptly called *Confessions*. Rousseau advocated natural rather than revealed sectarian religion. Because of his ideas, he was among the most controversial figures of his era.

• **Birthplace:** Geneva, on June 28, 1712; his mother died a few days after his birth.

• **Resting Place:** The Pantheon, Paris.

FROMMER'S FAVORITE
GENEVA EXPERIENCES

Wine Tasting in the Countryside Winding your way through the rolling vineyards just outside Geneva makes for an enjoyable day's outing. Many of the best Swiss wines never leave the country, and grapes grow on slopes overlooking Lake Geneva and the Rhône. Pick up a brochure called "Discover Geneva and Its Vineyards" from the tourist office and set out.

Sailing Lake Geneva The crescent-shaped lake (called Lac Léman locally) gives Geneva a resortlike ambience, stretching for 45 miles. In the summer it's alive with activity: sailing, rowing, canoeing, waterskiing, and more—and you can join in the fun.

Wandering Through Old Town Geneva's Vieille Ville has been called "Europe's best-kept secret." Exploring its ancient streets brings you to art galleries, antiques shops, booksellers, and tiny bistros. Follow the Grand'Rue, where Jean-Jacques Rousseau was born, and wander back into time.

to the Palais des Nations, which was inaugurated by the Aga Khan. The international organization continued minor activities through the war years until it was dissolved in 1946, just as the newly created United Nations met in San Francisco. Today the Palais des Nations is the headquarters of the United Nations in Europe. A modern wing was added in 1973.

Inside is a philatelic museum and the **League of Nations Museum,** although the building itself is the most interesting attraction. Daily tours leave from the visitors' entrance at 14, avenue de la Paix, opposite the Red Cross building. For information, get in touch with the Visitors' Service, United Nations Office, 14, avenue de la Paix (tel. 734-60-11, ext. 4539).

Admission: 8F ($5.85) adults, 3.50F ($2.55) children; under 6, free.

Open: June–Oct, daily 9am–5:15pm; Jan–May and Nov to mid-Dec, daily 9am–noon and 2–5:15pm. **Closed:** Mid-Dec to Jan 1. **Bus:** 8 or F.

MORE ATTRACTIONS

MUSEUMS

MUSEE DU PETIT PALAIS, 2, terrasse Saint-Victor. Tel. 46-14-33.

This 19th-century town house displays artwork from 1890 to 1930, from impressionism to surrealism. It's known chiefly for its collection of impressionists and post-impressionists, although the pointillists and Fauve artists are also represented. The private museum has such outstanding artists as Renoir, Cross, Picasso, Cézanne, Steinlen, Chagall, Utrillo, and Rousseau.

Admission: 10F ($7.30) adults, 3.50F ($2.55) children.

Open: Mon 2–6pm, Tues–Sun 10am–noon and 2–6pm. **Bus:** 1 or 3.

MUSEE D'HISTOIRE NATURELLE (Natural History Museum), 1, route de Malagnou. Tel. 735-91-30.

This modern museum has a variety of regional and exotic natural-science exhibits. Among the specimens are mammals, birds, reptiles, fish, mollusks, and insects. The earth-science galleries are devoted to mineralogy, fluorescent minerals, gemology, regional and Swiss geology, human history, and dinosaurs.

Admission: Free.
Open: Tues–Sun 10am–5pm. **Bus:** 6 or 12.

MUSEE DE L'HORLOGERIE (Watch Museum), 15, route de Malagnou. Tel. 736-74-12.

This town house chronicles the history of watches and clocks from the 16th century. It displays everything from sand timers to sundials, although most of the exhibits are concerned with the watches of Geneva, usually from the 17th and 18th centuries. The enameled watches of the 19th century are particularly outstanding (many have chimes that play when you open them).

Admission: Free.
Open: Wed–Mon 10am–5pm. **Bus:** 6.

THE BAUR COLLECTIONS, 8, rue Munier-Romilly. Tel. 46-17-29.

The collections, housed in a 19th-century mansion with a garden, constitute a private exhibit of artworks from China (dating from the 10th to the 19th century) and Japan (17th to 20th century). On display are ceramics, jade, lacquer, ivories, and delicate sword fittings.

Admission: 5F ($3.65) adults, free for children.
Open: Tues–Sun 2–6pm. **Bus:** 8.

MUSEE D'HISTOIRE DES SCIENCES (Museum of the History of Science), Villa Bartholoni, 128, rue de Lausanne. Tel. 731-69-85.

This museum near the lake contains scientific instruments and other articles relating to medicine, astronomy, physics, and mathematics.

Admission: Free.
Open: Tues–Sun 10am–6pm. **Bus:** 4 or 44.

MAISON TAVEL, 6, rue du Puits-St-Pierre. Tel. 28-29-00.

Built in 1303 and partially rebuilt after a fire in 1334, this is the city's oldest house and one of its newest museums. The building has undergone several transformations over the centuries, it opened as a museum in 1986. The front wall is typical of the 17th century, with its gray paint, white joints, and stone sculpted heads. A private home until this century, the house contains a courtyard with a staircase, a 13th-century cellar, and a back garden. The museum exhibits art from Geneva dating from the Middle Ages to the mid-19th century. The Magnin relief in the attic is outstanding, as is the copper-and-zinc model of Geneva in 1850, which is accompanied by a light-and-tape commentary. Objects of daily use are displayed in the old living quarters. Postcards, books, slides, and small guidebooks are available at the book stand.

Admission: Free.
Open: Tues–Sun 10am–5pm; tours on the second Sat of every month at 3pm. **Bus:** 2 or 22.

THE LIBRARY OF GENEVA

This structure has been a library since 1873. It was originally built in 1559 as an academy for Calvinist theologians. The east wing of the library dates from the 15th century and has some 1.2 million volumes. The building also contains two museums:

MUSEE JEAN-JACQUES-ROUSSEAU, promenade des Bastions. Tel. 20-82-66.

Located in the library's Salle Lullin, this museum is dedicated to the philosopher who is considered to have started the Romantic movement. Rousseau is said to have instigated the French Revolution with his criticism of the divine right of kings and his support of democracy. Rousseau, who wrote *The Social Contract, Emile,* and *Confessions,* believed that humanity is basically good, but that corruption came through such social institutions as governments and organized religions. The museum contains manuscripts, correspondence, prints, two busts by Houdon, and the death mask of Rousseau.

Admission: Free.

Open: Mon–Fri 9am–noon and 2–5pm, Sat 9am–noon. **Bus:** 3. **Tram:** 12.

MUSEE HISTORIQUE DE LA REFORMATION, promenade des Bastions. Tel. 20-82-66.

This museum is also in the Bibliothèque Publique (Salle Lullin) and is of particular note to those interested in Calvin and the Reformation.

Admission: Free.

Open: Mon–Fri 9am–noon and 2–6pm, Sat 9am–noon. **Bus:** 3. **Tram:** 12.

RELIGIOUS MONUMENTS

The old town, Vieille Ville, on the Left Bank, is dominated by the ✪ **Cathédrale de Saint-Pierre,** Cour St-Pierre (tel. 29-75-98), which was built in the 12th and 13th centuries and partially reconstructed in the 15th century. Recent excavations have disclosed that a Christian sanctuary was here as early as A.D. 400. In 1536 the people of Geneva gathered in the cloister of St. Pierre's and voted to make the cathedral Protestant. The church, which has been heavily renovated over the years, has a modern organ with 6,000 pipes. The northern tower was reconstructed at the end of the 19th century, with a metal steeple erected between the two stone towers. If you don't mind the 145 steps, you can climb to the top of the north tower for a splendid view of the city, its lake, the Alps, and the Jura Mountains. The tower is open daily from 11:30am to 5:30pm. Admission is 2F ($1.45).

To enter the St. Pierre archeological site, called **Site Archéologique de St-Pierre,** go through the entrance in the Cour St-Pierre, at the right-hand corner of the cathedral steps. The underground passageway extends under the present cathedral and the High Gothic (early 15th-century) **Chapelle des Macchabées,** which adjoins the southwestern corner of the church. The chapel was restored during World War II, after having been used as a storage room following the Reformation. Excavations of the chapel have revealed baptisteries, a crypt, the foundations of several cathedrals, the bishop's palace, 4th-century mosaics, and sculptures and geological strata.

The cathedral and the chapel are open June to September, daily from 9am to 7pm; March to May and in October, daily from 9am to noon and 2 to 6pm; in January, February, November, and December, daily from 9am to noon and 2 to 5pm. There is no admission charge, although donations are welcome. Sunday service is held in the cathedral at 10am, and an hour of organ music is presented on Saturday at 6pm from June through September. The archeological site is open Tuesday through Saturday from 10am to 1pm and 2 to 6pm; the admission charge is 5F ($3.65).

Next door to the cathedral is a Gothic church where Calvin preached, known as the **Temple de l'Auditoire,** or Calvin Auditorium. It was restored in 1959 in time for Calvin's 450th anniversary.

PARKS, GARDENS & SQUARES

If you walk along the quays, heading north as if to Lausanne, you'll come to some of the most beautiful parks in Geneva. **Parc Mon-Repos** is off avenue de France and **La Perle du Lac** is off rue de Lausanne. Directly to the right is the **Jardin Botanique (Botanical Garden),** which was established in 1902. It has an alpine garden, a little zoo, greenhouses, and exhibitions, and can be visited free daily from 7am to 6:30pm in the summer (in other months, daily from 8am to 5pm).

Back at lakeside, you can take a boat to the other side, getting off at quai Gustave-Ador. From there you can explore two more lakeside parks—**Parc de la Grange,** which has the most extravagant rose garden in Switzerland (especially in June), and, next to it, the **Parc des Eaux-Vives.**

When you leave the Botanical Garden on the Left Bank, you can head west, along avenue de la Paix, about a mile north from the pont du Mont-Blanc, to the Palais des Nations in the **Parc de l'Ariana.**

LES PAQUIS DISTRICT

One of Geneva's most animated and elegant districts, Les Pâquis faces the harbor from the Right Bank of Lake Geneva. To reach it, head north along the quai des Bergues, which leads into quai du Mont-Blanc. On your left, at the intersection of quai du Mont-Blanc and Gare Routière, stands the **Brunswick Monument,** the tomb of Charles II of Brunswick, who died in Geneva in 1873. The duke left his fortune to the city with the provision that it build a monument to him. Geneva accepted the fortune and modeled the tomb after the Scaglieri tombs in Verona. Les Pâquis is a sector of cozy bistros, nightclubs, ateliers, elegant boutiques, and banks. The word *pâquis* comes from the Latin *pascuum,* "pasture." The cows that grazed here have long gone, but from about A.D. 1330 the district consisted of a vast expanse of fields, pastures, and wastelands. It was very far from the heart of the city and its protective ditches, and exposed to permanent danger of invasion.

From the 14th century, as the city developed a stronger defense system, this unincorporated territory became safer, and more and more people came here to make homes. In the 15th century the Pâquis was home to potters and fishermen, and eventually homes and small industries began to take root.

In 1831 the French writer Chateaubriand settled at the **Hôtel des Etrangers,** 22, rue des Pâquis. From 1851 on development was fairly rapid, with the construction of **quai du Mont-Blanc** and of the **Rotonde,** the English church. An American church was also constructed, and in 1857 **quais Pâquis** and **Eaux-Vives** were erected. Construction on the Cornavin railway station began the following year. The **pont du Mont-Blanc** was erected in 1862. Soon, the lake promenade, the facade des Pâquis, and quai du Mont-Blanc became fashionable.

In 1873 construction began on the **Hotel National (Palais Wilson);** from 1925 to 1936 it would house the first secretariat of the League of Nations. The Kursaal was built between 1874 and 1879. One of the most infamous events in the history of the area was the assassination of Empress Elisabeth of Austria, in 1898, at the landing stage facing the Duke of Brunswick's mausoleum.

After wandering through the district with no particular fixed itinerary, visitors may tour Lake Geneva in a lake steamer. Steamers leave from quai du Mont-Blanc.

COOL FOR KIDS

Geneva is a city with many attractions of interest to the younger set. The following—all detailed above—are perhaps the "coolest of the cool":

Musée International de la Croix-Rouge et du Croissant-Rouge   Visiting the Red Cross Museum is like attending an adventure movie, as kids are enraptured by the sweep and drama of this heroic organization, which has always been near the "core of the action."

Musée d'Histoire Naturelle   One of the best natural-history museums of Europe delights children with its tropical birds, mammals, and exotic reptiles.

Jet d'Eau and Flower Clock   These scenic wonders are exciting introductions for children. After viewing both of them, parents can take their kids for a tour by steamer on Lake Geneva.

SPECIAL-INTEREST SIGHTSEEING

FOR THE LITERARY ENTHUSIAST   Voltaire lived at 25, rue des Délices—now the **Institut et Musée Voltaire** (tel. 44-71-33)—during his period of exile from France (1755 to 1760) and from time to time after that up to 1765; he wrote part of *Candide* here. The museum displays furniture, manuscripts, letters, and portraits, as well as a terra-cotta model of a seated Voltaire by Houdon. The museum is open Monday through Friday from 2 to 5pm., and admission is free. Bus: 6 or 7.

FOR THE MUSIC DEVOTEE   Once a private collection, the 350 instruments displayed at the **Musée des Instruments Anciens de Musique (Museum of Antique Musical Instruments)**, 23, rue Le-Fort (tel. 746-95-65), were purchased by the city of Geneva. Many of the instruments are still in working order and are occasionally played. Some are from the 16th century and are considered works of visual, as well as musical, art. The museum is open on Tuesday from 3 to 6pm, on Thursday from 10am to noon and 2 to 6pm, and on Friday from 8 to 10pm. Admission is 1F (75¢). Bus: 3 or 33.

WALKING TOUR — THE QUAYS & OLD TOWN

Start: Jet d'Eau.

Finish: Place du Bourg-de-Four.

Time: 2 hours.

Best Time: Any sunny day.

ALONG THE QUAYS   If, like most tourists, you arrive in the summer, you might begin your discovery of the city with a long promenade along the quays of Geneva. The one sight you can't miss is the:

1. Jet d'Eau, quai Gustave-Ador—the famous fountain that is the trademark of the city. Visible for miles from April to September, it throws water 460 feet into the air above the lake. The Genevese call the fountain the *jeddo*. It dates from 1891, but was improved in 1951. Many cities have sent engineers to Geneva to study the secret workings of the fountain, although it remains a carefully guarded state secret. The fountain pumps 132 gallons of water per second into the air.

Once you have seen the fountain, you'll be ready to explore the quays, with their gardens and ancient buildings. The aquatic population consists of seagulls, ducks, and swans. A fleet of small boats, called *mouettes genevoises,* shuttles visitors from one quay to another from spring until autumn.

From the fountain, head south along the quay until you reach the:

2. Flower Clock in the **Jardin Anglais** (English Garden), another Geneva landmark lying directly off quai du Général-Guisan. Its face is made of carefully landscaped beds of flowers, and it keeps perfect time! The Jardin Anglais is at the foot of the Mont Blanc Bridge, which spans the river at the point where the Rhône leaves Lake Geneva. The bridge was rebuilt in 1969.

Cross pont du Mont-Blanc and turn left (south) along quai des Bergues in the Right Bank of Geneva until you come to the next bridge, called pont des Bergues. If you cross this bridge you'll come to:

3. Ile Rousseau, with a statue of the philosopher sculpted by Pradier in 1834. The island, which was a stamping ground of the philosopher and the site of many of his reveries, is now home to ducks, swans, grebes, and other aquatic fowl. Situated in the middle of the Rhône, it was once a bulwark of Geneva's river defenses.

Return to quai des Bergues and continue to walk left along the quay until you reach place St-Gervais and the:

4. Tour-de-l'Ile. A château was built here in 1219, although the tower is all that remains today. The château had been used as a prison and place of executions by the counts of Savoy. A wall plaque commemorates a visit by Caesar in 58 B.C. Nowadays the headquarters of the Geneva tourist office is located on the island. You can also explore the old markets, which often exhibit the works of contemporary Genevese artists.

The walking tour of the quays is particularly good for children because the sites are outside and easily understandable. If the children get tired, however, you can take them to quai du Mont-Blanc, where they can board *le mini-train de Genève*. This 40-minute excursion will take them along the major parks and quays of Geneva. Departures April to October are daily every half hour from 9am to 5pm. Adults pay a fare of 6F ($4.40) and children pay 5F ($3.65).

THROUGH OLD TOWN At this point, you will be on the doorway of Geneva's Old Town or Vieille Ville, set on the cultural Left Bank. The district is one of the most remarkable in Switzerland.

After leaving the Tour de-l'Ile, you can continue across the Rhône until you reach place Bel-Air, on the Left Bank. From here, head south for a short distance along rue de la Monnaie, which quickly becomes rue de la Cité. When that street changes its name to rue de la Tertasse, continue south along this street until you reach:

5. Place Neuve, considered the cultural heart of Geneva. The square has a statue of General Dufour, who was a cofounder of the Red Cross. Monuments on this square include the Grand Théâtre, the Conservatory of Music, and the Rath Museum. The Grand Théâtre (opera house) was built in 1874 (see Section 9, "Evening Entertainment," below). The conservatory dates from 1858.

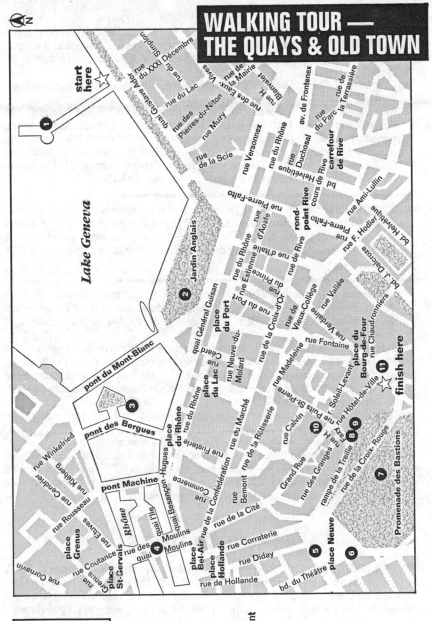

WALKING TOUR — THE QUAYS & OLD TOWN

start here

① ②

Lake Geneva

③ ④ ⑤ ⑥ ⑦ ⑧ ⑨ ⑩ ⑪

finish here

pont du Mont-Blanc
pont des Bergues
pont Machine

rue du XXXI Décembre
rue du Simplon
rue du Lac
rue des Pierres-du-Niton
rue Muzy
rue de la Scie
rue des Eaux-Vives
rue H. Blanvalet
rue de la Mairie
av. de Frontenex
rue du Parc
rue de la Terrassière
rue du Rhône
rue Duchosal
rue Helvétique
cours de Rive
carrefour de Rive
bd. Helvétique
rue Ami-Lullin
rond-point Rive
rue Pierre-Fatio
rue F. Hodler
bd. J. Dalcroze
Jardin Anglais
rue Pierre-Fatio
rue Versonnex
quai Général Guisan
place du Port
rue Estienne d'Orves
rue d'Italie
rue d'Aoste
rue du Prince
rue de Rive
rue du Rhône
rue de la Croix-d'Or
rue de Verdaine
rue du Vieux-Collège
rue Vallée
rue Chaudronniers
place du Bourg-de-Four
place du Lac
rue O. Girard
rue Neuve-du-Molard
rue Fontaine
rue de la Madeleine
rue Fontaine
place du Rhône
rue de la Confédération
rue du Marché
rue de la Rôtisserie
rue de la Croix-Rouge
Grand Rue
rue Calvin
r. Soleil-Levant
rue du Puits St-Pierre
rue Hôtel-de-Ville
rue de l'Hôtel-de-Ville
rue Winkelfried
rue Kléberg
rue Cendrier
rue Rousseau
rue des Étuves
rue Coutance
place Grenus
place St-Gervais
rue Comavin
Rhône
quai des Moulins
quai des Moulins
quai de l'Île
rue Besançon-Hugues
place Bel-Air
rue du Commerce
rue Bémont
rue de la Cité
rue de Hollande
rue Corraterie
rue Diday
rue de Hollande
bd. du Théâtre
place Neuve
rampe de la Treille
rue des Granges
Promenade des Bastions

Rhône

GENEVA

Walking Tour Area

① Jet d'Eau
② Flower Clock, Jardin Anglais
③ Île Rousseau
④ Tour de l'Île
⑤ Place Neuve
⑥ Rath Museum
⑦ Monument de la Réformation
⑧ Le Café-Restaurant Papon
⑨ Hôtel-de-Ville
⑩ Arsenal
⑪ Place du Bourg-de-Four

6. The Rath Museum, place Neuve (tel. 28-56-16), reached by tram no. 12 and bus no. 3 or 33, has temporary exhibitions of paintings and sculpture. It is open Tuesday through Sunday from 10am to noon and 2 to 6pm. Entrance is 5F ($3.65).

From place Neuve, continue southeast along rue de la Croix-Rouge, until you come to the:

7. Monument de la Réformation, in the park, promenade des Bastions. The Reformation Monument was built in 1917 along a 16th-century rampart, beneath the walls of the old town on promenade des Bastions. The monument, which is 100 yards long, represents John Knox, Calvin, Théodore de Bèze, and Guillaume Farel—the four Genevese reformers. Other statues include Cromwell, the Pilgrim Fathers, and on either end, Luther and Zwingli.

REFUELING STOP   One of the oldest and most venerated cafés of Geneva, **8. Le Café-Restaurant Papon,** 1, rue Henri-Fazy, lies near the Tour Baudet in the vicinity of the Hôtel-de-Ville. A restaurant, crêperie, tearoom, and café, it has been entertaining drinkers and diners under its vaulted ceilings since the 17th century.

Retrace your footsteps along rue de la Croix-Rouge until you return to place Neuve. From the square, take a sharp right and follow ramp de la Treille, which becomes rue Henri-Fazy. Turn right at rue de l'Hôtel-de-Ville and you'll approach the:

9. Hôtel-de-Ville (Town Hall), a short walk from the cathedral, dating from the 16th and 17th centuries. Its Baudet Tower was constructed in 1455. The building, which has a cobblestone ramp instead of a staircase, has witnessed some of the city's most important diplomatic events. The Red Cross originated here in 1864.

Across from the Town Hall is:

10. The Arsenal, an arcaded structure dating from 1634. In the courtyard of the building is a cannon cast in 1683.

Continue along rue de l'Hôtel-de-Ville until you reach:

11. Place du Bourg-de-Four, which was first a Roman forum and later a medieval town square. The Palais de Justice here was built in 1707, but it has housed courts of law only since 1860. While you're in this area, you will come across a fountain, many antiquaries' shops, and art galleries.

ORGANIZED TOURS

BUS TOURS   A 2-hour City Tour is operated daily all year by **Key Tours S.A.,** 7, rue des Alpes, place du Mont-Blanc (tel. 731-41-40). The tour starts from the Gare Routière, the bus station at place Dorcière, near the Key Tours office. From November through March a tour is offered only once a day at 2pm, but from April through October two tours leave daily, at 10am and 2pm.

A bus will drive you through the city to see the monuments, landmarks, and lake promenades. In the old town you can take a walk down to the Bastions Park to the Reformation Wall. After a tour through the International Center—where, you'll be shown the headquarters of the International Red Cross—the bus returns to its starting place. Adults are charged 20F ($14.60); children 4 to 12 accompanied by an adult pay 10F ($7.30).

BOAT TOURS   Many other excursions are offered, including a 2½-hour boat trip on the Rhône aboard the **Bâteau du Rhône,** with commentary in English. The trip takes you from Geneva to the Verbois dam and back. The group meets opposite pont de Sous-Terre, from April 1 to October 30 daily at 2:30pm and on Thursday, Saturday, and Sunday also at 10am. The boat trip costs 16F ($11.70) for adults and 10F ($7.30) for children 6 to 12 years of age.

First-class **lake cruises** are offered without guides and meals from June to the end of September. A 1-day cruise will take you on a complete tour of the lake, leaving from the Jardin Anglais pier at 8 and 10:15am daily and from the Mont Blanc pier at 9:15am and returning at 6:45pm. The cost of the cruise, which takes you past Nyon, Lausanne, Vevey, Montreux, Evian, and Thonon, is 45F ($32.85) for adults, half price for children 6 to 16.

You can go by boat to Montreux and the Château de Chillon on a **Castle Cruise** and then return by train. The boat leaves from the Mont Blanc pier daily at 9:15am, arriving at Chillon at 2:15pm, or from the Jardin Anglais pier at 10:45am, arriving at Chillon at 3:42pm. Trains for the 1-hour round-trip make the run every hour. Cost of the excursion is 53F ($38.70) for adults, half price for children 6 to 16. After Chillon, visitors must catch a bus to take them to the railroad station in Montreux, where they can board a train back to Geneva.

You can also take a tour called **Le Tour du Petit Lac,** which will take you around the lower part of the lake, past Nyon and Yvoire, in half a day. A ticket on this circuit costs 21F ($15.35) for second class, and 28F ($20.45) for first class. In the summer the tour departs every day at 9:15am from quai du Mont-Blanc and from the pier at the Jardin Anglais at 10:30am, 2:30pm, and 3pm.

A TOUR TO MONT BLANC   If you have time, I highly recommend a Mont Blanc excursion, which is an all-day trip to Chamonix by bus and a cable-car ride to the summit of the Aiguille du Midi (12,610 ft.). The tour is offered daily from April to October; January to March and in November and December on Tuesday, Thursday, Saturday, and Sunday. It leaves Geneva at 8:30am and returns at 5:30pm from October to April and at 6:30pm from May to September. Buses leave from the station, Gare Routière. You must take your passport with you.

Other climbs on this tour are Vallée Blanche by télécabin, an extension of the Aiguille du Midi climb, from April to October; to Mer de Glâce via electric rack railway to the edge of the glacier, from which you may descend to the ice grotto (the climb is not available in the winter); and to Le Brevent, an ascent by cable car to a rocky belvedere at 7,900 feet, facing the Mont Blanc range.

An English-speaking guide will accompany your bus tour. **Key Tours, S.A.,** 7, rue des Alpes (place du Mont-Blanc), Case Postale 490, CH-1211 Genève, Switzerland (tel. 022/731-41-40), operators of the excursions, require a minimum of eight people per trip. Tours range from 85F ($62.05) to 163F ($119), depending on which ascent you make.

6. SPECIAL & FREE EVENTS

The **Fêtes de Genève,** on August 1, when the Genevese celebrate their national holiday, is one of the most fun times in the city. It is followed 2 weeks later by a long weekend celebration, with fireworks on the lake, street dancing, and a parade of flower-covered floats.

Another celebration, on December 12, is known as **l'Escalade.** Geneva was attacked on that night in 1602 by Charles-Emmanuel, whose soldiers attempted—unsuccessfully—to scale the city ramparts. The heroine of the hour, a hearty matriarch who came to be known as Mère Royaume, poured a pot of boiling stew over the head of a marauding Savoy soldier and then cracked his skull with the kettle. Today residents celebrate the event by donning 17th-century costumes and staging torchlight parades through the old town.

7. SPORTS & RECREATION

Like most cities in health-conscious Switzerland, Geneva has many sports facilities. However, people also pursue activities outside the city. They are more interested in following their own personal sports program than they are in spectator sports, except for **soccer,** which is played in various stadiums (matches are announced in the tourist office's monthly "List of Events").

The big spectator event of the year, a soccer tournament known as the **Bol d'Or,** takes place some time in June (the Swiss National Tourist Office abroad will provide exact dates).

The world's most important **lake regatta** attracts approximately 600 sailboats and more than 3,500 competitors. The lake is virtually covered with white sails. It takes 7 hours for the luckiest to sail from one end to the other—and more than 24 hours for the unluckiest. But it's worth trying and participants talk about it for years. People come from all over the world to participate, including the winner of the America's Cup—Californian Dennis Conner, who piloted his *Stars & Stripes.*

BICYCLING Geneva is ideal for bicycle enthusiasts, who consider its countryside a paradise. What could be better than a ride through forest, vineyard, and cornfield? The most passionate cyclists climb Bernex's hill, the highest peak in the country, or cross the border into France (bring a passport). See Section 2, "Getting Around," above, for details about renting a bike.

GOLF The city has no public courses, but the private, 18-hole **Golf Club of Geneva,** at Cologny (tel. 735-75-40), will accept visitors who call or write in advance. The course is open from March to December.

HIKING/JOGGING In addition to the many trails that have been laid out in the parks, you can also jog along the quays and the lakeshore beaches. Best places for jogging are Parc Bertrand, Parc des Eaux-Vives, and Parc Mon-Repos.

SAILING This is perhaps the most popular sport in Geneva. All along the quays in the summer are kiosks offering sailboats for rent to visitors.

SKIING In the winter the people of Geneva flock to the resorts of the Haute Savoie in France, notably Chamonix and Megève. Each resort is about an hour's drive from Geneva. The smaller, lesser-known French resort of Flaine is even closer to Geneva. In Switzerland itself, the place nearest Geneva where there's good skiing is the Glacier of Les Diablerets or the resort of Champéry.

TENNIS Tennis can be played at several clubs, such as the **Geneva Tennis Club** at Parc des Eaux-Vives (tel. 735-53-50). Each September, world-famous tennis players meet in Geneva for the Barclay Open.

WATER SPORTS In the summer, swimmers will find fine beaches along the lake. The most popular is **Geneva Beach (Genève Plage),** where you can swim from

9am to 7pm for 5F ($3.65). You can also swim in the lake at bains des Pâquis and quai du Mont-Blanc.

8. SAVVY SHOPPING

THE SHOPPING SCENE

From boutiques to department stores, Geneva is a shopping paradise. The city, of course, is known for its watches and jewelry, but it's also a good place to buy embroidered blouses, music boxes from the Jura region, cuckoo clocks from German Switzerland, cigars from Havana (not allowed into the United States), chocolate, and Swiss army knives, among other items.

Geneva practically invented the wristwatch. In fact, watchmaking in the city dates from the 16th century. Be sure to avoid purchasing a Swiss watch in one of the souvenir stores. If jewelers are legitimate, they will display a symbol of the Geneva Association of Watchmakers and Jewelers. Here, more than in any other Swiss city perhaps, you should be able to find all the best brands, including Vacheron & Constantin, Longines, Omega, and Blancpain to name just a few. Sometimes there are discounts on such items as cameras. Most salespeople I've encountered spoke English and were helpful.

A shopping spree might begin at the **place du Molard.** Once this was the harbor of Geneva before the water receded. Merchants from all over Europe used to bring their wares to trade fairs here in the days before merchants emigrated to richer markets in Lyon.

If you're walking along rue du Rhône and are put off by the prices, go one block south to rue du Marché, which in various sections becomes rue de la Croix-d'Or and rue de Rive. Don't be afraid to comparison-shop in Geneva—many stores jack up prices for tourists.

Store hours vary in Geneva. Many stores are open Monday through Friday from 8am to 6:30pm and on Saturday from 8am to 5pm. Some shops don't open until 1:30pm on Monday.

SHOPPING A TO Z
AUCTIONS

The city has four of the world's most famous auction houses, with sales taking place mostly in May and November. During these periods, myriad social events accompany the auctions. Moreover, the city is an important center for the world art market and hosts prominent art and antiques dealers. Details and venues of sales appear in the tourist office's monthly "List of Events."

ANTIQUES

ART ET STYLE, 10, Grand'Rue. Tel. 21-45-97.
This antiques store looks and feels more like a museum than a commercial establishment. The high-ceilinged room is packed with furniture and 17th-century sculpture. The staff is eager to discuss merchandise and prices.

ERNEST SCHMITT AND CO. ANTIQUITES, 3, rue de l'Hôtel-de-Ville. Tel. 28-35-40.
This store beautifully displays English furniture in the ground-floor rooms of an

18th-century private house. Be sure to ask the owner to take you across the cobblestone courtyard to see the other showrooms.

CHINA

AUX ARTS DU FEU, 18, quai du Général-Guisan. Tel. 21-35-21.
This waterside store sells fine crystal, porcelain, china, silver, and decorative objects from around the world.

CHOCOLATES

CONFISERIE ROHR, 3, place du Molard. Tel. 21-63-03.
The aroma from this chocolate store practically pulls you in off the street. Among other specialties, you'll find chocolate-covered truffles, "gold" bars with hazelnuts, and poubelles au chocolat (chocolate "garbage pails").
There's another store at 42, rue du Rhône (tel. 21-68-76).

CLOTHING

CELINE, 23, rue du Rhône. Tel. 21-14-03.
This expensive shop sells all the clothing and accessories that any horsewoman or would-be equestrienne could use, as well as a selection of fashionably conservative skirts, blouses, and purses.

DEPARTMENT STORES

BON GENIE, 34, rue du Marché. Tel. 28-82-22.
Located on place du Molard, this department store sells mostly high-fashion women's clothing. Its storefront windows display art objects from local museums alongside designer clothes. There's also a limited selection of men's clothing.

GRAND PASSAGE, 50, rue du Rhône. Tel. 20-66-11.
The largest department store in Geneva, Grand Passage has just about everything under its roof: a travel bureau, an agency selling theater tickets, a hairdresser, a newspaper kiosk, a handful of boutiques, a restaurant, and a sandwich shop.

 FROMMER'S SMART TRAVELER: SHOPPING

1. Haggle in the open-air flea markets. Depending on how much the owner wants to sell, you can secure some good buys by steady and firm bargaining. Prices in stores are fixed.
2. Don't assume that because a product is made in Switzerland it's cheaper here. Check prices in stores at home before leaving, so that you'll know what is a good buy.
3. Browse through the stores on the left bank, where merchandise is considerably cheaper than it is on the right bank.

JEWELRY/WATCHES

BUCHERER, 26, quai du Général-Guisan. Tel. 21-62-66.
Located opposite Mont Blanc Bridge, this chrome-and-crystal store sells expensive watches and diamonds. The store offers such name brands as Rolex, Piaget, Baume & Mercier, Tissot, Rado, and Gerald Genta. The carpeted third floor is filled with relatively inexpensive watches. Once you're on that floor, you'll also find a large selection of cuckoo clocks, music boxes, embroideries, and souvenirs, as well as porcelain pill boxes and other gift items.

GÜBELIN JEWELERS, 1, place du Molard (60, rue du Rhône). Tel. 28-86-55.
Dating from 1854, this family-run establishment is known mainly for its brand-name watches, although it also sells 10-carat emeralds. You'll see two perpetual-motion clocks in the windows, giving chronological as well as astrological time, with fanciful enamel notations of the different time zones. You can also buy reasonably priced gifts, such as pen and pencil sets.

L. SCHERRER, 29, rue du Rhône. Tel. 21-70-96.
Located on the most prestigious street in Geneva, this elegant store sells a good selection of watches, diamonds, and gems. The polite staff caters to an elite clientele.

LEATHER

HERMES, 43, rue du Rhône. Tel. 21-76-77.
Like all Hermès boutiques, this store sells purses, leather accessories, diaries, jewelry, watches, ready-to-wear clothing, furs, and, naturally, the famous Hermès scarf and tie. Everything is beautifully handcrafted.

OUTDOOR MARKETS

Colorful **outdoor markets,** overflowing with flowers and fruit, take place several times a week at Rive, Coutance, Carouge, and other squares. A **flea market** is held every Wednesday and Saturday on the Plaine de Plainpalais; markets for books take place on place de la Madeleine on most days during the summer.

SHOES

BRUNO MAGLI, 47, rue du Rhône. Tel. 21-53-77.
This is one of the best-stocked shoestores in Geneva, with an elegant variety of Italian shoes, purses, and accessories.

TOBACCO

DAVIDOFF ET CIE, 2, rue de Rive. Tel. 28-90-41.
This is the most famous tobacco store in the world, with the best cigars you'll find in Europe. A massive, climate-controlled storage room in the basement holds dozens of Cuban cigars, which cannot be found in America. Russian exile Zino Davidoff (born in 1906) set up a revolutionary system of mixing grades of tobacco from his shop in Geneva. Today you'll see all kinds of cigar boxes and smoking paraphernalia.

TOYS

JOUETS WEBER (Franz Carl Weber), 12, rue de la Croix-d'Or. Tel. 28-42-55.
Located at the corner of rue de la Fontaine, this place is the best toy store in the

city. It has all kinds of children's toys, from slide shows to cartoon characters, as well as dolls and sports equipment.

9. EVENING ENTERTAINMENT

Geneva has more nightlife than any other city in Switzerland. Most activity centers around place du Bourg-de-Four, a stagecoach stop during the 19th century. In the old town there are lots of outdoor cafés in the summer, attracting the affluent and not-so-affluent Genevese. But if you get bored, you might consider going into France, which, because Switzerland limits bets to 5F ($3.65), attracts most of Geneva's serious gamblers. There's gambling at Divonne, France, 12½ miles away.

THE ENTERTAINMENT SCENE

Geneva has always attracted the culturally sophisticated, including Byron, Jean-Baptiste, Corot, Victor Hugo, Balzac, George Sand, and Franz Liszt. Ernest Ansermet founded Geneva's great Orchestre de la Suisse Romande, whose frequent concerts entertain music lovers at Victoria Hall. For opera there's the 1,500-seat Grand Théâtre, which welcomes Béjart, the Bolshoi, and other ballet companies, in addition to having a company of its own.

For a preview of events at the time of your visit, pick up a copy of the monthly "List of Events" issued by the tourist office.

THE PERFORMING ARTS

GRAND THEATRE, place Neuve. Tel. 21-23-18.

Modeled on the Paris Opéra, this building was opened in 1879. It burned down in 1951 and was subsequently rebuilt in the same style, except for the modern auditorium, which has a seating capacity of 1,488. From September to July it presents eight operas and two ballets, as well as recitals and chamber-music concerts.

Prices: Tickets, 18F–90F ($13.15–$65.70) for opera, 15F–75F ($10.95–$54.75) for ballet.

VICTORIA HALL, 14, rue du Général-Dufour. Tel. 28-81-21.

This 1,866-seat hall is the home of the celebrated Orchestre de la Suisse Romande. This is Geneva's most famous musical institution, whose musical interpretations have been heard throughout the world. For 50 years it was conducted by Ernest Ansermet.

Prices: Tickets, 18F–25F ($13.15–$18.25).

THE CLUB & MUSIC SCENE

CLUB 58, 15, Glacis de Rive. Tel. 735-15-15.

This private club does allow nonmembers to enter, although men are required to wear jackets. Club 58 is mainly a disco, but it has a restaurant attached. Occasionally, the club presents some top names in show business, such as Isaac Hayes, the Temptations, Sacha Distel, Gilbert Becaud, and others. It opens daily at 10pm; the restaurant opens at 8pm. Drinks in the club cost 22F ($16.05); restaurant drinks are 10F ($7.30).

Admission: 12F ($8.75) for men; women accompanying male nonmembers are admitted free.

LA GARÇONIERE, 22, place Bemont. Tel. 28-21-61.

Both straights and gays come to watch the burlesque transvestite act at La Garçonière. Two nightly shows are presented, at 11:30pm and at 1:30am. Open Sunday through Thursday from 10pm to 4am and on Friday and Saturday from 10pm to 5am. Drinks run 20F ($14.60).

Admission: Mon–Wed free, Sun–Thurs 10F ($7.30), Fri–Sat 15F ($10.95).

GRIFFIN'S CLUB, 36, bd. Helvótique. Tel. 735-12-18.

Griffin's is perhaps the most chic club in Geneva. Technically, it's private—you may or may not get in, depending on the mood of the management at the time of your visit. The popularity of nightclubs comes and goes, but the collection of celebrities who have traipsed here reads like a Who's Who from the tabloids. Jackets are required for men. Open daily from 10pm to 4am. Drinks cost 20F to 26F ($14.60 to $19); dinner begins at 110F ($80.30).

Admission: Free.

MAXIM'S CABARET, 2 rue Thalberg. Tel. 732-99-00.

This small, Lido-style cabaret and music hall has some very good acts and is a favorite of tourists. Open daily from 8:30pm to dawn, with shows at 11pm and 1am. Drinks start at 22F ($16.05); a fixed-price dinner goes for 100F ($73).

Admission: Free.

LA TOUR DANCING, 6, rue de la Tour de Boel. Tel. 21-00-33.

This difficult-to-locate club is on one of Geneva's most charming squares in the old town, in a building once belonging to the Genevese patriot Bezanson Hugues (1491–1532). The club has chiseled-stone and stucco walls with a wrought-iron dragon sticking out over the street. Inside, three levels of balconies overlook the central dance and performance area. Musical groups play rock and dance tunes daily from 10pm to 4am. No jeans or sneakers are permitted. The club, which has a small restaurant, is closed Monday. Drinks cost 20F ($14.60) and up.

Admission: Sun and Tues–Thurs free, Fri–Sat 12F ($8.75).

VELVET, 7, rue du Jeu-de-l'Arc. Tel. 735-00-00.

Night owls flock to this popular club for what the French call *le dancing à la mode.* Velvet is a combination restaurant, disco, and cabaret, usually featuring more than a dozen topless dancers. Shows begin nightly at 11pm. Open daily from 10pm to 4 or 5am. On Sunday night the restaurant part is closed. Drinks begin at 20F ($14.60).

Admission: Sun–Thurs free, Fri–Sat 12F ($8.75).

THE BAR SCENE

BAR DES BERGUES, in the Hôtel des Bergues, 33, quai des Bergues. Tel. 731-50-50.

Sheathed in mahogany, brass, and dark-green upholstery, this fashionable spot is decorated with a carefully illustrated series of late 19th-century menus from the Cercle des Arts et des Lettres. Although most clients come here for only a drink or two, the establishment also serves lunches and platters from the hotel's top-notch kitchens. Ask the barman for the list of daily specials. Beginning in the early evening, there's an international array of pianists. Open daily from 11am to midnight. Drinks begin at 14F ($10.20) each.

LE GENTILHOMME BAR, in the Hôtel Richemond, Jardin Brunswick. Tel. 731-14-00.

This is the most elegant bar in Geneva and one of the most prestigious in the world. Naturally, it attracts a chic crowd, ranging from Texas ranchers to Zurich bankers to glamorous women in $50,000 furs. The Napoléon III decor includes crystal chandeliers and velvet chairs. Open daily from 11:30am to 2:30pm and 7pm to 1am. Drinks cost 15F ($10.95) and up.

MR. PICKWICK PUB, 80, rue de Lausanne. Tel. 731-67-97.
This pub serves simple, English-style meals, but mostly the patrons come here to drink. The paneled rooms are filled in the evening with an attractive young crowd, who enjoy the dim lighting and American music. The place gets very crowded and can be fun. Irish coffee is a specialty, but most visitors order beer. In Geneva the pub is sometimes called the "Tower of Babble" because of all the languages spoken here (many employees of the United Nations hang out here). Open Monday through Friday from 10am to 1am, on Saturday from 3pm to 2am, and on Sunday from 3pm to 1am. A steak-and-kidney pie costs 15F ($10.95); a beer, 6F ($4.40).

A GAY BAR

LE TUBE, 3, rue de l'Université. Tel. 29-82-98.
This gay pub is recommended by the tourist office. Earlier in the evening it draws a mixed crowd, but every night after 9pm its clientele becomes predominantly gay. Open Sunday through Thursday to 1am and on Friday and Saturday until 2am. Beer costs 6F ($4.40).

10. NETWORKS & RESOURCES

FOR STUDENTS   The travel agency **SSR,** 3, rue Vignier (tel. 29-97-33), offers students discount opportunities for travel in Switzerland, France, and elsewhere. Open on Monday from 10am to 5:30pm and Tuesday through Friday from 9:30am to 5:30pm.

FOR WOMEN   The city's premier organization for women is **F-Information,** 1, rue des Barrières (tel. 21-28-28). Located in the heart of the old city, above the Taverne de la Madeleine, it is open on Monday, Tuesday, Thursday, and Friday from 2:30 to 6:30pm, on Wednesday from 9am to 6:30pm, and on Saturday from 11am to 3pm. It freely dispenses information (and occasionally legal advice) to women of all ages concerning social and employment opportunities.
    The city's most visible feminist bookstore is **L'Inédite Librairie Femmes,** 18, Cardinal Mermillod, in Carouge (tel. 43-22-33).

FOR GAY MEN AND LESBIANS   Many lesbian groups meet for political and social consciousness-raising at the **Centre Femmes** (Le Maison), 30, avenue Peshier, in the district of Champel (tel. 789-26-00). It's considered the most visible and best-organized outlet for gay women in French-speaking Switzerland. Several nights a week, different social and political gatherings are organized. These include dancing on alternate Saturdays, Wednesday-night vegetarian dinners, and Thursday-night theme parties. The organization maintains a **multilingual hot line** (tel. 43-42-15) for information about each week's activities.
    The equivalent for men is Geneva's gay switchboard, **Dialogai,** 57, avenue de Wendt, in the district of Servette (tel. 340-00-00). It provides multilingual information and advice to anyone who calls. On the basement-level premises are found a library, a

café and bar, and meeting rooms for Wednesday-night dinners and Saturday-night dancing parties. The organization publishes a list of the gay bars of Geneva and French-speaking Switzerland, offered free to anyone who asks, and is the best conduit anywhere to the male homosexual network of Geneva.

FOR SENIORS   Go to the tourist office and request a copy of "Season for Seniors." This booklet lists some 450 hotels in 200 Swiss towns and resorts, many outside Geneva, that offer special off-season rates for senior citizens (women over 62 and men over 65).

11. EASY EXCURSIONS FROM GENEVA

There are many attractions in the region around Geneva. Several of the most popular places—at least around the lake—have been covered in Chapter 9, on Lausanne and Lake Geneva. Refer to that chapter for highlights around the lake itself. This section will deal with the attractions that are closest to Geneva.

MONT SALEVE

The limestone ridge of Mont Salève (House Mountain) is 4 miles south of Geneva, in France. Its peak is at 4,000 feet, but you'll need a passport to reach it. If you have a car, you can take a road that goes up the mountain, which is popular with rock climbers. Bus no. 8 will take you to Veyrier, on the French border, where there is a passport and Customs control. A 6-minute cable-car ride will take you to a height of 3,750 feet on Mont Salève. From the top you'll have a panoramic sweep of the Valley of the Arve, with Geneva and Mont Blanc in the background.

CAROUGE

Carouge, a suburb of Geneva, is a historic European town. It dates from the 18th century, when it was built by the king of Sardinia to rival Geneva. Architects from Turin supplied the Piedmontese charm. At the Congress of Vienna, in 1815, Carouge was annexed to the canton of Geneva. Once Carouge was the playground of smugglers and gold washers who panned for the precious metal in the Arve. The Genevese themselves—at least those who wanted to escape from the puritanical city—came here in search of decadence.

Switzerland now considers Carouge a national landmark because of its architecture. Begin your exploration in the Market Square, with its old fountain, plane trees, and markets. A Roman stone was imbedded in the Church of the Holy Cross. As you walk around, you'll pass the court of the Count of Veyrier's palace, dating from 1783, the place du Temple with a fountain from 1857, and a Louis XVI carved door at 18, rue St-Victor.

COLOGNY

Byron and Shelley both lived in the residential suburb of Cologny, where they met at the Villa Diodati in 1816. Nine miles northeast of Geneva, the suburb is served by bus A from the city. The view of the lake and the city is especially good from the "Byron Stone" on chemin de Ruth (Ruth's Path) leading to the Byron fields.

The best time to go to Cologny is on Thursday afternoon (between 2 and 5pm), when you can visit the **Bodmeriana Library,** chemin du Guignard (tel. 022/736-23-70), which is a foundation established by a Zurich millionaire named Martin Bodmer. The private collection contains first editions, rare manuscripts, and objets d'art.

If you'd like to do what the Genevese themselves do on a good day, take bus C, departing from Rond-Point de Rive in Geneva, and head for the charming village of Jussy to explore the countryside around Geneva on foot.

HERMANCE

You can reach this fishing village, set on the lake, by taking bus no. 9 from Rond-Point de Rive in Geneva. Founded in 1245, the village has been restored. There is a medieval tower as well as the 15th-century Chapel of St. Catherine. The Genevese come here to visit the art galleries and café-restaurants. Before heading back, I suggest that you take a walk along the lake.

RUSSIN & DARDAGNY

If you'd like to see some of the vineyards of Geneva, you can visit Russin and Dardagny by taking a train from the Gare Cornavin in Geneva. In about 10 minutes you'll reach Russin, which is right in the center of a wine-growing region. Later on you can go on to Dardagny, a landmark village with a castle by the Valley of the Allondon. Take the Donzelle route through the vineyards, where you'll eventually get a train to take you back to Geneva.

COPPET

Located 9 miles north of Geneva in the canton of Vaud, this little town on the western shore of Lake Geneva is one of the most interesting destinations in the region.

WHAT TO SEE & DO

The **Château de Coppet** (tel. 022/776-10-28) attracted some of the greatest minds of the 18th and 19th centuries. The château, which sits on a hill beside the lake, midway between Lausanne and Geneva, was purchased in 1784 by Jacques Necker, the rich and powerful finance minister of Louis XVI. His daughter was Madame de Staël—a great French woman of letters, who was eventually sent into exile for her opposition to Napoleon. The château is still owned by Necker's descendants. The museum contains some mementos of Madame de Staël. It's open March to October, Tuesday through Sunday from 10am to noon and 2 to 5:30pm. Admission costs 5F ($3.65) for adults and 3F ($2.20) for children 6 to 16. Guided tours are conducted.

WHERE TO STAY & DINE

HOTEL DU LAC, CH-1296 Coppet. Tel. 022/776-15-21. Fax 022/776-53-46. 18 rms (all with bath). MINIBAR TV TEL

$ Rates: 128F–188F ($93.45–$133.55) single; 196F–251F ($143.05–$183.20) double. AE, DC, MC, V.

This elegant hideaway offers the most superb food and lodging in the area. Six miles from the Geneva-Cointrin Airport, the lovely lakeside retreat was established in 1628 and designated a *grand logis* by royal decree. Many famous guests have stayed here over the years. Its bedrooms are decorated with stone walls, beamed ceilings, and Oriental carpets. Ask about rates for your pet when you make reservations.

The Rôtisserie du Lac is one of the finest restaurants on Lake Geneva. In the summer tables are set out right by the lake. Bertrand Hubert serves both classic cuisine and cuisine moderne. You might begin with a warm salad of frogs' legs or a ravioli of snails with sweet garlic, then follow with grilled sole in a chive sauce. Omble chevalier, the famous lake fish of Geneva, is prepared here as you like it. Full meals cost 105F ($76.65) and more. A business lunch is offered on weekdays for 60F ($43.80). Lunch is served daily from noon to 2:15pm; dinner, daily from 7 to 10:15pm. The hotel also operates a nightclub, open Wednesday through Sunday from 9pm to 2am.

CHAPTER 11

LUCERNE & CENTRAL SWITZERLAND

Lucerne (Luzern in German) and its lake lie in the heartland of Switzerland, where the tops of the mountains are covered with eternal snow and their sides are flanked with glaciers. They are in William Tell country, where the seeds that led to the Swiss Confederation were sown. It was near Brunnen that the Everlasting League of 1315 was created, in the meadow of Rutli.

Despite the presence of many small resorts in the neighborhood, Lucerne is the district's largest and busiest city. The lake that nurtures it is the fourth largest in Switzerland, 24 miles long and (at its broadest) 2 miles wide. Geologists refer to it as the terminal basin for the nearby glaciers. The lake is known in German as the Vierwaldstättersee and in French as the Lac des Quatre Cantons. Either way, it's the lake of the four cantons: Lucerne, Uri, Unterwalden, and Schwyz (from which Switzerland derives its name).

Lucerne and its lake are among the most popular tourist destinations in all of Europe. Paddle-steamers service the many cable cars and lidos (beaches) set at the edge of the water, providing sweeping views of mountains—with names like Pilatus and Rigi—along the way. The region is rich in panoramas, folklore, and sports diversions, such as tobogganing, skiing, hill climbing, ice skating, and curling. The irregular geography of the brusquely vertical limestone and granite outcroppings give the shoreline one of the most romantic looks in Switzerland.

SEEING LUCERNE & CENTRAL SWITZERLAND

Lucerne is the traditional gateway to Lake Lucerne. It lies only a fast rail ride from Zurich, where most visitors arrive by plane. Once at Lake Lucerne, you can tour the mountain peaks by rail or funicular and cable-car connections and visit the resorts along the lake by steamer. Buses and trains link the historic towns in the heartland of Switzerland, including Schwyz and Altdorf.

WHAT'S SPECIAL ABOUT LUCERNE & CENTRAL SWITZERLAND

Great Towns/Villages

☐ Lucerne, capital of the Lake Lucerne district and base for some of the greatest alpine excursions.

☐ Schwyz, the "core of Helvetia," birthplace of the country.

☐ Altdorf, reputed site of the William Tell legend.

☐ Bürgenstock, choicest resort along Lake Lucerne, a 6-mile limestone ridge and hotel colony that's a deluxe citadel.

Natural Spectacles

☐ Mount Pilatus, a 7,000-foot summit overlooking Lake Lucerne from the west.

☐ Mount Rigi, extolled by Victor Hugo, at 5,900 feet one of the greatest mountain views of Europe.

☐ The St. Gotthard Pass, at 6,920 feet, providing a link between the Grisons and Valais Alps.

Museums

☐ Swiss Transport Museum, at Lucerne, one of the world's great transportation museums, containing railway cars, airplanes, cars, ships, even spaceships.

Ace Attractions

☐ Lake-steamer cruises on Lake Lucerne, leaving from all the major resorts.

IF YOU HAVE A WEEK

Days 1–4: You might see Lucerne in 1 day, but you'll need to stay there for more than 1 night if you want to visit the famous mountain peaks nearby, such as Rigi and Mount Pilatus.

Day 5: Anchor in for a night at one of the lake resorts, such as Weggis.

Day 6: Continue south to visit the historic town of Schwyz and the Holloch Caves.

Day 7: From Schwyz, drive south or take the train to Altdorf and Amsteg, spending the night at Andermatt before crossing the St. Gotthard Pass.

---

1. LUCERNE

31 miles S of Zurich, 55¾ miles E of Bern

GETTING THERE By Plane The international airport at Zurich is but an hour away by fast train (see below). It is a distance of 41 miles.

By Train Lucerne lies at the junction of four major rail lines, which connect it by fast train with every other major city of Switzerland. Travel time from Bern on one of the many express trains is 90 minutes; from Zurich, 50 minutes.

By Car From Bern, take Route 1 north until it becomes Route E17 east to Zurich. Follow E17 until it dips southeast to Lucerne and becomes Route E9.

From Zurich, you can take the N3 expressway south, but you'll have to turn off onto the signposted E60 heading southwest to Lucerne. This road becomes Route N4a and eventually an expressway again, the N14, as it continues west right into Lucerne.

SPECIAL EVENTS   The **Lucerne International Festival of Music** is held in August and September. For more information, contact the International Festival of Music administrative director, at Hirschmattstrasse 13, CH-6002 Luzern (tel. 041/23-35-62). There is also a **summer night festival**, as well as an annual **Carnival** before Ash Wednesday.

———————————

Lucerne is a tourist favorite partly because it lives up to the storybook image of a Swiss town. Located at the north end of the lake, the city abounds in narrow cobblestone streets, slender spires and turrets, covered bridges, frescoed houses, and fountains. Its residents are quick to tell you that you're "never very far from the snow"—Rigi and Pilatus mountains form the southern gate to the city, while the snow-capped Alps loom in the distance.

Lucerne's strategic gateway to the south and the rich markets of Italy lies between Rigi and Pilatus. The city's history has always been tied to the St. Gotthard Pass. During the 13th century, the routes leading to it were no more than mule paths. By 1820 the road had been widened enough to allow the easy transit of carriages. By 1882 Lucerne had a railway tunnel. Once a satellite vassal of the Hapsburgs, Lucerne became the first city to join the Swiss Confederation, in 1332. Unlike Geneva and Zurich, Lucerne did not support the Reformation and has always remained a stronghold of Catholicism.

The city is also a cultural center. Richard Wagner spent several of his most productive years in Tribschen, on the outskirts (there is a Wagner museum there). Arturo Toscanini was a founder of the Lucerne International Festival of Music, which takes place in August and September and is one of the most important musical events in Europe.

Fireworks are featured at the summer-night festival, a tradition dating back 250 years. The annual Carnival, shortly before Ash Wednesday, includes a parade of musicians in whimsical costumes producing ear-splitting sounds from trumpets, kettles, and drums. Numerous balls take place before and during the Carnival.

The residents of Lucerne are also sports-oriented. Every summer there are international rowing regattas on the Rotsee. Swimmers go to the lido (lake beach), and golfers head for the 18-hole golf course on the outskirts. Other sports include tennis, hiking, and mountaineering. Residents are especially fond of horse races, and there are plenty of international jumping contests.

Lucerne is at its best on Tuesday and Saturday mornings, when it becomes a lively market town. The markets are sheltered by stately arcades on both banks of the Reuss River.

ORIENTATION

ARRIVING   The Lucerne Bahnhof (train station), on Bahnhofplatz (tel. 21-33-11), lies on the south bank of the Reuss River. Taxis line up to take you to your destination. Many hotels are near the station; if your luggage is light, therefore, you might walk.

TOURIST INFORMATION   The **Lucerne Tourist Office** is at Frankenstrasse 1 (tel. 041/51-71-71), near the train station. It's open year round, Monday through Friday from 8:30am to 6pm and on Saturday from 9am to 5pm.

CITY LAYOUT   Most arrivals are at the railroad station, on **Bahnhofplatz,** where trains arrive from Zurich and other parts of Switzerland. The tourist information office is found here. This train depot is on the south bank of the **Reuss River.**

If you cross a bridge from the station square, you'll be on the north bank at the **Schwanenplatz** (Swan Square), which is the center of Lucerne. Also on the north bank of the Reuss is **Altstadt** (Old Town), containing many burghers' houses with oriel windows and old squares with fountains.

Kappellgasse is a major shopping street that leads to the Kornmarkt (Grain Exchange) on which stands the Altes Rathaus (Old Town Hall), from 1602. To the west of Kornmarkt is the **Weinmarkt** (Wine Market), a lovely old square with a splendid fountain.

The Kursaal, a casino-and-restaurant complex, stands at the Kurplatz on **Nationalquai,** the major quay of Lucerne, opening onto the lake.

From Kurplatz, **Löwenstrasse** leads to **Löwenplatz,** site of the Panorama, a famed canvas depicting the retreat of the French army during the Franco-Prussian War (1870–71). Nearby stands the even-more-famous **Löwendenkmal** (Lion Monument), the town's best-known and much-photographed monument.

GETTING AROUND

The city has a good network of **buses,** costing 1F to 1.50F (75¢ to $1.10), depending on the distance you ride (within the city limits). Purchase your ticket at automatic vending machines before you board. A **2-day ticket,** available in almost every hotel in Lucerne, costs only 5F ($3.65) and entitles you, if presented in combination with the Official Guidebook of the city, to unlimited rides on the Lucerne bus network. The guidebook is presented to guests registered at hotels in Lucerne.

Bicycles can be rented at the railroad station.

FAST FACTS

American Express The American Express office, at Schweizerhofquai 4 (tel. 50-11-77), is open Monday through Friday from 8:30am to noon and 2 to 6pm, and on Saturday from 8:30 to noon. No checks are cashed after 5pm.

Area Code The telephone area code for Lucerne is 041.

Laundry The clean and comfortable **Jet-Wasch,** Bruchstrasse 28 (tel. 22-01-51), has washers, dryers, irons, and ironing boards.

Post Office The city's main post office is at Bahnhofplatz 2 (tel. 26-91-11), a few steps from the railroad station. It's open Monday through Friday from 7:30am to 6:30pm and on Saturday from 7:30 to 11am.

WHAT TO SEE & DO

Don't miss the view from one of Lucerne's nine lookout towers. Part of the old fortifications erected along the north side of the medieval sector, they were all built in a different style between 1350 and 1408. At twilight they stand in dramatic silhouette against the sky. Known as the **Museggturme,** these ramparts are open daily from 8am to 8pm. Visitors can climb the 100 steps of the Schirmerturm for a view of the city and its spires.

WALKING TOUR —— Lucerne

Start Schwanenplatz.
Finish: Kurplatz.

Time: 2½ hours.
Best Time: Any sunny day.

The best way to see Lucerne is on foot, going along its lakeside quays, across its old squares, and through the streets of its old town.

Start in the heart of Lucerne at:

1. **Schwanenplatz,** or Swan Square, on the north bank of the Reuss River, reached by crossing the bridge, Seerbrücke, from Bahnhofplatz on the south bank, site of the train station.
   Adjoining the square on the west is:
2. **Kappellplatz,** site of St. Peter's Church. The church, the oldest in Lucerne, was built in 1178. In the center of the square is a fountain commemorating Carnival revelry in Lucerne.
   From here, continue west along a major shopping street, Kappellgasse, until you reach the:
3. **Kornmarkt,** the old Grain Exchange, which is today the site of the:
4. **Altes Rathaus** (Old Town Hall), a Renaissance building from 1602. The town hall has impressive masonry, a tremendous roof, and a tall rectangular tower. The tower is a good vantage point from which to survey the crowded market scene on Tuesday and Saturday morning. To the left of the town hall lies the:
5. **Picasso Sammlung,** a 17th-century building housing a Picasso collection (described below). The Am Rhyn town house, site of the museum, is entered at Fürrengasse 21.
   After leaving the museum, follow Rathausquai east toward Schwanenplatz again but only to cross the:
6. **Kappellbrücke** (Chapel Bridge), the symbol of Lucerne. It is a covered wooden footbridge, which you can use to cross the Reuss River, leading to the south bank. Built in 1333, the bridge is 560 feet long and crosses the river diagonally. It is one of the best-preserved wooden bridges in Switzerland, used originally for defense. There is also an octagonal Wasserturm (Water Tower), used variously as a prison, a torture chamber, and an archive. The bridge has more than 100 paintings, some of them done in 1599 by Heinrich Wagmann, illustrating the daily activities and dress of the people.
   You emerge onto Bahnhofstrasse; you can continue right (west) until you see the next covered bridge across the Reuss, the:
7. **Spreuerbrücke** (Mills Bridge), the second most famous bridge of Lucerne. Built in 1407 and restored in the 19th century, this wooden bridge spans an arm of the Reuss. Its gables are painted with the *Dance of Death,* a mural by Kaspar Meglinger dating from the 17th century. The mural commemorates a plague that swept through the city.
   Cross the bridge and take a sharp right to reach:
8. **Mühlenplatz** (Mills Square), dating from the 16th century. This was the old site of Lucerne markets. From Mühlenplatz walk down Kramgasse (to the east) to reach:
9. **Weinmarkt** (Wine Market), a lovely old square with a fountain, west of Kornmarkt. Long ago the mystery play *Confraternity of the Crown of Thorns* was performed here. Among the colorful old dwellings on the square is the Müllersche Apotheke, a "drugstore" from 1530.
   Directly northwest of Weinmarkt lies:

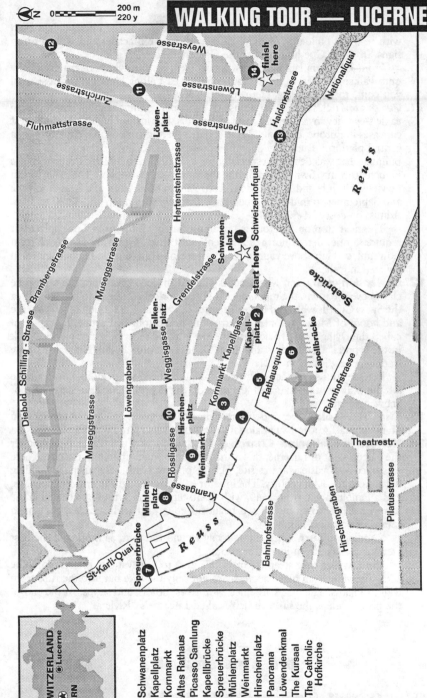

WALKING TOUR — LUCERNE

0 ──── 200 m
     ──── 220 y

start here

finish here

Reuss

Weystrasse
Löwenstrasse
Alpenstrasse
Zürichstrasse
Fluhmattstrasse
Löwen-platz
Hertensteinstrasse
Haldenstrasse
Nationalquai
Schweizerhofquai
Schwanen-platz
Grendelstrasse
Falken-platz
Kapellgasse
Kornmarkt
Kapell-platz
Weggisgasse
Rathausquai
Kapellbrücke
Seebrücke
Bahnhofstrasse
Löwengraben
Hirschen-platz
Rössligasse
Weinmarkt
Theatrestr.
Kramgasse
Museggstrasse
Brambergstrasse
Diebold Schilling - Strasse
Museggstrasse
Mühlen-platz
Bahnhofstrasse
Hirschengraben
Pilatusstrasse
St-Karli-Quai
Spreuerbrücke

Reuss

SWITZERLAND
⭑ Lucerne
BERN

1 Schwanenplatz
2 Kapellplatz
3 Kornmarkt
4 Altes Rathaus
5 Picasso Samlung
6 Kapellbrücke
7 Spreuerbrücke
8 Mühlenplatz
9 Weinmarkt
10 Hirschenplatz
11 Panorama
12 Löwendenkmal
13 The Kursaal
14 The Catholic Hofkirche

10. Hirschenplatz (Stag Square), another landmark square of Lucerne. It is filled with restored buildings, many of them with painted facades and wrought-iron signs. In 1779, Goethe stayed at the Goldener Adler.

From Hirschenplatz head west along Weggisgasse, which opens eventually onto Falkenplatz. From Falkenplatz continue east along Hertensteinstrasse until you come to Löwenplatz. Here you can view the:

11. Panorama (tel. 50-22-50). Because of its name, you might think that this is an eagle's-eye view over the lakes and mountains, but instead it's one of the largest canvases in Europe, covering 11,836 square feet and curving in a circle around a central platform. Painted in 1889 by Edouard Castres and contained in a round building that was designed especially for it, it depicts the bloody retreat of the French army into Switzerland during the Franco-Prussian War. The painting can be viewed in July and August, daily from 9am to 6pm; from mid-March to June and September to mid-November, daily from 9am to noon and 12:30 to 5pm. Admission costs 3F ($2.20).

The next stop on this tour is not immediately visible from Löwenplatz but requires a brief detour north along Denkmalstrasse. Within about a block from Löwenplatz, high above your head, you'll see one of the most famous statues in Switzerland, the:

12. Löwendenkmal (Lion Monument). Carved in deep relief into the sandstone cliff above the town, the monument is an allegorical reference to the bravery of the Swiss Guards who died in the Tuileries of Paris in 1792 trying to save the life and honor of Marie Antoinette. During his grand tour of Europe, Mark Twain called the Dying Lion of Lucerne "the saddest and most poignant piece of rock in the world." Designed by the great Danish sculptor Bertel Thorvaldsen, the statue was dedicated in 1821.

Retrace your steps back to Löwenplatz, then head south along Löwenstrasse all the way to the lake and the site of the Kurplatz, a few steps east of Schwanenplatz.

13. The Kursaal, a casino-and-restaurant complex, is on Kurplatz on Nationalquai. Above Nationalquai the twin towers of the Catholic:

14. Hofkirche (Collegiate Church of St. Leodegar) are visible. Named after the patron saint of Lucerne, this is the most important church in the city. There was once a monastery at this site, but the present Gothic-Renaissance building dates from the 17th century. The interior has rich wrought-iron work, carvings, and a famous organ from 1640, with 4,950 pipes. Concerts are presented in the summer. The church also has a beautiful courtyard with arcades, containing tombs of patrician families.

Standing at **Kurplatz** is a good way to end the tour, as it takes in the best view of the lake from its northern rim.

You can also take steamers from this area to visit various resorts along the lake. The view from here encompasses not only the lake but also the Alps from Rigi to Pilatus. The quays are lined with trees, hotels, and shops. At the end of the promenade is the **Lido** (beach), called Lucerne's "Riviera."

OTHER MAJOR SIGHTS

AM RHYN-HAUS, Fürrengasse 21. Tel. 51-17-73.
A small but choice collection of the works of Pablo Picasso is displayed on two

levels, including paintings, drawings, original prints, sculpture, and ceramics from the last 20 years of the artist's life. The collection was a gift from Siegfried and Angela Rosengart, who presented the city of Lucerne on its 800th anniversary with eight masterpieces by Picasso, one for each century. Outstanding works include *Woman and Dog Playing* (1953), *Woman Dressing Her Hair* (1954), *The Studio* (1955), *Rembrandtesque Figure and Cupid* (1969), and a sculpture, *Woman with a Hat* (1961).

Admission: 2F ($1.46).

Open: Apr–Oct, daily 10am–6pm; Nov–Mar, Fri–Sun 11am–noon and 2–5pm. **Bus:** 1.

GLETSCHERGARTEN (Glacier Garden), Denkmalstrasse 4. Tel. 51-43-40.

This so-called glacier garden has 32 "potholes" that were worn into the sandstone bed of an Iron Age glacier, during the era when ice covered the surface of Lake Lucerne. Discovered and cleared of their debris in 1872, the holes measure up to 30 feet wide and almost as deep. A museum at the site contains a famous 18th-century relief map of the Alps, prehistoric remains of plant and animal life, and a Swiss homeland museum.

Admission: 5F ($3.65).

Open: May to mid-Oct, daily 8am–6pm; Mar–Apr and mid-Oct to mid-Nov, daily 9am–5pm; mid-Nov to Feb, Tues–Sun 10:30am–4:30pm. **Bus:** 1.

KUNSTMUSEUM (Fine Arts Museum), Robert-Zünd-Strasse 1. Tel. 23-92-42.

The Fine Arts Museum includes many paintings by Swiss artists, dating from the 16th century to the present. Ferdinand Hodler (1835–1918) is among those represented, as well as Duffy and Utrillo.

Admission: 4F ($2.90).

Open: Tues and Thurs–Sat 10am–noon and 2–5pm, Wed 10am–9pm, Sun 10am–5pm. **Bus:** 1.

VERKEHRSHAUS DER SCHWEIZ (Swiss Transportation Museum), Lidostrasse 5. Tel. 31-44-44.

✪ The museum is the best of its kind in Europe and very popular with foreign visitors. It's located beyond the Haldenstrasse cable-car station. All forms of transportation, old and new, are on display, including railway cars, airplanes, automobiles, ships, and spaceships. Also on display is the oldest ship in the country. Built in 1847, the steamboat *Rigi* has been converted into a restaurant. The most popular exhibition is a scale model of a Swiss railway crossing the Gotthard (a dozen trains move simultaneously).

The **Longines Planetarium** is at the eastern end of the complex. Here you can experience the constellations, an eclipse of the sun and the moon, as well as space travel. Also attached to the transport museum is the **Hans Erni House,** containing artwork by this well-known native son.

Admission: 12 F ($8.75) adults, 6F ($4.40) children.

Open: Mar–Oct, daily 9am–6pm; Nov–Feb, Mon–Sat 10am–4pm, Sun 10am–5pm. **Bus:** 2.

TRACHTENMUSEUM (National Costume Museum), Utenberg. Tel. 36-80-58.

Folk costumes from every canton in the Confederation, as well as from several other European countries, are displayed in this former villa situated in parklike grounds on the outskirts of Lucerne.

Admission: 4F ($2.90).

Open: Easter Sun to Oct, daily 9am–5:30pm. **Closed:** Nov–Easter. **Bus:** 14.

Directions: Take Dreilindenstrasse to the highway. Follow the highway for about half a mile and, at the junction, turn right off the road to Dietschiberg, swinging onto the Utenberg route.

RICHARD WAGNER MUSEUM, Wagnerweg 27, Tribschen. Tel. 44-23-70.

Wagner lived here from 1866 to 1872 and composed several works, including *Die Meistersinger*. Located about 2 miles from the city, in the suburb of Tribschen, the museum contains some original scores and memorabilia, including letters and pictures. There is an exhibit of antique musical instruments in the summer.

Admission: 4F ($2.90).

Open: Tues–Wed and Sat 9am–noon and 2–6pm, Sun 10:30am–noon and 2–5pm. **Boat:** Motorboats leave every hour from in front of the railroad station (rail passes are valid for this trip). **Bus:** 6 or 7 to Wartegg.

NEARBY ATTRACTIONS

There are dozens of half-day and full-day excursions from Lucerne—so many that I recommend you allow at least 5 days to see the city and its environs. There are several points of interest around Lake Lucerne. Most of them can be reached by paddle steamer along the lake. While en route, you can enjoy the breathtaking view of the water and mountains. **Lake Lucerne (Vierwaldstättersee)** winds its way 24 miles into the alpine ranges of the heart of Switzerland. Many excursions can be combined with a trip to the top of a mountain by cable car or funicular. Summer is the peak season.

The **Lake Lucerne Navigation Company** (tel. 40-45-40) offers 18 boats, of which 5 are paddle steamers. You can buy your ticket at the landing station opposite the Hauptbahnhof in Lucerne. A steamer trip from Lucerne to the farthest point, Flüelen, takes 3½ hours. Most boat schedules allow for a 2-hour stop at most destinations before the boat (or a different one) returns to Lucerne. A complete lake tour with stops takes about 8½ hours. First-class, round-trip fare from Lucerne to Flüelen is 37F ($27); second-class fare is 23F ($16.80). In midsummer an early-morning paddle steamer departs from the quay at 9am. Watch the return schedules carefully, so that you're not caught at the far end of the lake when night falls. Most returning boats leave before 5 or 6pm from Flüelen, depending on the season. All the main steamer services have a restaurant on board.

The **William Tell Express** offers an opportunity to see regions of German- and Italian-speaking Switzerland in one full-day excursion. Linking Lucerne with Lugano and Locarno, between May 8 and October 20, it transports participants on a combination of both paddle steamer and deluxe train. A three-course meal is included on the boat. Make your reservations at the number listed above, preferably several days in advance. Round-trip fare, with the meal included, is 190F ($138.70).

WHERE TO STAY

Lucerne is one of the most visited cities of Switzerland, with a wide range of hotels. But they're mostly expensive and moderate; there's a shortage of good budget hotels. Reservations are very important in the summer, when hordes of Europeans and North Americans pour into this town.

VERY EXPENSIVE

CARLTON HOTEL TIVOLI, Haldenstrasse 57, CH-6002 Luzern. Tel. 041/ 51-30-51. Fax 041/51-19-29. 100 rms (all with bath). MINIBAR TV TEL Bus: 24.
$ Rates (including continental breakfast): 170F–255F ($124.10–$186.10) single; 320F–415F ($233.55–$302.90) double. Single and double rooms can be joined together. AE, DC, MC, V.
This five-star hotel is located on a tree-lined promenade on the north side of the lake in an area filled with resort hotels and private homes. The tasteful rooms have big windows, plenty of space, and modern furniture.
Dining/Entertainment: The terrace restaurant serves good food, and a piano bar features live music daily, beginning at 7pm.
Services: Room service, laundry, baby-sitting.
Facilities: Tennis courts, marina.

GRAND HOTEL NATIONAL, Haldenstrasse 4, CH-6002 Luzern. Tel. 041/50-11-11; or 212/593-2988 in New York City, or toll free 800/223-5652 in the U.S., 800/882-4777 toll free in New York State. Fax 041/51-55-39. 79 rms (all with bath). MINIBAR TV TEL **Bus:** 24.
$ Rates (including continental breakfast): Summer, 240F–310F ($175.20–$226.25) single; 360F–495F ($262.75–$361.30) double. Winter, 190F–240F ($138.70–$182.50) single; 290F–370F ($211.65–$270.05) double. AE, DC, MC, V.
Built "in the style of the French kings," this legend among Swiss hotels has a huge facade of gray stone, with a mansard roof and dozens of gables. Constructed in 1870, when tourists were just beginning to discover Lake Lucerne, it looks like a wing of the château at Versailles. Guests have included monarchs and diplomats from all over Europe, including César Ritz. Umberto Erculiani of Italy is the current owner; between 1977 and 1980 he reconstructed this grand palace and installed modern conveniences. The bedrooms are among the most comfortable in the city, with thick carpets and old-fashioned charm. Many have private balconies with a view of the lake. The hotel is a member of the prestigious Steigenberger Reservations System.
Dining/Entertainment: The piano bar has elegant paneling that glitters with cut crystal. It is one of the town's most alluring rendezvous points.
Services: In-house movies, massage.
Facilities: Indoor swimming pool, sauna.

PALACE HOTEL, Haldenstrasse 11, CH-6006 Luzern. Tel. 041/50-22-22, or toll free 800/223-6800 in North America. Fax 041/51-69-76. 157 rms (all with bath). MINIBAR TV TEL **Bus:** 2.
$ Rates (including buffet breakfast): 180F–345F ($131.40–$251.80) single; 240F–545F ($175.20–$397.80) twin. AE, DC, MC, V. **Parking:** 25F ($18.25).
This large Belle Epoque hotel by the lake is one of the best in Switzerland. It has two towers and a mansard roof. The lobby has Ionic columns, high ceilings, and a massive chandelier. Each of the guest rooms has an individual decor and is filled with luxuries and conveniences.
Dining/Entertainment: The Mignon Restaurant is one of the most elegant and formal places to dine in town. Candlelight and piano music add to the atmosphere. The menu includes classic French dishes and cuisine moderne variations. The main dining room is the Gourmet. The Victorian bar has globe lights and leather-upholstered barrel chairs.
Services: Baby-sitting, room service.

Facilities: Lakeside terrace for snacks, garage.

SCHWEIZERHOF LUCERNE, Schweizerhofquai 3, CH-6002 Luzern. Tel. 041/50-22-11. Fax 041/51-29-71. 120 rms (all with bath). TV TEL **Bus:** 24.

$ Rates (including continental breakfast): 230F–310F ($167.90–$226.25) single; 340F–440F ($240.85–$321.15) double. AE, DC, MC, V.

★ The Hauser family has owned this 19th-century "palace" since 1861. It consists of three symmetrical white buildings interconnected by arched passageways lining the lake for at least two blocks. The lobby has pink marble columns and pilasters and a cream-colored ceiling with plaster details. The bedrooms are spacious and well furnished.

Dining/Entertainment: The restaurant, La Rotonde, is one of the most elegant and refined dining rooms in the city. At lunch, it offers a simple businessperson's menu for 40F ($29.20). A la carte dinners start at 90F ($65.70). The menu features classic continental cuisine. An American bar is decorated with rich woods, Louis XV–style armchairs, and leather bar stools.

Services: Room service, baby-sitting.
Facilities: Old-fashioned public rooms.

EXPENSIVE

GRAND HOTEL EUROPE, Haldenstrasse 59, Ch-6002 Luzern. Tel. 041/30-11-11. Fax 041/31-10-31. 190 rms (all with bath). MINIBAR TV TEL **Bus:** 2.

$ Rates (including continental breakfast): 133F–160F ($97.10–$116.80) single; 231F–285F ($168.60–$208) double. AE, DC, MC, V. **Closed:** Nov–Mar.
Parking: Free.

A neoclassical pediment graces the white facade of this elegant 19th-century hotel one block from the north shore of the lake. There is a row of red awnings sheltering the public rooms, which face a garden. The salons contain large tapestries, Oriental rugs, and comfortable couches and chairs. Most of the rooms are spacious and well furnished.

Dining/Entertainment: One hotel restaurant, Français, serves Swiss and continental specialties, as does Tiziano.
Services: Room service, laundry.
Facilities: Lakeside terrace.

HOTEL ASTORIA, Pilatusstrasse 29, CH-6003 Luzern. Tel. 041/24-44-66. Fax 041/23-42-62. 140 rms (all with bath). MINIBAR TV TEL

$ Rates (including continental breakfast): 160F ($116.80) single; 190F–240F ($138.70–$175.20) double. AE, DC, MC, V.

This first-class modern hotel has prominent horizontal rows of windows and a desirable location in the center of Lucerne. The subdued interior is decorated with metal and stucco. Each of the well-furnished rooms has a radio and other amenities; 30 new rooms were added in the back for those who want a more tranquil location.

Dining/Entertainment: The Restaurant Green-Life serves French and Swiss specialties, as does the Boulevard Restaurant. Other drinking and dining facilities include a 65-seat Thai Restaurant, the Coffee Shop Astoria, and a snack bar. The popular Green-Life Bar has green upholstered walls, a metal ceiling, and a central fireplace.

Services: Room service, baby-sitting, laundry.
Facilities: Facilities for the handicapped.

HOTEL DES BALANCES & BELLEVUE, Weinmarkt, CH-6002 Luzern. Tel.

041/51-18-51. Fax 041/51-64-51. 59 rms (all with bath). MINIBAR TV TEL **Bus:** 1.
$ Rates (including continental breakfast): 130F–170F ($94.90–$124.10) single; 250F–290F ($182.50–$211.65) double. AE, DC, MC, V.

This quiet hotel, separated from the city by the Reuss River, faces the most colorful square in town. The elaborate gray-stone building has lots of curlicue wrought-iron balconies; the interior has high ceilings and Oriental rugs. Most rooms are pleasant, and some have been modernized. Guests are permitted to drive to the hotel even if barricades have temporarily turned the inner city into a pedestrian zone.

Dining/Entertainment: There is a great view of the city from the popular riverside café. The hotel has two restaurants, the Bistro, with an adjoining Bar, and La Vague, with a piano bar.

Services: Laundry, porter, baby-sitting, concierge, room service.

Facilities: Public parking in a nearby garage.

HOTEL FLORA, Seidenhofstrasse 5, CH-6002 Luzern. Tel. 041/24-44-44. Fax 041/23-83-60. 145 rms (all with bath). MINIBAR TV TEL
$ Rates (including continental breakfast): 160F ($116.80) single; 280F ($204.35) double. AE, DC, MC, V.

If you don't have your heart set on an old-fashioned hotel, this is a good choice. It's large and near the railway station. The modern decor imparts a warm atmosphere, with Swiss touches. Each of the comfortable rooms contains a radio and other amenities. One of the restaurants presents a folklore show in the evenings. The show is set to music, with yodelers and alpine horns. The disco has comfortable banquettes and hanging pin lights.

HOTEL HERMITAGE, Seeburgstrasse 79, CH-6006 Luzern-Seeburg. Tel. 041/31-37-37. Fax 041/31-69-55. 20 junior suites (all with bath). MINIBAR TV TEL **Bus:** 24.
$ Rates (including continental breakfast): 220F–320F ($160.60–$233.55) single or double. AE, DC, MC, V.

In 1990, a run-down older hotel was demolished and in its place arose this brand-new lakeside building, whose pink-painted walls contain only junior suites. Each suite has a lakefront view, a private balcony, and a tastefully modern decor featuring rattan furniture. Set in a flowering suburb 2½ miles from the center of Lucerne, the hotel (rated four stars by the Swiss government) has a café-terrace beside the water and two restaurants, the Hermitage and the more expensive Quatre Saisons. The English-speaking staff is helpful and justifiably proud of the hotel's new design.

HOTEL MONOPOL & METROPOLE, Pilatusstrasse 1, CH-6002 Luzern. Tel. 041/23-08-66. Fax 041/23-60-01. 105 rms (all with bath). MINIBAR TV TEL
$ Rates (including continental breakfast): 120F–150F ($87.60–$109.50) single; 210F–260F ($153.30–$189.75) double. AE, DC, MC, V.

Built in 1898, this grand hotel has a carved limestone facade, wrought-iron balconies, half-columns, and elaborately detailed windows. The rooms are individually furnished; some are modern and others have paneling, alcove beds, and chalet chairs. The amenities include a radio.

Dining/Entertainment: The Taverne is lined with rustic vertical beams; a pianist entertains daily from 7 to 11pm. The Arbalète is a more formal French restaurant with lighthearted decor of crimson walls and modern chandeliers. There is also the Boulevard Café.

Services: Room service, baby-sitting, laundry.

Facilities: Special facilities for invalids.

HOTEL MONTANA, Adligenswilerstrasse 22, CH-6002 Luzern. Tel. 041/ 51-65-65. Fax 041/51-66-76. 116 rms (all with bath). MINIBAR TEL **Bus:** 2, then the funicular.

$ Rates (including continental breakfast): 170F ($124.10) single; 290F ($211.65) double. Extra bed 50F ($36.50). AE, DC, V. **Closed:** Nov–Mar.

This beautifully detailed 19th-century hotel is on a quiet hillside overlooking the lake. A private cable car transports guests to the lakeside promenade. The interior is filled with old-fashioned grandeur. The lobby has Oriental rugs, brocaded antique chairs and settees, and polished paneling. The rooms are comfortably furnished with traditional styling; some have TVs.

Services: Room service, laundry.

Facilities: Hotel cable car, free parking in front of the hotel.

HOTEL SCHILLER, Pilatusstrasse 15, CH-6002 Luzern. Tel. 041/23-51- 55. Fax 041/23-34-04. 70 rms (all with bath). TEL

$ Rates (including continental breakfast): 125F–150F ($91.25–$109.50) single; 180F–210F ($131.40–$153.30) double. AE, DC, MC, V.

Although it's surrounded by other antique buildings near the station, this one stands out because of its 19th-century details and colorful awning above the entrance. The interior has many fine touches—dark-green walls, framed prints, and a few bronze statues. Many of the rooms are modern and streamlined, with angular furniture and comfortable beds. Some are equipped with TVs and minibars. The hotel is on a busy commercial street, a 5-minute walk from the train station.

Dining/Entertainment: A rustic restaurant, La Parrilla Steakhouse, has heavy beams and an open hearth where steaks are grilled. There is also a sidewalk café as well as a bar, Casablanca.

Services: Baby-sitting, laundry.

Facilities: Banqueting room.

HOTEL UNION LUZERN, Löwenstrasse 6, CH-6002 Luzern. Tel. 041/51- 36-51. Fax 041/51-67-76. 105 rms (all with bath). MINIBAR TV TEL **Bus:** 1.

$ Rates (including continental breakfast): 95F–150F ($69.35–$109.50) single; 170F–270F ($124.10–$197.05) double. AE, MC, V.

The copies of medieval frescoes that adorn the facade of this leading four-star hotel creates one of the most impressive sights in Lucerne. Inside, the high ceiling of the 19th-century lobby is supported by columns of reddish stone. A massive crystal chandelier was custom-designed for the space. The hotel has been renovated and furnished with conservatively modern furniture. High standards of comfort and service are maintained in the rooms.

Dining/Entertainment: There are two restaurants, an attractive bar, and a ballroom that you should at least have a look at.

Services: Room service, laundry, baby-sitting.

Facilities: Public garage 150 yards away.

HOTEL ZUM REBSTOCK, Sankt Leodegar Platz, CH-6000 Luzern. Tel. 041/51-35-81. Fax 041/51-39-17. 38 rms (all with bath). TV TEL **Bus:** 24.

$ Rates (including buffet breakfast): 110F–130F ($80.30–$94.90) single; 185F– 230F ($135.05–$167.90) double. AE, DC, MC, V.

Claudia Moser manages one of the most charming four-star hotels in town. The half-timbered building has green shutters with a brown-tile roof. In 1443 it was the headquarters of the wine-growers guild; later it was used as a recruitment center for the Swiss mercenaries who came from this region. The rooms are small but charming. Most have a blue-and-white decor; some are pink and green. There is a thick-walled restaurant as well as a garden terrace.

LUZERNERHOF, Alpenstrasse 3, CH-6004 Luzern. Tel. 041/51-46-46.
Fax 041/51-55-66. 75 rms (all with bath). MINIBAR TV TEL **Bus:** 1.
$ Rates (including continental breakfast): 110F–130F ($80.30–$94.90) single; 200F–240F ($146–$175.20) double. AE, DC, MC, V.
This comfortable, modern hotel is in a silver-colored building with brick detailing around its corners. Each of its spacious, well-furnished bedrooms has wall-to-wall carpeting and classic chairs. The hotel has a restaurant, a grillroom, a garden restaurant, and a sidewalk café. The Regina Bar is open until late.

MODERATE

CONTINENTAL & PARK, Morgartenstrasse 4–13, CH-6002 Luzern. Tel. 041/23-75-66, or toll free 800/221-65-09 in North America. Fax 041/23-30-69. 68 rms (all with shower or bath). TV TEL **Bus:** 1.
$ Rates: 69F–112F ($50.35–$81.75) single; 127F–184F ($102.70–$134.30) double. AE, DC, MC, V.
The attractive facade of this six-story hotel includes masonry and dark-gray detailing, with a row of evenly spaced gables; the exterior of the ground-floor restaurant is framed in burgundy. The hotel is near the railroad station and the lake. Its rooms are modern and comfortable; amenities include a radio. The hotel has two handsomely furnished restaurants, Le Beaujolais and Locanda Ticinese, both offering good Swiss cuisine.

HOTEL AMBASSADOR, Zurichstrasse 3, CH-6004 Luzern. Tel. 041/51-71-51. Fax 041/51-71-78. 31 rms (all with bath). MINIBAR TV TEL **Bus:** 1.
$ Rates (including buffet breakfast): 108F–130F ($78.85–$94.90) single; 184F–238F ($134.30–$173.70) twin. AE, DC, MC, V.
Opened in 1987, the modern, four-star Ambassador, an 8-minute walk from the train station, is regarded as one of the finest moderately priced hotels in Lucerne. Its rooms contain comfortable furniture, radios, hairdryers, and other amenities. A breakfast buffet is the only meal offered, but there are many fine restaurants nearby. The hotel offers room service, as well as baby-sitting and laundry service. It has an indoor swimming pool and a sauna.

HOTEL DES ALPES, Rathausquai, CH-6002 Luzern. Tel. 041/51-58-25. Fax 041/51-74-51. 41 rms (all with bath). MINIBAR TV TEL **Bus:** 1.
$ Rates: (including continental breakfast): 85F–115F ($62.05–$83.95) single; 140F–186F ($102.20–$135.75) double. **Closed:** Jan. AE, DC, MC, V.
The tall, narrow facade of the Hôtel des Alpes has elegantly restrained baroque details. The public rooms retain some of their old-fashioned charm, but most of the bedrooms have been streamlined and filled with modern furnishings. The riverside café has a terrace facing the Reuss River and Lucerne's famous covered bridge. Parking is available across the river at the nearby train station.

HOTEL JOHANNITER, Bundesplatz 18, CH-6003 Luzern. Tel. 041/23-18-55. Fax 041/23-16-50. 50 rms (all with shower or bath). MINIBAR TV TEL **Bus:** 1.
$ Rates: (including buffet breakfast): 98F ($71.55) single; 159F–189F ($116.05–$137.95) double. AE, DC, MC, V. **Parking:** 9F ($6.55).
Rated three stars, this traditional Swiss hotel has a complicated gabled roofline and an

attractively modernized interior. Gerhard Fahrni offers comfortable rooms with modern furniture; amenities include a radio. The restaurant serves typical Lucerne cuisine and several continental specialties. The hotel stands behind the railway station, about six blocks from the lake.

HOTEL KOLPING, Friedenstrasse 8, CH-6004 Luzern. Tel. 041/51-23-51. Fax 041/51-11-62. 123 rms (all with shower or bath). TV TEL **Bus:** 1.

$ **Rates** (including continental breakfast): 73F–86F ($53.30–$62.75) single; 130F–153F ($94.90–$111.70) double. DC, MC, V.

Centrally located, this pleasant hotel has a restrained facade of gray stone and stucco. Large tour groups sometimes stay here, and the staff tries to please. The modern interior has some rustic furniture. The chalet-style restaurant has blond paneling. The hotel is 3 minutes away from the lake and the Lion Monument.

HOTEL ROTHAUS, Klosterstrasse 4–6, CH-6003 Luzern. Tel. 041/22-45-22. 50 rms (all with bath). TEL **Bus:** 1.

$ **Rates** (including continental breakfast): 97F ($70.80) single; 157F–176F ($113.85–$128.45) double. AE, DC, MC, V.

This angular, modern hotel with red shutters is located in the center of town. It has a pleasant sitting room with contrasting Oriental rugs and a large armoire in reddish carved wood. The other public rooms have paneling and beams, with wood furniture and wrought-iron lighting fixtures. The rooms are comfortably furnished.

BUDGET

PENSION PANORAMA, Kapuzinerweg 9, CH-6006 Luzern. Tel. 041/36-67-01. 27 rms (none with bath). **Bus:** 4 or 5 to the third stop (Kapuzinerweg).

$ **Rates** (including continental breakfast): 40F–50F ($29.20–$36.50) single; 60F–80F ($43.80–$58.40) double. No credit cards.

One of the better bargains in Lucerne, this angular, five-story hotel, built in the 1970s, is on a hill with a sweeping view of the lake and the mountains. It's a 10-minute walk from the center of the old town. Kurt Matti and Barbara Roth offer simple but comfortable rooms. There is a communal bathroom for every four rooms.

PENSION VILLA MARIA, Haldenstrasse 36, CH-6002 Luzern. Tel. 041/31-21-19. 10 rms (5 with bath). **Bus:** 2

$ **Rates** (including continental breakfast): 80F–95F ($58.40–$69.35) single or double without bath, 95F–120F ($69.35–$87.60) single or double with bath. Extra bed 25F–30F ($18.25–$21.90). V. **Closed:** Nov–Mar.

Set in a charming garden near the north shore of the lake, this family-run villa was built in 1955 and is today owned by members of the Winkler family. Part of the experience is the welcome they offer into a chalet-inspired private home with comfortably cluttered public rooms decorated in shades of red, gold, and pink. The rooms are clean, spacious, and comfortable. The establishment lies about a half mile from the center of Lucerne.

SSR TOURISTENHOTEL, St. Karlquai 12, CH-6004 Luzern. Tel. 041/51-24-74. Fax 041/52-84-14. 88 beds. **Bus:** 2.

$ **Rates** (including buffet breakfast): 38F–56F ($27.75–$40.85) per person. Students with an ISIC or an International Student Card get a 10% discount. AE, DC, MC, V.

This attractive budget hotel with a sage-green facade lies beside the river, a few minutes from the train station. Guests have free use of the showers. The hotel attracts young people and families to its rooms, many of which sleep four. All units have hot and cold running water. The furnishings are in a basic, functional modern style. There is a dining room as well as a TV room on the premises.

WHERE TO DINE

Lucerne has some of the finest restaurants in Switzerland, in a wide range of prices, so don't confine yourself to your hotel at mealtime. Prices are fairly reasonable.

EXPENSIVE

ARBALETE, in the Hôtel Monopole & Métropole, Pilatusstrasse 1. Tel. 23-08-66.
   Cuisine: SWISS. **Reservations:** Recommended.
$ **Prices:** Appetizers 12F–16F ($8.75–$11.70); main courses 18F–32F ($13.15–$23.35). AE, DC, MC, V.
   Open: Dinner only, daily 6pm–12:30am.
Located on the first floor of the Hôtel Monopole & Métropole, this elegantly decorated restaurant has crimson walls and modern chandeliers. The menu might include clear lobster bouillon, gratiné of veal kidneys, turbot with anise sauce, and rolled filet of sole stuffed with shrimp.

CHEZ MARIANNE (Restaurant zum Raben), am Kornmarkt 5. Tel. 51-51-35.
   Cuisine: SWISS. **Reservations:** Recommended. **Bus:** 1.
$ **Prices:** Appetizers 12F–18F ($8.75–$13.15); main courses 22F–38F ($16.05–$27.75). AE, DC, MC, V.
   Open: Lunch daily noon–2pm; dinner daily 6:30–10pm.
   Marianne Kaltenbach is a celebrity in Switzerland because of her well-known cookbooks. Her restaurant, set in the center of the old town in a building dating from the Middle Ages, contains four elegant dining rooms. A favorite room has exquisitely crafted Louis Philippe chairs made of a glowing hardwood, built-in Gothic revival cupboards, mirrors, modern paintings, and a view of the river. Specialties include filet of pike with saffron-cream sauce, venison pâté with nuts and bitter-orange sauce, and boiled beef with horseradish.

OLD SWISS HOUSE, Löwenplatz 4. Tel. 51-61-71.
   Cuisine: SWISS. **Reservations:** Recommended. **Bus:** 1.
$ **Prices:** Appetizers 12F–18F ($8.75–$13.15); main courses 18F–38F ($13.15–$27.75); fixed-price meals 22F–28F ($16.05–$20.45) at lunch (11am–6pm), 55F–75F ($40.15–$54.75) at dinner. DC, MC, V.
   Open: Daily 9am–midnight.
This charming, half-timbered building near the Lion Monument is one of the most photographed attractions in the area (in 1964, Anheuser-Busch built an enlarged replica of it at Busch Gardens in Tampa, Florida). The restaurant is decorated in a 17th-century style, with porcelain and antique glass, hand-carved oak doors, wooden stairways, leaded- and stained-glass windows with heraldic panes from 1575, antique silver, and old pewter. There are also original oil paintings throughout the house. Perhaps the most outstanding item of the entire collection is a handmade porcelain stove from 1636, in the Knight's Room. The house has a long bar near the entry, private banquet rooms upstairs, and a dining room downstairs. In fair weather you can have lunch on the terrace. There is a city parking lot several hundred yards away.

Waitresses wear regional dress and speak several languages. Specialties include homemade cheese croquettes, onion soup, fresh fish from Lake Lucerne, veal prepared at your table, a deluxe Wiener Schnitzel, and veal escalope.

VON PFYFFER STUBE, in the Grand Hôtel National, Heldenstrasse 4. Tel. 50-11-11.
   Cuisine: SWISS. **Reservations:** Required. **Bus:** 24.
$ **Prices:** Appetizers 12F–18F ($8.75–$13.15); main courses 22F–38F ($16.05–$27.75); menu dégustation 95F ($69.35). AE, DC, MC, V.
   Open: Dinner only, daily 6:30–11pm.

The menu has changed since César Ritz and Auguste Escoffier worked here in 1870, but this is still one of the most prestigious restaurants in Lucerne. The dining room has paneling crafted from exotic hardwoods, plush Oriental carpets, modern drawings, and a carved limestone fireplace. Most of the dishes are French-inspired—ravioli stuffed with smoked salmon, roast seawolf (bass) with fresh herbs, saddle of lamb with fresh herbs, breast of duckling with beetroot, and grilled scampi with lobster sauce. An after-dinner menu offers a selection of cigars and vintage port, grandly served by attendants in white jackets.

MODERATE

CHINA RESTAURANT LI-TAI-PE, Furrengasse 14. Tel. 51-10-23.
   Cuisine: BEIJING/CHINESE. **Reservations:** Recommended but not required. **Bus:** 2.
$ **Prices:** Appetizers 7F–16F ($5.10–$11.70); main dishes 22F–46F ($16.05–$33.60); fixed-price meals 17F ($12.40) at lunch, 35F–58F ($25.55–$42.35) at dinner. AE, DC, MC, V.
   Open: Lunch Thurs–Sun 11:30am–2:30pm; dinner Tues–Sun 6:30–11pm.
   Closed: 2 weeks in midwinter, during Carnival time.

The best Chinese restaurant in Lucerne is run by German-born Margaret Chi Tsun, now in her 80s, whose late husband was once an aide to General Chiang Kai-shek. Located on a narrow street in the old town, the restaurant has two levels and is decorated with Oriental artifacts and somber lighting. The Peking-style menu includes crispy fried boneless chicken, beef in oyster oil, abalone with bamboo shoots, and diced duck with almonds. The specialty, whole Peking duck, must be ordered a day in advance.

EICHHOF, Obergrundstrasse 106. Tel. 41-11-74.
   Cuisine: SWISS. **Reservations:** Usually not required. **Bus:** 2.
$ **Prices:** Appetizers 14F–20F ($10.20–$14.60); main courses 28F–40F ($20.45–$29.20); fixed-price lunch (served 11:30am–2:30pm only) 24F–30F ($17.50–$21.90); mug of beer 3.80F ($2.75). AE, DC, MC, V.
   Open: Tues–Sat 9am–midnight; Sun 9am–5pm. **Closed:** Feb.

The Eichhof bears the name of a well-known local beer, which, not surprisingly, is used in some of the house recipes—as the one for pig's feet and pork shoulder. You can come just to drink, but if you're hungry the extensive menu includes wild game, duckling in green peppercorns with cream sauce, and rack of lamb provençal.

HOFSTUBE, in the Hotel Zum Rebstock, Sankt-Leodegar-Strasse 3. Tel. 51-35-81.
   Cuisine: SWISS/FRENCH. **Reservations:** Recommended. **Bus:** 1 or 4.
$ **Prices:** Appetizers 12F–16F ($8.75–$11.70); main courses 18F–36F ($13.15–$26.30); fixed price meals 22F–55F ($16.05–$40.35). AE, DC, MC, V.
   Open: Daily 11am–midnight.

This flourishing restaurant is in the Hotel zum Rebstock, next to a building used as a guildhall for Lucerne wine growers in the Middle Ages. The 1920s-style entrance hall is filled with valuable art deco pieces. There are two *gemütlich* dining rooms, one with elaborately carved timbers. Beyond the dining area is a large, illuminated courtyard, where additional tables are set up on warm summer nights. The menu, a classic blend of Swiss and French traditions, usually includes an impressive array of terrines, an elixir of morels, lake trout, tournedos "prepared in the style of 1900," suckling veal with spinach, and duckling in orange sauce.

RESTAURANT LAPIN, in the Hôtel de la Paix, Museggstrasse 2. Tel. 51-52-53.
  Cuisine: SWISS. **Reservations:** Recommended. **Bus:** 1.
$ **Prices:** Appetizers 12F–15F ($8.75–$10.95); main courses 18F–35F ($13.15–$25.55). AE, DC, MC, V.
  Open: Daily 7am–12:30am.

This restaurant is attractively angled so that its walls seem to radiate outward like a fan from the entrance. Accented with rustic panels of light-grained wood and roughly textured stone, it contains a bar with a picture window and comfortable banquettes for a predinner drink. Specialties include sirloin steak Café de Paris, lamb in the style of the Engadine, savory preparations of local fish, and many of the classic Swiss specialties, such as sausage with Rösti. In honor of the restaurant's name—*lapin*, French for "rabbit"—the chef prepares a terrine made with rabbit. (Note that the restaurant lies at the corner of the Alpenstrasse; if you begin your search at the wrong end of the street, you'll face a very long walk up some very steep hills.)

SCHWANEN RESTAURANTS, Schwanenplatz 4. Tel. 51-11-77.
  Cuisine: SWISS/FRENCH. **Reservations:** Recommended. **Bus:** 1.
$ **Prices:** Le Bec Rouge, appetizers 8.50F–21F ($6.15–$15.35); main courses 13.50F–45F ($9.85–$32.85); special menu 38F ($27.75). AE, DC, MC, V.
  Open: Lunch daily 11am–2pm; dinner daily 7–11:30pm.

Three different restaurants are under the same roof near the old bridge in the center of Lucerne. Le Bec Rouge, upstairs, is the most elegant and expensive of the three. It is attractively decorated and dimly lit, with a view of the lake. The service is refined. Fresh seasonal specialties are offered for very reasonable prices, considering the quality. Traditional dishes are offered, and small portions are available.

The less formal Brasserie Steak House, on the ground floor, has a distinct ambience. The menu includes steaks, salads, Swiss specialties, and a variety of spaghetti dishes. A meal in the brasserie averages 29F ($21.15). The third restaurant, La Romandie, specializes in cheese fondue, raclette, and meals from the French-speaking part of Switzerland. Main dishes here cost 12.50F to 33F ($9.15 to $24.10).

INEXPENSIVE

KUNST AND KONGRESSHAUS RESTAURANTS, Bahnhofplatz. Tel. 23-18-16.
  Cuisine: SWISS. **Reservations:** Not needed.
$ **Prices:** Appetizers 8F–12F ($5.85–$8.75); main courses 15F–26F ($10.95–$19). AE, DC, MC, V.
  Open: Lunch daily noon–2:30pm; dinner daily 6:30–11pm.

This modern, metallic building next to the train station contains three restaurants: the Tell Stube, a saloon, and a bistro and bar. They are connected with the largest convention hall in Lucerne. There is an equestrian statue in front, and the complex is surrounded by flower gardens and a park. The food is well prepared. Sausages and barbecues are served on the terrace for 6F ($4.40)

PEPPINO, Theaterstrasse 7. Tel. 23-77-71.
Cuisine: ITALIAN. **Reservations:** Recommended. **Bus:** 2.
$ Prices: Appetizers and pastas 14F–18F ($10.20–$13.15); main dishes 28F–38F ($20.45–$27.75); pizzas 13F–16F ($9.50–$11.70). AE, DC, MC, V.
Open: Lunch daily noon–2pm; dinner daily 6–10pm; snack menu daily noon–11:30pm.

The modern, spartan interior of this restaurant gives one a sense of solidity. You might choose to have just a drink in the stucco bar area or head into the dining room to the left of the entrance. There, in an Italian-inspired room with lots of sunlight and modern ceiling beams, you might order just a pizza or a more substantial meal. The menu includes 10 different pastas (rigatoni all'Emiliana is a specialty), seven kinds of pizza, and such main courses as a savory kettle of mussels and an array of veal dishes.

SCHIFFRESTAURANT WILHELM TELL, Landungsbrucke 9. Tel. 51-23-30.
Cuisine: SWISS. **Reservations:** Recommended. **Bus:** 2.
$ Prices: Appetizers 8F–17F ($5.85–$12.40); main courses 30F–40F ($21.90–$29.20); fixed-price menu 35F ($25.55). AE, MC, V.
Open: Lunch daily 12:30–2pm; dinner daily 6–10pm. **Closed:** Nov–Mar.

When it was built in 1908, this lake cruiser (*Schiff* is German for "ship") sailed boatloads of happy passengers from one end of Lake Lucerne to the other. After it was replaced by newer ships in the late 1960s, it was transformed into a floating restaurant. Now permanently moored at one of the quays, it's usually ringed with a colony of elegant swans, which feed off the scraps thrown overboard. Drinks and snacks are served on outdoor café tables in the bow area, where you can have a beer or coffee throughout the day. A formal restaurant is found under the low ceiling of the aft section, where fine food is served with alert attention. The ship's engine, brightly polished and set behind glass, is on display as a work of industrial art. The menu might include filets of perch or sole prepared seaman's style, cream of lobster soup, and flavorful grills of veal and beef.

WIENER CAFE, in the Grand Hôtel National, Haldenstrasse 4. Tel. 50-11-11.
Cuisine: SWISS. **Reservations:** Required, especially for Sun. brunch. **Bus:** 24.
$ Prices: Appetizers 8F–15F ($5.85–$10.95); main courses 18F–34F ($13.15–$24.80); lunch special 18F ($13.15); brunch 42F ($30.65). AE, DC, MC, V.
Open: Lunch daily 11:30am–2pm; dinner daily 6:30pm–midnight; tea daily 2–6:30pm; brunch Sun 11am–2pm.

The 19th-century passion for afternoon tea has been revived at this delightful restaurant with an ornately gilded ceiling. You can choose from 6 kinds of special Austrian-inspired coffees or one of 10 kinds of exotic teas, served the old-fashioned way, with a silver strainer in a porcelain pot. Fresh pastries are also served. Tea and coffee cost 4.50F ($3.60). The menu also includes a spicy version of bouillabaisse, chicken-based pot-au-feu, and a game terrine with goose liver. The Sunday brunch is very popular; reservations are required.

WIRTSHAUS GALLIKER, Schutzenstrasse 1. Tel. 22-10-02.
Cuisine: SWISS. **Reservations:** Required. **Bus:** 2.
$ Prices: Appetizers 4.50F–15F ($3.30–$10.95); main courses 15F–46F ($10.95–$33.60); pot-au-feu 35F ($25.55). AE, MC, V.

Open: Mon–Sat 10am–midnight. **Closed:** Last 3 weeks of July, first week of Aug.

⑤ Generous portions of unpretentious, well-prepared food are served amid a rustic decor. Regional specialties include calf's head vinaigrette with Rösti and farmer-style Bratwurst seasoned with caraway seeds. Fixed-price specials change weekly: On Tuesday, Thursday, and Saturday, it's pot-au-feu. The fruit desserts are popular.

SHOPPING

Lucerne is an excellent shopping center if you can wade through the junk and souvenir shops. Watches are a popular item. Many Zurich residents take the train to Lucerne for daylong shopping sprees.

SHOPPING A TO Z
CLOCKS & WATCHES

BUCHERER, Schwanenplatz. Tel. 50-99-50.

The largest watch and jewelry retailer of Switzerland offers 10,000 gift items, including clocks and souvenirs. Lucerne is the company's headquarters, and this store is the major outlet. Specialty watches include Rolex, Piaget, Baume & Mercier, and Rado.

JUWELIA, Denkmalstrasse 3. Tel. 51-53-29.

This is the place to buy clocks of all kinds, inexpensive watches, and music boxes. There are more than 100 models of cuckoo clocks, as well as clocks that need winding every 400 days. Cuckoo clocks come in 85 different styles, from the Black Forest as well from Switzerland itself, and play every kind of melody. Some of the watches are inexpensive; the flattest watch in the world is on display. The famous Swiss army knife is also sold here; you can have your name or initials engraved for free. The staff is charming and speaks several languages. The shop is located near the Lion Monument.

Another Juwelia shop is at Pfistergasse 11 (tel. 22-44-75), near the Hotel Baslertor and the second wooden bridge. Juwelia is also an agent for the Swiss Credit Bank.

HOFSTETTER & BERNEY CO. LTD., Alpenstrasse 1. Tel. 51-45-40.

This company sells watches, cuckoo and other clocks, jewelry, music boxes, crystal, gift items, and souvenirs. Another Hofstetter & Berney shop is at Schweizerhofquai 6 (tel. 51-31-06).

A. HURTER, Löwenstrasse 11. Tel. 51-24-79.

A complete line of moderately priced watches and clocks is offered. Specialties include Itraco and Hudson brands, mechanical and quartz—all made in Switzerland. One popular item is a woman's watch with jeweled insets; the insets match the semiprecious jewelry that goes with the watch. Open daily from 7:20am to 6pm.

EMBROIDERY

STURZENNEGER, Schwanenplatz 7. Tel. 51-19-58.

Established more than a century ago as one of the finest embroidery shops in Lucerne, Sturzenneger sells women's lingerie, monogrammed handkerchiefs, petit-point embroidered purses, folk items, and ready-to-wear outfits.

SOUVENIRS

CHALET SWISS SOUVENIRS, Haldenstrasse 23. Tel. 51-31-12.

The largest souvenir shop in the area is across from the Grand Hôtel National. Hans Peter Hunziker and his wife, Ida, sell the famous Swiss army knife, which they'll engrave on the spot for free. Music boxes are also sold; most have Reuge mechanisms, which are among the best in the country. Beer steins are popular items, as are cuckoo clocks. The shop also sells Hummel figures and Anri wood carvings.

GIFT SHOP CASAGRANDE, Kapellgasse 24. Tel. 51-51-01.

This shop offers an extensive selection of Lladró, Hummel, and Dresden porcelain, wood carvings, Swiss army knives, silver, and Waterford crystal. Reuge and other music boxes, tapestries, moderately priced watches, cuckoo clocks, and grandfather clocks are also sold. Carlo and Kyra Casagrande and their sons, John and Robert, have expanded their business during the past four decades, so that now they have three shops and a wood-carving factory turning out the world-famous Casy-Boys.

The shop is open during regular hours, on Sunday from April to October, and in the evening from mid-May to the end of September. You can arrange to have your purchases shipped to your home.

BOLLINA-SCHNEIDER, Haldenstrasse 11. Tel. 51-33-66.

This small shop specializes in Swiss souvenirs, among them beer steins, Anri wood carvings, Hummel figurines, cowbells, etchings, music boxes, T-shirts, and Swiss army knives. You'll have to hunt through the dust gatherers to find the good Swiss mementos. Piero Bollina is the articulate owner.

SPORTING GOODS

FRITZ GENHART SPORT, Löwenstrasse 14. Tel. 51-46-41.

You'll find a complete range of sporting goods here, including gear for skiing and mountain climbing. Clothing includes wool coats, sneakers, leather shorts, and a variety of T-shirts. You can also rent skis and ski boots. The store is near the Hotel Union. You can arrange to have your purchases mailed home.

EVENING ENTERTAINMENT

Lucerne is not famous for its nightlife, but there is enough to keep you busy. In the summer one of the most popular evening outings is to take the **Night Boat,** leaving from Pier 6, near the train station. For information call 041/47-44-46. The cruise sails daily, from May to September, at 8:45pm. Folk performers present a show that includes costumes, folk dances, yodeling, and alpine horn blowing. There's dancing afterward. Reserve tickets in advance with a travel agent or with the concierge of one of the larger hotels. The ride and show cost 40F ($29.20); the price includes a free drink. Just the ride without the show costs 31F ($22.65); dinner costs 53F to 75F ($38.70 to $54.75). Depending on the price you pay, your meal might range from a bubbling bowl of cheese fondue with a drink to a three-course Swiss dinner. Drinks can get expensive. The cruise ends at 11pm.

THE CLUB & MUSIC SCENE

HAZYLAND, Haldenstrasse 21. Tel. 51-19-61.

A member of a national disco chain, Hazyland presents live bands every weekend, ranging from pop and rock to punk. Young people in their early 20s are attracted to the red-velvet interior. There are strobe lights and a medium-size dance floor. The club is opposite the Grand Hotel National. Open daily from 9pm to 2:30am. Beer costs 13F ($9.50).

Admission: Free.

RESTAURANT STADTKELLER, Sternenplatz 3. Tel. 51-47-33.
At the Stadtkeller—located in a 400-year-old building in the heart of the old town—you can drink, eat, and listen to an alpine band perform a Swiss folkloric show with plenty of cowbells and alpine horns. Between early March and November, live music is performed every day of the week during the lunch and dinner hours, from 12:15 to 1:30pm and 8 to 11pm. (The rest of the time, the bar inside is popular with local residents.) When music is playing, there's a cover charge. Full à la carte meals are available for between 38F and 55F ($27.75 and $40.15). During midwinter, the musical repertory changes to jazz, pop, and rock and roll. Drinks begin at 10F ($7.30) each.

Admission: Cover charge of 10F ($7.30), added to your final tab.

THE BAR SCENE

Popular and crowded, **Barstube Zur Gerbern,** Sternenplatz 7 (tel. 51-55-50), is an informal bar and pub with probably the highest percentage of gay clients of any bar in Lucerne, as well as many enlightened heterosexuals. Video movies are projected against one wall to a clientele proud of its open-mindedness. Open daily from 7pm to 2:30a.m. Beer (depending on its size) costs 5.50F to 8.50F ($4 to $6.20).

MORE ENTERTAINMENT

Since the largest bet allowed by the government is 5F ($3.65), gambling in Switzerland is not infused with the passion that sometimes characterizes the wager of larger sums. Most Swiss casinos, therefore, have diversified into entertainment. The casino in Lucerne, the **Kursaal,** at Haldenstrasse 6 (tel. 51-27-51), contains a cabaret, a disco, several bars and restaurants, and a somewhat sedate gambling room with eerie lighting and a handful of roulette tables. The entire complex is open daily from 6pm to 2am. Visit as many of its clubs and bars as possible for the strongest concentration of nightlife options under one roof in Lucerne. For a break, stroll through the gardens and admire one of the most famous flower clocks in Switzerland.

The Kursaal's **Red Rose Cabaret** is a tastefully evocative strip club, offering nonstop performances by a handful of international *artistes* every evening between 9pm and 2am. Entrance is from the sidewalk (not from the interior of the complex). Admission is 6F ($4.40), and drinks cost 11F to 17F ($8.05 to $12.40). The wallpaper is bordello red. To make everything more convenient for the foreign visitor, there's a currency-exchange booth in the lobby.

The red-and-gold **Black Jack Club** plays an electronic mix of British and American disco, which alternates with performances by live bands. (On Sunday night there's only recorded disco.) It's open every night from 9pm to 2am. Admission ranges from 6F to 12F ($4.40 to $8.05), depending on the night; Monday through Thursday, women enter free. Drinks start at 11F ($8.05) each.

Folkloric shows are presented in another quadrant of this complex—**Le Chalet,** a large, rustic room with heavy timbers that reverberate with yodels, alpine horns, and flag-throwing. Shows begin around 8pm and usually require a reservation for dinner. A ticket to the show costs 35F ($25.55) for entrance and two drinks, and 45F to 85F ($32.85 to $62.05) for entrance, two drinks, and a full dinner.

The **Roulette Bar,** with its sheathing of beige marble and art nouveau café tables, is another dining and drinking option in the complex. Meals are served from 7pm on, and the menu specializes in grilled meats. Beer costs 4F ($2.90); whisky costs 9F to 13F ($6.55 to $9.50). It's open daily from 6pm to 2am.

Finally, the **Seegarten** is a restaurant with a view of the lake. On a summer afternoon the terrace is usually filled.

EASY EXCURSIONS

Lake Lucerne is known for its beautiful scenery and the many old-world villages along its shores. Many poets have praised the area's beauty. You may be lucky enough to stay in a hotel room that commands a view of the lake.

Lake steamers and mountain railways can get you to most points of interest around Lake Lucerne. Boat cruises are free if you have a Eurail or InterRail pass. Mountain railways can whisk you to elevations of 10,000 feet or more in a very short time. Our first adventure will be a major mountain excursion to Mount Pilatus, a 7,000-foot summit overlooking Lucerne.

MOUNT PILATUS ✪ Mount Pilatus is located 9 miles south of Lucerne. Its name derives from an old legend associated with it. During medieval times, it is said, the city fathers of Lucerne banned travel up the mountain because they thought that its slopes were haunted by the ghost of Pontius Pilate; they feared that Pilate would be angered by intrusive visitors and cause violent storms. For many years after the ban was finally lifted only a few souls were brave enough to climb the mountain. (Queen Victoria made the trip in 1868.) Today the ascent to Pilatus is one of the most popular excursions in Switzerland.

In the summer, between May and late September, the cog railway operates between Alpnachstad, at the edge of the lake, and the very top of Mount Pilatus. From the quays of Lucerne, take a lake steamer for a scenic 90-minute ride to Alpnachstad. (If you have a rail pass, remember that it will be valid on this steamer.)

At Alpnachstad, transfer to the electric cog railway, which runs at a 48% gradient—the steepest cogwheel railway in the world. Departures are every 45 minutes. At Pilatus-Kulm you can get out and enjoy the view. There are two mountain hotels and a belvedere offering views of Lake Lucerne and many of the mountains around it. In descending from Mount Pilatus, some visitors prefer to take a pair of cable cars—first a large cabin-style téléphérique, then a small gondola. The cable cars end at Kriens, a suburb of Lucerne. There you can take tram no. 1, which will carry you into the heart of Lucerne. The round-trip fare on the cog railway costs 44F ($32.10). The extended excursion, which includes the ascent by cog railway and the descent by cable cars, costs 48.20F ($35.20).

A similar excursion to Pilatus is possible in the winter, but because the cog railway is buried in snow, you must alter your plans. During the cold months you'll have to ascend and descend by cable car, which many visitors find exhilarating. From the center of Lucerne, take tram no. 1 from the Bahnhof to the outlying suburb of Kriens. At Kriens, transfer to a cable car that glides over meadows and forests to the village of Fräkmüntegg, 4,600 feet above sea level. The trip takes a half hour. At Fräkmüntegg, switch to another cable car, this one much more steeply inclined than the first. Considered a stunning feat of advanced engineering, it swings above gorges and cliffs to the very peak of Mount Pilatus. Unlike the cog railways, these cable cars operate year round. The complete ride by cable car costs 44F ($32.12) round-trip.

For information, call 041/95-14-21 or 041/45-55-42. The staff at the tourist office is well informed about these excursions, as are the desk personnel at most of the city's hotels.

RIGI ✪ For another panoramic view from a hilltop belvedere, go to Rigi, 15 miles east of Lucerne. The view from Rigi is different from that atop Mount Pilatus, so if you see both you won't be replicating your experience. Pilatus offers the more panoramic vista, but the view from Rigi is more beautiful. By most accounts, Rigi (5,900 ft.) is the most famous mountain view in the country. However, you might be disappointed if the weather is not clear. Rigi is called the "island mountain," because it appears to be surrounded by the waters of Lakes Lucerne, Zug, and Lauerz. It's accessible by two cog railways and a cableway.

The most adventurous of visitors who made the "grand tour" in the 19th century spent the night at Rigi-Kulm to see the sun rise over the Alps. Victor Hugo called it "an incredible horizon . . . that chaos of absurd exaggerations and scary diminutions." Later, Mark Twain also climbed to the top to see the sun rise across the Alps. But he was so exhausted, as he relates in A Tramp Abroad, that he collapsed into sleep, from which he didn't wake until sunset. Not realizing that he had slept all day, he at first recoiled in horror, believing that the sun had switched its direction and was actually rising in the west. This experience continues to be one of nature's loveliest offerings in all of Europe. For those wanting to partake of the tradition, many hotels are perched on the mountainside.

You can travel to the mountain by taking a 55-minute trip by lake steamer from Lucerne to Vitznau, a small resort on the northern shore of the lake. The rack railway from Vitznau to Rigi-Kulm was the first cog railway in Europe, built in 1871. You can also approach the mountain from Arth-Goldau, which is on the southern shore of Zug Lake. The Arth-Goldau cog railway to Rigi-Kulm opened in 1876. The maximum gradient is 21%. Both cog railways cost 40F ($29.20) for the round-trip. It's possible to go up one way and come down the other if you want to see both sides of the mountain. The trip from Vitznau takes 40 minutes and the trip from Arth-Goldau lasts 35 minutes. There are a dozen departures a day in season. For more information, call 041/83-18-18.

DIETSCHIBERG ✪ The best view of Lucerne and its lake can be enjoyed from Dietschiberg, at 2,065 feet. Board the cable car on Haldenstrasse in Lucerne. The trip takes about half an hour. You can also see Pilatus and Rigi from a belvedere platform.

GÜTSCH One sweeping panorama of the region that's easily accessible from downtown Lucerne (and doesn't involve a full day's excursion) is the mountain plateau of Gütsch, 1,715 feet above sea level. Board a short funicular on Baselstrasse for the 10-minute ride. At the top is a belvedere platform beside the Hotel Château Gütsch, which takes in the city, the lake, and the snow-capped Alps. The funicular departs in both directions every 10 minutes throughout the year, beginning at 8:30am and terminating every night at 9pm in the winter, 11:30pm in the summer, and 10pm in the spring and autumn. Every day from 12:45 to 1:15pm there's a lunch break for the operators (a 45-minute lull in operations). The ride costs 3F ($2.20) round-trip. For more information, call 22-02-72 in Lucerne.

MOUNT TITLIS ✪ Mount Titlis, which is visited as an excursion from the little resort of Engelberg, is the highest point from which you can get a view over central Switzerland. The summit is always covered by snow and ice; there's an "ice cave," in addition to a glacier trail. The view from the belvedere, at 9,900 feet, takes in the Jungfrau and the Matterhorn, as well as Zurich and Basel on a clear day. There is a summer ski run with a ski lift. There are also two restaurants: the **Panorama Restaurant Titlis,** at 10,000 feet, and the **Gletscher-Restaurant Stand,** at 8,040 feet.

To get to the summit, you take a funicular and three cable cars. The last stage of the cable-car trip is the most spectacular, as you are taken right over the glacier. Visitors with respiratory problems may want to forgo this trip because of the thinness of the air at such elevations. The terminal at the summit (which is referred to in some timetables as Kleintitlis, or Little Titlis) has an observation lounge and a large sun terrace.

To get to Titlis from Lucerne's Bahnhof, take a train to Engelberg and transfer to the cable car as described above. Departures from the Lucerne train station are every 30 to 60 minutes, depending on the season. The complete round-trip fare, paid at the Lucerne Bahnhof, is 52F ($37.95).

---

2. BÜRGENSTOCK

10 miles SE of Lucerne

GETTING THERE   By Train   About a dozen trains make the 40-minute trip from Lucerne to Kehrsiten-Bürgenstock every day. From Kehrsiten-Bürgenstock you transfer to a steeply ascending cog railway (its gradient is 45%) that departs every 25 to 45 minutes throughout the day for the 7-minute ascent to Bürgenstock.

By Lake Steamer   In the summer frequent lake steamers leave from the quays in the center of Lucerne, taking 30 minutes to reach the pier at Kehrsiten. From there passengers transfer to the cog railway.

By Car   The road to Bürgenstock is winding and treacherous, so it's better to go via the lake steamer or train as outlined above. However, if you insist on driving, head south from Lucerne on Route N8 to Stansstad and from there take a steep and narrow, often-dangerous, road east for 3 miles until you reach Bürgenstock.

ESSENTIALS   The **Bürgenstock Tourist Office** (tel. 041/61-55-45) is open Monday through Friday from 8am to 6pm. The **telephone area code** for Bürgenstock is 041. There are no **street names,** so follow hotel directional signs.

The most luxurious resort in the region, Bürgenstock is situated high above Lake Lucerne on a 6-mile limestone ridge. Audrey Hepburn, Sophia Loren, and many other movie stars have lived here, swelling the resort's international reputation for glamour. Bürgenstock is lower in altitude than other resorts in the region, reaching only 1,640 feet on its northern side; the southern edge of town gently slopes through fertile pastureland to the Stans Valley.

While in Bürgenstock you can walk along **Felsenweg,** a cliff path skirting the Hammetschwand. Take the Hammetschwand elevator to 3,580 feet, where you'll have a vista of the Bernese Alps and the lakes of central Switzerland.

WHERE TO STAY & DINE

THE BÜRGENSTOCK HOTELS, CH-6366 Bergenstock. Tel. 041/63-25-45. Fax 041/61-76-88. 106 rms (all with bath), 66 suites. MINIBAR TV TEL
$ Rates (including continental breakfast): Grand and Palace Hotels; 220F–290F ($160.60–$211.65) single; 380F–430F ($277.35–$313.85) double; from 550F ($401.45) suite. Park Hotel; 190F–290F ($138.70–$211.65) single; 280F–430F ($204.35–$313.85) double; 380F–580F ($277.35–$423.35) junior suite. AE, DC, MC, V. **Closed:** Grand and Palace Hotels, Oct to late May.

⭐ This is one of the most exclusive hotels in Europe, and also the largest privately owned hotel complex in Switzerland. Set in a 12-acre private park, it consists of three separate buildings—the Grand Hotel (opened in 1873), the Palace Hotel (opened in 1904), and the Park Hotel (opened in 1888 but demolished and rebuilt in a plushly modern format in 1991). The public rooms of each of the three hotels abound in art treasures, including works by Rubens, van Dyck, Tintoretto, and Brueghel. Most were collected by the father of the present owner, Fritz Frey. (The director of the enormous properties is Dirk Post.) The furniture is worthy of a modern-day Versailles, and many different fireplaces throw off a welcome glow. In the summer a battalion of gardeners keeps the grounds immaculate and flowering—one of the most beautiful luxury oases in the Alps.

Dining/Entertainment: Each of the three hotels contains its own restaurant. They include the Spycher, the Trotte, and the most exclusive and elegant of all, the Club. Three bars are on the premises, ranging from stylishly up-to-date to richly antique and old-fashioned. Jackets and ties for men are expected in many of the bars and restaurants.

Services: Room service, baby-sitting, "solve-anything" concierge, complimentary transportation from the cog-railway station.

Facilities: Two swimming pools (both outdoor and indoor), health center with sauna, solarium, exercise machines, a nine-hole golf course, two tennis courts.

HOTEL FÜRIGAN, CH-6366 Bürgenstock. Tel. 041/63-22-22. Fax 041/61-27-24. 80 rms (all with bath), 4 suites. MINIBAR TV TEL
$ Rates (including continental breakfast): 115F–125F ($83.95–$91.25) single; 210F ($153.30) double; from 290F ($211.65) suite. AE, DC, MC, V.
Located on a wooded hillside high above the lake, this resort hotel has white walls and a red-tile roof with gables and towers. A private funicular whisks guests to the private beach beside Lake Lucerne. The bedrooms are comfortable and offer good views. There are several terraces, four restaurants, and a bar that offers dance music. Tennis, a fitness center, a sauna, and a solarium are provided. The hotel operates an Italian restaurant on the lake.

HOTEL WALDHEIM, CH-6366 Bürgenstock. Tel. 041/63-23-83. Fax 041/61-64-66. 58 rms (all with bath). TV TEL
$ Rates (including continental breakfast): 67F–87F ($48.90–$63.50) single; 134F–156F ($97.80–$113.85) double. Half board 22F ($16.05) extra. No credit cards.
There has been a hotel at this site since 1895. The present, modern building was built after the previous hotel burned in 1958. The new version has an elegantly paneled lounge, an elevator, and a narrow terrace with a view of the snowy mountains. Facilities include a heated swimming pool, a solarium, and a children's play area. Most of the rooms have balconies; amenities include a radio. The hotel is accessible by a single-lane road that winds through an alpine meadow dotted with huts and 19th-century chalets.

The Waldheim offers a less expensive alternative to dining at the Bürgenstock Hotel Estate. The restaurant has a terrace and is open daily from 11am to 2pm and 6 to 9:30pm. Full meals begin at 35F ($25.55).

3. WEGGIS

18½ miles E of Lucerne

GETTING THERE By Bus Several buses depart from the quays of Lucerne for Weggis every day, requiring about 30 minutes for the transfer. Once you reach Weggis, a local bus run by the village transports you (in the summertime only) from the lakefront to the upper reaches of the town.

By Lake Steamer Several ferryboats make the 35-minute trip every day from Lucerne's quays to Weggis.

By Car From Lucerne, drive east on Route 2, along the northern rim of Lake Lucerne, cutting south on Route 2b at the signposted turnoff to Weggis.

ESSENTIALS The **Weggis Tourist Office** (tel. 041/93-11-55) is open Monday through Saturday from 8:30am to noon and 2 to 6pm. The **telephone area code** for Weggis is 041. There are no **street names,** but directional signs are posted throughout the resort.

The lakeside resort of Weggis is on the sunny side of Mount Rigi, one of three holiday centers—Vitznau and Gersau are the others—that offer the kind of mild climate found in favored parts of Italy. Weggis and the other resorts are about an hour's walk (or a 5-min. drive) apart. Mark Twain stayed here in 1897.

Of the three resorts, Weggis is the most preferred. It's usually the first port of call for steamers from Lucerne and is also easily accessible from the international St. Gotthard railway line, although it's not on the main traffic route.

Many excursions are possible from early spring to late autumn. You can take the aerial cableway up to **Rigi-Kaltbad** (4,756 ft.), a mountain health resort behind Weggis. In addition, mountain transport links Weggis with the Rigi Railways.

WHERE TO STAY & DINE

EXPENSIVE

HOTEL BEAU-RIVAGE, CH-6353 Weggis. Tel. 041/93-14-22. Fax 041/93-19-87. 45 rms (all with bath). MINIBAR TV TEL

$ **Rates** (including continental breakfast): 110F–140F ($80.30–$102.20) single; 180F–270F ($131.40–$197.05) twin. Half board 35F ($25.55) extra. AE, DC, MC, V. **Closed:** Nov–Mar.

One of the attractions of this hotel is its expanse of lawn, which reaches down to the lake. The view of the mountains from here is exhilarating. The symmetrical yellow hotel has a series of wrought-iron balconies, a prominent nameplate in red letters, and a Swiss flag. The rooms are comfortably furnished.

Dining/Entertainment: There is a restaurant with wood paneling, as well as a comfortable bar.

Services: Room service, laundry, baby-sitting.

Facilities: Heated swimming pool, lakeside terrace, sunbathing lawn.

HOTEL ALBANA, CH-6353 Weggis. Tel. 041/93-21-41. Fax 041/93-29-59. 85 rms (all with bath). MINIBAR TV TEL

$ **Rates** (including continental breakfast): 100F–140F ($73–$102.20) single; 160F–260F ($116.80–$189.75) double. Half board 35F ($25.55) extra. AE, DC, MC, V. **Closed:** Nov–Mar.

The most prestigious hotel at Weggis was built in the art nouveau style in 1896 and has been run by the Wolf family since 1910. One of the public rooms, with a grand piano and a 10-foot ceramic stove, looks almost baronial. Heavy brass chandeliers hang from the frescoed ceiling, and very large rococo mirrors reflect the wood paneling. The bedrooms are modernized; many have good views of the nearby lake.

Dining/Entertainment: The best food at the resort is served at the Panorama Restaurant, which has large windows and a terrace above the lake. International cuisine is offered, with a wide selection of fish and meat dishes. The excellent chef cooks with a light touch and uses quality produce. A la carte meals start at 40F ($29.20). The restaurant is open daily from noon to 2pm and 6:45 to 9:30pm.

Services: Room service, baby-sitting, laundry.
Facilities: Lake terrace.

MODERATE

HOTEL CENTRAL AM SEE, CH-6353 Weggis. Tel. 041/93-12-52. Fax 041/93-14-96. 55 rms (all with bath). TV TEL
$ Rates (including continental breakfast): 70F–90F ($51.10–$65.70) single; 130F–180F ($94.90–$131.40) double. Half board 30F ($21.90) extra. No credit cards.
This old-fashioned resort hotel has six large gables and many smaller ones. It's on a shady peninsula with a swimming pool near the lake and a good view of the lake steamers. The interior has fancy furniture and an elevator, and the bedrooms are comfortable.

HOTEL RÖSSLI, CH-6353 Weggis. Tel. 041/93-11-06. 68 rms (all with bath). TV TEL
$ Rates (including continental breakfast): 70F–90F ($51.10–$65.70) single; 130F–180F ($94.90–$131.40) double. Half board 30F ($21.90) extra. AE, DC, MC, V.
Closed: Oct–Feb.

Ⓢ This Victorian hotel with elaborate shingles has the most desirable lakefront position at the center of the resort, facing a tranquil square with flowers, statues, and a fountain. The hotel has ornate wood balustrades, russet-colored shutters, a modern fifth-floor addition, and another extension. The renovated interior is comfortable and modern, with a decor of wrought iron, wicker chairs, and hanging lamps. The Nölly family offers comfortable rooms with attractive furniture, and a sidewalk café in front.

HOTEL WALDSTAETTEN, CH-6353 Weggis. Tel. 041/93-13-41. Fax 041/93-13-43. 62 rms (all with bath). TV TEL
$ Rates (including continental breakfast): 80F–120F ($58.40–$87.60) single; 150F–225F ($109.50–$164.25) double. Half board 30F ($21.90) extra. MC, V.
This three-story hotel is surrounded by a well-planned garden with lots of trees with red leaves. The rooms have low-slung beds and contrasting solid colors. Amenities include a radio. Some of the rooms have balconies with views of the lake.

4. VITZNAU

16 miles E of Lucerne

GETTING THERE By Train The only rail line servicing Vitznau is a local alpine train connecting it to such panoramic points as Rigi-Kulm and Rigi-Kaltbad.

By Bus Buses depart for Vitznau from the quays of Lucerne every 45 minutes year round, requiring about 45 minutes to arrive, stopping in the villages of Brunnen and Gersau along the way.

By Lake Steamer Throughout the year, ferries depart nonstop for Vitznau from the quays of downtown Lucerne every 45 minutes in the summer and every 90 minutes in the winter. The trip takes 45 minutes.

By Car The resort is reached by first passing through Weggis (see Section 3, above), then continuing along Route 2b south to Vitznau, a very short drive along the lake.

ESSENTIALS The **Vitznau Tourist Board,** in the town center (tel. 041/83-17-83), is open Monday through Saturday from 8:30am to noon and 2 to 6pm. The **telephone area code** for Vitznau is 041.

Vitznau is located on a different bay of Lake Lucerne, at the foot of the Rigi. At 1,446 feet, it offers an alpine panorama that is mirrored in the lake. It's an hour's drive from Zurich and 30 minutes from Lucerne. The lake steamer from Lucerne takes an hour.

Sports holidays are especially popular in Vitznau from April to October. Facilities include swimming in the lake, indoor and outdoor pools, and tennis courts. There are also many inviting hiking trails in the meadows, woodlands, and mountains.

Vitznau is the lower terminal of the Rigi cogwheel-railway line. Pause to enjoy the beauty of the resort before heading up to the mountain.

The Vitznau-Rigi railway starts at Vitznau along the shores of Lake Lucerne, on the south side of Mount Rigi. The railway terminates at Kulm peak, after passing through the mountain stations of Rigi-Kaltbad-First, Rigi Staffelhöehe, and Rigi Staffel. In the summer old-fashioned steam trains travel on this stretch of electric rack-and-pinion railway. Departures are every 30 minutes.

WHERE TO STAY & DINE

PARK HOTEL VITZNAU, Kantonstrasse, CH-6354 Vitznau. Tel. 041/83-13-22. Fax 041/83-13-97. 79 rms, 20 suites. MINIBAR TV TEL

$ Rates (including continental breakfast): 230F–340F ($167.90–$248.15) single; 390F–500F ($284.65–$364.95) double; from 650F ($474.45) suite. Half board 75F ($54.75) per person extra. MC, V. **Parking:** 12F ($8.75).

This luxurious summer hotel resembles a Belle Epoque castle, with a central tower and a steep, brown-tile roof. The hotel is owned by Rudolf-August Oetker, one of the most respected hoteliers in Europe, who also operates Brenner's Park in Baden-Baden, Hôtel du Cap in Cap d'Antibes, and the formidable Bristol in Paris. The Park Hotel Vitznau is one of the two or three most idyllic retreats along the "Lucerne Riviera." The grand public rooms have high ceilings, and there is a sun terrace with parasols. The bedrooms are carpeted and well furnished with reproductions of French antiques; each room has a private terrace.

Dining/Entertainment: In the à la carte restaurant, Quatre Cantons, with a lakeside terrace, and in the main hotel restaurant, local and international specialties are offered, including high-quality fish dishes. The bar has a fireplace and overlooks the swimming pool and sunsets. A piano player entertains.

Services: Laundry service, shoe cleaning, room service, baby-sitting; lake and mountain excursions can be arranged.

Facilities: Two tennis courts, heated indoor and open-air pool, sauna, bathing beach with a bathing raft, motorboat for excursions and waterskiing, garden golf.

HOTEL SCHIFF, Kantonstrasse, CH-6554 Vitznau. Tel. 041/83-13-57. 16 rms (1 with bath).

$ Rates (including continental breakfast): 40F ($29.20) single; 65F ($47.45) double. No credit cards.

This excellent budget choice has a nautical theme. The interior resembles a harbor pub, with brass fittings and some antique engine controls. The sloping garden is built around a copy of the front of a lake cruiser, and there's a pleasant lakeside terrace. The Zimmermann family keep the hotel open year round.

Only one of the rooms has a private bath, but the facilities on each floor are perfectly adequate.

5. BRUNNEN

28 miles SE of Lucerne

GETTING THERE **By Train** Some of the local trains running between Zurich and Lugano or Locarno in Switzerland's deep south stop in Brunnen, although some require changes in such towns as Goschenen.

By Bus A mini-armada of buses commutes dozens of times every day from Schwyz to both the waterfront and the railroad station at Brunnen, requiring only about 12 minutes for the one-way passage. Other buses travel from Brunnen to the beginning of the cable car that ascends to Morschach.

By Lake Steamer Several lake steamers depart from the quays of Lucerne for Brunnen throughout the day, with more frequent service scheduled during midsummer. Travel time from Lucerne to Brunnen ranges from 2 to 2½ hours.

By Car From Lucerne, drive to the resorts of Weggis and Vitznau (see Sections 3 and 4, above), then continue southeast along Route 2b until you reach Brunnen.

ESSENTIALS The **Brunnen Tourist Office,** Bahnhofstrasse 32 (tel. 043/31-17-77), is open Monday through Saturday from 8:30am to noon and 2 to 6pm. The **telephone area code** for Brunnen is 043.

B runnen is a popular holiday resort in the canton of Schwyz. It's located at the foot of Fronalpstock, in a beautiful inlet at the southern end of Lake Lucerne, bordering Lake Uri. There is a fine view of the two lakes and the Alps from the quays. The resort is about an hour's drive from Zurich's Kloten International Airport.

WHAT TO SEE & DO

The area around Brunnen is the cradle of the Confederation and abounds with reminders of the country's history, including archives in Schwyz where the Confederation documents are displayed and the Federal Chapel in Brunnen.

This is also William Tell country. Around the year 1250 several families left Raron in the Valais and crossed the Alps to establish new homes in desolate Schächental/Uri. Records confirm that the Tell family helped found the settlement. According to folk legend, William Tell was the hero of a decisive battle in 1315 and reportedly died in 1350. Historians, however, have no proof of these events.

Nevertheless, the Swiss honor the man who shot an apple off the head of his brave young son with a bow and arrow in a test of prowess. You may visit the **Tell Monument;** many visitors also travel to Sisikon, just south of Brunnen, to see the **Tell Chapel,** which was restored in 1881. The chapel contains records from the early 16th century and paintings by Stückelberg.

NEARBY ATTRACTIONS

Brunnen is the starting point of **Axenstrasse,** the stunning panoramic road leading south to the St. Gotthard Pass. It goes along the rim of Lake Uri (Urnersee), in and out of subterranean passageways and galleries carved out of the mountain. Brunnen is also a base for excursions by ship, mountain railway, bus, and train to points around Lake Lucerne.

WHERE TO STAY & DINE

SEEHOTEL WALDSTÄTTERHOF, Waldstätterquai, CH-6440 Brunnen. Tel. 043/33-11-33. Fax 043/31-47-66. 101 rms (all with bath). MINIBAR TV TEL

$ **Rates** (including buffet breakfast): 140F–200F ($102.20–$146) single; 200F–310F ($146–$218.95) double. After 3 or more nights, half board is available for 35F ($25.55) extra. AE, DC, MC, V. **Parking:** 12F ($8.75).

One of the few five-star hotels opening onto the lake, the Waldstätterhof offers grand comfort in the old style. The symmetrical white building has a mansard roof and a series of balconies overlooking the lake. Plenty of modern comforts have been installed since the hotel opened in 1870. The public rooms are grand, and the dining room has fanciful chandeliers. The grounds are well kept and free of traffic. Facilities include a tennis court and beach. There also is a terrace restaurant. The Lake Lucerne steamers stop nearby and the famous Schiller Memorial Stone can be seen on the opposite shore of the lake. The hotel is open year round.

HOTEL BELLEVUE, Axenstrasse, CH-6440 Brunnen. Tel. 043/31-13-18. Fax 043/31-38-89. 48 rms (all with bath). MINIBAR TEL

$ **Rates** (including continental breakfast): 100F–110F ($73–$80.30) single; 170F–180F ($124.10–$131.40) double. AE, DC, MC, V. **Closed:** Feb and Nov.

This renovated baroque hotel at the edge of the lake is the center of nightlife in the town. It has a café and sun terrace, as well as a Tropicana Bar and Casino, where an orchestra plays dance music. Werner Achermann and his family offer well-maintained rooms, most with carpeting and some with TV. Other facilities include a reading and TV room, a restaurant with a view, and private parking.

HOTEL ELITE-AURORA, Axenstrasse, CH-6440 Brunnen. Tel. 043/31-10-24. 043/31-55-65. 65 rms (all with bath). TEL

$ **Rates** (including continental breakfast): 55F–80F ($40.15–$58.40) single; 110F–138F ($80.30–$100.75) double. AE, DC, MC, V. **Closed:** Nov 1–Mar 1.

Built in 1964, this lakeside hotel has a facade of beige wood, with large balconies, and a terrace by the water shaded by clipped sycamores. You must be a guest to enjoy the sixth-floor terrace with a panoramic view. The public rooms are dignified and modern, while the bedrooms are decorated in earth tones, with comfortable beds. The annex, Aurora, contains single units.

---

6. SCHWYZ

15 miles SE of Zug, 13 miles N of Altdorf

GETTING THERE By Train Schwyz lies directly astride one of the most important railroad lines in Europe, linking Zurich and the cities of Germany with Milan. Rail transport to everywhere in Europe is convenient and quick.

By Bus The only bus link between Schwyz and its neighbors goes between Brunnen, at the edge of Lake Lucerne, and Zug, connecting many different mountain towns (including Schwyz) along the way.

By Car Take the N3 express highway south from Zurich to the junction with Route 8, where you continue south along this secondary road.

ESSENTIALS The **Schwyz Tourist Office,** Postplatz 9 (tel. 043/21-34-46), is open Monday through Friday from 10am to noon and 2:30 to 6pm. The **telephone area code** for Schwyz is 043.

This pleasant little town in the heart of Helvetia is set amid orchards on a mountain plateau between Lake Lucerne and Lake Lauerz. Lying under the towering twin horns of Gross Mythen, it is also the repository of the country's most treasured archives. Its mountain "annex" is the little resort of Stoos, at 4,250 feet.

Since the 16th century, when foreign powers such as France and the Vatican needed mercenaries, they often recruited them here. The men of Schwyz were known for their prowess and courage. Those who survived the battles returned to build the sturdy and often quite opulent houses you can still see today.

Schwyz was in the forefront of the movement toward unity that ultimately led to the Swiss Confederation; it joined with the neighboring districts of Uri and Unterwalden to create the "everlasting league" on August 1, 1291. In the 14th century its name in dialectical form, Schweiz, was first used by foreigners to refer to the entire region (later it was applied to the country itself).

WHAT TO SEE & DO

The **Bundesbriefarchiv,** the archive of the federal charters, contains the original deed of the Swiss Confederation and other national documents. Built in 1936, the simple concrete structure has a frescoed facade. It stands on Bahnhofstrasse and is open daily from 9:30 to 11:30am and 2 to 5pm. For more information, call 24-20-64.

The **Church of St. Martin,** built in 1774 on Hauptplatz (the main square), is embellished in the baroque style, with a richly frescoed nave. Opposite it, the **Rathaus** (Town Hall) dates from 1642. Its facade is handsomely decorated with some of the most elaborate murals in town, each of which portrays epic and somewhat romanticized moments in Swiss history. To be admitted into the Rathaus, apply to the concierge. Immediately to the south of the town hall is a tower that contains the canton's historical museum.

WHERE TO STAY

HOTEL WYSSES RÖSSLI, Hauptplatz, CH-6430 Schwyz. Tel. 043/21-19-22. Fax 043/21-20-46. 27 rms (all with bath). MINIBAR TV TEL
$ Rates (including continental breakfast): 90F–105F ($65.70–$76.65) single; 165F–185F ($120.45–$135.05) double. AE, DC, MC, V.

This five-story hotel is ideally located across from the baroque church in the center of Schwyz. A hotel has stood on this spot since 1642. When the present hostelry was restored in 1978, some of the banqueting rooms were brought in intact from an 18th-century baroque house. The public rooms are rustic, but the bedrooms are modern, with radios. The bar is warm and intimate.

The formal Turmstube is one of the finest dining rooms in town, serving elegant continental cuisine. For an appetizer, there is caviar or foie gras from Strasbourg. Fish dishes include filet of sole with almonds or in a white wine sauce, as well as trout meunière. The menu has a special section called plats de résistance, with a wide range of meat dishes. The chef specializes in scampi flambéed with Pernod, beef Stroganoff, and fondue chinoise. A la carte meals start at 55F ($40.35); the menu gourmet costs 80F ($58.40). The restaurant is open daily from 11:30am to 2pm and 6 to 9pm.

WHERE TO DINE

RATSKELLER, Strehlgasse 3. Tel. 21-10-87.
   Cuisine: SWISS. **Reservations:** Required.
$ **Prices:** Appetizers 8F–15F ($5.85–$10.95); main courses 18F–36F ($13.15–$26.30); fixed-price meals 75F–120F ($54.75–$87.60). No credit cards.
   Open: Tues–Sat 10am–midnight, Sun 3pm–midnight.

The Ratskeller is in a historic building, a few steps from Hauptplatz. It contains a labyrinth of intimate Rhenish-style rooms with leaded-glass windows and paneling. The cellar has wrought-iron grills. The menu might include filet of beef with tarragon, mountain goat, venison with herbs, filet of lamb in a Roquefort sauce, and veal filet in a sherry sauce. Specialties change with the season.

AN EXCURSION TO THE HÖLLOCH CAVES

The mammoth Hölloch Caves are an intriguing excursion from the valley. To get there, take the Muotathal road southeast of Schwyz for about 9 miles. Park in the lot of the restaurant there; it's about a 10-minute walk to the caves. The Höllochgrotte is the largest grotto in Europe, with some 60 miles of passages; only half a mile is open to visitors. The caves, virtually unknown at the turn of the century, were explored extensively after World War II. You'll see stalagmites and stalactites, as well as other strange netherworld formations. What might be the eeriest section is the "grosse Pagoda."

A 1-hour tour of the caves is available in the summer, daily from 10am to 4pm. Five to six people are needed for each tour. If you're alone, your best chance of joining a group is to arrive at the caves in the early afternoon. A 1-hour tour costs 5F ($3.65) for adults and 2.50F ($1.85) for children. Tours are conducted in sunny weather only—rain fills the caves with water. The caves may also be explored on Friday and Saturday nights. Groups of 12 to 15 visitors must make a reservation in advance. The tour includes a preexploration dinner, an all-night tour of the caves, and breakfast the following morning. The cost is 55F ($40.15). The cave information office is at the pleasant restaurant near the entrance.

7. ALTDORF

34 miles SE of Lucerne

GETTING THERE   By Train   Several daily trains make the 27-minute trip to Altdorf from the region's biggest railway junction, Arth-Goldau, on their way south to Chiasso and, eventually, Milan. In Arth-Goldau, rapid connections can be made on express trains to Paris, Bern, Zurich, Lucerne, or Basel.

By Bus   The bus routes coming into Altdorf connect the town with mountain hamlets, which usually have no railway junctions of their own. In the summer, a handful of buses connect it with Zurich's Hauptbahnhof, sometimes with a transfer in Flüelin. Travel time from Zurich is about 1½ hours.

By Car   From Brunnen on Lake Lucerne, continue south along Route N4.

ESSENTIALS   The **Altdorf Tourist Office** (tel. 044/2-28-88) is open Monday through Friday from 9 to 11am and 2 to 6pm, and on Saturday from 9 to 11:30am. The **telephone area code** for Altdorf is 044.

Altdorf is the town where the William Tell legend is said to have taken place. A statue of the Swiss national hero stands in the main square. The key to the St. Gotthard Pass, Altdorf is north of the Alps and 2 miles south of where the Reuss River flows into Lake Uri. It is the capital of the canton of Uri and the starting point of the road over the Klausen Pass. The most scenic way to get to Altdorf from Lucerne is to ride a lake steamer to Flüelen and transfer to a bus. The total trip takes about 3 hours.

WHAT TO SEE & DO

The famous **William Tell statue** is in front of the early 19th-century **town hall** and a tower dating from the Middle Ages. The monument was created by Richard Kissling in 1895; it was this image, engraved on a postage stamp, that became familiar to people all over the globe.

NEARBY ATTRACTIONS The road to the Klausen Pass leads to **Bürglen,** one of the oldest hamlets in Uri. Snowdrifts block the pass from October to May. Bürglen, according to legend, was the birthplace of William Tell. The **Tell Museum** contains documents and mementos relating to the early history of Switzerland. The museum is in a Romanesque tower adjacent to the parish church. It's open from June to October, daily from 9:30 to 11:30am and 2 to 5pm. Admission is 3F ($2.20).

WHERE TO STAY & DINE

GOLDENER SCHLÜSSEL, CH-6460 Altdorf. Tel. 044/2-10-02. Fax 044/2-11-67. 24 rms (all with bath). MINIBAR TV TEL
$ Rates (including continental breakfast): 85F–95F ($62.05–$69.35) single; 130F–160F ($94.90–$116.80) double. AE, DC, MC, V. **Closed:** Jan and Mon in winter.
The best of the lot is this five-story, three-star hotel in the center of town, renowned for its menu. A historic inn dating from the 18th century, it faces a tiny medieval plaza and is distinguished by a wrought-iron sign bearing a golden key (*goldener Schlüssel*). The hotel's many amenities and accessories include a handful of original paintings.
At the hotel's restaurant, a fixed-price lunch costs 32F ($23.35) and a full dinner starts at 45F ($32.85). Daily specials might include minced veal with four types of mushrooms, scaloppine Florentine with saffron rice, ravioli with rosemary, and tournedos with shallots and marrow in a Pinot Noir sauce. Parking is available behind the hotel.

HOTEL BAHNHOF, CH-6460 Altdorf. Tel. 044/2-10-32. 28 rms (none with bath).
$ Rates (including continental breakfast): 40F ($29.20) single; 70F ($51.10) double. No credit cards.
Anna Niederberger and her family own this well-established tourist hotel that resembles an old-fashioned private house, with a modern addition in front. It has pleasantly dated furniture, and all rooms have a sink. The cheaper rooms are small but pleasantly paneled and comfortable.

---

8. AMSTEG

9 miles S of Altdorf, 4 miles S of Erstfeld

GETTING THERE By Bus The village can be reached by the postal coach from the Amsteg train station, 2 miles away, or by public bus from the express-train station of Erstfeld.

By Car   From Altdorf, continue south along Route N2 (also called Route E9).

ESSENTIALS   The **telephone area code** for Amsteg is 044.

This is a traditional stop on the St. Gotthard route and a good base for walks and mountain excursions. Amsteg is at the mouth of the Maderanertal. In the distance you can see a tall viaduct which holds the tracks of the St. Gotthard railway.

WHERE TO STAY & DINE

HOTEL STERN UND POST, CH-6474 Amsteg. Tel. 044/6-44-40. Fax 044/6-32-61. 20 rms (all with bath). MINIBAR TV TEL
$ Rates (including continental breakfast): 60F–90F ($43.80–$65.70) single; 115F–180F ($83.95–$131.40) double. AE, DC, MC, V. **Parking:** 5F ($3.65).

A former post house, this hotel has a steep tile roof and long rows of small-paned windows with flower boxes. The Tresch family has managed the "inn of the Golden Star" since 1734, when the family was in charge of customs and the region's private mail system. After the Swiss Federal Post was founded in 1850, the Tresches became postmasters, soon adding the word "Post" to the name of the hotel (the word *Stern* means "star" in German). In the days of the famous St. Gotthard Mail Coach (1850 to 1882), the Tresches had stables for more than 400 horses. P. A. Tresch, who manages the hotel today, is still responsible for the postal-coach (mail-bus) services in the area (there's a post office in a wing of the hotel).

The interior is elegantly furnished with a combination of 19th-century parlor antiques and chalet chairs. Some of the bedrooms are furnished with Victorian beds and lots of gingerbread (the beds are shorter than those elsewhere). The dining room has fern-green walls and large windows. The local trout is excellent and comes in six varieties. Many of the specialties are written tongue in cheek in the regional dialect, so you will need a staff member to assist you. The specialties include pork with potatoes and chestnuts. Full meals begin at 35F ($25.55).

9. ANDERMATT

31 miles SE of Lucerne

GETTING THERE   By Train   Andermatt lies directly on a secondary rail line connecting Chur with Lucerne, where further connections can be made on express trains to the rest of Switzerland. Travel time to Lucerne is about 1¾ hours.

By Bus   Three or four buses travel daily from the bus junction of Airola to Andermatt. To Airola, buses funnel in every day from Basel, Lucerne, Zurich, and Lugano, with connections to such other resorts as Brig and Oberwald.

By Car   From Amsteg, continue south along Route N2.

ESSENTIALS   The **Andermatt Tourist Office,** on Bahnhofplatz (tel. 044/6-74-54), is open Monday through Saturday from 9am to noon and 2 to 6pm. The **telephone area code** for Andermatt is 044.

At the crossroads of the Alps, Andermatt is a sports center known for its long, sunny days in winter. It's in the Urseren Valley, at the junction of two alpine roads—the St. Gotthard highway and the road to Oberalp and Furka.

WHAT TO SEE & DO

Andermatt is a good base for hikes across the mountain passes. In the winter skiers flock to Gemsstock, Natschen, Oberalp, and Winterhorn. There's also a 12½-mile-long cross-country ski track open from November to May. Safety devices help protect against snowdrifts and avalanches. Other sporting facilities include a Swiss ski school, an ice-skating and curling rink, an indoor swimming pool, and squash courts. Sleigh rides are also offered.

South of Andermatt, the ✪ **St. Gotthard Pass,** at 6,920 feet, provides a link between the Grisons and the Valais Alps. It's one of the most stunning and scenic passes in Switzerland used by merchants and messengers as far back as the early Middle Ages. The road through the pass was built in the 18th and 19th centuries atop a much older footpath; it is still the shortest route between the two watersheds that fall away on either side. A 9-mile-long railway tunnel burrows under the peak of the St. Gotthard massif; nearby, the St. Gotthard road tunnel, opened in 1980, is the longest one in the world. There is no toll along the 10-mile route, which is open year round (the road high above it closes during heavy snowfalls).

WHERE TO STAY & DINE

HOTEL DREI KÖNIGE UND POST, Gotthardstrasse 69, CH-6490 Andermatt. Tel. 044/6-72-03. Fax 044/6-81-85. 32 rms (all with bath). MINIBAR TV TEL

$ Rates (including continental breakfast): 66F–80F ($48.15–$58.40) single; 132F–160F ($96.35–$116.80) double. AE, DC, MC, V.

There has been an inn at this site since 1234. Goethe spent the night at one in 1775. The family-run hotel, built since then, was renovated in 1977. There's a café terrace in front of this white-walled chalet with buttressed eaves and brown shutters. The Renner family offers paneled rooms with balconies. Facilities include a sauna, whirlpool, and fitness center.

HOTEL KRONE, Gotthardstrasse, CH-6490 Andermatt. Tel. 044/6-72-06. Fax 044/6-78-38. 72 rms (all with bath). TEL

$ Rates (including continental breakfast): 66F–80F ($48.15–$58.40) single; 132F–160F ($96.35–$116.80) double. AE, DC, MC, V.

The finest place to stay in Andermatt also serves the best food. Located on the main artery of town, the hotel is one of the oldest establishments, dating from Victorian days. The chalet has richly paneled rooms as well as carpeted modern rooms. There's a cozy, paneled Victorian parlor with a sofa, chairs, and books one floor above the reception area; it also contains an upright piano and a large TV set. The bedrooms are medium-sized, with conservative decor.

The Krone bar is one of the most popular stops on the après-ski circuit. A French restaurant serves excellent food. The Kronenstübl is known for its grills and fondues. Food is served daily from 11am to 10pm.

CHAPTER 12

THE GRISONS

The eastern region of Switzerland, the Grisons, is still the largest and least developed of all the Swiss cantons. Its German name is Graubunden, to the Romansh-speaking population it's Grischun, and the Italians call it Grigioni. Grisons is the French (and English) name, although French isn't spoken in this canton.

This sparsely settled region is quite mountainous and has some 140 square miles of glaciers. Forests cover one-fifth of the canton's total area. Juf, nearly 7,000 feet above sea level, is the highest permanently inhabited village in the Alps. Even the 150 or so valleys of the Grisons lie at high altitudes, between 2,953 and 6,562 feet, and the region's highest peak, Bernina, reaches 13,285 feet. The alpine scenery here differs from that of other areas of Switzerland because of the altitude and topography; and the air is clear and invigorating, which has led to the establishment of many health centers in the Grisons. The height makes it cooler at night in the summer, but it enjoys the extra daytime warmth of other southern cantons.

The Grisons contains the sources of the Rhine and Inn (En in Romansh) rivers, which form the major valleys of the canton.

The territory of the Grisons was once a part of Rhaetia, peopled by Celtic tribes in pre-Christian times. In 15 B.C. the Romans conquered the Rhaetians, began colonization, and built alpine roads. The Germanic Franks entered the Roman provinces in the 3rd century and established themselves along the Rhine. They and their successors, the Ostrogoths, introduced Teutonic influences into the Roman territories they seized, gradually changing the language of the inhabitants to Germanic dialects, especially in the northern regions. As a result, German is spoken today by about half the Grisons population, mainly around Davos and Chur, the capital of the canton. About a sixth of the people of the Grisons—those living in the south—speak the language of their next-door neighbor, Italy.

The people of the upper valleys of the Rhine and the Inn were isolated enough to resist Germanic influences, and today they still cling to their ancestral tongue, Romansh—the language of a third of the Swiss living in the Grisons. Both the dialect spoken in the Engadine (Ladin) and the one spoken in the Vorderrhein Valley (Surveltisch) are derived from the Latin of Rhaetia. The centuries altered it, so that today it sounds rather like Spanish spoken with a German accent. In 1938 Romansh officially became the fourth of the Swiss national languages.

From the time of the Romans down through the Middle Ages, travelers could take either the High Road (Obere Strasse), which used the Juli Julier Pass and Septimer Pass, or the Low Road (Untere Strasse), via the Splugen Pass. These roads gave Rhaetia a monopoly on almost all transalpine traffic through the territory, and the Low Road (much enlarged) is still in use today. The Septimer Pass fell into disuse after a modernized road was constructed.

WHAT'S SPECIAL ABOUT THE GRISONS

Great Towns/Villages

☐ Chur, an old town with medieval houses, whose history goes back to 3,000 B.C.

☐ Davos, one of the Alps' finest ski centers, the setting of Thomas Mann's novel *The Magic Mountain*.

☐ Klosters, a charming, animated ski village preferred by the rich and famous, including Prince Charles.

☐ Arosa, one of the highest of the alpine resorts at 6,000 feet, a favorite of such movie stars as Sophia Loren.

Museums

☐ Bünder Kunstmuseum (Fine Arts Museum), in Chur, with paintings and sculptures by Grisons artists and others.

Religious Monuments

☐ The cathedral of Chur, erected between 1178 and 1282, with the largest Gothic triptych in Switzerland.

Natural Spectacles

☐ Parsenn-Weissflüh, at Davos, acclaimed by some as the finest ski area in Europe.

☐ The Weisshorn, at 8,704 feet, outside Arosa, offering a vast panorama of the Grison Alps.

Ace Attractions

☐ Natureisbahn, at Davos-Platz, the largest natural ice rink in Europe.

The Grisons was one of the last regions of Switzerland to benefit from busy commerce with the rest of the country. Cars were forbidden on all roads until 1927, and even today it's illegal to drive cars in Arosa after nightfall. This ban on the use of roads helped to popularize the Rhaetian railway, whose narrow-gauge trains travel along hairpin turns and through dozens of tunnels. Today this railway, as well as the postal buses which crisscross the district, provide panoramas of a harsh and sometimes-bleak landscape.

The peasants of this canton banded together in 1395 to form the Ligue Grise (Gray League), from which the name Grisons is derived. Two other such leagues were formed in the area to oppose Hapsburg domination. In 1803 the three leagues formed a single canton, which joined the Swiss Confederation. The belief system of the Protestant Reformation, however, was adopted by only part of the canton, and today sections of it remain staunchly Catholic.

Since the 1950s much of the Grisons has earned its living from tourists, who enjoy the ski resorts and the small villages, as well as the local red and "green" wines (*vetliner*), the exquisite embroidery, and the hand-woven linens still produced in the mountain homes.

SEEING THE GRISONS

Zurich has the airport nearest to the Grisons. From there it's an easy rail trip to the major resorts, such as Davos, all of which are reached by scenic lines. The *Engadine Express* runs from Chur to the Swiss National Park in the Lower Engadine. Arosa is easily reached from Chur. The twin resorts of Klosters and Davos are reached by train connections through Landquart.

IF YOU HAVE 4 DAYS

Day 1: Spend the day in Chur, the capital of the canton, exploring its medieval streets.

Day 2: Travel to Arosa, an elegant resort reached by a corniche along Schanfigg, where visitors can climb by cable car to the Weisshorn.

Days 3 and 4: Spend the third and fourth days either in Klosters or in Davos, taking in some alpine skiing and a host of mountain attractions.

---

1. CHUR

76 miles SE of Zurich, 37 miles W of Davos

GETTING THERE   By Train   The town is the end of some international lines, such as the standard-gauge railway from Sargans. It's also the starting point for the narrow-gauge line to St. Moritz, known as the Rhätische Bahn. The Chur–Arosa line and the *Glacier Express* also start here. Chur also has frequent rail connections from Zurich.

By Bus   Chur lies near the terminus of several bus lines, which link its railway facilities with some of the villages scattered throughout the nearby valleys. The two most prominent of these are Davos and St. Moritz, where bus connections can be made to Munich, across the German border.

By Car   About 90 minutes from Zurich, along Route N3 (later the N13), Chur is easily reached by expressway.

ESSENTIALS   The **tourist office** is located on Bahnhofplatz (tel. 081/22-18-18). The **telephone area code** for Chur is 081.

The capital of the Grisons, Chur is the oldest town in Switzerland. According to recent excavations, the area had been inhabited as early as 3,000 B.C. The Romans established a settlement in 15 B.C., naming it Curia Rhaetorum. In 450 B.C. a recently Christianized Chur became the see of a bishop. The town still has a bishop, but he no longer has the power of his medieval predecessors, who ruled virtually every aspect of life in Chur until 1526.

Set at an elevation of 1,955 feet, Chur lies near the head of the Rhine Valley, surrounded by towering mountains. The Plessur River, a tributary of the Rhine, flows through the center of town. Chur is at the natural junction of several of the most important routes from Italy over the alpine passes, and as a result incorporates both Italian and Rhaetian influences.

Favored by tourists, who appreciate the wilderness surrounding it, Chur is the largest mercantile center between Zurich and Milan. It is also an important rail center, the origination point for several of the most scenic railway lines in Switzerland: the narrow-gauge rail line to St. Moritz (the Rhätische Bahn), the Chur–Arosa line, the *Glacier Express,* the *Palm Express,* and the *Bernina Express.* You might also consider a trip to Splügen, said to have the prettiest mountain-pass village in the area.

THE GRISONS & THE ENGADINE

N

0 |====| 200 m
       220 y

Prättigau Valley

3 Klosters

Chur

1 Chur

Schanfigg Valley

Davos

Davos **4**

Tschuggen

Arosa

2
Arosa

Rothorn

Fluëla Pass

Stätzerhorn

Lenzerheide

Piz Scalottas   Valbella

Bärentritt

S-chanf

Zuoz   **1**

Savognin

Albulapass

Samedan
& Celerina   **2**

St. Moritz

Pontresina

Julierpass

3
St. Moritz

Bernina Valley

Juf

Silvaplana   **5**

Lake Silvaplana

6
Sils-Maria/
Sils-Baselgia

Septimer Pass

Bernina Pass

Morteratsch Glacier

Val Bregaglia

Diavolezza

Ski Areas

SWITZERLAND

BERN ★

The Grisons
& The Engadine

THE GRISONS:

1 Chur
2 Arosa
3 Klosters
4 Davos

THE ENGADINE:

1 S-chanf and Zouz
2 Samedan and Celerina
3 St. Moritz
4 Pontresina
5 Silvaplana
6 Sils-Maria/Sils-Baselgia

Chur also offers a variety of sports facilities. Summer sports include hiking, swimming, and riding. In the winter skiers have access to the top 20 ski areas surrounding Chur, some of which reach 9,000 feet and are only 1½ hours away.

WHAT TO SEE & DO

You'll want to spend as much time as possible in Chur, to see the legacies left by the many emperors, kings, armies, and traders who have marched through here. City officials have painted red-and-green footprints to facilitate self-guided tours of the medieval sector. You'll come across squares with flower-bedecked fountains and narrow streets, along with elegant houses and many towers.

The **cathedral of Chur,** on Hofplatz, was built between 1178 and 1282 on an ancient foundation and was renovated extensively in the 19th century. Inside, the high altar displays a 15th-century, gilded-wood triptych in the Gothic style—the largest of its kind in Switzerland. To visit the Dom Treasury, you'll have to apply to the sacristan at building no. 2 on the square. For a cost of 1.50F ($1.10), he'll show you many medieval reliquaries, among other treasures, including the relics of St. Lucius of the 2nd century.

Near the cathedral the baroque **Bishop's Palace** was built in 1732 and is still the residence of a bishop. The palace opens onto the Hofplatz—site of a Roman fort.

The town has at least two museums worth visiting:

RÄTISCHES MUSEUM (Rhaetic Museum), Quaderstrasse 15. Tel. 22-29-88.
This museum, in the late 16th-century Buolsches Haus, presents regional history and folklore exhibits and an archeological collection.
Admission: 3F ($2.20).
Open: Tues–Sun 10am–noon and 2–5pm.

BÜNDNER KUNSTMUSEUM (Fine Arts Museum), Postplatz. Tel. 22-17-63.
Known as the Villa Planta, this museum, set in a park, displays paintings and sculptures by many well-known Grisons artists. Some of the works are by Giovanni, Segantini, Angelica Kauffmann, Ferdinand Hodler, and Cuno Amiet, as well as by Alberto and Augusto Giacometti. You'll also find a large collection of works by Ernst Ludwig Kirchner (1880–1938), the German painter and leader of the Brücke school of expressionists.
Admission: About 3F ($2.20).
Open: Tues–Sun 10am–noon and 2–5pm.

WHERE TO STAY

EXPENSIVE

DUC DE ROHAN, Masanerstrasse 44, CH-7000 Chur. Tel. 081/22-10-22. Fax 081/22-45-37. 52 rms (all with bath). TV TEL
$ Rates (including continental breakfast): 90F–105F ($65.70–$76.65) single; 150F–190F ($109.50–$138.70) double. AE, DC, MC, V.

The four-star Duc de Rohan is the best and the most expensive hotel and restaurant in Chur. One part of the hotel is a white-walled neoclassical villa with elaborate lintels, while the other section is modern. The hotel has a large indoor swimming pool, a sauna, massage facilities, and a fitness club. Many of the public rooms contain rococo and 19th-century antiques set in pastel-colored niches. The bedrooms are comfortable and conservative.

MODERATE

HOTEL CHUR, Welschdörfli 2, CH-7000 Chur. Tel. 081/22-21-61. Fax 081/23-34-92. 58 rms (all with bath). MINIBAR TV TEL
$ Rates (including continental breakfast): 75F–110F ($54.75–$80.30) single; 130F–170F ($94.90–$124.10) double. AE, DC, MC, V.

This imposing building with arched windows and fifth-floor gables contains three restaurants and comfortable bedrooms. Each room has a radio; some of the rooms have Queen Anne chairs.

The Cava Grischa is an informal cellar with black-vested waiters, rustic paneling, and nighttime folk or modern music and dancing. The art nouveau Bistro is decorated with wrought iron and bentwood chairs, and offers crêpes and light snacks. Finally, the Welschdörfli is an elegant dining room, serving cuisine moderne and Grisons-style cooking.

HOTEL FREIECK, Reichsgasse 50, CH-7000 Chur. Tel. 081/22-17-92. Fax 081/23-34-19. 80 rms (all with bath). TV TEL
$ Rates (including continental breakfast): 100F ($73) single; 160F ($116.80) double. AE, DC, MC, V.

This tall building is decorated with drawings of grapevines, a sundial, and two lions. The renovated bedrooms contain simple furniture and comfortable low beds. The Stockman family, however, places more emphasis on the restaurants, which range from a rustic stucco room with massive beams and vaulting to a paneled contemporary room.

HOTEL STERN, Reichsgasse 11, CH-7000 Chur. Tel. 081/22-35-55. Fax 081/22-19-15. 56 rms (all with bath). TEL
$ Rates (including buffet breakfast): 90F–100F ($65.70–$73) single; 155F–165F ($113.15–$120.45) double. DC, MC, V. **Parking:** Free.

⭐ Like most members of the Romantik chain, the charming Hotel Stern is filled with authentic antiques. The outside looks like a giant strawberry mousse with white shutters. The interior has pine paneling—some of which dates from 1646—and vaulted or timbered ceilings. The public rooms and modernized bedrooms have antiques and wrought iron. Emil Pfister's staff will meet you at the train station if you call ahead.

The hotel has one of the finest dining rooms in town; you may want to try it even if you're not a guest. Meals costing 42F ($30.65) and more are served daily from 11:30am to 2pm and 6:30 to 9:30pm. The chefs specialize in regional fare, including capon Oberland (poached in bouillon), calves' liver in a red wine sauce, and pan-fried trout. A special gourmet menu is offered for 65F ($47.45).

INEXPENSIVE

HOTEL DREI KÖNIGE, Reichsgasse 18, CH-7002 Chur. Tel. 081/22-17-25. Fax 081/22-17-26. 52 rms (38 with bath). TEL TV
$ Rates (including continental breakfast): 45F ($32.85) single without bath; 82F ($59.85) single with bath; 75F–145F ($54.75–$105.85) double with bath. AE, DC, MC, V. **Parking:** 7F ($5.10).

Ⓢ This historic hotel is at the entrance to the old town. The building's foundation dates from at least the 14th century. Excavations in the hotel cellar unearthed a collapsed tunnel that had led to the bishop's palace at the opposite end of the old city. The Schällibaum family has managed the hotel since 1911; over the years they've welcomed royalty, high-ranking politicians, and world-famous artists. The Drei Könige Hall on the premises used to be part of a monastery and, later, the seat of government.

Except for a handful of budget accommodations under the eaves, most of the well-scrubbed rooms have comfortable furniture and the standard amenities. The hotel has one of the most popular restaurants in town (see "Where to Dine," below).

HOTEL ZUNFTHAUS ZUR REBLEUTEN, Pfisterplatz, CH-7000 Chur. Tel. 081/22-17-13. Fax 081/22-30-56. 13 rms (8 with bath).

$ Rates (including buffet breakfast): 55F ($40.15) single without bath, 90F ($65.70) single with bath; 95F ($69.35) double without bath, 145F ($105.85) double with bath. AE, DC, MC, V.

The hotel was built in 1483 in the middle of the old town. Set in front of a fountain, it has blue shutters and a beautiful window ornamentation. The inside is paneled, with elaborate chandeliers, leaded-glass windows, and hunting trophies. The white stucco bedrooms have comfortable beds. Ralph Cottiati's establishment, however, is known mainly for its good food.

WHERE TO DINE

EXPENSIVE

DUC DE ROHAN, Masanerstrasse 44. Tel. 22-10-22.
   Cuisine: SWISS. **Reservations:** Recommended.
$ Prices: Appetizers 4F–16F ($2.90–$11.70); main courses 10.50F–24F ($7.70–$17.50). AE, DC, MC, V.
   Open: Daily 9:30am–11:30pm.

Many Swiss consider the Duc de Rohan the best and most elegant restaurant in town. Located on the north side, it has top-notch chefs, good food, and polished service. Specialties include strips of beef grilled at your table with a homemade sauce, grilled trout, and goat with flap mushrooms. You can also help yourself to a salad buffet. Drinks are available in the keller, whose baronial granite fireplace juts into the rustically elegant bar and dining room.

MODERATE

OBELISCO, Vazerolgasse 12. Tel. 22-58-58.
   Cuisine: ITALIAN. **Reservations:** Required.
$ Prices: Appetizers 5F–19.50F ($3.65–$14.25); main courses 24F–30.50F ($17.50–$22.25). AE, DC, MC, V.
   Open: Lunch daily noon–2pm; dinner daily 6–10pm.

Named after the obelisk in the square outside, Obelisco is the best Italian restaurant in Chur. Located in the heart of the old town, the neobaroque pine restaurant has three dining rooms. You can begin with one of the more than a dozen pastas and choose among many classic Italian dishes, such as veal with tuna and saltimbocca. The Gennaro Garofalo family owns the restaurant.

ZUNFTHAUS ZUR REBLEUTEN, Pfisterplatz. Tel. 22-17-13.
   Cuisine: FRENCH/ITALIAN. **Reservations:** Recommended.

$ Prices: Appetizers 11.50F–18F ($8.40–$13.15); main courses 11.50F–80F ($8.05–$58.40); fixed-price meal 25F ($18.25). AE, DC, MC, V.
Open: Breakfast/lunch daily 7am–2pm; dinner daily 4pm–midnight.
This historic restaurant serves such specialties as roast breast of goose in a cabbage-and-kirsch sauce, pork filets with apples and hazelnuts, and calves' liver in wine with Rösti. An excellent appetizer is the stuffed trout in a saffron sauce.

INEXPENSIVE

DREI KÖNIGE, Reichsgasse 18. Tel. 22-17-25.
Cuisine: SWISS. **Reservations:** Not needed.
$ Prices: Appetizers 8F–14F ($5.85–$10.20); main courses 12F–28F ($8.75–$20.45); Weinstube meal from 28F ($20.45); Usteria meal from 42F ($30.65). AE, DC, MC, V.
Open: Weinstube, lunch daily 11am–2pm; dinner daily 5–9pm. Usteria, lunch daily noon–2pm; dinner daily 6:30–9pm.
The Weinstube, on the first floor, is covered with worn paneling, whose nicks and scratches only add to the character of the room. Don't expect haute cuisine here. A limited menu is offered from 2 to 5pm and 9pm to midnight. Meals are served amid hunting trophies, collections of medals, and old photographs.

Usteria, one floor above street level beside the reception desk, is the more formal of the hotel's restaurants. The Schällibaum family welcomes some of Chur's most prominent citizens. Sometimes the chef prepares a double entrecôte marchand de vin or a chateaubriand Henri-IV. You can also order more standard fare such as pot-au-feu served as an appetizer and polenta with cheese.

2. AROSA

19 miles E of Chur

GETTING THERE   By Train   Trains connect Chur and Arosa at the rate of one per hour during the day (trip time: 1 hour). Trains from Zurich take 3 hours to reach Arosa. Zurich is the nearest airport to Arosa.

By Car   To make the 19-mile drive from Chur in good weather, allow at least an hour, as the road is steep, with hairpin curves. Don't make the drive in icy weather. Instead, take the narrow-gauge railway that has been in operation since World War I.

Cars are restricted, except vehicles entering or leaving town. Even so, you won't be stranded without transportation, as a local bus travels across the resort, transporting visitors free.

ESSENTIALS   The **Arosa Tourist Bureau** is open Monday through Saturday from 9am to 6pm and on Sunday from 10am to 1pm and 2 to 5:30pm. The **telephone area code** for Arosa is 081. Only one of Arosa's streets has a name, Poststrasse, which runs as a traffic artery through the center of town; in the absence of **street names,** visitors can follow hotel and restaurant directional signs.

Arosa, one of the highest of the alpine resorts (6,000 ft. above sea level), lies in a sheltered basin at the top of the Schanfigg Valley. The most popular resort in the Grisons after Davos and St. Moritz, it consists of one main street (Poststrasse), which is lined with hotels and shops. Though parts of the village date from the 14th century, the look of the resort is modern and contemporary. If St. Moritz is too ultrachic for you, Arosa may be your answer. Both visitors and the hotels that house them tend to be low-key and family-oriented, often favoring ski jackets over dinner jackets. Arosa lures the family trade through such attractions as kindergartens for children.

GETTING AROUND   There's a local **city bus** that makes frequent runs throughout the day from Unterseeplatz (in the lower reaches of town) to the railroad station and to most of the chair lifts and cable-car departure points in the resort's heights.

Taxis are always available. In the winter, a "Night Express" taxi service runs continually from 8pm to 2am, charging 2F ($1.45) per trip. The vehicles are marked NIGHT EXPRESS and can be stopped for boarding or getting off anywhere along the way.

WHAT TO SEE & DO

Skiing is the big attraction in Arosa, but summer activities and other winter sports, such as tobogganing and horse-drawn sleigh rides on the Arlenwald road, are also popular. Tennis, squash, bowling, and golf can all be played year round at inside facilities. Walks can be taken over 18 miles of easy, sunny, and varied trails kept open in the winter.

SKIING   Arosa draws an international crowd to its slopes. It offers 40 miles of the best ski runs in the Grisons. It also has the Swiss Ski School, which, with 100 instructors, is one of the best ski schools in Switzerland.

Skiing is popular in the Obersee area at the eastern edge of the resort, whose focal point (reached by cable car) is the ✪ **Weisshorn** (8,704 ft.). During the day, cable cars leave for the Weisshorn at the rate of one every 20 minutes. You first make the ascent to the middle station, Larn Mittle, at 6,640 feet, from which there are splendid panoramas of Arosa. From the top at the final station there is one of the grandest views in eastern Switzerland, taking in a vast panorama of the Grison Alps. Even Chur can be viewed to the northwest, at the foothills of the Calanda mountain peak.

To the west, skiers take to Hörnli gondola, reaching **Hörnligrat** (8,180 ft.) in about 16 minutes. Drag lifts at Hörnligat fan out, taking skiers to the top of several different ski slopes.

Skiing lessons for classes at the Swiss Ski School cost 22F ($16.05) for half a day, 105F ($76.65) for 6 half-days for adults; 20F ($14.60) for half a day to 95F ($69.35) for 6 half-days for children. Private ski instruction is possible through the **Grison Association of Private Ski Instructors Arosa** (tel. 31-14-07) and a group of private professional instructors (tel. 31-34-48).

ICE SKATING   Ice-skating rinks are busy here; one is at Inner-Arosa and another is at the **Obersee Sports Grounds,** also used for ice hockey and Bavarian curling. The cost for skating is 4F ($2.90) for adults; children 6 to 16 pay 2.50F ($1.85).

WHERE TO STAY

Most of Arosa's hotels are modern and expensive. In the peak season—winter—reservations are imperative. In the summer it's much easier to find accommodations.

VERY EXPENSIVE

ALEXANDRA SPORT HOTEL, CH-7050 Arosa. Tel. 081/31-01-11. Fax
081/31-32-90. 150 rms (all with bath). MINIBAR TV TEL
$ Rates (including half board): 140F–190F ($102.20–$138.70) single; 270F–370F
($197.05–$270.05) double. AE, DC, MC, V.
Its innovative design sprawls in a semicircular curve of balconied rooms layered on top
of one another, with oversize windows and a view over Arosa and the snow-covered
mountains. The rooms are panoramic, modern, and comfortable, and are usually
occupied by sports enthusiasts, who spend their days skiing or hiking through the
neighboring hills. The town's ski lifts are just 500 yards away.
   Dining/Entertainment: Evening entertainment may include a fondue party
with folk music, a candlelight buffet, a night at the disco or tavern, a bowling
tournament, or a sleigh ride. The attractive restaurant is called Modern Art.
   Services: Free local bus transportation, room service, laundry service.
   Facilities: Heated swimming pool, sauna.

AROSA KULM HOTEL, CH-7050 Arosa. Tel. 081/31-01-31. Fax 081/31-40-
90. 212 rms (all with bath). MINIBAR TV TEL
$ Rates (including half board): 255F–415F ($186.10–$302.90) single; 410F–730F
($299.25–$532.85) double. AE, DC, V. **Closed:** Apr–July and Sept–Dec.
This modern hotel is the incarnation of the original Arosa Kulm Hotel, a simple
guesthouse built here in 1882. The hotel is surrounded by rushing streams and hills,
and the indoor swimming pool has panoramic mountain views, as do most of the
bedrooms. The decor combines warm tones, pine paneling, and comfortable
furnishings. Low season is in summer, in January, and from mid-March. High season
is February and Easter, and at Christmas prices go even higher than those mentioned
above.
   Dining/Entertainment: The hotel offers rustic restaurants, a Weinstube, and
nightclubs with a sophisticated clientele.
   Services: Room service, laundry.
   Facilities: Outdoor tennis courts, heated swimming pool; a wide range of fitness,
massage, and cosmetic programs.

HOTEL PARK, CH-7050 Arosa. Tel. 081/31-01-65. Fax 081/31-44-74. 158
rms (all with bath). MINIBAR TV TEL
$ Rates (including half board): 200F–300F ($146–$218.95) single; 400F–600F
($291.95–$437.95) double. AE, DC, MC, V. **Parking:** Free. **Closed:** May–Nov.
The giant rectangular shape of this luxury five-star hotel has a richly decorated interior
filled with velvet and leather, intimate lighting, and the aura of comfort. The indoor
pool has a panoramic view of the snow-covered Alps, and the bedrooms are richly
upholstered in corduroys, velvets, and brocades.
   Dining/Entertainment: On the premises you'll find a bowling alley, pinball
machines, a disco, an intimately lit bar, and several restaurants.
   Services: Bus service to ski lifts, room service, laundry service.
   Facilities: Indoor tennis court, two squash courts, a swimming pool, two saunas,
a whirlpool, massage and cosmetic treatments.

TSCHUGGEN GRAND HOTEL, CH-7050 Arosa. Tel. 081/31-02-21. Fax
081/31-41-75. 145 rms, 4 suites. MINIBAR TV TEL
$ Rates (including half board): 200F–295F ($146–$215.30) single; 370F–710F

($270.05–$518.25) double; from 990F ($722.60) suite. No credit cards. **Closed:** Summer.

⭐ The modern high-rise could be in the pages of *Architectural Digest,* with its potted palms, distressed tortoise-shell wallpaper, and brass-framed mirrors. It's one of the most glamorous hotels in the Swiss Alps. The rooms are handsomely decorated and beautifully kept. Each week, there are two *soirées élégantes,* for which evening dress is compulsory. The winter season starts at the first of December, with Arosa's traditional ski weeks, and continues until the end of March.

Dining/Entertainment: The intimate Bündnerstube is filled with festive guests. For meals, try the Restaurant Français or the panoramic roof-garden restaurant. There's also a dancing room with an orchestra.

Services: Massage, room service, laundry service.

Facilities: Penthouse indoor swimming pool with outside terrace, sauna, suntan salon, ski shop, bowling center, hairdressing salon, kindergarten with nurse.

EXPENSIVE

GOLFHOTEL HOF MARAN, CH-7050 Arosa. Tel. 081/81-01-85. Fax 081/81-45-28. 65 rms (all with bath). MINIBAR TV TEL

$ Rates (including half board): Summer, 130F–180F ($94.90–$131.40) single; 250F–350F ($182.50–$255.45) double. Winter, 160F–220F ($116.80–$160.60) single; 300F–420F ($218.95–$306.55) double. AE, DC, MC, V.

Set high in an alpine meadow, away from the center of downtown Arosa, this mountain chalet is rustically decorated with beamed ceilings, carpeting in autumnal colors, and comfortable armchairs. Many of the bedrooms have balconies suitable for year-round tanning. All accommodations have radios.

Dining/Entertainment: The hotel has a nightclub and a good restaurant serving both regional and international specialties.

Services: Transportation to the town center and ski lifts.

Facilities: Two tennis courts with an on-the-spot tennis pro; well-marked mountain trails; skating rink; nine-hole golf course.

HOHE PROMENADE, CH-7050 Arosa. Tel. 081/31-26-51. Fax 081/31-44-04. 38 rms (all with bath). MINIBAR TV TEL

$ Rates (including half board): Summer, 100F–125F ($73–$91.25) single; 186F–256F ($135.75–$186.85) double. Winter, 120F–150F ($87.60–$109.50) single; 220F–280F ($160.60–$204.35) double. No credit cards. **Closed:** Apr–June and Sept–Dec.

This eight-story, balconied hotel looks down over a valley surrounded by jagged mountains. The center of Arosa is 5 minutes away on foot, but some of the ski lifts are even closer. The bedrooms have tile bathrooms and radios, and the restaurant is decorated with wood beams. The hotel is owned by the Ackermann family.

HOTEL EDEN, CH-7050 Arosa. Tel. 081/31-02-61. Fax 081/31-40-66. 83 rms (all with bath). MINIBAR TEL

$ Rates (including continental breakfast): 105F–147F ($76.65–$107.30) single; 198F–278F ($144.50–$202.90) double. AE, DC, MC, V. **Closed:** Apr–Dec.

The Hotel Eden, in the center of Arosa, is surrounded by pine trees, near the cable car and ski lift. It has five floors of weathered balconies and sun-streaked planking over white walls. The public rooms have marble floors, Oriental rugs, hanging lamps, and wall-to-wall carpeting. Each of the spacious bedrooms has a radio (a TV is available upon request); the rooms with southern exposure have balconies. High season is from

December 17 to January 9 and February 4 to March 11. Write to the Leu family well in advance for reservations.

Dining/Entertainment: There's a piano bar with live music; only breakfast is served.

Services: Room service, laundry.

Facilities: Covered skating rink, ski school, heated whirlpool, fitness room, children's playroom.

HOTEL EXCELSIOR, CH-7050 Arosa. Tel. 081/31-16-61. Fax 081/31-16-64. 102 rms (all with bath). MINIBAR TV TEL

$ Rates (including half board): 140F–210F ($102.20–$153.30) single; 270F–400F ($197.05–$291.95) double. No credit cards. **Closed:** Apr–Dec.

Set in a quiet neighborhood near the center of town, this modern hotel blends attractively into the conifer-dotted lawn surrounding it and has a series of cantilevered balconies above wall-sized panoramic windows. Each accommodation contains comfortable furnishings. There's a wide price difference between rooms with and without southern exposure and balconies. The most expensive rates are charged over Christmas and New Year's, when a minimum stay of 14 days is required.

Dining/Entertainment: The hotel has a cozy Weinstube, plus a restaurant and a bar with a dance floor and live music. Oscar Rederer, the owner, offers a farmer's buffet on Tuesday and a gala dinner on Thursday. The Bündnerstübli serves à la carte Swiss specialties.

Services: Room service, laundry service.

Facilities: Swimming pool.

HOTEL PANORAMA RAETIA, CH-7050 Arosa. Tel. 081/31-02-41. 58 rms (all with bath). TV TEL

$ Rates (including half board): 110F–150F ($80.30–$109.50) single; 220F–300F ($160.60–$218.95) double. AE, DC, MC, V. **Closed:** Apr–Dec. **Parking:** Free.

These hillside chalets overlook the main street of Arosa. Some consider this tasteful hotel to have the best location in the resort. The main salon has panoramic views of the Alps. The rooms are comfortably furnished.

Dining/Entertainment: The Panorama Restaurant has a good view (as its name suggests) and serves excellent Swiss and continental food. The Grill Restaurant serves a creative à la carte cuisine. The Bündnerstube offers such regional dishes as cheese fondue. There is a bar with a red-tile dance floor.

Services: Room service, laundry service.

Facilities: Parking spaces.

SPORTHOTEL VLASANA, CH-7050 Arosa. Tel. 081/31-02-75. Fax 081/31-41-59. 138 rms (all with bath). MINIBAR TV TEL

$ Rates (including half board): Summer, 127F–177F ($92.70–$125.55) single; 230F–320F ($167.90–$233.55) double. Winter, 164F–220F ($119.70–$293.40) double. No credit cards. **Closed:** Apr–June and Oct–Dec.

This comfortably renovated hotel has arched windows, five tiers of balconies, and an interior that's usually flooded with sunlight during good weather. It's conveniently located for cross-country skiers, hikers, and downhill racers. Each room has wood trim and colorful accents of Grisons-style sgraffito, as well as a radio and safe-deposit box. Both the owners and the clientele, as the hotel's name implies, tend to be athletic and spend most of their days outdoors.

Dining/Entertainment: An intimately lit bar has a coffered ceiling and pine walls and often provides live musicians. The hotel also has an attractive restaurant and a Weinstube with roughly hewn walls.

Services: Kindergarten, laundry service.

Facilities: Four tennis courts, an outdoor and indoor pool, sauna and massage facilities, a children's playground.

WALDHOTEL-NATIONAL HOTEL, CH-7050 Arosa. Tel. 081/31-13-51.
Fax 081/31-32-10. 162 rms (all with bath). TV TEL

$ Rates (including half board) Summer, 167F–233F ($121.90–$170.05) single; 275F–385F ($200.70–$281) double. Winter, 190F–266F ($138.70–$194.15) single; 320F–448F ($233.55–$327) double. AE, DC, V. **Closed:** Apr–June and Sept–Dec.

Set in a forest, this generously proportioned and comfortable hotel was designed with symmetrical wings extending from a central core. In the public rooms, accessories include apricot-colored stencils decorating the arched ceilings, a beautifully carved and embellished booth resembling a church pulpit, and decorative ovens sheathed in ceramic tiles. The bedrooms are comfortably and attractively furnished, with a price level that is determined by the view.

Dining/Entertainment: The hotel has a beautifully paneled restaurant, with weekly parties and dinners for guests.

Services: Room service, laundry service.

Facilities: Heated swimming pool, massage and stress-reduction treatments, chair lift and cable car.

MODERATE

HOTEL ALPENSONNE, CH-7050 Arosa. Tel. 081/31-15-47. Fax 081/31-34-70. 40 rms (all with bath). MINIBAR TEL

$ Rates (including half board): Summer, 98F–128F ($71.55–$93.45) single; 184F–257F ($134.30–$187.60) double. Winter, 118F–145F ($86.15–$105.85) single; 224F–310F ($163.50–$286.25) double. V. **Closed:** May.

Five floors of well-proportioned, chalet-style comfort make this small hotel worth trying. In the middle of Arosa near the ski lifts, it offers panoramic views from many of the bedrooms. Each of them is clean and simple, with white stucco walls partially sheathed in planks of knotty pine. Some contain TV. The hotel, operated by the Bareit family, has a dining room and a restaurant.

HOTEL CENTRAL, CH-7050 Arosa. Tel. 081/31-02-52. Fax 081/31-42-71. 72 rms (all with bath). MINIBAR TV TEL

$ Rates (including half board): Summer, 89F–124F ($64.95–$90.50) single; 180F–252F ($131.40–$183.95) double. Winter, 114F–159F ($83.20–$116.05) single; 228F–319F ($166.40–$232.85) double. AE, DC, MC, V.

This quiet and unpretentious hotel occupies one end of a large architectural complex a short walk from the train station. Many of the comfortable bedrooms have balconies crafted from weathered wood and are attractively furnished with a collection of upholstered settees and wooden chalet chairs. There is a collection of antique pewter in the wood-paneled restaurant. In the summer guests enjoy the view from the terrace. A fitness center with exercise machines, whirlpool, and sauna offers relaxation to guests who come here to climb hills or ski. Andy Abplanalp, Jr., the helpful owner, often organizes mountain picnics and excursions. Christmas is the high season.

HOTEL STREIFF, CH-7050 Arosa. Tel. 081/31-11-17. Fax 081/31-29-92. 58 rms (40 with bath). TEL

$ **Rates** (including half board): Summer, 70F–98F ($51.10–$71.55) single without bath, 94F–130F ($68.60–$94.90) single with bath; 128F–178F ($93.45–$129.92) double without bath, 180F–252F ($131.40–$183.95) double with bath. Winter, 80F–112F ($58.40–$81.75) single without bath, 108F–150F ($78.85–$109.50) single with bath; 160F–220F ($116.80–$160.60) double without bath, 208F–290F ($151.80–$211.65) double with bath. No credit cards.

Away from the main street, but still centrally located, this hotel is set off from the road by a narrow but attractive series of terraced gardens. Trails, cable cars, and chair and ski lifts are all nearby. Mr. and Mrs. Christen Streiff provide radios in all the comfortably furnished and snug bedrooms.

INEXPENSIVE

HOTEL ALPINA, CH-7050 Arosa. Tel. 081/31-16-58. Fax 081/31-37-52. 35 rms (all with bath). TEL
$ **Rates** (including half board): Summer, 85F–120F ($62.05–$87.60) single; 170F–240F ($124.10–$175.20) double. Winter, 100F–130F ($73–$94.90) single; 200F–260F ($146–$189.75) double. AE, DC, MC, V. **Closed:** May and Nov.
Finally, I've found a budget hotel in Arosa that looks from the outside like the type of old-fashioned chalet one always associates with Switzerland. The balconies have hand-carved railings and trimwork. There's a terraced garden, and near the entrance a Swiss flag flaps in the mountain breeze. My favorite room is up under the eaves. All the bedrooms have flowered wallpaper. The public rooms are filled with furniture painted in alpine designs, baroque clocks, and Voltaire-style chairs and couches.

HOTEL MERKUR, CH-7050 Arosa. Tel. 081/31-16-66. Fax 081/31-45-61. 52 rms (40 with bath). TEL
$ **Rates** (including half board): Summer, 95F ($69.35) single without bath, 135F ($98.55) single with bath; 180F ($131.40) double without bath, 255F ($186.10) double with bath. Winter, 110F ($80.30) single without bath, 150F ($109.50) single with bath; 215F ($156.95) double without bath, 295F ($215.30) double with bath. No credit cards. **Closed:** May and Nov.
Hans Tobler's charming, family-run hotel is next to a bus stop in the middle of the village. Some of the soundproof bedrooms have white pine boards, balconies, and mountain views. All rooms have radios. The pine-paneled restaurant serves regional à la carte meals in the summer. In the winter hotel guests have candlelight meals in the rôtisserie.

VETTER, CH-7050 Arosa. Tel. 081/31-17-02. 28 rms (15 with bath). TEL
$ **Rates** (including half board): 66F–90F ($48.15–$65.70) single without bath; 124F–173F ($90.50–$126.25) double without bath, 143F–200F ($104.40–$146) double with bath. No credit cards. **Closed:** May and Nov.

Centrally located, a few steps from the railroad station, this hotel offers glassed-in verandas, open porches, and wooden balconies. The interior is a mix of wrought iron and wood beams, enlivened by pithy bits of wisdom stenciled in German above a masonry fireplace. Everything is clean and comfortable. Many of the accommodations lack a private bath; hallway facilities, however, are adequate.

WHERE TO DINE

Most guests book into the Arosa resort hotels on a board basis. Nearly all the major restaurants are in hotels—hence the shortage of well-known independent dining spots. However, if you can break away from your hotel for a main meal, you may want to try the cuisine at one of the places cited below.

ARVEN RESTAURANT AND CHAMANNA, in the Hotel Merkur. Tel. 31-16-66.

Cuisine: SWISS. **Reservations:** Recommended.

$ Prices: Appetizers 12F–16F ($8.75–$11.70); main courses 22F–36F ($16.05–$26.30). No credit cards.

Open: Arvan, lunch daily 11:30am–2pm; dinner daily 6:30–9:30pm. Chamanna, dinner daily (winter only) 6:30–9:30pm. **Closed:** May and Nov.

⭐ Most critics consider these two cozy eateries in the Hotel Merkur among the five or six best restaurants in the resort. The more formal Chamanna Rôtisserie—with its coffered ceiling and half-timbers—offers basically the same menu as the Arven but is open only for dinner in ski season. Lunch at the Arven is usually uncrowded, because most skiers are out on the slopes. You might begin with escargots or spaghetti carbonara, then move on to lamb medallions in mustard sauce, flounder meunière, grilled scampi, or trout. In the winter you might order the filet goulash Stroganoff or the cheese fondue.

CHEZ ANDRE, in the Hotel Central. Tel. 31-15-13.

Cuisine: SWISS. **Reservations:** Recommended.

$ Prices: Appetizers 10F–15F ($7.30–$10.95); main courses 20F–35F ($14.60–$25.55); fixed-price meals 28F ($20.45) at lunch, 42F ($30.65) at dinner. AE, DC, MC, V.

Open: Lunch daily 11:30am–2pm; dinner daily 5:30–10pm.

This centrally located restaurant is one of the best in Arosa. Customers may have drinks in the modern bar before dining in one of two pine-sheathed dining rooms. A typical meal might begin with either filet of smoked trout or artichoke stuffed with goose liver, followed by grilled brochette of scampi, veal piccata with Emmenthal, beefsteak tartare, or a robustly seasoned filet of veal. Occasional gourmet menus are also featured.

THE GRILL ROOM, in the Arosa Kulm Hotel. Tel. 31-01-31.

Cuisine: SWISS. **Reservations:** Required.

$ Prices: Appetizers 15F–18F ($10.95–$13.15); main courses 24F–38F ($17.50–$27.75); menu gastronomique 95F ($69.35). AE, DC, V.

Open: Dinner only, daily 7–10pm. **Closed:** Apr–July and Sept–Dec.

This inner room of the Kulm Hotel is one of the most stylish restaurants in Arosa. An all-black room with a single horizontal red stripe, the restaurant has a Japanese simplicity. A piano and violin provide live music for dancing. The modern French menu changes frequently, according to the availability of the seasonal ingredients. You might begin with a half lobster stuffed with caviar, sweetbreads braised with flap mushrooms and served in puff pastry, or medallions of roebuck with juniper berries. There is an elaborate array of desserts.

STÜVA (Trattoria Toscana). Tel. 31-03-31.

Cuisine: SWISS. **Reservations:** Required.

$ Prices: Appetizers 10F–15F ($7.30–$10.95); main courses 18F–28F ($13.15–$20.45). AE, V.

Open: Lunch daily 11am–2pm; dinner daily 6pm–midnight. **Closed:** Apr to mid-Dec.

This log building belongs to the nearby Kulm Hotel, but it takes its true flavor from its managers, Armando Solaro and Raffaelo Limone. Mr. Solaro worked for several years as the personal chef of the Aga Khan—an experience that helps him serve his international clientele. The restaurant is within a few steps of the Inner-Arosa Tschuggen chair lift, near the top of the village. One side of the cozy room overlooks the spectator seats around one of the village's ice-skating rinks. In sunny weather, you can dine outside. The daube de boeuf specialty is marinated for a full day before it's served with spinach and fresh vegetables. Other continental specialties are also well prepared.

EVENING ENTERTAINMENT

Since many guests come to Arosa only for the après-ski activities, the action often continues until the morning hours. Arosa has the usual run of taverns, pubs, and piano bars. A visit to any of these can be preceded, in the winter, with a horse-drawn sleigh ride along the famous Arlenwald Road. Inquire at the tourist office for details.

KURSAAL. Tel. 31-21-15.

At the Kursaal you'll find, clustered under one roof, a **casino** (the highest bet legally permitted is 5F, $3.65), an **Espresso Bar,** an Italian restaurant called **Da Giancarlo,** and a **disco** named Nuts. The Kursaal is open daily: the Espresso Bar, from 9pm to 3am; Da Giancarlo, from 11pm to 3am; and Nuts, from 9pm to 2am. Drinks run 13F ($9.50), and meals begin at 50F ($36.50).

Admission: Free.

AROSA KULM HOTEL. Tel. 31-01-31.

The Kulm hotel houses several nightspots. The Tavern is the least formal of its restaurants, sought out by skiers after a day on the slopes. Best of all for a change of pace there are two bowling alleys, set off in an isolated corner. Most customers however, come to drink. The **Tavern** serves fondue, raclette, selections from a salad bar, roast beef, and beer. The stylish and sometimes overcrowded **Kulm Night Club** is one floor below the reception desk. There's almost always a live band.

The hotel's **Espresso Bar/Conditorei** serves some of the most elaborate pastries in town. Live musicians, often a Hungarian violinist and pianist, play from 3 to 5pm daily in the winter. A slice of some kind of confection may cost 3.50F ($2.55) and more, accompanied by a steaming mug of coffee or hot chocolate.

The Tavern is open daily from 5pm to 2am; the Kulm Night Club, daily from 9pm until dawn; and the Espresso Bar/Conditorei, daily from 8am to 6pm. Drinks cost about 20F ($14.60); beer is 13F ($9.50).

HOTEL PARK. Tel. 31-01-65.

The Hotel Park is another lively spot in peak season. The manager likes to keep his guests entertained, and throughout the winter he stages gala dinners, raclette or fondue parties, Bauern (peasant) buffets, a festival du poisson with a splendid offering of fish, and what is called a "spaghettata." You'll have to call to see what's happening and to make a reservation.

POSTHOTEL. Tel. 31-01-21.

Jacques Rudisser's **Fondue and Raclettekeller** is especially popular in the winter; its specialties include fondue vaudoise, valaisanne, chinoise, and bourguignonne. Another option is the **Pizzeria da Giacomo** for pizzas and pastas, with meals costing 38F ($27.75) and up. Or you might choose the rustically alpine **Post Stübli** or stick around for dinner at the **Restaurant Post** or at the Chinese restaurant, **Peking.** Finally, you may end your night by dancing to live music in the **Postbar.** Open from 5pm. Fondue costs 22F ($16.05), and drinks run about 12F ($8.75).

SPORTHOTEL VALSANA, Tel. 31-02-75.

If the night is right and your companions are compatible, this can be a lively and gregarious spot. A lovely bar and dance floor lie between harlequin-painted columns. There's a stage for the presentation of live music (every evening after 8pm). Drinks are 12F ($8.75); beer, 5F ($3.65).

---

3. KLOSTERS

8 miles N of Davos, 27 miles E of Chur, 18 miles E of Landquart

GETTING THERE By Train There are frequent express trains between Zurich and the railway junction at Landquart. From Landquart, connecting trains depart about once an hour for Klosters on secondary rail lines.

By Car From Zurich, head south on the N3 expressway until you reach Landquart, at which point you cut southeast along Route 28.

ESSENTIALS The **Klosters Tourist Board,** in the center of town (tel. 081/69-18-77), is open Monday through Saturday from 8am to noon and 2 to 6pm. The **telephone area code** for Klosters is 081. Some roads in the center have **street names;** others outside the town do not, but establishments can easily be found by following directional signs.

Life at this 4,000-foot-high village in the Prattigau Valley has changed greatly from the time that a cloister was founded here in 1222. Many visitors prefer the intimacy and hospitality of Klosters to the more touristlike atmosphere of Davos. Unlike some of its neighbors (most notably St. Moritz), Klosters has few unattractive structures. All its buildings are constructed in the chalet style, giving the town a pleasing architectural harmony. Local residents claim that the popular sport of tobogganing originated here.

The main road to Davos runs through Klosters, and the two resorts have been known to compete aggressively for the tourist business. Famous past visitors include Sir Arthur Conan Doyle and Robert Louis Stevenson, who is said to have finished *Treasure Island* here. In the heyday of tax benefits, Klosters became known as "Hollywood on the Rocks." It still attracts an international crowd of movie people, likely to include Gore Vidal, Gene Kelly, and Kirk Douglas. It has also been given a royal seal of approval by the king and queen of Sweden, who visit regularly; but invariably generating more publicity are Prince Charles and Lady Diana, who have made it their favorite resort.

GETTING AROUND A city bus, **bus A,** makes frequent runs from Klosters-Dorf (the railroad station) to the base of the town's ski lifts, passing virtually every building in town on the way.

WHAT TO SEE & DO

Some of the finest downhill skiing in the world is here, with slopes for beginners as well as for the most advanced skiers. A kindergarten will look after the very young while you hit the slopes. The most populous part of Klosters is centered around the railway station and is called **Klosters-Platz** (square). A smaller, less populated neighborhood (site of the resort's excellent ski school) lies about a mile to the north and is called **Klosters-Dorf** (village).

The region contains two principal areas for skiing or hiking, the more popular of which is the **Gotschna-Parsenn.** To reach it, board the Gotschnagrat cableway in Klosters-Platz; the cable car carries more than 50 skiers up to the 7,545-foot Gotschnagrat elevation. In the peak season, especially around February, expect lines of passengers awaiting a ride up. A series of cableways, a chair lift, and 18 ski lifts hook up with the Davos-Parsenn skiing areas, where your highest point will be Weissflühgipfel (9,260 ft.). The Parsenn area enjoys world renown and has some of the longest runs in Europe. It offers more than 14 different cableways and ski lifts, plus more than 85 miles of well-kept runs.

The other major area, **Madrisa,** dates from the 1960s. To reach it, you go to Dorf via a bus, which leaves from Klosters-Platz every 30 minutes. From Dorf, the Klosters–Albeina gondola will take you to a height of 6,323 feet. Then by drag lift, known as the Schaffüggli, you rise to 7,850 feet.

Nontransferable Rega (season) tickets are priced according to the number of days you plan to ski.

Horse sleighing, curling, and **skating** are popular sports for those who don't ski. Ask at the tourist office about the various venues for these activities.

In the summer, Klosters is in the center of fine **hiking** grounds. The Madrisa and Gotschna-Parsenn cable cars will carry you to starting points on both sides of the valley for hikes on well-marked trails through woods and alpine meadows. In Klosters you can enjoy tennis, squash, and swimming in a heated pool.

WHERE TO STAY

VERY EXPENSIVE

HOTEL PARDENN, Monbielerstrasse, CH-7250 Klosters. Tel. 081/69-11-41. Fax 081/69-40-06. 75 rms (all with bath). MINIBAR TV TEL
$ Rates (including half board): Summer, 170F–210F ($124.10–$153.30) single; 320F–400F ($233.55–$291.95) double. Winter, 190F–240F ($138.70–$175.20)

MOUNTAIN EMERGENCIES

If hikers or skiers are injured or stranded in the mountains or on the slopes, their companions should immediately go for assistance. Local residents know whom to call in an emergency, but here are some emergency telephone numbers for the region:

Parsenn Rescue Service, Lehenweg 7, Klosters (tel. 67-33-93).
Weissflühjoch first-aid station (tel. 46-38-01).
Branabuel/Jakobshor Rescue Service first-aid station (tel. 43-59-59).
Rinerhorn first-aid station (tel. 49-12-58).
Ski-route SOS telephones: Pischa (tel. 46-17-28), Strela (tel. 42-67-57), and Gotschna (tel. 69-13-91).

single; 360F–460F ($262.75–$335.75) double. AE, DC, MC, V. **Closed:** May and Nov.

This rambling, modern structure has hosted the Princess of Wales and her children. The terrace overlooks the well-landscaped lawn. Inside is a green-marble circular staircase. Many accommodations have pine paneling, while others contain flowery carpets and Louis XV–style armchairs.

Dining/Entertainment: The restaurant features a central grill with a copper chimney.

Services: Room service, laundry.

Facilities: Sauna, massage facilities, indoor swimming pool.

PIZ BUIN HOTEL, Alte Bahnhofstrasse 1, CH-7250 Klosters. Tel. 081/ 69-81-11. Fax 081/69-51-01. 53 rms (all with bath). MINIBAR TEL TV

$ **Rates** (including half board): Summer, 170F–240F ($124.10–$175.20) single; 310F–400F ($226.25–$291.95) double. Winter, 240F–315F ($175.20–$229.90) single; 350F–490F ($255.45–$357.65) double. AE, MC, V.

This five-star hotel is the most modern and elegant one in Klosters. It's located in the heart of the village, just a stroll away from the Gotschna lift, which takes you straight to the skiing and hiking area of Parsenn. The hotel, built in 1984, is designed like a chalet. The large yet cozy rooms are all equipped with two beds and a balcony.

Dining/Entertainment: The hotel's three restaurants offer modern, vegetarian, and typical Swiss menus. You can also entertain yourself at the house bar and the Funny Place dance club.

Services: Room service, laundry.

Facilities: Swimming pool, whirlpool, sauna, solarium, gym room, massage and cosmetic treatments, and eucalyptus, Kneipp, and Turkish baths.

EXPENSIVE

CHESA GRISCHUNA, Bahnhofstrasse 12, CH-7250 Klosters. Tel. 081/ 69-22-22. 27 rms (all with bath). MINIBAR TV TEL

$ **Rates** (including half board): 170F–195F ($124.10–$142.35) single; 320F–380F ($233.55–$277.35) double. AE, DC, MC, V.

Closed: Mid-Apr to early June.

Set behind a lavishly decorated facade and rebuilt in 1938 on the foundation of a much older building, this four-star hotel has hosted some of the most illustrious personalities of Europe. The hotel is really famous for its chic restaurant, although its cozy, pine bedrooms are worth mentioning as well. The overflow from the main house is lodged at a comfortable annex nearby. In the summer the Guler family hangs flower boxes from almost every horizontal surface of the hotel. See "Where to Dine," below, for a recommendation of its restaurant.

Services: Room service, baby-sitting, laundry.

Facilities: Comfortable modern annex for overflow guests.

SILVRETTA PARKHOTEL, CH-7250 Klosters. Tel. 081/69-61-21. Fax 081/69-23-23. 160 rms (all with bath). MINIBAR TV TEL

$ **Rates** (including half board): Summer, 150F ($109.50) single; 280F ($204.35) double. Winter, 170F ($124.10) single; 320F ($233.55) double. AE, DC, MC, V.

This four-star hotel opened in 1990, opposite Silvretta Park with its cross-country ski runs and ice rink for skating, hockey, and curling. It's within walking distance of the Gotschna lift connecting the Parsenn skiing area with Klosters. Designed in a typical

Swiss-chalet style, it offers modern rooms in a rustic style. Amenities include a safe and a balcony or terrace.

Dining/Entertainment: The Stübli has a cozy Swiss atmosphere and serves regional specialties; the Rôtisserie offers gourmet specialties. There is also a piano bar, as well as a nightclub.

Services: Massage, hairdresser.

Facilities: Health center, swimming pool, sauna, Turkish sauna, whirlpool.

HOTEL WALSERHOF, CH-7250 Klosters. Tel. 081/69-42-42. Fax 081/69-14-37. 21 rms (all with bath). MINIBAR TV TEL
$ Rates (including half board): 155F–195F ($113.10–$142.35) single; 290F–350F ($211.65–$255.45) double. AE, DC, MC, V. **Parking:** Free.

This modern chalet, about a quarter of a mile north of the town center, was built in 1981 and quickly gained a reputation for charm and comfort. Its stylish rooms have pine furniture and a marble-lined bath; many have a balcony.

Dining/Entertainment: The restaurant is excellent and attracts famous customers (see "Where to Dine," below).

Services: Room service, laundry.

Facilities: Parking spaces.

MODERATE

HOTEL RUSTICO, CH-7250 Klosters. Tel. 081/69-12-93. Fax 081/69-49-06. 25 rms (all with bath). TV TEL
$ Rates (including half board): 80F–98F ($58.40–$71.55) single; 158F–196F ($115.30–$143.05) double. DC, MC, V. **Closed:** May and Nov.

Located across the river from the busiest part of town, this bargain hotel is run by Marion Theus and Jürg Benkert. Set on a major road, the 120-year-old former private house offers simple rooms and a small restaurant with regional dishes. You can also order vegetarian food here. There is a pool lounge with an open fireplace. The hotel has been known to fill up with tour groups in midwinter. It has a sauna.

HOTEL VEREINA, CH-7250 Klosters. Tel. 081/69-11-61. Fax 081/69-15-39. 120 rms (all with bath). TEL
$ Rates (including half board): Summer, 130F–150F ($94.90–$109.50) single; 220F–290F ($160.60–$211.65) double. Winter, 150F–190F ($109.50–$138.70) single; 300F–380F ($218.95–$277.35) double. AE, DC, MC, V. **Closed:** Mar–June and Sept–Dec.

A favorite in Klosters, owing to the efforts of the owners, Eva and Stephan Diethelm, this stucco palace is crowned with a baroque dome and decorated with arched windows and a mansard roof. It's surrounded by a 2-acre park containing fountains and ornamental trees. The Vereina is close to nearly every sports facility in town and only a few minutes' walk from the railroad station. The rooms are comfortably and attractively furnished; more than two-thirds of them contain a minibar and TV.

Dining/Entertainment: Something's always happening in the pub and the piano bar. A softly lit, elegant restaurant serves fine food and wine. There is also a popular pizzeria, open daily from noon to 2pm and 6 to 11pm, with a guitar player on weekends.

Services: Kindergarten Monday through Friday from 9am to 4pm.

Facilities: Tennis courts, table-tennis tables, children's playground, glass-enclosed swimming pool.

BAD SERNEUS KUR-UND-SPORTHOTEL, CH-7250 Klosters. Tel. 081/69-14-44. Fax 081/69-52-92. 58 rms (all with bath). TV TEL
$ **Rates** (including half board): 98F–120F ($71.55–$87.60) single; 200F–240F ($146–$175.20) double. AE, DC, MC, V. **Closed:** Nov.

This yellow house with black shutters is solidly built and well located. The public rooms have wood beams, regional-style stenciling, and fireplaces. The bedrooms are filled with pine armoires and warm-colored fabrics. The hotel also offers a swimming pool, a sauna, and massage facilities. Many guests stroll in the flower-filled meadow and visit the nearby mineral springs.

HOTEL PENSION BUEL, CH-7242 Klosters-Dorf. Tel. 081/69-26-69. Fax 081/69-49-41. 18 rms (all with bath or shower). TEL
$ **Rates** (including half board): 88F–110F ($64.25–$80.30) single; 140F–180F ($102.20–$131.40) double. No credit cards. **Closed:** Apr–June and Oct–Dec.

This family-run, L-shaped stucco hotel is clean and rustic. The dining room has a knotty-pine ceiling and chalet chairs; one of the sitting rooms has a stone fireplace and a flagstone floor. Your English-speaking host, Walter Hongler, rents out pleasantly furnished rooms.

INEXPENSIVE

HOTEL RUFINIS, Hauptstrasse, CH-7252 Klosters-Dorf. Tel. 081/69-13-71. Fax 081/69-28-02. 8 rms (4 with bath). TEL
$ **Rates:** 25F–45F ($18.25–$32.85) per person, single or double without bath, 44F–70F ($32.10–$51.10) per person, single or double with bath. Breakfast 11F ($8.05) extra. No credit cards.

Near the entrance to the resort, this attractively decorated chalet is owned by Thomas Jost (whose photography has been exhibited throughout the region). In addition to a pleasant restaurant (see "Where to Dine," below), the hotel offers a stone-trimmed terrace flanked by both an outdoor swimming pool and a view of the mountains. It has a lovely English garden as well as a balcony terrace for breakfast. The bedrooms also have great views.

WHERE TO DINE

EXPENSIVE

ALTE POST, Klosters-Aeuja. Tel. 69-17-16.
Cuisine: SWISS. **Reservations:** Required.
$ **Prices:** Appetizers 12F–18F ($8.75–$13.15); main courses 22F–38F ($16.05–$27.75); menu dégustation 85F ($62.05). DC, MC, V.
Open: Lunch Wed–Sun 11:30am–2:30pm; dinner Wed–Sun 6–10pm. **Closed:** Apr–June.

Master chef John M. Ehrat-Flury pampers the palate with regional specialties in this roadside chalet outside town. His secret lies, in part, in the use of fresh ingredients. In the right season, he prepares superb game and fish dishes. Guests dine in the restaurant or the intimate grillroom, in which meats are grilled over an open fire. It's a fun, informal place and has long been a celebrity favorite. Guests enjoy such fare as smoked trout with juniper, suprême of salmon with pink peppercorns, and fresh mushrooms in a nest of homemade noodles.

CHESA GRISCHUNA, Bahnhofstrasse 12. Tel. 69-22-22.
Cuisine: INTERNATIONAL. **Reservations:** Required.

$ Prices: Appetizers 13F–29F ($9.50–$21.15); main courses 35F–49F ($25.55–$35.75); fixed-price meals 32F ($23.35) at lunch, 54F ($39.40) at dinner. AE, DC, MC, V.

Open: Lunch daily noon–2:30pm; dinner daily 7–9:30pm. **Closed:** May.

⭐ This restaurant is so popular that celebrities often book tables a year in advance. Some of its famous patrons have included Truman Capote, Rex Harrison, Audrey Hepburn, the Aga Khan, Winston Churchill, Deborah Kerr, and Queen Juliana of the Netherlands. The restaurant has attractively decorated alpine walls and a scattering of unusual portraits. Part of the reason for its persistent popularity is the warm welcome of the Guler family, and part, certainly, is the food. Specialties include a crêpe suedoise stuffed with shrimp, chicken livers in puff pastry on a bed of leeks, grilled salmon with white butter and tomato sauce, and rack of lamb. In the summer, guests may dine outdoors.

HOTEL WYNEGG RESTAURANT, Landstrasse 205, CH-7250 Klosters. Tel. 081/4-13-40.
Cuisine: SWISS. **Reservations:** Required.

$ Prices: Appetizers 10.50F–18F ($7.65–$13.15); main courses 25F–38F ($18.25–$27.75). AE, MC, V.

Open: Winter, lunch daily noon–2pm; dinner daily 6–10pm. **Closed:** Summer.

Set on the ground floor of a 20-room hotel built in 1878, this restaurant is noted for its kitchens, partly because of the hard work of owner Ruth Guler, the niece of the owner of the prestigious Chesa Grischuna. The hotel came into prominence when Prince Charles arrived here recently, choosing this modest place for a discreet afternoon of drinking with one of his cousins. The establishment—clean, cozy, and straightforward—offers simple but well-prepared meals, which might include local air-dried beef, hearty soups, entrecôtes, and veal steak with Rösti.

The rooms are strictly no-frills, but the half-board price is reasonable: 85F to 95F ($62.05 to $69.35) per person daily.

WALSERSTUBE, in the Walserhof Hotel, Klosters-Platz. Tel. 69-42-42.
Cuisine: SWISS. **Reservations:** Required in peak season.

$ Prices: Appetizers 12F–18F ($8.75–$13.15); main courses 24F–38F ($17.50–$27.75); fixed-price meals 65F ($47.45), 85F ($62.05), and 105F ($76.65). AE, DC, MC, V.

Open: Lunch daily 11am–2pm; dinner daily 6–11pm. **Closed:** Mon June–Nov and Apr–May.

⭐ The Walserstube's Beat Bolliger entertains everybody from celebrities to regular folks. His cuisine is a winning combination of fresh ingredients and the best culinary skills. As you sit under the restaurant's massive wood beams and alpine carvings, you might begin with a duckling foie gras or something less fattening (a yogurt mousse with seasonal fruit). In season, asparagus is featured and prepared in a variety of elegant ways. Lobster appears under soups, and is served with profiteroles. The fish is special here, including salmon with onions, a fricassee of lobster, and trout grilled and served with ratatouille. You can also order excellent meat dishes, among them Scottish lamb seasoned with thyme.

MODERATE

HOTEL RUFINIS, Hauptstrasse, Klosters-Dorf. Tel. 081/4-13-71.
Cuisine: SWISS. **Reservations:** Recommended.

$ Prices: Appetizers 8F–12F ($5.85–$8.75); main courses 14F–40F ($10.20–$29.20). No credit cards.

Open: Lunch daily 11am–2pm; dinner daily 6–10pm. **Closed:** Mon in summer.

This rustic restaurant is in a modern chalet, a 2-minute walk from Madrisa cable car. Nicely presented regional specialties are served by a regionally costumed staff. The restaurant's three rooms are charmingly handcrafted, with exposed wood and stone. You might begin with a salmon terrine, soup, or the salad buffet. Main dishes are likely to feature calves' liver in red wine sauce, veal saltimbocca, tournedos with tarragon sauce, trout with mushrooms and cognac, and the inevitable fondue. Customers may also enjoy excellent ice creams and pastries on the terrace.

EVENING ENTERTAINMENT

It's quite customary for many guests of Klosters hotels to head to nearby Davos for nightlife. Others prefer the more subdued nighttime fun in Klosters itself—a good sampling of bars, taverns, restaurants, and a few nightclubs that stir to life when the season comes and snowflakes fill the air.

BLACK BIRD BAR, in the Hotel Vereina. Tel. 69-13-23.
One of the resort's most popular bars is managed by Armin Kaufmann, a local artist who displays some of his works here. It's not a place for real dancing, but that activity has been known to occur if the spirits are high. If you want a snack, there's an adjoining pizzeria. Open Monday through Saturday from 9pm to 2am. Drinks run 8F ($5.85).

CHESA BAR, in the Hotel Chesa Grischuna, Bahnhofstrasse 12. Tel. 69-22-22.
The fact that this nightspot is immediately below one of the most chic restaurants in all of Switzerland doesn't prevent it from being a lot of fun. Amid walls stenciled with Engadine designs, there's a warm, cozy drinking enclave, where a pianist contributes to the ambience nightly from 5 to 7pm and 9pm to 2am, when the bar closes. The bar has an entrance leading directly from the sidewalk. Drinks cost 12F to 15F ($8.75 to $10.95).

FUNNY PLACE, in the Piz Buin Hotel. Tel. 69-61-01.
This is one of the town's most attractive, electronically sophisticated nightspots. Open from 10pm. Closed in May and November. Drinks run 15F ($10.95).

KIR-ROYAL NIGHT CLUB, in the Silvretta Parkhotel. Tel. 69-61-21.
Young people and others can enjoy the DJ here, along with occasional live bands. There is also a piano bar, with talented international musicians. The bartender mixes generous cocktails—everything from a Sidecar to a creamy brandy Alexander. Open daily from 9pm to 3am. Drinks run 7.50F to 11F ($4.75 to $8.05).
Admission: Free.

---

4. DAVOS

15 miles E of Chur, 7 miles S of Klosters

GETTING THERE   By Train   Trains from Zurich usually require a transfer in the provincial railway junction of either Landquart or Filisur, where secondary rail lines continue on to Davos. Throughout the day, trains travel to Davos from both of these towns every hour. The nearest airport is Zurich's Kloten, but the trip involves three different trains and two transfers. For information about train schedules, call the railroad station (tel. 43-50-50).

By Bus   Bus lines connect Chur with Munich, stopping at Davos and at several other mountain towns along the way, but they usually require transfers.

By Car   Drive to Klosters (see Section 3, above), then continue south on Route 28 to Davos.

ESSENTIALS   The **telephone area code** for Davos is 081. Not all roads in Davos have **street names,** but there are signs pointing the way to all the hotels and restaurants so you'll have no trouble finding your way around. Public **children's playgrounds** are found in the Kurpark in Davos-Platz and opposite the lower terminal station of the Parsenn funicular at Davos-Dorf.

Along with St. Moritz and Zermatt, Davos has some of the finest sports facilities in the world, as well as a diversified choice of après-ski entertainment. The variety of activities makes it a favorite holiday spot for both the chic and wealthy and for the hundreds of ordinary folk just out to have a good time in the mountains.

The name Davos (first Tavauns, later Dafaas) entered written history in 1160 in a document in the episcopal archives of Chur. In 1289 a group of families from the Valais established homes here. In 1649 the town bought its freedom from Austria.

The two sections, Davos-Platz and Davos-Dorf, were once separate entities, but in the past 20 years or so, construction on the land between the two has served to join them, making Davos today somewhat larger than St. Moritz.

The canton of Davos is the second largest in Switzerland. The high valley that contains it is surrounded by forest-covered mountains that shelter it from rough winds. The area thus has a bracing climate, which has proved ideal for a summer-and-winter resort. Davos first entered the world limelight as a health resort in the 19th century, when Dr. Alexander Spengler prescribed mountain air for his tuberculosis patients. He brought the first summer visitors here in 1860 and the first winter ones 5 years later. There are still several sanatoriums in the area.

Thomas Mann used Davos, at the foot of the Zauberberg (Magic Mountain), as the setting for his famous novel *The Magic Mountain.* He saw the resort (when his wife went there briefly in 1913 for her health) as a symbol of the general malaise that afflicted Europe on the eve of World War I. Robert Louis Stevenson wrote the last seven chapters of *Treasure Island* there between 1881 and 1882, as he, too, tended his consumptive wife. Another writer, Sir Arthur Conan Doyle, engaged in a daring run on skis over the Furka Pass to Arosa. (Unfortunately, the much-celebrated villa-hotel where all three writers stayed, Am Stein, contains only private apartments and cannot be visited.)

The German painter Ernst Ludwig Kirchner (1880–1938) lived at Davos from 1917 until his death. He is considered a leading exponent of the expressionist movement.

ORIENTATION

INFORMATION   The **Davos-Dorf tourist office** is at Promenade 67 (tel. 081/43-51-35).

CITY LAYOUT   The town's two sections, **Davos-Platz** (5,118 ft.) and **Davos-Dorf** (5,128 ft.), are linked by a boulevard that is flanked by fashionable boutiques, shops, hotels, and cafés. This thoroughfare is the famous **Promenade,** which takes the one-way traffic flow from Dorf to Platz (beware, however, if you're driving, as buses go in both directions). The lower artery, **Talstrasse,** runs along the railroad tracks, linking the train station in Davos-Platz with the station in Davos-Dorf.

GETTING AROUND

Yellow-and-white **buses** run along the major arteries from Davos-Dorf to Davos-Platz, making scheduled stops near all the main hotels and restaurants. In the winter the buses depart daily every 10 minutes from 7am to 11:20pm; in the summer departures are every 20 minutes. A single ride costs 1.20F (90¢); a book of tickets for 12 rides sells for 12F ($8.75).

The **postal bus** leaves from the Davos-Platz railroad station. Organized excursions are available on the postal buses; for information, go to the nearest post office.

WHAT TO SEE & DO

Among the old buildings to be seen in Davos-Platz are the parish **Church of St. John the Baptist,** with a nave dating from 1280–85. The church, now restored, was completed in 1481. It stands east of the train station along Talstrasse. A window in the choir is by Augusto Giacometti. The adjoining Rathaus (Town Hall) has been extensively restored. Its paneled Grosse Stube (Great Chamber) dates from 1564.

In Davos-Dorf you can see the 14th-century **Church of St. Theodulus.** At Museumstrasse 1 is the **Altes Pfründhaus** (Old Prebend House), the town's only surviving example of a medieval burgher's domicile, now sheltering a local museum.

You don't come to Davos to visit museums, but there is an interesting one on the top floor of the post office, the **Kirchner Museum,** Promenade 43 (tel. 6-64-84). It's devoted to Ernst Ludwig Kirchner, who lived in this part of Switzerland. This leader of the "Brücke" group of expressionists, who gathered in Dresden in 1880, committed suicide in 1938. Entrance to the museum is 4F ($2.90) for adults, 2F ($1.45) for children. In the winter the museum is open Tuesday through Sunday from 4 to 6pm; in May, June, September, and October, it's open on Wednesday, Saturday, and Sunday from 4 to 6pm; in July and August, it's open on Tuesday, Wednesday, Saturday, and Sunday from 4 to 6pm.

SKIING   Recreational skiing began here in 1888, but Davos first appeared on the world sports stage in 1899, when a large ice rink was opened for the world figure-skating and the European speed-skating championship competitions. In the same year the Davos-Schatzalp funicular and the Schatzalp toboggan run were inaugurated. Now Davos is considered one of the best ski regions in the world.

On both sides of the valley, you're faced with five large ski areas, of which the most noted is the ✪ **Parsenn-Weissflüh.** Some experts say this is the finest ski area in Europe. To reach it, you take the Parsennbahn (railway) from Davos-Dorf to **Weissflühjoch** (8,740 ft.), the gateway to the major ski area, with a huge number of runs in every category, especially a few descents leading back to Davos that are suitable for only the most skilled skiers.

From Weissflühjoch, where there is a restaurant, take the cableway to **Weissflühgipfel** (9,260 ft.). It takes about an hour from Davos-Dorf.

From there you can reach the celebrated Kublis run to the north. The inauguration of the Parsenn funicular in 1931 opened up the greatest snowfields in Switzerland.

Davos shares its snow with nearby Klosters, where you can also ski, but cable cars and T-bar lift service may keep you happy with the ski opportunities nearer to Davos. Beginners are advised to stick to Rinerhorn, the Strela slopes, or perhaps Pischa, where, if you're graded "intermediate" by your ski school instructor, you may be directed to Jakobshorn.

OTHER SPORTS   Several winter sports besides skiing are offered here as well. For information on curling, call the **Davos Curling Club,** Promenade 46, Davos-Platz (tel. 43-67-30), or the **Davos-Village Curling Club,** Derby Hotel, Davos-Dorf (tel. 47-11-66). An hour of curling costs 15F ($10.95) per person; you can purchase a season ticket for 120F ($87.60).

If you're interested in ice skating on the   ✪ **Natureisbahn,** Davos-Platz, the largest natural ice rink in Europe, phone 43-73-54. Admission costs 4F ($2.90) for adults, 2.50F ($1.85) for children. Davos-Platz also has a huge artificial ice rink open daily from 9:30am to 4:30pm. These hours could change, so call for more information.

Many Davos sports facilities can be used both in the winter and in the summer, so Davos isn't only for winter holiday crowds. It has first-class **tennis** courts, **sailing** and **windsurfing** on Lake Davos, **swimming,** and **horseback riding.** The wide mountain valleys offer opportunities for walking on about 200 miles of signposted paths. There's an 18-hole **golf** course; for information, call the clubhouse (tel. 46-56-34). There's also a large indoor ice rink if you want to keep your skills and your skates sharp during the summer months.

Davos has an impressive **Tennis & Squash Center** at Clavadelerstrasse (tel. 43-31-31), in Davos-Platz, which is open daily from 7am to 11pm. Prices depend on when you play, day or night. Court rental costs 34F ($24.80) from 4:30 to 9:30pm.

Want to go **swimming**? Call 43-64-63 for information on either indoor swimming in the winter or outdoors swimming in the summer. Adults are charged 4.50F ($3.30), and children pay 3F ($2.20), including changing-room facilities. With use of the mixed sauna included, adults pay 11F ($8.05).

WHERE TO STAY

IN DAVOS-PLATZ

Very Expensive

STEIGENBERGER BELVEDERE, Promenade 89, CH-4270 Davos-Platz. Tel. 081/44-12-81. Fax 081/43-11-71. 146 rms (all with bath). MINIBAR TV TEL

$ Rates (including half board): 230F–270F ($167.90–$197.05) single; 410F–574F ($299.25–$418.95) double. AE, DC, MC, V. **Closed:** Apr 15–May 31 and Oct 15–Dec 1.

✪ This light-gray neoclassical building on the main road of Davos-Platz is a world-famous resort hotel originally built around 1875. It was purchased in the 1980s by the Steigenberger chain, one of the most prestigious in Europe. The beautiful interior has a series of intricately carved fireplaces, ornate ceilings, a well-polished bar, and supremely comfortable contemporary and Victorian arm-

MOUNTAIN EMERGENCIES

If hikers or skiers are injured or stranded in the mountains or on the slopes, their companions should immediately go for assistance. Local residents know whom to call in an emergency, but here are some emergency telephone numbers for the region:

Parsenn Rescue Service, Lehenweg 7, Klosters (tel. 67-33-93).
Weissflühjoch first-aid station (tel. 46-38-01).
Branabuel/Jakobshor Rescue Service first-aid station (tel. 43-59-59).
Rinerhorn first-aid station (tel. 49-12-58).
Ski-route SOS telephones: Pischa (tel. 46-17-28), Strela (tel. 42-67-57), and Gotschna (tel. 69-13-91).

chairs. Guests have a choice of modern, Belle Epoque, or regionally decorated rooms, many with furniture crafted from a local wood called *Arvenholz*. It's worth visiting the pool for the beautiful murals even if you don't swim; a Tahitian lagoon with flamingoes and lifelike jungle plants sway in the imaginary breeze, and seem to grow right out of the pool.

Dining/Entertainment: The hotel's elegant main dining room, the Belvedere, serves local and international specialties. The hotel bar presents live entertainment nightly. During the peak winter season the hotel opens its Italian specialty restaurant, Romeo and Julia.

Services: Laundry, baby-sitting, room service, hairdresser, masseur.
Facilities: Indoor pool, massage and sauna facilities, clay tennis courts.

Expensive

**CENTRAL SPORTHOTEL, Promenade, CH-7270 Davos-Platz. Tel. 081/
44-11-81.** Fax 081/43-52-12. 92 rms (all with bath). MINIBAR TV TEL **Bus:** To stop 10.
$ Rates (including half board): Summer, 85F–105F ($62.05–$76.65) single; 150F–195F ($109.50–$142.35) double. Winter, 185F–230F ($135.05–$167.90) single; 320F–410F ($233.55–$299.25) double. AE, DC, MC, V. **Parking:** 8F ($5.85).
This rambling, 19th-century hotel with a white-and-gray exterior was built in what looks like several different styles. Most of the spacious accommodations have wooden balconies, large windows, and cabriole-legged armchairs and settees.

Dining/Entertainment: The disco—one of the liveliest in town—is in a dark-wood room with regional designs. Guests dine in the wood-paneled Bündnerstübli or in the regional restaurant. There is also a piano bar.

Services: Room service, laundry.
Facilities: Swimming pool, sauna.

HOTEL EUROPE, Promenade, CH-7270 Davos-Platz. Tel. 081/43-59-21.
Fax 081/43-13-92. 82 rms (all with bath). MINIBAR TV TEL **Bus:** To stop 10.
$ Rates (including half board): Summer, 110F–132F ($80.30–$96.35) single; 200F–244F ($146–$178.10) double. Winter, 190F–225F ($138.70–$164.25) single; 340F–430F ($248.15–$313.85) double. AE, DC, MC, V.

This longtime favorite is near the tourist office and the Schatzalp-Strela funicular. It was built in 1868, and is thus the oldest of the resort's big hotels. In 1914 it became the Kurhaus health spa, and later it was the Palace Hotel. The present building, which has been called the Hotel Europe since 1956, is a flat-roofed, white stucco structure. The formal interior is decorated with Oriental rugs and hunting trophies, and the renovated bedrooms are well furnished.

Dining/Entertainment: The dining room, with its polished paneling and hunting trophies, has a distinctive ambience. The bar has a dance floor and offers live music.

Services: Room service, laundry.

Facilities: Indoor swimming pool, fitness room, sauna, outdoor tennis court.

KONGRESS HOTEL DAVOS, Promenade 94, CH-7270 Davos-Platz. Tel. 081/47-11-81. Fax 081/46-48-61. 102 rms (all with bath). MINIBAR TV TEL **Bus:** To stop 10.

$ Rates (including half board): Summer, 97F–112F ($70.80–$81.75) single; 170F–200F ($124.10–$146) double. Winter, 160F–180F ($116.80–$131.40) single; 290F–330F ($211.65–$240.85) double. No credit cards. **Closed:** Apr–June and Oct–Dec.

This first-class hotel is a bit far from the center of town. Most guests, however, are willing to sacrifice proximity for the view. The hotel, which opened in 1982, is inside the Convention Center of Davos, in the same building as the indoor swimming pool complex. Virtually all the sports facilities of Davos are close by. In addition, a public bus stops in front of the hotel for frequent rides to the ski runs. The bedrooms are smartly furnished, with radios. The hotel is managed by the Frey family.

Dining/Entertainment: The hotel has a good restaurant, serving both regional and continental specialties. There is also a bar.

Services: Room service, laundry.

Facilities: Sauna, garage, parking lot.

MOROSANI POSTHOTEL, Promenade 42, CH-7270 Davos-Platz. Tel. 081/44-11-61. Fax 081/43-16-47. 90 rms (all with bath). MINIBAR TV TEL **Bus:** To stop 9.

$ Rates (including half board): Summer, 95F–133F ($69.35–$97.10) single; 188F–263F ($137.20–$191.95) double. Winter, 180F–234F ($131.40–$170.80) single; 336F–436F ($245.25–$318.25) double. AE, DC, MC, V. **Closed:** May and Nov.

Set at the gateway to the Promenade in Davos-Platz, this landmark has been efficiently run for more than a century by the Morosani family. The hotel consists of three buildings connected by means of a rustically decorated underground tunnel. The cozy lobby has an open fireplace, and each room has a radio, along with other amenities. From Christmas to New Year's, the hotel requires a minimum stay of 12 nights.

Dining/Entertainment: The hotel has a restaurant and a bar. It even has a resident orchestra.

Services: Room service, laundry.

Facilities: Indoor swimming pool, playground, sauna.

Moderate

HOTEL DAVOSERHOF, Bahnhofstrasse Platz, CH-7270 Davos-Platz. Tel. 081/3-68-17. 25 rms (all with bath). MINIBAR TV TEL **Bus:** To stop 11.

$ Rates (including half board): Summer, 90F–105F ($65.70–$76.65) single; 190F

($138.70) double. Winter, 157F ($114.60) single; 304F ($221.90) double. AE, DC, MC, V. **Closed:** May.

Run by the Petzold family, this hotel (whose facade is accented with Grisons designs) is in the center of Davos-Platz, just a short distance from the main road. Two restaurants, the bar and dance floor, and the terrace are all attractively decorated with rustic paneling and antiques. Some rooms—those furnished in an alpine-chalet style with pinewood pieces—have more character and charm than others, which tend to be simple and unadorned. However, all are reasonably comfortable and well maintained.

HOTEL OCHSEN, Talstrasse, CH-7270 Davos-Platz. Tel. 081/43-52-22.
Fax 081/43-76-71. 62 rms (all with bath). TV TEL
$ **Rates** (including half board): Summer, 83F–93F ($60.60–$67.90) single; 146F–166F ($106.55–$121.15) double. Winter, 130F–150F ($94.90–$109.50) single; 230F–270F ($167.90–$197.05) double. AE, DC, MC, V.

This salmon-colored building is only a few minutes on foot from the train station. The lobby is tastefully decorated with leather furnishings and Oriental rugs. The bedrooms contain colorful draperies and upholstery; many of them are quite large. The hotel's restaurant is filled with chalet chairs.

Inexpensive

ZUR ALTE POST, Berlistutz 4, CH-7270 Davos-Platz. Tel. 081/43-54-03.
Fax 081/43-51-25. 30 rms (all with shower). MINIBAR TV TEL
$ **Rates** (including half board): Summer, 59F–69F ($43.05–$50.35) single; 118F–138F ($86.15–$100.75) double. Winter, 79F–103F ($57.65–$75.20) single; 170F–210F ($124.10–$153.30) double. MC, V. **Closed:** Apr–July and Nov–Dec. **Parking:** Free.

The Camenzind-Flühmann family offers guests a good value in its little hotel next to the town hall. The paneled dining room, Tavaasar Schtuba, has intricately carved beams and chalet chairs. The food is good country fare and includes filet goulash Stroganoff, pork cutlets, and piccata with saffron rice. The rooms are furnished with pinewood pieces and have views of the mountains.

IN DAVOS-DORF

Very Expensive

FLÜELA HOTEL, Bahnhofstrasse 5, CH-7260 Davos-Dorf. Tel. 081/47-12-21. Fax 081/46-44-01. 73 rms (all with bath), 12 suites. MINIBAR TV TEL
$ **Rates** (including half board): 205F–287F ($149.65–$209.50) single; 410F ($299.25) double; from 574F ($418.95) suite. AE, DC, MC, V. **Closed:** May–Oct.

More than a century after its opening, this thick-walled, solidly built hotel is still managed by the Gredig family. Its unadorned beige facade conceals an elegantly rustic five-star interior with comfortable and cozy bedrooms. In recent years, many rooms have been redone; some have been enlarged into suites.

Dining/Entertainment: Drinking and dining facilities often lure many nonresidents. In the Stübli, raclettes and fondues are served until 5pm; after that, guests are treated to Swiss and nouvelle cuisine. Flüela Post offers a wide selection and is open both to guests and nonresidents.

Services: Hairdresser, room service, laundry.

Facilities: Pool, sauna, Turkish bath, riding school.

Expensive

DERBY HOTEL, Promenade, CH-7260 Davos-Dorf. Tel. 081/47-11-66.
Fax 081/46-46-38. 88 rms (all with bath). MINIBAR TV TEL
$ Rates (including half board): Summer, 75F–95F ($54.75–$69.35) single; 140F–
180F ($102.20–$131.40) double. Winter, 165F–210F ($120.45–$153.30) single;
325F–420F ($237.20–$306.55) double. AE, MC, V. **Closed:** Apr–June and
Oct–Dec.
Well equipped and comfortable, this stylish, turn-of-the-century hotel has an arched,
wrought-iron entrance and lyre-backed chairs in the sitting rooms, where a pianist
usually plays near the bar. The bedrooms are modern and balconied, often with
separate sleeping alcoves curtained off from the rest of the accommodation.
  Dining/Entertainment: The hotel contains the elegant Paluda Grill and a
second intimate restaurant, as well as a rustic bar with a dance floor.
  Services: Room service, laundry, massage.
  Facilities: Fitness room, sauna, indoor swimming pool, playroom, curling, three
tennis courts.

**HOTEL MEIERHOF, Dischmastrasse, CH-7260 Davos-Dorf. Tel. 081/47-
12-85.** Fax 081/46-39-82. 80 rms (all with bath), 9 suites. MINIBAR TV TEL **Bus:**
To stop 5.
$ Rates (including half board): Summer, 100F–130F ($73–$94.90) single; 180F–
240F ($131.40–$175.20) double. Winter, 185F–240F ($135.05–$175.20) single;
350F–450F ($255.45–$328.45) double; from 480F ($350.35) suite. AE, DC, MC,
V. **Closed:** Apr–June and Sept–Dec. **Parking:** 16F ($11.70).
This 19th-century, family-run hotel is surrounded by lawns and a terrace. The
luxurious, regionally inspired interior has been renovated with wood paneling, warm
colors, and antiques. A more modern wing has an indoor swimming pool with a
complete range of fitness facilities, as well as an underground garage. The bedrooms
are furnished in a cozy alpine style with pinewood pieces.

Moderate

**HOTEL DISCHMA, Promenade 128, CH-7260 Davos-Dorf. Tel. 081/46-
33-23.** Fax 081/46-32-88. 32 rms (all with bath). MINIBAR TV TEL **Bus:** To
stop 5.
$ Rates (including half board): Summer, 85F ($62.05) single; 160F ($116.80)
double. Winter, 125F–132F ($91.25–$96.35) single; 210F–224F ($153.30–
$163.50) double. AE, DC, MC, V.
This modern, rustic, year-round hotel is set in the middle of Davos-Dorf. The
renovated rooms all have radios. The hotel has two good restaurants. There's dancing
in the cellar until 3am, with live bands providing all kinds of music.

**HOTEL MEISSER, Dorfstrasse, CH-7270 Davos-Dorf. Tel. 081/46-23-
33.** Fax 081/46-56-79. 22 rms (all with bath). MINIBAR TEL
$ Rates (including half board): 120F–130F ($87.60–$94.90) single; 220F–230F
($160.60–$167.90) double. AE, DC, MC, V. **Closed:** Nov.
The facade of this sunny, brown-and-white hotel is accented by stone detailing and
regional designs. The hotel is only a few steps from the funicular up the famous ski
mountain, Parsenn. Its paneled dining room has a scattering of regional antiques. Each
room is well maintained and comfortably furnished. Ralf and Kathrin Meisser offer

some accommodations with a private balcony. The hotel also has a sauna and solarium.

MONTANA SPORTHOTEL, Promenade, CH-7260 Davos-Dorf. Tel. 081/ 46-34-44. 80 rms (76 with bath). TEL **Bus:** To stop 4.

$ Rates (including half board): 110F ($80.30) single without bath, 125F–160F ($91.25–$116.80) single with bath; 250F–320F ($182.50–$233.55) double with bath. AE, DC, MC, V. **Closed:** Apr–Dec.

Located near the Parsennbahn, this Edwardian-era hotel has a gabled roof and terrace. Inside are massive beams and marble columns. The bedrooms usually have exposed wood, wall-to-wall carpeting, and lots of light. The dining room has one of the most beautiful ceilings in Davos. Some guests have been coming here for 50 years, ever since the Hüsler family took over.

PARSENN SPORTHOTEL, Promenade, CH-7260 Davos-Dorf. Tel. 081/ 46-32-32. Fax 081/46-38-67. 40 rms (all with bath). TV TEL

$ Rates (including half board): 128F–140F ($93.45–$102.20) single; 240F–264F ($175.20–$192.70) double. No credit cards. **Closed:** Apr–Dec.

This is a large and substantial Engadine chalet, whose facade is covered in intricate stencils. Built around the turn of the century, it sits beside a large parking lot and near a cluster of gas stations in Davos-Dorf, not far from the base of several ski lifts. The ceilings of the public rooms are beamed or vaulted, sheltering a simplified mountain-rustic decor with few frills. The bedrooms are comfortable—some are newer than others, furnished in a pinewood chalet style. Skiers often congregate in the public rooms before dinner, between 6 and 9pm, in the warmly decorated restaurant and beerhall. Lunch is served daily from noon to 2pm. The restaurant remains open throughout the afternoon for a limited menu and closes around 11pm.

Inexpensive

HOTEL ANNA MARIA, Promenade, CH-7260 Davos-Dorf. Tel. 081/46-35-55. 32 rms (all with bath). TEL **Bus:** To stop 5.

$ Rates (including half board): Summer, 55F–65F ($40.15–$47.45) single; 112F–124F ($81.75–$90.50) double. Winter, 80F–92F ($58.40–$67.15) single; 152F–164F ($110.95–$119.70) double. **Closed:** May–June and Sept–Dec.

Anna Maria is a boardinghouse run by the Buchmann family, off the main road of town. You'll drive along a gently winding road until you reach the tall building whose redwood balconies have southern exposure and overlook the mountains. The rooms are cozy. In the summer guests can use the heated outdoor swimming pool.

IN DAVOS-SCHATZALP

BERGHOTEL SCHATZALP, CH-9720 Davos-Platz. Tel. 081/44-13-31. Fax 081/43-13-44. 93 rms (all with bath). MINIBAR TEL **Transportation:** The Schatzalp funicular, from Davos-Platz, is the only public transportation to the hotel.

$ Rates (including half board): Summer, 180F–220F ($131.40–$160.60) single; 300F–360F ($218.95–$262.75) double. Winter, 230F–270F ($167.90–$197.05) single; 400F–460F ($291.95–$335.75) double. AE, DC, MC, V. **Closed:** Apr–July and Oct–Dec.

The extravagant Berghotel Schatzalp is an ideal choice for those who want to get away from it all. Built in 1900 as a sanatorium, it has an arched, wrought-iron door and long colonnades. It is said to receive four more hours of sun every day than the center of Davos. Many of the bedrooms have exquisitely carved Swiss beds. TV is available upon request.

The staff of the funicular takes your luggage straight to your room. The last car usually leaves at 11pm in the summer and at 2am in the winter. Guests can even take the toboggan run straight to Davos. You also have direct access to the Strela cable cars 165 feet away, taking you to the Strela ski resort in 10 minutes or to the Parsenn district in 20 minutes. A reservation is necessary in the high winter season.

Dining/Entertainment: The Belle Epoque dining room is painted with alpine scenes. The terrace-restaurant is called Snow Beach.

Services: Laundry.

Facilities: Heated swimming pool, massage, sauna, therapy facilities, kindergarten, wine cellar.

IN DAVOS-LARET

HÜBLI'S LANDHAUS, Kantonsstrasse, CH-7265 Davos-Laret. Tel. 081/ 46-21-21. Fax 081/46-33-42. 28 rms (15 with bath).
$ Rates (including half board): 85F–95F ($62.05–$69.35) single without bath, 110F–135F ($80.30–$98.55) single with bath; 160F–170F ($116.80–$124.10) double without bath, 210F–260F ($153.30–$189.75) double with bath. AE, DC, MC, V.

Built a century ago as a relay station, Hübli's is one of the region's best little hotels for the money. The dynamic owners put most of their energy into the excellent restaurant (see "Where to Dine," below), although there is a selection of cozy bedrooms, connected to the restaurant by a tunnel. A majority of the rooms contain private baths and have earth-tone fabrics and furniture. In the height of midwinter the hotel provides free transportation to the ski lifts of Davos for any of its guests.

WHERE TO DINE

VERY EXPENSIVE

DAVOSERSTÜBL, in the Hotel Davoserhof, Bahnhofstrasse Platz, Davos-Platz. Tel. 43-68-17.
Cuisine: ITALIAN/CONTINENTAL. **Reservations:** Required. **Bus:** To stop 11.
$ Prices: Appetizers 12F–24F ($8.75–$17.50); main courses 18F–52F ($13.15–$37.95); business lunch 37F ($27); fixed-price dinner 105F ($76.65). AE, DC, MC, V.
Open: Lunch daily noon–2pm; dinner daily 6–11pm. **Closed:** Mon. in summer.

Paul Petzold offers some of the finest dining in Davos. Customers enjoy a memorable cuisine moderne in an intimate, paneled room filled with flowers. Dishes include lobster bisque, filet trout, a magret of duckling with raspberry vinegar, and filet of beef with shallots.

EXPENSIVE

BÜNDNERSTÜBLI, Dischmastrasse 8, Davos-Dorf. Tel. 46-33-93.

Cuisine: SWISS. **Reservations:** Required. **Bus:** To stop 5.

$ Prices: Appetizers 6.50F–15F ($4.75–$10.95); main courses 15F–40F ($10.95–$29.20); fixed-price meals 55F–60F ($40.15–$43.80). AE, DC, MC, V.

Open: Tues–Sun 3–11pm. **Closed:** May–June.

The walls and the ceiling of this cozy place are covered with local pine giving it a rustic look. The menu, appropriately, reads like a history book of local recipes, some of whose names will require a staff member to translate. One example is "Maluns," potatoes served with applesauce and local cheese. Other dishes are fondue with grated potatoes, a richly flavored barley soup, and a daily farmer's menu with large portions of reasonably priced, well-prepared food.

RESTAURANT PÖSTLI, in the Morosani Posthotel, Promenade 42, Davos-Platz. Tel. 2-11-61.

Cuisine: SWISS. **Reservations:** Required. **Bus:** To stop 9.

$ Prices: Appetizers 12F–16F ($8.75–$11.70); main courses 22F–32F ($16.05–$23.35). AE, DC, MC, V.

Open: Lunch daily 11am–2pm; dinner daily 6pm–1am. **Closed:** Apr–Nov.

This elegant room offers live music from 4:30 to 5:30pm and 8:30pm until closing time. Many guests follow dinner here with a later sojourn to the Pöstli Club (see "Evening Entertainment," below). The restaurant has a bar as well as a more formal seating area. Your choice in tasty platters is extensive—a different fresh fish daily or something classic, such as Tafelspitz (boiled beef Viennese style). Other selections are veal liver with polenta, venison in a hunter's sauce, filet of U.S. beef with mushrooms, and rack of lamb with braised cabbage. Most main dishes are for two people, but dishes can be ordered in large or small portions.

MODERATE

RESTAURANT GENTIANA, Promenade 53, Davos-Platz. Tel. 43-56-49.

Cuisine: SWISS. **Reservations:** Required. **Bus:** To stop 5.

$ Prices: Appetizers 6F–15F ($4.40–$10.95); main courses 19.50F–46F ($14.25–$33.60); fondue from 18F ($13.15). AE, MC, V.

Open: Daily 11am–11pm. **Closed:** Wed in summer.

Housed in a gold-colored building opposite the Hotel Schweizerhof in the center of town, this restaurant is one of the few authentic bistros in Davos. It is known for its eight different types of fondue dishes, as well as for its unusual list of dishes prepared with snails. Unpretentious and bustling, the establishment serves ample portions of air-dried beef and ham, as well as inexpensive daily specials. Its choice of desserts includes local pears in cinnamon syrup, honey-flavored ice cream, and chocolate mousse. Wines are sold by the carafe. Don't overlook the pair of upstairs dining rooms, whose focal point is a blue-toned painting by German artist Ernst Ludwig Kirchner, a former resident of Davos.

INEXPENSIVE

ROTER LÖWEN (Red Lion Bar), Promenade 40, Ratia Center, Davos-Platz. Tel. 43-79-01.

Cuisine: ITALIAN. **Reservations:** Not needed.

$ Prices: Appetizers 5.50F–14F ($4–$10.20); main dishes 14F–35F ($10.20–$25.55); lunch plates 13.50F ($9.85); city lunch 19.50F ($14.25). AE, MC, V.

Open: Lunch daily 11am–2pm; dinner daily 5:30–9:30pm.

Some of the best and most moderately priced Italian food in the resort is served at this well-patronized trattoria beside the bus station at Postplatz. Specialties include spaghetti Alfredo, gnocchi del padrone, and scaloppine con marsala. The pastas are excellent and can easily make a meal in themselves.

NEARBY DINING

GASTHAUS ISLEN. Tel. 43-58-56.
   Cuisine: INTERNATIONAL. **Reservations:** Recommended. **Directions:** See below.
$ **Prices:** Appetizers 8F–12F ($5.85–$8.75); main courses 12F–32F ($8.75–$23.35). AE, MC, V.
   Open: Lunch daily noon–2pm; dinner daily 6–9:30pm. **Closed:** Mon in midsummer, and from mid-April to the end of May.
The weather-blackened chalet containing the Iseln was built in the early 1600s; it is probably the oldest building in the Davos region today. Claus Wertmann, the innkeeper, serves international, Swiss, Italian, and Provençal dishes, either inside or on the wide, sun-flooded outdoor deck. The specialties include grills, such as filet steak, veal steak, or entrecôte; a sophisticated array of pastas; and a deliciously garlicky version of fish soup.
   From Davos, diners usually elect to walk for 20 minutes up a gentle slope beside an alpine brook (follow the hiker's signs to Iseln). Otherwise, the Rhaetische Bahn trains from Davos to Chur will drop you off in the center of Iseln, a 2-minute ride from Davos.

GASTHOF LANDHAUS, Route Cantonale, Davos/Tiefencastel, Frauenkirche (Laret). Tel. 43-63-35.
   Cuisine: SWISS. **Reservations:** Recommended. **Bus:** The yellow postal bus running from Davos to Lenzerheide will deposit you near this restaurant if you ask the driver.
$ **Prices:** Appetizers 8F–14F ($5.85–$10.20); main courses 23F–38F ($16.80–$27.75). MC, V.
   Open: Lunch daily 11:30am–2pm; dinner daily 6–10pm; café with a limited menu daily 7:30am–midnight. **Closed:** After 2pm Tues and all day Wed in summer only.
This 300-year-old chalet (renovated in 1973) has an alpine decor of pinewood ceilings and numerous cubbyholes for intimate and escapist dining. The decor includes lots of mountain memorabilia, such as stag horns, rifles, and wrought iron. The menu includes fondues, peppersteak, wild venison (in season) with juniper berries, omelets, salads, and pastas.

HÜBLI'S LANDHAUS, Kantonsstrasse. Tel. 46-21-21.
   Cuisine: SWISS. **Reservations:** Recommended.
$ **Prices:** Appetizers 10F–15F ($7.30–$10.95); main courses 20F–32F ($14.60–$23.35); menu simple 75F ($54.75); menu surprise 130F ($94.90). AE, DC, MC, V.
   Open: Lunch Fri–Wed noon–2pm; dinner daily 6:30–11pm. **Closed:** Thurs in summer; Apr 15–June 15 and Oct 15–Dec 10.
Within the solid white walls of what was built a century ago as a relay station for the Swiss postal service (directly north of Davos-Dorf, on Route 28 heading toward Klosters), you'll find a handful of simple dining rooms that serve superb cuisine. The specialties prepared by Felix and Anne-Marie Hübli change with the seasons. The menu might offer a salad of quail with fresh asparagus, fresh morels with noodles and sweetbreads, fricassee of lobster with asparagus, and roast duckling with blackberries.

Among the choice desserts are a parfait of Peruvian mangoes and a variety of sorbets, made fresh every evening with such exotic fruits as gooseberry and rhubarb.

EVENING ENTERTAINMENT

Davos rivals St. Moritz for the brightest lights in the Alps, with lots of après-ski fun. Drinks cost 9F ($6.55) and up, depending on what kind of entertainment has been booked, particularly around New Year's and the Christmas holidays.

CABANNA CLUB, in the Hotel Europe, Promenade, Davos-Platz. Tel. 43-59-21.

This disco has videos and live bands. You can find schedules in the hotel or at the tourist office. Open daily from 9pm to 1am. Drinks cost 13F ($9.50).

Admission: 14F ($10.20) in winter. Free in summer.

CAVA GRISCHA-KELLERBAR-DANCING, in the Hotel Europe, Promenade 63, Davos-Platz. Tel. 43-59-21.

This is the most popular folkloric nightclub in Davos, filled with live music and foaming glasses of beer. Chances are that soon after you enter you'll be swaying to the rhythmic melodies of the flügelhorn, the alpine guitar, and the accordion. Few customers seem to escape from here without a dance or two. Open nightly throughout the year, from 9pm to 3am. Beer runs 9F ($6.55).

Admission: Free.

HOTEL DISCHMA, Promenade 128. Tel. 46-33-23.

The place attracts mostly younger people, with its dark-timbered walls and danceable band music. The restaurant serves meals for 50F ($36.50) until 11pm. Drinks cost about 12F ($8.75).

Admission: Free.

JACOBSHORN CLUB, in the Hotel Davoserhof, Bahnhofstrasse Platz. Tel. 43-68-17.

This disco attracts a younger crowd of drinkers and dancers, who enjoy the colored spotlights and the logs burning in the massive fireplace. Dinner is served until closing time. Open daily from 5pm to 2am; happy hour is from 5 to 8pm. Drinks run 13F ($9.50).

MONTANA-STÜBLI, in the Hotel Montana, Promenade, Davos-Dorf. Tel. 46-34-44.

The Hüsler family offers a cozy, distinguished ambience to an older crowd, who dine to the music from the piano bar. It's a rustic room, lined with pine. The atmosphere is intimate, and the food is excellent. Open in the winter only, daily from 8pm. Drinks go for 9F ($6.55).

PALÜDA GRILL, in the Derby Hotel, Promenade, Davos-Dorf. Tel. 47-11-66.

The clientele in this rustic room tends to be a distinguished, older crowd. There is a dinner-dance every evening in the winter. The bar area offers raclette, apéritifs, and escargots during happy hour, with beer on tap. The specialties offered in the restaurant include fondue bourguignonne, flambées, seafood, and T-bone steaks. There's a large open grill. Happy hour is from 6 to 7pm; dinner and dance, from 7:30pm. Meals begin at 35F ($25.55); drinks, 12F ($8.75).

PÖSTLI CLUB, in the Morosani Posthotel, Promenade 42, Davos-Platz. Tel. 44-11-61.

The Pöstli Club opens only in the winter; many aficionados consider it the number-one spot in Davos. It's decorated in a typical Grisons style, and live bands from all over the world are brought in to entertain. Open daily from 9pm to 3am. Drinks cost 12F ($8.75).

Admission: Sun–Thurs free, Fri–Sat 6F–9F ($4.40–$6.55).

SPORTHOTEL CENTRAL, Promenade, Davos-Platz. Tel. 44-11-81.

A predominantly under-30 crowd dances in this vaulted room with wood paneling and dozens of gaily striped chairs and banquettes. Musical groups include local artists, such as the Dominoes. Music daily from 9pm. Drinks cost 12F ($8.75).

Admission: Free.

THE ENGADINE

The Valley of the Inn (or En, as the locals call it in Romansh) stretches for 60 miles, from the Maloja Plateau (5,955 ft.) to Finstermünz, and all the villages except Sils lie at a higher altitude than the plateau. The highest is St. Moritz, at 6,036 feet. (See the map on p. 423.)

The Lower Engadine is reached from Davos over the Flüela Pass (7,818 ft.) and by the Ofen Pass (7,050 ft.). Four major passes lead into the Upper Engadine: Maloja (5,955 ft.), Julier (7,493 ft.), Albula (7,585 ft.), and Bernina (7,621 ft.). The upper valley contains several lakes, including that of St. Moritz.

The Engadine is enclosed by great mountain ranges with meadows and forests on the steep hillsides. The villages are built of stone, originally as a protection against the fires that swept the narrow windy valleys. The whitewashed houses in the villages, known for their larders, often have sgraffito decorations, with mottoes and heraldic devices. The population is of Rhaeto-Romanic heritage and is mostly Protestant.

From the Maloja Pass the road runs northeast through the Upper Engadine, where the clear mountain skies and dry, light breezes make the area popular both in the summer and in the winter. Since the 19th century, when Upper Engadine became fashionable for its "air cure," it has developed into a winter-sports resort, highlighted by St. Moritz.

In the Lower Engadine, where the valley is narrower and more forested, the mineral springs of Scuol and the Swiss National Park, which is a 55-mile wildlife sanctuary, are the two major attractions.

Some of the Engadine's ancient customs have died out, but two that are upheld throughout the area are the Chalanda Marz (the first of March) and the Schlitteda.

The **Chalanda Marz,** celebrated by the youth of Engadine, originated with the old Roman New Year festival and has been observed since the Romans ruled the Rhaetian valleys. Early on the morning of March 1, schoolboys congregate at the center meeting place of each Engadine village. With bells large and small, the boys create a hullabaloo to frighten the winter monster and lure spring from its snowy bed. The boys are divided into "herds" that go from house to house soliciting goodies such as fruit, sweets, and chestnuts. Romantic songs of spring are sung, in which the girls of the village are requested to join. Money—which usually goes toward school trips—is accepted from visitors and locals in lieu of edible treats.

An especially beautiful custom is the observance of **Schlitteda,** a romantic horse-drawn sleigh ride in January for the unmarried village youth. The couples dress in the festive scarlet costume of the region, known as *schlittunza*. In a decorated sleigh, they set out for a nearby village on a ride that usually takes about 2 hours.

WHAT'S SPECIAL ABOUT THE ENGADINE

Great Towns/Villages

☐ St. Moritz, considered one of the world's great resorts, playground of the rich and famous.

☐ Pontresina, the best center for hiking and mountaineering in the Upper Engadine.

☐ Zuoz, filled with old-world charm, the best-preserved village in the Upper Engadine.

Museums

☐ Engadine Museum, St. Moritz, devoted to the culture of the Engadine, with sgraffito displays.

☐ Segantini Museum, St. Moritz, featuring works of the famed Engadine artist Giovanni Segantini.

Ace Attractions

☐ Maloja Pass, south of Sils, the historic pass connecting the Engadine with the Lake Como region in Italy.

☐ Muottas Muragli (on the road to Samedan), at an altitude of 8,048 feet, offering a panoramic vista of the Upper Engadine Gap.

☐ The main square of Zuoz, famed for its Engadine houses, which played an important role in the history of the Grisons.

Special Events/Festivals

☐ Schlitteda, a romantic horse-drawn sleigh ride through the Engadine in January for the unmarried village youth.

When they reach their goal they're served a hot spiced-wine drink and pastries to strengthen them for their trip home after music and dancing. Back home after a romantic ride through the Engadine night, each couple dines at the girl's home. Musicians in traditional costumes accompany the young couples in another sleigh and are greeted in the villages they pass through by townspeople dancing in the square.

In the summer music lovers are drawn to the **Engadine Concert Weeks,** during which chamber music concerts are given throughout the area, arranged by the Upper Engadine Tourist Office.

SEEING THE ENGADINE

From Zurich the *Glacier Express* climbs over the Alps from St. Moritz to Zermatt in the Valais. The *Engadine Express* also goes from Chur through the Swiss National Park into the Lower Engadine. St. Moritz is the major rail terminus for the valley. From there you can make bus or rail links to other villages of the Engadine.

IF YOU HAVE 5 DAYS

Day 1: Visit the small towns of S-chanf and Zuoz, selecting one for an overnight stopover.

Day 2: Explore the attractions in and around Samedan and Celerina; stay overnight in either resort.

Day 3–5: Anchor into St. Moritz to sample its many attractions. If you'd like to live within your budget, settle in nearby Pontresina instead. From either resort, branch out on mountain and village excursions, exploring Silvaplana and Sils Maria on day trips.

1. S-CHANF & ZUOZ

30 miles SE of Davos, 12 miles NE of St. Moritz

GETTING THERE By Train About 17 trains travel every day from St. Moritz, which arrive first at Zuoz and then at S-chanf, 30 and 35 minutes later, respectively.

By Car From St. Moritz, drive northeast along Route 27.

ESSENTIALS The **Zuoz Tourist Office** is on Via Maistra (tel. 082/7-15-10); it's open Monday through Friday from 8:30am to noon and 2 to 5:30pm. The **telephone area code** for both Zuoz and S-chanf is 082.

These two Engadine resorts provide attractive, less expensive alternatives to St. Moritz, located to the southwest.

WHAT TO SEE & DO

IN S-CHANF At 5,100 feet, this village with a most unusual name is a summer-and-winter resort at the entrance to the Swiss National Park. It's an ideal starting point for excursions and tours in the Upper and Lower Engadine and in the park. **Valley Trupchun** is the park hunting ground, where you will find all the game of the Grisons.

S-chanf is a peaceful village with easy access to several busy sports centers, including St. Moritz. It lies on the Engadine cross-country ski marathon trail.

⭐ **IN ZUOZ** This old-world village, once the chief population center of the Engadine, is located by the Inn River, amid alpine meadows and lush forests. Most of the 1,200 inhabitants of Zuoz speak Romansh.

This is the best-preserved village in the Upper Engadine, with the most striking collection of Engadine houses to be found anywhere in the valley. The houses are always festively decorated. The best-known is the famed **Planta House** (two houses, actually), on the main square of the village, with an outdoor staircase and a rococo balustrade. The Planta family, historically important in the Grisons, built most of the spectacular structures in town. The church also merits a visit. Inside, look for the severed-bear's-paw theme—a heraldic symbol of the Plantas that also appears on a fountain in the main square. Augusto Giacometti designed some of the church's modern stained-glass windows.

A fledgling summer resort, Zuoz offers tennis, hill climbing and mountaineering, horse-drawn carriage rides, fishing, swimming, horseback riding, and summer skiing.

At 5,740 feet above sea level, this minor winter-sports center has a ski school for beginners, including children, as well as for those more advanced in the sport. Experienced skiers will gravitate to the heights of the Piz Kesch region or else journey by train to St. Moritz. Numerous cross-country tracks lead through Zuoz in all directions, and the village is the finishing point of the Engadine ski marathon. Curling, ice skating, and sledding are other winter sports pursued here.

WHERE TO STAY & DINE

IN S-CHANF

HOTEL SCALETTA, via Maistra 52, CH-7525 S-chanf. Tel. 082/7-12-71.
    Fax 082/73-138. 56 rms (16 with bath). TEL
$ Rates (including continental breakfast): 60F–70F ($43.80–$51.10) single without

bath, 80F–100F ($58.40–$73) single with bath; 120F–140F ($87.60–$102.20) double without bath, 180F ($131.40) double with bath. Half board 20F ($14.60) extra. AE, V.

S Originally built in 1624 as a relay station for horses struggling over the Engadine passes, today this hotel is covered in baroque sgraffito. It is centrally located, opposite a tiny square, a few steps from the village church. The hospitable owner, Jorg Bauder, bought the hotel in 1984 and renovated it. Each of the pine rooms has a sink and cozy alpine furniture. The hotel restaurant, the Arvenstube, serves Swiss meals, which cost 30F ($21.90) and up.

PARKHOTEL AURORA, Via Maistra, CH-7525 S-chanf. Tel. 082/7-21-19. Fax 082/7-12-64. 52 rms (38 with bath). TEL
$ Rates (including half board): 53F–68F ($38.70–$49.65) single without bath, 73F–94F ($53.30–$68.60) single with bath; 109F–141F ($79.55–$102.90) double without bath, 155F–203F ($113.15–$148.15) double with bath. AE, DC, MC, V.
The best in town, this renovated hotel is designed with paneled and vaulted ceilings, rustic niches, and Oriental rugs. Even the double-lane bowling alley has wood paneling and an alpine decor. Mrs. Dora Langen, the hostess, is very hospitable. The hotel is open year round; its rooms are snug and comfortable. The hotel restaurant serves Engadine and continental specialties.

IN ZUOZ

POSTHOTEL ENGIADINA, CH-7524 Zuoz. Tel. 082/7-10-21. Fax 082/7-33-03. 40 rms (all with bath). TV TEL
$ Rates (including half board): 120F–152F ($87.60–$110.95) single; 184F–296F ($134.30–$216.05) double. AE, DC, MC, V. **Closed:** Apr–June and Oct–Dec.
This beautifully preserved, pink baroque structure is more than a century old; it is owned and managed by the Arquint family. The public rooms remain faithful to the style of the original construction but have been charmingly updated with murals. There is also a parlor with antiques, art deco chandeliers, and an unusual collection of antique clocks. The bedrooms are attractively furnished with traditional styling.
Dining/Entertainment: The hotel has a bar with a dance floor, plus two restaurants serving Swiss and Italian specialties.
Services: Laundry.
Facilities: Heated swimming pool, tennis courts, sauna, curling rinks, solarium.

---

2. SAMEDAN & CELERINA

2 miles NE of St. Moritz, 3 miles NW of Pontresina

GETTING THERE By Plane From December through April, various "air taxis" connect Zurich's airport with the small field at Samedan Airport. For details about flights, phone 082/6-54-33.

By Train Almost 20 trains depart from St. Moritz every day, stopping after 4 minutes in Celerina and after 7 minutes in Samedan. Trains also run from Chur to Samedan.

By Bus Buses running from St. Moritz to Lugano are not scheduled to stop at Celerina and Samedan; usually, however, if you let the driver know that you'd like to get off at either point, he will stop for you. Buses making the run between Pontresina and St. Moritz (there are two to five buses a day, depending on the season) stop regularly at Samedan.

By Car   From St. Moritz, head northeast along Route 27.

ESSENTIALS   The **Celerina Tourist Office** (tel. 082/3-39-66) provides information about the area; it's open Monday through Saturday from 8:30am to noon and 2 to 6pm. The **telephone area code** for both Celerina and Samedan is 082.

These twin resorts are virtually at the doorstep of St. Moritz and have been referred to as suburbs of St. Moritz, but that's a somewhat-demeaning label, as Samedan and Celerina have individual characters.

Samedan, originally a Roman settlement, survived to become a principal village of the Upper Engadine. Over the years many well-known Swiss families have made their homes here. Seek out the Planta House (the same family who made its mark on Zuoz) and note its large roof and impressive library of Romansh works.

Celerina, a hamlet on the Inn River (about 5,675 ft.), has long been overshadowed by its more celebrated neighbors. But for those in search of local color, Celerina (Schlarigna in Romansh) is an ideal choice as a winter or summer resort. Known for its charming Engadine houses, this little village on a sunny plain is sheltered from bitter winds.

WHAT TO SEE & DO

IN SAMEDAN   The village (5,160 ft.) has its own ski lift and ice-skating rink, plus a ski school. In the summer it's ideal for mountain walks and for climbing. Visitors can fish or play tennis and golf. When there's snow it's possible to take a horse-drawn sleigh to St. Moritz in less than an hour, and all mountain transportation can be reached in a short time.

IN CELERINA   Celerina has an old Romanesque church, **St. John's (San Gian),** with a painted ceiling dating from 1478.

The Cresta run, a mecca for bobsledders, starts from St. Moritz and terminates near Celerina. The village also has ice rinks for curling and skating, a toboggan run, and a ski school. Winter Celerinade packages for skiing, cross-country, and curling are offered, as well as Summer Celerinade guided mountain bike tours with a picnic included.

Several interesting **conducted tours** are offered in the summer through the tourist office. An experienced guide will take you on an exploration tour through the Swiss National Park, or you can join a botanical excursion to see alpine flowers in bloom. Strenuous geological and mineralogical tours are also offered, and you can make an exciting journey from the Diavolezza over the glacier to Morteratsch, but only with an experienced guide. The latter tour is offered only in the spring and summer.

Celerina is known for its belvederes and stunning views. One such view is of **Piz Nair** at 10,000 feet. To reach it, you can take a cable car from St. Moritz, departing every 20 minutes daily from 8:30am to 4pm. You'll ride from St. Moritz to Corviglia. Round-trip passage between the two sites costs 14F ($10.20) per person. At Corviglia, you board another cable car between Corviglia and Piz Nair. The round-trip passage from Corviglia to Piz Nair is 25F ($18.25) per person. The circular panorama takes in the Bernina summits and provides a breathtaking panorama.

You can also visit **Muottas Muragl** (8,040 ft.). From the lower station at Punt Muragl, funicular departures are about every 30 minutes. The round-trip fare is 15F

($10.95). You'll have stunning views of the Upper Engadine gap, and in the distance you can see the peaks of the Bernina massif, each with "Piz" in its name. You'll probably see ibex and marmots as you take mountain walks.

WHERE TO STAY

IN SAMEDAN

HOTEL QUADRATSCHA, CH-7503 Samedan. Tel. 082/6-42-57. Fax 082/6-51-01. 40 rms (all with bath). MINIBAR TV TEL
$ **Rates** (including half board): 115F–160F ($83.95–$116.80) single; 220F–300F ($160.60–$218.95) double. AE, DC, V.
Built as a private house in 1870, this became a hotel in the 1970s. The lobby retains most of the paneling and elaborate murals of the original 19th-century construction, and one of the dining rooms, the Arvenstube, has one of the most beautifully crafted wood ceilings in town. The simply furnished bedrooms have balconies and a view of the mountains. Facilities include a sauna, a solarium, and massage facilities.

HOTEL BERNINA, CH-7503 Samedan. Tel. 082/6-54-21. Fax 082/6-36-06. 85 rms (all with bath). MINIBAR TV TEL
$ **Rates** (including half board): 115F–140F ($83.95–$102.20) single; 216F–280F ($157.65–$204.35) double. AE, DC, MC, V. **Closed:** Apr to mid-June and Oct to mid-Dec.
Built in 1865, the Hotel Bernina maintains much of its original grandeur. The entire edifice is painted beige and gray, with Italianate detailing over the windows. The comfortable bedrooms are furnished in a rustic Engadine style, with patterned carpeting and big windows. On the premises, guests can use a tennis court or enjoy a summer terrace and a private park. The restaurant picks its ingredients straight from the vegetable garden.

HOTEL DONATZ, CH-7503 Samedan. Tel. 082/6-46-66. Fax 082/6-54-51. 38 rms (all with bath). TV TEL
$ **Rates** (including half board): 110F–120F ($80.30–$87.60) single; 205F–215F ($149.65–$156.95) double. AE, DC, MC, V. **Closed:** May.
This sunny hotel has green shutters and wood-paneled public rooms. A restaurant, La Padella, serves regional specialties in an alpine setting. Paneled bedrooms are brightly carpeted and comfortable. Each room contains a radio. René Donatz is the owner.

IN CELERINA

CRESTA PALACE HOTEL, Hauptstrasse, CH-7505 Celerina. Tel. 082/3-35-64. Fax 082/3-35-64. 98 rms (all with bath). MINIBAR TV TEL
$ **Rates** (including half board): 120F–250F ($87.60–$182.50) single; 220F–460F ($160.60–$335.75) double. AE, DC, MC, V. **Closed:** Apr–June and Sept–Dec.
This grand building dates from the turn of the century. The inside contains several public rooms, including a bar and an elegant restaurant, as well as a swimming pool, a sun terrace where breakfast is served, and a skating rink. The bedrooms are brightly colored and often include rustic pine furnishings.

HOTEL CRESTA KULM, Hauptstrasse, CH-7505 Celerina. Tel. 082/3-33-73. Fax 082/3-70-01. 50 rms (all with bath). MINIBAR TV TEL
$ **Rates** (including half board): 145F–160F ($105.85–$116.80) single; 280F–320F ($204.35–$233.55) double. AE, DC, MC, V. **Closed:** Apr–June and Sept–Dec.
The famous Cresta run and the St. Moritz–Celerina bobsled run come to an end in

front of this first-class hotel, run by Jürg and Genevieve Küng. Set off the main road, the sunny building is unusually designed, with irregularly shaped windows and a white concrete facade. The interior is filled with modern curves and well-crafted stone floors, white stucco walls, and comfortable furniture in the attractive bedrooms. The rooms have radios.

HOTEL MISANI, Hauptstrasse, CH-7505 Celerina. Tel. 082/3-33-14. 32 rms (8 with bath).

$ Rates (including continental breakfast): 45F ($32.85) single without bath, 55F ($40.15) single with bath; 75F ($54.75) double without bath, 85F ($62.05) double with bath. AE, DC, V. **Closed:** Apr–June and Oct–Dec.

This dark-pink house with white shutters is only a 3-minute walk from the ski lifts and cable car. The interior has some regional antiques, lots of full-grained paneling, and sunny, comfortable bedrooms. Part of the hotel encloses Stuvetta—one of the finest restaurants in town. Food is served daily from noon to 2pm and 6:30 to 9pm. Engadine dishes include savory snails, the chef's special steak, raclette, trout meunière, and many veal dishes. A four-course fixed-price meal costs 23F ($16.80), and à la carte dinners cost 20F to 30F ($14.60 to $21.90). Parking is nearby. Laundry facilities are provided and room service is available.

WHERE TO DINE

ARVENSTÜBLI/STUVETTA, in the Hotel Quadretscha, Samedan. Tel. 6-42-57.
Cuisine: SWISS. **Reservations:** Recommended.
$ Prices: Appetizers 10F–16F ($7.30–$11.70); main courses 18F–32F ($13.15–$23.35). AE, DC, V.
Open: Dinner only, daily 7–10pm.
The restaurant's paneling and elaborate pinewood ceiling are remnants from a villa originally built on this site in 1870. Today a polite staff serves a darne of salmon, a "turban" of sole with shrimp, a platter containing three different filet mignons, quail with truffles, and an array of succulent grills. If for any reason the Arvenstübli is full or closed, dinner is served in an adjacent room, the Stuvetta.

LE PAVILLON, in the Hotel Bernina, Samedan. Tel. 6-54-21.
Cuisine: SWISS. **Reservations:** Recommended.
$ Prices: Appetizers 12F–16F ($8.75–$11.70); main courses 18F–28F ($13.15–$20.45). AE, DC, MC, V.
Open: Daily 9am–midnight. **Closed:** Mid-Apr to mid-June and Oct 1 to mid-Dec.
This pleasant restaurant, which has a garden terrace and a bar with dancing, serves such delectable items as fresh goose liver and, when available, fresh mushrooms made into several delicious dishes. The service is as good as the food.

3. ST. MORITZ

50 miles S of Davos, 46 miles SE of Chur, 126 miles SE of Zurich

GETTING THERE **By Train** St. Moritz is linked by rail (through a complicated series of tunnels) to the rest of Switzerland via Chur, with other links to such non-Swiss population centers as Milan and Munich. Travel time by rail from Chur is 2

hours. St. Moritz is also the end point of the world-famous *Glacier Express,* which links Zermatt, in the southwest, with St. Moritz, in the southeast, on a 7½-hour trip through 91 tunnels and over nearly 300 bridges.

By Bus   St. Moritz is linked by bus to Chur, Davos, and Pontresina, each of which is easily reachable via bus connections from Munich.

By Car   From Zurich, take Route N3 (later N13) to Chur and, once there, head southwest along Route 3.

ESSENTIALS Information   The St. Moritz tourist office, **Kur- and Verkehrsverein,** via Maistra 12 (tel. 082/3-31-47), will answer any questions you might have. The office is open Monday through Friday from 9am to noon and 2 to 6pm, and on Saturday from 9am to noon.

Fast Facts   The **telephone area code** for St. Moritz is 082. **Day-nursery care** for children costs 30F ($21.90) for a whole day with lunch; inquire at the tourist office for the nursery locations. The St. Moritz **post office,** via Chasellas 12 (tel. 3-15-78), is open Monday through Friday from 7:45am to noon and 1:45 to 6:15pm, and on Saturday from 7:45 to 11am; you can arrange **postal-bus excursions** here. The St. Moritz **telegraph office,** via Serlas 23 (tel. 3-30-10), is open daily from 7:30am to 11pm. A **city bus** runs back and forth across the town, linking all the major hotels and restaurants.

St. Moritz is the *ne plus ultra* of winter glamour—a haven for German and Italian aristocracy and the jet-setters who come in February and March. Long a favorite of movie stars, it also attracts internationally prominent people in politics, the world of finance, and the arts. St. Moritz may well be the most fashionable resort in the world.

Not all its visitors, however, are prestigious. Author Peter Viertel wrote that St. Moritz attracts "the hangers-on of the rich . . . the jewel thieves, the professional backgammon players and general layabouts, as well as the high-class ladies of doubtful virtue (if such a thing still exists)."

On the southern side of the Alps in the Upper Engadine, at an altitude of 6,000 feet, St. Moritz (San Murezzan in Romansh) was originally known for its mineral springs, which were discovered, probably by the Celts, some 3,000 years ago. From Roman times through the Middle Ages, visitors came here in the summer to experience the curative powers of the spring waters. The hamlet first appears in written history in an official document referring to the sale of the Upper Engadine by a count to the bishop of Chur in 1138. It was first referred to as a spring by the Swiss-born alchemist and physician known as Paracelsus.

Use of the spring waters was a summer pursuit. It was not until 1834 that the first winter guest stayed in the area. The earliest skiers appeared on the Upper Engadine scene in 1859 (the natives thought they were nutty), and in 1864 a pension owner, Johannes Badrutt, brought a group of English people to St. Moritz to spend the winter, starting what has grown into a flood of tourism.

WHAT TO SEE & DO

THE ENGADINE MUSEUM, via dal Bagn 39. Tel. 3-43-33.
This museum offers a glimpse of the history of St. Moritz and the Engadines. You'll

learn about sgraffito (designs in plasterwork) on Engadine buildings and local styles of architecture, and see a collection of Engadine antiques and regional furniture. The elegantly decorated state room shows how nobility in the area lived. Artifacts from the Bronze Age, when Druids lived in the land, are also on display, including the 3,000-year-old encasement of the spring of Mauritius. St. Moritz stands on a former "mystic place" of the Druids.

Admission: 4F ($2.90) adults, 2.50F ($1.85) children.

Open: Mon–Sat 9:30am–noon and 2–5pm, Sun 10am–noon. **Closed:** May and Nov.

THE SEGANTINI MUSEUM, via Somplaz 30. Tel. 3-44-54.

Housed here are works by the artist Giovanni Segantini (1858–99), who lived in the Engadine (Maloja) during the last years of his life. The artist's work is famous for his technique, Divisionism; his most important work is a triptych called *Birth, Life, Death,* which is exhibited at the museum among other important pictures.

Admission: 5F ($3.65) adults, 1.50F ($1.10) children.

Open: Summer, Tues–Sat 9am–12:30pm and 2:30–5pm, Sun 10:30am–12:30pm and 2:30–4:30pm; winter, Tues–Sat 10am–12:30pm and 3–5pm, Sun 10:30am–12:30pm and 3–5pm. **Bus:** 1.

SPORTS

The tourist office has complete details about the various activities in the area. Although skiing is the premier sport, other winter-sports activities, including curling, ice skating, tobogganing, bobsledding, and an early form of ice hockey, were enjoyed by most winter visitors in the last part of the 19th century.

SKIING   The world's oldest **ski school** is at Moritz-Dorf, founded in 1927. A total of five **ski complexes** encircles St. Moritz, the nearest being Corviglia–Piz Nair, which has some challenging, mile-long runs back to the base. There's an abundance of snow in winter on **250 miles of downhill ski runs, 100 miles of cross-country ski trails,** and the **Olympic ski-jumping hill.**

There are five mountains, all of which can be skied on one lift pass. **Corvatsch,** with 5,800 feet of height, is known for its bowl skiing. **Corviglia** has broad runs attracting fledgling and intermediate skiers and is the base for skiing **Piz Nair,** the highest skiable mountain, 10,837 feet, with a vertical drop of 4,748 feet. Nearby, in Pontresina, a neighbor resort to be visited in the next section, are the steep **Piz Lagalb** and **Diavolezza,** with skiing for all levels of experience, including a run over the Morteratsch glacier.

In all, St. Moritz has a total of 25 mountain railways and 58 ski lifts. A 6-day, general **ski pass** costs 156F ($113.85). Various other ski passes are also sold. Telephone 3-88-88 for more information.

The groomed and tracked **cross-country runs** in the Upper Engadine valley include a tame 1-mile loop near the cross-country center; trails are laid out between the valley resorts. A 1-mile segment is lit for night skiing. The Engadine cross-country ski marathon is a major annual event.

Instruction in cross-country skiing, available in groups on Monday, Wednesday, and Friday from 10am to noon, costs 22F ($16.05) for a half day and 58F ($42.35) for 3 half days. A day's excursion costs 28F ($20.45). Call 3-62-33 for more information.

OTHER WINTER SPORTS   Horse racing on the frozen lake of St. Moritz is also popular, or you can take taxi rides on the bobsled natural-ice run. There are 30 curling rinks, winter golf played on the frozen lake, and tobogganing on the Cresta run. Indoor tennis and squash can be played as well.

If you're interested in **curling** but don't know how, you can have a first training session free (40 min.). Individual lessons thereafter cost 40F ($29.20) for 45 minutes. Call 3-45-88 for details.

A **bobsled ride** costs 130F ($94.90), but you get your picture taken (for you to keep), a drink, and a certificate in addition to the ride. Call 3-41-10.

SPAS The spa section of this resort is called **St. Moritz-Bad,** where you can take mud and carbon-dioxide mineral-water baths, physical therapy, and physiotherapy while you enjoy the stimulating alpine climate in a modern **Health Spa Center** in Bad (tel. 3-31-47), next to the Parkhotel Kurhaus. The spa opened in 1976. From Roman times to now, "taking the waters" has been a popular pursuit for those seeking natural curative treatment for relief from pain and stress. The charge for a mineral-water bath is 22F ($16.05); for a peat-mud bath, 35F ($25.55). For additional treatments, you can get a special price list.

SUMMER SPORTS In the summer visitors are offered cultural programs and sports activities. **Windsurfing** at St. Moritz and on the lakes of nearby resorts has boomed in popularity—the Engadine surf marathon in July draws competitors from all over the world. A 2-hour lesson costs 30F to 40F ($21.90 to $29.20) per person. Call 4-92-29 for information. **Sailing** on the area's 25 lakes is also possible.

Greens fees on the 18-hole **golf** course are 60F ($43.80) per day. Rates at the 25 **tennis** courts vary from 16F ($11.70) to 29F ($21.15) per hour. For tennis and squash information, consult the **Corviglia Tennis Center** (tel. 3-15-00).

Fishing may be done only by persons over 16, with special permission. Call 3-34-04 for details.

There's **summer skiing** on Crovatsch, costing 30F ($21.90) for all day. Only half-day passes on the Diavolezza, costing 26F ($19) per person, are sold, because the afternoon sun turns the mountainside into slush at midday. Call 4-82-42.

WHERE TO STAY

St. Moritz offers several different types of accommodations, with dozens of hotels, pensions, and chalet-style apartments. But because it's expensive, you may prefer one of several neighboring resorts, such as Pontresina, Silvaplana, Sils Maria, Samedan, or Celerina, all of which are covered in this chapter. The following hotels are in the heart of St. Moritz.

VERY EXPENSIVE

BADRUTT'S PALACE HOTEL, via Serlas 27, CH-7500 St. Moritz. Tel. 082/2-11-01. Fax 082/3-77-39. 270 rms (all with bath), 18 suites. MINIBAR TV TEL **Bus:** 1.

$ Rates (including half board): Summer, 250F–400F ($182.50–$291.95) single; 440F–700F ($321.15–$510.95) double. Winter, 450F–750F ($328.45–$547.45) single; 800F–1,400F ($583.90–$1,021.85) double; from 1,500F ($1,094.85) suite. AE, DC, MC, V. **Closed:** Apr–June and Sept–Dec. **Parking:** 18F ($13.15).

Few hotels in Switzerland command the attention and fame of this monument to grandeur. Set in the center of town, behind a chiseled stone facade and a series of fortified towers, the Palace was built at the turn of the century by Caspar Badrutt, who reportedly was the first hotelier in Europe to install private bathrooms in the more expensive suites. Over the years the chic and famous have come through the doors of the Palace, including the Shah of Iran, Greta Garbo, Barbara Hutton, Noël Coward, Aristotle Onassis, and the Duke of Alba.

The hotel's Great Hall soars in Gothic dimensions above. twin black-marble fireplaces, clusters of antique furniture, and massive bouquets of flowers. Twice a year, during annual closings, an army of Swiss, Italian, and Portuguese employees replaces, upgrades, renews, and cleans virtually every square inch of this remarkable hotel. The accommodations have French and Swiss furnishings. Each contains the amenities and comforts available in most luxury hotels.

Dining/Entertainment: If you're rich enough, and appropriately dressed, most of the hotel's drinking and dining facilities will welcome you. Many of them are separately described in "Where to Dine" and "Evening Entertainment," below.

Services: Room service, laundry.

Facilities: Spacious grounds, sports facilities.

CARLTON HOTEL, via Badrutt, Dorf, CH-7500 St. Moritz. Tel. 082/2-11-14. Fax 082/3-20-12. 99 rms (all with bath), 6 suites. MINIBAR TV TEL **Bus:** 1.

$ Rates (including half board): Summer, 180F–270F ($131.40–$197.05) single; 330F–540F ($240.85–$394.35) double. Winter, 240F–400F ($175.20–$291.95) single; 440F–800F ($321.15–$583.90) double; from 900F ($656.90) suite. AE, DC, MC, V. **Closed:** Apr–June and Sept–Dec. **Parking:** 5F ($3.65).

⭐ Now owned by Grand Hotel Tschuggen of Arosa, this elaborate, ocher-colored château was originally built for Nicholas II, the last tsar of Russia. With a view of the lake and the mountains, it's one of the loveliest hotels in St. Moritz. One particularly spectacular sitting room has tall, narrow fireplaces with neoclassical designs. The well-furnished rooms have new bathrooms (complete with hairdryer, bidet, and makeup mirror).

Dining/Entertainment: The elegant Tschiné offers various continental and regional specialties. You can also dine in the rustically decorated Restaurant Pruveda. International musicians perform at the hotel's bar.

Services: Hairdresser, kindergarten, free bus to the ski lifts and the center of town, room service, laundry.

Facilities: Swimming pool, sauna, solarium, massage.

HOTEL SCHWEIZERHOF, via dal Bagn 54, Dorf, CH-7500 St. Moritz. Tel. 082/2-21-71. Fax 082/3-83-00. 85 rms (all with bath), 10 suites. MINIBAR TV TEL **Bus:** 1.

$ Rates (including half board): Summer, 250F–300F ($182.50–$218.95) single; 400F–510F ($291.95–$372.25) double. Winter, 260F–350F ($189.75–$255.45) single; 420F–540F ($306.55–$394.15) double; from 800F ($583.90) suite. AE, DC, MC, V. **Parking:** 15F ($10.95).

This four-star establishment—owned since it was built in 1896 by the von Gugelberg family—is considered one of the 10 best hotels in town. It has attractively modernized rooms, many furnished in pastel colors. The better units face south, opening onto views of the lake. What makes this hotel exceptional, aside from its central location, is its personal service, along with an array of drinking and dining choices.

Dining/Entertainment: Buffet breakfast and dinners are served in the Segantini Dining Room, with tables set beneath a Giovanni Segantini painting. Those seeking more elaborate meals can head for La Terrine, an intimate French restaurant open nightly from 7pm to midnight. Open only in the winter, it serves such fare as lobster bisque, superb hors d'oeuvres, a cassolette of veal shank, delectable sole and turbot dishes, and lamb provençal style. Meals cost 68F ($49.65) and up. The other specialty restaurant, Acla, is recommended separately, as are the Schwyzerhof-Stübli in the cellar and the Pianobar. The alpine hut, called the Clavadatsch, offers meals in the mountains, warmed by a fireplace in the corner.

Services: Kindergarten daily 9am–6pm, room service, laundry.

Facilities: Fitness center, massage parlor, sauna.

KULM HOTEL, via Veglia 18, Dorf, CH-7500 St. Moritz. Tel. 082/2-11-51. Fax 082/3-17-38. 200 rms (all with bath). MINIBAR TV TEL **Bus:** 1.
$ Rates (including half board): Summer, 175F–285F ($127.75–$208) single; 140F–630F ($102.20–$459.85) double. Winter, 245F–420F ($178.85–$306.55) single; 450F–900F ($328.45–$656.90) double. AE, MC, V. **Closed:** Apr–June and Sept–Nov.

These three elegant buildings, the oldest of which was erected in 1760, were taken over in 1856 by Joseph Bedrutt, who was the first to encourage British vacationers to come to the Alps. In 1878 it became the first building in Switzerland to have electricity, and it was the center of the Olympic Games in 1928 and 1948. Over the years the Kulm has hosted royalty from all over the world, including the kings and queens of industry and entertainment. The public rooms are beautifully paneled, with vaulted ceilings. A large part of the city's world-famous bobsled run, Cresta run, and the curling rinks of St. Moritz are on property belonging to this hotel.

Dining/Entertainment: Today the Sunny Bar is one of the most popular spots in town (usually with live music). Its restaurants, Français and Rôtisserie des Chevaliers, serve some of the finest continental specialties in St. Moritz.

Services: Room service, laundry.

Facilities: Indoor swimming pool with mountains, sauna, gym, massage facilities, ice-skating rink, curling rink, tennis courts with pros, children's playground and playroom.

SUVRETTA HOUSE, via Suvretta, CH-7500 St. Moritz. Tel. 082/2-11-21. Fax 082/3-85-24. 230 rms (all with bath). TV TEL
$ Rates (including half board): Summer, 175F–285F ($127.75–$208) single; 350F–710F ($255.45–$518.25) double. Winter, 225F–375F ($164.25–$273.70) single; 450F–900F ($328.45–$656.90) double. No credit cards.

Set about a mile from the resort, this five-star hotel has a comfortable and somewhat-sedate clientele, a grand but unusually simple decor, and a highly individual style. It was built in 1912 on a plateau surrounded by mountains and lakes. Its Edwardian facade has two neomedieval towers and a grandly baroque central gable that has become the hotel's trademark. Except for areas of richly grained oak paneling and Engadine sgraffito, the interior is covered with simple, no-nonsense plaster and pierced with endless series of vaulted arches. It is surrounded with more land than any other hotel in St. Moritz.

Dining/Entertainment: With the push of a button, a wall of the French restaurant, Le Miroir, slides away to expose the popular nightclub La Voilière. Dining facilities, housed in mountain huts, can also be found on the ski slopes. Men must wear dinner jackets or dark suits in the winter and jackets and ties in the summer.

Services: 24-hour room service, laundry.

Facilities: Indoor swimming pool, two bowling alleys, three tennis courts, ice-skating rink, games room, private ski lift.

EXPENSIVE

HOTEL ALBANA, via Maistra 6, CH-7500 St. Moritz. Tel. 082/3-31-21. Fax 082/3-15-43. 75 rms (all with bath). MINIBAR TV TEL **Bus:** 1.
$ Rates (including half board): Summer, 175F–285F ($127.75–$208) single; 350F–710F ($255.45–$518.25) double. Winter, 225F–375F ($164.25–$273.70) single; 450F–900F ($328.45–$656.90) double. AE, DC, MC, V. **Parking:** 15F ($10.95).

A hotel was first established here in 1644; the current hotel has been managed by the Weinmann family since 1971. This is a popular hotel, painted a salmon color with white trim and decorated with regional designs and an occasional hunting trophy. The bedrooms usually have ceiling beams or elaborate paneling and occasionally a regional armoire. The bedrooms have radios and safes.

Dining/Entertainment: The bar area has stenciled illustrations. There are also two restaurants, serving Swiss, French, and international dishes.

Facilities: Sauna, fitness room, whirlpool, solarium.

HOTEL CRYSTAL, via Traunter Piazzas 1, CH-7500 St. Moritz. Tel. 082/2-11-65. Fax 082/3-64-45. 138 rms (all with bath). MINIBAR TV TEL **Bus:** 1.

$ Rates (including half board): Summer, 140F–170F ($102.20–$124.10) single; 250F–320F ($182.50–$233.55) double. Winter, 185F–210F ($135.05–$153.30) single; 360F–410F ($262.75–$299.25) double. AE, DC, MC, V.

This large white building looks oddly futuristic when compared with the 19th-century structures around it. The interior combines comfortable alpine rusticity with knotty-pine cabinets and ceiling beams, along with wall-to-wall carpeting and informal furniture. The bedrooms are furnished with a combination of walnut and lighter grained woods.

Dining/Entertainment: The in-house Grotto restaurant serves Italian specialties. A nearby piano bar provides midafternoon entertainment.

Services: Room service, laundry.

Facilities: Free access to the Kulm Hotel swimming pool.

HOTEL STEFFANI, Sonnenplatz 1, CH-7500 St. Moritz. Tel. 082/2-21-01. Fax 082/3-40-97. 69 rms (all with bath). MINIBAR TV TEL **Bus:** 1.

$ Rates (including continental breakfast): Summer, 110F–180F ($80.30–$131.40) single; 180F–340F ($131.40–$248.15) double. Winter, 190F–220F ($138.70–$160.60) single; 280F–440F ($204.35–$321.15) double. AE, DC, MC, V.

Built in 1869 by Lorenzo Steffani, the hotel is run by the Märky family. The elegant guests find lots of carved wood here, especially in one of the restaurant areas. The rooms are comfortably and cozily furnished.

Dining/Entertainment: Some of the hotel's many restaurants and nightclubs are covered separately under "Where to Dine" and "Evening Entertainment," below.

Services: Room service, laundry, baby-sitting, hairdresser.

Facilities: Fitness room, indoor swimming pool, sauna, solarium.

MONOPOL-GRISCHUNA, via Maistra 17, Dorf, CH-7500 St. Moritz. Tel. 082/3-44-33. Fax 082/3-71-37. 71 rms (all with bath). MINIBAR TV TEL **Bus:** 1.

$ Rates (including half board): 110F–220F ($80.30–$160.60) single; 200F–430F ($146–$313.85) double. AE, DC, MC, V.

Set above the busy street, this 25-year-old stucco building offers elegant public rooms furnished with French pieces, a few oil paintings, and well-polished wood detailing. The spacious bedrooms are colorfully designed around Louis XV and Louis XVI or rustic furniture.

Dining/Entertainment: This hotel has its own nightclub and a restaurant called the Grischuna.

Services: Room service, laundry.

Facilities: Covered pool, roof terrace.

NEUES POSTHOTEL, via dal Vout 3, Dorf, CH-7500 St. Moritz. Tel.

082/2-21-21. Fax 022/3-89-73. 88 rms (all with bath). MINIBAR TV TEL **Bus:** 1.
$ Rates (including half board): Summer, 140F–170F ($102.20–$124.10) single; 260F–320F ($189.75–$233.55) double. Winter, 160F–190F ($116.80–$138.70) single; 280F–360F ($204.35–$262.75) double. AE, DC, MC, V.

In the heart of St. Moritz, this year-round four-star hotel was built in 1908 and today places more emphasis on hospitality than on stylish furniture and a sense of chic. Peter and Elli Graber maintain a hotel with a blazing midwinter fireplace and comfortably furnished, and sometimes quite spacious, bedrooms. Those on the uppermost floor have private balconies and a view of the lake. The two different sections of the hotel, built on either side of a steeply inclined street, are connected by a covered passageway that soars high above the cobblestone pavements.

Dining/Entertainment: The hotel restaurant has lake views (if requested in advance) and large portions.
Services: Room service, laundry.
Facilities: Sauna, whirlpool.

MODERATE

HOTEL BELLEVUE, via del Bagn 18, Bad, CH-7050 St. Moritz. Tel. 082/2-21-61. Fax 082/3-81-63. 74 rms (all with bath). TV TEL **Bus:** 1.
$ Rates (including half board): Summer, 110F–130F ($80.30–$94.90) single; 190F–230F ($138.70–$167.90) double. Winter, 118F–138F ($86.15–$100.75) single; 205F–245F ($149.65–$178.85) double. AE, DC, MC, V.

This is an angular, white-and-buff building with an occasional balcony and a panoramic view to justify its name. The interior is functionally attractive, with patterned carpeting, the obligatory pinewood paneling, and comfortable bedrooms with wood furniture. The hotel's restaurant serves both Swiss and continental specialties.

HOTEL EDEN, via Vegia 12, CH-7500 St. Moritz. Tel. 082/3-61-61. Fax 082/3-91-91. 34 rms (all with bath). TV TEL **Bus:** 1.
$ Rates (including buffet breakfast): Summer, 75F–85F ($54.75–$62.05) single; 140F–170F ($102.20–$124.10) double. Winter, 105F–120F ($76.65–$87.60) single; 180F–240F ($131.40–$175.20) double. No credit cards. **Closed:** Apr–July and Dec.

A pleasant hotel whose architecture might remind you of a Tuscan villa, this establishment was built more than a century ago and has been in the Degiacomi family for almost 40 years. It doesn't cost as much as either of its more glamorous neighbors, the Kulm and Badrutt's Palace, whose exterior it overlooks. The Eden, which opens onto a tiny but charming plaza in the center of town, is filled with pinewood paneling and family antiques. Each of the simple and modernized bedrooms has conservative furniture.

HOTEL LANGUARD-GARNI, via Maistra, CH-7500 St. Moritz. Tel. 082/3-31-37. 28 rms (all with bath). TEL **Bus:** 1.
$ Rates (including breakfast): 85F–110F ($62.05–$80.30) single; 120F–240F ($87.60–$175.20) double. No credit cards. **Closed:** May and Nov.

Built a century ago as the private home of the owner of the nearby Kulm Hotel, this much-enlarged and altered property lies just off the main street of town. It's run by a conservative Swiss staff and the Trivella family, who display their family's ski awards (one of their sons, Roberto, was a champion in 1978) in a glass case by the reception desk. The hotel's pine-paneled interior is clean and very charming, with a breakfast room that overlooks the valley and the lake. Breakfast is the only meal served. Some of the accommodations have private balconies, private baths, radios, direct-dial phones, and safes.

HOTEL WALDHAUS AM SEE, via Dimiej 6, CH-7500 St. Moritz. Tel. 082/3-76-76. Fax 082/3-88-77. 36 rms (all with bath). MINIBAR TV TEL

$ **Rates** (including half board): 80F–110F ($58.40–$80.30) single; 190F–320F ($138.70–$233.55) double. V. **Closed:** Nov.

Built in 1880 as a tavern, the castlelike structure was later expanded into a private home by a Swiss industrialist. You can dine in one of three lovely rooms, the largest of which has access to a sheltered sun terrace and views over the lake. Halen and Claudio Bernasconi-Mettier, the hosts, offer comfortably conservative rooms with a radio.

INEXPENSIVE

HOTEL BERNINA, via del Bagn 5, Bad, CH-7500 St. Moritz. Tel. 082/3-60-22. Fax 082/3-19-40. 30 rms (16 with bath). TEL **Bus:** 1.

$ **Rates** (including half board): Summer, 75F ($54.75) single without bath, 95F ($69.35) single with bath; 150F ($109.50) double without bath, 180F ($131.40) double with bath. Winter 90F ($65.70) single without bath, 110F ($80.30) single with bath; 180F ($131.40) double without bath, 210F ($153.30) double with bath. AE, MC, V. **Closed:** Mid-Apr to early June.

Set close to the lake in St. Moritz-Bad, the Hotel Bernina has a pleasant, earth-colored lobby, with warm textiles and lots of wood. The unpretentious hotel and restaurant have been managed by the Hermann family for several generations. The rooms are simply but comfortably furnished.

HOTEL NATIONAL, via de l'Ova, Cotschna 1, CH-7500 St. Moritz. Tel. 082/3-32-74. 50 rms (42 with bath). **Bus:** 1.

$ **Rates** (including half board): 65F ($47.45) single without bath; 85F ($62.05) single with bath; 120F ($87.60) double without bath, 150F ($109.50) double with bath. AE, V. **Closed:** Apr–June and Sept–Dec.

Erich Wissel's hotel is one of the better bargains in St. Moritz. The outside has neoclassical details and wrought-iron balconies, while the interior has a scattering of Oriental rugs, informal furniture, and comfortable bedrooms. The hotel is opposite a large indoor swimming pool. This family-run place was built at the turn of the century, and it still evokes a bygone age. Its restaurant serves various specialties from the different sections of Italy, including the Ticino. Laundry and room service are provided.

WHERE TO DINE

Although meals may be included in the cost of your hotel, you may want to sample the selections at other hotels and restaurants. There are also dozens of fashionable Konditoreien (coffeehouses).

VERY EXPENSIVE

CHESA VEGLIA, via Veglia 2, Dorf. Tel. 3-35-96.
Cuisine: INTERNATIONAL. **Reservations:** Required. **Bus:** 1.

$ **Prices:** Appetizers 10F–18F ($7.30–$13.15); main courses 36F–98F ($26.30–$71.55). AE, DC, MC, V.

Open: Summer, daily 11am–midnight; winter, daily 11am–2am. **Closed:** Beginning of Apr to June and mid-Sept to beginning of Dec.

⭐ *Chesa* means "house" in Romansh, and that's exactly what this Engadine-style building once was. Built in 1658 of stone, stucco, and wood, it retains much of its original paneling and carving, as well as entire rooms comprised of architectural remnants from local houses. It is the only authentic Engadine house left in St. Moritz. You'll enter through a massive arched oak door.

Inside you'll find three restaurants, each on a different floor. The Chadafo Grill cooks your meat over a wood fire visible from the dining room. The Patrizier-Stube serves regional specialties. The Hayloft—the least expensive of the three—is a pizzeria, with a wood-stoked oven. Local musicians will probably be playing folk music while you eat. If you're visiting for a gourmet repast, expect a wide choice of international dishes, from Italian (saltimbocca) to Hungarian (goulash) to Russian (chicken Kiev). Try the grilled scampi or trout meunière. The desserts are equally elegant, including soufflés and mousses. It's owned and operated by the Palace Hotel.

RESTAURANT/THE GRILL ROOM, in Badrutt's Palace Hotel, via Serlas 27. Tel. 2-11-01.

Cuisine: SWISS. **Reservations:** Required. **Bus:** 1.

$ **Prices:** Appetizers 30F–100F ($21.90–$73); main courses 50F–80F ($36.50–$58.40); fixed price meals from 75F ($54.75) at lunch, from 95F ($69.35) at dinner. AE, DC, MC, V.

Open: Main dining room, lunch daily 12:15–3pm; dinner daily 7:30–10pm. Grill room, lunch daily 12:30–2:30pm; dinner daily 8–11pm.

This pair of posh restaurants is presided over by a sophisticated staff of 70 employees who have waited table for such luminaries as the Shah of Iran and his wife, Fara Diba, the Aga Khan, and Alfred Hitchcock. Representative menu listings include fresh oysters, smoked trout, risotto with exotic mushrooms, julienne of veal with white wine sauce, saddle of roebuck, and an array of desserts.

Some guests prefer the more lavish meals amid the green and gold baroque decor of the high-ceilinged grillroom, on the lobby level of the hotel. Menu items include hearts of artichoke with a salad of truffles, terrine of shellfish with smoked salmon and watercress sauce, lobster cocktail with aged cognac, fettuccine with foie gras and two varieties of exotic mushrooms, and poached quail with grapes. Appropriate attire in either restaurant is strongly recommended.

TRATTORIA, in Badrutt's Palace Hotel, via Serlas 27. Tel. 2-11-01.

Cuisine: SWISS/ITALIAN. **Reservations:** Required. **Bus:** 1.

$ **Prices:** Appetizers 35F–100F ($25.55–$73); main courses 60F–90F ($43.80–$65.70). AE, DC, MC, V.

Open: Dinner only, daily 7:30–midnight.

This is one of the few places in Badrutt's Palace where jackets and ties are not required for men. The cozy Stube with live piano music and a separate street entrance offers sophisticated meals and a well-polished feeling of alpine warmth. It opens for drinks in the late afternoon. Typical dishes include trout soup with shrimp, skewered brochette of lamb with mint, and sautéed veal kidneys with flap mushrooms. If you order sufficiently in advance, the chef will prepare a succulent version of bouillabaisse or paella.

EXPENSIVE

LANDGASTHOF MEIEREI, via Dimlej 52. Tel. 3-20-60.

Cuisine: SWISS. **Reservations:** Required. **Directions:** See below.

$ **Prices:** Appetizers 10F–16F ($7.30–$11.70); main courses 18F–32F ($13.15–$23.35). No credit cards.

Open: Lunch daily 11:30am–3pm; dinner daily 6:30–9:30pm.

Built a century ago as a relay station for the Swiss Postal Service, today it houses four dining rooms, which have served the Shah of Iran, playboy industrialist Günther Sachs, Picasso, the Aga Khan, and King Farouk of Egypt. Considering the glamorous clientele that the place has attracted, its menu is earthy and simple.

No diner is allowed to drive a car along the difficult-to-navigate service roads that reach it. You can hire a taxi or a horse-drawn sleigh. My recommendation is that you park your car in the public parking lot near the edge of the lake, just below the Hotel Waldhaus am See, and walk the 20-minute lakeside promenade to the restaurant. The footpath has been carefully paved, and there are only a few slopes to negotiate. Before you set out, it's advisable to phone the restaurant to confirm that they're open.

LA MARMITE, Corviglia Bergstation. Tel. 3-63-55.

Cuisine: SWISS. **Reservations:** Recommended. **Transportation:** Funicular.

$ **Prices:** Appetizers 12F–16F ($8.75–$11.70); main courses 18F–39F ($13.15–$28.45). AE, DC, MC, V.

Open: Lunch daily noon–4pm; dinner daily 6–10pm. **Closed:** Apr 20 to early June and mid-Oct to Nov. 20.

This woodsy establishment is the best high-altitude restaurant in the Grisons. It can be reached only by funicular. The Mathis family offers excellent service and a sophisticated menu. There's also a less expensive cafeteria on the premises that in midwinter is usually crowded with skiers. Dishes might include creamed venison soup, fresh duck liver with truffles, calves' foot in a truffle sauce, and a bone-warming bouillon, perfect for a cold day, flavored with marrow, vegetables, sherry, and meat. If you're in the mood, you might ask for the six-course caviar menu or a seafood omelet. Desserts might be figs soaked in grappa, although a buffet of some 25 to 30 desserts is available if you prefer something less potent.

RESTAURANT ACLA, in the Hotel Schweizerhof, via dal Bagn 54, Dorf. Tel. 2-21-71.

Cuisine: SWISS/INTERNATIONAL. **Reservations:** Recommended. **Bus:** 1.

$ **Prices:** Appetizers 10F–15F ($7.30–$10.95); main courses 16F–32F ($11.70–$23.35); fixed-price lunch 18F ($13.15). AE, DC, MC, V.

Open: Daily 11am–midnight.

Situated in the elegant Hotel Schweizerhof, this "little house on the mountain"—as its name is translated from Romansh—serves Swiss specialties and international dishes in a rustically appealing and rather formal ambience. The restaurant's more popular name, at least among the locals, is "Chez Molly." You're given the famous Tafelspitz (the boiled beef of Vienna), blinis with caviar and smoked salmon, and the "original" Viennese fried chicken. Trout is from the Inn, and you can also order poached fresh salmon and filets of sole bonne femme.

RESTAURANT CHESA PIRANI, La Punt–Chamues. Tel. 7-25-15.

Cuisine: SWISS. **Reservations:** Recommended. **Transportation:** See below.

$ **Prices:** Appetizers 22F–35F ($16.05–$25.55); main courses 40F–60F ($29.20–$43.80); fixed-price meals 75F–140F ($54.75–$102.20). AE, MC, V.

Open: Lunch, in winter only daily 11am–3pm; dinner daily 6–11pm. **Closed:** Mon in summer; late April to mid-June and Nov.

This fine restaurant is 12 miles from the center of St. Moritz in an Engadine-style chalet originally built in 1750. The Hitzbergers offer excellent cuisine and service.

You'll be shown into one of a series of dining rooms, none of which holds more than four or five tables. Mr. Hitzberger prepares original recipes, which include an avocado salad with shrimp and a sour-vinegar sauce, hearty cabbage soup, and a terrine of foie gras. Dessert might be a champagne sorbet.

To get to the restaurant, you can drive or take a taxi. Or you can take one of the frequent daily Rhaetische Bahn trains from St. Moritz toward Ternez-Chur. Tell the conductor that you want to get off in La Punt; it's about a 15-minute ride from St. Moritz.

RESTAURANT STEFFANI, in the Hotel Steffani, Sonnenplatz 1. Tel. 2-21-01.
   Cuisine: SWISS. **Reservations:** Not needed. **Bus:** 1.
$ **Prices:** Appetizers 10F–15F ($7.30–$10.95); main courses 18F–31F ($13.15–$22.65); fixed-price meal 38F ($27.75). AE, DC, MC, V.
   Open: Daily 11:30am–11:30pm.

Half-board guests of the hotel usually dine upstairs in the elegant grillroom, but in many ways I prefer the warm, wood-lined decor and the polite service of the street-level tavern. Specialties include tagliatelle Alfredo, poulet chasseur with polenta, alpine goat with rosemary, at least six different kinds of pasta, trout, lobster, and pepper steak.

MODERATE

AL REDUIT, piazza Mauritius, Dorf. Tel. 3-66-57.
   Cuisine: SWISS. **Reservations:** Not needed. **Bus:** 1.
$ **Prices:** Appetizers 8F–14F ($5.85–$10.20); main courses 15F–26F ($10.95–$19). AE, DC, MC, V.
   Open: Mon–Sat 11am–midnight, Sun 4pm–midnight.

A typical trattoria and pizzeria, this popular late-night spot offers good food in a rustic setting with red-and-white-checked tablecloths. It is located in a shopping arcade near the Hotel Albana. Most diners come for one of 15 different kinds of pizza, but you can also order more substantial fare, such as a variety of pastas. Meats are cooked to perfection on an open grill. If the weather's right, you can also select a table on one of the best sun terraces in town.

GROTTO, in the Hotel Crystal, via Traunter Piazzas 1. Tel. 2-11-65.
   Cuisine: ITALIAN. **Reservations:** Recommended. **Bus:** 1.
$ **Prices:** Appetizers 10F–15F ($7.30–$10.95); main courses 18F–29F ($13.15–$21.17). AE, DC, MC, V.
   Open: Lunch daily noon–4pm; dinner daily 5–10pm. **Closed:** Nov.

Grotto is the best place in St. Moritz for Ticino food. Many of the hors d'oeuvres are laid out on a buffet. Main courses might include rabbit with thyme, an array of pasta dishes, codfish with polenta, and fondue Piedmont style. You can begin with a steaming-hot bowl of minestrone. Desserts are smooth and rich, including a classic zabaglione.

LE MANDARIN, in the Hotel Steffani, Sonnenplatz 1. Tel. 2-21-01.
   Cuisine: CHINESE. **Reservations:** Not needed. **Bus:** 1.
$ **Prices:** Appetizers 10F–16F ($7.30–$11.70); main courses 16F–29F ($11.70–$21.15). AE, DC, MC, V.
   Open: Lunch, midwinter only, daily 11:30am–2pm; dinner, year round, daily 6:30–11pm. **Closed:** Late Apr to early June.

As one of the few Chinese restaurants in the region, Le Mandarin does a thriving business, especially later in the evening. The decor is predictably Chinese, with black lacquer screens and hanging lanterns. The menu has a wide selection of hors d'oeuvres and soups, followed by such dishes as squid with peppers, sautéed fish in hot sauce, and butterfly prawns. Duck is prepared in a variety of ways. The house specialty is Peking duck; it is prepared for groups of three or more customers. The pork and veal dishes are especially delectable.

RESTAURANT ENGIADINA, piazza da Scoula 2. Tel. 3-32-65.
   Cuisine: SWISS. **Reservations:** Recommended. **Bus:** 1.
$ **Prices:** Appetizers 8F–14F ($5.85–$10.20); main courses 16F–24F ($11.70–$17.50). AE, DC, MC, V.
   Open: Summer, lunch Mon–Sat 10am–2pm; dinner Mon–Sat 5–9:30pm. Winter, Mon–Sat 10am–10pm, Sun 4–10pm.

⑤ In the direct center of St. Moritz-Dorf, across the street from the town hall, the Melchers run an old-fashioned family dining room that is uncharacteristic for St. Moritz. You get good value for your money here. Pleasant, comfortable, and simple, it consists of two hunters'-style rooms filled with trophies and alpine accents, such as pinewood tables and paneling. There's even an outdoor wooden deck for drinking and dining if the weather is right. Selections include carpaccio, petite marmite, fondues (with cheese or champagne), grilled steaks, goulash, and snails in garlic butter.

ROTISSERIE DES CHEVALIERS, in the Hotel Kulm, via Veglia 18, Dorf. Tel. 2-11-51.
   Cuisine: FRENCH. **Reservations:** Required. **Bus:** 1.
$ **Prices:** Appetizers 10F–40F ($7.30–$29.20); main courses 35F–60F ($25.55–$43.80). AE, MC, V.
   Open: Lunch daily noon–3pm; dinner daily 7pm–midnight. **Closed:** Mid-Sept to Nov and mid-Apr to June.
This exquisitely paneled grillroom, in one of the most historic hotels in St. Moritz, is decorated with mementos of the Cresta bobsled run. The smaller of the two menus lists changing daily specialties, which include seasonal food such as fresh asparagus, along with terrine of goose liver, grilled sea bass flambé, and a unique stuffed veal Hotel Kulm.

VELTLINER-KELLER, via del Bagn 11. Tel. 3-40-09.
   Cuisine: SWISS/ITALIAN. **Reservations:** Required. **Bus:** 1.
$ **Prices:** Appetizers 7F–18F ($5.10–$13.15); main courses 22F–35F ($16.05–$25.55). No credit cards.
   Open: Daily 9am–midnight.
Although it functions as a café and tavern throughout the day, it is at its best for dining in the evening, when the rustically informal premises welcomes many of the town's professional ski-and-sea crowd. The menu includes mushroom salads, trout with mushrooms, spaghetti, and a wide selection of meats and fish, along with a tasty risotto. Desserts include just about every in-season fruit in Europe.

INEXPENSIVE

HANSELMANN, via Maistra 8. Tel. 3-38-64.
   Cuisine: SWISS. **Reservations:** Accepted only for lunch. **Bus:** 1.
$ **Prices:** Appetizers 8F–14F ($5.85–$10.20); main courses 15F–26F ($10.95–$19); breakfast 12F–18F ($8.75–$13.15); fixed-price lunch 23F ($16.80). No credit cards.
   Open: Daily 7am–7pm.
Since it was originally established in the mid-1800s, this tavern and tearoom has

grown to occupy a much-embellished building decorated with sgraffito. Today it's one of the best and most inexpensive places in town for breakfast or lunch. It is owned by Fritz Mutschler, grandson of the original founder. For breakfast, you might choose an omelet (from a German-language menu), an egg-and-cheese dish, or a country platter piled high with Black Forest ham and Valais rye rolls. Other dishes include Welsh rarebit and smoked salmon with buttered toast. The upstairs restaurant opens at 11:30am. The place is also popular with the après-ski crowd.

RESTAURANT CASCADE, via Somplaz 6, Dorf. Tel. 3-10-42.
   Cuisine: ITALIAN. **Reservations:** Required in winter. **Bus:** 1.
$ Prices: Appetizers 5.50F–21F ($4–$15.35); main courses 15F–40F ($10.95–$29.20). AE, DC, MC, V.
   Open: Mon–Sat 11am–11pm, Sun 3–11pm.
Next door to the Hotel Steffani, this restaurant offers Italian recipes from the Ticino. With its etched-glass mirrors and bentwood chairs, it is popular with a young, informally dressed crowd for drinks as well as food (see "Evening Entertainment," below). Dishes include carpaccio, saltimbocca, and gnocchi Piedmont style, but mainly it specializes in pastas and entrecôtes.

SHOPPING

The shops of St. Moritz are as chic and expensive as any stores in Paris, London, or New York. Smart shoppers have long known that the best time to buy in St. Moritz is during the winter and summer clearance sales. You can stroll along the inner village streets and find all the shops easily. Some of the most important ones are on via Maistra (the main shopping street) and in the Palace-Arcades.

In spite of its bland architecture, the **Galleria Caspar Badrutt,** via Maistra, has many facilities and stores, including a fitness center (Caribbean Sunshine), a pharmacy, an elegant hairdressing salon, and an art gallery. The stores sell everything from men's wear to perfumes, from lingerie to furs by Balenciaga or fashions by Saint Laurent.

EVENING ENTERTAINMENT

The nightlife here in the winter is the most glamorous in Switzerland. It centers around the Palace, but there are dozens of other bars, restaurants, and taverns. In some chic discos the dress code ranges from black-tie to jeans. Nightlife is very expensive, and although cases of French champagne are consumed, no one looks askance if you order a beer.

THE CLUB & MUSIC SCENE

KING'S CLUB, in Badrutt's Palace Hotel, via Serlas 27. Tel. 2-11-01.
   Every grand hotel has a disco, where guests mingle with the rich and famous. This particular club is distinguished by its jungle paintings, neomedieval stone work, and contemporary dance music. Jackets and ties are not required. Open in season daily from 10pm to 6am. Drinks begin at 15F ($10.95).
   Admission: 30F–50F ($21.90–$36.50), depending on the entertainment and the season.

VIVAI DISCO, in the Hotel Steffani, Sonnenplatz 1. Tel. 2-21-01.
   Its basement-level portal is etched in Engadine line drawings, but inside all is

intimately lit and modern. The music is contemporary. The club has a separate entrance off the square in front of the hotel. Beer runs 15F ($10.95).

Admission: 12F–22F ($8.75–$16.05).

SUNNY BAR, in the Hotel Kulm, via Veglia 18, Dorf. Tel. 2-11-51.

Decorated with signs of the zodiac, this is one of the most popular dance clubs in town. Open daily until 3am. Drinks cost about 11F ($8.05).

Admission: Free.

THE BAR & CAFE SCENE

HANSELMANN, via Maistra 8. Tel. 3-38-64.

Immediately after skiers return from the slopes, they come here for either breakfast or lunch. The tearoom has its busiest hours from 4:30 to 6pm. The place is famous for its pastries, cakes, and chocolates. After a day in the open air, a crowd gathers to have hot chocolate, espresso, tea, or even a cup of grog with rum. The more expensive desserts include a large Engadiner Nusstorte (a delectable pastry of walnuts, butter, and honey), the Baumkuchen (a cake), and caviar toast. Hanselmann's also has a retail counter where you can choose chocolates or other confections to take home. Open daily from 7:30am to 7pm. Desserts begin at 12F ($8.75).

GRAND BAR, in Badrutt's Palace Hotel, via Serlas 27. Tel. 2-11-01.

The tables are tiny, the drinks are expensive, and the stand-up bar is inconveniently set up on the wrong side of the stage. Still, this is considered the place to be. Murals that might have been executed by Jean Cocteau add a visual element. The quality of your evening might depend on the musical artist of the moment, but in its past the place has seen some winners. You'd be well advised to reserve a table in advance. Open daily from 10pm to 4 or 5am. Closed April to June and September to December. Drinks run 24F ($17.50).

SCHWYZERHOF-STÜBLI, in the Hotel Schweizerhof, via dal Bagn 54, Dorf. Tel. 2-21-71.

Skiers often head directly to the club's separate entrance after a day on the slopes. The Stübli—unlike the conservative hotel that contains it—often gets quite rowdy. Many guests, in spite of the crowds, order dinner, served on top of the bar. The place looks much older than it probably is, with a coffered alpine ceiling and pinewood paneling, along with trestle tables. Open daily from 4pm to midnight. Drinks cost 8F ($5.85); raclette, 18F ($13.15).

THE PIANOBAR, in the Hotel Schweizerhof, via dal Bahn 54, Dorf. Tel. 2-21-71.

Priding itself on the refinement of its clientele, its drinks, and its music, this piano bar is suitable for a mellow and calming round or two of drinks, served with panache by the barman, Edi. Musicians change regularly; often they're imported from outside Switzerland. Open daily from 8pm to 2am. Drinks cost 16F ($11.70).

LA CAVA STEFFANI, in the Hotel Steffani, Sonnenplatz 1. Tel. 2-21-01.

Contained beneath the vaulted ceilings of the lowest level of the Hotel Steffani, this dimly lit and warmly decorated après-ski hangout is decorated with antique skis, crisscrossed ski poles, Engadine-style chairs, and flickering candles. Menu items include fondue chinoise, picatta with spaghetti, rumpsteak, two varieties of ravioli, and entrecôte. Open daily from 4pm to midnight. Dinner costs about 33F ($24.10); a glass of wine, 4F ($2.90).

CRESTA BAR, in the Hotel Steffani, Sonnenplatz 1. Tel. 2-21-01.

Small, cramped, and nearly concealed behind a thick door near the hotel's reception desk, this club isn't particularly noteworthy in any way, except that its pair of rooms are mobbed with skiers at the end of a midwinter's day. Open daily from 4pm to midnight. Beer runs 6F ($4.40).

CASCADE BAR, via Somplaz 6. Tel. 3-15-22.

Richly decorated with such art nouveau accessories as stained and etched glass, this place can be both rowdy and fun. The posters are unabashedly explicit, at least for Paris of 1903. Music lovers will appreciate the unsolicited groups of men singing in spontaneous choruses everything from barbershop quartets to operatic trios. Cordon Rouge chills invitingly in Plexiglas buckets on the zinc bartop. A restaurant is attached. Open daily from 1 to 11pm. Drinks range from 3.50F to 14F ($2.55 to $10.20).

---

4. PONTRESINA

4 miles E of St. Moritz, 53 miles SE of Chur, 130 miles SE of Zurich

GETTING THERE **By Train** From Zurich, via Chur, there is a train arriving in Pontresina every hour throughout the day until 10pm. There is also a train arriving every hour from St. Moritz.

By Bus In the winter there is a "sportbus" running between St. Moritz and Pontresina every 30 minutes daily from 7:30am to 6:30pm. Tickets can be purchased at the post office or directly on the bus.

By Car From St. Moritz, head northeast along Route 27, then cut southeast at the junction with Route 29.

ESSENTIALS The **Pontresina Tourist Office** (tel. 082/6-64-88) is open Monday through Friday from 8am to noon and 2 to 6pm, and on Saturday from 8am to 5pm. The **telephone area code** for Pontresina is 082. In lieu of **street names,** follow hotel or restaurant directional signs.

Pontresina (5,916 ft.) doesn't have the fame of St. Moritz, but it offers some of the best hiking and mountaineering in the Engadine. Its long hours of sunshine in the winter, and its access to all the noted ski sites in the greater St. Moritz area, make Pontresina an attractive alternative to the more expensive town. Situated in the Upper Engadines on the road to the Bernina Pass, at the mouth of the Bernina Valley, it is surrounded by larches, stone pines, and the Alps. From Pontresina you have views of what is called the "glacier amphitheater" of the Roseg Mountains.

Originally a 19th-century summer resort, Pontresina has become a leading ski resort, known for its famous ski runs and cross-country skiing tracks. The village today is filled with hotels and shops and has much old Engadine architecture.

WHAT TO SEE & DO

Several tours are available. The ☼ **Diavolezza** tour, which starts at 9,076 feet and passes over two glaciers on the way down, is one of the major attractions of the Engadines. You go by road toward Bernina as far as the lower station of the Diavolezza cable car, which can carry you up to 9,076 feet by drag lift for skiing. There's a famous ski run down to the valley or down the glacier to Morteratsch. If you go with a guide for this glacier walk, allow about 3 hours. In season the Diavolezza cable car is likely to be crowded—the journey up will take about half an hour. The round-trip fare is 22F ($16.05).

Alp Languard, at an altitude of 8,500 feet, is directly above Pontresina; you reach it by ski lift. The round-trip costs 13F ($9.50).

The area's chief attraction is ✪ **Muottos Muragl,** a mountain whose peak is reached by funicular. The excursion begins in Pontresina, where you board a bus that travels 2 miles uphill in the direction of Samedan, to a final destination at the base of the funicular, a place known as Punt Muragl. The funicular ride takes 30 minutes to reach a platform set at 8,048 feet above sea level. From it you'll see the Upper Engadine Gap, with the mountain ranges of Piz Julier and Piz Rosatsch on either side. If the day is clear you can also see the lakes between Maloja and St. Moritz. The excursion, including bus rides, costs 16F ($11.70) round-trip. For information in Pontresina, call 082/3-39-42 or inquire at the reception desk of your hotel.

WHERE TO STAY

VERY EXPENSIVE

GRAND HOTEL KRONENHOF, CH-7540 Pontresina. Tel. 082/6-01-11. Fax 082/6-60-66. 104 rms (all with bath). MINIBAR TEL
$ **Rates** (including half board): Summer, 170F–280F ($124.10–$204.35) single; 320F–480F ($233.55–$380.35) double. Winter, 190F–300F ($138.70–$218.95) single; 360F–540F ($262.75–$394.15) double. AE, DC, MC, V. **Closed:** Mar–June and Sept–Dec.

✪ This is indubitably the grandest hotel in town. Set in the center of town, behind iron gates and a circular driveway, the Kronenhof is decorated with Corinthian columns and vaulted, frescoed ceilings. Its oldest section dates from 1848; the impressive details are from 1898. The bedrooms are comfortable and attractively furnished.

Dining/Entertainment: The dining room is as grand as you'd expect. The hotel restaurant, the Kronenstübli, is recommended separately (see "Where to Dine," below). Televisions are provided in rooms upon request.

Services: Room service, laundry.

Facilities: Ice-skating rink, indoor and outdoor swimming pool, curling contests, films, gala dinners for half-board guests, access to local ski schools.

EXPENSIVE

HOTEL LA COLLINA & SOLDENELLA, CH-7504 Pontresina. Tel. 082/6-01-21. Fax 082/6-79-95. 55 rms (all with bath). MINIBAR TV TEL
$ **Rates** (including half board): 125F–155F ($91.25–$113.15) single; 260F–340F ($189.75–$248.15) double. AE, DC, MC, V. **Closed:** Apr–June and Oct–Dec. This elegant, white-walled château is decorated with a few regional antiques, beamed ceilings, and Oriental rugs. The bedrooms are conservatively modern, spacious, and colorful. The hotel restaurant serves both regional and continental specialties.

HOTEL SCHWEIZERHOF, CH-7504 Pontresina. Tel. 082/6-01-31. Fax 082/6-79-88. 98 rms (all with bath). MINIBAR TV TEL
$ **Rates** (including half board): 145F–175F ($105.85–$127.75) single; 270F–360F ($197.05–$262.75) double. AE, DC, MC, V. **Closed:** Apr–June and Oct–Dec. The Schweizerhof was built in 1910, but it was so drastically modernized in 1975 that old-time visitors hardly recognize it; much of its roofline (including the towers and turrets) was removed. Yet it remains a huge, comfortable, and expansive hotel; it's a

member of the Best Western chain. The lobby has a wall of hewn stone and a ceiling of weathered wood slats, and the dining room has Engadine stencils and arches. The rooms are well furnished and comfortable.

HOTEL WALTHER, CH-7504 Pontresina. Tel. 082/6-64-71. Fax 082/6-79-22. 102 rms (all with bath). MINIBAR TV TEL

$ Rates (including half board): 175F–215F ($127.75–$156.95) single; 340F–420F ($248.15–$306.55) double. AE, DC, MC, V. **Closed:** Apr–June and Oct–Dec.

This is a 19th-century palatial hotel, surrounded by lawns. Some aspects of the hotel suggest a Wagnerian fantasy of Disneyland. The bedrooms are available in various sizes, but each is well furnished and maintained.

Dining/Entertainment: Despite the medieval aspects of the facade, the piano bar couldn't be more contemporary. There is also a regal restaurant with good service and food.

Services: Room service, laundry.

Facilities: Tennis courts, indoor swimming pool, Jacuzzi, sauna, massage room, children's playroom.

MODERATE

HOTEL BERNINA, CH-7504 Pontresina. Tel. 082/6-62-21. Fax 082/6-70-32. 80 rms (all with bath or shower). TV TEL

$ Rates (including half board): 115F–136F ($83.95–$98.90) single; 220F–260F ($160.60–$189.75) double. AE, DC, MC, V. **Closed:** Apr–June and Oct–Dec.

The members of the Schmid family welcomes you to their hotel with old-fashioned hospitality. The dining room is decorated with panels of local wood, and the hotel's popular restaurant has excellent à la carte specialties. It's a place where the locals from the ski schools meet in the winter.

HOTEL GARNI CHESA MULIN, CH-7504 Pontresina. Tel. 082/6-75-75. Fax 082/6-70-40. 50 rms (all with bath). MINIBAR TEL TV

$ Rates (including buffet breakfast): Summer, 80F–95F ($58.40–$69.35) single; 140F–170F ($102.20–$124.10) double. Winter, 90F–105F ($65.70–$76.65) single; 160F–190F ($116.80–$138.70) double. AE, DC, MC, V.

Mr. and Mrs. Schmid and their staff go out of their way to make guests feel welcome in this quiet, centrally located hotel. The public rooms are filled with plants, which serve to accentuate the wood paneling. The large, airy bedrooms have radios and down comforters. The hotel has a good snack restaurant, a sauna, a solarium, a terrace, and a garage.

SPORTHOTEL, CH-7504 Pontresina. Tel. 082/6-63-31. Fax 082/6-77-85. 120 rms (all with bath). TV TEL

$ Rates (including half board): 114F–140F ($83.20–$102.20) single; 214F–278F ($156.20–$202.90) double. AE, DC, MC, V. **Closed:** Apr–June and Oct–Dec.

This Victorian hotel offers the best breakfast buffet in town. Its comfortable bedrooms, all with good views, are colorful and tasteful. The beamed dining room has alpine chairs and Engadine illustrations of animals and plants; the rest of the place is cozily paneled and filled with softly upholstered armchairs. The manager speaks English.

WHERE TO DINE
EXPENSIVE

KRONENSTÜBLI, in the Grand Hotel Kronenhof. Tel. 6-01-11.

Cuisine: SWISS. **Reservations:** Required.

$ **Prices:** Appetizers 10F–28F ($7.30–$20.45); main courses 35F–55F ($25.55–$40.15); menu dégustation 110F ($80.30). AE, DC, MC, V.

Open: Daily 10am–10pm.

⭐ The restaurant at the Grand Hotel Kronenhof is one of the most popular spots in the resort. It's filled with valuable pieces of brass and pewter; the wood paneling is from the mid-19th century. You might enjoy the suprême de turbot et baudroie aux fleurs de safran or mignons de veau à la mousse de foie gras. There is a weekly carte with chef's specialties, inspired by modern cuisine. For dessert you might try the fried ice cream.

RESTAURANT SARAZENA, in the town center. Tel. 6-63-53.

Cuisine: FRENCH/CHINESE. **Reservations:** Required.

$ **Prices:** Appetizers 10F–18F ($7.30–$13.15); main courses 20F–38F ($14.60–$27.75); fixed-price Chinese menu 45F ($32.85); fixed-price continental menu 45F ($32.85). AE, DC, MC, V.

Open: Lunch Tues–Sun noon–2pm; dinner Tues–Sun 6–9:30pm. **Closed:** Lunch in Jan; late Apr to late May and for most of Oct and Nov.

This French and Chinese restaurant has an outdoor terrace as well as a dining room where Chinese symbols of good luck and red paper lanterns hang beneath solid masonry vaults. Chinese food is served in the evening only, including prawns in Szechuan sauce, abalone with mushrooms and bamboo, pork with asparagus and bamboo, and sweet-and-sour chicken.

There's also a continental menu, listing such dishes as a duet of veal and pork with béarnaise sauce, scallops with spinach and mornay sauce, and flambéed veal kidneys with mustard sauce. If you're interested in light meals, pizzas, or a pasta dinner, be sure to sit in the first (outermost) dining room. Meals there include raclette, scampi with pepper, rumpsteak, and scaloppine milanese.

RESTAURANT SCHWEIZERHOF, in the Hotel Schweizerhof. Tel. 6-01-31.

Cuisine: SWISS. **Reservations:** Recommended.

$ **Prices:** Appetizers 10F–18F ($7.30–$13.15); main courses 18F–28F ($13.15–$20.45); fixed-price meals 45F–110F ($32.85–$80.30). AE, DC, MC, V.

Open: Daily 11am–11pm. **Closed:** May and Nov.

The dining room is full of regional charm, with primitive paintings and an open fireplace, where the meats are grilled. Specialties include fresh lobsters and oysters, filet of beef, ravioli maison, lobster bisque in champagne, noodles with a salmon-cream sauce, and smoked river trout, along with such game dishes as roebuck (in season). Dessert might be a satisfying portion of flambéed raspberries with cream.

INEXPENSIVE

RESTAURANT LOCANDA, in the Hotel Bernina. Tel. 6-62-21.

Cuisine: CONTINENTAL/ITALIAN. **Reservations:** Recommended.

$ **Prices:** Appetizers 8F–14F ($5.85–$10.20); main courses 15F–22F ($10.95–$16.05). AE, DC, MC, V.

Open: Dinner only, daily 6–9:30pm.

Ⓢ This restaurant provides intimate, vaulted rooms, where guests gather on snowy nights for raclette and fondues. Of course, other fare, such as pastas, fresh trout, steaks, and various Schnitzels, are also offered. The service is polite.

EVENING ENTERTAINMENT

It's no longer necessary to head over to St. Moritz for evening entertainment. Pontresina has enough nighttime diversions of its own. Life here is decidedly more informal than in St. Moritz.

THE NORDESKA BAR, in the Sporthotel Pontresina. Tel. 6-63-31.
This bar has a small dance floor, a warmly rustic decor, and a crowd of young, convivial patrons. Drinks run 12F ($8.75).

SARAZENA DDC CLUB, in the Sarazena Restaurant. Tel. 6-63-53.
The initials "DDC" stand for "Dancing, Disco, Cabaret," for which you'll pay a cover whenever live music is playing. You can drink in the gallery above the beamed bar, or you can dance to recorded or live music. The lights are kept dim. Snacks are available, including goulash soup, sandwiches, or a platter containing an entrecôte with french fries. Open Tuesday through Sunday from 9pm to 2am. Drinks cost about 12F ($8.75), and beer goes for 10F ($7.30).
   Admission: 18F ($13.15).

5. SILVAPLANA

4 miles SW of St. Moritz

GETTING THERE   By Train   Silvaplana is not serviced by any railroad. Local residents usually take the bus or drive to the railway station at St. Moritz for most of their transportation needs.

By Bus   The postal bus makes daily runs from the St. Moritz railroad station to the center of Silvaplana. The *Palm Express* bus also travels through Silvaplana from Lugano and Locarno in Italian-speaking Switzerland.

By Car   From St. Moritz, head southwest along Route 27.

ESSENTIALS   The **Silvaplana Tourist Office** (tel. 082/4-81-51) is open Monday through Friday from 8:30am to noon and 2 to 6pm, and on Saturday from 8am to noon. The **telephone area code** for Silvaplana is 082. There are no **street names,** but signs point the way to the hotels and restaurants.

Situated on Lake Silvaplana, in sight of Lake Champfèr, the little village of Silvaplana (5,900 ft.) is at the foot of Piz (Mount) Corvatsch (11,338 ft.), at the beginning of the Julier Pass.
   Built around a late Gothic parish church, whose stone walls were completed in 1491, the hamlet of Silvaplana is one of the most unspoiled resorts in the Engadine.

WHAT TO SEE & DO

Swimming, hill climbing, riding, fishing, and even windsurfing on Lake Silvaplana are available in the summer.
   Whether you're a skier, a mountaineer, a nature lover, or just a sightseer, you may want to visit **Corvatsch.** From Silvaplana, go across the narrow neck of water where Lake Champfèr and Lake Silvaplana join and take an aerial cable car at Surlej. In just 15 minutes you'll reach the mountain station, from which you have a view of the lakes,

meadows, forests, and villages of the Upper Engadine. From the lookout terrace you take in a panorama of what appears to be an infinity of mountain peaks, with the giant glacier of the Bernina group looking close enough to touch.

From November to May skiers find nearly 50 miles of ski runs covered with deep, powdery snow, while in the summer you can ski on the granular ice of the glacier. (Ski lifts carry skiers to the glacier throughout the year.) The town's ski school is open throughout the year.

WHERE TO STAY
EXPENSIVE

HOTEL ALBANA, CH-7513 Silvaplana. Tel. 082/4-92-92. Fax 082/4-81-81
48 rms (all with bath). MINIBAR TV TEL
$ Rates (including half board): Summer, 155F ($113.15) single; 280F–320F ($204.35–$233.55) double. Winter, 180F ($131.40) single; 310F–370F ($226.25–$270.05) double. AE, DC, MC, V. **Closed:** May and Nov.
This four-star hotel is the best in town. It is designed with beamed ceilings, stone fireplaces, and half-timbered walls, and has regional stenciling throughout. The modern bedrooms are appealing.

MODERATE

HOTEL JULIER-CHESA ARSA, CH-7513 Silvaplana. Tel. 082/4-96-44.
Fax 082/4-81-43. 88 rms (62 with bath). TEL
$ Rates (including half board): 91F–101F ($66.40–$73.70) single without bath, 109F–144F ($79.55–$105.10) single with bath; 156F–166F ($111.85–$121.15) double without bath, 192F–262F ($140.15–$191.25) double with bath. AE, DC, MC, V. **Closed:** May and Nov.
Located at the entrance to the road leading to the Julier Pass, this is a three-star, four-story building with a warmly traditional interior. The bedrooms contain knotty-pine furniture and bright colors; the public rooms have half-timbering and a few antiques.

HOTEL SONNE, CH-7513 Silvaplana. Tel. 082/4-81-52. Fax 082/4-80-21.
65 rms (38 with bath). TEL
$ Rates (including half board): 120F ($87.60) single without bath, 140F ($102.20) single with bath; 230F ($167.90) double without bath, 260F ($189.75) double with bath. AE, DC, MC, V.
This four-story building is decorated with flower boxes, monochromatic regional designs, and neoclassical details. The rustically modern interior has settees in the salon and old-fashioned wallpaper and paneling in the dining rooms. The rooms are well maintained and comfortably furnished. The hotel also has a well-maintained garden and a bar with dancing. It remains open year round.

HOTEL STAILA, CH-7513 Silvaplana. Tel. 082/4-81-47. Fax 082/4-91-51.
17 rms (14 with bath). TEL
$ Rates (including half board): Summer, 95F ($69.35) single without bath, 120F ($87.60) single with bath; 180F ($131.40) double without bath, 200F ($146) double with bath. Winter, 110F ($80.30) single without bath, 130F ($94.90) single with bath; 200F ($146) double without bath, 230F ($167.90) double with bath. MC, V.
Closed: Easter to early June and Oct to early Dec. **Parking:** 6F ($4.40).
Originally built in a much smaller form in 1710, today this is a substantial and solid Engadine house, whose facade is covered with monochromatic regional stencils. It has

pinewood pancling and Victorian antiques. Located near where the postal bus stops to deliver visitors to Silvaplana, it offers old-fashioned sitting rooms (including one with a TV) and well-insulated bedrooms with radios. Its cozy restaurant serves local and international specialties. Laundry service is provided. Its name in Romansh means "star" (*stella* in Latin).

INEXPENSIVE

HOTEL CHESA GRUSAIDA, CH-7513 Silvaplana. **Tel. 082/4-82-92.** 18 rms (all with bath). TEL

$ Rates (including half board): 87F–102F ($63.50–$74.45) single; 102F–204F ($74.45–$148.90) double. AE, DC, MC, V. **Closed:** May and Nov.

This little hotel is an Engadine house with white walls and a gently sloping roof. Located in the middle of a grassy lawn, it's popular with skiers. The rustic interior is crisscrossed with ceiling beams. The restaurant serves well-prepared meals, consisting of both regional and continental specialties. The rooms are comfortable and cozily furnished.

WHERE TO DINE

RESTAURANT ALBANA, in the Hotel Albana. **Tel. 4-92-92.**
Cuisine: SWISS. **Reservations:** Recommended.

$ Prices: Appetizers 12F–18F ($8.75–$13.15); main courses 22F–38F ($16.05–$27.75); menu dégustation 85F ($62.05). AE, DC, MC, V.
Open: Daily 7am–midnight. **Closed:** Early May to mid-June and mid-Oct to mid-Dec.

Albana is the best dining choice in Silvaplana. It has a richly appealing decor of wrought iron, heavy timbers, and striped fabrics. The chef prepares such specialties as medallions of pork with grapes and nuts, sweetbreads in an artichoke sauce with a purée of asparagus, filet of lamb with black truffles, and filet of red mullet with saffron and fresh morels.

The hotel also maintains a less glamorous second-floor dining room, the Spunta, which offers Engadine dishes and full meals for 45F ($32.85) and up.

6. SILS-MARIA/SILS-BASELGIA

6 miles S of St. Moritz, 3 miles S of Silvaplana, 4 miles NE of Maloja

GETTING THERE **By Train** There is no direct train service. You'll have to take the train to St. Moritz (see Section 3, above), then go by taxi or postal bus.

By Bus Postal buses go back and forth between Sils-Maria and St. Moritz every 30 minutes during the day.

By Car From St. Moritz, continue south along Route 27.

ESSENTIALS The **Sils Maria Tourist Office** (tel. 082/4-51-40) is open Monday through Friday from 8am to 6pm and on Saturday from 9 to 11am and 3 to 5pm. The **telephone area code** for the area is 082. There are no **street names,** but you can follow the hotel and restaurant directional signs.

At an altitude of 6,000 feet, beside the lakes of the Upper Engadine, are two townships at the beginning of the Inn Valley—Sils-Baselgia, a hamlet with several hotels, and the larger town of Sils-Maria. Many budget-minded travelers stay here and then take the bus to the ski facilities in the greater St. Moritz area, but this resort has attractions of its own as well. There are some excellent hotels in this resort area, with reasonable prices.

WHAT TO SEE & DO

Nietzsche spent his summers in Sils-Maria between 1881 and 1889. Besides the Edelweiss Hotel, there's a small house where he lived while he wrote *Thus Spake Zarathustra*. This has been turned into a museum, with some mementos of the German philosopher on display.

A funicular takes you to **Furtschellas** (about 7,500 ft.), where skiers can use ski lifts and 25 miles of runs without having to line up and wait their turn. The Sils resort also offers facilities for trails, curling, sailing, windsurfing, horseback riding, and tennis. If you're here in the summer, take an enjoyable horse-drawn bus trip up the Fex Valley.

NEARBY ATTRACTIONS If you're touring in the area, consider a visit to **Grevasalvas,** a hamlet containing about a dozen farmhouses, to the east of Sils-Maria, about 6 miles southwest of St. Moritz. The remake of *Heidi* was filmed here. Overlooking Lake Sils, it commands views of the Bernina and Bergell mountain chains from its lofty perch at 6,000 feet. Residents take their cars into Grevasalvas, but visitors must park outside and make the 30-minute trek on foot. The most intrepid hikers will climb to **Lej Nair,** an alpine lake about 3,300 feet above Grevasalvas, reached via a steep, potentially dangerous pathway that should be taken only with an experienced guide.

WHERE TO STAY

IN SILS-MARIA

HOTEL WALDHAUS, CH-7514 Sils-Maria. Tel. 082/4-53-31, or toll free 800/44-UTELL in North America. Fax 082/4-59-92. 130 rms (all with bath), 10 suites. MINIBAR TV TEL
$ Rates (including half board): 190F–270F ($138.70–$197.05) single; 340F–490F ($248.15–$357.65) double; from 600F ($437.95) suite. AE, MC, V. **Closed:** Apr–June and Oct–Dec.

⭐ This comfortable, Edwardian palace was built in 1908. It has hosted such guests as Albert Einstein, Thomas Mann, and Richard Strauss. You'll reach it by riding or climbing to the top of the forested Laret Hill. The reception area has a wrought-iron staircase railing and Oriental carpets, giving it an undeniable grandeur. The oversize bedrooms are filled with elegant furniture, including some antiques, and usually have good views of the surrounding mountains. The best rooms have private balconies, offering the finest views in the Engadine.

Dining/Entertainment: The traditional Swiss food here is among the best in the region. A band usually plays in the bar area.

Services: Winter bus service provided by the hotel transports guests to and from the alpine ski slopes.

Facilities: Covered swimming pool, children's facilities.

HOTEL PENSIUN PRIVATA, CH-7514 Sils/Segl-Maria. Tel. 082/4-52-47. 28 rms (all with bath). TEL
$ Rates (including half board): 105F–125F ($76.65–$91.25) single; 195F–220F ($142.35–$160.60) double. No credit cards. **Closed:** Apr–June and Oct–Dec.

Ⓢ This five-story, ocher building is centrally located, near the village church. The Giovanoli family offers comfortably furnished and well-maintained rooms. Both regional and continental food is served.

IN SILS-BASELGIA

HOTEL MARGNA, CH-7517 Sils-Maria-Baselgia. Tel. 082/4-53-06. Fax 082/4-51-40. 88 rms (all with bath). MINIBAR TV TEL
$ **Rates** (including half board): 160F–200F ($116.80–$146) single; 300F–390F ($218.95–$284.65) double. No credit cards. **Closed:** Apr–June and Oct–Dec.
Built in 1817, this pink stucco structure with wrought-iron details has an interior with vaulted ceilings and paneling as well as a terrace and garden. The bedrooms are comfortably and cozily furnished. Sepp and Dorly Mussgens have two good restaurants and a rustic cellar bar. The facilities include a sauna and a fitness room.

CHESA RANDOLINA, CH-7515 Sils-Baselgia. Tel. 082/4-52-24. 42 rms (28 with bath). TEL
$ **Rates** (including half board): 100F ($73) single without bath, 135F ($98.55) single with bath; 190F ($138.70) double without bath, 230F ($167.90) double with bath. No credit cards. **Closed:** End of Apr to early June and end of Oct until just before Christmas.
This rambling, stucco building used to be a farmhouse, but now it's a hotel owned by the Clavadetscher family. The front doorway has a massively arched area covered with gray-and-white regional designs; a herringbone pattern is built into the rustic front door. The interior is filled with knotty-pine furniture; it has wall paneling and brightly colored carpeting. The rooms are comfortably furnished.

WHERE TO DINE

WALDHAUS RESTAURANT, in the Hotel Waldhaus, Sils-Maria. Tel. 4-53-31.
Cuisine: SWISS/ITALIAN. **Reservations:** Recommended.
$ **Prices:** Appetizers 12F–18F ($8.75–$13.15); main courses 22F–36F ($16.05–$26.30); fixed-price meals 45F–65F ($32.85–$47.45). AE, MC, V.
Open: Lunch daily noon–2:15pm; dinner daily 7–9:30pm. **Closed:** Mid-April to early June and mid-Oct to mid-Dec.
Housed in the Hotel Waldhaus, in a forested area a slight distance from the center of Sils-Maria, this restaurant is considered the finest in the village. The dining room has a very high ceiling and offers grand views of the larchwood forest. You might enjoy turbot with hollandaise sauce or tournedos, perhaps a salmon ragoût or filet of sole poached in white port. A Lake Sils specialty is a sautéed pork steak prepared from an old Engadine recipe. Every other Saturday night the management serves specialties from one of the Swiss regions, including the Ticino.

CHESA MARCHETTA, on the main street, Sils-Maria. Tel. 4-52-32.
Cuisine: SWISS. **Reservations:** Required.
$ **Prices:** Appetizers 5F–12F ($3.65–$8.75); main courses 18F–28F ($13.15–$20.45). AE, MC, V.
Open: Dinner only, daily 7:30–9pm. **Closed:** Apr 15–June 15 and Oct 15–Dec 15.

Ⓢ This restaurant, run by Christina and Maria Godly, is housed in an old building with steeply angled eaves and a stone foundation on the town square in the center of the village. The menu is small and select, offering only a few well-prepared specialties, such as homemade pasta, polenta, meat fondue, and other regional dishes.

AN EXCURSION TO THE MALOJA PASS

South of Sils you reach the famous Maloja Pass (or Maloja Crossing), a historic gap between towering alpine ridges that for centuries has facilitated passage from the Engadine to the Lake Como region of Italy. At the pass belvedere stands the old Maloja Kulm Hotel. Even if you don't plan to spend the night here, stop and rest for a while. From the hotel's observation platform, you'll have a sweeping view of the Bergell Valley.

WHERE TO STAY & DINE

HOTEL MALOJA KULM, CH-7516 Maloja. Tel. 082/4-31-05. Fax 082/4-34-66. 32 rms (18 with bath). TEL

$ Rates (including half board): 90F ($65.70) single without bath, 108F ($78.85) single with bath; 180F ($131.40) double without bath, 220F ($160.60) double with bath. No credit cards.

This historic hotel has a Victorian hipped roof on one section and on the other the kind of flagstone roof you might have noticed elsewhere in the Grisons. Inside, you'll see animal skins decorating the paneled and stucco walls; there are stone floors. A panoramic alpine restaurant and bar serve wholesome meals. The management has added a modern wing for additional accommodations. The rooms are comfortably furnished.

CHAPTER 14

LUGANO, LOCARNO & THE TICINO

- **WHAT'S SPECIAL ABOUT THE TICINO**
1. **BELLINZONA**
2. **LOCARNO**
3. **ASCONA**
4. **LUGANO**
5. **MORCOTE**

If you don't normally think of palm trees in Switzerland, you haven't seen the Ticino. Also called the Tessin, it's the Swiss Riviera—the retirement fantasy of thousands of Swiss living in the more northerly cantons. Although Italian is the major language, German and French (as well as English) are also widely spoken.

A visitor could spend at least 2 weeks just touring through the valleys of the canton. Officially, the Ticino begins at Airolo (the southern exit of the St. Gotthard Tunnel), but most visitors head for the district's major resorts of Locarno, Lugano, and fast-rising Ascona. Lugano and Locarno share the magnificent shores of the Lakes Lugano and Maggiore with Italy. Relations between Switzerland and Italy, however, weren't always peaceful. The Ticino was basically carved out of the Duchy of Milan by Swiss soldiers and staunchly defended in several bloody battles.

The name of the canton is taken from the Ticino River, a tributary of northern Italy's Po River. The balmy climate produces much subtropical vegetation, which thrives in gardens famous throughout Switzerland for their verdancy. The district's weather is almost addictive between March and November. The rest of the year can be cold and damp.

The nearness of Italy manifests itself in the Ticino's architecture and cuisine. Many buildings are made of stone and are proportioned like structures in Lombardy or Tuscany. Also, in many cases, a trattoria will be owned by a Swiss-German husband and a Swiss-Italian wife, so that their cuisine ends up being a concession to each other's culinary traditions.

SEEING THE TICINO

For many visitors entering from the south, Lugano is the gateway to the district because of its superior rail and air links with neighboring Italy. The capital of the Ticino, Bellinzona, is the gateway for visitors from the north, entering the Ticino through the St. Gotthard Tunnel. The major towns are linked by either rail or bus. Motorists take the N2 expressway, completed in 1986, which runs from the St. Gotthard Tunnel right through the Ticino. It's also possible to travel on Lake Lugano or Lake Maggiore by steamers and motor launches.

IF YOU HAVE 4 DAYS

Days 1 and 2: Head for either Lugano or Ascona on Lake Maggiore for 2 activity-filled days of taking in their attractions.
Days 3 and 4: Travel south to Lugano and explore its old town and many

WHAT'S SPECIAL ABOUT THE TICINO

Great Towns/Villages

☐ Lugano, the premier tourist resort of Italian-speaking Switzerland, opening onto Lake Lugano.

☐ Locarno, opening onto Lake Maggiore, known for its exceptional climate and semitropical vegetation.

☐ Morcote, one of the most idyllic villages of Switzerland, with arcaded houses and old streets built on mountain slopes.

☐ Ascona, opening onto Lake Maggiore, a former fishing port that celebrities have turned into a lakeside resort.

Museums

☐ Villa Favorita, outside Lugano, a 17th-century mansion with one of Europe's most important art collections.

Natural Spectacles

☐ Mount Salvatore, outside Lugano (at 2,992 ft.), offering a view of Lake Lugano and the Bernese and Valais Alps.

☐ Mount Brè, outside Lugano (at 3,061 ft.), with a spectacular view of Lake Lugano and the Alps.

☐ Mount Generoso, outside Lugano (at 5,581 ft.), with its celebrated panorama extending over the Alps to Italy's Lombardy Plain.

---

attractions, including the Villa Favorita, and spend the final day visiting two of the most outstanding villages in the Ticino: Gandria and Morcote.

1. BELLINZONA

14 miles E of Locarno, 22 miles N of Lugano

GETTING THERE By Train Bellinzona is the easiest destination to reach in the Ticino. Every train from the north of Switzerland stops here, as Bellinzona lies on the Brussels–Basel–Zurich–Milan international line. Indeed, every day regional and international trains stop at the rate of one every 30 minutes.

The nearest airport is at Lugano-Agno, 30 minutes from Bellinzona by train.

By Car Travelers from Zurich and other places in the north of Switzerland should continue along the N2 expressway through the St. Gotthard Tunnel into the Ticino. N2 continues southeast to Bellinzona.

ESSENTIALS The **Bellinzona Tourist Bureau,** on via Camminata (tel. 092/25-21-31), is open Monday through Friday from 8am to noon and 2 to 6:30pm. The **telephone area code** for Bellinzona is 092.

The opening of the St. Gotthard tunnel has made this once-remote Swiss town on Italy's side of the Alps very accessible. Bellinzona is known for the beauty of its old city and the nearby hills, as well as for the hospitality of its inhabitants.

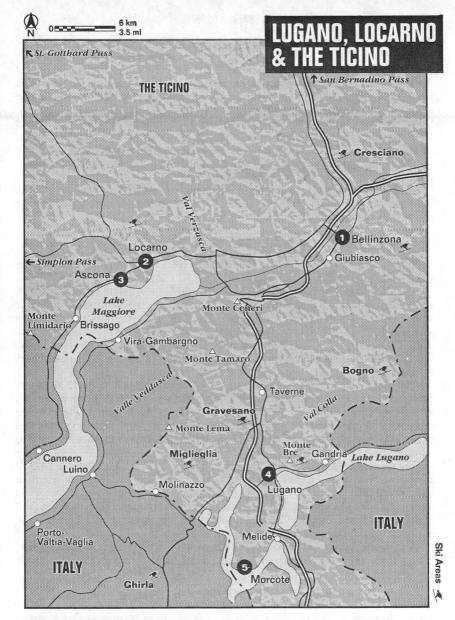

LUGANO, LOCARNO & THE TICINO

N
0 ⊢⊢⊢⊢⊢⊣ 6 km
3.5 mi

↖ St. Gotthard Pass

THE TICINO

↑ San Bernadino Pass

⚞ Cresciano

Val Verzasca

Locarno
2

① Bellinzona
⊙ Giubiasco

← Simplon Pass

Ascona **3**

Lake Maggiore

Monte Limidario

Brissago

⊙ Vira-Gambargno

△ Monte Ceneri

△ Monte Tamaro

Bogno ⚞

Valle Veddasca

⊙ Taverne

Gravesano

Val Colla

△ Monte Lema

Miglieglia

Monte Bre

Gandria   Lake Lugano

Cannero Luino ⊙

Molinazzo

4
Lugano

⊙ Porto-Valtia-Vaglia

Melide

ITALY

ITALY

5
Morcote

Ghirla

Ski Areas ⚞

① Bellinzona
② Locarno
③ Ascona
④ Lugano
⑤ Morcote

Because of its location astride the best of the ancient military and trade routes between Rome and its colonies in the north, the town is believed to be of Roman origin. It was later occupied, along with the rest of the Ticino, by both the Celts and the Ligurians. Records of the town date from A.D. 590. As the strategic key to the passes of St. Gotthard, San Bernardino, and Lucomagno, Bellinzona loomed large in the history of Lombardy. In the 8th century it was owned outright by the bishop of Como, and ownership went back and forth between Como and Milan in the 13th and 14th centuries. By 1798 it had become the capital of its own canton, Bellinzona, within the Swiss confederation. Five years later it was incorporated into the newly formed canton of the Ticino, where it has remained ever since, serving as the canton's capital.

Saturday morning is a good time to visit here to see the lively outdoor market, between 7 and 11:30am. Peddlers, vendors, country people, artisans, and townsfolk converse in Italian over the wares.

WHAT TO SEE & DO

Bellinzona has three castles dating from 13th to the 15th century: the Schwyz, the Unterwald, and the Uri.

The **Castle of Uri (Castello Grande** or San Michele, in Italian), built in 1280, is the most ancient and the largest castle in town. To reach the castle, take an elevator from piazza del Sole in the town center. In addition to the elevator, there are signposted paths from piazza Collegiata and piazza Nosetto for those who'd like to walk. The castle was restored in 1991 with a historical section and a small numismatic museum. The castle contains a restaurant, a banquet room, and a congress hall. Open April to September, daily from 9am to 5:30pm. Admission is free.

The most outstanding of the three medieval fortifications is the **۞ Schwyz Castle (Castello di Montebello).** It has a 13th-century château with a courtyard, as well as several 15th-century additions. Today it's a museum of history and archeology. To get there by car, start from viale Stazione and follow the steep ramp up to this huge citadel. Open Easter to mid-September, daily from 9am to noon and 2 to 5pm. Admission is free.

The **Castle of Unterwald (Castello di Sasso Corbaro)** was built in 1479. It can be reached by the same road that goes up to the Schwyz. The view from the terrace here is the finest in Bellinzona. You'll see not only the lower valley of the Ticino but Lake Maggiore as well. The museum contains regional costumes, arts, and crafts. Open Easter through October, Tuesday through Sunday, from 9am to noon and 2 to 5pm. Admission is free.

Also worth visiting is the collegiate **Church of Sts. Peter and Stephen,** dating from the 16th century. It's a fine Renaissance structure, with a richly embellished baroque interior.

WHERE TO STAY & DINE

HOTEL UNIONE, via Général Guisan 1, CH-6500 Bellinzona. Tel. 092/ 25-55-77. Fax 092/25-94-60. 42 rms (all with bath). TV TEL
$ Rates (including continental breakfast): 95F–100F ($69.35–$73) single; 150F–170F ($109.50–$124.10) double. AE, DC, MC, V.

The best hotel in town is a plain-looking, white building with a pink-marble extension with balconies. It's surrounded by gardens, some with fountains. The three-star hotel offers modern rooms with flowered carpets and beige tiles.

Fine Italian specialties are served at the restaurant—ravioli filled with the house pâté, saltimbocca with saffron-flavored risotto or truffles (in season). There is a cold buffet in the summer. The fixed-price menu costs 32F ($23.35). The restaurant is open Monday through Saturday from noon to 2pm and 7 to 9pm; it's closed from December 20 to mid-January.

AN EXCURSION TO GIORNICO

The most charming stop along the St. Gotthard road is in the village of Giornico. The hamlet is surrounded by vineyards and bisected by the Ticino River. A pair of old arched bridges connects the two sides of Giornico with a small island in the river. The island has several buildings, with weathered stone roofs.

There are two Romanesque churches on the right bank. Near the entrance of the **Church of San Nicolao** are columns supported by sculptures of mythical beasts. The church dates from the 12th century, and the crypt contains several interesting sculptures. The other church, **Santa Maria di Castello,** is higher up, among the vineyards.

A monument in the village commemorates a dramatic Swiss military victory over the forces of Milan. In 1478 some 600 Swiss defeated 10,000 Milan soldiers in a battle that took place in Giornico.

---

2. LOCARNO
14 miles W of Bellinzona, 25 miles N of Lugano

GETTING THERE By Plane The nearest air link is Lugano (see Section 4, below), 45 minutes away by train.

By Train The Locarno–Domodossola electric railway links Locarno with the Italian town of Domodossola. From there you can continue to Brig in the Rhône Valley, through the Simplon Tunnel. Railway lines connect Brig with Lake Geneva and Bern through the Lotschberg Tunnel. Direct trains from Lausanne or Bern take 4 hours to reach Locarno. From the other direction, through the St. Gotthard Tunnel, Locarno is 14 miles west of Bellinzona by rail.

By Bus Locarno sits atop the bus routes that connect Ascona with Lugano, and that continue on to many different mountain villages to the northeast until eventually arriving at Chur.

By Car After passing through the St. Gotthard Tunnel and reaching Bellinzona on the N2 expressway, take Route 13 west to reach Locarno.

ESSENTIALS The **Locarno Tourist Bureau,** on largo Zorzi (tel. 093/31-03-33), is open Monday through Friday from 8am to 7pm and on Saturday from 9am to noon and 1 to 5pm. The **telephone area code** for Locarno is 093.

This ancient town at the north end of Lake Maggiore is a holiday resort known for its mild climate. The rich Mediterranean vegetation includes camellias, magnolias, mimosa, wisteria, azaleas, and oleander in the spring. Olives, figs, and pomegranates also flourish in this climate.

Locarno entered world history in 1925 because of an international conference there that resulted in a series of agreements known collectively as the Locarno Pact. It was in Locarno that the former enemies of World War I, in seeking to reorder the affairs of Europe, committed themselves to a peaceful coexistence. (Locarno was chosen over Lucerne, reportedly, because the mistress of the French representative wanted the meeting to be held on Lake Maggiore.) The "spirit of Locarno," however, did not last long; within a decade the participants were arming again for war.

If you take the electric railway between Locarno and the Simplon Pass, you'll pass through the Centovalli, named for the hundred valleys that slope toward the river. There are many charming villages on the banks of this river. At Carnedo, in Italy, the railway climbs up to the plateau of Santa Maria Maggiore, a wide, barren, and solitary district that stretches for about 6 miles at 2,800 feet above sea level. A steep descent leads down to the railway junction of Domodossola. This international railway serves as a link between the Gotthard and the Simplon lines. The bridges are considered to be technological wonders.

WHAT TO SEE & DO

Start your tour at **piazza Grande,** the main square of town. On the north side, the arcades are filled with shops. You can find antiques, art, Swiss and Italian handcrafts, and high fashion from Milan.

From piazza Grande, follow the curvy **via Francesco Rusca** to the old town. Along the way you can visit the **Castello Visconti,** via Francesco Rusa 1 (tel. 21-59-72). This structure is all that survives from a late medieval castle in which the dukes of Milan lived. It was severely damaged in 1518. Today the castle contains a **Museum Civico,** which displays many Roman artifacts excavated in the area. It's open April through October, Tuesday through Sunday from 10am to noon and 2 to 5pm.

The most important sight in Locarno is the **Church of the Madonna del Sasso,** on a wooded crag above the resort. Hearty visitors and devout pilgrims can climb to the church, which is at an elevation of 1,165 feet. However, I recommend the funicular, which leaves every 15 minutes from 7am to 11pm. Round-trip fare is 4.60F ($3.40) for adults, 2.30F ($1.75) for children. The church was founded in 1480 after a friar, Bartolomeo da Ivrea, reportedly saw a vision of the Virgin. It was reconstructed in 1616. The basilica contains much artwork, including Bramantino's *Flight into Egypt* (1536).

WHERE TO STAY

Locarno has many good hotels that accommodate travelers on their way to or from Italy. You can also spend a pleasant holiday along the lake here.

EXPENSIVE

GRAND HOTEL LOCARNO, via Sempione 17, CH-6000 Locarno-Muralto. Tel. 093/33-02-82. Fax 093/33-30-13. 80 rms (all with bath). MINIBAR TV TEL
$ Rates (including buffet breakfast): 140F–170F ($102.20–$124.10) single; 220F–300F ($160.60–$218.95) double. Half board 35F ($25.55) extra. AE, DC, MC, V. **Closed:** Late Nov to Mar.
This very grand hotel opened in 1876 to celebrate the inauguration of the St. Gotthard railway line; nearly half a century later it provided accommodations for some of the most important leaders of Europe during the Locarno conference. The hotel, most of which was renovated in the 1980s, sits amid gardens in the middle of town, facing the lake. The salons on the main floor are capped with elaborate Belle Epoque frescoes of

flowers, cherubs, and mythological figures. Bedrooms contain reproductions of furnishings that are consistent with the exterior's neoclassical theme, and a scattering of modern pieces as well. The hotel is large, well managed, and comfortable, with the best rooms facing the lake.

Dining/Entertainment: The Liberty Bar has a sophisticated collection of single-malt whiskies. There's also a nightclub and a restaurant.

Services: Room service, baby-sitter, hairdresser.

Facilities: Heated outdoor swimming pool in the garden, tennis court, shops (including an art gallery).

HOTEL ARCADIA AL LAGO, Lungolago G. Motta, CH-6600 Locarno. Tel. 093/31-02-82. Fax 093/31-53-08. 90 rms (all with bath). MINIBAR TV TEL
$ Rates (including buffet breakfast): 95F–160F ($69.35–$116.80) single; 160F–245F ($116.80–$178.85) double. AE, DC, MC, V. **Closed:** Jan.

Completely modern, this hotel has dozens of balconies and sunny bedrooms with angular wood furniture and carpeting. It is separated from the water and a lakeside promenade by a whimsical wrought-iron fence.

Dining/Entertainment: The hotel has a piano bar and a good restaurant serving Swiss and Italian specialties.

Services: Room service, laundry, baby-sitting.

Facilities: Sauna, solarium, fitness room, swimming pool in the garden, roof terrace for sunbathing.

HOTEL ESPLANADE, via Esplanade, CH-6600 Locarno-Minusio. Tel. 093/33-21-21. Fax 093/33-44-70. 72 rms (all with bath). MINIBAR TV TEL
Bus: 23 or 31.
$ Rates (including continental breakfast): 105F–140F ($76.65–$102.20) single; 190F–250F ($138.70–$182.50) double. Half board 36F ($26.30) extra. AE, DC, MC, V.

Italian Renaissance style is evident in the double towers connected by long rows of covered loggias. This very large, ocher hotel in Minusio has an elegant interior with high ceilings. There's a sun terrace, as well as a large park filled with flowers. The bedrooms are comfortably and attractively furnished.

Dining/Entertainment: Music is played in the evening on a grand piano in one of the salons. The restaurant serves Swiss and international specialties.

Services: Laundry.

Facilities: Outdoor swimming pool, outdoor tennis court with a tennis instructor.

HOTEL LA PALMA AU LAC, viale Verbano 29, CH-6600 Locarno-Muralto. Tel. 093/33-01-71. Fax 093/33-39-74. 78 rms (all with bath). MINIBAR TV TEL
$ Rates (including continental breakfast): 180F–210F ($131.40–$153.30) single; 250F–330F ($182.50–$240.45) double. AE, DC, MC, V.

This sparkling-white building has vivid green awnings and long modern balconies. Sun chairs and chaise longues are set up on the lawn, which extends right down to the lake. The updated public rooms are decorated with oil paintings and tapestries, and retain their 19th-century grace. The elegantly furnished bedrooms have an Italian flair.

Dining/Entertainment: There are several restaurants, including the Coq d'Or, and a barbecue snack bar on the beach. Dance music is played at the bar.

Services: Room service, laundry.

Facilities: Swimming pool, sauna, private lido (beach).

HOTEL MURALTO, piazza Stazione 8, CH-6600 Locarno. Tel. 093/33-01-81. Fax 093/33-43-95. 82 rms (all with bath). TV TEL

$ Rates (including buffet breakfast): 105F–165F ($76.65–$120.45) single; 190F–280F ($138.70–$204.35) double. Half board 35F ($25.55) extra. AE, DC, MC, V.

This hotel is white, with long rows of silvery windows. Chairs and parasols are set out on the modern balconies, which are visible from the lake promenade. The sunny rooms are clean and gracefully furnished with reproductions of antiques. Amenities include a radio. My favorite part of this hotel is the tiled sun terrace, which is ringed with semitropical plants. The hotel restaurant serves Swiss and Italian specialties.

HOTEL ORSELINA, Orselina, CH-6600 Locarno. Tel. 093/33-02-32. Fax 093/33-62-21. 72 rms (all with bath). MINIBAR TV TEL

$ Rates (including continental breakfast): 148F–165F ($108.05–$120.45) single; 260F–330F ($189.75–$240.85) double. Half board 20F ($14.60) extra. No credit cards. **Closed:** Dec–Feb.

⭐ Guests enjoy a dramatic view from this peaceful oasis in a suburb north of town accessible by funicular from Orselina. It resembles a Spanish parador situated on a hillside. The lake is visible in the distance. The rooms are well furnished and comfortable. The best rooms have a balcony facing south.

Dining/Entertainment: The specialties of the Ticino are served in the loggia, which offers fresh breezes from the lake. You can also eat in the lounge, which has a fireplace and massive beams.

Services: Room service, laundry.

Facilities: Indoor and outdoor swimming pools.

HOTEL REBER AU LAC, viale Verbano 55, CH-6600 Locarno-Muralto. Tel. 093/33-02-02. Fax 093/33-79-81. 90 rms (all with bath), 12 suites. TV TEL

$ Rates (including continental breakfast): 153F–200F ($111.60–$146) single; 262F–340F ($191.25–$248.15) double; from 510F ($372.25) suite. Half board 40F ($29.20) extra. AE, DC, MC, V. **Parking:** 15F ($10.95).

This comfortable first-class hotel has been owned by the same family since 1886. It offers a lakeside terrace and a large garden with semitropical plants. The bedrooms are attractively furnished with modern styling.

Dining/Entertainment: The Spanish bar and grillroom is decorated in shades of scarlet. The French restaurant has Corinthian columns and a high ceiling. The piano bar, Contenotte, has sophisticated colors and a psychedelic dance floor.

Services: Room service, laundry.

Facilities: Outdoor heated pool, private pier, tennis courts.

MODERATE

HOTEL BEAU-RIVAGE, viale Verbano 31, CH-6600 Locarno. Tel. 093/33-13-55. Fax 093/33-94-09. 50 rms (all with bath). TV TEL

$ Rates (including continental breakfast): 82F–146F ($59.85–$106.55) single; 160F–205F ($116.80–$149.65) double. Half board 28F ($20.45) extra. AE, MC, V. **Closed:** Nov–Mar.

A Doric colonnade supports the sun terrace over the main entrance. Above the colonnade the white facade has white wrought-iron balconies decorated with flowers. The interior is elegantly simple, with vaulted ceilings, salmon-colored marble floors, and a few neoclassical gilt-edged mirrors. The bedrooms are furnished with attractive modern styling; many have private balconies overlooking the lake. A panoramic terrace restaurant serves Italian and international food. Outside parking is available in back of the hotel; laundry and room service are provided.

HOTEL BELVEDERE, via ai Monti della Trinità 44, CH-6601 Locarno. Tel. 093/31-03-63. Fax 093/31-52-39. 52 rms (all with bath). MINIBAR TV TEL **Directions:** Take Locarno's only funicular, departing from via Ramogna near the lakefront, to its second stop (Belvedere), a few steps from the hotel.

$ **Rates** (including continental breakfast): 152F–162F ($110.95–$118.25) single; 204F–224F ($148.90–$163.50) double. Half board 20F ($14.60) extra. AE, DC, MC, V. **Closed:** Feb.

Set on a steep hillside in the upper heights of Locarno, this ocher-colored, neoclassical hotel was built around 1910 on the foundations of a 300-year-old house. Reopened in 1990 after 4 years of total restoration, it offers modernized comforts and sweeping views of the lake from each of its streamlined and contemporary bedrooms. All but four of its bedrooms have a private balcony, extending the living quarters, Italian style, into the open air. On the premises are the Tre Palme restaurant-bar and the L'Affresco Terrace Restaurant.

HOTEL GARNI NESSI, via Varenna 79, CH-6604 Locarno. Tel. 093/31-53-23. Fax 093/31-92-09. 19 rms (all with bath), 1 suite. MINIBAR TV TEL

$ **Rates** (including continental breakfast): 80F–85F ($58.40–$62.05) single; 150F–160F ($109.50–$116.80) double; 280F ($204.35) suite. AE, MC, V.

One of the most striking modern hotels in town, the concrete-sided Nessi was influenced by the latest trends in Milanese design. Windows, loggias, and furniture are all laid out in Mondrian-inspired crossings of horizontal and vertical lines, and the bedrooms are stylish and comfortable. Only breakfast is served. In the garden outside is a rectangular swimming pool; a solarium and bar are also available.

REMORINO HOTEL-GARNI, via Verbano 29, CH-6648 Minuslo-Locarno. Tel. 093/33-10-33. Fax 093/33-74-29. 27 rms (all with bath). MINIBAR TV TEL **Bus:** 23 or 31.

$ **Rates** (including buffet breakfast): 65F–100F ($47.45–$73) single; 130F–200F ($94.90–$146) double. No credit cards. **Closed:** Nov–Feb.

The Remorino is in a secluded residential area a short walk from the center of town and 2 minutes from the lakeside promenade. The hotel offers modern comfort and rooms with a balcony overlooking the lake and the Alps. Amenities include a strongbox and a radio. There is a garden with an outdoor swimming pool; plus a solarium.

INEXPENSIVE

HOTEL DELL'ANGELO, piazza Grande 1, CH-6601 Locarno. Tel. 093/31-81-75. Fax 093/31-82-56. 50 rms (all with bath). TV TEL

$ **Rates** (including continental breakfast): 70F–100F ($51.10–$73) single; 120F–160F ($87.60–$116.80) double. AE, DC, MC, V.

This centrally located, newly renovated hotel is clean and attractive, with an inviting atmosphere. The bargain rooms are simply furnished. The more expensive rooms have more amenities, including a radio. The hotel's terrace opens onto a view of the lake, and its grill-restaurant features moderately priced regional and Italian specialties. A wood-fired oven turns out luscious pizzas in the evening.

ROSA SEEGARTEN, viale Verbano 25, CH-6600 Locarno. Tel. 093/33-87-31. Fax 093/33-50-02. 32 rms (all with shower). TEL

$ **Rates** (including continental breakfast): 70F–100F ($51.10–$73) single; 124F–190F ($90.50–$138.70) double. Half board 28F ($20.45) extra. **Closed:** Nov–Mar.

For a bargain in Locarno, try this old-fashioned, cream-colored hotel on the lake, a 3-minute walk from the train station. Half board is encouraged. Meals are served on a lakeside terrace under a grape arbor. The inside dining room has white walls and wood tones. All rooms have a toilet, and amenities include a radio.

WHERE TO DINE

EXPENSIVE

LA CENTENARIO, Lungolago 15, Muralto. Tel. 33-82-22.
  Cuisine: SWISS/ITALIAN. **Reservations:** Required.
$ **Prices:** Appetizers 18F–40F ($13.15–$29.20); main courses 35F–45F ($25.55–$32.85); fixed-price meals 45F–125F ($32.85–$91.25). AE, DC, MC, V.
  Open: Lunch Tues–Sat noon–2pm; dinner Tues–Sat 7–10pm. **Closed:** First 3 weeks of Feb, first 2 weeks of July.

The dining room, with austere white walls and straight-back chairs, has a simplicity that contrasts with the colorful creations of Gérard Perriard. The menu is based on fresh ingredients from the market. Specialties include sea bass with fennel, foie gras of duck with salad, filet of roebuck with mushrooms, roast guinea fowl with sauerkraut and truffles, and shrimp St. Jacques. For an unusual first course, ask for a cold consommé of quail eggs garnished with caviar.

RESTAURANT CITTÀDELLA, via Cittàdella 18. Tel. 31-58-85.
  Cuisine: SWISS/ITALIAN. **Reservations:** Required.
$ **Prices:** Appetizers 12F–16F ($8.75–$11.70); main courses 22F–32F ($16.05–$23.35); pizzas from 15F ($10.95); gourmet menu 85F ($62.05). AE, MC, V.
  Open: Lunch Wed–Sun 11:30am–2pm; dinner Wed–Sun 5pm–midnight. **Closed:** 3 weeks in June.

Located in the center of the old town, this restaurant complex is separated from the cobblestone street by a granite arcade draped with vines. The downstairs pizzeria has timbered ceilings, stucco walls, and an informal ambience. Upstairs is a chic enclave of cuisine moderne. Specialties include a goose-liver terrine and a salad of large shrimp with nuts and mango. One dish is a mixed grill with saltwater and freshwater fish—it's delicious.

MODERATE

MÖVENPICK OLDRATI, Lungolago. Tel. 33-85-44.
  Cuisine: SWISS/ITALIAN. **Reservations:** Not needed.
$ **Prices:** Appetizers 10F–16F ($7.30–$11.70); main courses 18F–28F ($13.15–$20.45); daily specials from 35F ($25.55). AE, DC, MC, V.
  Open: Daily 11am–11pm.

This two-restaurant complex is one of the most elegant members of a popular chain. The more formal of the two restaurants is at the top of a staircase carpeted with an Oriental runner and covered in fabric woven like an American needlepoint sampler. Sidewalk tables are also available. The chef specializes in curry dishes. Many Italian dishes are offered, such as good pasta courses and saltimbocca. For an appetizer, try a terrine or the air-dried beef of the Grisons. The sole meunière is a favorite main dish.

RESTAURANT CERVO, via Toretta 11. Tel. 31-41-31.
  Cuisine: SWISS/ITALIAN. **Reservations:** Recommended.
$ **Prices:** Appetizers 7F–15F ($5.10–$10.95); main courses 25F–45F ($18.25–$32.85); two-course fixed price lunch 20F ($14.60). No credit cards.
  Open: Lunch Tues–Sun noon–2pm; dinner Tues–Sat 6:30–9:30pm.

You'll recognize the Cervo (Italian for stag) by the wrought-iron bracket on its facade holding a replica of a deer head. The small hotel has brown shutters and flower boxes. The interior is well kept and rustic. The separate restaurant serves Italian specialties, including gnocchi, Ticino minestrone, saltimbocca, risotto with mushrooms, and a special dessert "del padrone."

RISTORANTE ZURIGO, viale Verbano, CH-6600 Locarno. Tel. 093/33-16-17.

Cuisine: SWISS/ITALIAN. **Reservations:** Recommended.

$ Prices: Appetizers 7F–15F ($5.10–$10.95); main courses 25F–45F ($18.25–$32.85); fixed-price meals 22F ($16.05). AE, DC, MC, V.

Open: Daily 7am–midnight; lunch daily 11:30am–2:30pm; dinner daily 6–9pm.

One of the finest places to dine on a summer night is on this restaurant's flagstone terrace, which is dotted with chestnut trees and festive lights. A loyal clientele enjoys savory Italian food right on the lakefront. The restaurant is part of a turn-of-the-century Mediterranean-style hotel with balconies and shutters. The dining room is decorated in green and white. Specialties include a platter piled high with three types of pasta. The menu also includes risotto verde, saltimbocca, and grilled beefsteak. For dessert, the zabaglione is superb.

The Zurigo also offers 25 comfortably furnished rooms, each with bath, for reasonable prices. Single rooms range from 85F to 100F ($62.05 to $73); double rooms cost 130F to 190F ($94.90 to $138.70).

INEXPENSIVE

RESTAURANT CARBONARA, piazza Stazione. Tel. 33-67-14.

Cuisine: SWISS/ITALIAN. **Reservations:** Not needed.

$ Prices: Appetizers 9F–13F ($6.55–$9.50); main courses 25F–35F ($18.25–$25.55); pizza and pasta 9F–14F ($6.55–$10.20); fixed-price meals 22F–26F ($16.05–$19). AE, DC, MC, V.

Open: Lunch daily 11:30am–2pm; dinner daily 6:30–10pm.

There is a well-stocked bar near the entrance of this restaurant. The dining room is separated by a glass partition. The stucco walls are decorated with original paintings and copper pots. Specialties include veal kidney with grappa and mushrooms, saltimbocca, and a large pasta menu, featuring macaroni with four different types of cheese. Other dishes include braciola alla pizzaiola, grilled shrimp, and 15 types of pizza. There is a cellar bar decorated in a stark modern style, with an entrance from the street.

EVENING ENTERTAINMENT

Nightlife in Locarno may not impress you. So drag out your dinner, have a nightcap in a bar at your hotel, and save your money. If you go out, you'll find that drinks are expensive. You're better off turning in early and getting an early start on sightseeing the following day. For a nightcap, I recommend the following:

ARCADIA BAR AND CAFE, in the Hotel Arcadia, Lungolago G. Motta. Tel. 31-02-82.

Built in 1983, this attractive bar is decorated with black-and-pink marble flooring, palm trees, and rattan chairs that evoke a balcony in the Caribbean. Large windows offer a panoramic view of the gardens. Piano music is played daily from 8pm to midnight. Open Tuesday through Sunday. Drinks run 15F ($10.95).

CAFE DEBARCADERO, Lungolago G. Motta. Tel. 31-52-52.

This bar-café-restaurant is on the lake, next to the landing and ticket office for cruises on Lake Maggiore. Café tables are set up under an awning. The dining room is sunny and unpretentious, with comfortable wooden chairs. Open daily from 7am to midnight. Drinks cost about 13F ($9.50); beer goes for 5F ($3.65).

EASY EXCURSIONS

After visiting the Church of the Madonna del Sasso, continue by cable car to **Alpe Cardada,** at 4,430 feet. The 1-mile trip takes 10 minutes. From Cardada, a chair lift goes to the summit of **Cimetta,** at 5,480 feet, from which a magnificent sweep of Lake Maggiore and the Alps unfolds. There's good skiing here, with several ski lifts. The total round-trip fare from Orselina—reached by cable railway—to Cardada and then to Cimetta is 22F ($16.05). Service in season is daily from 7:30am to 8pm. For information, call 093/31-26-79.

The other popular excursion is the **Ronco Tour.** The trip can also be made from the competitive resort of Ascona.

For additional full-day and half-day trips, inquire at the tourist office in Locarno. Many of the trips will take you through valleys and up steep, hairpin mountain roads that only very skilled drivers should attempt. The most fascinating is a trip to the **Val Verzasca,** 20 miles away. The tranquil vacationland has tile-roofed houses and old churches with campaniles.

Before starting out, however, get a good map. Leave Locarno on Route 13 to Bellinzona. At Gordola, a village at the entrance to the valley, continue on to Sonogno. Along the way you'll see the **Verzasca Dam,** which was built in the 1960s to prevent flooding in the area. The dam made a lake, called the Lago di Vogorno. Skirting the lake, you'll pass through seven tunnels. Eventually you'll arrive at **Brione,** at the head of the Valle d'Osola. The hamlet has a four-towered castle but is known mainly for its church, with its frescoes dating from the 14th century. The post road terminates at **Sonogno,** a mountain hamlet at an elevation of 3,020 feet.

---

3. ASCONA

2½ miles SW of Locarno, 26 miles NW of Lugano

GETTING THERE   By Train   Ascona has no railway station of its own, so most passengers disembark at nearby Locarno, transferring on a bus or taxi the short distance to Ascona. Locarno has good connections to the region's major railway junction of Bellinzona. From Bellinzona connections are easy on express trains to either Milan or Zurich.

By Bus   A handful of buses connect Ascona with the railroad junction of Locarno, a short distance to the northeast.

By Car   Continue west from Locarno along Route 13.

ESSENTIALS   The **Arosa Tourist Board,** on via Papio (tel. 093/35-55-44), is open Monday through Saturday from 8am to 7pm and on Sunday from 10am to noon and 4 to 7pm. The **telephone area code** for Ascona is 093.

Once a tiny fishing port, Ascona has swiftly developed into a resort to rival nearby Locarno. Located snugly on Lake Maggiore, it has long been a popular rendezvous point for painters, writers, and celebrities. Lenin found the place ideal, as did Isadora

Duncan and Carl Jung. Rudolf Steiner, Hermann Hesse, and Paul Klee lived here. Today Ascona is one of the most popular destinations in the Ticino.

New developments have obscured much of the old town cherished by these famous people, but the heart of Ascona is still worth exploring. It has colorful little shops, art galleries (some good, some of the souvenir variety), and antique stores.

Because of its mild climate, Ascona has subtropical vegetation. Flowers bloom year round. Facilities include a golf course, a lido (beach), and a Kursaal (casino).

WHAT TO SEE & DO

The **Collegio Pontificio Papio,** lying off via Cappelle, has one of the most beautiful Renaissance courtyards in Switzerland. Dating from 1584, the building has two-story Italianate loggias. The **Church of Santa Maria della Misericordia** is part of the cloisters of the Collegio Pontificio Papio. Built at the end of the 14th century, it contains one of the largest late Gothic frescoes in Switzerland.

Casa Serodine (also called Casa Borrani), which lies off piazza G. Motta, was built in 1620 and has one of the most richly embellished facades of any secular structure in the country.

NEARBY ATTRACTIONS The **Isole di Brissago,** off the shore of Lake Maggiore, contains a botanical garden of Mediterranean and subtropical flora. There are also the remains of a small Roman bath. The gardens can be reached by boat from the center of Ascona. Round-trip fare and admission cost 8F ($5.85). Inquire at the Ascona tourist office if the gardens are open, and where to board the boat.

You can also visit the little village of **Ronco** along the corniche road west, an 11-mile trip. This very Mediterranean-type village is on a slope in one of the most charming settings in all of Ticino. Erich Maria Remarque, the German author of *All Quiet on the Western Front,* lived here and is buried in the cemetery of the little church.

WHERE TO STAY

Bus 31 from Locarno services most of the hotels below.

VERY EXPENSIVE

ALBERGO CASA BERNO, CH-6612 Ascona. Tel. 093/35-32-32. Fax 093/36-11-14. 62 rms (all with bath). MINIBAR TV TEL **Transportation:** Taxi.
$ Rates (including continental breakfast): 120F–180F ($87.60–$131.40) single; 240F–360F ($175.20–$262.75) double. Half board 20F ($14.60) extra. AE. **Closed:** Nov–Feb.
Built into a hillside, this large hotel has several wings with balconies. Its rooms are comfortably furnished—some of them with elegant Louis XVI–style chairs. Each room has a balcony with a southern exposure. The hotel is between Monte Verita and Ronco-sur-Ascona; the street has no name.
Dining/Entertainment: There are two restaurants and a bar.
Services: Massage, hairdresser, room service, laundry.
Facilities: Outdoor swimming pool, sauna.

CASTELLO DEL SOLE, viale Muraccio 142, CH-6612 Ascona. Tel. 093/ 35-02-02. Fax 093/36-11-18. 85 rms (all with bath). MINIBAR TV TEL **Bus:** 31 from Locarno.
$ Rates (including continental breakfast): 230F–320F ($167.90–$233.55) single; 360F–500F ($262.75–$364.95) double. No credit cards. **Closed:** Mar 30–Oct.

★ The grandest hotel in Ascona is surrounded by a large park and green meadows. This peaceful haven is near the Maggia River, at the point where it flows into Lake Maggiore. It has the atmosphere of a private estate, 1½ miles from the center of town. There is an antique palazzo, with many courtyards. The spacious public rooms have vaulted ceilings, granite columns, and marble terraces. The rooms have balconies and beautiful furniture.

Dining/Entertainment: Many of the ingredients used in the Barbarossa restaurant are grown on the hotel's farm. Savory specialties include grilled meat. Buffets are offered in the summer. The hotel also produces its own wine.

Services: Massage, room service, laundry.

Facilities: 18-hole golf course, beachfront, five outdoor tennis courts, two indoor tennis courts, indoor and outdoor swimming pools, sauna.

HOTEL ASCOLAGO, via Albarelle, CH-6612 Ascona. Tel. 093/35-30-55.
Fax 093/35-42-26. 45 rms (all with bath). MINIBAR TV TEL **Bus:** 31 from Locarno.
$ Rates (including continental breakfast): 115F–170F ($83.95–$124.10) single; 220F–330F ($160.60–$240.85) double. Half board 40F ($29.20) extra. AE, MC. **Parking:** 15F ($10.95).

This unusual hotel has an angular facade, with a roofline inspired by the lines of a Chinese pagoda. It's ideally located in the center of town, in a park with flowers and sculpture. A portico by the entrance looks as if it had been designed by Le Corbusier. The interior is less stylish. The bedrooms are modern, with thick carpeting, radios, and safes.

Dining/Entertainment: There is a large, paneled restaurant on the ground floor; tables are set out on the terrace in the summer. There's also a bar.

Services: Room service, laundry.

Facilities: Indoor swimming pool, sauna, parking garage.

HOTEL EDEN ROC, via Albarelle, CH-6612 Ascona. Tel. 093/35-01-71.
Fax 093/35-15-71. 51 rms (all with bath), 8 suites. MINIBAR TV TEL **Bus:** 31 from Locarno.
$ Rates (including continental breakfast): 230F–330F ($167.90–$240.85) single; 360F ($262.75) double; from 540F ($394.15) suite. AE, DC, MC, V. **Parking:** 15F ($10.95). **Closed:** Jan–Mar.

Located on the lake's shoreline, this hotel has terraced flowerbeds leading gently down to the water. The interior is lighthearted and modern. The bedrooms are sunny and spacious, with balconies and radios. Some rooms are frilly and romantic; others are more modern.

Dining/Entertainment: The hotel offers gourmet dining from an international kitchen. Guests prefer outdoor terrace tables overlooking the lake. Piano-bar entertainment is also provided.

Services: Room service, baby-sitting, laundry, massage.

Facilities: Swimming pool, lakeside terrace, garage.

EXPENSIVE

HOTEL ACAPULCO AU LAC, Porto Ronco, CH-6612 Ascona. Tel. 093/35-45-21. Fax 093/36-19-51. 52 rms (all with bath). MINIBAR TV TEL **Bus:** 21 to Port Ronco.
$ Rates (including continental breakfast): 105F–155F ($76.65–$113.15) single; 156F–230F ($113.85–$167.90) double. Half board 33F ($24.10) extra. AE, DC, MC, V. **Parking:** Free. **Closed:** Dec–Feb.

This elegant hotel is set on a hill so steep that you park your car on the roof before heading down to the reception desk. Each pleasant bedroom has its own balcony or terrace, as well as a private bath and a radio. The lounge area is filled with rattan furniture and summer colors.

Dining/Entertainment: The gaily decorated rustic restaurant overlooks the water, and the cozy Fiesta Bar has outdoor terraces.

Services: Room service, laundry.

Facilities: Marina, beach, heated indoor swimming pool, waterskiing facilities.

HOTEL SASSO BORETTO, via Locarno, CH-6612 Ascona. Tel. 093/35-71-15. Fax 093/35-50-18. 48 rms (all with bath). MINIBAR TV TEL **Bus:** 31 from Locarno.

$ Rates (including continental breakfast): 127F ($92.70) single; 200F ($146) double. Half board 35F ($25.55) extra. AE, DC, MC, V. **Parking:** 15F ($10.95). **Closed:** Nov–Mar 20.

The entire balconied structure of this establishment seems to be set on top of concrete columns. Glass windows frame the ground floor, which is surrounded by red-brick terraces and Mediterranean trees. Most of the establishment's bedrooms are decorated in warm, monochromatic tones of brown and beige. The larger ones are decorated with Italian flair; the smaller ones are less dramatic but cozy and comfortable nonetheless.

Dining/Entertainment: There are several restaurants and garden cafés, as well as a modern bar.

Services: Room service, laundry.

Facilities: Swimming pool, sauna, underground garage.

MODERATE

SEESCHLOSS-CASTELLO, piazza G. Motta, CH-6612 Ascona. Tel. 093/35-01-61. Fax 093/35-18-04. 44 rms (all with bath). MINIBAR TV TEL **Bus:** 31 from Locarno.

$ Rates (including continental breakfast): 120F–180F ($87.60–$131.40) single; 200F–300F ($146–$218.95) double. Half board 25F ($18.25) extra. AE, DC, MC, V. **Parking:** 15F ($10.95). **Closed:** Dec–Feb.

The tower was built in 1250 by a countess of Milan from the Ghiriglioni family. It served as the fortified dwelling of the family, which eventually controlled most of the navigation on the lake. Today palms and palmettos surround the flagstone terrace leading to the stone entryway. Pull the wrought-iron bell handle for assistance. The lobby is filled with antiques, and the rooms are small, clean, and comfortable. There's a heated swimming pool in the backyard.

TAMARO DU LAC, piazza G. Motta, CH-6612 Ascona. Tel. 093/35-02-82. Fax 093/35-29-28. 52 rms (all with bath). TV TEL **Bus:** 31 from Locarno.

$ Rates (including continental breakfast): 87F–130F ($63.50–$94.90) single; 154F–230F ($112.40–$167.90) double. Half board 25F ($18.25) extra. AE, DC, MC, V. **Closed:** Nov–Mar.

A welcome is painted in Latin above the huge arch leading into the flagstone reception hall. Farther on is a skylit central courtyard, with vines growing over the massive vaults of the arcade surrounding it. This former hospice and abbey is managed by Annette and Paolo Witzig. They have decorated the interior with antiques and some romantic artifacts.

ALBERGO ELVEZIA, piazza G. Motta, CH-6612 Ascona. Tel. 093/35-15-14. 28 rms (all with bath). TV TEL **Bus:** 31 from Locarno.

$ Rates (including continental breakfast): 80F–115F ($58.40–$83.95) single;

140F–210F ($102.20–$153.30) twin. Half board 30F ($21.90) extra. AE, DC, MC, V.

This hotel has a cobblestone terrace facing the lake and an indoor dining room just behind it. The upper-story terrace is ringed with vines. The ground-floor restaurant is rustic, with Oriental rugs, wooden tables, and chandeliers. Meals begin at 35F ($25.55) and include many Italian specialties, such as good pasta (especially one made with four different kinds of cheese), scampi prepared several ways, osso buco, and veal piccata. The Crociani family offers rooms with small refrigerators.

INEXPENSIVE

HOTEL LA PERLA, via Collins 14, CH-6612 Ascona. Tel. 093/35-35-77.
38 rms (all with bath) TV TEL **Bus:** 31 from Locarno.

$ Rates (including continental breakfast): 65F–90F ($47.45–$65.70) single; 140F–180F ($102.20–$131.40) double. Half board 15F ($10.95) extra. AE, DC, MC, V.

This white-walled hotel is located in a residential area away from the lake. Its rooms have balconies with a good view of the mountains; amenities include a radio. Among the facilities provided are a swimming pool and a garage. Most of the surrounding homes date from the 19th century.

WHERE TO DINE

The harbor of Ascona is lined with many fine restaurants. Most guests dine outside during the summer, by the lake. There are also many fine restaurants on the cobblestone streets of the old town.

EXPENSIVE

GIARDINO, in the Hotel Giardino, via Segnale. Tel. 35-01-01.
Cuisine: FRENCH. **Reservations:** Required. **Bus:** 31 from Locarno.

$ Prices: Appetizers 10F–35F ($7.30–$25.55); main courses 35F–45F ($25.55–$32.85); fixed-price meals 95F–130F ($69.35–$94.90). AE, DC, MC, V.
Open: Dinner only Wed–Sun 7–10pm. **Closed:** Winter.

The finest dining room in Ticino is in the elegant Hotel Giardino. Many gourmets drive all the way from Milan to enjoy the excellent cuisine. You'll be warmly welcomed by the staff. The albergo (hotel) was originally located in Brissago; some of the furniture came from a nearby cloister. When the hotel was relocated to Ascona, the furniture was moved to the new site.

MODERATE

AL PONTILE, piazza G. Motta 31. Tel. 35-46-04.
Cuisine: FRENCH/ITALIAN. **Reservations:** Required.

$ Prices: Appetizers 7F–18F ($5.10–$13.15); main courses 15F–40F ($10.95–$29.20); fixed-price lunch 17F–20F ($12.40–$14.60). AE, MC, V.
Open: Lunch daily noon–2pm; dinner daily 6:30–9:30pm.

Many of the restaurants along the quays look alike and have similar menus, but the decor here, with a darkly rustic interior and hanging straw lamps, seems a little warmer and more intimate than elsewhere. The menu might include quail with risotto, osso buco, and saltimbocca, in addition to a variety of good pasta dishes. Fish dishes include scampi, sole, and salmon. For dessert, I recommend one of the homemade pies.

AL TORCHIO, contrada Maggiore 1. Tel. 35-71-26.
   Cuisine: SWISS/ITALIAN. **Reservations:** Not accepted.
$ **Prices:** Appetizers 9F–12F ($6.55–$8.75); main courses 15F–32F ($10.95–$23.35). AE, DC, MC, V.
   Open: Lunch daily noon–2pm; dinner daily 5:30–10pm; café daily 9am–1am.
The first room of this rambling restaurant has a rustic decor, red candles, and imaginative designs painted on the plaster walls. On a warm night you might continue past the American-style salad bar in the back and turn left into the vine-covered courtyard. The menu might include calves' liver Venetian style, osso buco, a winter fondue, and spaghetti with clams. For dessert, try the gelato misto (a mixed selection of ice cream) or a sorbet with vodka. Jazz is presented every Friday evening in the cellar.

RISTORANTE BORROMEO, via Collegio 16. Tel. 35-12-98.
   Cuisine: SWISS/ITALIAN. **Reservations:** Recommended.
$ **Prices:** Appetizers 10F–16F ($7.30–$11.70); main courses 22F–35F ($16.05–$25.55); fixed-price meals 30F–38F ($21.90–$27.75). AE, DC, MC, V.
   Open: Lunch daily noon–2pm; dinner daily 6–9pm.
This former monastery and Catholic school is now one of the most popular restaurants in the region. Local residents flock to its three rustic rooms with high ceilings. The menu might include risotto milanese with saffron, a mixed grill, piccata marsala, trout, scampi, and osso buco.

RISTORANTE DA IVO, via Collegio 141. Tel. 35-10-31.
   Cuisine: SWISS/ITALIAN. **Reservations:** Required. **Bus:** 31 from Locarno.
$ **Prices:** Appetizers 18F–29F ($13.15–$21.15); main courses 25F–48F ($18.25–$35.05); business lunch 30F ($21.90); menu gastronomique 85F ($62.05). No credit cards.
   Open: Lunch Wed–Sun noon–2pm; dinner Wed–Sun 6:30–10pm. **Closed:** Jan–Feb.
You'll have to wind your way through the streets of the old town to get to this sophisticated restaurant featuring the nouvelle cuisine of Ivo Balestra. The large, rustic house has a fireplace, light-grained paneling, cream-colored walls, and a wide selection of folk art. The menu is based on fresh ingredients from the market. Specialties might include suckling lamb with cabbage, turbot à l'orange with pink peppercorns, baby veal with white truffles in puff pastry, and salmon flan with leaf lettuce. The tagliatelle alla panna is an excellent pasta dish.

INEXPENSIVE

OSTERIA NOSTRANA, via Albarelle. Tel. 35-51-58.
   Cuisine: SWISS/ITALIAN. **Reservations:** Not needed. **Bus:** 31 from Locarno.
$ **Prices:** Appetizers 10F–14F ($7.30–$10.20); main courses 15F–28F ($10.95–$20.45). AE, DC, MC, V.
   Open: Daily 9am–midnight.
⑤ One of the most active harborfront restaurants in Ascona has sidewalk tables overlooking the lake and its fashionable promenade. The rustically comfortable dining room offers 11 different types of spaghetti (try the carbonara), lasagne verde, cannelloni, tortelloni, and tagliatelle. There is also a typical Italian pizzeria, offering 12 kinds of crisp homemade pizza (try the calzone).

EVENING ENTERTAINMENT

DANCING CLUB CINCILLA, via Brissago. Tel. 35-51-71.

This popular disco has an urban ambience and a good DJ. The darkly painted interior is carpeted. Proper dress is required. Open daily from 9pm to 3:30am. Drinks run 15F ($10.95).

Admission: Free.

HAPPYVILLE NIGHT CLUB, via Borgo. Tel. 35-11-58.

A cast of seven actors perform a song, dance, and striptease routine. There is also band music. The cabaret has comfortable banquettes and a tiny dance floor. Shows begin at 11:30pm and 1:30am. The club is open until 4am; closed in midwinter. Drinks cost about 15F ($10.95).

Admission: 6F ($4.40).

---

4. LUGANO

20 miles S of Bellinzona, 143 miles S of Zurich

GETTING THERE By Plane Crossair, Aeroporto Lugano (tel. 50-50-01), provides air links between Lugano and several major cities in Switzerland (Zurich, Bern, Basel, Geneva), in Italy (Rome, Florence, Venice), and in France (Paris, Nice).

By Train Lugano is a major stop along the rail lines that connect Milan with Zurich. As such, it receives trains from all parts of Switzerland throughout the day and night.

By Bus Lugano is linked by bus to dozens of hamlets in the Ticino that lack rail connections. There are also long-range buses that come from Italian cities: Como (trip time: 30 min.), Venice (trip time: 5 hr.), and Milan (trip time: 90 min.). From the rest of Switzerland, however, most visitors arrive by train.

By Car Pass through the St. Gotthard Tunnel and continue south along Route N2, via Bellinzona, all the way to Lugano.

ESSENTIALS The **telephone area code** for Lugano is 091.

Lugano is a Swiss town with an Italian flavor. The Italian influence is evident in the city's cafés, sunny piazzas, cobblestone streets, and arcades.

Lugano is built along the shore of Lake Lugano, which the Italians call Lake Ceresio. The peaks of San Salvatore and Monte Brè loom on opposite sides of town. The low mountains protect it from cold alpine winds; the climate is ideal from March to November. As the cultural center of the Ticino, Lugano has attracted many artists and tourists.

ORIENTATION

ARRIVING Flight passengers arrive at the airport at **Lugano-Agno,** where taxis await visitors for the 10-minute ride to the center of Lugano. Rail passengers arrive at the **Lugano railroad station,** piazzale della Stazione, which is in the center of the city, west of piazza Indipendenza. If your luggage is light, you can walk to many of the hotels; if not, you can take one of the taxis waiting outside the station.

For **travel information** in or out of town, call 22-65-02 daily at the Lugano railway station. You can also visit the travel agency for the Swiss Federal Railways at piazza Rezzonico 7 (tel. 23-75-01), Monday through Friday from 9am to 5pm.

INFORMATION The **Lugano Tourist Office** is at riva Albertolli 5 (tel. 21-46-64), open Monday through Friday from 8am to 6pm and on Saturday from 9am to 5pm.

CITY LAYOUT The center of town is **piazza Riforma,** dominated by a neoclassical city hall constructed in 1844. From here you can explore the ancient streets of the old town.

Lugano is built along several **lakeside quays,** of which riva Albertolli, riva Vincenzo Vela, and riva Antonio Caccia are the most important. They run from piazza Cassarate to piazza Paradiso.

The other two important squares of Lugano, also by the lake, are **piazza Riziero Rezzonico** and **piazza Alessandro Manzioni,** the latter with gardens.

The major park of Lugano, also opening onto the lake, is **Parco Civico,** site of the Casino, the Palazzo del Congressi, and the town's large swimming pool.

Directly east of the center is **Castagnola,** a suburb and site of the Villa Favorita, with its celebrated collection of art.

Towering over Lugano are two hills, **Monte San Salvatore,** at 2,992 feet, and **Monte Brè,** at 3,061 feet. They're ideal for full- or half-day excursions.

GETTING AROUND

BY PUBLIC TRANSPORTATION An explanation of fares and ticket machines can be found in a brochure distributed by the tourist office and the Public Transport Board, Azienda Comunale dei Trasporti, via Carducci (tel. 20-72-24).

You must purchase a ticket before boarding a bus or a train. If you're caught without one, you may have to pay a 30F ($21.90) fine. You can purchase a **1-day ticket** for 1.50F ($1.10) from automatic ticket machines for 4F ($2.90); this ticket allows you unlimited travel for 24 hours from the moment you purchase it. It includes the Funicular Lugano–Main Street SBB, but not the Line 12 Lugano–Brè.

BY TAXI Call 51-21-21 or 54-44-66.

FAST FACTS

Drugstore The **Farmacia San Luca,** via Pioda 9 (tel. 23-84-55), is conveniently located in the center of Lugano. You'll find what you need for most minor ailments. English is spoken.

Emergencies Call 117 for **police,** 118 for the **fire department,** 22-91-91 for an **ambulance,** 111 for **a doctor or a dentist,** 58-61-11 for **first aid,** and 140 for **road service.**

Hospital The major hospital is **Ospedale Civico,** via Tesserete (tel. 58-61-11).

Lost Property To report or retrieve lost property, go to the Polizia comunale, piazza Riforma (tel. 20-70-76).

Luggage Storage/Lockers Luggage can be stored at the Lugano railway station, piazzale della Stazione (tel. 23-66-91), for 24 hours in special compartments or at the luggage counter found there. The counter is open daily from 6:30am to 7pm.

WHAT TO SEE & DO
IN TOWN

Parco Civico is the city park along Lake Lugano. It contains the Palazzo dei Congressi (the convention center), the Casino, and the Villa Ciani art museum. Outdoor concerts are presented in the summer.

Villa Ciani, Parco Civico (tel. 23-61-62) contains works by modern Swiss and Quattrocento (15th-century) artists, as well as other European masters. See especially the works of Lucas Cranach the Elder, Vela, Serodine, Mola, Piazzetta, Monet, Pissarro, Rousseau, and Derain. In addition, you'll find works by Hodler and Augusto and Alberto Giacometti. Marini, Martini, and Messina are represented in the sculpture gallery. The museum is open Tuesday through Sunday from 10am to noon and 2 to 6pm. Admission is 3F ($2.20).

The **Cattedrale di San Lorenzo** (St. Lawrence), via Cattedrale, in the old town, was originally a Romanesque church. It was reconstructed in the 13th and 14th centuries and overhauled in the 17th and 18th centuries. It has three outstanding Renaissance doorways and a baroque interior. Look for the 16th-century tabernacle at the end of the south aisle; it was designed by the Rodari brothers of Maroggia.

The other important church is **Chiesa di Santa Maria degli Angeli** (Church of St. Mary of the Angels), piazza Luini, located on the south side of the resort. This convent church was built at the end of the 15th century and is celebrated throughout the Ticino for its frescoes by Bernardino Luini, the Lombard painter. His huge fresco *The Crucifixion* dates from 1529. Many critics have compared the beauty of his work to that of Leonardo da Vinci. John Ruskin found an "unstudied sweetness" in Luini's work. The church was occupied by Franciscans until 1848.

SPORTS

Water sports are popular in Lugano; you can also bicycle or play golf and tennis.

Boating   You can rent rowboats and motorboats along the lakefront.

Sailing   Circolo Velico, Lago di Lugano, Foce Cassarate (tel. 51-09-75), charges 25F to 35F ($18.25 to $25.55) per hour.

Scuba   Try **Lugano-Sub,** G. Bucher, corso Elvezia 3 (tel. 22-96-29).

Swimming   The **Lido** (tel. 51-40-41) is a sandy stretch of beach along the lake. You can also relax on the lawn or eat at the cafeteria on the terrace. Use of the beach and a changing cabin costs 4F ($2.90) for adults, 2F ($1.45) for children 2 to 14. The beach is open in the summer daily from 9am to 7pm.

You can also swim in the lake at the **public bath,** riva Caccia (tel. 54-20-35), and at **Lido San Domenico,** Castagnola (tel. 51-65-66). Admission is 2F ($1.45) for adults, 1F (75¢) for children. At **Lido Piscina Comunale,** Paradiso (tel. 54-75-62), the charge is 4F ($2.90) for adults, 1.50F ($1.10) for children.

In addition, many hotels have heated pools, some with salt water.

Waterskiing   Club Nautico-Lugano, via Calloni 9 (tel. 68-61-39), charges 120F ($87.60) per hour, instruction included. It's located between Lugano and Melide. **Club Sci Nautico Ceresio** (tel. 54-19-21) charges 150F ($109.50) per hour and also offers instruction. **Saladin,** piazza B. Luini (tel. 23-57-97), charges 60F ($43.80) for a half hour and 120F ($87.60) for an hour.

Windsurfing   You can windsurf on the lake at Club Nautico-Lugano (address and phone listed above), Hôtel du Lac, Paradiso (tel. 54-19-21), and Circolo Velico (address and phone listed above). The cost ranges from 15F to 25F ($10.95 to $18.25) per hour.

NEARBY ATTRACTIONS

VILLA FAVORITA, Castagnola. Tel. 51-61-52.

⭐ This 17th-century building contains one of the world's great private art collections. The collection belongs to Baron Hans Heinrich Thyssen-Bornemisza, who shares it with the public in his luxuriously furnished villa. The art ranges from the Middle Ages to the 19th century and includes many Flemish and German works. There are paintings by Cranach the Elder, Dürer, Holbein the Younger, Memling, and Van Eyck (see his masterpiece, *The Annunciation*). The Italian school is well represented by Titian, Raphael, Fra Angelico, Caravaggio, and Correggio. Special exhibitions are presented each year. Castagnola is east of Lugano.

Admission: 12F ($8.75).

Open: Apr 20–Oct 29, Tues–Sun 10am–5pm. **Closed:** Oct 30–Apr 19. **Bus:** 2.

SCHMID MUSEUM, Brè. Tel. 51-66-93.

The former home of architect Wilhelm Schmid is now a museum displaying many of his works and documents. The architect was deeply involved in the "new objectivity" of the 1920s and 1930s. Paintings from that period are on display, as are ceramics, work tools, and decorated furniture. Some of Schmid's books and papers deal with the political events that drove him out of Nazi Germany in 1936 and back to his native Switzerland. After Schmid's widow died, the home became public property. The suburb of Brè is 5½ miles from Lugano.

Admission: Free.

Open: Easter to mid-Oct, Tues–Sun 10am–noon and 3–5pm. **Closed:** Mid-Oct to Easter. **Bus:** Costs 2.40F ($1.80). **Funicular:** Costs 6F ($4.40).

SWISS MINIATURE VILLAGE, via Cantonale, Melide-Lugano. Tel. 68-79-51.

Small replicas of the major buildings in Switzerland are displayed along a labyrinth of asphalt paths. There's also a miniature of the twin castles in Sion. You can purchase an official guidebook for detailed explanations. This attraction is especially popular with children.

Admission: 8F ($5.85) adults, 5F ($3.65) children under 14.

Open: Mid-July to Aug 20, daily 8:30am–10pm; Mar to mid-July and Aug 21–Oct, daily 8:30am–6pm. **Closed:** Nov–Feb. **Transportation:** Train from Lugano Village.

VILLA HELENEUM, via Cortivo 24, Lugano-Cassarate. Tel. 51-73-53.

This landmark building is along the famous walk to Gandria. It contains the **Museum of Extra-European Cultures,** which exhibits objects from Oceania (New Guinea, New Britain, New Ireland, the Solomon Islands, Vanuatu, New Caledonia, Polynesia), Indonesia (Sumatra, Kalimantan, Nias, Timor), and Africa (Dan, Senufo, Ibo, Yoruba). The collection was donated by Serge Brignoni, an exponent of the surrealist movement. The museum opened in 1989. There is also a center for ethnographic studies, as well as a library annexed to the museum.

Admission: 6F ($4.40) adults, 3F ($2.20) children.

Open: Tues–Sun 10am–5pm. **Bus:** 11.

WHERE TO STAY

Lugano has hotels in all price categories. Many are located in the suburbs of Paradiso, Cassarate, and Castagnola.

VERY EXPENSIVE

GRAND HOTEL VILLA CASTAGNOLA AU LAC, viale Castagnola 31, CH-6900 Lugano. Tel. 091/51-22-13. Fax 091/52-72-71. 99 rms (all with bath). MINIBAR TV TEL **Bus:** 1.

$ Rates (including buffet breakfast): 170F–230F ($124.10–$167.90) single; 260F–350F ($189.75–$255.45) double. Half board 45F ($32.85) extra. AE, DC, MC, V. **Closed:** Feb.

⭐ The beauty of this ocher, Mediterranean-style villa, across the street from the lake, is enhanced by its exotic trees and plants. The hotel attracts an older crowd. The public rooms have marble or parquet floors; some have large fireplaces in consonance with their baronial decor. There are flagstone terraces, and elegant nooks where you can have tea or apéritifs. The bedrooms are furnished with traditional styling.

Dining/Entertainment: In an elegant setting, both in and out of doors, the hotel offers a refined continental cuisine.

Services: Room service, laundry.

Facilities: Indoor swimming pool, two tennis courts, private beach, fitness center.

HOTEL ADMIRAL, via Geretta 15, CH-6902 Lugano-Paradiso. Tel. 091/54-23-24; for reservations and information, 212/593-2988 in New York City, or toll free 800/223-5652 in the U.S., 800/882-4777 in New York State. Fax 091/54-25-48. 92 rms (all with bath). MINIBAR TV TEL **Bus:** 9 or 10.

$ Rates (including breakfast): 120F–175F ($87.60–$127.75) single; 180F–270F ($131.40–$197.05) double. Half board 40F ($29.20) extra. **Parking:** 15F ($10.95). No credit cards.

The first-class Admiral was built in 1975 out of concrete and glass and is today one of the finest hotels on the outskirts of Lugano. The seven-story high-rise is near the Lugano-Sud exit from the main highway. Many of the public rooms have red leather accents and wood trim. The showplace salon has French-style armchairs, Oriental rugs, and large windows with a view of the garden. The comfortable rooms are equipped with radios, refrigerators, a trouser press, a hairdryer, and cosmetic bars. The hotel is open year round and is a member of the prestigious Steigenberger Reservation Service.

Dining/Entertainment: There are two restaurants, a cafeteria, and a bar.

Services: Underwater massage, room service, laundry.

Facilities: Indoor swimming pool, outdoor swimming pool on the roof, two saunas, fitness center.

EXPENSIVE

EUROPA GRAND HOTEL AU LAC, via Cattori 1, CH-6902 Lugano. Tel. 091/55-01-71. Fax 091/54-27-57. 104 rms (all with bath). A/C MINIBAR TV TEL **Bus:** 1, 2, or 9.

$ Rates (including buffet breakfast): 140F–210F ($102.20–$153.30) single; 210F–310F ($153.30–$226.25) double. Half board 50F ($36.50) extra. AE, DC, MC, V. **Parking:** 20F ($14.60).

There is a flower garden in front of the pure-white facade of this hotel. The modern interior is informal, with a streamlined elegance. The well-furnished rooms are equipped with balconies, radios, and cosmetic bars.

Dining/Entertainment: There is a café boulevard open all day, as well as an international cabaret at the Night Club Europa. The à la carte restaurant, Les Quatre Saisons, serves a refined French and Italian cuisine in an elegant atmosphere.

Services: Room service, laundry.

Facilities: Indoor swimming pool, parking, shops.

GRAND HOTEL EDEN, riva Paradiso 7, CH-6900 Lugano-Paradiso. Tel.

091/55-01-21. Fax 091/54-28-95. 130 rms (all with bath). A/C MINIBAR TV TEL **Bus:** 1, 2, or 9.
$ **Rates** (including continental breakfast): 180F–240F ($131.40–$175.20) single; 320F–420F ($233.55–$306.55) double. Half board 55F ($40.15) extra. AE, DC, MC, V.

The finest hotel in Lugano, the Eden is large and contemporary, with balconies overlooking the lake. Rated five stars, it has a sun terrace built over the lake, with café tables and chaise longues. The rooms are handsomely furnished. Amenities include a radio, a video, and a safe.

Dining/Entertainment: The hotel's restaurant serves a sophisticated international cuisine, with an emphasis on Swiss, Italian, and French dishes. There is also a high-class bar.

Services: Room service, laundry.
Facilities: Large swimming pool.

HOTEL BELLEVUE AU LAC, riva Caccia 10, CH-6902 Lugano. Tel.
091/54-33-33. Fax 091/54-12-73. 70 rms (all with bath). MINIBAR TV TEL **Bus:** 1 or 2.
$ **Rates** (including continental breakfast): 120F–180F ($87.60–$131.40) single; 220F–300F ($160.60–$218.95) double. Half board 35F ($25.55) extra. AE, MC, V. **Closed:** Nov–Mar.

Because of the angle of this four-story hotel, only a few rooms have full views of the lake. The other rooms have balconies and a pleasant view of the garden and sun terrace. The Foery family offers sunny rooms equipped with a radio and a refrigerator.

Dining/Entertainment: The half-board plan includes a sangría party, a candlelight dinner, and weekly barbecues. The hotel has a bar.

Services: Room service, laundry.
Facilities: Outdoor swimming pool.

HOTEL BELMONTE, via Serenella 29, CH-6976 Lugano-Castagnola. Tel.
091/51-40-33. Fax 091/52-61-39. 42 rms (all with bath). MINIBAR TV TEL **Bus:** 1.
$ **Rates** (including breakfast): 120F–160F ($87.60–$116.80) single; 180F–260F ($131.40–$189.75) double. Half board 35F ($25.55) extra. AE, DC, MC, V. **Closed:** Dec–Feb.

Palm trees grow in front of this grand hotel with balconies and large windows. Many rooms have a view of the lake. Chaise longues are set up on the flagstone border around the pool. The Belmonte is in the suburb of Lugano-Castagnola, a 2-minute trolley-bus ride from the center.

Dining/Entertainment: The Belmonte hires some of the best-trained continental chefs for an excellent cuisine. There is also a bar.

Services: Room service, laundry.
Facilities: Outdoor swimming pool.

HOTEL MONTALBANO, via Montalbano, CH-6900 Lugano. Tel. 091/55-
88-11. Fax 091/54-25-38. 44 junior suites. MINIBAR TV TEL **Transportation:** Hotel minibus provided, including airport pickups.
$ **Rates** (including buffet breakfast): 295F–325F ($215.30–$237.20) single; 365F–395F ($266.40–$288.30) double. AE, DC, MC, V. **Parking:** 16F ($11.70).

This modern hotel with two sienna wings resembles a Caribbean resort. It's managed by the same group that owns the Villa Principe Leopoldo, across the street. The exclusive residential neighborhood Collina d'Oro (Golden Hill) is in the hills above Lugano; the grounds are shaded by trees. Rated five stars, the Montalbano offers rooms with curved walls, sophisticated lighting fixtures, and the kind of furniture found in an urban art gallery.

Dining/Entertainment: There is a fine restaurant, serving a selection of international dishes.

Services: Room service, laundry.

Facilities: Two outdoor swimming pools, fitness center, sauna rooms, indoor golf, children's playground.

HOTEL PULLMAN COMMODORE, riva Caccia 6, CH-6900 Lugano. Tel. 091/54-39-21. Fax 091/54-37-44. 58 rms (all with bath). A/C MINIBAR TV TEL **Bus:** 1 or 2.

$ **Rates** (including continental breakfast): 160F–180F ($116.80–$131.40) single; 210F–240F ($153.30–$175.20) double. Half board 50F ($36.50) extra. AE, DC, MC, V. **Parking:** 20F ($14.60).

Situated on the lakeside promenade in the center of town, this modern, four-star hotel has two huge wings extending toward the water. The balconies are decorated with flowers and there is a series of sun terraces in the middle. The public rooms have plush armchairs. The comfortable bedrooms are well furnished in summertime colors, with wood and brass accents. The hotel is a member of the Pullman chain.

Dining/Entertainment: The Nettuno restaurant is spacious and sunny, with glossy-white, Chinese Chippendale-style chairs. The Moby bar is a popular meeting place.

Services: Room service, laundry.

Facilities: Covered garage.

HOTEL SPLENDIDE ROYAL, riva A. Caccia 7, CH-6900 Lugano. Tel. 091/54-20-02. Fax 091/54-89-31. 150 rms (all with bath). MINIBAR TV TEL **Bus:** 1, 2, or 9.

$ **Rates** (including continental breakfast): 190F–260F ($138.70–$189.75) single; 330F–450F ($240.85–$328.45) double. Half board 55F ($40.15) extra. AE, DC, MC, V.

The splendor of the 19th century is evident in the elegant architecture of this mansard-roofed hotel. Built in 1888, the Splendide Royal has welcomed many famous people (and even a few infamous ones). Maria, Queen of Romania, and Vittorio Emanuele di Savoia have both stayed here. The public rooms are decorated with columns, crystal-and-gilt chandeliers, Venetian furniture, and Oriental rugs. Some of the most magnificent bedrooms have ceiling frescoes. The swimming pool is shaped like an oyster, and there is a rock garden.

Dining/Entertainment: The lovely restaurant, La Veranda, overlooks riva Caccia and the lake. There's also a bar.

Services: Room service, laundry.

Facilities: Covered swimming pool.

VILLA PRINCIPE LEOPOLDO, via Montalbano 5, CH-6900 Lugano. Tel. 091/55-88-55. Fax 091/55-88-25. 24 junior suites. MINIBAR TV TEL **Transportation:** Hotel provides minibus for guests, including airport pickups.

$ **Rates** (including buffet breakfast): 400F–440F ($291.95–$321.15) single; 500F–540F ($364.95–$394.35) double. AE, DC, MC, V. **Parking:** 20F ($14.60).

This elegant villa was built in the early 1900s as the home of Prince Leopold, of Austria's von Hohenzollerns. After World War I it was sold to a Swiss industrialist. In 1986 the villa was transformed into a hotel with an understated Italian style. Today it's one of the chicest hotels in Lugano. There is a modern addition with a two-story atrium and a cascade of illuminated water. The junior suites have beige travertine trim, and each room has a terrace overlooking the lake and Paradiso. The staff is polite. The hotel is in the upper heights of Lugano, along a winding road in the exclusive Collina d'Oro neighborhood.

Dining/Entertainment: The restaurant consists of three garden rooms. There is also an elegant bar. The menu includes tagliolini with squid, tagliatelle with pesto, grilled lobster, and rack of lamb pré-salé. Piano music is provided in the bar daily from 8 to 11pm. Full meals start at 55F ($40.15) and are served daily from noon to 3:30pm and 7 to 11pm. Reservations are required.

Services: Room service, laundry.

Facilities: Fitness center, solarium, Jacuzzi, sauna.

MODERATE

CARLTON HOTEL VILLA MORITZ, via Cortivo 9, CH-6976 Lugano-Catagnola. Tel. 091/51-38-12. Fax 091/51-38-14. 52 rms (all with bath). TEL **Bus:** 11.
$ Rates: 82F ($59.85) single; 156F ($114.05) double. AE, V. **Parking:** 8F ($5.85). **Closed:** Nov–Feb.

Peace and quiet are assured at this hotel as it's located in a park a good distance from the main road. The Wernli family manages several 19th-century buildings clustered near a swimming pool surrounded by flagstones. The hotel also benefits from being on the sunny side of Mount Brè. The bedrooms are comfortably furnished with traditional styling. The public rooms are modern, with stone accents around the bar. Public buses transport guests to the center of Lugano in 10 minutes. There is an underground garage nearby. Laundry facilities are provided.

HOTEL ARIZONA, via Massagno 20, CH-6900 Lugano. Tel. 091/22-93-43. Fax 091/23-81-43. 50 rms (all with bath). MINIBAR TV TEL **Directions:** See below.
$ Rates (including buffet breakfast): 100F–120F ($73–$87.60) single; 160F–180F ($116.80–$131.40) double. AE, DC, MC, V.

Alternating bands of reddish brick and white concrete adorn the facade of this attractive modern hotel at the north end of the city. The Brunner family offers bedrooms with irregular shapes and large windows facing south. There is a sun terrace, as well as a swimming pool on the roof. The renovated restaurant and bar offer guests a quiet place to eat and drink.

To get to the hotel, take the Lugano-Nord exit of the autobahn, then turn left at the first traffic light in the direction of Massagno. Follow the signs to Lugano, which will direct you to turn right at via San Gottardo. Follow the signs to the hotel.

HOTEL COLORADO, via Maraini 19, CH-6901 Lugano. Tel. 091/54-16-31. Fax 091/54-90-65. 34 rms (all with bath) MINIBAR TV TEL **Bus:** 9.
$ Rates (including continental breakfast): 90F–135F ($65.70–$98.55) single; 130F–195F ($94.90–$142.35) double. AE, DC, MC, V.

Both its name and its architecture might inspire nostalgia in North American guests. The Colorado has eight stories with balconies. The comfortable rooms are equipped with a radio and other amenities. The Tavernetta Grill offers modern cuisine, as well as regional and international specialties. Full meals begin at 32F ($23.35). There's also a bar, as well as another dining room. Room service, laundry, and baby-sitting are provided.

HOTEL DELFINO, via Casserinetta 6, CH-6900 Lugano. Tel. 091/54-53-33. Fax 091/54-55-52. 48 rms (all with bath). TV TEL **Bus:** 1 or 2.

$ **Rates** (including continental breakfast): 90F–100F ($65.70–$73) single; 160F–190F ($116.80–$138.70) double. AE, DC, MC, V. **Closed:** Dec–Mar.

Built in 1972, this hotel is especially attractive at night, when the exterior is illuminated with spotlights. The modern balconies are decorated with cascading plants. The interior has elegant touches, such as a hardwood reception desk decorated with elaborate carvings and antique pewter. Oriental rugs and a baroque chest make the place even more appealing. Facilities include a swimming pool. There is a dining room with chandeliers, as well as a bar. The hotel is on a side street a few blocks from the lake.

ROMANTIK HOTEL TICINO, piazza Cioccaro 1, CH-6901 Lugano. Tel. **091/22-77-72.** Fax 091/23-62-78. 20 rms (all with bath). A/C MINIBAR TV TEL **Bus:** 1 or 2.

$ **Rates** (including buffet breakfast): 170F–200F ($124.10–$146) single; 270F–320F ($197.05–$233.55) double. AE, MC, V. **Closed:** Jan.

The central courtyard of this former convent has been covered with a glass ceiling for year-round comfort. In front of the narrow hotel is one of the most charming squares in the old town. Antique cupboards and chests are in the stairwell. Each of the small bedrooms is uniquely furnished, usually with 19th-century provincial pieces. Amenities include a radio; a TV is available on request. The restaurant serves regional specialties from Switzerland and Italy.

INEXPENSIVE

ALBERGO DOMUS, riva Paradiso 24, CH-6900 Lugano-Paradiso. Tel. **091/54-34-21.** 30 rms (24 with bath). MINIBAR TV TEL **Bus:** 1 or 9.

$ **Rates** (including continental breakfast): 50F ($36.50) single without bath, 80F–90F ($58.40–$65.70) single with bath; 90F ($65.70) double without bath, 120F–150F ($87.60–$109.50) double with bath. AE, DC, MC, V. **Closed:** Dec–Feb.

This red-brick building with balconies is on the main road from Lugano to Paradiso. The attractive and spacious interior is decorated with potted palms and Oriental rugs. The uncluttered bedrooms have large windows and a lighthearted, southern decor. The restaurant provides a good cuisine of the Ticino and international dishes.

HOTEL MARINA, via Generale Arcioni 20, CH-6900 Lugano-Cassarete. **Tel. 091/51-45-12.** 30 rms (all with bath). MINIBAR TV TEL **Bus:** 2.

$ **Rates** (including continental breakfast): 80F–100F ($58.40–$73) single; 135F–155F ($98.55–$113.15) double. AE, DC, MC, V.

This three-star hotel has a flat roof and symmetrical rows of concrete balconies. The entrance hall is attractively austere, with a marble floor. The public rooms have pastel colors, tile floors, and flowered curtains. The congenial Schreiber family offers spacious rooms with large windows, wooden furniture, and homey knickknacks.

POST HOTEL SIMPLON, via Generale Guisan, CH-6900 Lugano-Paradiso. Tel. 091/54-44-41. Fax 091/54-12-21. 32 rms (all with bath). TEL

$ **Rates** (including continental breakfast): 60F–75F ($43.80–$54.75) single; 110F–140F ($80.30–$102.20) double. Half board 18F ($13.15) extra. AE, DC, MC, V. **Closed:** Jan–Feb.

This inexpensive hotel is located in the outlying suburbs of Lugano Paradiso. The rooms are comfortable and the staff is polite. The hotel's restaurant serves a typically Ticino cuisine.

WHERE TO DINE
EXPENSIVE

RISTORANTE AL PORTONE, viale Cassarate 3. Tel. 23-59-95.
   Cuisine: SWISS/ITALIAN. **Reservations:** Required.
$ **Prices:** Appetizers 18F–34F ($13.15–$24.80); main courses 38F–46F ($27.75–
   $33.60); fixed-price dinner 112F ($81.75). AE, DC, MC, V.
   Open: Lunch Tues–Sat noon–3pm; dinner Mon–Sat 7:30pm–midnight. **Closed:**
   Aug.

⭐ If you enjoy Italian-style modern cuisine, head for this sophisticated restaurant managed by chef Roberto Galizzi and his wife, Doris. As with all cuisine moderne, many of the combinations sound bizarre, but the taste is usually sensational. The veal liver with champagne and the sole "in the style of Roberto" are veritable palate pleasers. The desserts are also exceptional.

MODERATE

**ALBERGO RESTAURANT TICINO, in the Romantik Hotel, piazza
   Cioccaro 1. Tel. 22-77-72.**
   Cuisine: SWISS/ITALIAN. **Reservations:** Recommended. **Bus:** 1 or 2.
$ **Prices:** Appetizers 8F–15F ($5.85–$10.95); main courses 18F–32F ($13.15–
   $23.35). AE, MC, V.
   Open: Lunch daily 11:30am–3pm; dinner daily 6:30–11pm.
This hotel restaurant serves some of the best food in town. The dining room has vaulted ceilings and art deco lighting sconces. Fresh ingredients are used in the careful preparation of familiar dishes. The fixed-price menu might include scampi curry, chateaubriand, Ticino minestrone, and osso buco. Porcini mushrooms with risotto and polenta is a tasty local dish. The grilled rock lobster is a treat.

DA BIANCHI, via Pessina 3. Tel. 23-42-03.
   Cuisine: SWISS/ITALIAN. **Reservations:** Recommended. **Bus:** 1 or 2.
$ **Prices:** Appetizers 8F–15F ($5.85–$10.95); main courses 18F–28F ($13.15–
   $20.45); fixed-price meals 45F ($32.85). No credit cards.
   Open: Lunch Mon–Sat noon–2:30pm; dinner Mon–Sat 6:30–10pm. **Closed:**
   Aug.
One of the oldest and most venerated restaurants in Lugano, Da Bianchi is situated on a narrow street in the old town. It has a forest-green facade, accented by turn-of-the-century pillars carved from red stone. The walls have paneling and gold brocade, and the decor includes red carpeting, red upholstered chairs, rounded Belle Epoque ironwork, and a carriage lamp hanging over the door. The service is courteous and attentive. Many fine Italian dishes are served, such as scampi with curry, filet of sole in white wine, veal cutlet milanese, and risotto with fresh mushrooms. The specialty is three pastas served on a single platter. Some dishes are accompanied by deep-fried potatoes with pine nuts.

GAMBRINUS, piazza Riforma. Tel. 23-19-55.
   Cuisine: SWISS/ITALIAN. **Reservations:** Required. **Bus:** 1 or 2.
$ **Prices:** Appetizers 8F–15F ($5.85–$10.95); main courses 25F–48F ($18.25–
   $35.05). AE, DC, MC, V.
   Open: Daily 9am–midnight.
Two carved cherubs hold a fluted column above the door of this 18th-century building on via Giacomo Luvini, in a recessed corner of piazza Riforma, the main square. Be careful not to collide with the waiter bringing dishes of food to the outdoor café.

Inside is a central bar, with window tables. Specialties include saltimbocca, trout meunière, risotto marinara, air-cured beef from Davos, and pasta dishes.

LOCANDA DEL BOSCHETTO, via Boschetto 8. Tel. 54-24-93.

Cuisine: SWISS/ITALIAN. **Reservations:** Recommended. **Bus:** 1 or 2.

$ Prices: Appetizers 12F–16F ($8.75–$11.70); main courses 22F–35F ($16.05–$25.55). AE, DC, MC, V.

Open: Lunch daily noon–2pm; dinner daily 7–10pm. **Closed:** Mon in Jan.

Some residents of Milan say that it's cheaper to make the trip here than to eat at home. Guests can watch chef Vincenzo De-Martino cook beef and fish over the glowing coals. He produces a simple but flavorful cuisine, which includes a mixed grill of local fish, spaghetti with clam sauce, grilled calves' liver, and several succulent beef dishes. The well-known restaurant is in a wooded area near the highway. There are two dining rooms and a covered porch.

MÖVENPICK RISTORANTE PARCO CIANI, in the Palazzo dei Congressi, piazza Indipendenza. Tel. 23-86-56.

Cuisine: MEDITERRANEAN/INTERNATIONAL. **Reservations:** Recommended. **Bus:** 2 or 10.

$ Prices: Appetizers 5F–14F ($3.65–$10.20); main courses 15F–30F ($10.95–$21.90); plat du jour 15F–18F ($10.95–$13.15). AE, DC, MC, V.

Open: Daily 9am–midnight.

An abundant Italian harvest adorns this village restaurant—vines hang from the rafters and ripened corn is displayed in clusters. One of the dining rooms has modern bentwood armchairs, while the other has reproductions of Empire-style antiques. Located at the edge of a city park, the modern concrete building has irregular balconies and large windows. The menu includes wild game in season, veal-and-rice dishes, tortellini, three kinds of risotto, and a medley of broiled fresh fish and meats.

RISTORANTE GALLERIA, via Vegezzi 4. Tel. 23-62-88.

Cuisine: SWISS/ITALIAN. **Reservations:** Recommended. **Bus:** 1 or 2.

$ Prices: Appetizers 10F–16F ($7.30–$11.70); main courses 18F–32F ($13.15–$23.35); fixed-price meals from 35F ($25.55). AE, DC, MC, V.

Open: Lunch Mon–Sat noon–2pm; dinner Mon–Sat 7–10:30pm. **Closed:** Aug.

The red facade with gilt trim has an old-fashioned covered passageway leading to the door. The informal bar is on the left; the dining room, on the right, has white stucco arches, a beautifully textured wood ceiling with heavy beams, and original prints and lithographs by well-known artists, mostly Italian. Local bankers and businesspeople eat lunch here; at night a fun-loving crowd moves in. Café tables are set out on the mosaic floor under the arcade. Specialties include brochette Galleria, kebabs, fondue bourguignonne or chinoise, risotto with salmon, and five kinds of scampi.

RISTORANTE OROLOGIO, via Nizzola 2. Tel. 23-23-38.

Cuisine: SWISS/ITALIAN. **Reservations:** Recommended. **Bus:** 1 or 2.

$ Prices: Appetizers 8F–35F ($5.85–$25.55); main courses 26F–35F ($19–$25.55). AE, DC, MC, V.

Open: Lunch Sun–Fri 11:30am–2pm; dinner Sun–Fri 6:30–10pm. **Closed:** 3 weeks in Aug.

The high-quality Orologio occupies the ground floor of this buff-colored building with restrained detailing and leaded glass windows. The restaurant has 19th-century French-provincial chairs and an ice chest displaying salads and condiments. Amusing illustrations advertise the dishes—a mermaid draws your attention to the fish courses. Vincenzo Campanile and his family offer five kinds of spaghetti, four kinds of scampi, osso buco, smoked fish, Ticino minestrone, and a springtime celebration of seasonal vegetables.

INEXPENSIVE

LA TINERA, via dei Gorino 2. Tel. 23-52-19.
    Cuisine: SWISS/ITALIAN. **Reservations:** Not needed. **Bus:** 1 or 2.
$ Prices: Appetizers 8F–12F ($5.85–$8.75); main courses 15F–24F ($10.95–$17.50). No credit cards.
    Open: Lunch Mon–Sat 11:30am–2pm; dinner Mon–Sat 6:30–9:30pm.

A familiar array of Italian specialties are served for budget prices. The menu includes fresh pasta, risotto, and some good meat dishes. The restaurant is in the center of town, off piazza Riforma.

RISTORANTE MONTE CENERI, via Nassa 44. Tel. 23-33-40.
    Cuisine: SWISS/ITALIAN. **Reservations:** Not needed. **Bus:** 1 or 2.
$ Prices: Appetizers 8F–12F ($5.85–$8.75); main courses 12F–35F ($8.75–$25.55); fixed-price meal 28F ($20.45). No credit cards.
    Open: Lunch daily 11:30am–2pm; dinner daily 6:30–10pm.

A favorite among the locals, this family-run restaurant is one of the best bargains in town. Pet dogs also seem to be welcome. The dining room has an ornate plastic ceiling, red-checked tablecloths, and large windows. The Campanile family offers typical Italian specialties, such as fresh mushrooms, polenta, and risotto. Try one of the fondues or the special of the day. A local favorite is a platter of fresh mushrooms with polenta.

NEARBY DINING & LODGING

MOTTO DEL GALLO, CH-6807 Taverne. Tel. 091/93-28-71.
    Cuisine: MEDITERRANEAN. **Reservations:** Required. **Transportation:** Take the unnumbered bus marked "Taverne."
$ Prices: Appetizers 19F–29F ($18.85–$21.15); main courses 39F–43F ($28.45–$31.40); business lunch 45F ($32.85); menu gastronomique 95F ($69.35). AE, DC, MC, V.
    Open: Lunch Mon–Sat noon–2pm; dinner Mon–Sat 7:30–10:30pm. **Closed:** First 2 weeks in Jan.

For a visual treat, visit this baroque house, practically bursting with atmosphere. There is a collection of antiques, and the tables are covered with lace. The restaurant is in a 15th-century hamlet that alone is worth the trip—8 miles from Lugano on the road to Bellinzona. The menu includes homemade pastas, risotto with champagne, a succulent choice of fresh fish, and a salad of fresh foie gras. Main dishes include baked beef heart with levisticum (wild celery), rabbit with truffles and zucchini, and alpine-style lamb and fish dishes, many laced with mountain cheese. The chefs, Nico and José de la Iglesias, sometimes make an appearance in the dining room. Their partner is Tenca Piero, the maître d'. If you're looking for a romantic place to spend the night, suites for two cost 170F to 180F ($124.10 to $131.40), including breakfast.

SHOPPING

Lugano does not have much to offer shoppers. Two stores, however, are exceptions. **Bottega dell'Artigiano,** via Canova 18 (tel. 22-81-40), offers textiles, wood carvings, pottery, and metalware, all made in the Ticino. The service is cordial. The small shop filled with displays is run by the Cooperative per l'Artigianato Ticinese.

Dreamland Franz Carl Weber, via Nassa 5 (tel. 23-53-21), is the best toy store in the Ticino and part of a nationwide chain.

CASINO KURSAAL, Parco Civico. Tel. 23-32-81.
Since the Kursaal—unlike the Casino Municipale, above—is on Swiss soil, the highest bet allowed on its premises is 5F ($3.65). Most people, however, go there for the entertainment, which consists of a variety of cabaret, striptease, and magic acts. The best time to go is after 10pm. The club usually stays open until 3am. Drinks cost about 15F ($10.95).
Admission: 12F ($8.75).

EVENING ENTERTAINMENT

For a pleasant evening stroll, start at the famous **piazza Riforma** in Lugano, a huge flagstone square. You'll be surrounded by arcaded buildings, flowers, and cafés.

CASINOS

CASINO MUNICIPALE, Campione, Italy. Tel. 091/68-79-21.
This casino lies on Italian soil, across the lake from Lugano, only 20 minutes away by ferry. The casino is a glittering establishment, filled with an international clientele and such games as blackjack and chemin de fer, along with the inevitable slot machines. Here, in Italy, gambling stakes are unlimited. Oddly, however, despite the casino's location, the currency is Swiss. The casino is in the village of Campione, which is surrounded by Switzerland. Long ago the imperial fiefdom of Campione was presented to a Milanese monastery; it has remained Italian ever since. The men of Campione were famous for their stonework, and many buildings in Milan are a testament to their skill. Take a moment to admire the handiwork of some of the local buildings. Drinks run 12F ($8.75). Open daily from 9pm to 3am.
Admission: Free.

A CAFE

There are many cafés around piazza Riforma, but my favorite is the **Café Olimpia** (tel. 22-74-88), in an elegant stone building with hundreds of chairs set out front. Live bands occasionally perform. The menu includes daily specials, pastas, curries, and meat dishes. The pizzas, at 12F ($8.75), are especially popular at night. Inside is a wooden bar room with a charming, old-fashioned decor, as well as a formal dining room. The café is open daily from 7am to midnight, but hot meals are served only from noon to 3pm and 6:30 to 11pm. Full meals begin at 13F to 40F ($9.50 to $29.20).

EASY EXCURSIONS

Many excursions are offered on Lake Lugano, Lake Como, and Lake Maggiore. The **Societa Navigazione del Lago di Lugano** (tel. 51-52-23) offers cruises during the day and evening. Gandria and Morcote are the most popular destinations. If you plan to vacation in the Ticino, you can purchase a ticket for unlimited boat trips for 3 days; it costs 40F ($29.20).
The area around Lugano has many belvederes from which you can survey the mountain scenery. The most exciting excursion is a funicular ride to ◉ **Monte**

San Salvatore. From the top of the mountain you'll have a great view of all three lakes, as well as of the Swiss and French Alps, including the Matterhorn and Monte Rosa. Board the funicular in Paradiso. Departures are daily from 9am to 5pm from mid-March to mid-November. A round-trip ticket costs 14F ($10.20).

For an impressive view, take the funicular from Cassarate to the peak of ✪ **Monte Brè,** called the sunniest mountain in Switzerland. You'll see the Valaisan and Bernese Alps, including the Matterhorn and Monte Rosa. From Lugano you can take a trolley-bus to Cassarate, where you board a funicular. A round-trip ticket costs 13F ($9.50).

You can also take a cogwheel train from Capolago to ✪ **Monte Generoso,** at 5,590 feet. The panoramic view includes the lakes of the Ticino and parts of northern Italy. From Lugano take a boat or train to Capolago and board the train. A round-trip ticket costs 32F ($23.35).

GANDRIA

Gandria is a small, romantic oasis at the foot of Monte Brè 3 miles east of Lugano. This is one of the most popular excursions visitors make from Lugano. Some go by boat, departing from the central quays in Lugano; trip time is 30 minutes. After exploring the town, walk back along the famous lakeside path to Castagnola (it takes about an hour). Frequent trams connect suburban Castagnola with the center of Lugano.

Gandria abounds in intricate lanes, courtyards, and lush vegetation. It's built on terraces above Lake Lugano and has hundreds of steps linking the tiers. An afternoon spent climbing these stairs can exhaust an athlete, but this doesn't stop hordes of tourists from descending on Gandria. Most visitors come for the day, to shop for souvenirs and dine.

Where to Stay

HOTEL MOSMANN, CH-6978 Gandria. Tel. 091/51-72-61. Fax 091/52-71-32. 33 rms (all with bath). TEL

$ Rates: 70F–90F ($51.10–$65.70) single; 120F–150F ($87.60–$109.50) double. Half board 20F ($14.60) extra. AE, DC, MC, V. **Closed:** Dec–Feb.

The comfort and inviting atmosphere of this family-run hotel make up for its less than luxurious amenities. Try to get a room overlooking the lake. There is a beautiful lakeside terrace. The restaurant serves well-prepared Ticino specialties.

Where to Dine

LOCANDA GANDRIESE, on the lakeshore. Tel. 51-41-81.
   Cuisine: SWISS/ITALIAN. **Reservations:** Not needed.
$ Prices: Appetizers 8F–14F ($5.85–$10.20); main courses 15F–26F ($10.95–$19). No credit cards.
   Open: Lunch daily noon–2pm; dinner daily 6–10pm.

The lakeside terrace is so popular that it's hard to get a table in fair weather. The old-fashioned dining room has a fireplace where polenta is cooked in a cast-iron pot. The menu might include carpaccio, spaghetti bolognese, lasagne, and several veal dishes.

ANTICO, in the center of town. Tel. 51-48-71.
   Cuisine: SWISS/ITALIAN. **Reservations:** Not needed.
$ Prices: Appetizers 8F–14F ($5.85–$10.20); main courses 18F–26F ($13.15–$19). AE, DC, MC.
   Open: Lunch daily noon–2pm; dinner daily 6–10pm.

One of the most acclaimed restaurants in Gandria has an elaborate lakeside terrace with a glass enclosure that protects guests from the wind and cool temperatures. Many people come here in the afternoon only for coffee and an elaborate dessert. The menu might include grilled crayfish, Ticino minestrone, arrosto misto (mixed boiled meats) served with polenta, fondue bourguignonne, and steak tartare.

---

5. MORCOTE

7 miles S of Lugano, 25 miles S of Bellinzona

GETTING THERE By Bus Several buses depart from Lugano every day for Morcote (trip time: 30 min.).

By Lake Steamer Throughout the summer about a dozen boats make the trip every day from Lugano to Morcote, with many intermediary stops along the way. Depending on the schedule, trip time is between 1½ and 2½ hours. In the winter boats continue to run, but on a less frequent schedule.

By Car From Lugano, head south along Route 4.

ESSENTIALS For **travel information,** go to the Lugano Tourist Office (see Section 4, above). The **telephone area code** for Morcote is 091.

Morcote is considered one of the most idyllic villages of Switzerland. Its arcaded houses and old streets are built on the southern slopes of Monte Arbostora, at 2,755 feet. Cypresses and vineyards grow on the mountain.

WHAT TO SEE & DO

The **Church of the Madonna del Sasso** dates from the 13th century; it was reconstructed later, however, and given a baroque overlay. It has some beautiful 16th-century frescoes. A staircase with more than 400 steps lead down to the village and the lake. The cemetery contains the remains of many famous people.

Scherrer Park contains typical Ticino trees and plants, as well as sculpture and architecture. Some of the sculpture is from the Far East. Admission is 5F ($3.65). It's open on Wednesday and Friday through Monday from 9am to 5pm.

WHERE TO STAY

ALBERGO CARINA, CH-6922 Morcote. Tel. 091/69-11-31. Fax 091/69-19-29. 28 rms (all with bath). MINIBAR TV TEL
$ Rates (including continental breakfast): 90F–150F ($65.70–$109.50) single; 160F–220F ($116.80–$160.60) double. Half board 35F ($25.55) extra. AE, DC, MC, V. **Closed:** Dec–Feb.
The Albergo Carina has an Italian-style facade, with pink-and-cream trim and lime-green shutters. Such lighthearted contrast of colors also marks the lobby, which is decorated with Oriental rugs. The hotel's several terraces are filled with potted plants and small tables. A structure of whimsical design, it was once owned by the architect Gaspare Fossati (d. 1883), a native of Morcote, who was known for his renovations of Saint Sophia in Constantinople (present-day Istanbul). Some of the awards he received from the Ottoman sultan are displayed in the lobby. The Carina offers elegant bedrooms filled with provincial furniture, some of it antique; a swimming pool; and a lakeside restaurant.

HÔTEL RIVABELLA, CH-6922 Morcote. Tel. 091/69-13-14. 18 rms (11 with bath). TEL

$ Rates: 50F ($36.50) single without bath, 90F ($65.70) single with bath; 100F ($73) double without bath, 180F ($131.40) double with bath. Half board 20F ($14.60) extra. No credit cards. **Closed:** Nov–Mar.

If you want to escape from the most congested part of Morcote, try this Italian-style country house farther down the lakefront. Beneath the terrace built out over the water sailboats and motorboats are moored. Flower boxes on the rustic covered porch are filled with begonias and geraniums. The Tamborini family offers comfortable rooms with pleasant furniture.

WHERE TO DINE

LA VOILE D'OR, Olivella au Lac, CH-6922 Morcote. Tel. 091/69-10-01.
   Cuisine: SWISS/ITALIAN. **Reservations:** Required.
$ Prices: Appetizers 14F–18F ($10.20–$13.15); main courses 22F–38F ($16.05–$27.75). AE, DC, MC, V.
   Open: Lunch daily noon–2:30pm; dinner daily 7–10pm.

Chef Martino Meier has elevated Ticino cooking to a high art. His restaurant is one of the best in Switzerland. An oasis of lawns, flowers, and elegant terraces, it offers an intimate atmosphere and impeccable service. For an appetizer, try the foie gras or a lobster cocktail. Specialties include duck à l'orange, beef Wellington, and blue trout meunière; the filet of sole Caruso is very good. Game dishes, such as roebuck, are featured in season.

The hotel is also an excellent choice. Most of the 15 rooms have a balcony and such amenities as a radio, phone, and minibar. Guests can swim in either of the two pools, waterski, or windsurf. There's also a piano bar. Services include a nanny. Singles rooms range from 150F to 170F ($109.50 to $124.10); double rooms, 250F to 340F ($182.50 to $248.15). Breakfast is included. Half board is an extra 45F ($32.85) per person. The hotel is closed in January and February.

RISTORANTE DELLA POSTA, in the center of town. Tel. 69-11-27.
   Cuisine: SWISS/ITALIAN. **Reservations:** Not needed.
$ Prices: Appetizers 10F–15F ($7.30–$10.95); main courses 14F–28F ($10.20–$20.45). No credit cards.
   Open: Lunch Thurs–Tues 11:30am–2:30pm; dinner Thurs–Tues 5–11pm.
   Closed: Nov to mid-Mar.

This restaurant is on a terrace built out over the lake. Waiters scurry with food-laden trays from the kitchen across the street. The setting is charming, but the traffic makes it somewhat hectic. Specialties include risotto with mushrooms, osso buco with polenta, lake fish, and real Italian pizza.

CHAPTER 15

LIECHTENSTEIN

- **WHAT'S SPECIAL ABOUT LIECHTENSTEIN**
- **1. ABOUT LIECHTENSTEIN**
- **2. VADUZ**
- **3. THE UNTERLAND**
- **4. THE OBERLAND**

Liechtenstein, whose history goes back to the 14th century, is a land of fairytale castles, chalets decorated with geraniums, Rhine meadows, and small villages high in the Alps. One of the castles is inhabited by the reigning prince.

Nestled snugly beside Austria and separated from Switzerland by the Rhine River, it is one of the smallest independent sovereign states of Europe, along with San Marino in Italy and Andorra in the Pyrenees between Spain and France. The entire country is only about 16 miles long and 4 miles wide.

Liechtenstein is famous for its finely engraved postage stamps, which are treasured by collectors the world over. The stamps illustrate the country's religion (predominantly Roman Catholic), monarchy, art, history, landscape, nature, and leisure activities. Stamps provide 25% of the government's income, and new series are issued frequently. There is a postal museum in Vaduz, the capital of the principality.

Although it's commonly regarded as remote, Liechtenstein is actually very accessible from eastern Switzerland. Many good roads link the two countries, which have no border formalities or Customs stops. There are border guards along the Austrian frontier, but they rarely stamp visitors' passports.

SEEING LIECHTENSTEIN

European express trains cross Liechtenstein but don't stop there, so passengers from Switzerland take trains to the nearby town of Buchs, in the Swiss canton of Gallen or Sargans, and then take a connecting postal bus into Vaduz. If you're in Austria, you can go by train to Feldkirch, then by postal bus across the border into Liechtenstein.

IF YOU HAVE 3 DAYS

Days 1–3: Spend the first day in and around Vaduz, seeing the state art collection, the postage museum, and other sights. Visit the Unterland on the second day and the Oberland on the third day.

1. ABOUT LIECHTENSTEIN

ORIENTATION

GEOGRAPHY The Rhine River forms Liechtenstein's western boundary; the Swiss canton of St. Gallen is on the other bank. To the east is the Austrian province of Vorarlberg, and to the south is the Grisons of Switzerland. Liechtenstein is cradled by the Drei Schwestern (Three Sisters) mountains.

WHAT'S SPECIAL ABOUT LIECHTENSTEIN

Great Towns/Villages

☐ Vaduz, capital of the Principality of Liechtenstein, which is a holdover from the Holy Roman Empire.

☐ Gamprin-Bendern, a cliché of *Heidi*-type, picture-postcard charm, with the Rhine flowing by.

☐ Triesen, a settlement in Roman times, the oldest in the principality, lying at the foot of the Falknis cliffs.

Museums

☐ The Liechtenstein State Art Collection, whose Rubens collection is considered one of the best in the world.

☐ The Postage Stamp Museum, in Vaduz, attracting philatelists from around the world.

Monuments

☐ Schloss Vaduz, the prince's castle, dating from the 12th century; may be viewed only from the outside.

Shopping

☐ Purchasing the rare and finely engraved postage stamps, which depict special features of the principality.

Ace Attractions

☐ The Oberland, or Upper Country, a region of meadows and hills rising from the Rhine Valley.

PEOPLE About 28,500 citizens live in 11 communes (comparable to Switzerland's cantons). Most—more than 85%—are Roman Catholic and of German ancestry. They enjoy one of the highest standards of living in the world and pay very little in taxes. Unemployment is rare, and the annual export revenue per citizen is 75,000F ($54,742).

The country's prosperity, however, is a relatively recent development. Many old-timers remember the hardships of World War I, when the country was virtually cut off from food supplies because of blockades. The social and economic growth since the end of World War II has exceeded that of any other Western nation. Today, Liechtenstein is one of the most highly industrialized countries in Europe. The industry is hardly noticeable, however, because the factories and workshops are dispersed among orchards, meadows, and woodlands. There are no smokestacks, with their pollution from fumes. One of the industrial specialties is the production of false teeth.

Liechtenstein has a rich cultural life, supported by royal patrons and the cooperation of neighboring countries. Though open to foreign influences, through commerce and cultural exchanges as well as through tourism, Liechtenstein maintains its unique national identity by severely restricting citizenship. Any foreigner wishing to become a citizen must first be approved by a majority of the commune he intends to live in; then his application must be approved by parliament, and then by the monarch. The process is meant to be discouraging.

LANGUAGE Most residents of Liechtenstein, who are largely of Austrian origin, speak a German dialect. English is also understood throughout the country.

HISTORY The first traces of tribal settlements were left by the Celts in 4000 B.C. The Romans occupied the Rhine Valley in 15 B.C. The area that is now called

Liechtenstein was part of the Roman province of Rhaetia. Emperor Augustus established a military and trade route here. The Romans were followed by the Alemanni, Germanic tribes who settled here from A.D. 300 to 700. In 850, Charlemagne signed the Rhaetican Register, making all the alpine region a part of what subsequently became the Holy Roman Empire.

The land destined to become Liechtenstein was carved up into royal estates. Charlemagne's descendants owned rich estates near Lake Constance and the Lower Alps. These estates were broken up through hereditary claims and resulted in the formation of the County of Vaduz, on the east side of the Rhine. The County of Vaduz (called Oberland, or the Upper Country) and the Lordship of Schellenberg (called Unterland, or Lower Country) were united in 1437 to form a dependency. The little state fought several wars during the Middle Ages and shifted its allegiance from Switzerland to Austria. It also weathered religious strife and the plague. The country was passed from count to count and lord to lord through inheritance and sometimes outright sale. Several of the rulers levied heavy taxes that reduced the populace to misery.

Finally, Prince John Adam Andrew of Liechtenstein purchased the estates of Schellenberg and the County of Vaduz, and in 1719 the two territories were given the title "Imperial Principality (Fürstentum) of Liechtenstein." This made the country a member of the Holy Roman Empire. When travelers cross from Switzerland into Liechtenstein, tour guides often tell them they are leaving one of the world's oldest democracies and entering the last remaining outpost of the Holy Roman Empire.

As part of the Holy Roman Empire, Liechtenstein had to provide 5 men for the Imperial Army; the figure was later raised to 80 under the German Confederation. A contingent of soldiers from Liechtenstein served a tour of duty in 1866, during the Seven Weeks' War between Prussia (Germany) and Austria. In 1869 the principality's army was disbanded permanently by Prince John II. The prince ruled for 71 years, until his death in 1929. He used part of his vast fortune to improve conditions in the principality.

Until the end of World War I the country had a close alliance with Austria, but in 1921 it signed a postal treaty with Switzerland, followed in 1924 by adoption of Swiss currency and inclusion in the Swiss Customs Union. Since 1959, Switzerland has acted as Liechtenstein's diplomatic representative abroad.

This political marriage with Switzerland proved a smart move by the principality. During World War II, Liechtenstein, like Switzerland, remained neutral and escaped occupation by Nazi Germany. Austria, on the other hand, was absorbed in the German Reich in 1938.

That same year, Franz Josef II of Liechtenstein ascended the throne, succeeding his great-uncle as the principality's 12th ruler. When he died, at 83, in 1989, he was the world's longest-reigning monarch. Franz Josef enjoyed great popularity because of his modesty and devotion to the people of Liechtenstein, which, he once said, "is a happy country because it is small."

Immediately after his death, his oldest son, Hans-Adam II (b. 1943), succeeded him upon the throne, together with his wife, Marie Algaë.

GOVERNMENT The Principality of Liechtenstein is a constitutional hereditary monarchy with a unicameral parliament (Diet). The state power is vested in the prince and the people. The prince's powers are passed on through hereditary succession to the throne and are independent of the will of the people. The people also have political power and must work together with the prince, according to the constitution.

Members of the parliament are chosen for 4 years by general elections. The right to vote is universal (women received the right to vote in 1984), secret, and direct.

Public referendum is an important right of all citizens. Any law passed by the Diet that is not declared urgent may be put to referendum. The constitution also assures freedom of speech, freedom of the press, and freedom of assembly.

Liechtenstein has a prime minister and four councilors, appointed by the prince for a 4-year term. They act as a link between the prince and the Diet. In 1969 the principality celebrated its 250th anniversary.

GETTING THERE

BY PLANE   The nearest airport is Kloten International Airport outside Zurich, about 80 miles to the west of Vaduz. There is both train and bus transportation into Liechtenstein from Zurich.

BY TRAIN   Many express trains pass *through* Liechtenstein, but none stops there. You can take a train from Zurich to Sargans in Liechtenstein or to Buchs in Switzerland. From either place there are good bus connections to Vaduz and the other communes in Liechtenstein.

BY BUS   Bus connections into Liechtenstein are possible from Buchs in Switzerland and from Feldkirch in Austria. Tickets are sold in all bus stations and post offices (including those at Buchs and Sargans); individual tickets can also be bought aboard buses going into Liechtenstein.

BY CAR   From Zurich head southwest along Route N3 until you reach the junction with Route N1, then take N1 north to the turnoff for Vaduz.

GETTING AROUND

BY TRAIN   There is only one local train, going from Nendeln to Schaan and Schaanwald.

BY BUS   Buses are the most efficient means of getting around Liechtenstein. Major towns have good bus service to the outlying communes. There are stations in Sargans (10½ miles from Vaduz); Buchs, Switzerland (4½ miles from Vaduz); and Feldkirch, Austria (3 miles from Vaduz).

FAST FACTS

Area Code   The telephone area code for Liechtenstein is 075.

Currency   The Swiss franc is legal tender in Liechtenstein; the exchange rate is the same as in Switzerland (see Section 2, "Information, Documents & Money," in Chapter 2).

Documents Required   All travel documents recognized by Swiss authorities are valid in Liechtenstein. However, you'll encounter the formalities of any western European border crossing if you enter through Austria.

Holidays   The public holidays are New Year's Day, Epiphany (Jan 6), Candlemas (Feb 2), Shrove Tuesday, Feast of St. Joseph (Mar 19), Holy Friday, Easter Monday, May Day ("Labor Day", May 1), Ascension Day, Whit Monday, Corpus Christi, Feast of the Assumption/National Day (Aug 15), the Nativity of Our Lady (Sept 8), All Saints' Day (Nov 1), Immaculate Conception (Dec 8), Christmas (Dec 25), and St. Stephen's Day (Dec 26).

Information For further information about the principality, contact the **Liechtenstein National Tourist Office,** Städtle 37 (P.O. Box 139), FL-9490 Vaduz, Fürstentum (tel. 075/2-14-43).

Mail The postage rates are the same as in Switzerland (see "Fast Facts: Switzerland" in Chapter 2). But you must, of course, use Liechtenstein stamps.

Medical Doctors and dentists take turns handling emergency calls (the names of those currently available are published in the Saturday and Sunday newspapers). Your hotel will put you in touch with an English-speaking doctor or dentist. Phone 144 for an ambulance.

Telephone Liechtenstein's telephone system is integrated with that of Switzerland. You can call Liechtenstein from Switzerland by dialing area code 075 followed by the local number. The rates are the same as in Switzerland (see "Fast Facts: Switzerland" in Chapter 2).

---

2. VADUZ

80 miles E of Zurich, 24 miles E of Chur

GETTING THERE See "Getting There" in Section 1, "About Liechtenstein," above.

ESSENTIALS The **Liechtenstein National Tourist Office** is at Kirchstrasse 7 (tel. 075/2-14-43).

Vaduz (pronounced *Va*-dootz) is the capital of the Principality of Liechtenstein.

Vineyards surround this little town (pop. about 4,900) at the foot of the royal family's castle. The rural commune known for its good wines, is also very hospitable and sociable to tourists.

WHAT TO SEE & DO

Traffic is allowed one way on the main street, **Städtle.** Also at the center of Vaduz is the **Rathaus** (Town Hall). The post office is across the street.

Vaduz offers a wide range of sports and entertainment. Facilities include a miniature golf course, tennis courts, and a large swimming pool.

The prince's castle, ✪ **Schloss Vaduz** dates from the 12th century. The oldest parts are the keep and the buildings on the east side. The castle was burned down by Swiss troops in 1499 and rebuilt at the beginning of the 16th century. It has round bastions at the northeast and southwest corners. Once a bleak and gloomy fortress, the castle is now much improved. The private interior contains lavish furnishings, antiques, and priceless artwork. Although the public is not welcome inside, the exterior of the fortress is worth seeing. The climb along the wooded footpath takes 20 minutes and starts between the Hotel Real and the Hotel Engel. There is a sweeping vista from the grounds around the castle.

In the upper village, on the road to the castle, is the **Red House.** This was the seat of the vassals of the counts of Werdenberg during the Middle Ages. The house was acquired along with the vineyard by the Monastery of St. Johann in the Toggenburg.

LIECHTENSTEIN STATE ART COLLECTION, Städtle 37. Tel. 2-23-41.

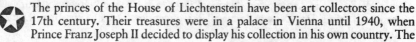 The princes of the House of Liechtenstein have been art collectors since the 17th century. Their treasures were in a palace in Vienna until 1940, when Prince Franz Joseph II decided to display his collection in his own country. The

collection occupies two floors of a gallery above the tourist office. The works by Rubens are considered among the greatest in the world. They include the *Toilet of Venus* and a cycle of nine large paintings illustrating the history of a Roman consul. Many of the pictures on exhibit are reproduced on Liechtenstein's famous stamps. The art collection is the country's most outstanding attraction and the highlight of many a visitor's trip to Liechtenstein.

Admission: 3F ($2.20) adults, 1.50F ($1.10) students and children 6–16.

Open: Summer, daily 10am–noon and 1:30–5:30pm; winter, daily 10am–noon and 2–5:30pm.

POSTAGE STAMP MUSEUM, Städtle 37. Tel. 6-62-59.

Philatelists and other admirers come from all over the world to see the Liechtenstein stamps. The collection includes the stamps of the Universal Postal Union, printing plates, and postal documents. Liechtenstein's first stamp dates from 1912. The museum was opened in 1930.

Admission: Free.

Open: Daily 10am–noon and 2–6pm.

LANDESMUSEUM, Städtle 43. Tel. 2-23-10.

The building that houses the Liechtenstein National Museum was once the Stag Inn (a stop on the stagecoach route), then the prince's own tavern and customshouse. In the early 19th century, it was called the Eagle Inn, and until 1905 it was the seat of government, with the state prison in the basement. Now the renovated structure houses the collection of the Liechtenstein Historical Society. Some artifacts date from prehistoric times. Other items include Roman implements, Alemannic burial articles, records of the early Christian era, medieval coins and weapons, rare stamps, and some antique Rhineland jewelry.

Admission: 2F ($1.45) adults, 1F (75¢) children.

Open: May–Oct, daily 10am–noon and 1:30–5:30pm; Nov–Apr, Tues–Sun 2–5:30pm. **Closed:** Dec 24–25 and Dec 31–Jan 1.

WHERE TO STAY

Most of Liechtenstein's hotels are in the capital.

VERY EXPENSIVE

PARK HOTEL SONNENHOF, Mareestrasse 29, FL-9490 Vaduz, Fürstentum. Tel. 075/2-11-92. Fax 075/2-00-53. 29 rms (all with bath). MINIBAR TV TEL

$ Rates: 140F–190F ($102.20–$138.70) single; 220F–370F ($160.60–$270.05) double. Half board 45F ($32.85) extra. AE, DC, MC, V. **Parking:** 20F ($14.60).

The finest hotel in the principality is among the finest in Europe. Diplomatic receptions are held here frequently. Built in the late 19th century, the hotel has been modernized into a streamlined chalet, with balconies and awnings. The garden is beautiful, and the rooms are handsomely decorated and furnished.

Dining/Entertainment: Unfortunately, only hotel guests are admitted to the dining room. Celebrated chef Emil Real is the brother of another distinguished chef, Felix Real, who owns the Hotel Real. Emil Real is a native of Italy and has worked at Maxim's in Paris. (In 1971 he and his brother were flown to Iran by the shah to cook at the extravaganza in Persepolis celebrating the Persian throne's 2,500-year history.) His English-speaking wife, Jutta, is the charming hostess.

Services: Room service, laundry.

Facilities: Swimming pool.

MODERATE

HOTEL ENGEL, Städtle 13, FL-9490 Vaduz, Fürstentum. Tel. 075/2-03-13. Fax 075/8-11-59. 17 rms (all with bath). MINIBAR TV TEL
$ Rates (including continental breakfast): 85F–105F ($62.05–$76.65) single; 105F–128F ($76.65–$93.45) double. AE, DC, MC, V.
This small, three-story hotel is owned by Roland Huber (not the same Roland Huber who has the well-known jewelry shop next door). Huber and his wife are among the most gracious hoteliers in Vaduz. The hotel is modern outside and decorated with rustic artifacts inside. The balconies are covered with flowers in the summertime. There is a grillroom with an antique winescrew. In addition, the hotel has the only Chinese restaurant in the country, and a covered terrace.

HOTEL REAL, Städtle 21, FL-9490 Vaduz, Fürstentum. Tel. 075/2-22-22. Fax 075/2-08-91. 12 rms (all with bath). MINIBAR TV TEL
$ Rates (including continental breakfast): 135F–160F ($98.55–$116.80) single; 145F–190F ($105.85–$138.70) double. AE, DC, MC, V.
This well-maintained hotel is on the main street, below the wooded bluff on which the palace of the prince is built. The modern facade is decorated with flower boxes in the summer. The rooms are clean and comfortable and have been renovated in an elegant, modern style.

HOTEL SCHLÖSSLE, Fürst-Franz-Josef-Strasse 68, FL-9490 Vaduz, Fürstentum. Tel. 075/2-56-21. Fax 075/2-07-10. 33 rms (all with bath). MINIBAR TV TEL
$ Rates (including continental breakfast): 90F–98F ($65.70–$71.55) single; 150F–170F ($109.50–$124.10) double. AE, DC, MC, V.
This hotel has an ocher facade with medieval-style Teutonic turrets, a clock tower with gingerbread trim, and a small carillon of bells hanging above the statue of a Liechtenstein couple in regional garb. The bedrooms have charming painted furniture. The hotel is on the main route from Vaduz to the prince's castle.

INEXPENSIVE

HOTEL VADUZERHOF, Städtle 3, FL-9490 Vaduz, Fürstentum. Tel. 075/2-84-84. Fax 075/2-84-86. 23 rms (9 with bath). MINIBAR TV TEL
$ Rates: 42F–67F ($30.65–$48.90) single; 66F–94F ($48.15–$68.60) double. AE, DC, MC, V. **Closed:** Jan.
(S) There are several places to eat and drink at in this small hotel in the center of town. A canopy above the front door is crowned with flowers. The furniture in the bedrooms is pleasant.
Fine food is served at the Trattoria Toscana (see "Where to Dine," below) and the Zum Güggel. The menu might include poached salmon with hollandaise, trout meunière, chicken curry, and veal steak with morels. Try the interesting local dishes. A light lunch costs 12F ($8.75); à la carte dinners start at 25F ($18.25). The restaurant is open daily from 11am to 2pm and 6 to 11pm. The hotel also offers a cozy wine Stube. The outdoor café has metal tables ringing an old tree in the hotel's center.

WHERE TO DINE

EXPENSIVE

RESTAURANT REAL, Städtle 21. Tel. 2-22-22.

Cuisine: CONTINENTAL. **Reservations:** Required.
$ **Prices:** Appetizers 14F–22F ($10.20–$16.05); main courses 25F–38F ($18.25–$27.75); "menu of the month" 105F ($76.65). AE, DC, MC, V.
Open: Lunch daily 11:30am–2pm; dinner daily 6:30–10pm.

⭐ Celebrated chef Felix Real is the second famous Real brother who runs a restaurant in town. His older brother, Emil, owns the Park Hotel Sonnenhof (see "Where to Stay," above). The royal family are frequent guests; their castle looms above the restaurant, which is on the main street of Vaduz. There are café tables and plastic rattan chairs outside. The dining rooms have paneling and lighting fixtures shaped like grape garlands. You will appreciate the well-polished ambience of understated prosperity. The menu might include coquilles St. Jacques with Noilly Prat and leeks, duck-liver salad followed by a choice of six lobster dishes, wild game specialties, filet of wild trout with Riesling, and salmon with champagne.

MODERATE

CHINATOWN, in the Hotel Engel, Städtle 13. Tel. 2-03-13.
Cuisine: CHINESE. **Reservations:** Recommended.
$ **Prices:** Appetizers 8.50F–12F ($6.20–$8.75); main dishes 24.50F–40F ($17.90–$29.20); fixed-price meals 35F–68F ($25.55–$49.65). AE, DC, MC, V.
Open: Lunch daily noon–2pm; dinner daily 6–10pm.
The only Chinese restaurant in the principality is on the second floor of this previously recommended hotel. There's a terrace for fair-weather dining. Chinese cooks were brought in from Hong Kong, and many of the dishes show a Cantonese influence. Fish and poultry dishes are excellent.

RESTAURANT TORKEL, Hintergasse 9. Tel. 2-44-10.
Cuisine: SWISS. **Reservations:** Recommended.
$ **Prices:** Appetizers 8F–14F ($5.85–$10.20); main courses 18F–32F ($13.15–$23.35). AE, DC, MC, V.
Open: Lunch Tues–Sat noon–2pm; dinner Tues–Sat 7–9pm.

🅢 The prince owns this charming country inn on the site of an old wine press. It's in the royal vineyards on the outskirts of town; park your car and follow the signs a short distance to a low-lying building. Specialties include veal dishes, filet goulash Stroganoff, and "Torkelsteak." Noodle and Rösti dishes are also offered. Wine is available from the royal cellars.

TRATTORIA TOSCANA, in the Hotel Vaduzerhof, Städtle 3. Tel. 2-84-84.
Cuisine: ITALIAN. **Reservations:** Not needed.
$ **Prices:** Appetizers 5F–18F ($3.65–$13.15); main courses 22.50F–38F ($16.45–$27.75). AE, DC, MC, V.
Open: Lunch daily 11am–2pm; dinner daily 6–10pm. **Closed:** Jan.
The finest Italian food is served in a paneled dining room decorated with bright colors. For an appetizer, try straciatella, minestrone, or antipasti—served hot or cold. Main dishes might include Tuscan-style lamb cutlets or scaloppine marsala. The pasta dishes are excellent, especially the tagliatelle with seafood.

INEXPENSIVE

OLD CASTLE INN, Aeulestrasse 22. Tel. 2-10-65.
Cuisine: ITALIAN/GERMAN. **Reservations:** Not needed.
$ **Prices:** Appetizers 8F–12F ($5.85–$8.75); main courses 14F–24F ($10.20–$17.50). No credit cards.
Open: Daily 11am–1am.

Locals gather at the long, half-timbered bar to drink and gossip, while Italian and German folk music or rock music is being played. You'll be able to see the castle from the green leatherette banquettes that surround the wood tables. Outside there's a terrace with a striped canopy and geraniums around the border. The special Italian menu might include antipasti and risotto with mushrooms. There's also a good selection of Wurst and steak dishes, or you might choose one of the sandwiches. The paprika Schnitzel with pommes frites and a salad is a good bargain. The menu also includes minestrone, spaghetti, lasagne, and veal liver Venice style.

SHOPPING

Most visitors stop here just to purchase stamps. But if the bus isn't pulling out, you may have time to shop. The best craft store is **L'Atelier,** Städtle 36 (tel. 2-46-88). You'll recognize it by the chic orange neon sign. Hélène de Marchi sells lamps, dolls, stoneware, pewter, sculpture, and many other handmade items. You'll also find famous European glass, sterling-silver jewelry, precious stones, and hand-painted silks. The store is open Monday through Friday from 9:30am to noon and 2 to 6:30pm, and on Saturday from 9am to noon and 1 to 4pm.

EVENING ENTERTAINMENT

The cost of a night on the town is low, compared with similar entertainment in other European cities. Most clubs in Liechtenstein are open Sunday through Thursday from 8:30pm to 1am and on Friday and Saturday from 8:30pm to 2am. Admission is usually free. Drinks cost 11F ($8.05); beer, 5F ($3.65).

In Vaduz a good bet is the **Hotel Engel,** Städtle 13 (tel. 2-10-57), which features live music in winter (see "Where to Stay," above).

3. THE UNTERLAND

Formed by the Rhine Valley, Liechtenstein's Unterland, or Lower Country, is at the foot of the Drei Schwestern (Three Sisters) mountains. It contains eight villages along the slopes of the Eschnerberg and five parishes: Ruggell, Schellenberg, Eschen-Nendeln, Gamprin-Bendern, and Mauren-Schaanwald. The landscape is a rugged mix of wooded hills, meadows, and clean brooks. The few pockets of agricultural and industrial development have not been allowed to damage the environment.

The **Eschnerberg Historical Trail** is an extensive network of footpaths. The Eschnerberg hills were a refuge for prehistoric settlers, offering an islandlike setting in the marshy Rhine Valley. The marshes have since been drained. A hike along these trails is both pleasant and informative. You'll learn the history of the people who have lived in this region.

All the villages recommended below are on the postal-bus route from Vaduz. The tourist office (see Section 1, above) will provide a map outlining the various routings and transportation connections possible.

RUGGELL

The record of this village dates from the year 933, when there was a farm here. The documents refer to a *run,* which means "cleared land" in the Rhaeto-Romanic dialect. Today the well-known farming district is dotted with small industries. Some 225 acres of this meadowland is designated as a protected area to prevent the extinction of the plant and animal life that is unique to the area. Ruggell is the northernmost village of Liechtenstein and at the lowest elevation.

SCHELLENBERG

This second-smallest parish in the principality (pop. 577) also has the smallest surface area. It was already settled when the New Stone Age began. Some of the Iron Age artifacts displayed in the National Museum in Vaduz were unearthed here. The Herren (nobles) von Schellenberg built two castles here in the Middle Ages. One of the castles, the **Obere Burg Schellenberg,** has been restored and offers a good view. Schellenberg is a starting point for the **Eschenerberg Historical Trail.**

MAUREN-SCHAANWALD

These two villages are a mile apart, in a parish covering only 3 square miles. Mauren is one of the most beautiful sights in Liechtenstein. It was called Muron in 1178 and today is known as the "Village of the Seven Hillocks." The remains of Roman baths and a 2nd-century farmhouse or outbuilding have been excavated here. The village is also known for its fine church, dating from 1787. The meadows and woodlands between Mauren and Schaanwald have been designated a bird sanctuary. The preserve contains a conservation pond and a nature trail. The villages are on the Schaan–Feldkirch road leading to Austria.

GAMPRIN-BENDERN

This small parish along the Rhine has picture-postcard charm. The two hamlets on the west spur of Eschnerberg are rich in archeological discoveries. Excavations have shown that the area was inhabited continuously from about 2500 B.C. to the Roman era. Discoveries around Gamprin have yielded many clues about the culture of the New Stone Age. The remains of a farm and a small church dating from A.D. 55 have been found on the hill on which the **Bendern church** stands today. This church belonged to the convent of Schanis (St. Gallen) from 809 to 1177 and to the monastery of St. Luzi (Chur) from 1200 to 1816. After the Reformation, the St. Luzi monks built a larger structure, which included the abbot's quarters. Recently restored, this building now serves as a vicarage for the Bendern church.

It was at Bendern's **Kirchhügel** that the men of the lowlands swore loyalty to the Prince of Liechtenstein in 1699. It is very scenic and includes a fitness track, a history trail, and a camp ground. The **Mariengrotte (Mary's Grotto),** at Bendern, is the only shrine of its kind in the country.

ESCHEN-NENDELN

Eschen was first mentioned in the Carolingian land registry in 850 under the name Essane, derived from the Celtic word *esca,* meaning "by the water." The water refers to the Esche, a nearby brook. Flint artifacts from the Middle Stone Age, about 5000 B.C., have been found here, and New Stone Age settlements have been excavated at Malanser and Schneller. The upper part of Eschen, Schönbühl, is one of the country's most attractive residential areas.

The parish includes the village of Nendeln, in which the foundation of a Roman villa and a prehistoric settlement have been discovered. Nendeln lies 3 miles northeast of Schaan, on Route 16.

There are several buildings worth visiting in the area. The **Pfründhaus** is a prebend structure. The **Holy Cross Chapel,** on the Rofenberg, was formerly a place of public assembly. The restored church at Eschen has the original walls of the old church laid bare. Other churches include **St. Sebastian's Chapel** and **Rochus Chapel.** Liechtenstein's first industrial enterprise was a tile factory founded at Nendeln in 1836. For a century, it was the only industrial plant in the Unterland.

There is a pool in Eschen, and a health trail in Nendeln. You can also enjoy the peaceful mountain footpaths of the Eschnerberg trail.

WHERE TO STAY & DINE

HOTEL LANDHAUS, Churer Strasse 263, FL-9485 Nendeln, Fürstentum. Tel. 075/3-20-11. Fax 075/3-43-67. 10 rms (all with bath). TEL
$ Rates (including continental breakfast): 65F ($47.45) single; 95F–105F ($69.35–$76.65) double. No credit cards.

Located on the road from Vaduz to the Austrian border, this hotel has a dark, modern facade and a large antique wine press in the yard. The large ground floor is decorated according to the season. Older residents tend to congregate here on Sunday morning.

The international menu includes beef goulash with Spätzli, spaghetti carbonara, sole meunière, Wiener Schnitzel, and steak au poivre. Fixed-price meals start at 28F ($20.45). The exotically painted bar is good for a drink in the evening.

4. THE OBERLAND

The Oberland, or Upper Country, of Liechtenstein was the former estate of the Count of Vaduz. It consists of Vaduz and five parishes or communes: Planken, Schaan, Triesen, Triesenberg, and Balzers. Although the area is in the south of Liechtenstein, it is still known as the Upper Country because of topography. The Unterland (Lower Country), to the north, consists of meadows and hills gently rising from the Rhine Valley, whereas the Oberland, from Planken on south, consists of higher country, reaching up to the Liechtenstein Alps.

In the shadow of the Drei Schwestern mountains, the Oberland abounds in woodlands and mountain trails, alpine flowers, and protected animal species. Settlements founded by Swiss immigrants some 700 years ago still retain their ancient traditions. There are plenty of opportunities for recreation throughout the region, but the alpine portion is the best place for winter sports.

All the villages and hamlets below are reached by postal bus from Vaduz. Pick up a map at the tourist office in Vaduz (see Section 1, above), where you can also learn about possible routings and schedules.

PLANKEN

The name of this hamlet, which is located 3 miles from Nendeln, derives from the Rhaeto-Romanic word *planca* or *plaunca,* meaning "pasture" or "meadow upland." The smallest parish in Liechtenstein (pop. 285), Planken occupies a natural terrace in a woodland. The area was settled in the 13th century by Swiss immigrants from the Valais.

Planken is the starting point for excursions to the **Drei Schwestern** (Three Sisters) area. From here you have an outstanding view of the Rhine Valley and the Swiss mountains. The panorama extends from Pizol to Lake Constance. A chapel dedicated to St. Joseph contains copics of old masters and a bronze cross by Georg Malin in the chancel.

SCHAAN

Located on the Arlberg railway line, Schaan is the country's main communications center. It's located at the foot of the Drei Schwestern, just 2 miles west of Vaduz. The Carolingian land registry (circa A.D. 831) lists Liechtenstein's second-largest parish under the name Scana. Archeologists have discovered the remains of a Roman fort, two Roman legionnaires' helmets from the 1st century A.D., and an Alemannic decorative shield from the 6th or 7th century. The 12th-century Romanesque church is worth a visit.

There is a sports center near a forest, offering tennis courts, a health center, an indoor swimming pool, public baths, and a children's playground. You can also hike in the mountains.

The **Theater a Klrchplatz** is one of the important cultural centers of the region. It presents international artists.

WHERE TO STAY & DINE

HOTEL SYLVA, FL-9494 Schaan, Fürstentum. Tel. 075/2-39-42. Fax 075/2-97-92. 11 rms (all with bath). TV TEL
$ Rates (including continental breakfast): 95F–110F ($69.35–$80.30) single; 140F–160F ($102.20–$116.80) double. No credit cards.

This little chalet in the woods is so inviting that you may want to anchor here for the night and make the easy commute to Vaduz. It's about a block above the main road. A mother and daughter, Friederecke and Sylva Eberle, offer well-furnished rooms, a pool, and a sauna.

The restaurant serves some of the best food in the area. The warmly decorated dining room has large windows, Oriental rugs, and a garden terrace. Specialties include sliced and fried duck liver, lobster salad with tarragon vinegar, a panaché of fish cooked with champagne, medallions of pork with Calvados, and filet of lamb with shallots. For dessert, try the apple crêpe with ice cream. The fixed-price gourmet menu costs 78F ($56.95); a standard three-course meal runs 42F ($30.65). The restaurant is open daily from 7am to 11pm.

SCHAANERHOF, In der Ballota 3, FL-3494 Schaan, Fürstentum. Tel. 075/2-18-77. Fax 075/8-16-27. 31 rms (all with bath). MINIBAR TV TEL
$ Rates (including continental breakfast): 78F ($56.95) single; 144 F ($105.10) double. AE, MC, V.

This modern hotel has a pink-and-white facade and balconies on several sides. The interior is comfortable and warm. There is a sleek bar near the reception area. The bedrooms are comfortably furnished and well maintained. Facilities include an indoor swimming pool.

DUX HOTEL, FL-9494 Schaan, Fürstentum. Tel. 075/2-17-27. 10 rms (all with shower or bath). MINIBAR TEL
$ Rates (including continental breakfast): 50F–65F ($36.50–$47.45) single; 100F ($73) double. AE, DC, MC, V. **Closed:** Feb and the last 2 weeks of Sept.

This Iberian-style country house is very superior for a tourist-class hotel. Built in 1924, it has a large sun terrace and long wrought-iron balconies. The rugged mountains loom in the background, and there are several old oak trees on the lawn. The comfortable rooms have wood ceilings and modern amenities, including a radio. The recently renovated hotel is accessible for wheelchairs. Facilities include a solarium and sauna. There are tennis courts and a fitness center nearby. Regional and continental cuisine is served in the hotel's three restaurants. Fondue is one of the specialties.

HOTEL LINDE, Feldkircherstrasse 1, FL-9494 Schaan, Fürstentum. Tel. 075/2-17-04. Fax 075/2-09-29. 23 rms (all with shower or bath). MINIBAR TEL
$ **Rates** (including continental breakfast): 48F–68F ($35.05–$49.65) single; 85F–100F ($62.05–$73) double. AE, MC, V. **Parking:** Free.

Ⓢ The semibaroque facade has a single ornate gable and a pumpkin-colored extension. Well-pruned hedges shield the sun terrace from the street traffic. The clean and comfortable rooms have wallpaper with large patterns and bright colors.

TRIESEN

This former Roman settlement, 2 miles south of Vaduz, is at the foot of the Falknis cliffs in a beautiful area between the Rhine and the Liechtenstein alpine areas. Vaduz is within walking distance to the north.

Be sure to tour the old quarter of the Upper Village, the **Sts. Mamerten and Maria Chapel,** and the large **Kosthaus,** built more than a century ago.

Sports facilities include tennis courts, a swimming pool, and a children's playground. There are also bicycle paths, hiking trails, and a nature reserve with a small lake. Hikes and mountain tours are offered along a wild gorge to the high alp of **Lawena.** There are two large camping areas.

WHERE TO STAY

HOTEL RESTAURANT MEIERHOF, FL-9495 Triesen, Fürstentum. Tel. 075/6-12-82. Fax 075/8-23-59. 20 rms (all with shower or bath). TV TEL
$ **Rates** (including continental breakfast): 85F ($62.05) single; 120F ($87.60) double. AE, DC, MC, V.
Roland Kindle and his family manage one of the best hotels in the principality. The conservatively designed modern building has an annex. The rooms are cozy and comfortable; many have balconies. Facilities include a swimming pool. The cuisine is excellent. Guests can dine on the terrace, which is decorated with geraniums in the summer. The paneled dining room has a tavern ambience. There is also a Stübli. The hotel is on the main Triesenberg road.

HOTEL/RESTAURANT SONNE, FL-9495 Triesen, Fürstentum. Tel. 075/2-15-05. 4 rms (none with bath).
$ **Rates** (including continental breakfast): 40F ($29.20) single; 70F ($51.10) double. No credit cards.

Ⓢ The Stalder family can offer very personal service because they rent only four rooms. The entrance has a granite arch, and the paneled main hallway has many deer heads. The menu might include filet Stroganoff, entrecôte, and several Italian dishes, such as spaghetti al pesto and piccata milanese. A la carte meals begin at 35F ($25.55).

WHERE TO DINE

RESTAURANT ADLER. Tel. 2-13-57.
Cuisine: CONTINENTAL. **Reservations:** Not needed.
$ **Prices:** Appetizers 8F–12F ($5.85–$8.75); main courses 14F–28F ($10.20–$20.45). No credit cards.

Open: Lunch daily 11am–2:30pm; dinner daily 6–11pm.

The locals favor this pizzeria and bar along the main road. The menu includes fettuccine, ravioli, gnocchi with Gorgonzola, filet of beef Stromboli (with pepperoni, artichokes, and olives), and osso buco. Veal is also prepared Valdostan style (that is, as in Italy's Valle d'Aosta) with cheese.

TRIESENBERG

The largest parish of Liechtenstein has stretches of woodland, scrub, farmland, and pasture. High above the Rhine Valley is a village with about 2,000 inhabitants, reached by taking a hill road out of Vaduz. The road is filled with steep bends but offers extensive views. The farming community is developing into a center for light industry and tourism.

Triesenberg, like Planken, was settled in the late 13th century by Swiss immigrants from the Valais. Many of the parish residents wear colorful regional garb. Modern materials and methods are used to build the houses, but the style dates from the early 14th century. The influence of the Valais is evident. The restored town hall is elegant, and the community center contains a local museum and exhibition of wood engravings.

At 2,600 feet, Triesenberg is a good base for excursions to the Liechtenstein Alps. Fine highways and well-tended hiking trails lead from Triesenberg to the alpine resorts: Masescha (4,100 ft.), Silum (5,000 ft.), Gaflei (5,000 ft.), Malbun (5,250 ft.), and Steg (4,600 ft.). Steg is on the way to Malbun and features the Valuna-Lopp cross-country skiing center and a ski lift. The half-mile-long Gnalp-Steg tunnel connects the valley with the alpine area.

WHERE TO STAY & DINE

HOTEL KULM, FL-9497 Triesenberg, Fürstentum. Tel. 075/2-87-77. Fax 075/8-28-61. 20 rms (all with bath). MINIBAR TEL

$ Rates (including continental breakfast): 70F ($51.10) single; 100F ($73) double. Half board 22F ($16.05) extra. AE, DC, MC, V.

Spring blossoms cascade down the balconies of this centrally located hotel with a pink and light-grained wood facade. It offers a wide view of the valley. There's a sidewalk café in front. The interior is a mix of rustic and modern styles. The furniture is comfortable in the well-maintained bedrooms.

HOTEL MARTHA BÜHLER, FL-9497 Triesenberg, Fürstentum. Tel. 075/ 2-57-77. Fax 075/8-15-20. 15 rms (all with shower), 3 suites. TV TEL

$ Rates (including continental breakfast): 61F–82F ($44.50–$59.85) single; 77F– 98F ($56.20–$71.55) double; 150F ($109.50) suite for two. Half board 20F ($14.60) extra. AE, DC, MC, V.

⑤ One of my favorite hotels in the upper reaches of Liechtenstein was founded in 1976 by Martha Bühler, the first woman from Liechtenstein to compete in the Winter Olympic Games, in Grenoble (1968) and Sapporo (1972). In the winter, Mrs. Bühler offers free weekly ski lessons to guests. The establishment is next to a baroque tower and offers a sweeping view of the valley. The public rooms are filled with elaborate wood detailing and warmly inviting colors and textures. The paneled rooms are cozy and well furnished. Each room has a balcony. The restaurant serves a limited menu of well-prepared meals. Snacks start at 12F ($8.75), while a full dinner costs 35F ($25.55) and up.

HOTEL STEG, FL-9497 Steb/Triesenberg, Fürstentum. Tel. 075/2-21-46. 10 rms (none with bath).

$ Rates (including continental breakfast): 35F ($25.55) single; 60F ($43.80) double. No credit cards.

This well-kept hotel, run by the Lamperts, is north of Triesenberg on the road to Steg. The chalet offers good cuisine and unpretentious comfort. The restaurant serves traditional alpine food, including veal, steak, and pork, along with two kinds of spaghetti and several cheese and meat salads. Full dinners start at 25F ($18.25).

MASESCHA

Hikers and mountaineers prefer this small resort 2 miles north of Triesenberg. The hamlet is perched high above the Rhine Valley. You can admire the cliffs, woods, lush meadows, and clear mountain brooks of this alpine world. In the village you should see **Theodul's Chapel,** a restored medieval church.

MALBUN

Fast rising as a winter ski area, Malbun, 9 miles north of Vaduz, is the center of winter sports in Liechtenstein, with ski lifts, chair lifts, a ski school, and hotels with indoor swimming pools. You can take the chair lift up to the **Bettlerjoch Peak,** at 6,900 feet. The Prince of Wales and Princess Anne learned to ski here many years ago. In the summer this is an ideal starting point for mountain walks.

WHERE TO STAY & DINE

HOTEL MALBUNERHOF, Malbun, FL-9497 Triesenberg, Fürstentum. Tel. 075/2-29-44. Fax 075/8-18-32. 30 rms. (all with bath). TEL

$ Rates (including continental breakfast): 75F–110F ($54.75–$80.30) single; 130F–200F ($94.90–$146) double. Half board 25F ($18.25) extra. No credit cards.

This four-star chalet is near the ski lifts. The timbered lounge has a fireplace and stucco walls decorated with farm implements. Facilities include a swimming pool, a sauna, and a bowling alley. The rooms are comfortable. The restaurant serves excellent meals in a homey atmosphere. There is a disco, as well as a comfortable bar containing chairs with padded armrests.

HOTEL MONTANA, Malbun, FL-9497 Triesenberg, Fürstentum. Tel. 075/ 2-73-33. Fax 075/8-22-72. 15 rms (all with bath). MINIBAR TEL

$ Rates (including continental breakfast): 75F–110F ($54.75–$80.30) single; 100F–140F ($73–$102.20) double. Half board 20F ($14.60) extra. AE, DC, MC, V.

Peter and Renate von Seemann manage this well-maintained building with wood balconies and a white stucco facade. There is a sun terrace, with a restaurant, on one side. The paneled interior is filled with bright upholstered chairs and functional wooden furniture in the bedrooms.

ALPENHOTEL, Malbun, FL-9497 Triesenberg, Fürstentum. Tel. 075/2-11-81. 29 rms (15 with bath). TEL

$ Rates (including continental breakfast): 40F ($29.20) single without bath, 80F ($58.40) single with bath; 80F ($58.40) double without bath, 120F ($87.60) double with bath. Half board 20F ($14.60) extra. No credit cards. **Closed:** Late Oct to mid-Dec and Easter to mid-May.

One of the oldest hotels in Malbun, the Alpenhotel has been in the same family for more than 75 years. It is filled with charming details, such as chandeliers made from deer antlers. The wooden ceilings are painted with alpine floral designs, and the heavy timbers are carved with regional reliefs. Jacob and Elsa Vögeli-Schroth are eager to please. The modern annex contains rooms equipped with a private bath. Facilities include a covered swimming pool. The attractive restaurant serves savory food.

BALZERS

If you're looking for Heidi tending her flock and picking edelweiss, perhaps you'll spot her here. Balzers could have been her home in the storybook. The southernmost parish in Liechtenstein contains Balzers and Mals, both first listed in the Carolingian land registry after the year 850. Artifacts indicate that people have lived here since about 3000 B.C. Archeologists have identified a Rossener jug, figurines from the Celto-Etruscan era, and early Roman coins, graves, and buildings.

The parish, 3 miles east beyond Triesen, was once a stop on the old Lindau–Milan post road; a tablet on the tower of the old cemetery honors an emissary from Milan who died making the trek. Balzers was the first official philatelic center in Liechtenstein, established in 1817.

Balzers is dominated by the privately owned **Gutenberg Castle**. It was built above a prehistoric mound during the Middle Ages and belonged to the Hapsburgs until 1824. You should also visit the **Mariahilf Chapel** and **St. Peter Chapel,** the restored **Old Vicarage,** and the old schoolhouse, which contains a local museum and library.

Sports facilities include a public indoor swimming pool. The nature reserves contain unusual plant species.

WHERE TO STAY & DINE

HOTEL POST, FL-9476 Balzers, Fürstentum. Tel. 075/4-12-08. Fax 075/4-25-68. 17 rms (all with bath). TEL
$ Rates (including continental breakfast): 70F–85F ($51.10–$62.05) single; 100F–120F ($73–$87.60) double. AE, DC, MC, V.

Although it's a little out of the way, this bargain hotel is clean and attractive. It was built in the 18th century but has been recently modernized. Sycamore trees shade the garden. There is a restaurant and bar. English is spoken.

APPENDIX

A. METRIC CONVERSIONS

LENGTH

1 millimeter (mm)	=	.04 inches (*or* less than 1/16 in.)
1 centimeter (cm)	=	.39 inches (*or* just under 1/2 in.)
1 meter (m)	=	39 inches (*or* about 1.1 yards)
1 kilometer (km)	=	.62 miles (*or* about 2/3 of a mile)

To convert kilometers to miles, multiply the number of kilometers by .62. Also use to convert kilometers per hour (kmph) to miles per hour (m.p.h.).

To convert miles to kilometers, multiply the number of miles by 1.61. Also use to convert from m.p.h. to kmph.

CAPACITY

1 liter (l)	=	33.92 fluid ounces	=	2.1 pints	=	1.06 quarts
	=	.26 U.S. gallons				
1 Imperial gallon	=	1.2 U.S. gallons				

To convert liters to U.S. gallons, multiply the number of liters by .26.

To convert U.S. gallons to liters, multiply the number of gallons by 3.79.

To convert Imperial gallons to U.S. gallons, multiply the number of Imperial gallons by 1.2.

To convert U.S. gallons to Imperial gallons, multiply the number of U.S. gallons by .83.

WEIGHT

1 gram (g)	=	.035 ounces (*or* about a paperclip's weight)
1 kilogram (kg)	=	35.2 ounces
	=	2.2 pounds
1 metric ton	=	2,205 pounds = 1.1 short ton

To convert kilograms to pounds, multiply the number of kilograms by 2.2.

To convert pounds to kilograms, multiply the number of pounds by .45.

TEMPERATURE

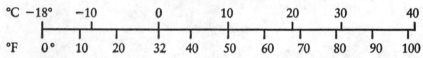

°C −18°   −10   0   10   20   30   40

°F   0° 10   20   32   40   50   60   70   80   90   100

To convert degrees Celsius to degrees Fahrenheit, multiply °C by 9, divide by 5, and add 32 (example: 20°C × 9/5 + 32 = 68°F).

To convert degrees Fahrenheit to degrees Celsius, subtract 32 from °F, multiply by 5, then divide by 9 (example: 85°F − 32 × 5/9 = 29.4°C).

B. SIZE CONVERSIONS

The following charts should help you to choose the correct clothing sizes in Switzerland. However, sizes can vary, so the best guide is simply to try things on.

WOMEN'S DRESSES, COATS, AND SKIRTS

American	3	5	7	9	11	12	13	14	15	16	18
Continental	36	38	38	40	40	42	42	44	44	46	48
British	8	10	11	12	13	14	15	16	17	18	20

WOMEN'S BLOUSES AND SWEATERS

American	10	12	14	16	18	20
Continental	38	40	42	44	46	48
British	32	34	36	38	40	42

WOMEN'S STOCKINGS

American	8	8½	9	9½	10	10½
Continental	1	2	3	4	5	6
British	8	8½	9	9½	10	10½

WOMEN'S SHOES

American	5	6	7	8	9	10
Continental	36	37	38	39	40	41
British	3½	4½	5½	6½	7½	8½

MEN'S SUITS

American	34	36	38	40	42	44	46	48
Continental	44	46	48	50	52	54	56	58
British	34	36	38	40	42	44	46	48

MEN'S SHIRTS

American	14½	15	15½	16	16½	17	17½	18
Continental	37	38	39	41	42	43	44	45
British	14½	15	15½	16	16½	17	17½	18

MEN'S SHOES

American	7	8	9	10	11	12	13
Continental	39½	41	42	43	44½	46	47
British	6	7	8	9	10	11	12

MEN'S HATS

American	6⅞	7⅛	7¼	7⅜	7½	7⅝
Continental	55	56	58	59	60	61
British	6¼	6⅞	7⅛	7¼	7⅜	7½

CHILDREN'S CLOTHING

American	3	4	5	6	6X
Continental	98	104	110	116	122
British	18	20	22	24	26

CHILDREN'S SHOES

American	8	9	10	11	12	13	1	2	3
Continental	24	25	27	28	29	30	32	33	34
British	7	8	9	10	11	12	13	1	2

INDEX

GENERAL INFORMATION

DESTINATIONS

NOW, SAVE MONEY ON ALL YOUR TRAVELS!
Join Frommer's™ Dollarwise® Travel Club

Saving money while traveling is never a simple matter, which is why the **Dollarwise Travel Club** was formed 31 years ago. Developed in response to requests from Frommer's Travel Guide readers, the Club provides cost-cutting travel strategies, up-to-date travel information, and a sense of community for value-conscious travelers from all over the world.

In keeping with the money-saving concept, the annual membership fee is low —$20 for U.S. residents or $25 for residents of Canada, Mexico, and other countries—and is immediately exceeded by the value of your benefits, which include:

1. Any TWO books listed on the following pages.
2. Plus any ONE Frommer's City Guide.
3. A subscription to our quarterly newspaper, *The Dollarwise Traveler*.
4. A membership card that entitles you to purchase through the Club all Frommer's publications for 33% to 40% off their retail price.

The eight-page *Dollarwise Traveler* tells you about the latest developments in good-value travel worldwide and includes the following columns: **Hospitality Exchange** (for those offering and seeking hospitality in cities all over the world); **Share-a-Trip** (for those looking for travel companions to share costs); and **Readers Ask . . . Readers Reply** (for those with travel questions that other members can answer).

Aside from the Frommer's Guides and the Gault Millau Guides, you can also choose from our Special Editions. These include such titles as *California with Kids* (a compendium of the best of California's accommodations, restaurants, and sightseeing attractions appropriate for those traveling with toddlers through teens); *Candy Apple: New York with Kids* (a spirited guide to the Big Apple by a savvy New York grandmother that's perfect for both visitors and residents); *Caribbean Hideaways* (the 100 most romantic places to stay in the Islands, all rated on ambience, food, sports opportunities, and price); *Honeymoon Destinations* (a guide to planning and choosing just the right destination from hundreds of possibilities in the U.S., Mexico, and the Caribbean); *Marilyn Wood's Wonderful Weekends* (a selection of the best mini-vacations within a 200-mile radius of New York City, including descriptions of country inns and other accommodations, restaurants, picnic spots, sights, and activities); and *Paris Rendez-Vous* (a delightful guide to the best places to meet in Paris whether for power breakfasts or dancing till dawn).

To join this Club, simply send the appropriate membership fee with your name and address to: Frommer's Dollarwise Travel Club, 15 Columbus Circle, New York, NY 10023. Remember to specify which single city guide and which two other guides you wish to receive in your initial package of member's benefits. Or tear out the next page, check off your choices, and send the page to us with your membership fee.

FROMMER BOOKS
PRENTICE HALL PRESS
15 COLUMBUS CIRCLE
NEW YORK, NY 10023
212/373-8125

Date_____

Friends: Please send me the books checked below.

FROMMER'S™ GUIDES

(Guides to sightseeing and tourist accommodations and facilities from budget to deluxe, with emphasis on the medium-priced.)

☐ Alaska	$14.95	☐ Germany	$14.95
☐ Australia	$14.95	☐ Italy	$14.95
☐ Austria & Hungary	$14.95	☐ Japan & Hong Kong	$14.95
☐ Belgium, Holland & Luxembourg	$14.95	☐ Mid-Atlantic States	$14.95
☐ Bermuda & The Bahamas	$14.95	☐ New England	$14.95
☐ Brazil	$14.95	☐ New Mexico	$13.95
☐ Canada	$14.95	☐ New York State	$14.95
☐ Caribbean	$14.95	☐ Northwest	$16.95
☐ Cruises (incl. Alaska, Carib, Mex, Hawaii, Panama, Canada & US)	$14.95	☐ Portugal, Madeira & the Azores	$14.95
☐ California & Las Vegas	$14.95	☐ Scandinavia	$18.95
☐ Egypt	$14.95	☐ South Pacific	$14.95
☐ England & Scotland	$14.95	☐ Southeast Asia	$14.95
☐ Florida	$14.95	☐ Southern Atlantic States	$14.95
☐ France	$14.95	☐ Southwest	$14.95
		☐ Switzerland & Liechtenstein	$14.95

☐ USA $16.95

FROMMER'S $-A-DAY® GUIDES

(In-depth guides to sightseeing and low-cost tourist accommodations and facilities.)

☐ Europe on $40 a Day	$15.95	☐ Israel on $40 a Day	$13.95
☐ Australia on $40 a Day	$13.95	☐ Mexico on $35 a Day	$14.95
☐ Costa Rica; Guatemala & Belize on $35 a day	$15.95	☐ New York on $60 a Day	$13.95
☐ Eastern Europe on $25 a Day	$16.95	☐ New Zealand on $45 a Day	$14.95
☐ England on $50 a Day	$13.95	☐ Scotland & Wales on $40 a Day	$13.95
☐ Greece on $35 a Day	$14.95	☐ South America on $40 a Day	$15.95
☐ Hawaii on $60 a Day	$14.95	☐ Spain on $50 a Day	$15.95
☐ India on $25 a Day	$12.95	☐ Turkey on $30 a Day	$13.95
☐ Ireland on $35 a Day	$13.95	☐ Washington, D.C. & Historic Va. on $40 a Day	$13.95

FROMMER'S TOURING GUIDES

(Color illustrated guides that include walking tours, cultural and historic sites, and other vital travel information.)

☐ Amsterdam	$10.95	☐ New York	$10.95
☐ Australia	$10.95	☐ Paris	$8.95
☐ Brazil	$10.95	☐ Rome	$10.95
☐ Egypt	$8.95	☐ Scotland	$9.95
☐ Florence	$8.95	☐ Thailand	$10.95
☐ Hong Kong	$10.95	☐ Turkey	$10.95
☐ London	$10.95	☐ Venice	$8.95

(TURN PAGE FOR ADDITONAL BOOKS AND ORDER FORM)

0391

FROMMER'S CITY GUIDES

(Pocket-size guides to sightseeing and tourist accommodations and facilities in all price ranges.)

☐ Amsterdam/Holland	$8.95	☐ Minneapolis/St. Paul	$8.95
☐ Athens	$8.95	☐ Montréal/Québec City	$8.95
☐ Atlanta	$8.95	☐ New Orleans	$8.95
☐ Atlantic City/Cape May	$8.95	☐ New York	$8.95
☐ Barcelona	$7.95	☐ Orlando	$8.95
☐ Belgium	$7.95	☐ Paris	$8.95
☐ Berlin	$8.95	☐ Philadelphia	$8.95
☐ Boston	$8.95	☐ Rio	$8.95
☐ Cancún/Cozumel/Yucatán	$8.95	☐ Rome	$8.95
☐ Chicago	$9.95	☐ Salt Lake City	$8.95
☐ Denver/Boulder/Colorado Springs	$7.95	☐ San Diego	$8.95
☐ Dublin/Ireland	$8.95	☐ San Francisco	$8.95
☐ Hawaii	$8.95	☐ Santa Fe/Taos/Albuquerque	$10.95
☐ Hong Kong	$7.95	☐ Seattle/Portland	$7.95
☐ Las Vegas	$8.95	☐ St. Louis/Kansas City	$9.95
☐ Lisbon/Madrid/Costa del Sol	$8.95	☐ Sydney	$8.95
☐ London	$8.95	☐ Tampa/St. Petersburg	$8.95
☐ Los Angeles	$8.95	☐ Tokyo	$8.95
☐ Mexico City/Acapulco	$8.95	☐ Toronto	$8.95
☐ Miami	$8.95	☐ Vancouver/Victoria	$7.95

☐ Washington, D.C. $8.95

SPECIAL EDITIONS

☐ Beat the High Cost of Travel	$6.95	☐ Motorist's Phrase Book (Fr/Ger/Sp)	$4.95
☐ Bed & Breakfast—N. America	$14.95	☐ Paris Rendez-Vous	$10.95
☐ California with Kids	$16.95	☐ Swap and Go (Home Exchanging)	$10.95
☐ Caribbean Hideaways	$14.95	☐ The Candy Apple (NY with Kids)	$12.95
☐ Honeymoon Destinations (US, Mex &		☐ Travel Diary and Record Book	$5.95
Carib)	$14.95	☐ Where to Stay USA (From $3 to $30 a	
☐ Manhattan's Outdoor Sculpture	$15.95	night)	$13.95

☐ Marilyn Wood's Wonderful Weekends (CT, DE, MA, NH, NJ, NY, PA, RI, VT) $11.95
☐ The New World of Travel (Annual sourcebook by Arthur Frommer for savvy travelers) $16.95

GAULT MILLAU

(The only guides that distinguish the truly superlative from the merely overrated.)

☐ The Best of Chicago	$15.95	☐ The Best of Los Angeles	$16.95
☐ The Best of France	$16.95	☐ The Best of New England	$15.95
☐ The Best of Hawaii	$16.95	☐ The Best of New Orleans	$16.95
☐ The Best of Hong Kong	$16.95	☐ The Best of New York	$16.95
☐ The Best of Italy	$16.95	☐ The Best of Paris	$16.95
☐ The Best of London	$16.95	☐ The Best of San Francisco	$16.95

☐ The Best of Washington, D.C. $16.95

ORDER NOW!

In U.S. include $2 shipping UPS for 1st book; $1 ea. add'l book. Outside U.S. $3 and $1, respectively.
Allow four to six weeks for delivery in U.S., longer outside U.S.

Enclosed is my check or money order for $_____

NAME _____

ADDRESS _____

CITY_____ STATE_____ ZIP_____

0391